WITHDRAWN

Presented to

Kingwood Branch Library

By

Donated by the National Charity
League – Kingwood Chapter

Harris County
Public Library

your pathway to knowledge

Gale Contextual Encyclopedia of American Literature

Gale Contextual Encyclopedia of American Literature

VOLUME 4

R–Z

GALE
CENGAGE Learning

Detroit • New York • San Francisco • New Haven, Conn • Waterville, Maine • London

**Gale Contextual Encyclopedia
of American Literature**

Project Editors: Anne Marie Hacht and Dwayne
D. Hayes

Editorial: Ira Mark Milne

Rights Acquisition and Management: Kelly Quin,
Robyn Young, and Tracie Richardson

Composition: Evi Abou-El-Seoud

Manufacturing: Wendy Blurton

Imaging: John Watkins

Product Design: Jennifer Wahi and Pam Galbreath

For product information and technology assistance, contact us at
Gale Customer Support, 1-800-877-4253.
For permission to use material from this text or product,
submit all requests online at **www.cengage.com/permissions.**
Further permissions questions can be emailed to
permissionrequest@cengage.com

Cover photographs reproduced by permission. Steinbeck, John, photograph. The
Library of Congress; Angelou, Maya, photograph. AP Images; Fitzgerald, F. Scott,
photograph. The Library of Congress; Twain, Mark, photograph. The Library of Congress;
Poe, Edgar Allan, public domain; London, Jack, photograph. The Library of Congress;
Hughes, Langston, 1943, photo by Gordon Parks. The Library of Congress; Dickinson, Emily.
The Library of Congress; Hemingway, Ernest, photograph. AP Images; Hemingway, Ernest,
photograph. AP Images; Lee, Harper, photograph. AP Images; Tan, Amy, 1993, photograph.
AP Images; Walker, Alice, photograph. AP Images.

While every effort has been made to ensure the reliability of the information presented
in this publication, Gale, a part of Cengage Learning, does not guarantee the accuracy of the
data contained herein. Gale accepts no payment for listing; and inclusion in the publication
of any organization, agency, institution, publication, service, or individual does not imply
endorsement of the editors or publisher. Errors brought to the attention of the publisher
and verified to the satisfaction of the publisher will be corrected in future editions.

Editorial Data Privacy Policy. Does this publication contain information about you as
an individual? If so, for more information about our editorial data privacy policies,
please see our Privacy Statement at www.gale.com.

Library of Congress Cataloging-in-Publication Data

Gale contextual encyclopedia of American literature / editorial, Anne Marie
Hacht, Dwayne D. Hayes.
    p. cm.
    Includes bibliographical references and index.
    ISBN 978-1-4144-3130-7 (set) -- ISBN 978-1-4144-3131-4 (v. 1) --
ISBN 978-1-4144-3132-1 (v. 2) -- ISBN 978-1-4144-3133-8 (v. 3) --
ISBN 978-1-4144-3134-5 (v. 4) -- ISBN 978-1-4144-3139-0 (e-book)
    1. American literature--Encyclopedias. 2. American literature--Bio-bibliography.
3. Authors, American--Biography--Dictionaries. 4. American literature--History and
criticism--Encyclopedias. I. Hacht, Anne Marie. II. Hayes, Dwayne D.

PS21.G36 2009
810'.9--dc22   2008051753

978-1-4144-3130-7 (set)   1-4144-3130-9 (set)
978-1-4144-3131-4 (vol. 1)   1-4144-3131-7 (vol. 1)
978-1-4144-3132-1 (vol. 2)   1-4144-3132-5 (vol. 2)
978-1-4144-3133-8 (vol. 3)   1-4144-3133-3 (vol. 3)
978-1-4144-3134-5 (vol. 4)   1-4144-3134-1 (vol. 4)

This title is also available as an e-book.
ISBN-13: 978-1-4144-3139-0 ISBN-10: 1-4144-3139-2
Contact your Gale, a part of Cengage Learning sales representative for ordering information.

Printed in the United States of America
1 2 3 4 5 6 7 13 12 11 10 09

Contents

VOLUME 2

F-G

H

VOLUME 3

L

N-Q

VOLUME 4

R

S

Introduction

How to Use This Book

The *Gale Contextual Encyclopedia of American Literature* is a resource for students who seek information beyond the simple biographical details of an author's life or a brief overview of the author's major works. This book is designed to offer a comprehensive view of how an author's work fits within the context of the author's life, historical events, and the literary world. This allows for a greater understanding of both the author's work and the cultural and historical environment in which it was created.

The *Gale Contextual Encyclopedia of American Literature* is divided into entries, each focused on a particular writer who has made significant contributions to literature. In some cases, these individuals may be known primarily for actions and contributions outside the realm of literature. John F. Kennedy and Martin Luther King Jr., for example, are two figures famous for their political activism; Rachel Carson is known primarily as a biologist and ecologist; Cotton Mather is remembered for his connection to the infamous Salem Witch Trials. However, all of these figures have, aside from their other accomplishments and activities, created significant works of literature that have stood the test of time and affected readers beyond the borders of their own cultures.

This book is best used not just to locate the facts of a writer's life and work, but as a way to understand the social, literary, and historical environment in which the writer lived and created. By understanding the context of the writer's work, you are more likely to recognize key themes and stylistic traits as elements of larger trends in the literary world, as well as understand the impact of historical events from a new and unique perspective.

Sections Found within Each Entry in This Book

Each entry in this book is divided into three main parts: Works in Biographical and Historical Context; Works in Literary Context; and Works in Critical Context. These sections are discussed below.

In addition, each entry includes: a Key Facts section, containing birth/death date information as well as a list of major works; a Responses to Literature section, containing discussion and writing activities related to the author in question; a

Further Reading section that includes bibliographic citations as well as reputable sources of additional material about the author in the form of books, periodicals, or Web sites; a Literary and Historical Contemporaries sidebar, listing several famous contemporaries of the author; and a Common Human Experience sidebar, offering examples of other literary or artistic works that share themes or techniques with those of the subject of the entry.

Works in Biographical and Historical Context In this section, you will find information about how events and concerns in the author's life helped to shape the author's work. For example, Kurt Vonnegut's experiences in a German prison camp in Dresden during the Allied bombing of that city in 1945 led him to write *Slaughterhouse-Five* (1969), while events surrounding Watergate (the political scandal that brought about the resignation of President Richard Nixon) led him to write *Jailbird* (1979). This section also includes information on historical events or trends that had an effect on the author. For example, the scientific and technological advancements of the late twentieth century greatly influenced the subject matter of the popular fiction of Michael Crichton, which often centered on the theme of modern technology run amok.

Works in Literary Context In this section, you will find information about how the author's work fits within the context of literature in general. This may include a description of a stylistic trait exhibited in the author's writing; for example, Mark Twain is known for his brilliant use of colloquial speech, and information on this technique—as well as examples of how the author used it—can be found in his entry. This section may also include a discussion of the writer's work as it exists within a specific genre, such as Southern Gothic fiction or modernist poetry. Finally, the Works in Literary Context section may contain discussion of specific themes commonly found in the author's work. The writings of James Baldwin, for example, frequently address the theme of race relations.

Works in Critical Context In this section, you will find a survey of critical and popular opinion related to the author and the author's most important works. The emphasis is on contemporary opinions, or those formed by readers and critics at the time the author's work was first published. In some cases, critical or popular opinion from the time of publication may not be available; this may be due simply to the passage of time, or due to the writer's lack of fame during his or her own lifetime. This section also includes information on how critical or popular opinion of an author has changed over time. Herman Melville's masterwork *Moby-Dick* (1851) met with a tepid reception upon publication, but is now considered one of the finest achievements in American literature. Kate Chopin's novella *The Awakening* (1899) earned her critical scorn and ruined her career, but the work is now considered a breakthrough in women's literature. Conversely, some works that enjoyed widespread acclaim initially are less well regarded or even forgotten today. Joel Chandler Harris's *Uncle Remus* books (published between 1880 and 1905) based on African American folk tales were popular with white and black readers in the North and South at the time; today, many critics accuse Harris (a white journalist) of misappropriating elements of African American culture, and his work has fallen out of favor. Likewise, James Branch Cabell was one of the most celebrated writers of the 1920s, made internationally famous because of the scandal stirred up by the obscenity charges attached to his 1919 novel *Jurgen*; today, his work is rarely read.

Other Information Contained in This Book

In addition to the entries for individual authors, this book also contains a chronology that indicates some major historical events related to the development of American literature. At the end of the book, you will find a glossary of terms—primarily literary and historical in nature—that are used in various entries throughout the book, along with a brief explanation of each term, a general index, and a nationality/ethnicity index.

Advisory Board

Alicia Baker Elley

taught undergraduate and high school literature, composition, and technical writing classes for over ten years. She is currently district librarian for the Harmony Independent School District in Texas.

Maureen Reed

has taught literature, history, and American Studies courses at Minnesota State University Moorhead, Lewis and Clark College, and Portland State University. She earned a Ph.D. in American Studies from the University of Texas at Austin and held a Fulbright Lectureship in American Studies at the University of Regensburg in Germany.

Roger K. Smith

has been a teacher of English, writing, and other humanities courses at such institutions as Ithaca College, Rutgers University, and Edward R. Murrow High School (Brooklyn). He holds a BA from Swarthmore College and an MA from New York University.

Patrick Walsh

holds a Ph.D. in history from the University of Texas at Austin. He has taught English and Multidisciplinary Studies at Concordia College and Minnesota State University, in Moorhead, Minnesota. A Fulbright Lecturer in American Studies at the University of Passau in Germany, he now teaches at the Catlin Gabel School in Portland, Oregon.

Chronology

This chronology contains a brief overview of some of the major events in the history of American literature. This includes the development of technologies and tools that advanced the writing and publishing process, as well as some significant historical events that had an impact on the development of literature.

1500–1700

1576   English explorers begin searching for the Northwest Passage, a hoped-for water route around North America to Asia.

1607   Jamestown settlement established in Virginia.

1620   The Pilgrims traveling from England aboard *The Mayflower* reach Cape Cod and form a settlement at Plymouth, Massachusetts.

1624   The Dutch establish a city called New Amsterdam on the island of Manhattan. The city later became known as New York City, a major center of American commerce and publishing.

1630   Massachusetts Bay Colony Governor John Winthrop begins keeping his journal of life in New England. William Bradford, governor of Plymouth, begins his own book, later titled *History of Plymouth Plantation*.

1650   Anne Bradstreet publishes her first volume of poetry.

1689   Enlightenment thinker John Locke anonymously publishes *Two Treatises of Government*, a work that attacks the idea of the "divine right" of kings and argues for a government that operates with the consent of the governed. The work exerts a strong influence over eighteenth-century French philosophers and America's founding fathers.

1692–1693
   The Salem Witch Trials are conducted. One hundred fifty people are arrested and accused of witchcraft, twenty-nine are convicted, and eighteen are executed.

1700–1800

1702   Cotton Mather publishes *Magnalia Christi Americana*, described as an ecclesiastical history of New England. It is one of the first works that attempts to define the American experience.

1718   The city of New Orleans, Louisiana, is founded by French and Canadian settlers.

1732   Benjamin Franklin begins writing *Poor Richard's Almanac*.

1740   Religious leader Jonathan Edwards begins writing his *Personal Narrative*.

1754–1763
   The French and Indian War is fought between France and Great Britain and their respective Native American allies. The conflict is part of a broader power struggle between France and Great Britain that is waged in Europe (the Seven Years War).

1762   Jean-Jacques Rousseau publishes *The Social Contract*, a landmark work of political philosophy.

1767   Daniel Boone explores territory west of the Appalachian Mountains.

1770   British soldiers fire into a crowd of rowdy, protesting colonists in Boston, killing five. The event, which helps spark the American Revolution, becomes known as the Boston Massacre.

1773   The British Parliament enacts the Tea Act; in protest, a group of men dressed as Native Americans dump a shipment of tea from Great Britain into Boston Harbor, an event called the Boston Tea Party.

1774   The British Parliament passes measures collectively known as the Intolerable Acts in an effort to punish Massachusetts for the Boston Tea Party.

1775   Patrick Henry gives his famous "Give me liberty, or give me death" speech; Paul Revere goes on his "midnight ride" to warn colonists to take arms against approaching British soldiers; Minutemen fight the British in Lexington and Concord, the first battles of the American Revolution.

1776   Thomas Paine publishes *Common Sense*; Thomas Jefferson writes, and Congress adopts, the Declaration of Independence.

1781   British general Charles Cornwallis surrenders to American General George Washington at Yorktown, ending the American Revolution.

1789   A mob storms the Bastille prison in Paris, France, setting off the French Revolution.

1794   Thomas Paine publishes *The Age of Reason*.

1800–1900

1800   John Chapman, also known as "Johnny Appleseed," travels through the Ohio Valley region giving settlers apple seeds.

1803   President Thomas Jefferson negotiates with France to purchase the Louisiana Territory for $15 million; Jefferson sets Meriwether Lewis and William Clark off on an expedition of the newly acquired territory and the lands west of it for the purpose of determining whether a water route existed between the Missouri River and the Pacific Ocean.

1812–1815
        Great Britain and the United States fight the War of 1812.

1819   Washington Irving publishes *The Sketch Book* containing such well-known short stories as "The Legend of Sleepy Hollow" and "Rip Van Winkle."

1820   Congress passes the Missouri Compromise, by which slavery is prohibited in the northern Louisiana territory, Maine is admitted to the Union as a free state, and Missouri is admitted as a slave state. The delicate balance between the interests of slave and free states is preserved for the next three decades.

1821   Sequoyah develops a Native American alphabet and uses it to help Cherokees read and write their own language.

1831   Nat Turner leads a slave rebellion in Virginia in which fifty-five white people are killed; Turner is captured and executed; several eastern Native American tribes are removed from their homelands and forced to march to Oklahoma Territory, a harsh, deadly journey dubbed "the trail of tears."

1832   Samuel Morse invents the telegraph.

1836   Texas declares its independence after revolting against Mexico; Ralph Waldo Emerson publishes *Nature*.

1841   Brook Farm, a utopian cooperative, is established in West Roxbury, Massachusetts, by Unitarian minister George Ripley.

1845   The United States annexes Texas.

1846–1847
        Mexican-American War waged; the United States wins the short war, and gains much of what is now the western United States, including present-day California, Arizona, Nevada, Utah, New Mexico, Colorado, and Wyoming.

1848   Women's Rights Convention held in Seneca Falls, New York.

1849   After gold is discovered in California in 1848, a rush of prospectors—known as forty-niners—flood into California in hopes of striking it rich.

1850   Nathaniel Hawthorne publishes *The Scarlet Letter*; after much bitter debate, Congress passes the Compromise of 1850, which includes multiple provisions designed to maintain a balance between the relative power of slave and free states in Congress.

1851   Herman Melville publishes *Moby-Dick*.

1852   Harriet Beecher Stowe publishes *Uncle Tom's Cabin*.

1854   Henry David Thoreau publishes *Walden*.

1855   Walt Whitman publishes his first version of the poetry collection *Leaves of Grass*.

1859   Abolitionist John Brown attacks the U.S. arsenal at Harper's Ferry, West Virginia, in an attempt to gain weapons to start a slave insurrection; he is captured, tried, and hanged.

1861–1865
        United States Civil War fought between the Union and the pro-slavery Confederate States of America. The war is effectively ended with the surrender of Confederate general Robert E. Lee to Union general Ulysses S. Grant, in Appomattox, Virginia, in 1865; President Abraham Lincoln is assassinated in 1865.

1869   The Fifteenth Amendment to the Constitution grants African Americans the right to vote.

1876   Alexander Graham Bell invents the telephone.

1879   Thomas Edison invents the electric light bulb.

1884   Mark Twain publishes *Adventures of Huckleberry Finn*.

1890   *The Poems of Emily Dickinson* is published posthumously, by the poet's sister.

1895   Stephen Crane publishes *The Red Badge of Courage*.

1898   The United States and Spain fight the Spanish-American War. The United States quickly wins the war, and gains Puerto Rico, Guam, and the Philippines. The war establishes the United States as a major world power.

1900–Now

1901   A major oil strike is made at Spindletop, Texas.

1903   Orville and Wilbur Wright launch the first successful manned airplane flight in Kitty Hawk, North Carolina; Henry Ford founds the Ford Motor Company.

1909   The National Association for the Advancement of Colored People (NAACP) is formed.

1914   World War I begins in Europe.

1917   The United States enters World War I on the side of the Entente Powers.

1918   Germany and its allies are defeated, and World War I ends.

1920   The Nineteenth Amendment to the Constitution grants women the right to vote.

1925   F. Scott Fitzgerald publishes *The Great Gatsby*.

1926   Ernest Hemingway publishes *The Sun Also Rises*; the Radio Corporation of America (RCA) organizes the National Broadcasting Company (NBC): the first radio network set up for public entertainment and information.

1927   American pilot Charles Lindbergh flies solo across the Atlantic Ocean from New York to France.

1929   The U.S. stock market crashes, causing financial panic; William Faulkner publishes *The Sound and the Fury*.

1929–1939
        The Great Depression, a global economic downturn, causes widespread unemployment and deflation.

1932   Amelia Earhart becomes first woman to fly solo across the Atlantic Ocean.

1936   Eugene O'Neill wins Nobel Prize in Literature.

1938   Thorton Wilder publishes the play *Our Town*; Pearl S. Buck wins Nobel Prize in Literature.

1939   World War II begins in Europe with the German invasion of Poland.

1940   Richard Wright publishes *Native Son*; Carson McCullers publishes *The Heart Is a Lonely Hunter*.

1941   Japanese fighter pilots attack the United States naval base at Pearl Harbor, Hawaii. The United States declares war on Japan and, subsequently, on Japanese ally Germany, effecting U.S. entry into World War II; the U.S. begins the Manhattan Project, a secret program to develop an atomic bomb.

1942   President Franklin Roosevelt signs an executive order authorizing the forced relocation of Japanese Americans to internment camps for the duration of the war.

1945   The United States drops atomic bombs on the Japanese cities of Hiroshima and Nagasaki, killing more than 100,000 people. Japan surrenders. Germany surrenders.

1947   Jackie Robinson becomes the first African American major-league baseball player; Tennessee Williams publishes the play *A Streetcar Named Desire*.

1948   Congress approves the Marshall Plan for the reconstruction and assistance of Europe; Jewish state of Israel proclaimed; first television broadcast of *Texaco Star Theater*, hosted by Milton Berle—the first major television program in America.

1949   William Faulkner wins Nobel Prize in Literature.

1950   Senator Joseph McCarthy claims that the United States State Department has been infiltrated by communists; President Harry Truman sends U.S. troops to Korea after communist North Korea invades pro-Western South Korea; Isaac Asimov publishes *I, Robot*.

1951   J. D. Salinger publishes *The Catcher in the Rye*.

1953   Senator Joseph McCarthy becomes chairman of the Senate Committee on Government Operations and launches his notorious investigations into purported communist activity in the United States.

1954   The Supreme Court case *Brown v. the Board of Education of Topeka* declares segregation in public schools unconstitutional; Ernest Hemingway wins Nobel Prize in Literature.

1955   Dr. Martin Luther King Jr. leads the Montgomery Bus Boycott.

1957   Jack Kerouac publishes *On the Road*; Theodore Seuss Geisel (Dr. Seuss) publishes *The Cat in the Hat*; the Soviet Union launches *Sputnik 1*, sparking the U.S./Soviet space race.

1959   Lorraine Hansberry publishes the play *A Raisin in the Sun*.

1960   Harper Lee publishes *To Kill a Mockingbird*; birth control pills are made available to the public.

1962   Cuban Missile Crisis occurs: a tense standoff between nuclear superpowers the United States and the Soviet Union; John Steinbeck wins Nobel Prize in Literature.

1963   President John F. Kennedy assassinated in Dallas, Texas.

1964   Congress passes the Civil Rights Act, prohibiting racial discrimination in public places.

1965   President Lyndon Johnson escalates hostilities against North Vietnam, ordering bombing raids; Dr. Martin Luther King Jr. leads a civil rights march from Selma to Montgomery, Alabama; African American rights activist Malcolm X assassinated; Voting Rights Act passed by Congress.

1968   Martin Luther King Jr. assassinated; presidential candidate Robert Kennedy assassinated.

1969   Kurt Vonnegut publishes *Slaughterhouse-Five*; astronaut Neil Armstrong becomes first human to set foot on the moon.

1974   President Richard Nixon resigns in the wake of the Watergate scandal.

1975   Vietnam War ends.

1976   Saul Bellow wins Nobel Prize in Literature.

1978   Isaac Bashevis Singer wins Nobel Prize in Literature.

1979   Radical Islamists storm the American embassy in Iran and take fifty-two hostages, most of whom are held for 444 days.

1981   The IBM personal computer first becomes available.

1984   Sandra Cisneros publishes *The House on Mango Street*.

1986   Cormac McCarthy publishes *Blood Meridian*.

1989   The Berlin Wall is torn down.

1990   First commercial dial-up access to the Internet becomes available; the Soviet Union collapses, and independent nations are formed of its former territory.

1993   Toni Morrison wins Nobel Prize in Literature.

1998   President Bill Clinton impeached by the U.S. House of Representatives.

2001   In a coordinated suicide mission, radical Islamists associated with terrorist organization al-Qaeda hijack commercial airliners and crash them into the World Trade Center in New York City and the Pentagon building in Virginia, killing nearly 3,000 people; Jonathan Franzen publishes *The Corrections*.

2003   The United States invades Iraq and topples the regime of Saddam Hussein.

2009   Barack Obama sworn in as president of the United States, the first African American ever elected to that office.

R

Ayn Rand

BORN: *1905, St. Petersburg, Russia*

DIED: *1982, New York, New York*

NATIONALITY: *American*

GENRE: *Fiction*

MAJOR WORKS:

The Fountainhead (1943)

Atlas Shrugged (1957)

Overview

Rand occupies a unique position in the history of American literature. In many ways she was a paradox: a writer of popular romances whose ideas were taken seriously, as well as a fierce individualist who attracted many followers. Politically and aesthetically, she defied the cultural currents of her times. She is chiefly remembered for her controversial novels *The Fountainhead* (1943) and *Atlas Shrugged* (1957), which promote her philosophy of "Objectivism." Her experience with communism and the collectivist political system in Russia determined her philosophy and politics.

Works in Biographical and Historical Context

A Rough Childhood in Revolutionary Russia
Born Alisa Rosenbaum in St. Petersburg, Russia, in 1905, Ayn Rand's father Fritz was a successful chemist and pharmacist, and Rand enjoyed an idyllic early childhood. She taught herself to read, and had, by age nine, decided on a career as a writer. Her heroes at that age were writers Sir Walter Scott and Victor Hugo.

The Russian Revolution in 1917 brought an end to Rand's happy years as a child. The Russian czar (emperor) had been deposed by a communist revolution that aimed to make all citizens of Russia equal. The new communist government pursued an aggressive policy of collectivization—seizing control of agriculture and indus-try. Rand's father's business was seized, and the family was plunged into poverty. Rand's firsthand experience of communism shaped her politics for life. Her family had previously lived through the privations of World War I and then struggled to adapt itself to the new communist regime. For Rand, life in Russia at that time was dreary, and the future held little hope, particularly for one who rejected the system in power. Despite her childhood dreams of writing, she chose to major in history at the University of Petrograd (the once and future St. Petersburg).

To the United States   Obtaining a passport to visit family, Rand emigrated to the United States in 1926. There, Alice Rosenbaum became Ayn Rand. (Her first name should be pronounced to sound like the -ine in *wine*; the last name she adopted from the Remington-Rand typewriter she used to write her first movie scenarios in America.) Despite her raw language skills, she soon headed for Hollywood, where she hoped to make her living. On her second day in town, she was befriended by her favorite American director, Cecil B. DeMille, who took her to watch the shooting of *The King of Kings* (1927). He gave her work first as an extra and then as a junior writer. Rand's 1929 marriage to Charles Francis "Frank" O'Connor, also an extra in *The King of Kings*, ensured that she would be allowed to stay in America. Shortly after her marriage, Rand got a job in the wardrobe department of RKO Studios. She hated the work, but it supported her financially while she improved her English and perfected her writing craft. Her progress was remarkable: she was to become one of a very few writers to attain artistic success in a language other than her native one.

Rand's first novel was written in order to keep a promise she had made to a family friend at a farewell party given for her before she left Russia. Her friend had begged her to tell Americans that Russia was a huge cemetery and that its citizens were slowly dying. In *We the Living* (1936) Rand detailed the deterioration of spirit and body under the communist system. In particular, she

Ayn Rand   *Rand, Ayn, 1962, photograph. AP Images.*

wanted to show that communism wreaks special havoc on the brightest, most creative thinkers. In her work, all three of the major characters, even the ardent communist, are destroyed. By making one of her major characters a hero of the revolution, one who had believed fervently in the cause, Rand was able to communicate basic flaws in the communist system.

Rand's primary reputation is as a novelist, but her first professional success was as a playwright. In all, Rand wrote four plays, two of which were produced on Broadway. Her best-known drama, *Night of January 16th* (1936), is significant for its ingenuity as well as for its historical sidelights. Rand developed the innovative theatrical device of using audience members at each performance to serve as the jury in this courtroom drama, and she wrote alternative endings for the cast to use in response to either the guilty or the not guilty verdict.

Anthem (1938), a novella, is Rand's shortest work. A parable-like dystopian tale, it portrays a totally collectivized world after some great war or holocaust. Originally titled "Ego," the work illustrates the negative effects on society of the suppression of individual ego and talent for the supposed good of all: When, in the name of all, no individual is allowed to stand above the others, then all stand in darkness.

Success with Fountainhead   Rand had done extensive research before she began writing her next novel, *The Fountainhead* (1943), which was originally titled "Secondhand Lives." This novel is the story of Howard Roark, a modern architect, and his fight for the preservation of his aesthetic vision. Although she worked for some time in the office of Eli Jacques Kahn, a famous New York architect, Rand's main purpose in the novel was not, as some critics have alleged, to extol the profession of architecture. Rather, the central purpose of the work, as in the ones before it, is to champion individualism versus collectivism. In *The Fountainhead* the focus

is not on the political system, as it was in *We the Living*, but on what Rand called collectivism in the soul. *The Fountainhead* is a defense of a positive rational egoism. Protagonist Howard Roark explains to Dominique Francon at one point in the book, "To say 'I love you' one must know first how to say the 'I.'" The egoism Rand defines in this novel is an integral part of the individualism she championed, just as the selfishness she describes is a virtue as opposed to the selflessness she abhorred.

Positive reviewers appreciated the powerful writing, intensity, and dramatic plot of the book. The success of *The Fountainhead* brought Rand to the attention of individuals who shared her perception of life. It also precipitated a lucrative movie deal. In 1950, Rand met a young man named Nathaniel Branden, an admirer of her work, and the two began a long personal and professional relationship that became an affair (both were married).

Objectivism Matures   In *Atlas Shrugged* (1957) Rand believed she accomplished her goal of creating the ideal man in her protagonist, John Galt. In this novel Galt and a number of followers succeed in stopping the world economy by removing themselves and their productive capacities from exploitation by forces they regard as looters and leeches. All of Rand's novels dramatize the primacy of the individual, but this is particularly evident in *Atlas Shrugged*, where the unique and precious individual human life is the standard by which good is judged. If something nourishes and sustains life, it is good; if it negates or impoverishes the individual's pursuit of happiness, it is evil. The secondary themes in Rand's fiction unfold as the logical consequence of her major theme, but it was not until *Atlas Shrugged*, the fullest explication in fiction of her philosophy, that Rand worked out all the political, economic, and metaphysical implications of that theme. Rand would label her philosophy Objectivism.

Rand was fifty-two when she published this, her last novel, but the end of her career as a fiction writer was in fact just the beginning of her career as a public philosopher, speaker, and cult figure. The publication of *For the New Intellectual: The Philosophy of Ayn Rand* (1961) was the first of a series of nonfiction books that anthologized her essays on such diverse subjects as the American public school system, Romanticism, and racism. Rand continued to refine and explore her philosophy of Objectivism in her own magazine, *The Objectivist*, published between 1966 and 1971. Branden was intimately bound up in Rand's professional ventures throughout the 1950s and 1960s, but the two ended their relationship abruptly in 1968.

Counter-countercultural Icon   During the 1960s and 1970s, many leading intellectuals in the United States—people like historian Howard Zinn, writer Susan Sontag, and poet Amiri Baraka—spoke critically of capitalism and extolled the virtues of communism. Argentine communist revolutionary leader Ernesto "Che" Guevara was a hero on college campuses, communes (communities in which property and work are shared) sprang up across the country, and even Chinese dictator Mao Zedong was seen by many American intellectuals as a liberator. Rand, on the other hand, was an unapologetic, forceful supporter of capitalism and enlightened self-interest. Rand was a proponent of unregulated capitalism, which she defined as the only social system based on the recognition of individual rights, the only system that bans force from social relationship, and the only system that fundamentally opposes war. Rand's defense of capitalism on moral grounds is unique. She based this on her view that only capitalism is consonant with man's rational nature, protective of his survival as man, and fundamentally just.

Rand possessed great charisma and an intense intellectuality that affected both admirers and detractors. Her last years were clouded by ill health (she lost a lung to cancer) and grief (her husband died in 1979). She died in March 1982.

Works in Literary Context

Rand's entire body of work is a protest against any individual submission. Her novels and stories are a defense of individual rights, of human creativity, of freedom of thought. Her defense of capitalism based on moral grounds is extremely articulate. "Capitalism," observed Rand, "has been called a system of greed—yet it is the system that raised the standard of living of its poorest citizens to heights no collectivist system has ever begun to equal."

Defense of Capitalism   In her nonfiction writings as well as in her fiction, Rand characterized the main areas of conflict in the field of human rights: individualism versus collectivism; egoism versus altruism; and reason versus mysticism. In Rand's philosophy, all of these areas are interconnected. Reason is the tool by which the individual discerns what is life-sustaining and ego-nourishing. Collectivism, altruism, and mysticism work against individual freedom, a healthy ego, and rationality. Collectively, Rand's philosophy is called Objectivism, an extreme form of individualism that has been defined by Rand as "the concept of man as a heroic being, with his own happiness as the moral purpose of his life, with productive achievement as his noblest activity, and reason as his only absolute."

Rand's championing of individual rights and minimal government is part of her appeal to the Libertarian political movement, although she herself denounced Libertarians, calling them hippies of the right and advocates of anarchism. Neither, however, would she ally herself with most conservatives because of what she called their mysticism, their staunch support of religion. Among her most persistent concerns about America was her belief that capitalism was being sold out by the very people who should be its strongest advocates. Rand felt that rather than supporting capitalism for the morality of its central vision, most capitalists defended it only on practical bases.

LITERARY AND HISTORICAL CONTEMPORARIES

Rand's famous contemporaries include:

Duke Ellington (1899–1974): Although usually classified as a jazz musician, Ellington preferred the term "American music" to describe his style. Throughout his long and influential career, Ellington was known primarily as a composer and bandleader of a handpicked orchestra that included some of the most talented musicians in the industry.

Mohandas Gandhi (1869–1948): An advocate for Indian independence from British colonial rule, Gandhi's name has become synonymous with non-violent protest and advocacy for peace; his methods inspired Martin Luther King and other civil rights activists in the 1960s.

Joseph Stalin (1878–1953): A participant in the Russian Revolution of 1917 that installed a new communist government, Stalin managed to seize outright control of the Soviet Union in 1924 following the death of that country's first leader, Vladimir Lenin. Stalin proceeded to rule with an iron fist for the next three decades, forcing his country through a series of violent modernization programs and killing millions through starvation, imprisonment, and forced migration.

George Orwell (1903–1950): The pen name of Eric Arthur Blair. Orwell wrote several pieces on the nature of totalitarianism and repression, most notably *Animal Farm* (1945) and *Nineteen Eighty-Four* (1949), which forecast a grim dystopian future where history and even language are constantly modified to fit the needs of an all-controlling government called "Big Brother."

Vladimir Nabokov (1899–1977): This Russian-born American novelist is famous for *Lolita* (1955) and *Pale Fire* (1962).

Works in Critical Context

Few authors of the twentieth century have had such a polarizing effect on critics and audiences as Rand. Her books tend to earn either violent dismissals or enthusiastic praise. "Ayn Rand is dead. So, incidentally, is the philosophy she sought to launch dead; it was in fact stillborn"— this, William F. Buckley's derogatory obituary in the *National Review*, sounded a note of wishful thinking on the part of Rand's persistent critics. But rather than quelling interest in her or her philosophy, Rand's death initiated a new era of academic interest and fueled the continued promotion of her philosophies by her followers. In the five years following her death there were as many books published about Rand as there were during all the years of her life. Her unpublished writing continues to be published posthumously; her novels continue to sell well as do some of her nonfiction works, and

BIBLIOGRAPHY

Books

"Atlas Shrugged," in *Novels for Students*. Michael LaBlanc and Ira Mark Milne, eds. Vol. 10. Detroit: Gale, 2001.

Branden, Nathaniel. *The Moral Revolution in Atlas Shrugged*. Poughkeepsie, N.Y.: Atlas Society, 2000.

Den Uyl, Douglas J. *The Fountainhead: An American Novel*. New York: Twayne, 1999.

Erickson, Peter F. *The Stance of Atlas: An Examination of the Philosophy of Ayn Rand*. Portland, Ore.: Herakles Press, 1997.

Gladstein, Mimi Reisel. *Atlas Shrugged: Manifesto of the Mind*. New York: Twayne, 2000.

————. *The New Ayn Rand Companion*. Westport, Conn.: Greenwood Press, 1999.

"The Fountainhead," in *Novels for Students*. David Galens, ed. Vol. 16. Detroit: Gale, 2002.

Periodicals

Chambers, Whittaker. "Big Sister Is Watching You." *National Review* 4 (December 28, 1957): 594–596.

Cody, John. "Ayn Rand's Promethean Heroes." *Reason* 5 (November 1973): 30–35.

Cox, Stephen. "Ayn Rand: Theory versus Creative Life." *Journal of Libertarian Studies* 8 (Winter 1986): 19–29.

————. "The Evolution of Ayn Rand." *Liberty* 11 (July 1998): 49–57.

Den Uyl, Douglas J. and Douglas Rasmussen. "Nozick on the Randian Argument." *Personalist* 59 (April 1978): 184–201.

Dwyer, William. "The Argument against 'an Objective Standard of Value.'" *Personalist* 55 (Spring 1974): 165–181.

COMMON HUMAN EXPERIENCE

Rand was not the only author to use fiction as a means to discuss and disseminate philosophical ideas. Here are some other works with similar goals:

The Plague (1947), a novel by Albert Camus. French philosopher Camus used this novel to expound his thoughts on destiny, human nature, and sociology.

The Flies (1943), a play by Jean-Paul Sartre. Sartre was, with Camus, a leading existentialist of his day. This play explores his thoughts on existentialism and religion.

Strange Case of Dr. Jekyll and Mr. Hyde (1886), a novella by Robert Louis Stevenson. In this tale of horror, Stevenson explores his own ideas about the duality of human nature and the mind long before such ideas were readily accepted into the mainstream.

further publishing ventures are planned by her literary executor, Leonard Peikoff.

Atlas Shrugged Critical outrage greeted the publication of *Atlas Shrugged*, especially from the battlements of the conservative establishment. Whittaker Chambers called it "remarkably silly," "bumptious," and "preposterous." He remarked: "Out of a lifetime of reading, I can recall no other book in which a tone of overriding arrogance was so implacably sustained. Its shrillness is without reprieve. Its dogmatism is without appeal." In the *Saturday Review*, Helen Beal Woodward, who concedes that "Ayn Rand is a writer of dazzling virtuosity," reacted negatively to the "stylized vice-and-virtue characters" and "prolixity." Woodward found *Atlas Shrugged* a book "shot through with hatred." Such critical attacks had no effect on the reading public, who have made *Atlas Shrugged* literary phenomenon: more than 5 million copies of the book have been sold since its publication.

Responses to Literature

1. How did Rand's social and political themes change between *We the Living* and *The Fountainhead*?

2. Watch the movie adaptation of *The Fountainhead*. How much of Rand's Objectivist philosophy comes through in the movie? What changes could be made to the film to make it more faithful to the book and still keep it entertaining?

3. Research the history of objectivism. Has it ever gained widespread popularity? Who are some of its most notable adherents?

4. How does Rand make use of opposite characters to contrast her opinions on domination and submission? What are those opinions?

✸ Dudley Randall

BORN: *1914, Washington, D.C.*

DIED: *2000, Southfield, Michigan*

NATIONALITY: *American*

GENRE: *Poetry*

MAJOR WORKS:

"The Ballad of Birmingham" (1965)

Poem Counterpoem (with Margaret Danner) (1966)

More to Remember (1971)

Overview

Dudley Randall was known as much for his work as an editor and publisher as for his poetry; his role was key in the publishing and popularization of contemporary African American poetry. Called Detroit's "First Poet Laureate," Randall was the founder of Broadside Press, a

Dudley Randall   *The Dudley Randall Literary Estate*

Michigan-based publishing company that helped launch the careers of many black poets, including Etheridge Knight and Haki R. Madhubuti.

Works in Biographical and Historical Context

First a Poet   Randall's interest in poetry has been lifelong. Born in Washington, D.C., the son of a minister and a teacher, he wrote his first poem when he was four years old, moved to Detroit when he was nine, and saw his poems first published in the *Detroit Free Press* when he was thirteen. A bright student, Randall graduated early. After working in Ford's River Rouge foundry for five years and serving in the army, he returned to school and earned a master's degree in library science from the University of Michigan. Randall, who became the reference librarian for Wayne County, also became fluent in Russian, visited Europe, Africa, and Soviet Russia, and later translated many Russian poems into English.

Randall's first book of poetry, *Poem Counterpoem* (1966), was perhaps the first of its kind; the volume contains ten poems each by Margaret Danner and Randall. The poems are alternated to form a kind of double commentary on the subjects they address in common.

Cities Burning (1968) focuses on the poet's urban environment and political turmoils of the 1960s. The third and more inclusive collection *More to Remember: Poems of Four Decades* (1971) displays Randall's artistic breadth in poems that address universal themes and explore "contradictions in human psychology and the black arts movement," according to R. Baxter Miller. Later collections *After the Killing* (1973), *Broadside Memories: Poets I Have Known* (1975), *A Litany of Friends: New and Selected Poems* (1981), and *Homage to Hoyt Fuller* (1984) show Randall's polished craftsmanship.

Publishing   Broadside Press—Randall's other contribution to black poetry in America—began in 1963. Randall had composed the poem "The Ballad of Birmingham" after a bomb exploded in an Alabama church, killing four children. The attack was a response to the civil rights movement, in which African Americans sought to achieve basic rights already afforded to their white counterparts. Birmingham was specifically targeted by civil rights activists—led by Martin Luther King Jr.—in an attempt to overturn unfair segregation laws through nonviolent protests. "Folk singer Jerry Moore of New York had it set to music, and I wanted to protect the rights to the poem by getting it copyrighted," the publisher recalled in *Broadside Memories: Poets I Have Known* (1975). Leaflets, he learned, could be copyrighted, so he published the poem as a broadside, a single sheet of paper that could be printed and sold for a minimal price. Randall's "Dressed All in Pink," composed after John F. Kennedy's assassination, also recorded by Moore, became number two of the Broadside series, which was to include close to one hundred titles by 1982.

Randall became a book publisher when poets at a Fisk University conference nominated him to collect and publish poems about slain civil rights leader Malcolm X. The result was *For Malcolm: Poems on the Life and Death of Malcolm X* (1967). By that time, aware that major publishers were seldom accepting works by young black poets, Randall became dedicated to publishing works by emerging black authors. Indeed, Randall's encouragement was essential to the writing careers of several black poets. Etheridge Knight, for example, was in prison when he contributed three poems to the Broadside anthology *For Malcolm*, and Randall's visits "convinced a hesitant Knight of his talent," Suzanne Dolezal reports in an article for *Detroit* magazine. Randall published first books for Knight and for Haki R. Madhubuti, two poets who now enjoy international acclaim.

With remarkable energy and commitment, Randall supported the modern black movement for self-determination. To achieve editorial freedom and flexibility, Randall declined partnerships as well as incorporations. Having devoted Broadside Press to poetry, he feared that stockholders would demand profits and lower quality or chase after profits into the realm of prose. While his income from the press went into publishing new volumes, he paid royalties to other poets. He confessed, "I

LITERARY AND HISTORICAL CONTEMPORARIES

Dudley Randall's famous contemporaries include:

Toni Morrison (1931–): A Nobel Prize–winning author known for her powerfully written books about the African American experience such as *The Song of Solomon* (1977) and *Beloved* (1987).

Henry Kissinger (1923–): Winner of the Nobel Peace Prize in 1973 for his efforts in brokering an end to the Vietnam War, Kissinger, who served as President Nixon's secretary of state, is known as the consummate diplomat, willing to do anything to achieve the best possible outcome for his cause.

Adrienne Rich (1929–): A celebrated American poet, Rich's subjects dwell most often on feminist and lesbian issues, critiquing the male-dominated world of art and politics for the last three decades.

Hunter S. Thompson (1937–2005): An inveterate individualist, Thompson defined the new genre of so-called gonzo journalism with his articles and books beginning in the 1960s, in which he, in defiance of conventional journalistic ethics, often became as much a part of the story as those he was ostensibly reporting on.

Malcolm X (1925–1965): A controversial civil rights leader in the 1960s, Malcolm X (he dropped his last name as a remnant of his ancestors' slavery) was seen by many as the antithesis of Martin Luther King—confrontational and potentially violent as opposed to King's pacifistic resistance.

am not well qualified to operate in a capitalistic society. I came of age during the Great Depression, and my attitude toward business is one of dislike and suspicion." Dedicated to ideals, he remembered well the pragmatic lessons of the Harlem Renaissance. When the Depression came in the 1930s, white publishers dropped black authors, who only a few years earlier were exotically popular. He recommended therefore that Afro-Americans "build a stable base in their own communities," and he devoted most of his professional life to providing the foundation.

Altogether, the press produced nearly sixty volumes of poetry and criticism under Randall's tenure, all showcasing black writers, who rewarded his dedication by remaining loyal to Broadside even when larger publishing houses with generous promotion budgets beckoned. Gwendolyn Brooks insisted that Randall, not Harper & Row, would publish her autobiography; Sonia Sanchez preferred Broadside to the Third World Press, the small press founded by Madhubuti. Poet Nikki Giovanni explained to Dolezal: "Broadside was neither mother nor father of the poetry movement, but it was certainly

midwife. [Dudley] . . . allowed his poets to find their own voices. That was the charm of Broadside."

As a poet and publisher, Randall helped revitalize black poetry in America. Yet by 1977, his determination to supply low-priced books to stores already in debt to him brought the small press, also deeply in debt, to the crisis point. The Alexander Crummell Memorial Center, a church in Highland Park, Michigan, bought the press, retaining Randall as its consultant. Though the poets he once encouraged found other publishers since the sale, Randall continued to be concerned for new poets and anticipated the publication of more new works after the press started publishing again, which indeed it did.

When Randall died in 2000, an obituary in the *Detroit News*, comparing him to the famous founder of seminal R&B music label Motown, described him as "the other Berry Gordy, the one who never left the west side of Detroit, never made millions and never became a glitter-sprinkled celebrity. Yet he, too, beamed black voices around the world."

Works in Literary Context

A child during the Harlem Renaissance of the 1920s, Randall became a poet of the next generation and, later, he helped to pioneer a third poetic era during the 1960s. Exploring racial and historical themes, introspective and self-critical, his work combines ideas and forms from Western traditional poetry as well as from the Harlem Renaissance movement. Often incisive humor and cryptic satire inform his work.

More to Remember: Poems of Four Decades "displays [Randall's] artistic breadth" in poems that address universal themes and explore "contradictions in human psychology and the black arts movement," observes Miller. Miller also sees "Randall's aesthetic theory" in poems that depict "the artist as a modifier of both literary tradition and classical form." Randall defined this aesthetic himself in *Negro Digest*: "Precision and accuracy are necessary for both white and black writers. . . . 'A black aesthetic' should not be an excuse for sloppy writing." Randall also warned that "what we tend to overlook is that our common humanity makes it possible to write a love poem, for instance, without a word of race, or to write a nationalistic poem that will be valid for all humanity."

The Humanity of Poetry Randall shied away from the label "pacifist," yet he was strongly antiwar; see especially the title poem of his 1973 collection *After the Killing* and the "War" section of *A Litany of Friends*. He did, however, accept the designation "humanist." He told of meeting Arna Bontemps in the 1960s at the Black Writers' Conference sponsored by the University of Wisconsin: Randall, upon asking permission to join a group seated in the cafeteria, was told by Bontemps, "Yes, Dudley, since you're the only humanist here."

Randall enlarged the humanness of poetry written in English. His democratic instincts were offended by what he called "poet snobs." In a forthright, unpublished poem about the period of his depression, he caustically contrasted some poets' affectation of slovenliness with his own genuine reluctance to care for his body when he was despairing of life itself. With ribald wit he lists the authentic "credentials of dirtiness" and defends his subsequent choice to dress well for public appearances. He felt strongly that poets should be interested in other people. "Shy and self-centered" in his early years, he gradually gained what he referred to as "negative capability" (adapting John Keats's phrase) by thinking of whatever person he meets instead of himself. Randall admired writers in whom he saw this capacity.

Works in Critical Context

The influence of Randall "has been one of the strongest—some say the strongest—in the black poetry movement of the last 15 years," observes Suzanne Dolezal. According to R. Baxter Miller, "Beyond Randall's contributions as a poet, his roles as editor and publisher have proven invaluable to the Afro-American community." Dolezal also acknowledges both his editorial work and his poetry:

> Randall provided a forum for just about every major black poet to come along during those years. And dozens of anthologies include his own rapid, emotional lyrics about Detroit's bag ladies, lonely old drunks, strapping foundry workers and young women with glistening, corn-rowed hair.

Critics regard Randall's poetry as a bridge between the works of earlier black writers and of the writers of the 1960s. "Exploring racial and historical themes, introspective and self-critical, [Randall's] work combines ideas and forms from Western traditional poetry as well as from the Harlem Renaissance movement," Miller notes. In an essay on Randall in *Black American Poets between Worlds, 1940–1960*, he elaborates: "Although attracted to the poetry of antiquity, including classical conventions, he also gives his energetic support to modern originality. ... Black American literary art has benefited from his great talent and love for fifty years."

After the Killing Reviewing *After the Killing* (1973) for *Black World*, Frank Marshall Davis declares, "Dudley Randall again offers visual proof of why he should be ranked in the front echelon of Black poets." When the poet evades "clichés and hackneyed rhymes, he excels at his craft," says Miller. Brief notices about Randall's books in library trade journals were generally complimentary, in keeping with Davis's and Miller's assessments.

Responses to Literature

1. Randall's work as both a poet and publisher has been seen as a bridge between two eras of black poetry. Research the history of poets of the Harlem Renaissance and compare it to later black poets of the 1960s and 1970s. How did the themes of the two different eras differ? What issues remained the same?

COMMON HUMAN EXPERIENCE

Through his Broadside imprint, Randall helped the careers of many important African American poets, giving them a place to publish and get their work out. Some of the classic Broadside titles include:

Poems from Prison (1968), a poetry collection by Etheridge Knight. One of the seminal early Broadside publications, Knight's first book of poetry mixes the African American tradition of the "toast" with a political agenda aimed at breaking free of oppression.

Think Black (1969), a book of poetry by Haki R. Madhubuti. Born Don L. Lee, Madhubuti is an important and respected poet and lecturer in the African American community and was one of the leading voices of the new black literature of the 1960s.

Family Pictures (1970), a poetry collection by Gwendolyn Brooks. By the time she published her poetry with Broadside, Brooks had been writing compelling, important, critically acclaimed Afro-American poetry for a quarter-century. That she chose to publish with a small imprint like Broadside is telling of the publishing house's reputation in the world of African American poetry.

From a Land Where Other People Live (1973), a book of poetry by Audre Lorde. An outspoken activist for black and lesbian causes, Lorde's poetry was as direct as her essays and monographs in decrying the oppressions, both external and internal, within the minority groups she identified with.

---

2. Randall wrote of a "black aesthetic" in poetry. What did he mean by that term? What differentiates black poetry from contemporary white poetry?

3. Why do you think Randall decided to write a poem in response to the Birmingham church bombing? Research the history of the bombing in the context of the civil rights movement, then study Randall's poem. What message does it convey? How effectively does it convey that message?

4. Randall initially used "broadsides," or cheaply printed single sheets of poetry, to get his message out. What methods could be used with today's technology to effect the same ends? Would those methods be more or less effective than Randall's broadsides?

BIBLIOGRAPHY

Books

Barksdale, Richard K., and Keneth Kinnamon. "Part VI: Since 1945." In *Black Writers of America: A*

Comprehensive Anthology, edited by Barksdale and Kinnamon. New York: Macmillan, 1972, pp. 808–809.

King, Woodie, Jr., ed. *The Forerunners: Black Poets in America*. Washington, D.C.: Howard University Press, 1981.

Thompson, Julius E. *Dudley Randall, Broadside Press, and the Black Arts Movement in Detroit, 1960–1995*. Jefferson, N.C.: McFarland, 1999.

Periodicals

Melhem, D. H. "Dudley Randall: A Humanist View." *Black American Literature Forum* 17, no. 4 (1983): 157–167.

Rowell, Charles H. "In Conversation with Dudley Randall." *Obsidian* 2, no. 1 (1976): 32–44.

Waniek, Marilyn Nelson. "Black Silence, Black Songs." *Callaloo* 6, no. 1 (1983): 156–165.

Web sites

"Etheridge Knight (1931–1991)." The Poetry Foundation Web site. Retrieved November 24, 2008, from http://www.poetryfoundation.org/archive/poet.html?id=81870.

✸ John Crowe Ransom

BORN: *1888, Pulaski, Tennessee*

DIED: *1974, Gambier, Ohio*

NATIONALITY: *American*

GENRE: *Poetry*

MAJOR WORKS:
Poems About God (1919)
Chills and Fever (1924)
Grace after Meat (1924)
Selected Poems (1945)

Overview

John Crowe Ransom was an American poet noted as much for his contributions to criticism and social theory as for his well-regarded poetry. Ransom was a leading figure in the movement of Agrarianism, which painted modern industrialized society as ultimately destructive of basic human needs and feelings. As such, his work promoted a "back to the earth" philosophy. Ransom was also key in the development of the so-called New Criticism of poetry.

John Crowe Ransom   *Truman Moore / Time Life Pictures / Getty Images*

Works in Biographical and Historical Context

John Crowe Ransom was born in Pulaski, Tennessee, on April 30, 1888. He was the son of John James (a Methodist minister) and Ella (Crowe) Ransom, a music and French teacher. His formal education began slowly due to his father's moves among churches throughout the state. He was educated at home until he was ten, at which point he entered public school in October 1898.

In June 1903, he graduated at the head of his class from the Bowen School in Nashville, and in September he entered Vanderbilt University, from which he again graduated at the head of his class in 1909. In the years following his graduation, he taught intermittently before entering Oxford University in England as a Rhodes Scholar. In 1914, he returned to his alma mater as a faculty member in Vanderbilt's English department. In 1920, he married Elizabeth Kirkland, the daughter of the chancellor at Vanderbilt, and they had three children.

Ransom and the Fugitives   Around the year 1915, a group of fifteen or so Vanderbilt University teachers and students began meeting informally to discuss trends in American life and literature. Led by Ransom, then a member of the university's English faculty, these young "Fugitives," as they called themselves, opposed both the traditional sentimentality of Southern writing and the increasingly frantic pace of life as the turbulent war years gave way to the Roaring Twenties. They recorded their concerns in a magazine of verse entitled the *Fugitive*. Though it appeared little more than a dozen times after the first issue was published in 1922, *Fugitive* proved to be the vanguard of a new literary movement—Agrarianism—and offered a new way of analyzing works of art—the New Criticism. As one of the group's major spokesmen (along with fellow members Allen Tate, Robert Penn Warren, and Donald Davidson), Ransom eventually came to be known as the dean of twentieth century American poets and critics.

The majority of Ransom's most significant work was published between 1915 and 1928, when he was part of the Fugitive Group. In 1917, Ransom went overseas to serve in the First World War, which the United States had just entered. While in France, he revised a body of poems that were then published under the title *Poems About God* (1919). The characters in those early poems mirrored Ransom's struggle against the nature of the world.

Two collections of Ransom's poetry, *Chills and Fever* and *Grace after Meat*, were published in 1924 with the helpful intervention of writers Christopher Morley and T. S. Eliot, respectively. These and other collections feature fables and narratives that explore the dual nature of man and the inevitable disappointments of life. Critics praised both of these volumes, and it was these collections that propelled Ransom as a writer on par with Eliot and Ezra Pound.

An Accomplished Poet and Lecturer   In 1937, Ransom moved from Vanderbilt's English department to Kenyon College, where he was soon promoted to Carnegie Professor of Poetry. In 1939, he founded the *Kenyon Review*, which he edited for twenty years. The most comprehensive collection of his work was the revised version of *Selected Poems*, first published in 1945, and in enlarged editions in 1963 and again in 1969. The latter volume included eighty poems.

Ransom's writing earned him many prizes and honors, including a Guggenheim Fellowship (1931), the Bollingen Prize in Poetry (1951), the Russell Loines Award for Poetry from the National Institute of Arts and Letters (1951), a Creative Arts Medal from Brandeis University (1958–1959), the National Book Award for the 1963 edition of *Selected Poems*, election to the American Academy of Arts and Letters (1966), and the Emerson-Thoreau Medal (1968). After his retirement from Kenyon College in 1958, he taught and lectured at more than two hundred colleges and universities—including Harvard, Princeton, Yale, Chicago, Rice, Vanderbilt, Duke, Florida, Iowa, and Indiana. Over the course of his career, Ransom published just under 160 poems, but his work was recognized in 1964 with the National Book Award. He died in Gambier, Ohio, about three months after his eighty-sixth birthday.

Works in Literary Context

A Southern poet and man of letters, Ransom chronicled the clash of flesh and spirit and the decline of morality in the twentieth century. He helped develop two significant movements—New Criticism, the textual analysis of poetry, and Agrarianism, which addressed the industrial age as an eroding force on artistic expression.

New Criticism   A *Times Literary Supplement* critic once concluded that Ransom "has invented an idiom that both connects him with and separates him from the situations he describes. His language implies a judgment on the people around him, a distance between present and past, speaker and story. But it also implies an ironic depreciation of the poet; for this is only his judgment." Many of these same qualities and attitudes eventually found their way into the new philosophy of criticism developed by Ransom and others in the 1930s. Using the *Kenyon Review* (founded by Ransom in 1939) as their principal forum, he and his fellow proponents of the "New Criticism" rejected the romanticists' commitment to self-expression and perfection as well as the naturalists' insistence on fact and inference from fact as the basis of evaluating a work of art.

Instead, the New Critics focused their attention on the work of art as an object in and of itself, independent of outside influences. This includes the circumstances of its composition, the reality it creates, the author's intention, and the effect it has on readers. The New Critics also tended to downplay the study of genre, plot, and character in favor of detailed textual examinations of image, symbol, and meaning. As far as they were concerned, the ultimate value of a work of art (in both a moral and an artistic sense)

LITERARY AND HISTORICAL CONTEMPORARIES

Ransom's famous contemporaries include:

Ezra Pound (1885–1972): Pound was an iconoclastic expatriate American poet called the "center" of the Modernist movement. Pound controversially became an advocate for the Fascist Italian government during World War II.

Philo Farnsworth (1906–1971): A "boy wonder" inventor, Farnsworth developed the first electronic television, as well as the first television camera, in the 1920s. In 1928, he became the first person to hold a public demonstration of television.

T. S. Eliot (1888–1965): Winner of the Nobel Prize for Literature in 1948, Eliot was a major force in poetry, theater, and literary criticism during the first half of the twentieth century. He is most famous for his poem, "The Waste Land" (1922).

Charles Lindbergh (1902–1974): Lindbergh was a world-famous American aviator. Lindbergh established himself as a national hero when he became the first person to fly solo across the Atlantic in 1927. During the 1930s, he added controversy to his adulation with his vocal endorsement of a non-interventionist position regarding Nazi Germany and Adolf Hitler.

A. A. Milne (1882–1956): Milne was a British writer. Milne's name became synonymous with children's literature when he published the stories he told his son, Christopher Robin, of a talking teddy bear named Winnie the Pooh.

was a function of its own inner qualities. In short, explains author James E. Magner, Jr., in the book *John Crowe Ransom: Critical Principles and Preoccupations*, "[Ransom] wishes the world and the poem to be perceived as what they are and not as someone would have them to be."

Agrarianism A second movement that Ransom helped develop was Agrarianism, a direct descendant of the Fugitive philosophy—the Agrarians, in fact, were former Fugitives (the original group drifted apart around 1925) who banded together again in the late 1920s to extol the virtues of the rural South and to promote the establishment of an agrarian, or agriculturally-based, economy (as opposed to an industrial one). Industrial living cut one off from nature and from its inherent honesty, said the Agrarians, leading to a withering of art, spirituality, self-reliance, and happiness. Such a life was played out "miserably in a rectilinear jungle of factories and efficiency apartments," explained John L. Stewart in his study of the poet and critic. As far as Ransom and his fellow Agrarians were concerned, it was through working closely with nature that true satisfaction could be achieved. As Louis D. Rubin, Jr. has explained in *Writers of*

the Modern South, "for Ransom the agrarian image is of the kind of life in which leisure, grace, civility can exist in harmony with thought and action, making the individual's life a wholesome, harmonious experience. ... His agrarianism is of the old Southern plantation, the gentle, mannered life of leisure and refinement without the need or inclination to pioneer."

Though the rustic dream of the Agrarians more or less evaporated with the coming of the Depression, it left its philosophical imprint on Ransom's later work. As Richard Gray observed in his book *The Literature of Memory*, "the thesis that nearly all of [Ransom's] writing sets out to prove, in one way or another, is that only in a traditional and rural society—the kind of society that is epitomized for Ransom by the antebellum South—can the human being achieve the completeness that comes from exercising the sensibility and the reason with equal ease."

Works in Critical Context

Ransom won critical praise and numerous awards, including a National Book Award for *Selected Poems* and a Guggenheim Fellowship. His celebrated students include Allen Tate and Robert Penn Warren. Louis Untermeyer, writing in *Yale Review*, hailed Ransom as "an imaginative poet, a technician of brilliance, a storyteller of power, whose flavor is as individual as that of any American writing today."

As poet Isabel Gambel MacCafrey has written, "he provided a small but accurate mirror of the modern sensibility. ... He has been celebrated rightly, as the poet of perilous equilibrium, of dichotomies and ironies, of tension and paradox." Some critics, nevertheless, think Ransom's contributions as critic, editor, and teacher were of even greater importance to modern American letters than his poetry. He was, many believe, the most original theoretical literary critic produced in America in the twentieth century.

A Lasting Body of Work Ransom's theories were not greeted with universal enthusiasm. George Core, echoing the views of those who felt Ransom's own poetry was too cool, subdued, and philosophical, cited Ransom's "neglect of the emotive dimension of the poem" as "the most serious possible deficiency in [his] theoretical formulations about poetry." Despite these and other reservations, however, most critics agreed with James E. Magner that "Ransom has given the world a redirection. ... He has made the pragmatists clear their vision again and again, and made them focus upon the poem, whose reason for existence, he thinks, is to catch up the world beautifully in the texture of its worded being."

Hyatt H. Waggoner, commenting in his *American Poets from the Puritans to the Present*, concurred with Stewart that "Ransom's poetry will outlast his critical theory. His influence has been enormous ... all out of proportion, really, to his actual accomplishments as a critic. ... [But] he will be remembered as a distinguished minor poet who, chiefly in his early youth, wrote a small number of perfectly wrought, finely textured poems that are likely to be remembered a long time." On the other hand, Robert D. Jacobs stated in the *South Atlantic Quarterly* that "John Crowe Ransom may be called a minor poet, and by some an eccentric critic, but within his special province he is unique." Core, impressed by both Ransom the poet *and* Ransom the critic, agreed that his contributions to literature should not be minimized. He concluded: "The present fame of John Crowe Ransom is very great ... this much is clear: the essential reputation is certain and will endure."

Chills and Fever Writing in *The New Republic*, Brad Leithauser claimed that Ransom "came into his own" with *Chills and Fever*. Louis Untermeyer called the book "unquestionably the best volume of poetry to be published in 1924." Richard Tillinghast, writing in *The New Criterion*, said the book placed Ransom "as a highly visible figure in the early years of literary modernism." At the time the book came out, *The New York Times Book Review* critic, commenting on the "sophisticated obliqueness" of the the poetry in *Chills and Fever*, compared Ransom to T. S. Eliot. Not all critics saw the similarity as a good thing, however. James E. Magner, also comparing Ransom's style to that of T. S. Eliot, pointed out that "neither Ransom nor Eliot is particularly logical in his critical progression. ... Both critics intimate a part of a definition, make somewhat arbitrary divisions, and then discuss what they are interested in, with a casual unpredictability."

Responses to Literature

1. Research and summarize the views of some contemporary opponents and supporters of New Criticism. What effect did the New Criticism movement have on literature and poetry? What is the status of New Criticism today?

2. Contrast Ransom's treatment of death in "Janet Waking" and "Bells for John Whiteside's Daughter." What differences do you see? What similarities? What evidence of agrarianism can you find in these poems? Support your answer using evidence from the texts.

3. Research some of the other poets and writers involved in the Agrarian movement. How did their views compare to Ransom's? How well-regarded are they today?

BIBLIOGRAPHY

Books

Magner, James E., Jr. *John Crowe Ransom: Critical Principles and Preoccupations*. The Hague, Netherlands: Mouton, 1971.

Stewart, John L. *John Crowe Ransom*. Minneapolis, Minn.: University of Minnesota Press, 1962.

Buffington, Robert. *The Equilibrist: A Study of John Crowe Ransom's Poems, 1916–1963*. Nashville, Tenn.: Vanderbilt University Press, 1967.

Knight, Karl F., *The Poetry of John Crowe Ransom: A Study of Diction, Metaphor, and Symbol*. The Hague, Netherlands: Mouton, 1964.

Trudeau. Lawrence J., ed. "John Crowe Ransom (1888–1974)." *Poetry Criticism*. Vol. 61. Detroit: Thomson Gale, 2005.

Young, Thomas Daniel, ed. *John Crowe Ransom: Critical Essays and A Bibliography*. Baton Rouge, LA: Louisiana State University Press, 1968.

Young, Thomas Daniel. *John Crowe Ransom: An Annotated Bibliography*. New York: Garland, 1982.

COMMON HUMAN EXPERIENCE

The Agrarian movement was not limited solely to Ransom. Several notable poets emerged from the movement, which helped lead to a revival of Southern literature in general. Here are some other works which explore agrarian themes:

Selected Poems (1938), a book of poetry by John Gould Fletcher, a native of Arkansas. One of the eleven poets who, along with Ransom, published the manifesto *I'll Take My Stand*, Fletcher won the Pulitzer Prize for this collection of agrarian poetry.

"The Briar Patch" (1930), a poem by Robert Penn Warren. This poem was included in *I'll Take My Stand* when it was published in 1930. The poem, in accordance with the conservative views of the other Agrarians, defends racial segregation. Warren would later renounce this position and become a vocal supporter of the civil rights movement.

"Ode To the Confederate Dead" (1928), a poem by Allen Tate. Another leading light in the Agrarian movement, Tate's poem eulogizes the "defenders of the South," a commonly held view of Confederate soldiers by conservative Southerners during the first half of the twentieth century.

The Southern Tradition at Bay (1968), a book by Richard M. Weaver. Agrarian sentiments weren't limited strictly to poetry or literature. Weaver, an intellectual historian, wrote this analysis of the suppression of Southern literary traditions after the Civil War as his doctoral thesis in 1943. It was published a year after his death.

⊛ Marjorie Kinnan Rawlings

BORN: *1896, Washington, D.C.*

DIED: *1953, St. Augustine, Florida*

NATIONALITY: *American*

GENRE: *Fiction*

MAJOR WORKS:
The Yearling (1938)

Marjorie Kinnan Rawlings   *Photograph by Carl Van Vechten.*
Reproduced by permission of the Carl Van Vechten Trust

Overview

Marjorie Kinnan Rawlings is known chiefly for a single book, *The Yearling* (1938), which has been hailed as a classic work of literature for children and adults alike and a prime example of regional fiction. The book also won the Pulitzer Prize for Fiction in 1939.

Works in Biographical and Historical Context

Finding Solace in the Country   Rawlings was born and raised in Washington, D.C., where her father worked as a patent attorney. Even as a young girl, Rawlings enjoyed writing. With the encouragement of her mother, she frequently contributed to the children's pages of local newspapers, and won her first writing contest at age eleven. The countryside also held a special fascination for the author; she spent many summers on family farms, visits which she would later recall as some of her happiest moments.

Rawlings's happy childhood ended with the death of her father in 1914; she then moved with her mother and brother to Madison, Wisconsin, where she entered college. She graduated in 1918, and the following year she married another would-be writer, Charles Rawlings, and moved with him to his hometown in New York. There the couple wrote for newspapers and tried to publish their fiction and poetry. Rawlings was unhappy with life in New York, however; in an attempt to save their marriage, she and her husband purchased an orange grove in Cross Creek, Florida, and moved there in 1928. The move failed to keep the couple together, but the Florida scrubland gave Rawlings an inner peace and a new inspiration for her writing. "We need above all, I think, a certain remoteness from urban confusion," the author explains in her book of autobiographical sketches, *Cross Creek* (1948). "For myself, the Creek satisfies a thing that had gone hungry and unfed since childhood days. I am often lonely. Who is not? But I should be lonelier in the heart of a city."

Rawlings remained in Cross Creek and managed the citrus grove herself after her husband left and her marriage ended. There she began writing a series of stories based on her new home and neighbors, impoverished whites known as "Crackers." Her "Cracker Chidlings" were published in *Scribner's* magazine and brought her to the attention of Maxwell Perkins, an editor with Scribner's publishing house. These first pieces reflected "the point of view of an outsider who finds the locals quaint and amusing," Perkins stated, but by the time Rawlings published her first novel, *South Moon Under* (1933), her "almost condescending attitude had changed to one of understanding and admiration for the enduring spirit and simple life of the Florida natives."

More Than a Book for Young Boys   Shortly after *South Moon Under* was published, Maxwell Perkins suggested that Rawlings attempt a novel in the same vein as Mark Twain's *Adventures of Huckleberry Finn* (1884). Rawlings found the idea daunting, and wrote another, less well-received novel, *Golden Apples* (1935), before she could be convinced. By 1936 Rawlings had begun the story of a poor, lonely boy who is forced to kill his pet deer after it destroys the crops his family needs to survive. Although *The Yearling* is told entirely from the point of view of young Jody, "I think it will only incidentally be a book for boys," the author indicated in a letter to her editor, as quoted by Perkins. She continued:

> I hope there will be nostalgic implications for mature people for we never *feel* more sensitively than in extreme youth, and the color and drama of the scrub can be well conveyed through the eyes and mind of a boy.

Dreams and their fulfillment played a significant part in Rawlings's life, as she disclosed in *Cross Creek*: "It is more important to live the life one wishes to live, and to go down with it if necessary, quite contentedly, than to live more profitably but less happily." Rawlings wrote just one more novel in her lifetime, 1953's *The Sojourner*, another regional tale, this one set in upstate New York. Rawlings nonetheless maintained active connections with other literary figures of note, including F. Scott Fitzgerald and Ernest Hemingway, for the rest of her life.

After successfully defending herself in a libel suit brought by a neighbor who felt she had been unfavorably depicted in *Cross Creek*, Rawlings left the area, using her earnings from the success of *The Yearling* to purchase a home in the St. Augustine area. She died there in 1953 of a brain hemorrhage.

Works in Literary Context

Christine McDonnell remembers *The Yearling* from her childhood reading as "a tear-jerker, with lots of action: hunting, fighting, natural disasters," the critic comments in *Horn Book*. She continues:

> But as an adult reader, these are not the ingredients that interest me. Instead, I was fascinated, shocked actually, by the view of life that Marjorie Kinnan Rawlings reveals in this story, a view so strong, bleak, but reassuring, that I am surprised to find it in a book that has deeply affected so many children.

Regional Literature Rawlings is a regional writer. Her work is inhabited by the simple people and natural settings of the Florida backwoods which she adopted as her home. In her first novel, *South Moon Under*, Rawlings portrays the special relationship the hunters and farmers of the Florida scrub country have to the land and to nature— a salient theme throughout this and all her work. In *The Yearling*, twelve-year-old Jody Baxter, from whose point of view the story is told, is considered one of the most endearing boy-characters since Twain's Huckleberry Finn. In the autobiographical *Cross Creek*, reminiscent of Thoreau's *Walden* in technique, Rawlings describes the flora and fauna of her beloved home, underscoring her basic belief that in order to be happy, one must find an environment in concert with one's nature.

Often paramount in Rawlings's novels is the struggle against the challenges of an uncertain existence by the poor white—the Florida "cracker"—commonly epitomized in an archetypal young protagonist with frontier virtues. These patterns are evident in her first four novels and in much of her short fiction. While Rawlings may have been eclipsed by the greater luminaries of her generation, such as Ernest Hemingway, William Faulkner, and F. Scott Fitzgerald, she made a unique contribution to the genre of frontier regional literature. Having escaped the prevailing pessimism of many post-World War I writers, she compassionately portrayed Florida's backwoods inhabitants and their relationship to the wild frontier country of north central Florida. Although Rawlings's work has been criticized for being overly sentimental and for relying too little on plot development and convincing characterization, her almost journalistic

LITERARY AND HISTORICAL CONTEMPORARIES

Marjorie Kinnan Rawlings's famous contemporaries include:

John Dos Passos (1896–1970): An American author and poet, Dos Passos was called one of the "Lost Generation" of writers, alongside Hemingway and Fitzgerald. His *U.S.A.* trilogy of novels, published between 1930 and 1936, uses a variety of experimental and unusual techniques to articulate Dos Passos's vision of American idealism and brutal reality.

Benny Goodman (1909–1986): Jazz musician and band leader, Goodman was a leading figure in the exploding popularity of "swing" jazz in the 1930s and 1940s, effectively popularizing a largely black form of music with young, mainstream white audiences.

Joe Louis (1914–1981): Nicknamed "The Brown Bomber," Louis was a heavyweight boxing champion consistently ranked as one of the greatest boxers of all time. He held his title longer than any previous champion, fighting in twenty-seven championship fights. He also served in the Army during World War II in a morale-boosting capacity, thus becoming an early ambassador for racial desegregation both in the military and in sports.

Eleanor Roosevelt (1884–1962): The wife of President Franklin D. Roosevelt, Eleanor Roosevelt was more than a simple First Lady; her ideas on economic and political policies were taken seriously by her husband. After his death, Roosevelt became a leader in the emerging civil rights and women's liberation movements.

Thomas Mann (1875–1955): German writer Mann wrote dense, highly symbolic epic novels that examined human psychology utilizing both ancient mysticism and modern philosophies.

observation of place and dialect remains as a record of a vanishing frontier and the folkways of its inhabitants.

Works in Critical Context

"In a time when it was fashionable to be negative and despairing, [Rawlings's] books were affirmative," Gordon E. Bigelow states in *Frontier Eden*. "In a time of great social and economic distress, of moral confusion and uncertainty, her stories quietly reasserted a familiar American ethic." And while the author's "legacy to children's literature essentially consists of just one book," Agnes Regan Perkins concludes, *The Yearling* is a work "that even after fifty years still lives through its strong characters, its telling metaphor, and its vivid scenes."

The Yearling Although not intended as a juvenile book, *The Yearling* has developed into a children's

COMMON HUMAN EXPERIENCE

Although she resisted the label, Rawlings is most often thought of as a regional writer, a strong literary tradition in American fiction. Here are some other regional works:

H. P. Lovecraft: Tales (2005), a short story anthology by H. P. Lovecraft. The father of modern horror literature, Lovecraft was a dyed-in-the-wool New Englander, and many of his weird tales are set in an invented university and town in Massachusetts—Miskatonic and Arkham, respectively.

The Adventures of Tom Sawyer (1876), a novel by Mark Twain. Born in Missouri to a Tennessean father, Twain was strongly rooted in the American South, and many of his most famous stories, such as this novel of a young boy's antics in a fictional Mississippi town before the Civil War, were portraits of Southern life.

East of Eden (1952), a novel by John Steinbeck. Many of Steinbeck's earlier stories were set in his native Salinas Valley, California, and the same is true of this epic novel of the interplay between two Salinas families over the course of several generations centered on the turn of the twentieth century.

favorite, according to Agnes Regan Perkins in *Writers for Children*, "not only because of its touching story ... but also because of its strong characterization of the independent Florida [people known as] 'Crackers' and its vivid evocation of the wild beauty of the Florida scrub country." While Jody's adventures and his friendship with the fawn make the novel attractive to children, Rawlings's story contains deeper elements which appeal equally to adults.

Lloyd Morris elaborates in the *North American Review*:

[Rawlings] plunges us deeply into the hearts and the perceptions of a child, a wise man, and a brave woman. It recreates for us those funda-mental attitudes of the human spirit which make life endurable, and those inalienable experiences of love and beauty which enable us to live it without shame.

By the time Jody must sacrifice his pet, he has learned to accept the pain and responsibility that accompany adulthood. As a result, William Soskin notes in the *New York Herald Tribune Book Review*, *The Yearling* "is an education in life that is far removed from our dreary urban formulas. ... [This] story of a boy and an animal becomes one of the most exquisite I have ever read."

Responses to Literature

1. Despite its deep and mature themes, *The Yearling* has come to be known primarily as a children's book. Why do you think this is? What changes could be made to the story to make its appeal stronger to a more mature readership?

2. How do you feel about the death of Flag in *The Yearling*? Do you think the situation could have been handled differently? Why or why not?

3. Research the etymology, or word history, of the term "cracker" as a cultural designation. What theories are there on the word's origin? Has it always been a derogatory phrase? Explain how you think the meaning of the word might have changed over time.

4. Are there any regional writers associated with the area you live in? If so, what distinguishing features of the region do they highlight? If not, how would you write about your home region?

BIBLIOGRAPHY

Books

Bellman, Samuel I. *Marjorie Kinnan Rawlings*. New York: Twayne, 1974.

Bigelow, Gordon E. *Frontier Eden: The Literary Career of Marjorie Kinnan Rawlings*. Gainesville, Fla.: University of Florida Press, 1966.

———. *Frontier Eden: The Literary Career of Marjorie Kinnan Rawlings*. Gainesville, Fla.: University of Florida Press, 1966.

Bigham, Julia Scribner. Introduction to *The Marjorie Rawlings Reader*. New York: Scribners, 1956, pp. ix–xix.

Bingham, Jane M., ed. *Writers for Children*. New York City: Scribner, 1988, pp. 463–67.

Parker, Idella with Mary Keating. "Marjorie Rawlings' 'Perfect Maid.'" Gainesville, Fla.: University Press of Florida, 1992.

Silverthorne, Elizabeth. *Marjorie Kinnan Rawlings: Sojourner at Cross Creek*. Woodstock, N.Y.: Overlook, 1988.

Tarr, Rodger L. *Marjorie Kinnan Rawlings: A Descriptive Bibliography*. Pittsburgh, Pa.: University of Pittsburgh Press, 1996.

Periodicals

Bellman, Samuel I. "Marjorie Kinnan Rawlings: A Solitary Sojourner in the Florida Backwoods." *Kansas Quarterly* 2 (Spring 1970): 78–87.

———. "Writing Literature for Young People: Marjorie Kinnan Rawlings' 'Secret River' of the Imagination." *Costerus: Essays in English and American Language and Literature* 9 (1973): 19–27.

Bigelow, Gordon E. "Marjorie Kinnan Rawlings' Wilderness." *Sewanee Review* 73 (Spring 1965): 299–310.

⊛ Ishmael Reed

BORN: *1938, Chattanooga, Tennessee*

NATIONALITY: *American*

GENRE: *Fiction, poetry*

MAJOR WORKS:

Yellow Back Radio Broke-Down (1969)

Conjure: Selected Poems, 1963-1970 (1972)

Flight to Canada (1976)

Overview

A highly original satirist and writer of experimental fiction, Ishamel Reed is best known for novels that assail aspects of Western religion, politics, and technology. Reed is known as much for his criticism of mainstream society as of African-American society, which has led to harsh reactions against him from other black American writers.

Works in Biographical and Historical Context

Early Years in New York Ishmael Scott Reed was born in Chattanooga, Tennessee, on February 22, 1938.

Ishmael Reed   *Reed, Ishmael, photograph. AP Images.*

He moved with his mother to Buffalo, New York in 1942. He lived there for twenty years, during which time he attended night school at the State University of New York at Buffalo. While in night school, Reed wrote a short story called "Something Pure," in which Jesus returns as an advertising agent with a unique sales strategy that causes him to be ridiculed and scorned. The story attracted the attention of an English professor who subsequently helped Reed become a full-time student at the university. However, Reed eventually left SUNY-Buffalo in 1960 because of financial problems. He briefly worked for a local newspaper and then left Buffalo.

Reed moved east to New York City, where he began writing "visionary poetry"—a loosely-defined type of poetry that focuses on metaphysical and spiritual imagery—and became affiliated with the Umbra Workshop, a group of artists and intellectuals associated with the growing Black Power movement, part of the civil rights movement of the mid-1960s. Reed also founded the *East Village Other*, a popular underground newspaper. According to Henry Louis Gates Jr., "Reed's New York period was crucial in his evolution as an artist." Between 1965 and 1966, Reed wrote his first novel, *The Freelance Pallbearers* (1967), a parody of the confessional style that has characterized much black fiction since the slave narratives of the eighteenth century. The book was warmly received by critics upon its publication.

In his next work, *Yellow Back Radio Broke-Down*, Reed introduced his Neo-HooDoo concept. As Reed explained in *Conjure* (1972), "Neo-HooDoo believes that every man is an artist and every artist a priest." Reed saw Neo-HooDoo as an artistic movement that embraced "all styles and moods." The concepts of time and syncretism emerge as central to *Yellow Back Radio Broke-Down* and Reed's vision of Neo Hoo-Doo. The title essentially means that the racial and political difficulties of an Old West town called Yellow Back Radio are explained, or "broke[n] down," for the reader. A spoof of Western pulp fiction, *Yellow Back Radio Broke-Down* is about the forces of intuition and irrationality, represented here by the Loop Garoo Kid, the Neo-HooDoo hero, in conflict with those of rationalism and science, as embodied by Drag Gibson.

A Love of Parody and Satire Reed extended his Neo-HooDoo philosophy in *Mumbo Jumbo* (1972) and *The Last Days of Louisiana Red* (1974). Both novels are parodies of the mystery genre in which a detective, Papa LaBas (who represents the voodoo deity Legba), attempts through voodoo to combat spells cast by the white establishment, which seeks to anesthetize the artistic and political black communities. A subplot in *The Last Days of Louisiana Red* involves a black radical feminist group called the Moochers, who conspire with white males to subdue black men. This theme is prevalent throughout Reed's work and has prompted feminists to criticize him harshly. *The Last Days of Louisiana Red* also perceived as a conspiracy between white male publishers and black female writers to subjugate black men by incorporating negative depictions of them into their work. In 1989, Reed published a sequel to *The Terrible Twos*. In *The Terrible Threes*, he speculated on the future and presented a nation that descends into chaos after the neo-Nazi president of the United States discloses a White House plot to expel all minorities as well as poor and homeless people and to institute a fundamentalist Christian state.

In addition to his novels, Reed has also written many essays and nonfiction pieces about contemporary American society and politics. Thirty-five of these essays, written between 1978 and 1993, were collected and published as *Airing Dirty Laundry* (1993). Among Reed's subjects are how blacks are, in Reed's opinion, negatively depicted in the mass media; his thoughts on attacks on multicultural education in schools; and how contemporary black intellectuals—among them Toni Cade Bambara and Langston Hughes—have had a significant impact on white America, even though most whites have not heard of them.

Reed has also written several volumes of poetry. In such collections as *Conjure: Selected Poems, 1963-1970*, *Chattanooga: Poems* (1973), and *New and Collected Poetry* (1988), he combined black street slang with elements of mythology, voodoo, and pop culture. In addition to writing, Reed promotes young writers through his "Before Columbus" coalition, an "anti-Nazi"—the term is Reed's, presumably referring to his leftist politics—venture that publishes unknown writers of all ethnicities. Yet, despite his poetry and activism, it is his fiction that has attracted the most critical attention, and that attention has often been negative.

A Lightning Rod for Controversy   It can be safely stated that Reed's writings have provoked controversy over the entire course of his career. He has been the target of attacks from both liberals and conservatives, from fellow black writers, from feminists who have accused him of misogyny—hatred of women—and certain literary critics who find his style and subject matter too cynical. What some find distasteful, however, others find merit in, and Reed has garnered much support along with the criticism. Reed continues to receive invitations to give lectures and contribute to magazine columns or articles. He has been nominated for the Pulitzer Prize and the National Book Award and has received multiple NEA grants and a Guggenheim fellowship. Reed recently retired from his teaching position at the University of California, Berkeley and is currently focusing on a series of collaborations with jazz musicians.

Works in Literary Context

Reed's writing is distinguished by dynamic, playful language. For example, he prefers phonetic spellings, uses capitalization for emphasis, and substitutes numbers for words in the text. Although he writes about injustices brought about by Western civilization, he is primarily

drew criticism from advocates of the Black Aesthetic, a movement that had arisen from the political culture of Black Nationalism in the 1960s and that viewed black artists as activists for their ethnicity. Objecting to Reed's satire of black cultural nationalists in the novel, Houston A. Baker wrote: "Concerned primarily with his own survival, [Reed] turns on the culture and destroys it with satire."

His next novel, *Flight to Canada*, continued to use parody and satire to explore themes of race, politics, and American society. In it, Reed lampoons the slave narrative and, particularly, Harriet Beecher Stowe's novel *Uncle Tom's Cabin* (1852). Reed has continued to satirize in subsequent novels, occasionally analyzing the American political and economic systems. In *The Terrible Twos* (1982), Reed distorts Charles Dickens's *A Christmas Carol* into a dark satire on racism and greed during the Ronald Reagan-led 1980s, equating the selfishness and destructive tendencies of the United States with those traditionally displayed by two-year-old children.

Reed continued to play with these themes in his next novel, *Reckless Eyeballing* (1986), a caustic satire of literary politics. Through his writing, Reed criticized what he concerned with establishing an alternative black aesthetic, which he terms Neo-HooDooism. This concept is a combination of aspects of voodoo and other cultural traditions that Reed hopes will forge a multicultural aesthetic to purge African-Americans and Third World peoples of Western influence. Although his works and the Neo-HooDoo Aesthetic have offended some groups and provoked the ire of critics Houston A. Baker, Jr., Addison Gayle, Jr., and Amiri Baraka, Reed is widely regarded as a revolutionary force in American writing. Despite adverse reactions to his works, Reed is committed to satirizing American society—specifically its supposed cultural arrogance and subsequent neglect of those who are not "vital people," or members of the dominant culture or moneyed class.

The worlds of Reed's novels reflect a vaudeville and picaresque universe where folk traditions inform the language and philosophy, where chronology can be altered to prove argumentative points, where the absurd becomes routinely possible, all to reinterpret and analyze the nature of social structure and our cultural manifestations of evil. The achievement that the work brings in sequences of fantastic situations, cartoon events, and biting parody is a coherent investigation of historic motivations, pointing the reader toward a more humane analysis of our cultural journey. Reed's versatility as a writer allows him to work in many formal genres. The vision is consistent enough that genre becomes liberating more than limiting; while a reader may predict a new Reed work to be inventive, fun, and bordering on the fantastic, the nature and quality of the invention will always be new. His influence may come close to that of Kurt Vonnegut, Jr.—with every bit as idiosyncratic an attitude as his contemporary fantasist.

All of these elements—satire and parody, inventive fantasy, constant reinvention—are derived from Reed's Neo-HooDoo philosophy, which a bears a closer analysis. First, some definitions are in order. Hoodoo is the name for a type of African-American folk magic. Closely related to yet distinctly separated from the more familiar practice of Voodoo, both practices share a common ancestry dating back to the days of slavery. West African religious beliefs, outlawed by white slave owners, where folded into the approved Christian religion that all slaves were required to practice. This blending of two separate and seemingly incompatible belief systems is known as syncretism and has become a hallmark of Hoodoo and Voodoo practices ever since.

The Neo-HooDoo Concept

In his second novel, *Yellow Back Radio Broke-Down*, Reed begins to use at length Hoodoofolklore as a basis for his work. Underlying all of the components of Hoodoo, according to scholars, are two central ideas: that of syncretism and the Hoodoo concept of time. Even before the exportation of slaves to the Caribbean, Hoodoo was a syncretic religion, absorbing all that it considered useful from other West

African religious practices. In the hostile environment of slave-owning America, Hoodoo survived because of its syncretic flexibility—its ability to take even supposedly negative influences and make them into something that helps the believer.

Reed turns this concept of syncretism into a literary method that combines aspects of "standard" English with less "standard" language—the language of the streets, and of "disposable" culture, such as popular music and television. By mixing language from different sources in popular culture, Reed can create the illusion of real speech, since very few people speak "proper" English in their everyday lives. In *Black American Literature Forum*, Michel Fabre draws a connection between Reed's use of language and his vision of the world, suggesting that "his so-called nonsense words raise disturbing questions ... about the very nature of language." Reed emphasizes "the dangerous interchangeability of words and of the questionable identity of things and people" in other words, the flexible syncretism Reed's philosophy brings to the English language reflects the transitory nature of language.

Reed applied his Neo-HooDoo philosophy to his poetry as well. In *Conjure*, "Neo-Hoodoo Manifesto" defines all that Hoodoo is and thus sheds light on the ways Reed uses its principles in writing, primarily through his absorption of material from every available source and his willingness to reevaluate and reinterpret that material in the best tradition of syncretism.

Works in Critical Context

Reed's novels "are meant to provoke," writes *New York Times* contributor Darryl Pinckney. Of Reed's role as an innovative force in American literature, Derek Walcott noted: "He alters our notion of what is possible. His importance to our use and understanding of language will not be obvious for many years."

Reed's poetry has been largely ignored by critics in favor of his fiction. Caroline G. Bokinsky has noted that Reed's poems "echo the musical and rhythmical quality of the black dialect," but added that "Although the poems attain lyrical excellence, Reed's anger permeates the poetry."

Critics are rarely satisfied with Reed's Neo-HooDooism. Darryl Pinckney contended: "Reed's 'Neo-HooDooism' is so esoteric that it is difficult to say what he intends by it, whether it is meant to be taken as a system of belief ... or, as he has also suggested, as ... a method of composition." Feminists have attacked his harsh portrayals of women and objected to his allegations that there is a conspiracy between white men and black women to oppress black men. Reed's satire of black characters has drawn criticism from architects of the Black Aesthetic: critics have accused the author of needlessly attacking a noble cause by lampooning figures in the Black Power and Black Arts movements. Furthermore, commentators have called Reed's works "crazy," "cute," and "living proof that the bacteria of the pop culture has entered the literary world." Reed responded to such reactions in the introduction to his 1978 essay collection, *Shrovetide in Old New Orleans*:

> Many people have called my fiction muddled, crazy, incoherent, because I've attempted in fiction the techniques and forms painters, dancers, film makers, musicians in the West have taken for granted for at least fifty years, and the artists of many other cultures, for thousands of years. Maybe I should hang my fiction in a gallery, or play it on the piano.

The Terrible Threes Reactions to Reed's later works, such as *The Terrible Threes*, were typically mixed. Even the positive reviews tended to note that this particular work did not live up to Reed's past standards. Several critics warn that readers will find *The Terrible Threes* near-incomprehensible without first reading *The Terrible Twos*. Further, *New York Times Book Review* critic Gerald Early observes, "The major problem with *The Terrible Threes* is that it seems to vaporize even as you read it; the very telling artifices that held together Mr. Reed's novelistic art in previous works, that cunning combination of boundless energy and shrewdly husbanded ingenuity, are missing here. ... I like *The Terrible Threes*, but it seems more a work for Reed fans among whom I count myself."

Los Angeles Times Book Review contributor Jacob Epstein finds that "Reed's vision of the future (and our present and past) is original and subversive." John O'Brien, writing in *Washington Post Book World*, says, "Reed's eerie, weird, implausible world has a way of sounding all too real, too much like what we hear on the evening news." O'Brien concludes, "Reed has an unnerving sense of what will show up next on our televisions. He is without doubt our finest satirist since Twain."

Conjure *Conjure* is perhaps the best known of Reed's poetry collections, which in and of themselves have not received as much critical attention as his fiction. Critical response to the volume is emblamatic of the general feeling towards Reed's poetry—mixed at best. Caroline G. Bokinsky observed that the collection "contains ... poems that echo the musical and rhythmical quality of the black dialect," but added that "Although the poems attain lyrical excellence, Reed's anger permeates the poetry." In his *Modern Poetry* review, Neil Schmitz says that Reed's writing is "essentially newfangled American tall-talk." Reed concludes that "in *how* it is written ... Neo-HooDoo is not art ... but rather an episode an episode in a continuous anti-literary literary movement in American literature."

Responses to Literature

1. Research the political climate of the 1980s in America, then analyze the political satire in *The Terrible Twos*. How much has changed in American politics since the book was published?

2. Can you point out any examples of syncretism in Reed's poetry or fiction?

3. How does Reed use farce and irony to explore gender roles in *Reckless Eyeballing*?

4. Reed has been attacked by feminists, black artists, and literary critics, among others. Choose a particular criticism of Reed's work and write two arguments, one defending Reed from his critics, the other supporting the criticism.

BIBLIOGRAPHY

Books

"Beware: Do Not Read This Poem," in *Poetry for Students*, edited by Mary Ruby. Vol. 6. Detroit: Thomson Gale, 1999.

Martin, Reginald. *Ishmael Reed and the New Black Aesthetic Critics*, London: Macmillan, 1987.

Settle, Elizabeth A., and Thomas A. Settle. *Ishmael Reed: A Primary and Secondary Bibliography*. Boston, Mass.: G. K. Hall, 1982.

Dick, Bruce, and Amritjit Singh, eds. *Conversations with Ishmael Reed*. Jackson, Miss. University Press of Mississippi, 1995.

"Ishmael Reed (1938-)," in *Poetry Criticism*, edited by
Michelle Lee. Vol. 68. Detroit: Thomson Gale,
2006.

Periodicals

Black American Literature Forum, Volume 12, 1978;
spring, 1979; spring, 1980; fall, 1984.
Los Angeles Times Book Review, April 20, 1986; June 4,
1989; April 14, 1991, p. 10.
New York Times Book Review, August 6, 1972;
November 10, 1974; September 19, 1976; July 18,
1982; March 23, 1986; May 7, 1989; April 7, 1991,
p. 32; February 13, 1994, p. 28.

Web sites

Martin, Reginald. *An Interview with Ishmael Reed*.
Retrieved December 3, 2007, from http://
www.centerforbookculture.org/interviews/
interview_reed.html.

✱ Anne Rice

BORN: *1941, New Orleans, Louisiana*

NATIONALITY: *American*

GENRE: *Fiction*

MAJOR WORKS:

Interview with the Vampire (1976)

The Vampire Lestat (1985)

Overview

Anne Rice is best known as the author of the "Vampire
Chronicles," a series of novels depicting the lives of
modern-day vampires, as told from the perspectives of
the monsters themselves. Despite mixed critical opinion,
her tales of modern gothic horror have long enjoyed a
massive popular following. After writing about soulless
undead for over a quarter-century, Rice began expressing
her recent religious reawakening through a series of
books about the life of Jesus Christ.

Works in Biographical and Historical Context

A Tragedy Motivates Horror Writing Rice was
born in New Orleans, Louisiana, on October 4, 1941.
She was originally named Howard Allen O'Brien (her
father's first name was Howard and her mother's maiden
name was Allen), but she disliked this name from an early
age, and it was legally changed when she was seven
years old. Rice's father was a postal worker who enjoyed
sculpting and writing. Rice lost her mother, an alcoholic,
when she was fourteen, and the family moved to Texas.
Throughout her childhood, Rice attended a Catholic
church, but she abandoned the faith when she was eighteen because she felt it was too repressive.

Anne Rice *Rice, Anne, photograph. AP Images.*

She married her high-school sweetheart, the poet
Stan Rice, when she was twenty, and the couple moved
to San Francisco, where she earned a degree in political
science from San Francisco State University. San Francisco
in the 1960s was the epicenter of a countercultural movement that valued nonconformity and encouraged free
experimentation with sex and illegal drugs. Rice, however,
did not consider herself part of this movement. She held a
variety of jobs, including cook, waitress, and insurance
claims adjuster. She gave birth to a daughter and wrote
sporadically during these years; but when her daughter
died of leukemia at the age of five, Rice channeled her
grief into her first vampire novel, *Interview with the Vampire* (1976), which she completed in only six weeks.

The book was deemed a success, but Rice's depression
was severe enough to cause her to drink heavily. Though
she continued to write, and even completed *The Feast of All
Saints* (1980), which focused on the lives of mixed-race
people living in New Orleans in the 1840s, she was barely
productive until her son was born. Finally overcoming her
alcohol problem, Rice wrote more vampire novels, as well
as several volumes of erotica, and a new series involving a
sect of witches in New Orleans. The success of *Interview
with a Vampire* spurred more vampire books based on
secondary characters in her original book; these include
The Vampire Lestat (1985), *Queen of the Damned* (1988),
Tale of the Body Thief (1992), and *Memnoch the Devil*
(1995). Rice moved back to New Orleans in 1989.

LITERARY AND HISTORICAL CONTEMPORARIES

Rice's famous contemporaries include:

Clive Barker (1952–): Second only to Stephen King in popularity among modern horror writers, Barker is known for his phantasmagorical, nightmarish novels and movies, particularly the *Hellraiser* series. Recently he has turned his attention to writing books in the fantasy genre aimed at young adults.

Seamus Heaney (1939–): A Nobel Prize-winning poet and writer, Heaney most often dwells on his own Irish background and the issues of modern Ireland, particularly in his native Northern Ireland, a land of long-standing conflict between British and Irish, Protestants and Catholics.

Stevie Wonder (1950–): A musical child prodigy billed as "Little Stevie Wonder," and blind from birth, Wonder grew up to become one of the most successful pop composers and performers of the late twentieth century, recording over thirty top ten hits.

Tom Cruise (1962–): An American actor whose film credits include *The Outsiders* (1983), *War of the Worlds* (2005), and the film adaptation of *Interview with the Vampire* (1994).

Christopher Lee (1922–): This eminent British actor is best known for playing Count Dracula in a series of films in the 1950s and 1960s.

Return to Catholicism and Avoiding Katrina
Rice fled from the Catholic Church as a young adult and explained to *New York Times Magazine*'s Susan Ferraro: "It struck me as really evil—the idea you could go to hell for French-kissing someone. ... I didn't believe God existed. I didn't believe Jesus Christ was the Son. ... I didn't believe heaven existed either." Creating an ethical code to replace this lost religious code, Rice suggested that "even if we live in a godless world, we can search for love and maintain it and believe it." Emphasizing the importance of ethics, she added that "we can found a code of morality on ethics rather than outmoded religious concepts. We can base our sexual mores on ethics rather than on religious beliefs."

After years as an atheist, however, she experienced a religious reawakening in 1998. She writes about her return to religion, and the death of her spouse in 2002, in her autobiography, *Called Out of Darkness* (2008). After the death of her husband, Rice decided to leave New Orleans and move to California. She completed her move prior to the arrival of Hurricane Katrina in August of 2005, which destroyed a large part of New Orleans and scattered its residents. Though Rice announced no plan to return, she was vocal in support of relief for her longtime home.

Although she published one last installment of the "Vampire Chronicles" after her religious reawakening, it soon became clear to Rice that she had to leave behind the dark personas that populated those books. She stated, "This character [Lestat] who had been my dark search engine for twenty-seven years would never speak in the old framework again." Rice then turned her creative efforts towards a trilogy of books about the life of Jesus Christ. The first installment, *Christ the Lord: Out of Egypt*, was published in 2005, with the second volume following in 2008. Rice has vacillated on whether she will return to her vampire books for one final story, which would purportedly focus on religious redemption.

Works in Literary Context

In her fiction Rice depicts horrific events through an ornate prose style and a painstaking attention to detail. She blends accurate historical elements with such themes as alienation and the individual's search for identity. Each of her novels centers on characters from an isolated segment of a real or imagined society.

Gothic Horror Rice single-handedly revived the gothic vampire novel, in the process added a new chapter to a literary tradition that stretches back over two hundred years. Gothic writing had its start with the publication of Horace Walpole's *Castle of Otranto* in 1764. The book was a popular sensation, and over the next half-century the traditions of the gothic novel—crumbling medieval ruins, corruption in the heart of the church, melodramatic heroes and virginal heroines, and a darkly passionate atmosphere—had been firmly established, to the point that Jane Austen parodied them in her *Northanger Abbey* (1818).

Gothic literature was originally closely associated with the Romantic movement of the eighteenth and nineteenth centuries. Romantics looked to times past for inspiration, and gothic writers were particularly inspired by the crumbling ruins of medieval monasteries and castles. They extrapolated such visual inspiration to spin yarns of corruption and once-grand institutions crumbling into decrepitude. It was from this literary tradition that gothic horror emerged; the two prototypical stories—Mary Shelley's *Frankenstein* (1818) and John Polidori's *The Vampyre* (1819)—were both conceived on the same night, when several of Europe's leading Romantic authors passed the evening telling each other ghost stories.

Polidori's *The Vampyre* was the first tale to recast the ancient myth of the bloodsucking corpse as a more mysterious and romantic figure. Unlike earlier folkloric traditions, Polidori's monster was an aristocratic figure who moved among—and fed off of—high society. His vampire, Lord Ruthven, was closely associated with Lord Byron, a leading Romantic figure, to the extent that Byron was often falsely attributed as the author of Polidori's story. *The Vampyre* touched off a craze for vampire stories, plays, and operas that culminated with Bram Stoker's *Dracula* (1897).

Even as the vampire became an icon of the silver screen in the twentieth century, vampire-themed literature largely disappeared. All that changed with Rice's publication of *Interview with the Vampire* in 1976. Rice took the gothic traditions of nineteenth-century and shifted the focus from human victim to monster, thereby adding an additional layer of pathos and melodrama. Her success inspired a slew of imitators, and virtually created a new subgenre, that of paranormal romance.

Works in Critical Context

"Anne Rice, a novelist so prolific she needs two pseudonyms—Anne Rampling and A. N. Roquelaure—to distinguish the disparate voices in her books, has won both critical acclaim and a readership of cult proportions," writes Bob Summer in *Publishers Weekly*. Rice's exotic subject matter, brooding sensibility, and baroque prose style prompted Michiko Kakutani to note: "Anne Rice has what might best be described as a Gothic imagination crossed with a campy taste for the decadent and the bizarre." Critics have compared Rice's "Vampire Chronicles" favorably with Mary Shelley's *Frankenstein*, and several have commented on her ability to use language to convey different moods. Many reviewers have said that the popularity of Rice's books lies not only in her skill as a storyteller, but with the lurid fascination readers have with such creatures as vampires, mummies, and witches.

Interview with the Vampire When *Interview with the Vampire* was published in 1976, critics were intrigued by Rice's unusual treatment of vampires: "Rice brings a fresh and powerful imagination to the staples of vampire lore; she makes well-worn coffins and crucifixes tell new tales that compose a chillingly original myth," observes Nina Auerbach in the *New York Times Book Review*. "Because Rice identifies with the vampire instead of the victim (reversing the usual focus), the horror for the reader springs from the realization of the monster within the self," writes Susan Ferraro in *New York Times Magazine*. "Moreover, Rice's vampires are loquacious philosophers who spend much of eternity debating the nature of good and evil. ... They are lonely, prisoners of circumstance, compulsive sinners, full of self-loathing and doubt. They are, in short, Everyman Eternal." Presented with flawless, alabaster skin, colorful glinting eyes, and hair that shimmers and seems to take on a life of its own, Rice's vampires are described by H. J. Kirchhoff in a *Toronto Globe and Mail* review as "romantic figures, super-humanly strong and fast, brilliant and subtle of thought and flamboyant of manner."

Walter Kendrick praises the scope of *Interview with the Vampire* in the *Voice Literary Supplement*, stating that "it would have been a notable tour de force even if its characters had been human." Kendrick also suggests that

---

COMMON HUMAN EXPERIENCE

Rice is one of several authors who have written about vampires. Here are some other vampire works:

I Am Legend (1954), a novel by Richard Matheson. A landmark in the development of the modern vampire, and credited by some as the first modern "zombie" story, Matheson's science-fiction/horror novel imagined the world's population transformed into vampires, and the struggle of the last unaltered man on Earth. Although Matheson's vampires had the traditional vulnerabilities and powers, their origin was thoroughly grounded in science.

Carmilla (1872), a novella by Sheridan Le Fanu. The first female literary vampire, *Carmilla* was quite sensational in its day due to its heavily lesbian undertones.

Dracula (1897), a novel by Bram Stoker. Irish author Stoker wove together threads of traditional mythology, gothic vampire stories of the preceding decades, and Eastern European history to create the most famous of all vampire stories.

Twilight (2005), a novel by Stephenie Meyer. This is the first in a popular series of vampire-romance novels featuring star-crossed lovers Isabella Swan, a mortal, and Edward Cullen, a vampire. A highly successful film adaptation was released in 2008.

"Rice's most effective accomplishment, though, was to link up sex and fear again." Conroy maintains that "not since Mary Shelley's *Frankenstein* and Louisa May Alcott's penny dreadful novelettes has a woman written so strongly about death and sex." Similarly, in a *New York Times Book Review* article, Leo Braudy observes that "Rice exploits all the sexual elements in [vampire myths] with a firm self-consciousness of their meaning."

Responses to Literature

1. How would you characterize Rice's shift from vampire novels to religious novels? Are the two completely distinct literary phases, or can you draw connections or parallels between them?

2. Rice has said the vampires are the perfect metaphor for the lost soul. Do you agree with this assessment? What other metaphorical roles do vampires fulfill?

3. Write a short piece in which you tell the story from the point of view of a mythical monster like a vampire. What issues would your monster have to grapple with? How does your world view change when you see things through a monster's eyes?

4. Vampires both repel and attract those who read about them. Why do you think this is? Are people, in your opinion, more frightened or fascinated by vampires?

BIBLIOGRAPHY

Books

Beahm, George, ed. *The Unauthorized Anne Rice Companion.* Kansas City, Mo.: Andrews & McMeel, 1996.

Dickinson, Joy. *Haunted City: An Unauthorized Guide to the Magical, Magnificent New Orleans of Anne Rice.* Secaucus, N.J.: Carol Publishing Group, 1998.

Hoppenstand, Gary and Ray B. Browne, eds. *The Gothic World of Anne Rice.* Bowling Green, Ohio: Bowling Green State University Popular Press, 1996.

Keller, James R. *Anne Rice and Sexual Politics: The Early Novels.* Jefferson, N.C.: McFarland, 2000.

Ramsland, Katherine M. *Prism of the Night: A Biography of Anne Rice.* New York: Dutton, 1991.

———. *The Vampire Companion: The Official Guide to Anne Rice's The Vampire Chronicles.* New York: Ballantine, 1993.

———. *The Witches' Companion: The Official Guide to Anne Rice's Lives of the Mayfair Witches.* New York: Ballantine, 1994.

Riley, Michael. *Conversations with Anne Rice.* New York: Ballantine Books, 1996.

Smith, Jennifer. *Anne Rice: A Critical Companion.* Westport, Conn.: Greenwood Press, 1996.

Roberts, Bette B. *Anne Rice.* New York: Twayne, 1994.

Smith, Jennifer. *Anne Rice: A Critical Companion, Critical Companions to Popular Contemporary Writers.* Westport, Conn.: Greenwood Press, 1996.

Web sites

Van Biema, David. *Anne Rice's Spiritual Confession.* Originally published October 8, 2008. Retrieved November 8, 2008, from http://www.time.com/time/arts/article/0,8599,1848149,00.html.

◉ Adrienne Rich

BORN: *1929, Baltimore, Maryland*

NATIONALITY: *American*

GENRE: *Poetry*

MAJOR WORKS:

A Change of World (1951)

Snapshots of a Daughter-in-Law: Poems, 1954–1962 (1963)

Diving into the Wreck: Poems, 1971–1972 (1973)

Adrienne Rich   *Rich, Adrienne, 1986, photograph. AP Images.*

Overview

Adrienne Rich is praised for lyrical and highly crafted poems in which she explores a variety of socially relevant subjects, including feminism and lesbianism, and criticizes patriarchal societies where women traditionally assume secondary status to men. An early proponent of societal changes that reflect the values and goals of women, Rich is credited with articulating one of the strongest poetic statements of the modern feminist movement.

Works in Biographical and Historical Context

Poetic Frustration Rich was born in Baltimore, Maryland, to Dr. Arnold Rich, a respected pathologist and professor at Johns Hopkins University Medical School, and his wife Helen, a trained concert pianist and composer. In accordance with the educational beliefs of her father, Rich was educated at home under the tutelage of her mother until the fourth grade. She showed an early interest in writing and was encouraged by her father to peruse his extensive Victorian literature collection. Rich graduated from Radcliffe College in 1951, and her first volume of poetry, *A Change of World* (1951), published when Rich was only twenty-one, was selected by noted Anglo-American poet W. H. Auden for the Yale Series of Younger Poets. In his introduction to the collection, Auden praised her mastery of form, delicacy, and restraint from striving for intense individuality. Other critical comments support Auden's evaluation and note that this volume is a remarkable production for so young a poet. In a 1971 essay, "When We Dead Awaken: Writing as Re-Vision," Rich herself comments upon her early poetry: "I know that my style was formed first by male poets: ... Frost, Dylan Thomas, Donne, Auden, MacNeice, Stevens, Yeats. What I learned chiefly from them was craft."

The following year Rich was awarded a Guggenheim Fellowship and traveled to Europe and England. In 1953 she married Harvard University economist Alfred H. Conrad, and the couple settled in Cambridge, Massachusetts. Rich gave birth to a son in 1955 and that same year saw the publication of her second poetry collection, *The Diamond Cutters, and Other Poems*. By 1959 Rich was the mother of three sons and had very little time for writing. While she wrote sporadically when her children were young, Rich was very unhappy with the quality of work she produced. In her essay "When We Dead Awaken: Writing as Re-Vision" she later explained:

> I was writing very little. ... What I did write was unconvincing to me; my anger and frustration were hard to acknowledge in or out of poems because in fact I cared a great deal about my husband and my children.

Politics and Art Rich published her third volume, *Snapshots of a Daughter-in-Law*, in 1963. A collection of poems drawn from the fragments of writings she had compiled over eight years, it is considered her breakthrough work because of its overt delineation of female themes. In 1966 Rich moved with her family to New York City, where she became involved in the civil rights and antiwar movements. By 1969 she had become estranged from her husband, who committed suicide the following year. During the early 1970s Rich devoted much of her time toward the women's liberation movement and began identifying herself as a radical feminist. In 1973 her eighth poetry collection, *Diving into the Wreck*, won the National Book Award. Defying what she perceived to be the patriarchal organization upon which the competition was founded, Rich refused the award as an individual; however, she accepted it with nominees Audre Lorde and Alice Walker, acknowledging the award "in the name of all the women whose voices have gone and still go unheard in a patriarchal world." Rich came out as a lesbian in 1976, at which time she advocated a female separatist philosophy in her works. In the early 1980s she moved to Massachusetts with poet Michelle Cliff, where they coedited the lesbian feminist journal *Sinister Wisdom*.

In 1984, Rich and Cliff moved to California, where Rich continued to explore the personal and political through her verse. In the collections *Your Native Land, Your Life* (1986); *Time's Power: Poems, 1985–1988* (1988); and *An Atlas of the Difficult World: Poems, 1988–1991*

LITERARY AND HISTORICAL CONTEMPORARIES

Rich's famous contemporaries include:

Richard Dawkins (1941–): In his 1976 book *The Selfish Gene*, Dawkins proposed a gene-centered, rather than species-centered, view of evolution and coined the term "meme." Dawkins has of late become an outspoken advocate on behalf of atheism.

Sid Vicious (1957–1979): A member of the infamous punk group The Sex Pistols, Vicious epitomized the self-destructive, anarchistic side of that musical movement. Noted more for his drug-fueled lifestyle than for his prowess on the bass guitar, Vicious died of a heroin overdose shortly after being charged with the murder of his girlfriend.

Saul Bellow (1915–2005): A Nobel Prize-winning fiction writer, Bellow set much of his fiction in his home town of Chicago, often showcasing street-smart philosophers as main characters.

Judy Blume (1938–): A widely-read author of children's and young adult books, Blume has been both widely praised and condemned for her willingness to address themes previously thought taboo in young people's literature, such as teenage sexuality.

Anne Sexton (1928–1974): Considered an archetypal poet of the confessional school, Sexton's poetry was both deeply personal and broadly focused on women's issues. A long-time sufferer of clinical depression, Sexton's career was cut short when she took her own life in 1974.

(1991), Rich addresses new issues while continuing to develop feminist themes. The long sequence titled "Sources" in *Your Native Land, Your Life* is Rich's first major attempt to confront her Jewish heritage and the effects of the Holocaust on her life and work. In "Living Memory," a long poem in *Time's Power*, Rich faces the consequences of time and aging and also meditates on her bond to the American landscape. *An Atlas of the Difficult World* focuses on such issues as poverty, the Persian Gulf War, and the exploitation of minorities and women. Rich's use of personal experience, first-person narratives, and language prompted critics to compare this collection to the works of Emily Dickinson and Walt Whitman. *Hudson Review* critic Dick Allen observes, "Rich's book is truly a small atlas; but it is also the mature poetry of a writer who knows her own power, who speaks in the passionate, ambitious blending of the personal and the universal."

Rich was to be given the National Medal of Arts in 1997, but she refused to accept the award because she felt that the "cynical politics" of the administration of President Bill Clinton was incompatible with her definition of art. She and Cliff continue to live and work in California.

COMMON HUMAN
EXPERIENCE

Rich found herself in esteemed company when she turned her attentions to penning feminist poems—the tradition of feminist poetry and fiction can claim some of the most honored writers of the last quarter-century and includes the following works:

The Handmaid's Tale (1985), a novel by Margaret Atwood. Set in a grim future, this novel explores issues of class, patriarchal religion, and the subjugation of women.

The Color Purple (1982), a novel by Alice Walker. A book that examines not just feminist themes but the experience of African American women and their relationships, *The Color Purple* earned Walker the Pulitzer Prize and the National Book Award.

Cables to Rage (1970), a book of poetry by Audre Lorde. Like Rich, Lourde intertwined her feminist beliefs with her lesbian sexuality. This volume of poetry, her second, was, via the poem "Martha," the first in which Lourde publicly confirmed her homosexuality.

Works in Literary Context

Rich's work sustains her belief that "Poetry is above all a concentration of the power of language which is the power of our ultimate relationship to everything in the universe." Her poetry is strongly integrated with other dimensions of her life, and changes in form and tone from volume to volume reflect changes in her personal life and consciousness.

Feminist Poetry Rich's poetry has not always been described as "feminist." Discussion of her poetry is generally divided into discrete phases that reflect the evolutionary nature of her canon. The highly crafted verse structures and delineation of such themes as alienation and loss in her first two collections display Rich's early fondness with modernist poets. In "Aunt Jennifer's Tigers," a poem often praised for its mastery of sound, rhythm, and meter, Rich depicts a woman embroidering a tapestry in which tigers playfully inhabit a forest scene. She contrasts the restrained lifestyle of Aunt Jennifer, who feels inhibited by "The massive weight of Uncle's wedding band," with the power and vitality of the tigers, who "pace in sleek chivalric certainty." While commentators frequently cite "Aunt Jennifer's Tigers" as an example of the control and objectivity that Rich sought in her early work, they nevertheless maintain that the poem portrays a feminist perspective in its critique of male dominance.

In *Snapshots of a Daughter-in-Law*, considered her first transitional work, Rich departs from the formalism of her earlier volumes by employing free verse forms and overtly portraying women's themes. For example, in the title poem, which is composed of ten rapidly shifting, fragmentary sections, Rich explores a young woman's anger and frustration at her banal and limited existence within a patriarchal society.

Rich began the second phase of her poetic career with the collections *Necessities of Life* (1966), *Leaflets* (1969), and *The Will to Change* (1971). These works focus on the relationship between private and public life and reflect social themes that openly reject patriarchal culture and language. *Diving into the Wreck*, Rich's second major transitional work, is a radical feminist critique of contemporary society. Many of the poems in this volume assert the importance of reinventing cultural standards in feminist terms and focus on the need for women to achieve self-definition. In the title poem, Rich recognizes the necessity of creating an alternative, female language. Her next collections, *The Dream of a Common Language* (1978) and *A Wild Patience Has Taken Me This Far* (1981), have been commended for their lyrical celebrations of the accomplishments of women. In poems such as "For Julia in Nebraska" and "The Spirit of Place," Rich envisions a separate, utopian community of women as an alternative to contemporary society. Rich's emphasis on a distinct community of women is portrayed in "Twenty-One Love Poems," a sequence of poems that directly represents lesbian sexuality and relationships.

Works in Critical Context

Since the publication of *Diving into the Wreck* in 1973, most critics have analyzed Rich's work as an artistic expression of feminist politics. While some reviewers have praised her ability to write effectively in numerous verse forms, others have faulted the content of her poems as preachy. Critical commentary on Rich's work has reflected the polarizing subject matter of her verse; critics who adhere to Rich's politics frequently commend her poems unconditionally, while those who disagree with her radical feminism disavow her work. Additionally, there has been no conclusive appraisal of her canon as Rich continually revises her views and asserts new approaches to contemporary issues. Most critics concur, however, that Rich's intelligent and innovative portrayals of women have contributed significantly to the feminist movement. Wendy Martin has stated that "Rich's poetry serves a prophetic function by articulating the history and ideals of the feminist struggle. By ... envisioning the women of the future who will emerge from the feminist struggle, her poetry celebrates women's strength and possibilities."

Snapshots of a Daughter-in-Law Many critics find in Rich's book *Snapshots of a Daughter-in-Law: Poems, 1954–1962* the first indication of both the end of Rich's imitative efforts and the beginning of her concern with feminist issues. In *Southwest Review*, Willard Spiegelman calls *Snapshots* "the liminal volume, attempting a journey from one self, world, poetic form, to another." In *Writing*

Like a Woman, Alicia Ostriker also comments on the change in Rich's poetry evident in *Snapshots*. Calling the collection "Rich's break-through volume," Ostriker notes that the book's title poem "has the immediacy and force which Rich did not attempt earlier."

Responses to Literature

1. How does Rich emphasize female empowerment in such works as *Snapshots of a Daughter-in-Law*? Provide examples from her work to illustrate your points.

2. Research the works of other political feminist poets, such as Audre Lorde. How do their styles differ from Rich's? How are they similar?

3. Compare Rich's "city" in "Rusted Legacy" to other imaginary political cities, such as those in Plato's *Republic* and Thomas More's *Utopia*. Are there any similarities in the descriptions of these political cities? Why do you think the authors chose fictional cities as their mediums for communicating their message?

BIBLIOGRAPHY

Books

"Rusted Legacy." *Poetry for Students*. Ed. Anne Marie Hacht. Vol. 15. Detroit: Gale, 2002.

Templeton, Alice. *The Dream and the Dialogue: Adrienne Rich's Feminist Poetics*. Knoxville, Tenn.: University of Tennessee Press, 1994.

Werner, Craig Hansen. *Adrienne Rich: The Poet and Her Critics*. Chicago: American Library Association, 1988.

Periodicals

Boyers, Robert. "On Adrienne Rich: Intelligence and Will." *Salmagundi* no. 22–23 (Spring–Summer 1973): 132–148.

Gelpi, Albert. "Adrienne Rich: The Poetics of Change." *American Poetry Since 1960*, ed. Robert B. Shaw. Cheadle, Cheshire, U.K.: Carcanet Press, 1973, pp. 123–143.

Gelpi, Barbara C. and Albert Gelpi, eds. *Adrienne Rich's Poetry: A Norton Critical Edition*. New York: Norton, 1975.

Jarrell, Randall. "New Books in Review." *Yale Review* 46 (September 1956): 100–103.

Jong, Erica. "Visionary Anger." *Ms.* 2 (July 1973): 31–33.

Kalstone, David. *Five Temperaments*. New York: Oxford University Press, 1977, pp. 129–169.

McDaniel, Judith. *Reconstituting The World: The Poetry and Vision of Adrienne Rich*. Argyle, N.Y.: Spinsters Ink, 1979.

Ostriker, Alicia. "Her Cargo: Adrienne Rich and the Common Language." *American Poetry Review* 8 (July–August 1979): 6–10.

Vendler, Helen. "Ghostlier Demarcations, Keener Sounds." *Parnassus* 2 (Fall–Winter 1973): 5–10, 15–16, 18–24.

Werner, Craig Hansen. *Adrienne Rich: The Poet and Her Critics*. Chicago: American Library Association, 1988.

✸ Alberto Alvaro Ríos

BORN: *1952, Nogales, Arizona*

NATIONALITY: *American*

GENRE: *Fiction, poetry*

MAJOR WORKS:

Whispering to Fool the Wind (1982)

The Iguana Killer: Twelve Stories of the Heart (1984)

The Smallest Muscle in the Human Body (2002)

Overview

A poet and writer, Alberto Alvaro Ríos has been heralded as a major voice of Southwest poetry and even as the

Alberto Alvaro Ríos   *ASU / Tom Story*

LITERARY AND HISTORICAL CONTEMPORARIES

Ríos's famous contemporaries include:

Carl Hiaasen (1953–): A native Floridian, Hiaasen writes popular thriller-mysteries set in a quasi-satirical Florida, which are filled with greed, corruption, apathy, and quirky characters.

Michael J. Fox (1961–): While still in his early twenties, Fox became a major celebrity with his character on the popular sitcom *Family Ties* (1982–1989) and his starring role in the "Back to the Future" film trilogy (1985–1990). After being diagnosed with Parkinson's disease, Fox has become an outspoken advocate for research on the condition.

Bill Richardson (1947–): California native Richardson is a leading Hispanic figure in American politics. He has served as the Secretary of Energy under President Clinton, has been elected as both a Congressman and Governor of New Mexico.

Rita Dove (1952–): Dove, who became the second African American woman to win the Pulitzer Prize for Poetry in 1987, is most famous for her collection *Thomas and Beulah* (1986).

Rudolfo Anaya (1937–): A native of New Mexico, Anaya is known both for his adult fiction such as *Bless Me, Ultima* (1972) as well as his books for children.

most articulate poetic voice of the American language in the 1980s. It is as a poet that he has received the bulk of attention, but Ríos is also a writer of short stories, including a collection written for young adults.

Works in Biographical and Historical Context

Growing Up Biracial Born September 18, 1952, in Nogales, Arizona, Ríos is the son of a British mother, Agnes Fogg Ríos, and a Mexican father, Alberto Alvaro Ríos. Growing up on the Arizona-Mexico border, the young Ríos first learned Spanish. When he entered grade school, like most Chicanos of Mexican ancestry, he was forced to give up his first language. As Ríos recalls, "We got swats for speaking Spanish, even on the playground." By the time he was in junior high school, Ríos could no longer speak Spanish. As a result of his forced forgetting of that language, Ríos invented a third language—"one," he says, "that was all our own." Many of his most important early poems dramatize the essence of this uncanny third language.

In junior high, Ríos began writing, what he calls "mildly rebellious, abstract poems" in the back pages of his notebooks. He continued this practice in high school and college. Ríos attended the University of Arizona and earned his B.A. with honors in 1974. Not satisfied with a double major in English and creative writing, Ríos earned another B.A. with honors in psychology in 1975. Ríos then enrolled in law school at the same university but quit after a year to enroll in the M.F.A. program in creative writing, which he completed in 1979.

Early Poetry Ríos became a technically brilliant poet at the University of Arizona, but, like many ethnic American writers, he spent much time in creative-writing workshops, in arguments over the content of his work. His professors, who were not from Arizona, would want him to change the names of his characters because, according to Ríos, "they had never heard of a Sapito or a Graciela. These were the names of my relatives!"

In 1980, Ríos received a fellowship in creative writing from the National Endowment for the Arts. *Sleeping On Fists* (1981), a major chap-book, was completed during this period. Next came *Whispering to Fool the Wind* (1982). In Ríos's early poems, he draws from an oral culture that was passed on from his *nani* (grandmother), *abuelo* (grandfather), cousins, aunts, childhood friends, an Uncle Humberto, and a representative relative who Ríos names Carlos. Storytelling in verse, traditionally, is a difficult task because the details in prose fiction—a sense of being and time and of characters exchanging experiences—are seemingly at odds with the compactness of poetry. Nevertheless, Ríos was able to master this difficult procedure. Ríos's work reaches back to his own past and to that of others. In "Madre Sofía," for example, he writes about his impressions of a local gypsy fortune-teller who his mother once took him to see. Carlos appears, like a ghost, in several other poems in the book, as the representative border man.

Short Stories and Recognition Ríos did not limit himself to just poetry. His collection of bucolic fables, *The Iguana Killer: Twelve Stories of the Heart* (1984), won the prestigious Western States Book Award for fiction, sponsored by the Western States Art Foundation in Santa Fe, New Mexico. Written for what Ríos calls a "young adult" audience, *The Iguana Killer* explores the world of his childhood and border culture. In the title story, young Sapito, like a mythical British knight, uses an American baseball bat his grandmother sends him to become the greatest iguana killer in tropical Mexico.

In Ríos's *Five Indiscretions* (1985), nearly every poem is about desire, sexuality, and religion, and nearly every poem deals with courtships between men and women. A reviewer for *Library Journal* felt that the poems in this collection demonstrate Ríos's "deep social commitment and rare ability to identify with others." Ríos followed this with the 1988 collection *The Lime Orchard Woman*. More poems of life in two cultures that exhibit a magic-realist bent are found in *Teodoro Luna's Two Kisses* (1990), the first of Ríos's works to receive mainstream publication. These characteristics are also evident in *Pig Cookies and Other Stories* (1995), set in a small Mexican town where cookies have supernatural powers, and life takes other surprising twists and turns.

Ríos's works have been published in over one hundred magazines, and his poetry has often been anthologized. His poem "Chileño Boys," in *Five Indiscretions*, has been set to reggae music by David Broza for CBS records. In 1984, Ríos was the only Arizonan selected for the *Esquire* feature titled "The Best of the New Generation: Men and Women Under Forty Who Are Changing America."

Ríos is now a Regents' Professor of English at Arizona State University. In 2002, Ríos was nominated for the National Book Award for his collection, *The Smallest Muscle in the Human Body.* That same year he received the Western Literature Association's Distinguished Achievement Award. In January 2003, he was invited to write and deliver a poem at the inauguration of Arizona Governor Janet Napolitano. His most recent collection is *The Theater of Night* (2006).

Works in Literary Context

Ríos has been praised both for his mastery of imagery and his command of the technical precision of poetic language. If queried about his use of language, however, Ríos refrains from putting all his faith in vocabulary. As he explains to Leslie Wooten in the *Bloomsbury Review*:

> Words are wonderful suitcases that hold ideas for us. Even so, they don't know everything, and aren't always necessary, or aren't always the answer. The body remembers instinctively how to walk, run, eat, sleep, kiss, and much more. The words come after.

Magic Realism Ríos's literary style has been placed under the umbrella of magic realism, a term originally applied to Latin American authors, especially Gabriel García Márquez and Jorge Luis Borges. Magic realism combines dreamlike narrative that evokes myths and fairy tales with precise descriptions of everyday events. It has been said that Ríos's poetry is a kind of magical storytelling, and his stories are a kind of magical poetry. While most of the young-adult stories in *The Iguana Killer*, for example, are straightforwardly narrated, "The Way Spaghetti Feels" and "The Birthday of Mrs. Piñeda" border on the metafictional and magic-realist impulse in postmodernist fiction. Throughout *Whispering to Fool the Wind*, extraordinary and magical events are related with the greatest of accuracy without being forced on the reader. The character Pánfilo's head is deformed and "awkwardly" bent out of shape; a grandfather "who has served ants with the attitude of a waiter" is buried in his best suit; and poor, sad Uncle Humberto, a collector of

COMMON HUMAN EXPERIENCE

Here are some more works by writers who, like Ríos, hail from the American Southwest and ground their stories in the rich cultural heritage of that region:

Red Sky at Morning (1968), a novel by Richard Bradford. A coming-of-age tale set among the high northern New Mexico mountains during World War II, the main character of this novel is a teenage boy who moves with his family from Mobile, Alabama, to a land still very much caught between two worlds of Spanish and American.

The Short Stories of Fray Angelico Chavez (2003), a story collection by Fray Angelico Chavez. A Franciscan priest, poet, painter, and man of letters, this collection, published after Chavez's death, functions as both social commentary and humorous evocation of life in rural New Mexico.

. . . y no se lo tragó la tierra (1971), a novel by Tomás Rivera. One of the breakthrough works of Chicano literature, Rivera's dreamlike tale was also the first novel to focus on the life and plight of migrant workers in America.

The Man Who Could Fly and Other Stories (2006), a book by Rudolfo Anaya. Using the Hispanic folktales taken from his New Mexico upbringing, Anaya, a major figure in the Chicano literature movement, spins eighteen yarns in simple, straightforward language as if the tales were being told around a campfire.

butterflies, dies of excessive rage because one day, Graciela, a "hard seamstress," refuses to give him pins.

Works in Critical Context

Critics have been generally favorable to Ríos's poetry, showing greatest enthusiasm for his early work, generally. Of particular note to critics is his use of language in both his short stories and poetry. He has won several major awards, including six Pushcart Prizes.

The Iguana Killer Ríos's prize-winning collection of stories received highly favorable reviews. Jodi Daynard, in *The New York Times Book Review*, favorably compared Ríos's *The Iguana Killer* with William Golding's *Lord of the Flies* (1954), another book about children. E. J. Montini, in the *Arizona Republic*, claims, "It is the taking away of secrets, the cruel, sometimes crude manner in which they are exposed, that is at the heart of each story in *The Iguana Killer*." In brief, various reviewers were favorably impressed with Ríos's bicultural perspective, with his portrayal of young Chicanas, and with his use of surreal language.

Five Indiscretions *Five Indiscretions*, arguably Ríos's most ambitious book, has not received the acclaim and attention as of some of his other works. Some reviewers, however, have praised his ability to represent gender issues and his use of the American language. A writer for *Booklist*, for example, claims that "Ríos is especially impressive in conjuring the emerging sexuality of adolescent girls." Similarly, a reviewer for *Library Journal* notes that Ríos "offers the insights into the lives of women seldom found in the work of a male writer." And Lawrence Joseph, in *American Book Review*, argues that "*Five Indiscretions* displays the breadth and richness of the American language." He even claims that, in the future, "when the revolutions of the American language are clearer to us, most of the poetry of the 1980s will pale beside Ríos's."

Responses to Literature

1. Why do you think Ríos and his Spanish-speaking friends received "swats" from teachers for speaking Spanish in class? What are the prevailing attitudes today towards bilingual students? Is it an asset or a liability?

2. Research the history of magic realism. Who were some of the first authors to make use of the technique? Is it still commonly used today in fiction and poetry? Find some examples of this technique in Rios's work.

3. If you were to write poetry about the region you grew up in, what would you choose to highlight as representative of your homeland? What, do you think, are the "core values" of your family and close friends?

4. Do you think Ríos succeeded in writing a book that was truly for "young adults" in *The Iguana Killer*? Write a critique that analyzes Rios's ability to gear his style and subject matter toward younger readers.

BIBLIOGRAPHY

Books

McDowell, Robert. "Ríos, Alberto (Alvaro)."
　　Contemporary Poets. Edited by Thomas Riggs.
　　Seventh ed. Detroit: St. James Press, 2001.
"Ríos, Alberto." *Authors and Artists for Young Adults.*
　　Vol. 66. Detroit: Gale, 2006.
"Island of the Three Marias." *Poetry for Students.* Edited
　　by Jennifer Smith and Elizabeth Thomason. Vol. 11.
　　Detroit: Thomson Gale, 2001.

Periodicals

Barillas, William. "Words like the Wind." (interview).
　　Americas Review (Fall–Winter 1996): 116–129.
Wootten, Leslie. "Writing on the Edge" (interview).
　　Bloomsbury Review (January–February 1996): 11.
McInnis, Susan. Interview with Ríos. *Glimmer Train*
　　(Spring 1998): 105–121.

✸ Tomás Rivera

BORN: 　1935, Crystal City, Texas

DIED: 　1984, Fontana, California

NATIONALITY: 　American

GENRE: 　Fiction, poetry

MAJOR WORKS:
　... And the Earth Did Not Part (1971)

Overview

Tomás Rivera was a key figure in the emergence of the so-called Chicano Renaissance, a period beginning in the early 1970s, when the literature and poetry of Chicanos—citizens of the United States of Mexican ancestry—began to develop a unique identity, earning recognition from critics as a literary movement in its own right. Rivera was the first writer to document the experiences of Mexican American migrant farm workers.

Works in Biographical and Historical Context

Growing Up a Migrant Born in 1935 in Crystal City, Texas, Rivera was the son of migrant farm workers;

Tomás Rivera 　*Used by permission of Special Collection and Archives, University of California, Riverside Libraries, University of California, Riverside, CA*

both his parents were Mexican immigrants. The life of the migrant farm worker was and remains a hard one—pay is among the lowest of any occupation in the United States, and working conditions are often extremely harsh and difficult. Growing up, Rivera accompanied his parents on their seasonal progress across America as they followed crop yields through spring, summer, and autumn, across the vastness of Texas and up into the Midwest states of Iowa, Minnesota, Wisconsin, Michigan, and North Dakota. Rivera would later recall one of his earliest memories, that of waking up on a farm in northern Minnesota where his parents and relatives worked in the beet fields. The time would have been around the late 1930s, when an estimated four million agricultural migrant laborers moved across America's farmlands, season to season.

Children of migrant workers were often put to work. Furthermore, many schools would not admit migrant children due to a lack of a local residence. Despite the semi-nomadic lifestyle and the obstacles against him, Rivera's parents made sure their son received a full education; after graduating high school, Rivera attended Southwest Texas State College, earning a degree in English in 1958. After graduating, he became a teacher of English and Spanish in the public schools of San Antonio, Crystal City, and League City, Texas, from 1957 to 1965. As he earned a living with teaching, Rivera also pursued higher education for himself, eventually earning a master's degree in education in 1964. Now qualified to teach at college level, Rivera became an instructor in English, French, and Spanish at Southwest Texas Junior College, Uvalde, from 1965–1966. In 1968, he became an instructor in Spanish at the University of Oklahoma, Norman; the following year he earned a doctorate in romance languages and literature from the same university. He immediately became associate professor at Sam Houston State University in Huntsville, Texas, a position he held until 1971, when he became professor of Spanish at the University of Texas at San Antonio.

Chicano Writings Rivera became an early figure in the emerging Chicano literature movement with the publication of his 1971 novel, *... And the Earth Did Not Part*. The book drew upon Rivera's experience as a migrant worker and was the first such work to address that lifestyle in American literature. Before the book was even published, in fact, it had won the first Premio Quinto Sol prize from the Chicano publishing house, Quinto Sol. The following two authors to win the prize, Rudolfo Anaya and Rolando Hinojosa, along with Rivera, quickly became major voices in the Chicano Renaissance.

Rivera was also a poet, and he published *Always and Other Poems* in 1973. In addition to his fiction and poetry, he also wrote nonfiction essays in scholarly journals on Chicano literature. Through such essays as "Chicano Literature: Fiesta of the Living" (1979) and "Into the Labyrinth: The Chicano in Literature" (1971), he was one of the prime movers in the promotion of Chi-

cano authors and in the creation of the concept of Chicano literature, as well as in the establishment of Chicano literature as worthy of academic attention. Some of Rivera's works were published posthumously. These include the short story "The Harvest" (1989) and *The Searchers: Collected Poetry* (1990).

Rivera's academic career culminated with his accepting the position of Chancellor at the University of California, Riverside, in 1979. Rivera was working on a second novel entitled *The People's Mansion* when he died of a heart attack in 1984.

Works in Literary Context

Rivera's first and only novel, *... And the Earth Did Not Part*, was a milestone in Chicano literature. Describing the experience of the Mexican-American, Rivera's book set the stylistic blueprint for a decade's worth of Chicano writers and helped touch off what would eventually become one of the major literary movements of the latter part of the twentieth century.

Chicano Literature At the end of the 1960s, there was only one Chicano publisher, Quinto Sol Publications, located in Berkeley, California, and founded by University of California professor Octavio I. Romano in 1967. Getting its start with one of the longest running and most successful Chicano literary journals, *El Grito*, in 1969,

COMMON HUMAN EXPERIENCE

Rivera was one of several authors who burst upon the scene in the 1970s and early 1980s, forming the bedrock of the Chicano literature movement. Here are some works by other Chicano writers:

Bless Me, Ultima (1972), a novel by Rudolfo Anaya. One of the most challenged books in the United States, this tale, set in 1940s New Mexico, raises questions about the nature of God, the Catholic Church, and humanity's relationship with nature.

Estampas del Valle y otras obras (1973), a novel by Rolando Hinojosa. Winner of the 1972 Premio Quinto Sol Prize, this book depicts life among the Chicano communities of the Rio Grande Valley in the 1930s, 1940s, and 1950s—the time and place where the author grew up and came of age.

The House on Mango Street (1984), a novel by Sandra Cisneros. Set in a Chicago Chicano ghetto, the action of the story centers on a young girl's attempts to leave her impoverished surroundings, along with her intention to one day come back to help those she left behind.

Chicano: 25 Pieces of a Chicano Mind (1969), a book of poetry by Abelardo Delgado. One of the first landmark books of Chicano poetry, this collection draws upon the oral tradition within the culture to raise a call for cultural and social unity at a time when the movement was just beginning to define itself.

Quinto Sol issued the first anthology of Chicano literature, *The Mirror*. The stated objective of the collection was to feature writings "by Chicanos without any obligation to be largely and submissively grateful to Anglo-American foundations and editors."

Chicano authors were drawing the attention of mainstream publishers around this time, but they were not seen as a cultural movement—rather, they were seen as part of the general radical youth movements of the late 1960s and early 1970s. As such, there was little being done on the part of the big publishers to seriously promote any one Chicano author. Therefore, it was up to individual Chicano writers to make names for themselves, which they did through the media of small magazines and alternative presses.

It was partially in response to this situation that the Premio Quinto Sol award for Chicano literature was created. In 1970, the first award went to Rivera for ... *And the Earth Did Not Part*, a work that virtually defined Chicano fiction for years to come. Centering on a year in the life of a fourteen-year-old migrant worker, the story is told through vignettes, inviting the reader, in the tradition of Latin American literature, to engage with the story and actively piece together details of the characters and their backgrounds. The contrast of the injustice and horror of the migrant lifestyle against the tight bond of *la familia*, which is shown to be the one thing that keeps Chicano culture intact, forms the central theme of the book.

The path blazed by writers like Rivera would lead to a virtual explosion of Chicano and Chicana writers in the decades to come. By the mid-1990s, Chicana writers were the most visible of any single ethnic literary grouping in America. Mainstream magazines regularly ran features on writers like Sandra Cisneros, and mainstream publishers had long since begun paying attention to Chicano literature. The Chicano Renaissance has since given way to a larger, pan-Latin sensibility. Although country and culture of origin—from Chicano to Dominican to Mexican to Cuban or Puerto Rican and beyond—still form the primary backdrops for individual authors' stories, there is a sense of "Latino literature" now that did not exist when Rivera published his first book in 1971.

Works in Critical Context

According to Patricia De La Fuente, writing in *Western American Literature*, "Rivera possesses that rare ability in writers to convert everyday episodes in the lives of ordinary people into small masterpieces of sparse yet often lyrical prose." Critics have praised Rivera's writings, both his poetry and fiction, for their focus on the roles of ritual and cultural memory as central to the Mexican migrant farm worker culture of the mid-twentieth century.

... And the Earth Did Not Part Writing in *The Modern Language Journal*, William H. González wrote that ... *And the Earth Did Not Part* "is final proof of the literary wealth which is beginning to emerge from the ranks of the Chicanos." González continues, "Tomás Rivera has masterfully captured the simplicity and feeling of his people in the fight for existence . . . ." In a review published in *The South Central Bulletin*, Don Whitmore observes that "[i]n a seriously committed fashion and with gut language, Rivera manages to depict this struggle to maintain dignity amid alien forces."

Responses to Literature

1. Rivera wrote about the family unit, and its role in creating a sense of continuity and identity by remembering the past. Chicano literature, in effect, continues this process. What are some other ways in which groups of people create a sense of community amongst themselves?

2. Research the history of migrant workers in the United States. What have migrant workers, such as César Chávez, achieved in the last four decades? What challenges remain?

3. In the short story, "The Harvest," one of the characters reconnects with nature, discovering a deep

bond with the earth. Describe an event in your life in which you felt a new appreciation or understanding of nature.

4. Rivera believed that migrant workers were possibly worse off than slaves, who were considered an investment by their owners and, therefore, had at least some protection. Do you agree with this sentiment? Why or why not? What are some possible solutions to the migrant worker situation?

BIBLIOGRAPHY

Books

"A Place on Identity's Bookshelf." *The Hispanic American Experience.* Woodbridge, Conn.: Primary Source Microfilm, 1999.

"Chicano Novelists: Tomás Rivera, Rudolfo Anaya, and Rolando Hinijosa." *DISCovering Multicultural America.* Online ed. Detroit: Gale, 2003.

"The Harvest." *Short Stories for Students.* Vol. 15. Detroit: Thomson Gale, 2002.

Kanellos, Nicolás. "Chicano Literature." *Hispanic American Almanac.* Edited by Sonia G. Benson. Third ed. Detroit: Gale, 2003.

Lattin, Vernon E., Rolando Hinojosa, and Gary D. Keller. *Tomás Rivera, 1935–1984, The Man and His Work.* Tempe, Ariz.: Bilingual Review/Press, 1988.

Olivares, Julián, ed. *International Studies in Honor of Tomás Rivera.* Houston, Tex.: Arte Público Press, 1986.

"Rivera, Tomás (1935–1984)." *Benet's Reader's Encyclopedia of American Literature*, Vol. 1. New York: HarperCollins Publishers, 1991.

Sommers, Joseph. "Interpreting Tomás Rivera." *Modern Chicano Writers: A Collection of Critical Essays*, edited by Joseph Sommers and Tomás Ybarra-Frausto. Upper Saddle River, N.J.: Prentice Hall, 1979.

Periodicals

González, William H. *The Modern Language Journal* Vol. 57, No. 4 (April 1973): 229.

Whitmore, Don. *The South Central Bulletin* Vol. 33, No. 3 (October 1973): 160–161.

✵ Edwin Robinson

BORN: *1869, Head Tide, Maine*

DIED: *1935, New York, New York*

NATIONALITY: *American*

GENRE: *Drama, poetry*

MAJOR WORKS:

The Children of the Night (1897)

The Man against the Sky (1916)

Collected Poems (1921)

The Man Who Died Twice (1924)

Edwin Arlington Robinson   *Robinson, Edwin Arlington, photograph. AP Images.*

Overview

Edwin Robinson was arguably the first great American poet of the twentieth century. Ironically, his greatness came not through the experimental or modernist forms that were beginning to predominate around the time he wrote, but by sticking with well-established, straightforward forms and rhymes inspired by the Romantic poets of Britain.

Works in Biographical and Historical Context

Early Hardships and Guilt A descendant of the colonial poet Anne Bradstreet, Edwin Arlington Robinson was born in Head Tide, Maine, and he grew up in the nearby town of Gardiner, his model for the fictitious Tilbury Town, which figures prominently in his early verse. Fascinated by the sounds and rhythms of words, he began to write poetry at an early age. Robinson attended Harvard University for two years, but a decline in the family's financial situation forced him to return home. His elder brothers' bad financial investments, alcoholism, and drug addiction left the Robinson family nearly penniless. Despite these hardships, Robinson subsequently rejected a business career in favor of writing poetry. His inability to aid his family financially forced them to become dependent on friends for money and caused Robinson to develop a sense of personal failure and guilt that haunted him for the remainder of his life. These themes and problems show up repeatedly in his work—Robinson's portraits of nonconformists, derelicts, alcoholics, and suicides, as well as his preoccupation with human failure, are attributed by many commentators to his personal experiences with poverty and alienation.

A Presidential Favorite   Early in his career, Robinson mastered the poetic form for which he became well known: the dramatic lyric marked by firm structure based on stanzas, deft rhyming patterns, and colloquial, or everyday, speech. His first book of poems, *The Torrent and the Night Before* (1896), is a forty-four page pamphlet that Robinson printed and distributed to numerous critics at his own expense. In addition to dramatic lyrics, this work demonstrates a myriad of styles: blank and rhymed verse, villanelles and ballades, as well as traditional sonnets and quatrains. While *The Torrent and the Night Before* received a few positive reviews for its stark portraits of Tilbury Town, it was generally ignored by both critics and readers.

Robinson's next volume of verse, *The Children of the Night* (1897), consists of psychological portraits of such odd characters as Aaron Stark, a vindictive miser, and Luke Havergal, a deprived lover. The frequently anthologized poem "Richard Cory" is about a seemingly fortuitous gentleman who earned the respect of the townspeople, yet one night committed suicide. *The Children of the Night* attracted the attention of President Theodore Roosevelt after his son, Kermit, sent him a copy of the book from school. Roosevelt was impressed with Robinson's work and gave it lavish praise. In the summer of 1905, Roosevelt helped arrange employment for Robinson at the New York City Custom House so he could write without financial worry. Robinson's finances, however, remained less than solvent until the late 1920s.

Despite his financial issues, Robinson continued to create verse. The title poem of *Captain Craig* (1902), Robinson's third book, is a dramatic narrative of approximately two thousand lines about a derelict whose bombastic yet learned observations of humanity serve as a source of fascination for the unnamed narrator. The theme of personal ruin continued in his next work, *The Town down the River* (1910), in which Robinson began composing poems that centered on historical and public personages. A companion volume, *The Three Taverns* (1920), features such individuals as abolitionist John Brown, the biblical figure Lazarus, and the early American statesmen Alexander Hamilton and Aaron Burr. *The Man against the Sky* (1916) is generally considered Robinson's most successful single volume of verse. It continues the deft psychological portraits that marked his earlier efforts and reflects Robinson's belief in the moral superiority of seemingly worthless characters over their more materially successful neighbors.

America's First Pulitzer Prize-Winner   In 1922 Robinson earned the Pulitzer Prize for his *Collected Poems* (1921)—the first Pulitzer ever awarded for poetry. In addition to reprinting his earlier verse, this volume also includes new poems that are now considered essential to the Robinson canon: "Mr. Flood's Party," "The Tree in Pamela's Garden," and "Rembrandt to Rembrandt." *Avon's Harvest* (1921) is the first of several book-length dramatic dialogues in which Robinson further delineates the theme of guilt and dereliction. For most critics, *The Man Who Died Twice* (1924) best represents Robinson's preoccupation with personal ruin. The book was also one of Robinson's most accessible books and earned him his second Pulitzer Prize. Robinson's other book-length poems include *Roman Bartholow* (1923) and *Cavender's House* (1929), which centers on domestic tragedies depicting betrayal, unrequited love, and adultery.

Around the time *Collected Poems* was published, Robinson produced *Lancelot* (1920), which was preceded by *Merlin* in 1917 and followed by *Tristram* in 1927. Commonly referred to as his Arthurian trilogy, these book-length works were composed in blank verse and were well received, but are no longer thought to be as important as Robinson's earlier verse. Despite brief passages of substantial lyric beauty, the poems are generally faulted for their length and monotonous tone. *Tristram*, however, became a best seller, a rare distinction for a book of poetry, and earned Robinson his third Pulitzer Prize in 1928.

A Pure Poet   In an age when most prominent poets were engaged in many different pursuits, Robinson stood alone in his unmitigated devotion to writing poetry. Poet T. S. Eliot, for example, had a career in publishing; William Carlos Williams had a medical practice. Wallace Stevens held an executive position in an insurance company, while Robert Frost, seemingly the most "professional" poet, held teaching jobs and went on speaking tours. Robinson, on the other hand, did virtually nothing in his life save write poetry. He neither married nor traveled; he neither taught nor gave public readings; he neither had professional preparation nor any extended occupation other than poetry writing. On the occasion of his fiftieth birthday he was treated to an encomium in the *New York Times Book Review* (December 21, 1919), which published comments by sixteen writers, including this statement from Amy Lowell: "Edwin Arlington Robinson is poetry. I can think of no other living writer who has so consistently dedicated his life to his work."

This pure focus on poetry continued through the end of his life. Robinson's final poems explore the subjects found in his earlier verse, as well as some new ones. For example, *Nicodemus* (1932) is a collection of medium-length pieces that center on biblical themes, the inhabitants of Tilbury Town, and the New England landscape. *Talifer* (1933), another book-length effort, deviates from Robinson's previous domestic tragedies—in this rather light-hearted tale, two couples decide to exchange partners. *Amaranth* (1934) is an allegory concerning a disillusioned painter who enters an alternate world populated by artists with thwarted dreams. Robinson's last work, *King Jasper*, was published posthumously in 1935. While favoring his Arthurian trilogy in tone and structure, *King Jasper* consummates Robinson's aesthetic principles and thematic concerns. Although the work was not successful because of its ambitious scope, most commentators agree that its examination of humanity in a transitory world best concludes Robinson's career. Robinson was diagnosed with cancer in 1935 and died that same year, just hours after completing corrections on the final proofs of *King Jasper*.

Works in Literary Context

Edwin Robinson achieved a hard-won prominence in American literature during the early twentieth century. During a period of intense experimentation in verse, his poetry adheres to the terse diction, careful metrical forms, and philosophical themes found in the work of his British predecessors Robert Browning and Matthew Arnold. Nonetheless, Robinson's poetic style signaled an end to the baroque sentimentality of nineteenth-century American poetry. While he is best known for his powerful narrative poems that dramatize the tribulations of small-town individuals, Robinson was not a systematic philosopher. His works, despite their sad, ironic tone and often tragic conclusions, are considered to be life-affirming, revealing a transcendental belief in God and in the value of human existence. Robinson stated: "I prefer men and women who live, breathe, talk, fight, make love, or go to the devil after the manner of human beings. Art is only valuable to me when it reflects humanity or at least human emotions."

Location as Metaphor Perhaps the best known of Robinson's poems are those now called the Tilbury Town cycle, named after the small town that serves as a physical setting for many of Robinson's poems. Through the town and its residents, Robinson metaphorically explores the human condition. These poems expound on some of Robinson's most characteristic themes: "his curiosity," as Gerald DeWitt Sanders and his fellow editors put it in *Chief Modern Poets of Britain and America*, "about what lies behind the social mask of character, and . . . his dark hints about sexuality, loyalty, and man's terrible will to defeat himself."

Tilbury Town is first mentioned in "John Evereldown," a ballad collected in *The Torrent and The Night Before*. Tilbury Town reappears at intervals throughout Robinson's work. The title poem in *Captain Craig* concerns an old resident of the town whose life, believed wasted by his neighbors, proves to have been of value. *The Children of the Night* contains the story of Richard

LITERARY AND HISTORICAL CONTEMPORARIES

Robinson's famous contemporaries include:

Jack London (1876–1916): Despite his short life, American author London wrote several literary classics, including *The Call of the Wild* (1903) and *White Fang* (1906), both set in the Alaskan frontier wilderness.

Edvard Munch (1863–1944): A Norwegian symbolist painter at the end of the nineteenth century, Munch is best known for his 1893 painting *The Scream*.

William McKinley (1843–1901): McKinley was the twenty-fifth president of the United States. He may be most remembered for reluctantly taking the United States to war against Spain, which won the nation its first overseas possessions. McKinley was assassinated by anarchist Leon Czolgosz and succeeded by his vice president, Theodore Roosevelt.

Oscar Wilde (1854–1900): A noted wit, author, and playwright, Wilde embodied the Bohemian Victorian lifestyle at the close of the nineteenth century. Convicted of carrying on a homosexual relationship—a crime at the time—Wilde was sentenced to hard labor in prison. He died in poverty and obscurity three years after his release.

Henri Matisse (1869–1954): A French artist, Matisse was one of the most celebrated and respected painters of the first half of the twentieth century.

Cory, a poem in which Tilbury Town itself is personified. Finally, *The Man against the Sky* includes the story of the man "Flammonde," in one of the poet's most anthologized Tilbury verses.

A Focus on People and Their Pain While Robinson frequently wrote poems on conventional topics, his subject matter was new in his heavy emphasis on people. Unlike other Romantic poets, he generally avoided the celebration of natural phenomena, bragging to a friend about his first volume that one would not find "a single red-breasted robin in the whole collection." Instead, many of his short poems are character sketches of individuals, while his long narratives deal with complicated human relationships. Frequently they explore psychological reactions to a prior event, such as *Avon's Harvest*, Robinson's "ghost story" about a man destroyed by his own hatred, and *Cavender's House*, a dialogue between a man and his dead wife that deals with questions of jealousy and guilt. The people inhabiting Robinson's books include imaginary individuals as well as characters modeled on actual acquaintances. Whether real or imaginary, many of them evoke themes of personal pain, guilt, betrayal, unrequited love, adultery, and other domestic tragedies.

COMMON HUMAN EXPERIENCE

Robinson's Tilbury Town was one of several fictional small American towns developed by poets and authors in which to set their allegorical tales. Here are some other works that use a fictional place as a metaphor or even a character:

Spoon River Anthology (1915), a book of poetry by Edgar Lee Masters. Each poem in this collection is presented by one of over two hundred residents of the fictional Spoon River Valley. The poems are in the form of an epitaph, reflecting on the life of the deceased speaker.

Winesburg, Ohio (1919), a short story collection by Sherwood Anderson. Anderson based his fictional town and its residents closely on his own Ohio upbringing and wrote a whole cycle of short stories about the travails of a typical American Midwest town.

South Park (1992), a television series created by Trey Parker and Matt Stone. Starting out as a crudely-animated project by two college friends, the irreverant *South Park* went on to become a national success, thanks to its edgy, postmodern attitude. Parker and Stone set the series in the fictional town of South Park, Colorado, which recalls their own childhoods growing up in the Rocky Mountain territory of Colorado.

Lost (2004), a television series created by Damon Lindelof, J. J. Abrams, and Jeffrey Lieber. The show follows the lives of survivors on a mysterious tropical island after their plane crashes somewhere in the South Pacific. Because of its magical properties and ability to interfere in the characters' lives, the island itself is considered to be one of the show's main characters.

Despite these themes, Robinson never saw himself as a pessimist. For example, in 1897 he responded to the charge that he was a pessimist in a letter to the British magazine the *Bookman*, in which he explained, "This world is not a 'prison house,' but a kind of spiritual kindergarten where millions of bewildered infants are trying to spell God with the wrong blocks." Several critics, too, see his work as life-affirming. May Sinclair, writing an early review of *Captain Craig* for the *Fortnightly Review*, said of the Captain, "He, ragged, old, and starved, challenges his friends to have courage and to rejoice in the sun." Robinson's pessimism was similarly denied by fellow poet Robert Frost, who, in his introduction to Robinson's posthumously published *King Jasper* declared, "His theme was unhappiness itself, but his skill was as happy as it was playful. There is that comforting thought for those who suffered to see him suffer." Robinson may instead be called an impersonal romantic, breaking with the nineteenth-century tradition by objectifying and dramatizing emotional reactions while at the same time emphasizing sentiment and mystical awareness. His combination of compassion and irony has become a familiar stance in modern poetry, and his celebrated advocacy of triumphant forbearance in the face of adversity anticipates the existentialist movement.

Works in Critical Context

One of the most prolific major American poets of the twentieth century, Robinson is, ironically, best remembered for only a handful of short poems. Aside from a few that he complained were "pickled in [the] brine" of poetry anthologies—"Richard Cory," "Miniver Cheevy," and "Mr. Flood's Party"—most of his work is not widely known. The fifteen-hundred-page collected edition of his work contains the twenty volumes of poetry published during his lifetime, including the thirteen long narratives that critics have ignored or denigrated but which he regarded as among his best work. Indeed, the long poems that occupied his energies during the last dozen years of his life were not designed for popular appeal, and his stubborn insistence on traditional forms at a time of extraordinary technical experimentation led to the critical attitude that his work is anachronistic, a throwback to the nineteenth-century triumphs of Robert Browning, Alfred Tennyson, and Matthew Arnold. As Robert Frost, in his introduction to *King Jasper*, put it, Robinson was "content with the old-fashioned way to be new."

"Richard Cory" Allen Tate has said that "Mr. Robinson's genius is primarily lyrical" and indicates that "Richard Cory" is "a perfect specimen of Mr. Robinson's dramatic powers—when those powers are lyrically expressed." W. R. Robinson points to "Richard Cory" as an example of the cycle of poems set in the fictional Tilbury Town that links Robinson with "the repressive, utilitarian social climate" of small-town New England. Louis Untermeyer says that Robinson is "at his height" in such poems.

Critical reactions to "Richard Cory" hinge almost exclusively on how individual critics interpret and react to the ending (when the character unexpectedly commits suicide). Richard P. Adams sees the poem as antimaterialistic and says that Cory's suicide "leaves the reader free to decide, if he has his own courage to do so, that working and waiting and going without, and even cursing on occasion, may be a pretty good life after all." William H. Pritchard apparently agrees—he sees Robinson as "someone who relished ironic incongruities" such as the difference between the perceptions of Cory and the actual nature of his personality. Yvor Winters, on the other hand, does not hold such a high opinion of the poem, instead referring to it as a "superficially neat portrait of the elegant man of mystery," and calling Cory's suicide "a very cheap surprise ending." Winters feels that "all surprise endings are cheap in poetry, if not, indeed, elsewhere, for poetry is written to be read not once but many times."

Responses to Literature

1. After reading the poem "Richard Cory," write the suicide note you think the main character might have left behind. Would it be a long letter or a short note? What do you suppose he'd have to say to his friends and neighbors? What reasons do you think he'd provide for killing himself?

2. Compare Robinson's Arthurian tales with those of latter-day writers such as Howard Pyle and John Steinbeck. How do these twentieth-century takes on Arthurian mythology differ? How are they similar?

3. Robinson was fond of figuring the fictitious Tilbury Town in his poetry. In a short essay, explain why setting matters so much in works of fiction. Think of at least three examples of book plots, television shows, or films that depend on their setting to make sense.

BIBLIOGRAPHY

Books

Hogan, Charles Beecher. *A Bibliography of Edwin Arlington Robinson*. New Haven, Conn.: Yale University Press, 1936.

Joyner, Nancy Carol. *Edwin Arlington Robinson: A Reference Guide*. Boston: G. K. Hall, 1978.

Murphy, Francis. *Edwin Arlington Robinson: A Collection of Critical Essays*. Upper Saddle River, N.J.: Prentice-Hall, 1970.

Robinson, W. R. *Edwin Arlington Robinson: A Poetry of the Act*. Cleveland: Press of Western Reserve University, 1967.

Ruby, Mary, ed. "Richard Cory." *Poetry for Students*. Vol. 4. Detroit: Thomson Gale, 1999.

Smith, Chard Powers. *Where the Light Falls: A Portrait of Edwin Arlington Robinson*. New York: Macmillan, 1965.

White, William. *Edwin Arlington Robinson: A Supplementary Bibliography*. Kent, Ohio: Kent State University Press, 1971.

Periodicals

Adams, Richard P. "The Failure of Edwin Arlington Robinson." *Tulane Studies in English* 11 (1961): 97–1151.

Pritchard, William H. "Edwin Arlington Robinson: The Prince of Heartbreakers." *American Scholar* 40, no. 1 (Winter 1978–1979): 89–100.

✺ Marilynne Robinson

BORN: *1944, Sandpoint, Idaho*

NATIONALITY: *American*

GENRE: *Fiction*

MAJOR WORKS:
Housekeeping (1980)
Gilead (2005)

Marilynne Robinson   *Ulf Andersen / Getty Images*

Overview

Although her first and second novels were separated by two decades, Marilynne Robinson has consistently won effusive critical praise and recognition for her writing. Her novels are distinguished for their meditative tone and their focus on the inner lives of characters, written in the first person. Her narratives address family, small town living, isolation both physical and emotional, and everyday details of life. Robinson has also written several nonfiction works that reflect her concern with truth, sin, and redemption.

Works in Biographical and Historical Context

A Life of Writing Details of Robinson's life remain obscure, as most writings about her focus on her writing style rather than her biography. She was born in Sandpoint, Idaho, most likely in 1944—the years 1943 and 1947 have also been reported. After graduating from Coeur d'Alene High School in 1962, she attended Pembroke College in Warren, Rhode Island, where she graduated with a degree in history and religion in 1966. In 1977 Robinson received her PhD from the University of Washington.

LITERARY AND HISTORICAL CONTEMPORARIES

Robinson's famous contemporaries include:

Jane Smiley (1949–): Smiley is an American author whose novel *A Thousand Acres* (1991), a dramatic retelling of William Shakespeare's *King Lear* set in rural Iowa, won the Pulitzer Prize for Fiction.

Annie Proulx (1935–): An author known for her emphasis on place, Proulx has won numerous awards for works like *The Shipping News* (1993) and *Postcards* (1992).

Al Gore (1948–): Former vice president of the United States and presidential candidate in 2000, Gore has also earned an Academy Award for his work on the documentary *An Inconvenient Truth* (2006).

Michael Crichton (1942–2008): Crichton, a doctor-turned-novelist, was responsible for such popular best sellers as *The Great Train Robbery* (1975) and *Jurassic Park* (1990).

Jonathan Franzen (1959–): American author Franzen is best known as the author of the National Book Award–winning novel *The Corrections* (2001).

COMMON HUMAN EXPERIENCE

Like Robinson, other writers have explored multigenerational story arcs through fiction. Here are some examples:

The Master Butchers Singing Club (2003), a novel by Louise Erdrich. This novel tells the story of a German immigrant and his wife, spanning thirty years in the small North Dakota town in which they settle and raise a family in the years following World War I.

One Hundred Years of Solitude (1967), a novel by Gabriel García Márquez. Tracing seven generations of a family's struggle in a fictional Mexican town, García Márquez treats his multigenerational saga with metaphor, irony, and magical realism.

A Garden of Earthly Delights (1967), a novel by Joyce Carol Oates. Extensively revised in 2003, one of Oates's earliest novels centers on the Walpole family and their struggles with poverty and familial legacies over the course of generations.

In 1980 Robinson published her first novel, *Housekeeping*. Dedicated to her husband and children, the book was nominated for the Pulitzer Prize and won the PEN/Hemingway Award for best first novel. Following the publication of her novel, Robinson wrote essays for the *Paris Review*, *New York Times Review of Books*, and *Harper's*. She also began teaching at various colleges and universities, such as the University of Massachusetts, Amherst College, and the University of Kent.

Robinson abandoned fiction for two decades, focusing on nonfiction works such as *Mother Country* (1989), an exposé of the nuclear power industry and its opponents, specifically Greenpeace, an organization that successfully sued the British publisher of this book for libel and got the book banned in England. Nonetheless, the book was a National Book Award finalist in the United States. Robinson and her husband divorced, and she eventually joined the faculty of the Writers' Workshop at the University of Iowa.

In 2004 Robinson returned to fiction with *Gilead*, an epistolary novel—a story told through letters—that won the 2005 Pulitzer Prize. In September 2008, Robinson published her third and latest novel, *Home*, which serves as a sort of companion piece to *Gilead*. Robinson continues to live and work in Iowa City, Iowa.

Works in Literary Context

In addition to her command of the intricacies of language and texture, Robinson's fiction is notable for its focus on intergenerational relationships. From the mother-daughter, aunt-niece relationships in *Housekeeping* to the father-son and multigenerational histories of *Gilead* and *Home*, Robinson lays out an examination of how different generations within a family influence each other over time.

Family Relationships   All three of Robinson's novels dwell upon relationships within families, and in particular across generations. The legacies of grandparents and great-grandparents echo down through the years. Fathers and sons, mothers and daughters, aunts and nieces all make efforts to reach out and understand each other. *Gilead* is dominated by the difficulty in connecting between fathers and sons. *Housekeeping* examines the effect that different approaches taken by three aunts to the simple act of keeping house affects the lives of the nieces the women have been put in charge of caring for. In both *Gilead* and *Home*, the parable of the prodigal son is evoked—a biblical tale in which a son, who has moved away and lived foolishly, returns to the family. These generational conflicts are used as a means to explore the complex inner lives of the characters in all of Robinson's novels.

Works in Critical Context

With the publication of each of Robinson's novels, critics have been quick to offer praise for the author's mastery of prose style, language, landscapes, textures, and characterization. *Housekeeping* was likened by some to a long prose poem. Robinson was also given kudos for seeing beauty in the commonplace as well as her subtle description of essentially ordinary lives. While many critics noted that Robinson took her time publishing her second novel, *Gilead* was equally celebrated for its quiet power and its ability to touch on religious issues while remaining engaging as it considered universal ideas about life. When *Home* was published in 2008, critics, such as A. O. Scott in the *New York Times*, continued to praise the author's mastery of language, saying she "is somehow able to infuse what can sound like dowdy, common words … with a startling measure of their old luster and gravity." Writing in the *New Yorker*, James Wood calls *Home* "one of the most unconventional conventionally popular novels of recent times." Robinson's nonfiction books have received plaudits as being every bit as passionate and well written as her fiction.

Gilead　Upon its publication, *Gilead* received effusive praise from critics. Writing in *Booklist*, Donna Seaman calls the novel "a work of profound beauty and wonder." *New York Times* reviewer James Wood calls the book "a beautiful work—demanding, grave and lucid." An unnamed critic for *Kirkus Reviews* notes, "Robinson has composed, with its cascading perfections of symbols, a novel as big as a nation, as quiet as thought, and moving as prayer." In her review for *Michigan Quarterly Review*, Stacy Carson Hubbard stresses that "Ames's tale is not so much a celebration of goodness as it is a celebration of complexity and ambiguity." The novel, she writes, is "a meditation on the meaning of fatherhood, both literal and figurative." Hubbard concludes that Robinson's novel is a "remarkable and redemptive" work that "invites us, with a kind of understated ecstasy, to contemplate the mysteries of being in the world."

Thomas Meaney, writing in *Commentary*, praises the "masterly control" of the novel's narrative. Meaney explores Robinson's handling of the concept of predestination, and he concludes that "*Gilead* … argues that, in this world, moral responsibility lies squarely on the individual's shoulders." Gerald T. Cobb, writing for the journal *America*, concludes that "Robinson deftly combines the elegiac and the eulogistic into a compelling sense that this minister of a small town has a privileged view of life's horizons and depths." Comparing Robinson's *Gilead* to other contemporary writing, Scott A. Kaukonen writes in the *Missouri Review*: "In a culture where bombast passes for insight and where theological nuance suffers amid sound bites and power politics, *Gilead* refreshes like water from a deep, cold spring."

Responses to Literature

1. In what ways does the novel *Housekeeping* play upon the different possible meanings of its title? Provide specific examples from the text to support your statements.

2. All three of Robinson's novels have been set in the Midwest, the first set in her native state of Idaho, and the other two in the state in which she currently lives (Iowa). Research the term *regionalism* as it applies to literature. Do you think Robinson qualifies as a regional writer? Why or why not?

3. Read *Gilead* or *Home*. How does the tale of the prodigal son relate to either work? How does the author use the familiarity of the tale to her advantage in her own story?

4. What is the "generation gap"? Do you believe one exists today? What are some ways you feel connected to your parents' or grandparents' generations?

BIBLIOGRAPHY

Books

"Gilead." *Novels for Students*. Edited by Ira Milne. Vol. 24. Detroit: Gale, 2007.

Morddel, Anne. "Robinson, Marilynne." *Contemporary Novelists*. Edited by Neil Schlager and Josh Lauer. 7th ed. Detroit: St. James Press, 2001.

"Robinson, Marilynne (1943–)." *Student Resource Center*. Detroit: Thomson Gale, 2007.

"Robinson, Marilynne (1944(?)–)." *Major Twenty-First Century Writers*. Edited by Tracey Matthews. Vol. 4. Detroit: Gale, 2005.

White, Rosie. "Robinson, Marilynne." *Cambridge Guide to Women's Writings in English*. Edited by Lorna Sage, Germaine Greer, and Elaine Showalter. Cambridge, United Kingdom: Cambridge, 1999.

Periodicals

Hubbard, Stacy Carson. "The Balm in Gilead." *Michigan Quarterly Review* 44, no. 3 (Summer 2005): 541–545.

Kaukonen, Scott A. Review of *Gilead*. *Missouri Review* 28, no. 1 (2005): 226–228.

Web sites

Scott, A. O. "Return of the Prodigal Son." *New York Times Online*. Retrieved November 30, 2008, from http://movies.nytimes.com/2008/09/21/books/review/Scott-t.html?pagewanted=all. Last updated on September 19, 2008.

Wood, James. "The Homecoming." *New Yorker Online*. Retrieved November 30, 2008, from http://www.newyorker.com/arts/critics/books/2008/09/08/080908crbo_books_wood?currentPage=all. Last updated on September 8, 2008.

⊛ Richard Rodriguez

BORN: *1944, San Francisco, California*

NATIONALITY: *American*

GENRE: *Nonfiction*

MAJOR WORKS:

Hunger of Memory: The Education of Richard Rodriguez (1982)

Richard Rodriguez   © *Roger Ressmeyer / Corbis*

Overview

Rodriguez is principally known for his poetical autobiography, *Hunger of Memory: The Education of Richard Rodriguez* (1982), which addresses the issue of minority alienation in American society. Arranged as a collection of related autobiographical essays, *Hunger of Memory* earned Rodriguez a prominent place in Chicano literature for its reflections on the role of language in determining one's cultural identity. His combining of journalistic techniques with a conventional literary style have brought Rodriguez much acclaim as well, though his writings remain politically and socially controversial.

Works in Biographical and Historical Context

Growing Up Alienated   Richard Rodriguez was born in San Francisco on July 31, 1944, the son of Leopoldo and Victoria Moran Rodriguez. His father worked at several jobs before becoming a successful dental technician and introducing his family to middle-class life in California. Both parents emigrated from Mexico at a young age and met and married in the United States.

They spoke Spanish in the home, and when Richard moved with his family to Sacramento and entered Sacred Heart, a Catholic private elementary school, he was unable to speak English. It is from this point that he dates his alienation from his culture; it began as soon as he learned the "public" language that would separate him from his family. Catholic nuns who taught Rodriguez asked that his parents speak English to him at home. When they complied, related the author in a *Newsweek* article by Jean Strouse, the sound of his "private" language, Spanish, and its "pleasing, soothing, consoling reminder of being at home" was gone. Rodriguez's parents eventually came to feel emotionally distanced from the son they had raised, the son who was part of a world that offered far greater opportunities than they could ever hope for.

Rodriguez reached the goals his parents had sought for him. He graduated with a B.A. degree in English from Stanford University in 1967 and received an MA degree in religious studies from Columbia University in 1969. Rodriguez did graduate work at the University of California, Berkeley (1969–1972, 1974–1975), and at the Warburg Institute in London (1972–1973) as a Fulbright fellow studying English Renaissance literature. In London he abruptly decided to leave academic life. The choice was prompted by the feeling that he was "the beneficiary of truly disadvantaged Mexican Americans." "I benefited on their backs," he told *Publishers Weekly* interviewer Patricia Holt. In ten years of college and postgraduate education, Rodriguez received assistance grounded in merit but based in part on his minority status. (Affirmative action policies in the United States began in the 1960s. They were designed to give more opportunities in education and employment to members of racial minority groups that had in the past suffered from discrimination.) He left London and tried to reestablish the long-severed connection with his parents. He failed to recover his lost ethnicity, remaining "an academic ... a kind of anthropologist in the family kitchen."

Revolt   Rodriguez eventually began to fight the very policies that had helped him attain his academic credentials. His revolt against affirmative action began when he turned down several university-level teaching jobs. Writing to the chairmen of the many English departments who were courting him, Rodriguez declined the positions, explaining that he felt the only reason he was being selected was because of affirmative action. Furthermore, Rodriguez genuinely felt he was not a minority when, as Schreiber put it, "in fact the irreversibly successful effort of his life had been to become a fully assimilated member of the majority." Rodriguez spent the next six years writing *Hunger of Memory*, parts of which appeared in magazines before being brought together in book form.

The publication of *Hunger of Memory* gave Rodriguez considerable literary as well as political cachet. It explores Rodriguez's formative years, focusing on the theme of alienation. Claiming that language is the key factor for assimilation into American society, Rodriguez argues that to be a success in America requires the suppression and denial of one's cultural heritage and, in particular, one's native language.

Rodriguez's 1992 book, *Days of Obligation: An Argument with My Mexican Father*, is a collection of previously published autobiographical essays. In this book, Rodriguez revises some of his earlier views about the place and value of one's cultural roots. Also organized as a series of autobiographical essays, with his father's voice as philosophical antagonist, the work treats Rodriguez's continuing alienation, as well as the AIDS epidemic and his own homosexuality. Rodriguez concludes by "re-valuating" his Mexican heritage, acknowledging its importance for him both as an individual and as a writer. Though Rodriguez pleads for the total assimilation of the Chicano community into American society, scholars note that *Days of Obligation* reveals a renewed sensitivity to his Hispanic heritage. In 2002 Rodriguez published *Brown: The Last Discovery of America*, which brings his ideas on race in America into the twenty-first century. In particular, Rodriguez addresses the growing multiculturalism of American society.

Acknowledged as an influential voice from the Chicano community, Rodriguez has received many honors, including a gold medal for *Hunger of Memory* from the Commonwealth Club of California, the Christopher Prize for Autobiography, and the Cleveland Foundation's Anisfield-Wolf Award for civil rights. Today, Rodriguez lives in San Francisco, writing for periodicals and occasionally appearing as a guest journalist and commentator on PBS's "News Hour."

Works in Literary Context

Alienation, Assimilation, and Language   Rodriguez's positions on language and affirmative action have sparked most of the public discussions. In brief, he feels that all Americans must learn English, a public language, as opposed to Spanish, a private language used in the home. Condoning the brash Irish nuns who invaded his home to insist that the Spanish-speaking Rodriguezes use only English, he attributes his success to this wrenching move toward assimilation. He attacks affirmative action, feeling that government programs accelerate the success of middle-class Chicanos like himself to the detriment of the targeted group, barrio Chicanos. In his view, affirmative action should be based on class, not ethnic group. In an interview in *People* magazine given shortly after the publication of *Hunger of Memory*, he synthesized his feelings on ethnic identity:

> I refuse to accept my generation's romanticism about discovering "roots." The trouble with that is it somehow holds children accountable for maintaining their culture, and freezes them into thinking of themselves as Mexicans or as Chinese or as

LITERARY AND HISTORICAL CONTEMPORARIES

Richard Rodriguez's famous contemporaries include:

Isabel Allende (1942–): One of the first successful female writers of the Latin American literary "boom," Allende, a Chilean-American born in Peru, has written several best sellers, many in the genre of magical realism.

Ronald Reagan (1911–2004): As America's fortieth president from 1981 to 1989, Ronald Reagan took the popularity based on a successful movie career and the political capital earned as governor of California during the 1960s and 1970s to become perhaps the most successful conservative president of the twentieth century. During his presidency, the long saga of the cold war entered its final chapter; his economic program, dubbed "Reaganomics," remains a lasting and controversial force in the American economy.

Alice Walker (1944–): Best known for her 1982 novel *The Color Purple*, Walker is an outspoken activist in the cause of women's rights and racial equality.

Phyllis Schlafly (1924–): A conservative political activist, Schlafly is perhaps best known for her successful campaign against the Equal Rights Amendment, a proposed amendment to the U.S. Constitution that would have guaranteed equal legal rights regardless of gender. Schlafly argued that the passage of the ERA would lead to women being drafted into the army, among other things.

Gabriel García Márquez (1921–): Winner of the Nobel Prize in Literature, Colombian author García Márquez has worked as a journalist and screenwriter, but it is for his novels, including *One Hundred Years of Solitude* (1967) and *Love in the Time of Cholera* (1985), that he remains most famous.

Sandra Cisneros (1954–): Cisneros is a Chicano author whose novel *The House on Mango Street* (1984), a coming-of-age story set in Chicago, was a breakthrough success for Chicana literature.

blacks. But culture is an extraordinary progression of ancestral memories and individual experience. People have accused me of losing my heritage. That assumes heritage is this little suitcase I carry with me, with tortillas and a little Mexican cowboy suit inside, and that one day I lost it at a Greyhound depot. The fact is, culture survives whether you want it to or not.

Rodriguez says that his autobiography "is a book about language." Rodriguez discusses his use of language as an author in the final chapter, "Mr. Secrets," in which he analyzes the act of writing and its motivation. A writer's feelings, he says, "are capable of public intelligibility. . . . By finding public words to describe one's

COMMON HUMAN EXPERIENCE

Rodriguez is one of many authors and thinkers who have penned books exploring issues and offering thoughts pertinent to Chicanos and other Hispanic communities. Here are some other works that deal with similar themes:

The Autobiography of a Brown Buffalo (1972), by Oscar Zeta Acosta. Part autobiography, part novel, this book was written by a prominent Chicano lawyer and activist.

A Puerto Rican in New York and Other Sketches (1961), by Jesus Colon. A collection of essays on the Hispanic experience in America, Colon's focus is primarily on the plight of the working class Latino.

Barrio Boy (1971), a novel by Ernesto Galarza. Another fictionalized autobiography, this novel is based on Galarza's childhood at the dawn of the twentieth century, primarily centering on his arduous journey from Mexico, wracked at the time by revolution, to California, where he eventually earned a degree from Stanford University.

Labyrinth of Solitude (1950), a novel by Octavio Paz. One of Nobel laureate Paz's best-known works, this novel is a sophisticated examination of the cultural psyche of Latin America.

feelings, one can describe oneself to oneself. One names what was previously only darkly felt."

As reviewer Paul Zweig observed, *Hunger of Memory* "is not only about the language adventures of a Mexican American child ... it is also about the coming into being of the remarkable language in which it is written."

Through the concept of language Rodriguez explores the processes of alienation, assimilation, growing up, and, of course, education. Through growth in language Rodriguez increasingly alienates himself from his family, the comfortable childhood with warm Spanish sounds, as he enters an adult world of superficial communication. The wedge between him and his family was caused mainly by education, a linguistic process that he describes as "radical self-reformation."

Works in Critical Context

Reviewers have given Rodriguez more attention than any other Mexican American author. Even the *New York Times Book Review*, indifferent to the literary creation of the Chicano movement since its beginnings in the 1960s, gave front-page recognition to *Hunger of Memory* (February 28, 1982). Approximately fifty other periodicals, from professional newsletters to library journals to the *New Yorker* and *Atlantic Monthly*, reviewed Rodriguez's autobiography. Commentators generally agree that Rodriguez's literary style is clear, poetical, and engaging.

Other critics note his adept blending of journalistic and classical literary techniques. *Hunger of Memory* has been praised in particular for its exploration of the influence of language on life and its observations on the "public" and "private" domains of language in minority cultures. While praising Rodriguez's literary expertise, however, Chicano scholars dispute his social and political conclusions, contending that his works fail to consider all of the facts surrounding the issues, and that Rodriguez's conclusions subvert the value of minority cultures. Indeed, critics who support Rodriguez's views as realistic and insightful are primarily mainstream American commentators who see him as a unique talent bridging Chicano and American cultures. As Ilan Stavans reflects: "[Rodriguez] is the embodiment of that complex fate shared by those born twice American: hybrids always living in the hyphen, with one leg here and the other across the Rio Grande."

Hunger of Memory In the opinion of *New York Times* critic Le Anne Schreiber, Richard Rodriguez's autobiography, *Hunger of Memory*, is an "honest and intelligent account of how education can alter a life." *Hunger of Memory* was praised by several critics, especially for its discussion of the impact of language on life. Le Anne Schreiber found that "what matters most about this intensely thoughtful book is that Richard Rodriguez has given us the fruit of his long meditation upon language." Paul Zweig judged that "the chapters Mr. Rodriguez devotes to his early experiences of language are uncannily sensitive to the nuances of language learning, the childhood drama of voices, intonations." A *New Yorker* review commended Rodriguez as "a writer of unusual grace and clarity ... eloquent in all his reflections."

However, Some Mexican Americans, such as Arturo Madrid (*La Red/The Net*, April 23, 1982), saw in Rodriguez's book a betrayal of the goals of the Chicano people as evidenced by the government programs he attacked. Sarcastically deriding Rodriguez's angst, these detractors have been rarely moved by his style or convinced of the universality of his experience. They felt that he spoke only for himself to a white audience. Yet Antonio C. Marquez, a professor of Chicano literature, argued that

> there is a level of artistry in *Hunger of Memory* that should not be shunned simply because Rodriguez does not meet the Procrustean bed of "cultural awareness" of any other ideology. I contend that its ultimate value lies in its literary qualities and the uniqueness of the autobiographical form.

Days of Obligation In this collection, Rodriguez returns to many of the issues he probed in *Hunger of Memory*: language, history, and the immigrant history. Critics remarked that *Days of Obligation* lacks the intuitive, coherent structure of *Hunger of Memory* but averred that the book once again displays the author's skill in producing powerful autobiographical writing. For instance, *Washington Post Book World* critic Jonathan Yardley noted, "though the earnestness of Rodriguez's self-examination remains affecting and convincing, *Days of Obligation* ... never states in sufficiently clear terms either the nature of the argument or the author's own line of reasoning." Though admitting that the book can be "maddeningly presumptuous and determinedly obscure," *New York Times Book Review* contributor David L. Kirp exclaimed that "In its most powerful passages, *Days of Obligation* reveals the writer as a tightrope walker who balances pessimism and the defeat of predictable expectations against the discovery of the profoundly unanticipated." Concluded Gray, "The wrestling with his elusive and insistent past makes these sinuous ruminations worthy of inclusion in the long American tradition of spiritual autobiography."

Responses to Literature

1. What is the role of public education in Rodriguez's discussions of language in *Hunger of Memory*?

2. How does Rodriguez view the "loss of ethnicity"? How does his background account for his views?

3. Why do you think Rodriguez views language as so central to the identity and acceptance of minorities in American society?

4. How do you feel about Rodriguez's stance on affirmative action? Do you think it was right of him to turn down teaching positions? Why or why not? Do you agree with him that affirmative action should be class-based and not race-based?

BIBLIOGRAPHY

Periodicals

Crowley, Paul. "An Ancient Catholic: An Interview with Richard Rodríguez." *America* (September 23, 1995): 8.

Danahay, Martin A. "Breaking the Silence: Symbolic Violence and the Teaching of Contemporary 'Ethnic' Autobiography." *College Literature* 18 (October 1991): 64–79.

Madrid, Arturo. *La Red/The Net* (April 23, 1982).

Marzan, Julio. "Richard Rodriguez's *Hunger of Memory* and the Poetics of Experience." *Arizona Quarterly* 40 (Summer 1984): 130–141.

McNamara, Kevin R. "A Finer Grain: Richard Rodriguez's *Days of Obligation*." *Arizona Quarterly* 53 (Spring 1997): 103–122.

Postrel, Virginia, and Nick Gillespie. "The New, New World: Richard Rodriguez on Culture and Assimilation." *Reason* 26 (August 1, 1994): 35(7).

Shuter, Bill. "The Confessions of Richard Rodriguez." *Cross-Currents* 45 (Spring 1995): 95–105.

Walton, Antony. "Greater than All the Parts." *New York Times Book Review* (April 7, 2002): 7.

Web sites

Online News Hour. *Richard Rodriguez Essays.* Retrieved November 27, 2008, from http://www.pbs.org/newshour/essays/richard_rodriguez.html. Last updated on May 17, 2007.

⊛ Theodore Roethke

BORN: *1908, Saginaw, Michigan*

DIED: *1963, Bainbridge Island, Washington*

NATIONALITY: *American*

GENRE: *Poetry*

MAJOR WORKS:

Open House (1941)
The Lost Son and Other Poems (1948)
The Waking: Poems, 1933–1953 (1953)
The Far Field (1964)

Overview

Considered one of the leading poets of the twentieth century during his lifetime, Theodore Roethke's work matured over time from initially emulating the poetry of earlier Romantics to a highly individual lyrical naturalism.

Works in Biographical and Historical Context

Growing Up in Michigan Theodore Roethke was born in Saginaw, Michigan. His father, Otto Roethke,

Theodore Roethke   *Roethke, Theodore (wearing dark overcoat, tie, weary expression), photograph. The Library of Congress.*

LITERARY AND HISTORICAL CONTEMPORARIES

Theodore Roethke's famous contemporaries include:

Jack Kerouac (1922–1969): Known both for his own writing and the influence he has exerted over countless other writers and artists, Kerouac was one of the leading figures of the "Beat Generation" of anti-establishment thinkers in the 1950s.

Edward R. Murrow (1908–1965): A paragon of respectable, responsible journalism, Murrow became an international celebrity reporting from war-torn Europe during World War II, then went on to become a pioneering figure in television news at the dawn of that new medium.

Daphne du Maurier (1907–1989): Du Maurier was the British author of such sweeping gothic novels as *Rebecca* (1940), which is often cited as the first modern "romance" novel, despite the fact that du Maurier herself hated the label.

Chiang Kai-shek (1887–1975): Military leader of the Republic of China, Chiang Kai-shek fought for twenty years against rival factions, Communists, and invading Japanese, only to eventually be forced into exile, along with his supporters, on the island of Taiwan.

Dylan Thomas (1914–1953): Thomas was a Welsh poet whose lyrical, insightful verse, most famously in his meditative "Do not go gentle into that good night" (1951), along with his popular readings, brought him fame on both sides of the Atlantic.

---

had immigrated to America from Germany in 1872. The Roethkes prospered, and when Roethke's grandfather had made sufficient money, he built a greenhouse so that he could enter the florist business, which also prospered. As a child, Roethke followed his father about his work. Thus, Roethke almost literally, grew up among the plants of the greenhouse. His experience of this vegetable world affected him deeply: the greenhouse itself was to become the central image of *The Lost Son* (1948) and *Praise to the End!* (1951). Also on the property, beyond the greenhouse, was a large field where Roethke often played as a child. This field, too, became an important image in his poetry.

During his freshman year of high school, Roethke distinguished himself by giving a speech on the Junior Red Cross, which was published and later translated into twenty-six languages for international distribution. This recognition whetted his ambition. He already knew that he wanted to become a writer, although he had not yet considered becoming a poet. At the time, he later recalled, he wanted to be a prose writer; so he began studying essayists, such as Walter Pater, Henry David Thoreau, Ralph Waldo Emerson, and short story writers.

During Roethke's second year in high school, his father died of cancer, a "kink in the bowels," as the doctors said. Outwardly, Roethke accepted the event calmly, probably because he had been prepared for it by the long illness that preceded Otto's death. However, as Roethke's mature poetry suggests, the loss had a deep and lasting effect on him. His attitude toward his father had been ambivalent. On the one hand, Otto had often been a hard taskmaster, demanding perfection from his son and belittling him when he failed to live up to standards. On the other hand, Roethke could admire the life-giving quality in Otto, not just as his own father, but as the gardener who devoted himself to the perpetuation of life. In "The Lost Son," which is written from the point of view of a child, the father's arrival is associated with order. In "My Papa's Waltz" Roethke captures the earthy vitality of Otto, and also something of his own joy and bafflement, as the victim of his father's exuberant energy. Later, in "Otto," written forty years after his father's death, Roethke objectively records the vitality, order, and contradictions in his father's character.

A Most Unlikely Poet Theodore Roethke was hardly one who would have been expected to become a major American poet. Though as a child he read a great deal, he strove to be accepted by his peers who felt that "brains were sissies." The insecurity that led him to drink to be "in with the guys" continued at the University of Michigan, where he adopted a tough, bear-like image (he weighed well over 225 pounds) and even developed a fascination with gangsters—it was the height of the Prohibition era, when gangsters like Al Capone ruled virtual crime empires. Eccentric and nonconformist—he later called himself "odious" and "unhappy"—"[h]is adolescence must have been a hell of a bright awareness," speculated Rolfe Humphries, "frustrated because he did not know what to do with it, and it was constantly sandpapered by those around him."

Roethke's awareness evolved at Michigan into a decision to pursue teaching—and poetry—as a career. The first fifteen years of Roethke's writing career, from his beginnings as an undergraduate to the publication of *Open House* (1941), his first book, formed a "lengthy and painful apprenticeship" for the young writer. In cultivating his poetic expression, Roethke relied heavily upon T. S. Eliot's belief that "the only way to manipulate any kind of English verse, [is] by assimilation and imitation." With this model in mind, Roethke himself once wrote "imitation, conscious imitation, is one of the great methods, perhaps THE method of learning to write."

Roethke's task was no easy one. In addition to debts to such contemporaries as W. H. Auden, Louise Bogan, Babette Deutsch, and William Carlos Williams, his extensive and varied poetic tradition included William Wordsworth, William Blake, Walt Whitman, William Butler Yeats, T. S. Eliot, and Dante. Along with these influences, the source of much of Roethke's poetry was the notes he dutifully kept throughout his life. In his biography of Roethke, *The Glass House*, Allan Seager estimates that only three percent of the lines of poetry in Roethke's more than two hundred notebooks was ever published.

Developing His Own Voice   After the publication of *Open House*, Roethke became dissatisfied with his job at Penn State, and accepted a position at Bennington College, where he thought the atmosphere would be much more congenial to his career as a poet and teacher. While at Bennington, Roethke established several important relationships with his colleagues. With the encouragement of his new friends and colleagues, Roethke threw himself into a fit of poetic creation that was to produce the major poems of *The Lost Son*. A period of depression followed in the winter of 1945. He was taken to a hospital in Albany where he underwent shock treatments. Roethke resumed work on his poetry during the spring while he was recovering his strength. By February 1947, the poems were completed, and he returned to Penn State to teach the spring semester. That summer he went to Yaddo, where he became friends with Robert Lowell. Also, during the summer he was accepted for a teaching position at the University of Washington in Seattle. In September he went west.

Roethke had been disappointed in Knopf's handling of *Open House*; they had not advertised the book properly, he felt, and they had failed to bring out a second printing, even when the first small printing of one thousand copies had been sold out. In the meantime, he had established contacts at Doubleday; consequently, when the manuscript of *The Lost Son* was completed in the spring of 1947, he sent it to them, and it was accepted. Again Roethke waited anxiously for the reviews; this time they were even more laudatory than those for *Open House*. This was original poetry, and the reviewers recognized it as such.

Roethke soon settled into a routine of life and was happier than he had been in any of his previous teaching positions. He was popular with his students. Among these students were several who were to become poets in their own right: Carolyn Kizer, David Wagoner, James Wright. Under these favorable conditions, Roethke worked hard at both his teaching and his poetry. His serious work was on the poems that would make up *Praise to the End!* (1951), but he was also writing a sequence of children's poems about animals that were published as *I Am! Says the Lamb* in 1961. During the Fall of 1949, Roethke suffered another mental breakdown and spent several months in a sanitarium. Sometime during 1950 he finished the poems for *Praise to the End!* and it was published in November 1951.

At the Height of His Career   Roethke now had three volumes of poetry and a reputation. In 1951 he received *Poetry* magazine's Levinson Prize. In the spring of 1952, his friend Dylan Thomas visited the Seattle campus. There he stated that Roethke was the best poetry reader in America. Roethke cherished this praise from the master reader himself and often repeated it. Roethke was now at the height of his career and no longer had to worry about money as he had in the past. In June he went to Saginaw to see his family and work undisturbed, away from the distractions in Seattle. In December he went to New York to give a poetry reading. There he ran into one of his former Bennington students, Beatrice O'Connell, who was now living in New York teaching art in a public school in Harlem. They began to see each other daily, and they married within a month.

In September 1953, Doubleday brought out *The Waking*, a selection of Roethke's poems, written between 1933 and 1953. It also included eight new poems. The end of the year brought twin tragedies in the loss of both Dylan Thomas and Roethke's mother, but good news came several weeks later: he had won the Pulitzer Prize for *The Waking*.

Later Career and Accolades   Roethke spent the next several years teaching, traveling, and experiencing continued mental breakdowns. In the fall of 1958, Doubleday published *Words for the Wind*, a mixture of new and previously collected poems. The critical reception was overwhelmingly favorable, and he received both the Bollingen Prize and the National Book Award.

Roethke remained in Seattle for the last years of his life, teaching, working on the poems that would appear posthumously as *The Far Field*, and making frequent trips to receive awards and give readings. In June 1962, he was presented an honorary Doctor of Letters degree from his alma mater, the University of Michigan. In October he gave a reading for the Seattle World's Fair. By the summer of 1963, he had completed the first draft of the manuscript for *The Far Field* (1964). He intended to revise it further, but on August 1, while swimming in a friend's pool, he had a coronary occlusion from which he could not be revived. He was buried beside his mother and father in Oakwood Cemetery in Saginaw.

Works in Literary Context

Roethke is among the most celebrated American poets of the twentieth century. His work conveys through dynamic, descriptive imagery the physical essence of nature and the human body. The concrete language of Roethke's poetry serves to present his personal themes as universal experiences, resulting in a highly original, symbolic body of work.

Romanticism   Roethke saw himself as working within a great tradition, modifying and extending it after his own fashion. Specifically, Roethke was a Romantic. His work abounds in references to European poets William Blake, William Wordsworth, and William Butler Yeats, especially, but also retains the American quality of his Romanticism with Ralph Waldo Emerson and Walt Whitman as primary ancestors, and with Ted Stevens as a

COMMON HUMAN EXPERIENCE

For Roethke, nature, and in particular gardens and the tiny wonders they contain, are a central theme. Other poetic works that center on the small things in nature include:

"The Grass so little has to do" (1924), a poem by Emily Dickinson. Known for her whimsical, introspective poems, here Dickinson personifies a field of grass as a playful, carefree entity, free to play with birds and bees and dance to the rhythm of breezes.

"Ode to a Nightingale" (1819), a poem by John Keats. An ode is a stately long-form poem that meditates upon a single object or subject, often in praise-worthy terms. Here Keats turns his meditations to the simple nightingale as a metaphor for immortality.

"Tintern Abbey" (1798), a poem by William Wordsworth. Taken from the collection *Lyrical Ballads*, this final poem of the collection finds Wordsworth reflecting upon a ruined abbey and the natural beauty of the River Wye valley surrounding it as symbolic of his general feelings on nature.

strong contemporary influence. Without impugning his originality, one can read all Roethke's work as a continuing conversation with his precursors; he was a poetic ventriloquist of sorts, able to speak through masks of those whom he called "the great dead."

The work of recent critics has been invaluable in showing the breadth and continuity of the Romantic movement, from its origins in eighteenth-century Germany to the present. What seems constant, is the recognition that every man is cut off from nature; given this state of affairs, art becomes indispensable in the process of reconciliation between self and nature (subject and object). Every man has either to make his peace with nature or wage his own "war between the mind and sky," as Stevens puts it.

Nature and the Poetic Journey The motif of the journey is more crucial to the poetry of Theodore Roethke than to any other major American poet since Whitman. Roethke's is a simple journey, from beginning to destination. But to say that it is simple is not to imply that it is easy. The journey, as it is recorded in *The Collected Poems* (1966), is that of a modern-day *Pilgrim's Progress*, the allegorical seventeenth-century tale by John Bunyan, fraught with temptations of vanity and pride. But Roethke's journey is essentially more difficult. For Roethke there is no well-defined path, nor are there signposts or prominences to indicate his destination. His journey is through a particularly American wilderness, and although the general direction of the journey is never in question, Roethke must make his groping way relying

on his instincts or intuitions, "feeling" and learning by the very act of "going" itself, as he was to articulate the process in his poem "The Waking." The American pilgrim makes his way westward through the wilderness toward discovery and self-realization: this is the movement of both Roethke's poetry and his life.

Roethke's journey is also an evolutionary one, essentially that described and speculated on by his contemporary Loren Eiseley in *The Immense Journey* (1957). In his second published book, *The Lost Son* (1948), Roethke returns to his evolutionary past, where he joins the worms, slugs, and snails in the slime of primordial existence. From that point, Roethke's poetry moves forward, through the realization of his kinship with the higher animals, through the realization of his own humanity (in *The Waking*, 1953, and *Words for the Wind*, 1957), and finally to the transcendence of spiritual man in *The Far Field* (1964). It is a movement from unconscious life, through various stages of intermediate consciousness, to the highest form of self-realization man is capable of.

Works in Critical Context

At the time of his death Roethke's reputation was high in both America and Europe. Many considered him the best American poet of his generation. Since his death, there has been a steadily increasing interest in his poetry, both by critics and the reading public. Most have placed him in the top rank of all American poets.

Critics have often disagreed, however, in their attempts to classify Roethke's poetic style. His deeply personal images and the manner in which he utilizes nature to explore psychological territories, have prompted scholars to associate Roethke's verse with either the Confessional or the Romantic school of poetry. The implicit content of his poems prompted Richard Allen Blessing to note: "When Roethke is at his best, 'meaning' is a complex of forces, a musical expression growing ... out of the play of sound against sound, out of the energy of primitive rhythms ... out of the telescoping ... of images." In any case, many would agree with Stanley Kunitz's assessment:

> Roethke belongs to that superior order of poets who will not let us rest in any of their poems, who keep driving us back through the whole body of their work to that live cluster of images, ideas, memories, and obsessions that constitutes the individuating source of the creative personality.

The Lost Son Justin Parini, in his book *Theodore Roethke: An American Romantic*, writes, "In all, *The Lost Son* remains the central volume, this poet's most durable achievement, and the key to his work." Michael Harrington states that "Roethke found his own voice and central themes" in the work, and Stanley Kunitz saw a "confirmation that he was in full possession of his art and of his vision." Richard Allen Blessing echoes this praise when he writes:

To my mind, the transformation of Theodore Roethke from a poet of 'lyric resourcefulness, technical proficiency and ordered sensibility' to a poet of 'indomitable creativeness and audacity ... difficult, heroic, moving and profoundly disquieting' is one of the most remarkable in American literary history.

Responses to Literature

1. Using your library or the Internet, research the Confessional movement in modern poetry. Can you find samples from Roethke's poetry that serve as examples of confessional verse?

2. How did Roethke's work change over his lifetime? Contrast one of his early poems to a poem published after his death and note the differences in style and theme.

3. Why do you feel *The Waking* brought Roethke so much critical acclaim? What was the state of poetry at the time it was published?

4. Roethke asserted that in order to learn one's craft, one must start with copying the old masters before developing a singular voice. Do you agree with this sentiment? Why or why not?

BIBLIOGRAPHY

Books

Blessing, Richard Allen. *Theodore Roethke's Dynamic Vision*. Bloomington, Ind.: Indiana University Press, 1974.

Bogen, Don. *Theodore Roethke and the Writing Process*. Athens, Ohio: Ohio University Press, 1991.

Bowers, Neal. *Theodore Roethke: The Journey from I to Otherwise*. Columbia, Mo.: University of Missouri Press, 1982.

Chaney, Norman. *Theodore Roethke: The Poetics of Wonder*. Washington, D.C.: University Press of America, 1981.

"My Papa's Waltz." *Poetry for Students*. Edited by Marie Napierkowski and Mary Ruby. Vol. 3. Detroit: Thomson Gale, 1998.

Parini, Jay. *Theodore Roethke: An American Romantic*. Boston: University of Massachusetts Press, 1979.

Stein, Arnold, ed. *Theodore Roethke: Essays on the Poetry*. Seattle, Wash.: University of Washington Press, 1965.

Stiffler, Randall. *Theodore Roethke, The Poet and His Critics*. Chicago: American Library Association, 1986.

Sullivan, Rosemary. *Theodore Roethke: The Garden Master*. Seattle, Wash.: University of Washington Press, 1975.

Williams, Harry. *"The Edge is What I Have": Theodore Roethke and After*. Lewisburg, Pa.: Bucknell University Press, 1977.

Wolff, George. *Theodore Roethke*. Boston: Twayne, 1981.

Periodicals

Burke, Kenneth. "The Vegetal Radicalism of Theodore Roethke." *Sewanee Review* 58 (Winter 1950): 68–108.

Staples, Hugh. "The Rose in the Sea-Wind: A Reading of Theodore Roethke's 'North American Sequence.'" *American Literature* 36 (May 1964): 189–203.

❁ Eleanor Roosevelt

BORN: *1884, New York City, New York*

DIED: *1962, New York City, New York*

NATIONALITY: *American*

GENRE: *Nonfiction*

MAJOR WORKS:
This Is My Story (1937)
This I Remember (1949)
On My Own (1958)

Overview

Arguably the most well-known—and certainly the most politically active—First Lady of all time, Eleanor Roosevelt made a name for herself as, not only a staunch supporter and partner to her husband, President Franklin

Eleanor Roosevelt   *Roosevelt, Eleanor, photograph. Courtesy of the FDR Library.*

D. Roosevelt, but also in her own right as a crusader for human and civil rights and an early icon of the women's rights movement.

Works in Biographical and Historical Context

A Difficult Childhood   Born to a wealthy New York family, Anna Eleanor Roosevelt, as she was christened, did not have an easy childhood. Her father, though loving, was a chronic drunk; her mother was strict and severe and overly concerned with the family's image. She berated her daughter for her homely looks, calling her "Granny" and creating a deep sense of shyness and insecurity in young Eleanor. By the time she was ten years old, both of Eleanor's parents were dead—her mother from diphtheria, her father from a bad fall—and Eleanor and her siblings were sent to live with their grandmother, another strict and matronly figure who continued to feed Eleanor's insecurities.

Things finally began to turn around when Eleanor, at the age of fifteen, was sent to England to study at the exclusive Allenswood finishing school. There, under the attentive tutelage of the headmistress, Mademoiselle Marie Souvestre, daughter of a prominent liberal French philosopher, Eleanor experienced encouragement and popularity for the first time. She returned to America two years later with a determination to begin using her position to help better society.

Social Work and Marriage   Largely rejecting the social expectations that were placed upon young women of means at the turn of the twentieth century, Eleanor instead focused on outreach programs, teaching classes at an institute for the poor and disadvantaged, and visiting children in the nearby tenement slums of New York City. She also joined a watchdog group that kept tabs on working conditions in garment factories and department stores, both of which employed primarily young, poor women. "The feeling that I was useful was perhaps the greatest joy I experienced," she later said.

During this time, Eleanor also got to know her distant cousin, five times removed, Franklin Delano Roosevelt. The two fell in love and, despite the reservations of Franklin's mother, they married in 1905, when she was twenty and he twenty-three. Eleanor's uncle, President Theodore Roosevelt, gave the bride away at the wedding. Afterwards, Eleanor quickly came under the domineering personality of her mother-in-law, who virtually ran the Roosevelt household. Over the next ten years, Eleanor gave birth to six children, one of whom died in infancy. During this time, with Eleanor's strong support and encouragement, Franklin began to build his political career, moving first into state politics, then gaining a position in Washington in 1913 as assistant secretary of the navy. When the United States entered World War I in

April 1917, Eleanor became a tireless volunteer with the Red Cross.

When Franklin returned from an inspection trip to Europe in September 1918, Eleanor discovered evidence of an affair between him and his personal secretary. Devastated, she offered to divorce him, but out of consideration for their children, and Franklin's political career, he refused. The couple would remain married, but the intimacy had vanished. In its place was a newfound determination on Eleanor's part to live life on her own terms. She would never again be subjugated by her mother-in-law's will.

Redefining the Position of First Lady   In 1921, during a sailing trip to the family retreat in New Brunswick, Canada, Franklin was stricken with polio, a degenerative disease that left him unable to walk. His mother strongly favored retirement from public life to the life of a genteel convalescent, but Eleanor's will prevailed this time: she alone urged her husband to continue his political career, and she alone helped nurse him back to health. In anticipation of the role she would have to play in the public eye in order to assist Franklin's political ambitions, she also mastered public speaking and political administration.

Throughout the 1920s, Eleanor was highly active in Democratic politics, campaigning on behalf of New York Governor Al Smith during his unsuccessful runs for the White House in 1924 and 1928. She also, in partnership with two friends, established a nonprofit works program and purchased a progressive private academy for wealthy girls, where Eleanor personally taught classes several days a week. In 1928, Franklin was elected governor of New York, and four years later he was elected president in the midst of the Great Depression. Roosevelt's election to the presidency in 1932 meant, as Eleanor later wrote, "the end of any personal life of my own."

Franklin Roosevelt came into the White House with an ambitious plan of govenment-funded work and poverty relief programs called the New Deal. Eleanor was, if anything, even more ambitious in her views on what needed to be done to bring the country out of the Depression, and it was at this time that she began publicizing her views in earnest. She quickly became a polarizing figure in American society, earning either devoted support or bitter opposition. Although she had been writing a weekly column for the *Women's Home Companion*, in 1936 she switched to a syndicated newspaper column and a series of radio broadcasts, the income from which she donated to charity. From June 1941 until spring 1949, she wrote a monthly question-and-answer column called "If You Ask Me" for *Ladies' Home Journal*, in addition to the monthly column she wrote for *McCall's*. It is estimated that Roosevelt wrote 2,500 newspaper columns and 299 magazine articles between 1933 and 1945, her years at the White House. Her column, "My Day," which would run until her death in

1962, addressed political topics frankly and openly, going against the tradition of the First Lady as largely being concerned solely with the social side of the presidential lifestyle. Although her prose style was basically pedestrian, filled with clichés and a certain naiveté, it was well received by her supporters.

Championing Human Rights Roosevelt's politics were mainly concerned with championing the rights of those she felt weren't getting a fair chance from society. Her press conferences were only open to female reporters, at a time when the news media was still very much a male-dominated profession. She also opened up government posts to qualified women. She was an ardent supporter of many New Deal policies, particularly those that helped people who had already been living below the poverty line when the Depression struck, such as Southern sharecroppers and Appalachian farmers or big city garment workers. She became a tireless advocate for increased civil rights, saying, "It is a question of the right to work and the right to work should know no color lines."

Roosevelt's positions on civil rights were often far more liberal than her husband's, and much of what she lobbied for, such as anti-lynching laws and desegregation of the armed forces, would not come to pass during the Roosevelt administration. Franklin Roosevelt died of a cerebral hemorrhage in April of 1945, leaving Eleanor a widow after four decades of marriage. Once again, she bucked tradition, which would ordinarily call for a life of genteel retirement, instead throwing herself into work on behalf of the newly formed United Nations.

Diplomatic Achievements Roosevelt was appointed by the new president, Harry Truman, as the American delegate to the United Nations Commission on Human Rights. As chairman of the Commission, Roosevelt was instrumental in drafting the Universal Declaration of Human Rights, adopted by the UN General Assembly in 1948. She remained in her post at the UN through 1952. Increasingly finding herself a target of right-wing attacks during the presidential campaign of that year, she gave up her UN post after the election of Republican Dwight D. Eisenhower. She remained, however, a very public figure, working towards building international goodwill and friendship as a representative of the American Association for the United Nations. She also did not shy away from the political scene, continuing to write about her views on liberal causes and, in particular, speaking out against the anti-communist witch hunts of Senator Joseph McCarthy during the mid-1950s.

During the last decade of her life Eleanor Roosevelt traveled to numerous foreign countries and authored several books. She continued to articulate a personal and social outlook which, while never profound and sometimes banal and obtuse, still inspired millions. Under the Kennedy administration, beginning in 1961, she kept up her tireless diplomatic schedule, acting as delegate to the UN, adviser to the Peace Corps, and chairman of the

LITERARY AND HISTORICAL CONTEMPORARIES

Roosevelt's famous contemporaries include:

Karen Blixen (1885–1962): Writing under the pen name of Isak Dinesen, Danish Baroness Blixen is perhaps best known for her account of seventeen years spent living on a coffee plantation in Kenya entitled *Out of Africa* (1937).

Theodor Geisel (1904–1991): Better known by his whimsical pen name of Dr. Seuss, Geisel wrote and illustrated a slew of classic children's stories, including *The Cat in the Hat* (1957), *Green Eggs and Ham* (1960), and *How the Grinch Stole Christmas!* (1957).

Howard Hughes (1905–1976): Early on in life, Hughes used his personal fortune to bankroll blockbuster movies and participate in the budding world of aviation, often personally taking part in air races and cross-country flights. Later in life, Hughes became notorious as an eccentric, rich recluse.

Ellen Glasgow (1873–1941): Glasgow was a southern writer whose novels critique the traditional southern attitude to women and the injustices women have to endure. She created strong female characters who strive to create effective lives for themselves. Her most famous work is *Barren Ground* (1925).

Harry S. Truman (1884–1972): U.S. president from 1945 to 1953, Harry Truman was unpopular during his presidency, but is now regarded highly by presidential historians. Truman appointed Eleanor Roosevelt as a delegate to the United Nations General Assembly. Truman later called her "The First Lady of the World."

Adlai Stevenson II (1900–1965): Stevenson was a Democratic politician, widely admired for his outstanding intellect. He ran unsuccessfully for the presidency twice, in 1952 and 1956, and on both occasions he was supported by Eleanor Roosevelt.

President's Commission on the Status of Women. She died in New York City on November 6, 1962.

A year before her death, Roosevelt's three autobiographical books, *This Is My Story* (1937), *This I Remember* (1949), and *On My Own* (1958), were combined with an additional updated chapter in *Autobiography* (1961).

Roosevelt summed up her life in her *Autobiography* thusly: "About the only value the story of my life may have is to show that . . . in spite of a lack of special talents, one can find a way to live widely and fully."

Works in Literary Context

Autobiography The autobiography—an account of a person's life written by himself or herself—has a long

COMMON HUMAN EXPERIENCE

Roosevelt's writings provide an insight into a remarkable life during remarkable times. Her autobiographies are part of a long tradition of public figures reflecting on their life in politics and diplomatic circles. Here are a few examples:

The Second World War (1948–1955), a six-volume history by former British prime minister Winston Churchill. Generally credited as a figure of morale-boosting inspiration to his fellow Englishmen during the darkest years of World War II, Churchill guided his country through the war from 1940 to 1945, then wrote this history of the conflict. This massive opus, along with his other political memoirs, won Churchill the Nobel Prize for Literature in 1953.

An American Life (1990) is an autobiography by former U.S. president Ronald Reagan. It is a comprehensive record of his life, including his early years in Illinois, his life as a movie actor, his years as governor of California, and the eight years he served as president, from 1981 to 1989.

Long Walk to Freedom (1995) is an autobiography by former South African president Nelson Mandela. He tells of his early life and education, and of the twenty-seven years he spent in prison before being released in 1990 and becoming president in 1994.

Living History (2003), an autobiography by Hillary Rodham Clinton. Often compared—both favorably and unfavorably—to Eleanor Roosevelt, Clinton wrote this account of her early life and time as First Lady, but to the dismay of many readers, she did not dwell long or candidly on some of the more controversial aspects of her husband Bill Clinton's term as president.

tradition, going back to classical times. Many autobiographies have stood the test of time as great works of literature. Some of the most widely praised autobiographies include St. Augustine's *Confessions*, written in the fourth century, A.D,; Ben Franklin's, *The Autobiography* (first published in its entirety in 1868); Henry Adams's *The Education of Henry Adams* (first commercial publication 1918); and Jean-Jacques Rousseau's *Confessions* (1784).

In contrast to these great works, Roosevelt's writings are not considered particularly noteworthy from a literary standpoint—they often rely on clichéd banalities and can sometimes come across as naïve or overly optimistic. Yet, throughout her life and in the years since her death, Eleanor Roosevelt has continued to inspire countless millions of readers because of her status as a role model. In effect, Roosevelt led by example, and it is this element of her writing, rather than any technical proficiency, that has captivated readers for decades.

On the worth of autobiographies, Eleanor Roosevelt had this to say in 1950:

Autobiographies are, after all, useful only as the lives you read about and analyze may suggest to you something that you find useful in your own journey through life. ... There is nothing particularly interesting about one's life story unless people can say as they read it, "Why, this is like what I have been through. Perhaps, after all, there is a way to work it out."

Works in Critical Context

Critics have largely overlooked Roosevelt's writings, focusing instead on her public persona or her husband's accomplishments. Nevertheless, her autobiographies have proven invaluable for the insights they provide into the highest echelons of power during a critical time in American history, when the country was threatened by economic crisis from within and political and military adversaries abroad.

This I Remember Of the second in Roosevelt's trilogy of autobiographies, *This I Remember*, an account of the crucial years between 1921 and 1945, Jeanette P. Nichols writes in *Annals of the American Academy of Political and Social Science* that the book "is so simply told, so direct ... that it adds greatly to our insight into the catastrophic sequence of world depression and total war." Writing in *The American Political Science Review*, Harold F. Gosnell states that the "book is a very human account of what public life does to a man and his family." Gosnell also points out the more gossipy side of the narrative, noting that the "book contains many shrewd observations regarding important figures in our times."

Responses to Literature

1. Do you think the First Lady should be involved in presidential policy-making? If so, to what extent? If not, what should the role of the First Lady be?

2. Hilary Clinton has described having imaginary conversations with Eleanor Roosevelt. If you had an imaginary conversation with Roosevelt, what would you talk about? What do you think Roosevelt would have to say to you?

3. Research one of the causes—civil rights, women's rights, small farmers, American youth—that Roosevelt supported. How have conditions changed since Roosevelt's day? Has the situation improved or worsened? What do you think Roosevelt would think of the cause's situation today?

4. What, in your opinion, is the value of political autobiography? Should it be judged on the grounds of literature, as a memoir, or as political propaganda?

BIBLIOGRAPHY

Books

Cook, Blanche Wiesen. *Eleanor Roosevelt*. New York: Viking, 1992.

Glendon, Mary Ann. *A World Made New: Eleanor Roosevelt and the Universal Declaration of Human Rights*. New York: Random House, 2001.

Goodwin, Doris Kearns. *No Ordinary Time: Franklin and Eleanor Roosevelt: The Home Front in World War II*. New York: Simon & Schuster, 1994.

Hershan, Stella K. *A Woman of Quality*. New York: Crown, 1970.

Kearney, James R. *Anna Eleanor Roosevelt; the Evolution of a Reformer*. Boston: Houghton Mifflin, 1968.

Lash, Joseph P. *A World of Love: Eleanor Roosevelt and Her Friends, 1943–1962*. Garden City, N.Y.: Doubleday, 1984.

Scharf, Lois. *Eleanor Roosevelt: First Lady of American Liberalism*. Boston: Twayne, 1987.

Homberger, Eric. "Roosevelt, (Anna) Eleanor." *Cambridge Guide to Women's Writings in English*. Eds. Lorna Sage, Germaine Greer, and Elaine Showalter. Cambridge, U.K.: Cambridge University Press, 1999.

Periodicals

Nichols, Jeanette P. Review of *This I Remember*. *Annals of the American Academy of Political and Social Science*, Vol. 268, Aiding Underdeveloped Areas Abroad (March 1950): 212–13

Gosnell, Harold F. Review of *This I Remember*. *The American Political Science Review*. Vol. 44, No. 2 (June 1950): 496–97

✸ Wendy Rose

BORN: *1948, Oakland, California*

NATIONALITY: *American*

GENRE: *Poetry*

MAJOR WORKS:

Academic Squaw (1977)

Lost Copper (1980)

The Halfbreed Chronicles and Other Poems (1985)

Going to War with All My Relations: New and Selected Poems (1993)

Itch like Crazy (2002)

Overview

Wendy Rose's poetry has been praised for capturing the pain and confusion of the Native American experience and for making these experiences accessible to a non-Native American audience. An activist and academic as well as a poet and a painter, Rose has been an important figure in the so-called Native American Renaissance that began in the late 1960s.

Works in Biographical and Historical Context

A Young Activist Wendy Rose was born Bronwen Elizabeth Edwards in Oakland, California on May 7, 1948. She is of Miwok and Hopi ancestry, but because she was raised in a predominantly white community near San Francisco, she was alienated from her Native roots throughout her youth. Her mother, who was of Miwok heritage, refused to acknowledge her Amerindian heritage. Although Rose's father was a full-blooded Hopi, she was denied membership in her father's tribe because acceptance is determined through the mother's bloodline.

Rose had a lonely childhood. Her peers often teased her about her Native American background, which caused Rose to express herself through writing, painting, drawing, and singing. Her disconnection with the people around her led her to drop out of high school, at which point she became connected with some of the bohemian artistic circles in San Francisco. She joined the American Indian Movement—at the time an activist, sometimes radical, political organization—and later took part in their protest occupation of the island of Alcatraz in San Francisco Bay.

Finding Her Heritage Through Poetry As she navigated her way through the tumultuous environment of the 1960s, Rose continued to develop her interests in the arts. She also traveled to the Hopi homeland in Arizona to get more in touch with her father's roots. The trip deeply moved her and instilled in her a strong desire to connect with her ancestry through writing. In fact, her earliest poems date to this period, although some were not published for many years afterward. Her art began to focus on a common theme, that of self-identity as a Native American, and of fighting exploitation of her culture.

Rose's professional writing career began with the publication of poetry in journals and anthologies under the pseudonym Chiron Khanshendel. In fact, Rose has written under a variety of names, reflecting her ongoing quest to find an identity of her own. Her birth name, Bronwen Elizabeth Edwards, was far too European-sounding for her tastes and was rejected early on. Her earliest pen name, Chiron Khanshendel, was chosen for its symbolic nature—"Chiron" was the name of a wise centaur from Greek mythology and reflected Rose's of love of horses; Khanshendel was a made-up name that sounded suitably exotic. In the end, Rose went with a shortened version of Bronwen—"Wendy"—and took the surname of Rose after the last name of a man she had a relationship with in her youth.

LITERARY AND HISTORICAL CONTEMPORARIES

Rose's famous contemporaries include:

Sam Shepard (1943–): A playwright noted for his intense portraits of people living on the edge in the American West, Shepard has also distinguished himself as a film actor and director.

Winona LaDuke (1959–): Writer and activist LaDuke became the first Native American to run on a Presidential ticket in 1996, when she ran as Ralph Nader's vice-presidential pick on the Green Party ticket. She ran with Nader again in 2000, when the ticket polled nearly three million votes, a major showing for a third-party candidate.

Geary Hobson (1941–): Of Cherokee and Chickasaw ancestry, Hobson has published poetry, short stories, historical essays, and critiques in the field of Native American literature.

Stephen King (1947–): Known primarily as an author of horror stories, King is one of popular literature's greatest success stories, having sold hundreds of millions of books in a multitude of genres. Many of his books and stories have been adapted into movies.

Lou Diamond Phillips (1962–): A Filipino-American actor, Phillips became a star in the 1980s after starring as rock pioneer Richie Valens in *La Bamba* (1987) and the popular *Young Guns* (1988) Western and its sequel.

It was under the name of Chiron Khanshendel that Rose's first collection, *Hopi Runner Dancing*, appeared in 1973. In 1976, she graduated with a B.A. in anthropology from the University of California, Berkeley, where she also earned a master's degree in 1978, and later became a lecturer in Native American studies.

An In-Demand Poet Between 1966 and 1980, Rose published five volumes of poetry, including *Lost Copper* (1980), which was nominated for a Pulitzer Prize. After completing her master's and doctorate degrees, Rose focused on the world of academia, acting as a teacher, anthropologist, advisor, and lecturer. She has taught at the University of California, Berkeley, and California State University, Fresno, currently coordinates the American Indian Studies program at Fresno City College, and edits the *American Indian Quarterly*. She has continued to publish poetry as well, putting out six volumes between 1982 and 2002. In addition to writing, drawing, painting, teaching, and researching, Rose has been consultant, editor, panelist, and adviser for community and academic projects. She is a member of the American Federation of Teachers and has served on the local executive council of that organization. She has also been consultant-bibliographer for a federal recognition project, seeking formal recognition of the status of the North Fork Mono Tribe, and has served as facilitator for the Association of Non-Federally Recognized California Tribes. Rose is in demand for poetry readings, which have taken her to all parts of the country on trips that have also inspired new poems. Rose also occasionally exhibits her artwork around the United States and provides designs for various Native American organizations. Rose's poetry has been featured in an impressive number of American and contemporary literature anthologies. More than sixty anthologies, poetry collections, and prize volumes contain one or more of her poems—these include feminist collections such as *In Her Own Image* (1980), small regional publications such as *Dreaming of the Dawn* (1980), and comprehensive anthologies of American literature, American Indian literature, and literature by women, including *The Heath Anthology of American Literature* (1990), *The Sound of Rattles and Clappers* (1994), and *Women Poets of the World* (1983). Her work has been translated into French, German, and Danish. She continues to live and write at her home in Coarsegold, California.

Works in Literary Context

In addition to treating ecological and feminist issues, Rose's poetry incorporates her own experiences and those of other mixed-blood Native Americans who, separated from their tribal culture and alienated by the white society in which they live, are searching for a sense of identity and community. Paula Gunn Allen, in *The Sacred Hoop: Recovering the Feminine in American Indian Traditions*, states that "while her enforced distance from her people grieves and angers Rose, she writes poetry that does not fall into suicidal bitterness on the one hand or radical excess on the other. Rather, it hews a clear line toward her understanding of her position, illuminating in that clarity the position of all who are dispossessed."

Native and "Half-Breed" Literature Much of Rose's work employs elements of Native American songs and chants and is preoccupied with spirituality, communion with the natural world, and the encroachment of white culture on Native society. In such poems as "The well-intentioned question," from the Pulitzer Prize-nominated *Lost Copper* (1980), Rose documents her feelings of marginalization and her desire to be part of the Native community. Rose's background in anthropology and involvement with various Native American organizations inspires much of the imagery and history employed in her poetry. In *The Halfbreed Chronicles, and Other Poems* (1985), written while she was studying anthropology as an undergraduate at Berkeley, Rose's focus on the marginalized mixed-blood Amerindian was expanded to include other minorities, such as Japanese Americans and Native Americans from Mexico. She has stated: "You don't think of these people in the same sense as you usually think of half-breeds. But my point is that, in an important way, the way I grew up is symptomatic of something much larger than Indian-white relations. History and circumstance have made half-breeds of all of us."

Despite her success, Rose has expressed disappointment with the way in which her work—and the work of other ethnic artists—has been received. For example, she has complained that academia tends to view Native writings as a fad rather than as serious literature. She has also expressed her disapproval of the way in which her poetry has been embraced as an anthropological curiosity rather than as art. "The deferential treatment accorded to Indians in artistic and academic settings is just as destructive, ultimately, as out-and-out racism," Rose has said. "It is startling to find your book of poems in an anthropology section of a bookstore instead of in the poetry section."

Works in Critical Context

Although some commentators assert that Rose's use of language masks her feelings, others note a sense of urgency and bitterness in her work and maintain that it is fueled by raw, unbridled emotion. Jamake Highwater has commented in the *American Book Review*, "[Rose's] lines are haunted by an unresolved search for a personal as well as a tribal sense of identity. That search gives her words strength and spirit. It dissolves the barrier of race with which she cautiously surrounds [herself], and it gives us access to her pain. In that pain we are all related."

The Halfbreed Chronicles and Other Poems B. Almon, writing in *Choice*, states that *The Halfbreed Chronicles* is a "strong and well-crafted collection of poems on Native American subjects." Almon calls Rose's verse both "fresh (because it is vivid) and traditional (because it evokes fundamentals of life and earth in the Indian tradition)." The reviewer writing in *Publisher's Weekly* observes that the title of the collection "aptly points to the complexion of her poems. ... [S]he carves a place for herself amid the cultures surrounding her." Of Rose's poetic voice, the reviewer calls it "sometimes ironic, sometimes angry" and concludes, "the writing is at times prosaic, rhetorical or gimmicky, but the spirit rings true."

Lost Copper Critics have singled out Rose's lyrical command of language, particularly in her book *Lost Copper*. N. Scott Momaday said in his introduction to *Lost Copper* that the book was "not made up of poems, I think, but of songs." Writing in *Parnassus*, Kenneth Lincoln says that Rose's poetry in *Lost Copper*, "mixes metaphors and ideas and inks and emotions in bicultural compost, a living poetic mixture unlike any other." Lincoln concludes his review by saying, "This artist, finally, works with her hand on words, chips away at America's intractable rocks of ignorance regarding Indians." Jamke Hightower's review of *Lost Copper* asserts that despite her lyrical prowess, Rose's "language never quite manages to overcome her rage. Yet that very paranoia may be the ultimate virtue."

COMMON HUMAN EXPERIENCE

The last three decades have seen a growing presence of Native Americans in literature and poetry, which critic Kenneth Lincoln has referred to as the "Native American Renaissance." Here are some other works which document the Native American experience:

The Lone Ranger and Tonto Fistfight in Heaven (1993), a short story collection by Sherman Alexie. Several of the characters and plots from this collection of interconnected short stories about modern life on Indian reservations were later adapted by Alexie into the movie *Smoke Signals* (1998).

Ceremony (1977), a novel by Leslie Marmon Silko. One of the most widely-read books to come out of the Native American Renaissance, this novel tells the story of a mixed-race soldier who returns from World War II to life on the reservation, and the economic and psychological hurdles he encounters.

House Made of Dawn (1968), a novel by N. Scott Momaday. Widely credited as the first work of the Native American Renaissance, Momaday based this novel on actual events in his life, as well as events surrounding the killing of a New Mexico State Trooper by a Native American and the ensuing controversy. The novel won the Pulitzer Prize in 1969.

Life is a Fatal Disease: Collected Poems 1962–1995 (1997), a book of poetry by Paula Gunn Allen. An anthropologist and critic as well as poet, Allen's poetry is a combination of personal remembrances from her life growing up on a New Mexico pueblo and political calls to arms.

Responses to Literature

1. Rose has been an activist for Native American causes her whole adult life, beginning with her involvement in the occupation of Alcatraz Island. Research the history of the occupation—what were the aims of the group that occupied the island? How long did the occupation last? What, if anything, was accomplished by the occupation? Write a brief report on the event.

2. How does the title of Rose's poem "For White poets who would be Indian" (1980) make you feel? Record your initial thoughts on what you think the poem might be about. Then, read the poem and analyze it in light of your initial impressions.

3. One of Rose's overarching themes is a phenomenon known as whiteshamanism, a term coined by Cherokee activist Geary Hobson. Research the history of the term, and the closely-related concept of "cultural

imperialism." Then, write about your feelings on the subject. Do you agree with Rose that only Native Americans can truly understand the Native American lifestyle? Why or why not?

BIBLIOGRAPHY

Books

Allen, Paula Gunn. *The Sacred Hoop: Recovering the Feminine in American Indian Traditions.* Boston, Mass.: Beacon Press, 1986.

Coltelli, Laura. *Winged Words: American Indian Writers Speak.* Lincoln, Neb.: University of Nebraska Press, 1990.

Giroux, Christopher, ed. "Wendy Rose (1948–)." *Contemporary Literary Criticism.* Vol. 85. Detroit: Gale Research, 1995.

Swann, Brian, and Arnold Krupat, eds. *I Tell You Now: Autobiographical Essays of Native American Writers.* Lincoln, Neb.: University of Nebraska Press, 1987.

Periodicals

Jocks, Christopher Ronwaniente. "Spirituality for Sale: Sacred Knowledge in the Consumer Age," in *American Indian Quarterly*, Vol. 20, 1996, pp. 415–17.

Tongson-McCall, Karen. "The Nether World of Neither World: Hybridization in the Literature of Wendy Rose," in *American Indian Culture and Research Journal*, 1996, pp. 1–40.

"Going to War with All My Relations." *Publishers Weekly* 240.n6 (Feb 8, 1993): 81(1).

Web sites

Nelson, Cary. *Wendy Rose (1948–).* Retrieved November 22, 2008, from http://www.english.uiuc.edu/maps/poets/m_r/rose/rose.htm.

✿ Philip Roth

BORN: *1933, Newark, New Jersey*

NATIONALITY: *American*

GENRE: *Fiction*

MAJOR WORKS:
Goodbye, Columbus (1959)
Portnoy's Complaint (1969)

Overview

Philip Roth's impressive body of fiction has attracted widespread critical acclaim. Combining comedy and social criticism, Roth draws heavily upon his Jewish-American upbringing and his life as a successful author to explore such concerns as the search for self-identity, conflicts between traditional and contemporary moral values, and the relationship between fiction and reality.

Philip Roth   *Roth, Philip, photograph. AP Images.*

Though critics have sometimes attacked Roth's work as anti-Semitic or vulgar, he is generally considered one of the most important American novelists of the late twentieth and early twenty-first centuries.

Works in Biographical and Historical Context

Pursuit of Higher Education   Philip Roth was born on March 19, 1933, in a working-class neighborhood in Newark, New Jersey. His parents were Jewish immigrants Bess (Finkel) Roth and Herman Roth, an insurance agent who rose to become a company manager. Early experiences from Philip Roth's old neighborhood would shape much of his writing throughout his life. Four years before his birth, in 1929, the U.S. economy crumbled. Stock values plummeted, and banks began to fail, triggering the Great Depression. People lost their life savings and many lost their homes. At the same time, unemployment skyrocketed, leaving one out of every four workers without a job by 1932. A destitute spirit pervaded the nation, and people's thoughts focused on surviving day by day. Beginning in his adolescence, Roth experienced the slightly more prosperous times of World War II. By 1945, when the war ended, the U.S. economy was growing. The government supported a housing boom and unemployment insurance to protect people from falling into the poverty experienced during the Great Depression. In this more hopeful and confident culture, Roth began to look beyond the provincial existence of his hometown in Newark.

After high school, Roth attended the Newark branch of Rutgers University in 1950, but he transferred to Bucknell University in Pennsylvania in 1951, where he performed in plays and edited the literary magazine before graduating magna cum laude in 1954 with a Bachelor of Arts in English. He then went on to obtain a master's degree in English from the University of Chicago in 1955. After serving in the U.S. Army for a few months, until his discharge due to a back injury, he returned to the University of Chicago in 1956 and began taking doctoral-candidate courses as well as teaching and writing stories.

Middle-Class Jewish Life in Fiction By 1957, Roth had published several short stories that centered on middle-class American Jewish life. In 1959, at age twenty-six, he published his first book, *Goodbye, Columbus, and Five Short Stories.* The title piece, about two Jewish college students from different socioeconomic circumstances, questioned Jewish family and social relationships. The work earned high acclaim but its share of criticism, as well, for what was seen as anti-Semitic character portrayals—depictions of Jewish characters that were perceived as negative. Decidedly, Roth never shied from showing both positive and negative behavior associated with the Jewish-American community.

Roth is credited with propelling Jewish-American fiction into the realm of popular culture with his 1969 novel, *Portnoy's Complaint.* In this work, main character Alexander Portnoy gives a profane, guilt-ridden confession to a silent psychoanalyst, Dr. Spielvogel. Decrying his Jewish upbringing, Portnoy wrestles with his conflicting relationship with his mother, obsession with non-Jewish women, and sexual fetishes. He yearns to free himself from the restrictions of his cultural background. Following the book's publication, scholars and Jewish-Americans again labeled Roth an anti-Semite. They objected to what they considered Roth's degrading treatment of Jewish life and to the novel's sexually explicit content. However, *Portnoy's Complaint* also won praise for its ethnic humor, clever dialogue, and psychological insight. It remains Roth's best-known work to date.

Fiction and Reality: The Zuckerman Saga In much of his work, Roth explores the relationship between fiction and reality. As such, many of Roth's characters serve as a confessional for his own thoughts and experiences. In 1979, Roth began a series of novels based on the character Nathan Zuckerman. The first in the series, *The Ghost Writer* (1979), contains Roth's angst transferred to a fictional persona, Zuckerman—his alter ego. The series begins with Zuckerman as a very young, very vulnerable writer who discovers that life and art have a strange, interpenetrating relationship. As the protagonist continues on the path to best-selling author, he faces

challenges along the way that mirror those faced by Roth himself.

In 1987, Roth won the National Book Critics Circle Award and National Jewish Book Award for his novel *The Counterlife* (1986), a continuation of the Zuckerman saga and an examination of the relationship between fact and fiction. In 1997 Roth revived his alter ego in *American Pastoral*, for which he received the Pulitzer Prize for fiction the following year. In this novel, Zuckerman is an aging prostate-cancer survivor looking back at his idyllic childhood in a Newark that promised prosperity and the good life for its immigrant class and their future generations.

Known to be an extremely private man, Roth uncharacteristically displayed his personal relations in print for all to see in his 1998 Zuckerman tale, *I Married a Communist.* Roth had begun living with actress Claire Bloom in 1976, and they married in 1990. After their divorce in 1994, Bloom included some unflattering details about their relationship in her memoir, *Leaving a Doll's House* (1996). She told of Roth's mental breakdowns in 1988 and 1993 that left him close to suicide. When Roth released *I Married a Communist*, commentators speculated that Roth wrote the book to tell his side of the story.

Zuckerman returns again in *The Human Stain* (2000). In this novel, Zuckerman exiles himself to New England. He plays a more passive agent this time, as he listens to the twisting tales of an acquaintance, Coleman Silk. A seventy-one-year-old Zuckerman emerges from his eleven-year self-

COMMON HUMAN EXPERIENCE

Portnoy's Complaint is famous for its portrayal of Jewish-American family life. Other works that treat the Jewish-American experience include:

Maus (1986, 1991), a graphic novel by Art Spiegelman. Serious historical subjects—the Holocaust and the Jewish American experience—are treated with humor and satire in this graphic novel.

The Amazing Adventures of Kavalier & Clay (2000), a novel by Michael Chabon. This novel tells the story of Josef Kavalier and Sammy Clay, two Jewish teenagers who invent a comic superhero in the late 1930s.

Lost in Yonkers (1991), a play by Neil Simon. This dark comedy focuses on a dysfunctional Jewish family. The play describes the experiences of two teenage boys—Jay and Arty—who are forced to live with their stern, intimidating Grandma Kurnitz for ten months.

Call It Sleep (1934), a novel by Henry Roth. This classic novel of Jewish American life tells the story of a young boy living in a pre–World War I ghetto in New York.

imposed exile in *Exit Ghost* (2007). It shows Zuckerman facing twists in life and still grappling with his identity.

Recent Works With a career that spans fifty years, Roth remains a prolific and relevant writer. His 2004 political fable *The Plot Against America* presents an alternative history of America in which Hitler's allies control the White House and fascism rules. The story is told from the perspective of what would seem to be a young Philip Roth. The seven-year-old narrator, Phil, is the son of Bess and Herman, a Jewish-American couple struggling to support a family in a Newark, New Jersey neighborhood. He watches in fear as the country degrades into an anti-Jewish, oppressive dictatorship.

In his 2006 *Everyman*, an unnamed protagonist confronts the loneliness of growing old, despair over the loss of his sexual vitality, and anguish over how he has shattered the lives of those who love him. In 2008, Roth's *Indignation* seems to tell the tale of what could have happened in his life had he not been a writer and instead faced a string of bad luck. In this way, Roth continues to share the inner workings of his psyche with readers today.

Works in Literary Context

Roth has established himself among the leading contemporary American authors through his careful scrutiny and biting satire directed at post–World War II America. He is often discussed in the company of other Jewish-American authors Saul Bellow and Bernard Malamud, as well as earlier, non-Jewish writers, including Anton Chekhov

and Henry James. However, Roth has most notably been described as a modern-day Franz Kafka. Kafka, often considered one of the founders of modern literature, created protagonists clearly based on himself. In the same way, Roth's characters often represent himself in some way.

Jewish Identity Nearly all of Roth's fiction is concerned in some way with expressing the Jewish-American experience. The importance of his childhood memories of growing up in a first-generation Jewish community first became evident in *Goodbye, Columbus, and Five Short Stories*. The story examines the relationship between Neil Klugman, a lower-middle-class Newark native, and Brenda Patimkin, a product of the growing postwar class of wealthy Jews.

Conflict and repression as part of Jewish identity are highlighted themes in many of Roth's books, including *Portnoy's Complaint*. In that tale, a young Jewish man's infatuation with non-Jewish girls and his constant state of war with his overbearing mother constitute the plot. The place of Jews in America is also a key component in his alternative-history novel *The Plot Against America*, in which American Jews are subjected to a fate not far removed from European Jews in the 1940s. In his works, from *Goodbye, Columbus* through *Portnoy's Complaint* and the Nathan Zuckerman novels, Roth has continued to explore Jewish family life in the city and the conflicted characters that it creates.

Satire Through most of his work, Roth employs ridicule and humor to create his own brand of satire. Roth's exaggerations, as well as his anger and ridicule, are intended to criticize and correct. Satire can be relatively mild—an ironic look at something that is strange or not entirely deserving of admiration. Or it can be a full-force condemnation of an evil, with just a bit of humor. Roth's work covers the entire range. He targets the Northeastern Jewish middle-class world of his background, the Midwest and its WASP (White Anglo-Saxon Protestant) inhabitants, academia, literary criticism, and the government and related political nightmares. *Portnoy's Complaint* is Roth's most famous satire, especially notable for its portrayal of the Jewish mother character, Sophie Portnoy.

Works in Critical Context

Roth has received much of his criticism from those who feel his characters elicit anti-Semitism from non-Jewish readers. However, it is generally agreed that Philip Roth possesses a firm grasp of the nuances of the spoken word, of the details of everyday things, and of the absurdities that can transform the crises of human life into hilarious comedy.

Goodbye, Columbus After the publication of his first novel *Goodbye, Columbus* in 1959, critics reacted heatedly to his portrayal of Jewish-American life. It is for his humor and satire that Roth sometimes gets in trouble with his readers, particularly when he considers Jews. As Ted Solotaroff notes in "American Jewish Writers: On Edge Once More," most of Roth's stories in *Goodbye, Columbus* "are devoted to an aggressive and astute exposure … of Jewish ethnocentrism [and] self-righteousness that his young protagonists are trying to escape." That Roth is turned off by bad taste, hypocrisy, stupidity and ignorance, snobbery of the wealthy, and other universally acknowledged evils is not admissible in defense, according to some of his critics.

Supporters point out that Roth's protagonists are in revolt against the American middle class as much as against a specifically Jewish lifestyle. They are just as alienated and just as critical wherever they find themselves. This fact of universal negativity is often found irrelevant by critics, and Roth's pointed portrayal of Jewish-American characters and lifestyles is seen as inexcusably negative.

Portnoy's Complaint   Roth's depiction of the title character of *Portnoy's Complaint*, Alex Portnoy, stirred a great deal of controversy in social and religious circles. Portnoy's frustration with his situation is manifested in his frequent masturbation, which is described in graphic detail by Roth. Furthermore, the author's continuing satiric examination of Jewish-American life sparked further debate within that ethnic and religious community. American writer and critic Marya Mannes went so far as to call Portnoy "the most disagreeable bastard who ever lived." But, by and large, academic responses were more typical. Here, for example, is a representative sampling from Lois G. Gordon's "*Portnoy's Complaint*: Coming of Age in Jersey City": "The theme of the book [is] tension between the public and private man, between consciousness and unconscious motivation, between the adult ideal one strives for and the childhood fantasy."

While some commentators view Roth's work as anti-Semitic, perverse, or self-indulgent, others laud Roth's skill at rendering dialect. They praise his exuberance and inventiveness, and his outrageous sense of humor. John N. McDaniel remarks: "No other living writer has so rigorously and actively attempted to describe the destructive element of experience in American life—the absurdities and banalities that impinge upon self-realization."

Responses to Literature

1. After reading *Portnoy's Complaint*, discuss Alex Portnoy's struggle between his two selves—Jewish and non-Jewish. What are the characteristics he associates with each self and what does he think of those characteristics? Explore whether Portnoy embraces or shuns the different aspects of his personality.

2. In *The Human Stain*, Coleman Silk is accused of racism even though he himself is black. Research the term "racial passing" and explain why and how it

happens in immigrant populations. Examine whether Silk's character is an example of this phenomenon.

3. Compare Nathan Zuckerman in *Ghost Writer* to the narrator's final appearance in *Exit Ghost*. He returns to New York after eleven years of solitude. How have his reactions to the city changed? What, if anything, has changed in Zuckerman's interior observations and in the workings of his mind?

BIBLIOGRAPHY

Books

McDaniel, John N. *The Fiction of Philip Roth.* Haddonfield, N.J.: Haddonfield House, 1974.

Safer, Elaine B. *Mocking the Age: The Later Novels of Philip Roth.* Albany, N.Y.: State University of New York Press, 2006.

Periodicals

Gordon, Lois G. "*Portnoy's Complaint*: Coming of Age in Jersey City." *Literature & Psychology* no. 19 (1969).

Mannes, Marya. "A Dissent from Marya Mannes." *Saturday Review* (February 1969).

Web sites

Finney, Brian. *Roth's Counterlife: Destabilizing the Facts.* Retrieved November 7, 2008, from http://www. csulb.edu/~bhfinney/Roth.html.

Gray, Paul. *Novelist: Philip Roth.* Retrieved November 7, 2008, from http://www.cnn.com/SPECIALS/ 2001/americasbest/pro.proth.html.

The Library of Congress. *Great Depression and World War II 1929–1945.* Accessed November 13, 2008, from http://memory.loc.gov/learn/features/ timeline/depwwii/depress/depress.html.

Metcalf, Stephen. *Zuckerman Unbound.* Accessed November 13, 2008, from http://www.slate.com/ id/2176969/pagenum/all/.

Partisan Review. *Born Again.* Accessed November 13, 1008, from http://www.bu.edu/partisanreview/ archive/2000/4/webb.html.

Hellman, David. *Review: Philip Roth's 'Exit Ghost'.* Accessed November 13, 2008, from http:// www.sfgate.com/cgi-bin/article.cgi?f=/c/a/2007/ 10/07/RVBRS4R7B.DTL.

Berman, Paul. *The Plot Against America.* Accessed November 13, 2008, from http://www.nytimes. com/2004/10/03/books/review/03BERMAN. html?ex=1254456000&en=b407dc 3a06c7 e743& ei=5090&partner= rssuserland.

Solotaroff, Ted. *American-Jewish Writers on Edge Once More.* Accessed December 2, 2008, from http://query. nytimes.com/gst/fullpage.html?res=940DE1DE1238 F93BA25751 C1A96E948260&sec=&spon=&page wanted=.

Mary Rowlandson

BORN: *c. 1637, Somerset, England*

DIED: *1711, Whethersfield, Connecticut*

NATIONALITY: *American*

GENRE: *Nonfiction*

MAJOR WORKS:

*A True History of the Captivity & Restoration of
Mrs. Mary Rowlandson, A Minister's Wife in
New-England* (1682)

Overview

Mary Rowlandson was abducted from her home in the
English frontier settlement of Lancaster, Massachusetts,
on February 10, 1676, by a band of Indian warriors. She
spent three months in captivity and was eventually rescued. She witnessed the slaughter of relatives and friends,
her own wounding by a musket ball, near starvation, and
the death of her six-year-old daughter. The account of
her travails, *A True History of the Captivity & Restoration
of Mrs. Mary Rowlandson, A Minister's Wife in New
England* (1682), became the first and best-known New
England Indian captivity narrative to seize the public
imagination and shape European/Native American relations for generations to come. While the popularity of her
narrative has carried it through some thirty editions, little
is known of her life beyond the facts contained in her
account.

Works in Biographical and Historical Context

Puritans in the Wilderness Born to John and Joan
White of Somerset, England, around 1637, Mary Rowlandson was raised from infancy in New England. The
Whites were among the original settlers of Lancaster,
arriving there in 1653, when the town numbered only
nine families. In 1656, Mary married the English-born,
Harvard-educated Joseph Rowlandson, Lancaster's first
minister.

The settlers in Lancaster, called Puritans for their
religious beliefs, originated from Europe. In the early
1600s, the Puritans had grown increasingly discontent
with the religious environment in England. They finally
decided in 1629 to migrate to America to begin a new
existence based on their own religious ideals. They followed an earlier group—the Pilgrims who came over on
the *Mayflower* in 1620—and established the Massachusetts Bay Colony, where Mary Rowlandson settled. Here,
the Puritans constructed a society based on their Christian beliefs. Among these, they believed that God was
pleased by hard work and diligence and would give due
rewards to the faithful.

The Raid on Lancaster On February 20, 1676, at
sunrise, Mary Rowlandson was captured by a Wampa-

noag Indian war party. This occurred during King Philip's War between the Native Americans and the English
settlers (1675–1676). Taken with Mary Rowlandson
were her daughters—six-year-old Sarah, who was wounded
in the raid and died a week later, and ten-year-old
Mary—and her son, Joseph, then fourteen. Captives ordinarily became the possession of the particular person by
whom they were taken, but as Rowlandson's narrative
indicates, they were, on occasion, purchased or traded.
As a consequence of this practice, Rowlandson was separated from her two older children immediately, she
having been captured by a Narragansett, her son by a
Nipmuck, and her daughter by a member of another,
unidentified tribe.

For eleven weeks and five days Rowlandson lived and
traveled with the Narragansetts, with her Indian "master" and "mistress," as she designated them in her narrative. On May 3, 1676, after "much prayer had been
particularly made before the Lord on her behalf," Rowlandson was ransomed by the English in exchange for
goods. In late June, Joseph was released by the Nip-
mucks, and Mary was brought to Providence by an
unidentified Indian woman.

Alive to Tell the Tale Lancaster had by then been
destroyed, and the Rowlandsons spent the following year
in Boston, supported by their friends. In the spring of
1677, they moved to Wethersfield, Connecticut, where
Joseph Rowlandson was called to the ministry. He died
the following year at age forty-seven. Rowlandson married a Connecticut leader, Capt. Samuel Talcott, nine
months later. The past assumption that both Rowlandson
and her husband died in the late 1670s had left the means
of the first publication of her narrative unexplained, but
scholars now believe that Mary Rowlandson Talcott published her narrative well after her husband's death with
the encouragement of the Reverend Increase Mather. He
was the minister of the Second Church in Boston and a
prominent political leader in the Massachusetts Bay
Colony.

The first edition was printed in Cambridge, Massachusetts, in 1682. A London edition later that year
republished the narrative under the full title by which it
is now best known, *A True History of the Captivity &
Restoration of Mrs. Mary Rowlandson, A Minister's Wife
in New-England: Wherein is set forth, The Cruel and
Inhumane Usage she underwent amongst the Heathens
for Eleven Weeks time: And her Deliverance from them.
Written by her own Hand, for her Private Use: and now
made public at the earnest Desire of some Friends, for the
Benefit of the Afflicted.*

Although Rowlandson was not the first white settler to
be captured by Native Americans, her account originated
what scholars usually consider the first Euro-American
literary genre, the captivity narrative. This genre persisted
well into the nineteenth century and influenced the form
of the novel in America. It was one of the earliest examples

of women's autobiographical writing and, in some respects, a precursor to later slave narratives.

Rowlandson died on January 5, 1711, at the age of seventy-three.

Works in Literary Context

As the author of the earliest known Indian captivity narrative, Rowlandson figures importantly in the literary history of the United States as a definitive spokesperson for the experience of colonial captives and as the originator of a new and long-lived narrative genre.

The Captivity Narrative   A captivity narrative tells the story of a person held forcibly by a group of people and awaiting rescue. In the early American captivity tales, the person is usually a woman, and the captors are Native Americans. Puritan religion plays a key role in captivity tales. As a prevailing theme, the captive represents the whole of Puritan society. The suffering during captivity symbolizes how true believers must endure life's sinful temptation and testing by God. In this scenario, the Native Americans represent sin and evil in the world. Redemption and approval by God is represented by the ultimate rescue from captivity.

As such, the significance of Mary Rowlandson's captivity narrative lies largely in its expression of profoundly felt religious experience. Most of her Biblical citations are strikingly appropriate to her captivity experience—Psalms 106:46, for example: "He made them also to be pitied, of all those that carried them Captives."

Ultimately, Rowlandson offers her experience as a morally instructive one; there were lessons to be drawn. For example, on the first Sabbath of her captivity, Rowlandson recalls "how careless I had been of God's holy time, how many Sabbaths I had lost and misspent." When, after her release, she is troubled with small matters ("a shadow, a blast, a bubble, and things of no continuance"), she thinks upon her recent captivity: "It was but the other day that if I had had the world, I would have given it for my freedom ... I have learned to look beyond present and smaller troubles." Perhaps the chief spiritual significance for both the captive-narrator and her reader lay in interpreting the captivity as an illustration of God's providence. "God was with me, in a wonderfull manner, carrying me along and bearing up my spirit ... that I might see more of his Power," writes Rowlandson.

The genre continued on into the eighteenth and nineteenth centuries. In particular, narratives by slaves during the mid-1800s exhibited similar themes of suffering while awaiting redemption by God. Slave narratives are rife with Biblical allusion and imagery, just as in captivity tales. The autobiographies of Frederick Douglass and Harriet Jacob are amongst the great body of slave narratives in existence. Other prominent writers of captivity narratives include Ann Bleecker and James Riley, and more recently, John Ford and Thomas Berger.

Works in Critical Context

A True History of the Captivity & Restoration of Mrs. Mary Rowlandson, A Minister's Wife in New-England   Rowlandson's high social standing as a minister's wife and the notoriety of the Lancaster raid ensured the immediate success of her account of her captivity. The Puritans of Lancaster immediately accepted the symbolic representation of her captivity as a test of God, and the endurance of the trial a mark of spiritual fortitude for Rowlandson. Caroline Gleason writes: "Through her use of scripture and portrayal of the relationship between the Indians and Puritan colonists, Rowlandson reinforced the traditional concept of providence preached by the founding Puritans forty years earlier." Gleason goes on to say: "By quoting the scriptural story of Joseph, Rowlandson illustrated her belief that the Puritans were the chosen people of God."

Rowlandson's and other early American captivity narratives were used to fuel the ongoing war between the New England settlers and the nearby Native American tribes, ultimately resulting in the defeat and removal of Indian populations from the areas. In these times, the captivity narratives helped to create the growing mythology that the Indians were a symbol of the wrath of God.

COMMON HUMAN EXPERIENCE

In *A True History of the Captivity & Restoration of Mrs. Mary Rowlandson*, the author creates what is acknowledged as the first American captivity narrative. Here are some other works that offer tales of white settlers seized by Native Americans:

Humiliations Follow'd with Deliverances, captivity narratives of Hannah Swarton and Hannah Dustin as told by Cotton Mather (1697). Mather, the first child of Increase and Maria Cotton Mather, continues in his father's tradition by documenting these tales of American captivity.

The History of Maria Kittle, a fictionalized captivity narrative by Ann Bleecker (1793). Bleecker transposes her own story of maternal loss onto the already popular captivity narrative literary form, contributing to a tradition of captivity stories by women that feature strong, active, female protagonists.

A Narrative of the Life of Mrs. Mary Gemison, a captivity narrative told by James E. Seaver (1823). Seaver based the book on a series of interviews with Gemison, who was kidnapped by Seneca Indians when she was fifteen years old. The events took place in the 1750s during the French and Indian Wars.

The Searchers (1956), a film directed by John Ford. In this classic Western, John Wayne plays a man who dedicates his life to tracking down his niece, abducted at a young age by Comanches. The film was notable at the time for its relatively evenhanded portrayal of Native Americans, and its less-than-heroic portrayal of some whites.

Kathleen Canavan writes: "The story of Mary Rowlandson fit in very nicely with this new mythology. She was a minister's wife who ... was called upon to suffer terrible hardship by His hand and comes truly to know Him."

The narratives were also instrumental to religious leaders of the time in perpetuating the Puritan way of life. Some commentators suggest Rowlandson's narrative shows influence by one of these leaders, Reverend Increase Mather, and that his voice appears strong in her writing. "Of course, Mather's opportunity of access and influence do not necessarily translate into a hands-on involvement with the narrative," says Canavan. "But the curious shifts in narrative voice that punctuate Rowlandson's text echo the tenets of Mather's religious agenda for New England."

Responses to Literature

1. Puritan ideals play a strong role in Rowlandson's and other American colonial captivity narratives. In what ways do Rowlandson's religious beliefs give her strength through her captivity? How can you tell that she has conflicting feelings about her suffering? Give examples from the text.

2. Ann Bleecker produced a fictionalized Indian captivity narrative following the popular form set forth by Rowlandson. Read Bleecker's *The History of Maria Kittle* and compare the leading female character to Rowlandson. How do they deal with their sufferings in captivity and where do they derive their strength to go on each day?

3. One significant contribution made by Rowlandson is the view she provides to modern readers of early Colonial American life. Read *Of Plymouth Plantation* by William Bradford to find out more about early Puritan life. What are the main tenets of the religion and how did these play out in the lives of the early Puritans?

BIBLIOGRAPHY

Books

Breitweiser, Mitchell R. *American Puritanism and the Defense of Mourning: Religion, Grief, and Ethnology in Mary White Rowlandson's Captivity Narrative.* Madison, Wis.: University of Wisconsin Press, 1990.

VanDerBeets, Richard. *The Indian Captivity Narrative: An American Genre.* Washington, D.C.: University Press of America, 1983.

———. Introduction to *Held Captive by Indians: Selected Narratives, 1642–1836*, edited by VanDerBeets. Knoxville, Tenn.: University of Tennessee Press, 1973.

Periodicals

Adams, Richard P. "Hawthorne's Provincial Tales." *New England Quarterly* 30 (March 1957): 39–57.

Burnham, Michelle. "The Journey Between: Liminality and Dialogism in Mary White Rowlandson's Captivity Narrative." *Early American Literature* 28 (1993): 60–75.

Davis, Margaret H. "Mary White Rowlandson's Self-Fashioning as Puritan Goodwife." *Early American Literature* 27 (1992): 49–60.

Derounian, Kathryn Zabelle. "The Publication, Promotion, and Distribution of Mary White Rowlandson's Captivity Narrative in the Seventeenth Century." *Early American Literature* 23 (1988): 239–261.

———. "Puritan Orthodoxy and the 'Survivor Syndrome' in Mary Rowlandson's Indian Captivity Narrative." *Early American Literature* 22 (1987): 82–93.

Diebold, Robert K. "A Critical Edition of Mrs. Mary Rowlandson's Captivity Narrative." Dissertation, Yale University, 1972.

Dietrich, Deborah J. "Mary Rowlandson's Great Declension." *Women's Studies* 24 (1995): 427–439.

Pearce, Roy Harvey. "The Significances of the Captivity Narrative." *American Literature* 19 (March 1947): 1–20.

Web sites

Mather, Increase. *A Brief History of the War with the Indians in New-England* (1676). Accessed November 9, 2008, from http://national humanitiescenter.org/pds/amerbegin/power/text7/IndiansMather.pdf.

Gleason, Caroline. *The Chosen People of God: Mary Rowlandson's Captivity Narrative.* Retrieved November 14, 2008, from http://history. hanover.edu/hhr/hhr4-2.html.

Sage History: An American Experience. *Massachusetts Bay: A Puritan Commonwealth.* Accessed November 14, 2008, from http://www.sagehistory.net/colonial/topics/NewEngland.htm. Last updated on January 26, 2007.

Washington State University Online. *Early American Captivity Narratives.* Accessed November 14, 2008, from http://www.wsu.edu/~campbelld/amlit/captive.htm. Last updated on March 12, 2008.

Canavan, Kathleen J. *The Matron and the Minister: Duality of Voice in Mary Rowlandson's Captivity Narrative.* Accessed November 14, 2008, from http://www.nd.edu/~kcanava1/Mary%20Rowlandson.html.

✸ Susanna Haswell Rowson

BORN: *1762, Portsmouth, England*

DIED: *1824, Boston, Massachusetts*

NATIONALITY: *American*

GENRE: *Fiction, drama*

MAJOR WORKS:

Charlotte, A Tale of Truth (1791); republished as *Charlotte Temple* (1797)

Rebecca, or, The Fille de Chambre (1792)

Slaves in Algiers (1794)

Overview

Susanna Haswell Rowson was America's first best-selling author. Her novella *Charlotte, A Tale of Truth* (1791), later retitled *Charlotte Temple*, has gone through more than 150 editions, including nine editions in three languages other than English. Rowson's controversial portrayals of strong, independent women made her a groundbreaking figure in American literature.

Works in Biographical and Historical Context

Young Susanna and the American Revolution Susanna Haswell was born in February 1762 to Susanna

Susanna Haswell Rowson   *Hulton Archive / Getty Images*

Musgrave Haswell and William Haswell in Portsmouth, England. Her mother died soon after Susanna's birth. Her father came from a naval family, and when the Royal Navy sent him to the colony of Massachusetts in 1763, he left his small daughter with relatives. William Haswell settled in Nantasket (now Hull) and remarried. In 1766, he brought his daughter to join him in America. Rowson recalled the adventurous journey twenty-five years later in her novel *Rebecca, or The Fille de Chambre* (1792), describing how her ship arrived in Boston Harbor during a sleet and snow storm. This vivid childhood memory is the source of the shipwrecks or dangerous adventures at sea in six of Rowson's novels.

In Hull, Susanna Haswell benefited from her father's small library of books by British writers and philosophers such as David Hume, Edmund Spenser, John Dryden, and William Shakespeare, as well as from conversations with patriot James Otis, who, according to Samuel Knapp, called Susanna his "little pupil" and often invited her to his home. Her happy childhood was brought to an end by the onset of the American Revolution. Starting in 1775, settlers of the thirteen American colonies revolted against the rule of the British Empire and began the revolution that would later result in the creation of the United States of America. William Haswell's affiliation with Britain's Royal Navy invited the suspicion of local revolutionaries, and in October 1775, the family was taken prisoner, moved farther inland, and kept under house arrest for three years. Then, like so many other people suspected of siding with the British, they were taken to Nova Scotia, exchanged for American prisoners of war, and shipped to England.

At age sixteen, Haswell found herself in London among hundreds of other refugees from America, their families deprived of property and livelihood by the war. At first the Haswells waited for an end to the hostilities, hoping to return to America and resume their lives. Without income and deprived of their American land, they passed the time exploring London, its free parks and monuments. As the end of the war extinguished hope of return to America and diminished prospects of financial redress from the British government, responsibility for family finances fell on the shoulders of young Susanna, who took work as a governess to help support her family.

Writing and Acting, Struggling to Make a Living
While a governess, Haswell wrote her first novel, *Victoria* (1786), which drew heavily on her own experience of dislocation and privation after the American Revolution. Also in 1786, Haswell married the minor actor and singer William Rowson and began a new career as an actress. Marriage did not alleviate Rowson's need to earn her living. William Rowson was seldom given acting roles and never earned much money. To supplement their income Rowson wrote a second novel, *The Inquisitor* (1788), a loosely structured series of heartrending domestic scenes.

The novel for which Rowson is best known, *Charlotte Temple*, was first published in England in 1791. It is a sentimental story of a beautiful, innocent girl seduced and abandoned by a soldier. Such moralistic stories of the perils of straying into sin proved very popular in the nineteenth century, and Rowson's novel was one of the first to enjoy bestseller status. Such books reflect the strong cultural belief in Western Europe and the United States in the late eighteenth and early nineteenth centuries that women and girls should be like domestic "angels": pious, devoid of sexual feeling, and devoted to their husbands and children. In the fiction of this time, female characters who stray from this model of behavior, even when lured or tricked, usually wind up dead. The last novel Rowson published in England was *Rebecca, or, The Fille de Chambre* (1792). This tale of Rebecca Littleton, daughter of a retired army lieutenant, is Rowson's most autobiographical work. The preface to the 1814 edition tells readers that the heroine's adventures have been those of the author. Rebecca's vain and cruel employer, Lady Ossiter, deprives Rebecca of her inheritance; Lord Ossiter attempts to seduce her and drives her from the house. Rebecca's sea voyage recalls Rowson's own early journey and her idyllic New England village life shattered by the onset of the American Revolution. The novel repeats Rowson's favorite themes of devotion to one's parents and the virtues of the middle class, which may be one reason why it, like *Charlotte Temple*, became popular in America.

Back to America
The Rowsons, frustrated by their inability to earn a living in England, joined a full company of actors who sailed for America in July 1793. In February 1794, the troupe moved to Philadelphia, where Rowson soon became recognized as an accomplished comedienne. Rowson's first American play, *Slaves in Algiers* (1794), capitalized on the current attacks on American ships by Barbary pirates from Algeria and other parts of north Africa. Accounts told of American ships being overtaken and those on board enslaved. Rowson's interest lay not in Algeria, but in the idea of tyranny, and she appealed to her American audience by means of her patriotic American characters. She extended the idea of political liberty to include love of sexual liberty, and the play includes her most staunchly feminist statements.

Educating Young Women
In 1797, Rowson gave up her stage career and turned to women's education, a field that had always held her interest and was then generating popular concern and debate. That fall she opened a private school, Mrs. Rowson's Young Ladies' Academy on Federal Street, the first of its kind in Boston. The academy opened with one pupil, and within a year the school had grown to accommodate more than one hundred students. As an educator, Rowson was known for her strict discipline and for setting a rigorous course of study designed to motivate and hold students' interest. Despite her responsibilities as headmistress, Rowson still enjoyed writing fiction. Her novels had always been forms of moral instruction, but *Reuben and Rachel; or, Tales of Old Times* (1798), published the year after she opened the academy, added instruction in history.

Unhappy Home
For many years, William Rowson earned no steady income. Indeed, despite his constant association with the theater, he clearly lacked acting talent, and evidence indicates that he drank heavily. The couple raised William's illegitimate son. In 1803–1804 Susanna Rowson published a novel that revealed some of her situation. *Sarah, or The Exemplary Wife* (1813), first appeared serially in the *Boston Weekly* under the title "Sincerity." Claiming in the preface that many scenes had been "drawn from real life," Rowson attempted to hide their autobiographical connection by adding that they occurred "in another hemisphere, and the characters no longer exist," but even Elias Nason, Rowson's defender and biographer, admitted that much of the plot paralleled her own experiences, and that the quotation on the title page, "Do not marry a fool," related to her own sufferings.

As her health declined and she suffered the losses of people she loved, Rowson's creative output diminished. Her last works were produced intermittently between bouts of illness. *Exercises in History, Chronology, and*

Biography (1822) is a series of questions and answers, tracing the history of the world from the time of creation to the founding of the American Republic.

Rowson's last years were unhappy. Her three half brothers had predeceased her, and in 1821, her good friend Catherine Graupner died. Her husband mortgaged their Hollis Street house, and she was unable to pay it off. Still, she managed to write one more novel, which was published posthumously as *Charlotte's Daughter: or, The Three Orphans* (1828; better known as *Lucy Temple* after the 1842 edition). It opens eighteen years after the end of *Charlotte Temple*. The book seems an expression of Rowson's old age, reflecting her increasing interest in religion and charitable causes and her nostalgia for times and places of her youth. Rowson died in Boston on March 2, 1824.

Works in Literary Context

Women Writers and Fiction   The works of Rowson and other women writers experienced a surge of popularity in the early nineteenth century. For the first time, the concerns and perspectives of women were being voiced to mainstream readers. Some male writers voiced contempt for these works, denouncing them as popular but lacking any lasting literary value. Nathaniel Hawthorne, one of Rowson's contemporaries, wrote: "America is now wholly given over to a damned mob of scribbling women, and I should have no chance of success while the public taste is occupied with their trash."

In this climate, Rowson, for her part, encouraged other women writers through works such as *The Inquisitor*, in which she expresses concern for the woman as artist, describing booksellers who urge aspiring women writers to plagiarize and a public that often disapproves of their literary ambitions. She is credited with promoting portrayals of female independence on stage and in print, as shown in her drama, *Slaves in Algiers.*

As author of the first American bestseller, *Charlotte Temple*, and the first American writer to find an audience for fiction, Rowson paved the way for other prominent women fiction writers to follow. Writer Susan Warner's *The Wide, Wide World* (1850), became the first domestic novel that was an American bestseller. Harriet Beecher Stowe, author of the best-selling novel, *Uncle Tom's Cabin* (1852), was also among the best-paid writers of her day. Like Rowson, Stowe's writings have been praised as leading exemplars of both sentimental and regional fiction.

Moralism and Filial Piety   Rowson offered much of her work towards the education of women in upholding of morals, especially regarding filial piety—the respect and love for one's parents and older generations within the family—and the importance of friendship. In her novel, *Victoria*, the title character resists an attempted seduction only to be taken in by a sham marriage. Soon pregnant and abandoned, she gives birth to a son, becomes insane, and dies. The importance of filial piety

runs through the five subplots and several brief stories within stories.

Rowson's *A Trip to Parnassus* (1788), a lighthearted poetic evaluation of thirty-four actors and writers at the Covent Garden Theatre, established the writer as a strict moralist among theatrical people, with their sometimes-scandalous private lives. *The Test of Honour* (1789) appealed to lower-middle-class women, who embraced the young woman protagonist's independent spirit and moral sense, which is shown to be far superior to that of the wealthy aristocrat who refuses to let his son marry her.

Works in Critical Context

Though successful in her lifetime, Rowson was generally ignored by literary critics after her death. Recently, however, she has benefited from current critical reappraisals of American women writers. Her versatile efforts as novelist, essayist, lyricist, and teacher are increasingly appreciated as a notable contribution to early American culture.

Francis W. Halsey writes in 1905: "The situations Mrs. Rowson describes, the sympathies she evokes, appeal to what is elemental in our nature and what is also eternal ... they are wholesome, sane, and true." Dorothy Weil comments on Rowson's contributions with the following: "Mrs. Rowson met the major issues concerning women, and claimed freedom for her sex ... and taught her reader that she could be the equal of the male in most of the important spheres of life."

COMMON HUMAN EXPERIENCE

Throughout her varied career, Rowson dedicated her literary works to the young female reader. Here are some other works that speak to young women:

The Boarding School (1798), a nonfiction work by Hannah Webster Foster. Foster delves into the subject of boarding schools for girls and women, a controversial topic of the time in England and the United States.

Female Spectator (1744–1746), a combination of letters, stories, and essays by Eliza Haywood. This work reads as a female courtesy book, which Rowson's *Mentoria* resembles.

The Errors of Innocence (1786), a novel by Harriet Lee. This novel revolves around the consequences of a hasty marriage between a young woman and an apparently dying admirer of hers, and explores the tragic effects of false pity and extramarital love.

Rowson has stirred favorable scholarly interest since the late 1970s, her rise in critical reputation paralleling the women's movement. Readers have particularly responded to Rowson's consistent advocacy of equal education and personal, as well as political, freedom for women. Her enlightened views of women are reflected in strong, adventurous, thoughtful heroines whose positive attributes surpassed the weaknesses of Rowson's plots. After two hundred years *Charlotte Temple* still has its fans, and many of Rowson's other works invite further study.

Charlotte Temple By the time Rowson published *Charlotte Temple*, she was a practiced writer whose previous novels showed a competent handling of contemporary genres. Her prose, and to a lesser extent her poetry, had met with moderate success. But when *Charlotte Temple* was reprinted in America three years after its publication in England, Rowson, still early in her career, made literary history. Hardly read in England, the novel went through more than two hundred editions by the mid-nineteenth century in America, and spawned a "Charlotte cult." Charlotte's supposed tombstone in Trinity Churchyard, New York, became a pilgrimage site for generations of readers. Alvarez Saar, in her essay "Susanna Rowson: Feminist and Democrat," maintains that Rowson's work represents "a landmark in the development of feminist political ideology in American drama."

Responses to Literature

1. Rowson was a great admirer of William Shakespeare. Compare and contrast Rowson's character Charlotte to William Shakespeare's young characters Romeo and Juliet. What are the messages from both authors to young readers?

2. In *Victoria*, Rowson draws from real events from her life to create the story. Read the sections of the novel dealing with war. What do these sections reveal about the author's ideas regarding war and its effects on citizens?

3. After reading Rowson's *Slaves in Algiers*, discuss Rowson's heroine, Mary. What are some of Mary's attributes that seem ahead of the time in which the play was written? Compare Mary to a heroine in a present-day book or movie.

BIBLIOGRAPHY

Books

Davidson, Cathy N. *Revolution and the Word: The Rise of the Novel in America*. New York: Oxford University Press, 1986.

Halsey, Francis W. *An Introduction to Charlotte Temple: A Tale of Truth, by Susanna Haswell Rowson*. New York: Funk & Wagnalls Company, 1905.

Haywood, Eliza. *Female Spectator*. Whitefish, Mont.: Kessinger Publishing, LLC, 2008.

Schofield, Mary Anne and Cecilia Macheski, eds. "Susanna Rowson: Feminist and Democrat." *Curtain Calls: British and American Women and the Theater: 1660–1820*. Athens, Ohio: Ohio University Press, 1991

Weil, Dorothy. "Inferior to None." *In Defense of Women: Susanna Rowson (1762–1824)*. University Park, Pa.: The Pennsylvania State University Press, 1976.

Periodicals

Cherniavsky, Eva. "Charlotte Temple's Remains." *Discovering Difference: Contemporary Essays in American Culture*, edited by Christoph K. Kohmann. Bloomington and Indianapolis, Ind.: Indiana University Press, 1993, pp. 35–47.

Davidson, Cathy N. "The Life and Times of Charlotte Temple: The Biography of a Book." *Reading in America: Literature and Social History*, edited by Davidson. Baltimore, Md.: Johns Hopkins University Press, 1989.

Forcey, Blythe. "Charlotte Temple and the End of Epistolarity." *American Literature* 63 (1991): 225–241.

Greenfield, Susan. "Charlotte Temple and Charlotte's Daughter: The Reproduction of Woman's Word." *Women's Studies* 18 (1990): 269–286.

Hansen, Klaus P. "The Sentimental Novel and Its Feminist Critique." *Early American Literature* 26 (1991): 39–54.

Kornfeld, Eve. "Women in Post-Revolutionary American Culture: Susanna Haswell Rowson's American Career." *Journal of American Culture* 22 (Winter 1983): 56–62.

Web sites

California State University at Stanislaus Online. *Nathaniel Hawthorne (1804–1864)*. Accessed November 15, 2008, from http://www.csustan. edu/english/reuben/pal/chap3/hawthorne.html.

Charvat, William. *Charlotte: A Tale of Truth (also known as Charlotte Temple)*. Accessed November 15, 2008, from http://www.wsu.edu/~campbelld/amlit/ rowson2.html.

✸ Muriel Rukeyser

BORN: *1913, New York City*

DIED: *1980, New York City*

NATIONALITY: *American*

GENRE: *Poetry*

MAJOR WORKS:
U.S. 1 (1938)
The Life of Poetry (1949)
The Gates: Poems (1976)
The Collected Poems of Muriel Rukeyser (1978)

Muriel Rukeyser   *Rukeyser, Muriel, 1972, photograph. AP Images.*

Overview

Muriel Rukeyser was one of the twentieth century's most productive and articulate poet-activists, concerned with a range of social and political justice issues. She saw poets as gifted leaders with a mission to encourage all human beings to realize their greatest human potential.

Works in Biographical and Historical Context

A Passion for Social Justice   Muriel Rukeyser was born in New York City in 1913. She attended Vassar College, where she co-founded and edited the undergraduate literary magazine the *Student Review*. She also briefly attended the Roosevelt Aviation School and Columbia University. At a young age, her life was marked by a strong commitment to social activism. While working at the *Student Review* at Vassar, Rukeyser covered the 1932 Scottsboro trial in Alabama in which nine African American youths were accused of raping two white girls. She based her poem, "The Trial," on this experience. Rukeyser's career as a published poet began in 1935 when her collection of poems *Theory of Flight*, inspired largely by her flying lessons at aviation school, won the Yale Series of Younger Poets competition and was published by Yale University Press. The collection established Rukeyser as an energetic writer, concerned with social injustice and the search for ways to discover the fullest human potential. *Theory of Flight* was also, in many ways, a template for the type of poetry Rukeyser would write her entire life. The poems were mostly written in free verse with syntax that is more like prose than song. She very often wrote sequences or clusters of poems grouped by single situations, characters, or themes.

After college, Rukeyser wrote a steady stream of poetry and taught at Vassar and Sarah Lawrence College. She also wrote plays, television scripts, children's books, biographies, and essays, and translated poems from several languages. She was married briefly and, on her own, raised a son, whom she had had by another man. Yet, it is her poetry about political and social issues, as well as her attempts to synthesize poetry into her own journey of self-discovery, that form the basis of her literary life.

Poetry of the Personal and Political   Rukeyser's second book, the 1938 collection, *U.S. 1*—named after the highway that runs from Maine to Florida—cemented her reputation as a proponent of social causes. In *U.S. 1*, Rukeyser wrote movingly about the West Virginia Gauley Bridge tragedy, in which thousands of workers died of the lung disease silicosis, while their employer ignored the hazards of inhaling glass particles the workers encountered while tunneling. The poems from this cycle are commonly referred to as *The Book of the Dead*.

With her next book, *A Turning Wind: Poems* (1939), Rukeyser maintained her passion for social justice, but she also focused on more personal issues. She was awarded

LITERARY AND HISTORICAL CONTEMPORARIES

Rukeyser's famous contemporaries include:

Lyndon B. Johnson (1908–1973): Johnson, who served as president of the United States from 1963–1969, presided over much of the turbulent decade of the 1960s.

Arthur Miller (1915–2005): American playwright and essayist Miller was a fellow PEN member who was involved in a number of political events, but is most famous for his play *Death of a Salesman* (1949).

Denise Levertov (1923–1997): British poet and prose writer Levertov is well-known for her gripping poetry about social activism, the antiwar movement, and feminism.

Adrienne Rich (1929–): American poet and prose writer Rich is one of the most influential feminist poets to emerge from the 1970s.

Kurt Vonnegut, Jr. (1922–2007): Prolific and provocative, Vonnegut is known for fusing a number of different genres to create complex satires, including the powerful *Slaughterhouse-Five* (1969).

COMMON HUMAN EXPERIENCE

Rukeyser is notable for expressing her personal and emotional reality within the larger framework of real-life political and social context. Here are some other works that fuse the personal and political:

Paterson (1946–1963), a poem series by William Carlos Williams. *Paterson* is an epic series of poems that center on Paterson, New Jersey, exploring the changing American identity.

"America" (1956), a poem by Allen Ginsberg. Ginsberg's poem reflects on events and trends in American history and explores his own countercultural beliefs.

"Diving into the Wreck" (1973), a poem by Adrienne Rich. Rich's moving poem is a metaphorical exploration of her feelings towards the violence and patriarchy that gripped America during the 1960s.

"Coming to Jakarta: A Poem about Terror" (1989), a poem by Peter Dale Scott. This long poem is an evocation of Scott's own journey of discovery into his family's involvement with the CIA during the 1960s.

a prestigious Guggenheim fellowship in 1943, and continued to explore a balance of her political and personal subjects over her next few books. She made a conscious choice to focus on very personal topics with the 1944 collection *Beast in a View*. *Beast in a View* contains the poem "Ajanta," which many critics still regard as her finest work. The title refers to a series of painted caves in India, which represent the poetic journey she undertook to delve deep into her inner, mysterious life to pursue self-knowledge. She continued this psychological and literary journey in her next two major works of poetry, *The Green Wave* (1948) and *Body of Walking* (1958).

A Renewed Commitment to Activism   During the 1960s and 1970s, Rukeyser renewed her commitment to political and social activism. She was jailed briefly for protesting the Vietnam War on the steps of the U.S. Capitol in Washington, D.C. She also stirred up controversy by visiting Hanoi, Vietnam, at a time when the United States was waging a war against the North Vietnamese government and its forces, which were based in Hanoi. Her poetry during this time, published in the notable collections *The Speed of Darkness* (1968) and *Breaking Open: New Poems* (1973), reflect a strong undercurrent of political passion along with personal topics. Many of her poems reflect her personal and emotional journey in the larger context of the political and social movements she supported. Rukeyser was also considered a contemporary of many of the feminist poets who emerged during the 1970s, including Denise Levertov, Adrienne Rich, and Anne Sexton.

At almost sixty, nearing the end of her life and in deteriorating health, she became president of the American Center for PEN, an organization that supports the rights and free expression of writers throughout the world. As a representative of PEN, Rukeyser traveled to South Korea to voice her opposition to the death sentence of poet Kim Chi-Ha. When she was denied a meeting with the poet, she stood outside the prison gates in protest. Her last collection of poetry, *The Gates*, published in 1976, is based on that experience. *The Gates* also contains a deeply personal poem about recovering from a paralyzing stroke, "Resurrection of the Right Side," which is admired by many critics. Despite her failing health, Rukeyser did see *The Collected Poems of Muriel Rukeyser* go to publication in 1978. In 1979, she was honored at the annual New York Quarterly Poetry Day for her outstanding contribution to contemporary poetry. In 1980, Rukeyser died in New York City.

Works in Literary Context

Documentary Poetry   Although her work borrows from a number of genres and traditions, including lyric and experimental poetry, Rukeyser is widely recognized for helping to usher in a new modern poetic style:

documentary poetry. Documentary poetry is a dynamic type of poetry that informs as it reflects and provides real facts and knowledge while imagining their emotional and psychological dimensions. Rukeyser's most famous series of documentary poems is *The Book of the Dead* in *U.S. 1*. *The Book of the Dead* documents the silicosis poisoning of workers in West Virginia and draws upon actual legal testimony, first-person interviews, and facts about the event while exploring the emotional devastation of the tragedy. Documentary poetry derives its power from being able to articulate the "real" while elevating it to the artistry of poetry.

Works in Critical Context

While Rukeyser's poetry exhibits an exuberant passion and outrage over political injustices, critics' assessments of that passion have varied. Many critics have found her more political work to be overly preachy and technically lacking, even simplistic. Most critics agree that her lyrical and personal poetry is, technically and artistically, more sophisticated. Critics also generally agree on her ability to reflect the changing social and political landscapes of her time and to articulate her own passionate experience of them. As Richard Eberhart wrote, "The poems of Muriel Rukeyser are primordial and torrential. They pour out excitements of a large emotional force, taking in a great deal of life and giving out profound realizations of the significance of being."

"Ajanta" Published in the collection, *Beast in a View*, "Ajanta" is a long poem of self-discovery inspired by a set of Buddhist cave temples in Ajanta, India. Critics praised the work as a departure from much of Rukeyser's earlier, more political pieces, and it remains one of her most critically acclaimed poems. Critic Virginia R. Terris calls the work Rukeyser's "first statement of this sense of achievement of integration with herself," noting, "In this inner exploration, she is released from the bonds that have held her, her involvement with society. She recognizes, at last, that self-knowledge must precede all other kinds."

"Resurrection of the Right Side" One of her last poems, "Resurrection of the Right Side" is an account of Rukeyser's battle to recover after stroke. Praised by critics for its striking ability to engage the reader and document the physical and psychological dimensions of her battle, "Resurrection of the Right Side" is also considered a strong restatement of Rukeyser's poetic philosophy. When writing about the poem as a culmination of her attempt to find an authentic and inspired poetic voice, critic Davis S. Barber concludes, "Rukeyser's intimately personal but objective voice is also evident in her treatment in a major article of faith: her belief in the power of creativity."

Responses to Literature

1. How does Rukeyser re-imagine and transform classical myth in her poem "The Poem as Mask: Orpheus"?

2. What does Rukeyser say about political action in the poem "How We Did It"?

3. Read the poem "The Conjugation of the Paramecium." How does Rukeyser use the characteristics of documentary poetry in this work? Provide examples to illustrate your statements.

4. Rukeyser is known for declaring the importance of poetry in an advanced, democratic society. In your opinion, is poetry a fundamental part of human culture? How do you think human culture would be different without it?

BIBLIOGRAPHY

Bibliography

Books

Dayton, Tim. *Muriel Rukeyser's The Book of the Dead.* Columbia, Mo.: University of Missouri Press, 2003.

Herzog, Anne F. and Janet E. Kaufman, eds. *"How Shall We Tell Each Other of the Poet?": The Life and Writing of Muriel Rukeyser.* New York: St. Martin's Press, 1999.

Kertesz, Louise. *The Poetic Vision of Muriel Rukeyser.* Baton Rouge, La.: Louisiana University Press, 1979.

Rosenthal, M. L. "Muriel Rukeyser: The Longer Poems." *New Directions in Prose and Poetry* 16. Norfolk, Conn.: New Directions, 1953, pp. 201–229.

Periodicals

Barber, David S. "Finding Her Voice: Muriel Rukeyser's Poetic Development." *Modern Poetry Studies* 11, 1 & 2 (1982): 127–38.

Bernikow, Louise. "Muriel at 65: Still Ahead of Her Time." *MS*, 2 (April 1974): 35–36.

Eberhart, Richard. "Personal Statement." *The New York Times Book Review* (June 23, 1968): 24, 26.

Solotaroff, T. "Rukeyser: Poet of Plenitude." *Nation* 230 (1980): 277–278.

Terris, Virginia R. "Muriel Rukeyser: A Retrospective." *The American Poetry Review* 3 (May–June 1974): 10–15.

⊛ Kay Ryan

BORN: *1945, San Jose, California*

NATIONALITY: *American*

GENRE: *Poetry*

MAJOR WORKS:

Flamingo Watching: Poems (1994)

Elephant Rocks (1996)

Say Uncle (2000)

The Niagara River (2006)

Kay Ryan *Christopher Felver / Corbis*

Overview

Named the sixteenth Poet Laureate of the United States in 2008, Kay Ryan spent most of her adulthood teaching basic writing courses at a public community college, far from the mainstream poetry world. Her poetry reflects her outsider history by intertwining two main strands of modern American poetry to create her own distinctive style, which is characterized by short-lined free verse with playful use of internal and end-rhyme. Over the past few years, critics have taken note of Ryan's masterful ability to blend observation with meditation, as well as lightness and profundity.

Works in Biographical and Historical Context

A Desolate Upbringing Fosters a Rich Imagination Ryan was born on September 21, 1945, in San Jose, California. Her father was an oil driller, and her mother raised Kay and her older brother in small towns of the Mojave Desert and the San Joaquin Valley. Despite the fact that southern California was becoming a thriving center for the film industry, as well as a rich site for real

estate development, there were many places in the interior valley of the state that were still desolate and unpopulated, with struggling economies. Ryan's desert childhood in such a bleak and unforgiving environment had a profound impact on her distinctive vision, enabling her to craft a world of robust contemplation combined with poetic minimalism.

In 1963, after she graduated from Antelope Valley High School in Lancaster, California, Ryan enrolled at the University of California at Los Angeles. She received both her B.A. (1967) and M.A. (1968) in English literature from UCLA, but she did not take any creative writing classes. She then pursued her Ph.D. in literary criticism at the University of California at Irvine but did not complete the degree. Despite her studies in literary criticism, Ryan did not seek out a career in academia. Instead, she began teaching basic writing and remedial English at the College of Marin, a public community college, a position she maintained for over thirty years. Ryan also completed a brief teaching stint at San Quentin Prison.

A Poetic Calling Ryan began writing poetry as a young adult in the wake of her father's death, but she was reluctant to take up writing as a profession because of the way it made her feel exposed. She did not fully accept her vocation as poet until she was thirty. Then, on a four-thousand-mile bicycle trip across the United States with friends, Ryan had a transformational experience with language and contemplation. Ryan says she became a poet at the moment when she answered her own unvoiced question about poetry—Do you like it?—in the affirmative.

Ryan wrote the poems of her first collection, *Dragon Acts to Dragon Ends* (1983), in relative isolation. The book was self-published, financed through a subscription by friends. The poems in this volume are varied in type, with some displaying the earmarks of Ryan's later style. In the best poems of this book, including "Didactic," hidden internal rhymes provide a loose structural scaffolding for short, free-verse lines that play against the syntax.

Breaking Through Ryan's next book, *Strangely Marked Metal: Poems*, was published by a small press in 1985, and produced hardly a ripple upon publication. Despite her relative obscurity, Ryan began to quietly build a presence in the literary world over the next ten years. The appearance of her next book, *Flamingo Watching: Poems* (1994), was preceded by the publication of her poems in some of the leading American literary journals: *American Poetry Review, The Atlantic, The American Scholar, The New Republic,* and *The Paris Review.* As a result, *Flamingo Watching: Poems* was Ryan's first book to garner critical review.

By the time Ryan published *Flamingo Watching: Poems,* she had fully assimilated her influences and fashioned her signature style. Although she developed her poetic voice during a time when American poetry was characterized by experimentation and the impulse to break free from conventional structures, Ryan used traditional structure as part of her style. As a result, Ryan's verse attracts both admirers of formal and free verse. In achieving such a fusion, Ryan has made her work thoroughly modern without employing any specific Modernist or postmodernist strategies. Instead of fragmentation, obscure allusions, and sterile verbal tricks, her poems surprise readers with their playfully shifting patterns and densely concentrated meanings. Ryan's poetry seems to embody a determination to follow Emily Dickinson's injunction to tell the truth, but tell it "slant."

Rising to Prominence Many of the poems of Ryan's *Elephant Rocks* (1996) appeared in prestigious magazines and journals prior to their publication in book form. When the book appeared, it received far more critical attention than her previous works. In *Elephant Rocks*, Ryan continued to develop many of her themes and refine her ability to illuminate experience through poetry. She continued to fine-tune her poetic voice throughout her next volumes, *Say Uncle: Poems* (2000) and *The Niagara River* (2006).

Ryan's poetry began to draw a large audience in the late 1990s, when it began to appear with some frequency in *The New Yorker* and other leading journals. Since then, Ryan has received a National Endowment for the Arts Fellowship and the Maurice English Poetry Prize in 2001; the Union League Poetry Prize in 2000; a Guggenheim Fellowship and the Ruth Lilly Poetry Prize from The Poetry Foundation in 2004; and the Gold Medal for Poetry from the San Francisco Commonwealth Club in 2005. Ryan has also won four Pushcart Prizes and has been included in four volumes of the *Best American Poetry*. One of Ryan's poems has been permanently installed in a playground in Central Park in New York City. In 2008, Ryan was named the American Poet Laureate, one of poetry's most distinguished honors, sealing her reputation as one the most profound and engaging poets of the modern age.

Works in Literary Context

Ryan's poems are short, loaded with images, and frequently make use of humor. Ryan rarely writes in first person. Her poems often take the shape of a single observation that becomes an intense contemplation. Her poems tease the imagination with wordplay and sudden reversals, yielding richer implications with each reading. New tangents often hinge on a single word, as in the title poem of *Flamingo Watching: Poems*, in which the Ryan pokes fun at overly serious viewers who fail to appreciate the flamboyance of the flamingo.

A Fusion of Formalism and Free Verse Because of her distinctive style, Ryan belongs to no single historical or modern literary tradition. Less "free" than the mainstream free verse of her contemporaries, Ryan's poems combine the English lyrical poetic tradition of the trimeter and tetrameter—in which each line contains, respectively, three and four "feet," or pairs of syllables—

LITERARY AND HISTORICAL CONTEMPORARIES

Ryan's famous contemporaries include:

Philip Larkin (1922–1985): Larkin is a beloved and engaging English poet. He is best known for poetry that is highly structured but creative in its use of language.

John Ashbery (1927–): Ashbery is a dominating presence in twentieth century American poetry. His work is characterized by a complex, surrealistic use of language and syntax.

W. S. Merwin (1927–): Merwin is an American poet and Pulitzer Prize winner. His work is marked by a unique evolution throughout the twentieth century.

Joan Didion (1934–): Didion is an American novelist, fiction writer, essayist and screenwriter. A distinctive voice of modern America, Didion's novel *Play It As It Lays* (1970) and her collection of essays *Slouching Towards Bethlehem* (1968), are widely considered to be among the finest literature of California.

Louise Glück (1943–): Glück is an American poet and former U.S. Poet Laureate who won the Pulitzer Prize for Poetry with her collection *The Wild Iris* (1992).

---

with the more syncopated free-verse line of modern schools of poetry. Combining occasional end-rhyme and regular meter with free verse, Ryan balances the irregularity of her language with frequent internal rhymes and thick assonance, or the repetition of vowel sounds in different words. In a similar way, her poetry balances small observations or limited subject matter with depth of consideration. Instead of better-known poetry contemporaries, the best comparisons to Ryan's poetry come from a diversity of historical poets, including Emily Dickinson, Robert Frost, Marianne Moore, and Elizabeth Bishop.

Works in Critical Context

Because of her sudden rise to prominence, the body of literary criticism on Ryan is rather small. Nevertheless, she is widely praised as a creator of short, engaging poetry that is both rhythmically light and densely philosophical at the same time. As critic Andrew Fisardi observed, despite their heavy use of wordplay and rich imagery, Ryan's poems often drive towards "something useful and important."

"Doubt" In "Doubt," Ryan opens a contemplation of the significance and experience of doubt with the simple image of a chick breaking out of its egg. By asking if the chicken can "afford" doubt, she reiterates the importance of action and hope. Critic Charlotte Muse praises Ryan's "many small deft touches" as the poet builds to a

COMMON HUMAN EXPERIENCE

Ryan's poetry is centered on observation, commonly of everyday objects or images, that evolves through engaging wordplay to become a thoughtful contemplation on universal ideas. Here are some other works that focus on using wordplay and observation to contemplate ideas:

> "There's a Certain Slant of Light" (1890), a poem by Emily Dickinson. Dickinson's poem captures the emotions that accompany the dying light of the afternoon.
>
> "Nothing Gold Can Stay," (1923), a poem by Robert Frost. Like much of Frost's poetry, this seemingly simple observation about changing seasons is also a brooding meditation on impermanence.
>
> "Octopus," (1935), a poem by Marianne Moore. One of Moore's long poems, "Octopus" is a highly detailed contemplation of Mount Rainier.
>
> "Question," (1994), a poem by May Swenson. Swenson's poem uses quizzical rhyme and repetition to move through an examination of her body and the implications of its mortality.

conclusion that resonates with the craft of writing, noting, "This one suggests the disorientation that arises at the beginning a work; the not knowing where the vision or idea we've begun to spin comes from."

"Paired Things" "Paired Things" is a key poem in *Flamingo Watching: Poems* that questions the nature of pairings. In this densely layered short poem, Ryan uses hidden rhymes and meter to bring her observation of life. Critics praised this work as an example of the poetic fusion that Ryan is able to achieve. As critic Dana Gioia comments, "image and abstraction dance so consummate a *pas de deux* that one wonders why modern poetics ever considered the two imaginative impulses at odds."

Responses to Literature

1. In Ryan's poems, animals often appear less as biological entities than emblems for larger ideas. What do you think is the meaning of the animal in Ryan's poem "Turtle" from her collection *Flamingo Watching: Poems*?

2. Ryan rarely uses a first-person perspective in her poems. In "Hide and Seek" (from *The Niagara River*), how does Ryan's use of a second-person voice impact how you read this poem?

3. How does Ryan use the cliché "waiting for the other shoe to drop" in the poem "The Other Shoe" (from *The Niagara River*)? How does she change the meaning of the expression?

BIBLIOGRAPHY

Periodicals

Hewitt, Alison. "Kay Ryan, Outsider with Sly Style, Named Poet Laureate." *The New York Times* (July 17, 2008).

Frisardi, Andrew. "*Elephant Rocks*, by Kay Ryan." *Poetry* 170 (1977): 101.

Gioia, Dana. "Discovering Kay Ryan." *Dark Horse* 7 (Winter 1998–1999): 6–9.

Haven, Cynthia L. "Let There Be Lightness: Poet Kay Ryan knows what the world needs now." *San Francisco Magazine* (October 2004).

Muse, Charlotte. "*Elephant Rocks*, by Kay Ryan." *Able Muse* (1999).

Cynthia Rylant

BORN: *1954, Hopewell, Virginia*

NATIONALITY: *American*

GENRE: *Fiction, nonfiction, poetry*

MAJOR WORKS:

When I Was Young in the Mountains (1982)
A Blue-Eyed Daisy (1985)
A Fine White Dust (1986)
Soda Jerk (1990)
Missing May (1992)

Overview

Cynthia Rylant is an award-winning author of children's and young adult books whose work includes picture books, poetry, short stories, and novels. With a writing style that has been described as unadorned, clear, and lyrical, Rylant presents young people's experiences with sensitivity and perceptiveness.

Works in Biographical and Historical Context

A Rural Life Cynthia Rylant was born on June 6, 1954, in the rural town of Hopewell, Virginia. Her parents had a stormy marriage and separated when Rylant was just four years old and she moved with her mother to West Virginia, where she was cared for by her grandparents while her mother was earning a nursing degree. Her rustic upbringing was characterized by a great deal of hardship: in the small town where she lived, many houses had neither electricity nor running water. The Appalachian region has been one of the most impoverished regions throughout United States history, despite the abundance of natural resources in the area. In the 1960s, President Lyndon B. Johnson called attention to poverty in that area, and the result was the 1964 Appalachian Regional Development Act, which ushered in improvements in education and health care. Nonetheless,

Rylant grew up in areas that were characterized by poverty. The lack of amenities did not bother young Rylant; she felt secure, surrounded by equally poor, yet friendly, church-going neighbors. When the author was eight years old, she and her mother moved to the town of Beaver, West Virginia. Raised in a town without a library, Rylant was exposed to a very limited range of literature in her youth. As a result, she cultivated a rich imagination that enabled her to become a highly successful author. In her autobiography, *But I'll Be Back Again: An Album*, Rylant reflected on how her hardscrabble childhood cultivated her powerful imagination, calling the town of Beaver "without a doubt a small, sparkling universe that gave me a lifetime's worth of material for my writing."

The uncommon hardships that Rylant faced in her youth contributed to her ability to write strong and sympathetic young characters. In her autobiography, Rylant wrote,

> They say that to be a writer you must first have an unhappy childhood. I don't know if unhappiness is necessary, but I think maybe some children who have suffered a loss too great for words grow up into writers who are always trying to find those words, trying to find a meaning for the way they have lived.

Rylant did, indeed, face a great deal of unhappiness. Her father wrote occasionally when Ryant and her mother first moved, but the letters eventually stopped. Rylant was afraid to ask questions about her father because none of her relatives spoke about him. After years of silence, he finally contacted her. Rylant dreamed of a reunion with him, but before it could take place, her father, a Korean War veteran who suffered from both hepatitis and alcoholism, succumbed to those diseases. He died when she was thirteen. In her autobiography, Rylant reflected on that loss and observed, "That is all the loss I needed to become a writer."

After she graduated from high school, Rylant pursued her bachelor of arts degree at the University of Charleston (formerly the Morris Harvey College). In her first English class at college, Rylant discovered a part of herself that she had not recognized before, but she was intimidated by the prospect of trying to write like great classical writers. She graduated in 1975, and continued her English studies, earning her M.A. in English from Marshall University in Huntington, West Virginia, in 1976. Still unsure of her career path, Rylant took a job in the children's room of a public library in Huntington, West Virginia. There, she was exposed to children's literature, and decided that she was going to become a children's author. As a single parent, she also began studying library science at Kent State University in Kent, Ohio. She graduated with a master of library science degree in 1982, the same year that she published her first book.

A Strong Voice for Children Rylant's first book was *When I Was Young in the Mountains* (1982), a picture book about life in West Virginia's Appalachian Mountains. Critics praised the first effort for its single, yet evocative text. Diane Goode's illustrations for *When I Was Young in the Mountains* won a Caldecott book citation. In 1984, Rylant published an autobiographical collection of poetry about coming-of-age, *Waiting to Waltz ... A Childhood*. The collection weaves in events and symbols from the turbulent decade of the 1960s to vividly re-create the era and provide a full portrait of her adolescence. Rylant followed that with her first novel, published in 1985, *A Blue-Eyed Daisy*. Set in Appalachia, the novel work is told by eleven-year-old Ellie Farley, the youngest of five daughters, who contends with her apprehensions and conflicting emotions about growing up. For example, she overcomes her fear of contracting epilepsy after witnessing a classmate's seizure; copes with her unemployed, alcoholic father's imperfections and the possibility of his death after an accident; and battles the nervous anticipation of a party. With *A Blue-Eyed Daisy*, Rylant began to make a name for herself as an uncommonly talented children's author.

Rylant's 1986 novel, *A Fine White Dust*, was named a Newbery Honor Book. In this work, a deeply religious seventh-grader named Pete believes he has found a human incarnation of God in a roving preacher named Carson. While attending a revival meeting, Pete is mesmerized by Carson's charismatic presence and, after being "saved," agrees to become his disciple. Despite his hesitance to leave his family and friends, Pete believes that such a sacrifice is needed to fully embrace the holy life. Pete's mission is never fulfilled, however, because the preacher unexpectedly runs off with a young woman. Although he initially feels betrayed, Pete develops a more mature understanding of love and faith.

Rylant was also honored with a Newbery award for her 1992 novel *Missing May*. Summer, the novel's protagonist, is a six-year-old orphan who is passed from family to family until her elderly Aunt May and Uncle Ob in West Virginia decide to adopt her. Summer lives happily with Ob and May for six years until May suddenly dies. Summer and Ob have difficulty adjusting to life without May, and Ob becomes convinced that he feels the spirit of May around him and decides to contact her through a spiritualist. They journey to find a medium who will connect them to May's spirit, but they are disappointed. During the return trip, Ob transforms and decides that being alive—even without May—is important. When they arrive home, Summer is finally able to grieve for May with Ob's support. Critics and readers found *Missing May* to be a rewarding and comforting experience.

In addition to her novels, Rylant has also been a prolific writer of picture books, including a notable series about the misadventures of a boy named Henry and his dog, Mudge, that began with the 1987 story *Henry and Mudge*. Her other early-reader series include stories about an old man who adopts a cat named Tabby, which

LITERARY AND HISTORICAL CONTEMPORARIES

Rylant's famous contemporaries include:

Philip Pullman (1946–): Pullman is a British children's novelist. Pullman won the prestigious British Carnegie Medal for his 1996 children's novel *Northern Lights*, which was published in America as *The Golden Compass*.

Christa McAuliffe (1948–1986): McAuliffe was an American teacher and astronaut. McAuliffe, the first participant in NASA's Teacher in Space Project, inspired a generation of American children. She was killed in 1986 when the Space Shuttle *Challenger* broke apart shortly after takeoff.

Kate DiCamillo (1964–): DiCamillo is an American children's author. DiCamillo is an award-winning children's author whose 2000 novel, *Because of Winn Dixie*, was adapted into a feature film.

J. K. Rowling (1965–): Rowling is a British children's author. Rowling is internationally renowned for her *Harry Potter* fantasy novel series, which began with *Harry Potter and the Philosopher's Stone* (1997).

Eoin Colfer (1965–): Colfer is an Irish children's author. Colfer is author of the best-selling novel *Artemis Fowl* (2001) and its sequels.

COMMON HUMAN EXPERIENCE

Throughout her novels and stories, Rylant focuses on the landscape and towns of Appalachia to explore how the socioeconomic issues of that area impact the lives of real children. Here are some other works that explore life in Appalachia:

"Knoxville, Tennessee" (1973), a poem by Nikki Giovanni. Giovanni explores her childhood in the Appalachia region in this poem, which was also made into an illustrated children's picture book.

Storming Heaven (1988), a novel by Denise Giardina. This novel is a re-creation of the turbulent lives of West Virginia coal miners in the early twentieth century.

Sweet Holler Creek (1988), a novel by Ruth White. This young adult novel is the story of a coal mining family in Western Virginia.

Rocket Boys (1998), a memoir by Homer Hickam, Jr. This memoir about growing up in a West Virginia mining town was made into the 1999 film, *October Sky*.

Gap Creek (1999), a novel by Robert Morgan. Morgan chronicles the life of a young woman living in Appalachia at the end of the nineteenth century.

began with *Mr. Putter and Tabby Pour the Tea* in 1994; her popular Poppleton Pig series, which began in 1997 with *Poppleton*; her series about "High-Rise Private Eyes" Bunny Brown and Raccoon Jones, animals who solve mysteries, which began in 2000 with *The Case of the Missing Monkey*; and her series about a guinea pig, which began with *Little Whistle* (2000).

Since the publication of *Missing May*, Rylant has continued to publish award-winning literature for children and young adults, earning a loyal readership and ongoing positive critical response.

Works in Literary Context

Children's Realistic Fiction Instead of creating fantasy worlds or characters, Rylant has focused the majority of her children's novels and stories (with the exception of her easy reader series) in the genre of literary realism. With unadorned and clear language, Rylant creates portraits of contemporary childhood, dramatizing ordinary or everyday events to which young readers can easily relate. For instance, *The Relatives Came* (1985) is the story about a visit from an extended family living in another state that reflects the complex emotions of anticipation and sadness, and in *Missing May* (1992), Rylant explores the grieving process as a necessary part of growing up in her story about a girl who loses her beloved aunt. By focusing on realistic stories, Rylant is able to create rich and poignant characterizations that are accessible to young readers.

Children's Poetry Rylant has also produced several volumes of children's poetry. While her themes and settings are very realistic in nature, Rylant's poetry gives a unique voice to her series for children. In *Soda Jerk*, Rylant creates a series of short poems, told from the point-of-view of a boy who works as an attendant at a soda fountain. The poems provide commentary on issues ranging from his customer's lives to his fears about his future. In her 2001 collection, *Good Morning, Sweetie*, Rylant writes poems from the point-of-view of a toddler. In all of her collections, Rylant uses poetry as a way to create simple, but playful, images and her observations capture the inner voices and lives of young people.

Works in Critical Context

A winner of numerous awards, Rylant is universally praised for her simple, yet evocative language and her sympathetic portrayal of young characters.

A Blue-Eyed Daisy Rylant's first novel, the 1985 *A Blue-Eyed Daisy*, is an episodic coming-of-age story of a young girl in Appalachia. Critics overwhelmingly praised the novel for its blend of realism and inner contemplation, despite the fact that some critics found the episodic structure of the text a weakness. The *Bulletin of the Center for Children's Books* commented, "Like many realistic novels, [*A Blue-Eyed Daisy*] describes a year in a child's life; unlike many, it is written with enough grace and nuance and momentum to compensate amply for lack of a story line." Other critics, like Betsy Hearne, found the structure to be a great strength: "Episodic in nature, the story captures, as if in a frozen fame, the brief moments between childhood and adolescence." *A Blue-Eyed Daisy* was named Children's Book of the Year by the Child Study Association of America.

A Fine White Dust Rylant's 1986 novel about a young man struggling with issues of faith and religion earned numerous awards, including the Newbery Medal, a *Horn Book* honor, the Parent's Choice Award, and the *School Library Journal* best book citation. Critics hailed the novel, citing Rylant's ability to present complex emotional and spiritual issues in an accessible manner. *Publishers Weekly* noted that "Rylant's writing is deceptively simple, creating an emotional whirlpool for the reader. ... Her characters are adults and teenagers who are neither good nor bad, but richly, heart-breakingly human." Many critics praised the novel as among the finest written for children about spirituality, including Lucy Marx, who wrote "*A Fine White Dust* is the best written YA novel dealing with religion and will appeal to readers searching for themselves and God's place in their lives."

Responses to Literature

1. How does Rylant use humor in *Missing May*? What impact does humor have on this story about death and grief?

2. How does Pete reconcile his disappointment in Carson with his faith in *A Fine White Dust*?

3. Compare the descriptions of the Appalachian landscape that Rylant uses in her nonfiction book *Appalachia: The Voices of Sleeping Birds* with descriptions of the region in one of her many fictional books set there. How are they similar? How are they different?

BIBLIOGRAPHY

Books

Ruffin, Frances E. *Meet Cynthia Rylant*. New York: PowerKids Press, 2006.

Periodicals

Review of *A Blue-Eyed Daisy*. *Bulletin of the Center for Children's Books* 39, no. 11 (September 1985): 16.

Review of *A Fine White Dust*. *Publishers Weekly* 229, no. 26 (June 27, 1986): 93.

Antonucci, Ron. "Rylant on Writing: A Talk with 1993 Newbery Medalist Cynthia Rylant." *School Library Journal* 39, no. 5 (May 1993): 27–28.

Cooper, Ilene. "The *Booklist* Interview: Cynthia Rylant." *Booklist* 89, no. 19–20 (June 1–15, 1993): 1840–42.

Hearne, Betsy. Review of *A Blue-Eyed Daisy*. *Booklist* 81, no. 11 (February 1, 1985): 789.

Frederick, Heather Vogel. "Cynthia Rylant: A Quiet and Reflective Craft." *Publishers Weekly* 244, no. 29 (July 21, 1997): 178–79.

Marx, Lucy. Review of *A Fine White Dust*. *Children's Book Review Service* 15, no. 3 (November 1986): 34.

S

Zitkala-Sa
SEE *Gertrude Bonnin*

Louis Sachar

BORN: *1954, East Meadow, New York*

NATIONALITY: *American*

GENRE: *Juvenile fiction*

MAJOR WORKS:

Sideways Stories from Wayside School
(1978)

There's a Boy in the Girls' Bathroom
(1987)

Holes (1998)

Overview

An immensely popular writer of juvenile and young adult fiction, Louis Sachar wrote the "Wayside School" series, the "Marvin Redpost" series, the young adult book *Holes* (1998), as well as several other books. *Holes*, which won both the National Book Award and a Newbery medal, was later made into a major motion picture. He later published *Small Steps* (2006), a sequel to *Holes*. Sachar's books are nearly always humorous and very often poignant looks at growing up. His protagonists are generally outcasts who gain social and personal acceptance through their experiences with other people.

Works in Biographical and Historical Context

Early Life Shapes Work Sachar was born in East Meadow, New York, and at age nine moved with his family to Tustin in Orange County, California. Sachar's interest in "the outcast" could well have been influenced by his middle- and high-school years. The counterculture, which began in the mid-1960s and was embraced by young, white, middle-class students, emphasized personal freedom and freedom from the need to conform. This widespread rebellion of American youth was particularly strong in California.

Following high school, Sachar had started college in Ohio at Antioch when he received news of his father's sudden death. Returning to California to be near his mother, Sachar took the next semester off and worked in retail sales. With greater aspirations, Sachar returned to school, majoring in economics at Berkeley, where he also took creative writing classes. When searching for an easy class to replace a class in Russian literature he had dropped, Sachar signed up to be a teacher's aide in an elementary school. He loved working in the school, and later credited this experience with shaping his future interest in writing books for children.

Deciding to Write After graduation from Berkeley, Sachar took a job as shipping manager for a sweater factory in Connecticut while writing *Sideways Stories from Wayside School* (1978) in the evenings. Sachar organized his book around the stories of different kids in a school, naming his characters after children at the school where he had worked. After being fired from his shipping job seven months later, he decided to return to law school. He sent out the final manuscript of *Sideways Stories* to publishers at the same time that he applied to law schools. He received the news that the book was accepted for publication during his first week at the University of California Hastings College of Law. Thus began Sachar's personal struggle over the next several years between his desire to write and his chosen law career. He finished law school and passed the bar, writing three more children's books at the same time. Sachar finally resolved his dilemma by working part-time as a lawyer for several years, writing in the mornings and practicing law in the afternoons.

Louis Sachar   *Sachar, Louis, photograph. Reproduced by permission.*

Sachar's books in the "Wayside School" series are what he describes as "complete fantasy." Humorous and slightly outrageous, they chronicle events in a school with thirty stories but only one classroom on each floor. Other Sachar titles are more realistic. In *There's a Boy in the Girls' Bathroom* (1987), Sachar writes of Bradley Chalkers, a schoolroom outcast who is his own worst enemy, and Jeff Fishkin, the new kid who slowly befriends him. The theme in this book is that of an outcast who eventually learns to like himself and make friends. This theme is revisited in many of Sachar's books.

Critical Acclaim Sachar published his most critically acclaimed book, *Holes*, in 1998. In the novel, Stanley is wrongly accused of stealing a pair of sneakers and is sent to Texas's Camp Green Lake juvenile detention facility. There the harsh female warden assigns him the task—along with other boys held there—of digging five-feet-deep holes in the camp's dried-up lake bed. Stanley and his friend Zero manage to escape, and Stanley then works to get rid of the Yelnats curse that has plagued his family for three generations. The book proved immensely popular, and was adapted for film by Disney in 2003.

Sachar followed up the success of *Holes* with another young adult novel, *Small Steps* (2006). Sachar, who lives in Austin, Texas, continues to write every morning for two hours, but insists, "I never talk about a book until I'm finished writing it."

Works in Literary Context

Fantasy and Magic Realism While best known for *Holes*, Sachar began his career writing fantasy books for children. Fantasy creates an alternative world for its readers. In this sense, Sachar can be understood as a descendant of fantasy writers such as J. R. R. Tolkien (*The Lord of the Rings*) and C. S. Lewis (*The Chronicles of Narnia*). Sachar's first book, *Sideways Stories from Wayside School*, introduced readers to the Wayside School, a thirty-story school with one classroom on each floor where many fantastic adventures took place.

Sachar's book *Holes* uses elements of magic realism. Magic realism is a mode of fiction in which magical or fantastic elements are included in an otherwise realistic story. Some of the most famous writers of magic realism are Gabriel García Márquez, author of *One Hundred Years of Solitude* (1970), and Isabel Allende, author of *Of Love and Shadows* (1985).

Works in Critical Context

Sachar's work has proven to be popular with both critics and young readers. As one reviewer writes, "His underdog characters often triumph in the end, and most of his works have a deeper meaning hiding beneath the surface of his witty writing."

Marvin Redpost Books Readers were first introduced to the humorous Marvin Redpost character in *Marvin Redpost: Kidnapped at Birth?* (1992). The book emphasizes the red-haired Marvin's feeling of being different from everyone else, including not only his classmates, but his family as well. Another book, *Marvin Redpost: A Flying Birthday Cake*, introduces a new kid in school named Joe Normal, who turns out to actually be an alien. One reviewer calls it "a smart, funny twist on the new-kid theme." Sachar has been commended for wittily and effectively getting across his message in these books, which, in the words of another reviewer, "remind(s) us that everyone feels alienated at one time or another." Another reviewer commented on how well Sachar writes for the elementary school audience, writing that he "exhibits a keen sense of the way a typical third grader thinks, and he sprinkles the text with believable dialogue."

Holes The 1998 novel *Holes*, which tells the story of Stanley Yelnats, was somewhat of a departure from Sachar's previous work. In the words of a writer in the

U.S. News & World Report, the book transformed Sachar "from literary class clown to king of children's books." One critic calls *Holes* "the greatest critical success of Sachar's career." Philip Pullman, writing for London's *Guardian*, declares that "the plain uninflected telling has the quality of a fable, the bright clarity of the narrative being shadowed by an atmosphere hard to define but unmistakably powerful." Critic Toger Sutton concludes: "We haven't seen a book with this much plot, so suspensefully and expertly deployed, in too long a time." The book won many awards, including the coveted Newbery Medal.

Responses to Literature

1. Writers of young-adult fiction often excel in portraying the awkwardness and embarrassment felt by many adolescents in their daily lives. Read one of Sachar's books and analyze the way in which he depicts these moments for his characters.

2. Read the novel *Holes*. Then watch the film version. How does the film version differ from the book? What did the book portray better? What elements of the book does the film best succeed in portraying?

3. Read a children's or young adult book that includes a main character who feels like an outcast. In a paper, examine the theme of friendship. How does friendship transform the outcast character?

4. Read *Sideways Stories from Wayside School*. Imagine the school has a thirty-first story. Write your own fantasy story based on this classroom.

LITERARY AND HISTORICAL CONTEMPORARIES

Sachar's famous contemporaries include:

J. K. Rowling (1965–): This British young adult novelist is the author of the *Harry Potter* fantasy series and one of the most popular writers of all time. The author has won numerous awards, including the British Book Award and the New York Public Library Best Book of the Year.

Hillary Rodham Clinton (1947–): Forty-second First Lady of the United States, U.S. senator from New York, and Secretary of State, Clinton has championed education and children's issues throughout her career.

Judy Blume (1938–): American writer Judy Blume is an extremely popular author of books aimed at children ages eight to fourteen. Her stories focus on the emotional concerns and social relationships of adolescents.

Caryl M. Stern (1958–): Stern was appointed President and Chief Executive Officer of the U.S. Fund for UNICEF in 2007. She has spent her career fighting for civil rights and working to improve children's lives all over the world.

Al Gore (1947–): This American politician served as a U.S. representative, senator, and vice president in the Clinton Administration. He won the Nobel Peace Price in 2007 for his environmental work, which includes the documentary *An Inconvenient Truth* (2006).

BIBLIOGRAPHY

Books

Children's Literature Review, vol. 28, Detroit: Gale, 1992.

Children's Literature Review, vol. 79. Detroit: Gale, 2002.

Interview with Louis Sachar. *Something About the Author*, vol. 63. Detroit: Gale, 1991.

"Louis Sachar." *Contemporary Authors Online*. Detroit: Gale, 2009.

Periodicals

Cooper, Ilene. Review of *Someday Angeline*. *Booklist* (September 1, 1983).

———. Review of *Sixth Grade Secrets*. *Booklist* (November 1, 1987).

Hearne, Betsy. Review of *There's a Boy in the Girls' Bathroom*. *Bulletin of the Center for Children's Books* (April 1987): 155.

Phelan, Carolyn. Review of *Wayside School is Falling Down*. *Booklist* (May 1, 1989).

Pullman, Philip. "Teenages Kicks." *Guardian* (November 10, 1999).

Review of *Holes*. *Publishers Weekly* (June 27, 1998): 78.

Review of *Holes*. *Bulletin of the Center for Children's Books* (September–October 1998): 593–595.

Weeks, Brigitte. "Good for a Laugh." *Washington Post Book World* (May 7, 1995): 16, 18.

Web sites

"Louis Sachar." *CBC Magazine*. Retrieved November 15, 2008, from http://www.cbcbooks.org/cbcmagazine/meet/louissachar.html.

Louis Sachar Home Page. Retrieved November 7, 2008, from http://www.louissachar.com.

COMMON HUMAN EXPERIENCE

A recurring theme running through Sachar's work is that of a young outcast who eventually learns, through his relationships with other people, to like himself and others. Here are some other works that portray the struggles of young outcasts:

Bridge to Terabithia (1977), a novel written by Katherine Paterson. This Newbery Award winner tells the story of a fifth-grade boy who is transformed by his friendship with his neighbor Leslie Burke, and by the imaginary world the two create together.

The Outsiders (1967), a novel by S. E. Hinton. This novel describes a rivalry between two gangs, one representing the upper class and one representing the lower middle class. The book was later made into a movie and a short-lived television series.

Charlotte's Web (1952), a novel by E. B. White. This story of a runt piglet named Wilbur, who is befriended by a spider named Charlotte, is one of the best-selling children's books of all time.

Grendel (1971), a novel by John Gardner. In this work, Gardner reimagines the tale of Grendel, a beast defeated by the hero Beowulf in the Anglo-Saxon epic of the same name, from the point of view of the monster. Gardner shows the evil creature to be nothing more than a misunderstood outcast.

✸ William Safire

BORN: *1929, New York, New York*

NATIONALITY: *American*

GENRE: *Nonfiction*

MAJOR WORKS:
The New Language of Politics
  (1968)
Before the Fall (1975)
On Language (1980)

Overview

Although he served as a speechwriter and assistant to Richard Nixon, William Safire is best known for political columns and his weekly *New York Times Magazine* column dealing with English-language usage. His "On Language" columns have been collected into several books. David Thomas of the *Christian Science Monitor* states, "Safire may be the closest we have to a clearinghouse for hearing, seeing, and testing how we're doing with the language." Safire has been one of the most influential columnists in America from the 1970s into the twenty-first century.

Works in Biographical and Historical Context

Early Career and Political Speechwriting Safire was born William Safir on December 17, 1929, in New York City. After attending Syracuse University for two years, Safire landed a job as a copyboy for Tex McCrary, a *New York Herald Tribune* reporter, radio show host, and Republican politician. He soon worked his way up and became a foreign correspondent in Europe and the Middle East. After a two-year stint in the U.S. Army, he produced a television show for NBC and then, in 1955, became vice president of the Tex McCrary, Inc. public relations firm. He eventually became president of his own firm, Safire Public Relations, from 1961 to 1968.

Following in his mentor's footsteps, Safire became involved in Republican politics. He organized an Eisenhower rally in New York City in 1952, helped arrange the "kitchen debate" between Vice President Richard Nixon and Soviet Premier Nikita Khrushchev in 1959, and worked on both Nixon's 1960 presidential bid and other Republican campaigns in New York.

In 1965 Safire volunteered as a speechwriter for Nixon. After Nixon's election, he became an advisor and senior speechwriter for the president. When working on Nixon's reelection campaign, Safire was credited with Agnew's well-known phrase calling the liberal media "nattering nabobs of negativism." After the election, Safire accepted an offer of a column from the *New York Times* and left the White House in 1973.

The Watergate Scandal On June 17, 1972, five men were arrested after breaking into the Democratic campaign headquarters at the Watergate hotel in Washington, D.C. At first, connections between the burglary and the Nixon administration were murky, and Nixon was easily reelected against Senator George McGovern that year. However, it was later discovered that the burglars' actions were carried out under the orders of the Committee to Reelect the President and involved key officials in Nixon's administration. In 1974, Nixon's own involvement in the break-in cover-up became clear, and he resigned from office.

As the scandal unfolded, Safire was working on a memoir of his time in the Nixon administration; in fact, he was finishing the book when Nixon resigned. Safire's account of Nixon was fairly positive. Given the political climate, publisher William Morrow demanded the royalty advance on the book back from Safire. Eventually, the book was published by Doubleday, but it received mixed reviews, in large part because of Safire's sympathetic view of Nixon.

Safire's Writing Because of Safire's political leanings—he was a self-described conservative and libertarian who believed "the less government the better"—his being hired at the *New York Times* was met with scorn by many at the newspaper. However, his twice-a-week political

William Safire   *Diana Walker / Time Life Pictures / Getty Images*

column and weekly column "On Language" subsequently won the admiration of almost all naysayers.

Safire also explored political themes in several novels, including *Full Disclosure* (1977), which tells the story of a president in danger of losing his office; *Freedom* (1987), a novel about Abraham Lincoln's presidency; *Sleeper Spy* (1995), a political thriller; and *Scandalmonger* (2000). *Scandalmonger* was widely read as a response to the scandals of the Clinton administration. President Clinton's sexual affair with White House intern Monica Lewinsky came to light during the investigation of a legal case filed by another woman, Paula Jones, who claimed the president had sexually harassed her. Under oath, Clinton denied having sexual contact with Lewinsky, a claim later disproved by Lewinsky's testimony and DNA evidence. While many believed that the affair was Clinton's personal busi-

ness, Clinton was impeached in 1999. The Senate cleared him but he was subsequently cited for contempt of court. *Scandalmonger* examined the role of the media in bringing morally questionable actions of presidents to light. It detailed the career of a journalist who first broke the story of Alexander Hamilton's extramarital affair in order to further Thomas Jefferson's career and just a few years later broke the story of Jefferson's affair with his slave Sally Hemings.

Safire published several collections of his *New York Times Magazine* columns in the late 1990s and early 2000s, including *Spread the Word* (1999), *No Uncertain Terms: More Writing from the Popular "On Language" Column in the New York Times Magazine* (2003), and *The Right Word in the Right Place at the Right Time: Wit and Wisdom from the Popular "On Language" Column in the New York Times Magazine* (2004). As of 2008, Safire no longer wrote political columns, but he continued to write "On Language."

Works in Literary Context

Safire's political perspective informed much of his work, be it his political columns, novels, or work on the English language. While he was a fierce defender of Nixon, he did not hesitate to criticize those who he believed had been unethical. His wit, intelligence, and willingness to criticize political figures on both the left and the right won him the respect of many in the media.

Political Fiction   Safire wrote several novels with politics as a central theme. His longest and perhaps most important work of fiction was *Freedom* (1987). The story begins with the Emancipation Proclamation and follows President Abraham Lincoln during the early years of the American Civil War. The Lincoln portrayed by Safire was beset by many human failings, including depression and anxiety. However, Safire concluded in an interview with *U.S. News & World Report* that Lincoln had in fact been the country's greatest president, even "when you see his drawbacks and his failures and his shortcomings." *Freedom* was widely praised and quite popular, but some reviewers faulted Safire for including almost no African-American perspective in his work. Others drew parallels between Safire's flawed Lincoln and Safire's defense of Richard Nixon.

Published in the wake of the Monica Lewinsky scandal, Safire's novel *Scandalmonger* dealt with the use of politics to enhance a journalist's fame. A *Publishers Weekly* reviewer connects the work with then-current political events: "It's fascinating to learn that in the days of the founding fathers, politicians were just as licentious and newspapermen even more scurrilous than some players in contemporary media."

The Wonders of the English Language   Safire was one of the most influential columnists of the late twentieth and early twenty-first centuries. His columns have been reprinted in several books. His first collection, *On*

LITERARY AND HISTORICAL CONTEMPORARIES

Safire's famous contemporaries include:

Richard Nixon (1913–1994): This U.S. president's major foreign policy successes included establishing an easing of tensions with the Soviet Union and reestablishing diplomatic ties with China. He is best remembered, however, for his involvement in the Watergate scandal and subsequent resignation from the presidency in 1974.

Art Buchwald (1925–2007): This American satirist began working at newspapers in 1948. He became widely known for satirizing politics and social concerns.

Walter Cronkite (1916–): Voted "the most trusted man in America" in 1973, Walter Cronkite worked as a television news reporter. He was anchorman of the *CBS Evening News* from 1962 to 1981.

George H. W. Bush (1924–): This American politician first served as vice president under Ronald Reagan from 1980 to 1988, and then was elected president himself in 1988.

William F. Buckley, Jr. (1925–2008): A noted conservative author and founder of *National Review*, Buckley was also a popular spy novelist.

COMMON HUMAN EXPERIENCE

Much of Safire's work focuses on uncovering the meaning of political language and rhetoric. Here are some other works that examine the language of politics:

Nineteen Eighty-Four (1949), a novel by George Orwell. This masterpiece of a dystopia tells the story of Winston Smith, who works for the Ministry of Truth in a bleak, futuristic London, where he rewrites history each day. To do so, he uses an officially sanctioned language called Newspeak.

Moral Politics: How Liberals and Conservatives Think (1997), a nonfiction book by George Lakoff. Lakoff, a founder of the progressive think-tank the Rockridge Institute, has written several books about language. *Moral Politics* analyzes how differing moral concepts affect the language used by liberals and conservatives.

All the King's Men (1946) a novel by Robert Penn Warren. Warren's Pulitzer Prize–winning novel is based on the story of Huey Long, the populist Louisiana governor who was assassinated in 1935, and his idealistic aide.

Language, explores word origins, correct and incorrect language usage, and gives examples of responses from his readers. In subsequent collections, Safire concentrated on words and phrases used in politics, development of slang, misuse of words, and the evolutions of the meanings of words over time. Safire emphasized in all his work that language should never be taken at face value. In *The Right Word in the Right Place at the Right Time*, Safire tackles how words and phrases are used rhetorically by politicians to convey political ideas. He continued this theme in *The Definitive Guide to the New Language of Politics*, which defines words and phrases coined or used by presidents, such as "evil empire," "read my lips," "voodoo economics," and "perestroika."

Works in Critical Context

While critics often do not agree with Safire's political conclusions, many agree that his works—especially his nonfiction works—are extensively researched and well written. Bob Trimble writes in the *Dallas Morning News*, "If you are a fan of language or worried about your grammar, William Safire is your touchstone, whatever your political persuasion."

Freedom Safire's longest book, the novel *Freedom* (1987), met with much critical acclaim as well as popular success. Reviewers agreed the book had been well researched. However, some reviewers faulted Safire for essentially ignoring the African American perspective on the Emancipation Proclamation and Lincoln's handling of the Civil War. C. Vann Woodward notes that the whole book contains "only four or five pages on blacks, and most of that is what whites said or did about them, not what they said and did themselves."

Collections of Language Columns Safire's collections of his "On Language" columns, on the other hand, have met with unqualified praise. As one observer notes, Safire "earned respect for his sharp mind and his expert word play" despite being a conservative columnist at a fairly liberal newspaper. Reviewers lauded Safire for doing much more than examining the historical origins of words and phrases. In fact, writes an anonymous reviewer for *Publishers Weekly*, "He does more than elucidate the origins of slang or correct common grammatical mistakes: he alerts readers to the rhetorical maneuvers of our politicians and public figures as only a former speechwriter can."

Responses to Literature

1. Read an article dealing with national politics in a major newspaper such as *The New York Times* or *The Washington Post*. Highlight one political phrase. Write a paragraph in which you explore the meaning of the term and how politicians have used the phrase to relate a political idea in this new way.

2. Why do you think Safire's column "On Language" enjoys such wide popularity?

3. Select a column from one of Safire's collected works. Research the period in which it was written. Write a paper in which you summarize the column, discuss what was happening in America at the time, and analyze how Safire's work reflected current events.

4. Write a paper comparing Safire's book *Before the Fall* to another work critical of the Nixon administration. Can you identify author bias in either or both of the books? Provide specific examples from each work.

BIBLIOGRAPHY

Books

Bourgoin, Suzanne M., ed. *Encyclopedia of World Biography*. 2nd ed. Detroit: Gale Research, 1998.

"William Safire (1929–)." *Contemporary Literary Criticism*, vol. 10. Edited by Dedria Bryfonski. Detroit: Gale Research, 1979, pp. 446–447.

Periodicals

Batchelor, John Calvin. Review of *Freedom. Tribune Books* (August 9, 1987): 1.

Sanoff, Alvin P. "A Modern Vote for Abraham Lincoln." *U.S. News & World Report* (August 24, 1987).

Trimble, Bob. Review of *No Uncertain Terms. Dallas Morning News* (July 24, 2003).

Woodward, C. Vann. Review of *Freedom. New York Review of Books* (September 24, 1987): 23.

Web sites

"Columnist Biography: William Safire." *New York Times Online*. Retrieved November 9, 2008, from http://www.nytimes.com/ref/opinion/SAFIRE-BIO.html.

"William Safire, Bill Moyers Discuss Post-Government Journalism." The U.S. Department of State Web site. Retrieved November 9, 2008, from http://www.america.gov/st/freepress-english/2008/July/200807011307191xeneerg3.944033e-02.html.

✸ J. D. Salinger

BORN: *1919, New York, New York*

NATIONALITY: *American*

GENRE: *Fiction, short stories*

MAJOR WORKS:
The Catcher in the Rye (1951)
Nine Stories (1953)
Franny and Zooey (1955)

Overview

Best known for his controversial novel *The Catcher in the Rye* (1951), Salinger has been one of the most popular

J. D. Salinger   *Salinger, J. D., 1951, photograph. AP Images.*

and influential authors of American fiction to emerge after World War II.

Works in Biographical and Historical Context

New York Upbringing and Trouble in School Salinger's upbringing was not unlike that of Holden Caulfield, the Glass children, and many of his other characters. Raised in Manhattan, he was the second of two children of a prosperous Jewish importer and a Scots-Irish mother. He was expelled from several private preparatory schools before graduating from Valley Forge Military Academy in 1936. While attending a Columbia University writing course, he had his first piece of short fiction published in *Story*, an influential periodical founded by his instructor, Whit Burnett. Salinger's short fiction soon began appearing in *Collier's*, the *Saturday Evening Post*, *Esquire*, and other magazines catering to popular reading tastes.

Writing through World War II Salinger entered military service in 1942 and served until the end of World War II, participating in the Normandy campaign and the liberation of France. He continued to write and publish while in the army, carrying a portable typewriter with him in the back of his jeep. After returning to the United States, Salinger's career as a writer of serious fiction took off. He broke into the *New Yorker* in 1946 with the story

LITERARY AND HISTORICAL CONTEMPORARIES

Salinger's famous contemporaries include:

William Faulkner (1897–1962): An American author from Mississippi who was awarded the Nobel Prize in Literature in 1945.

Kurt Vonnegut (1922–2007): Best known as the author of *Slaughterhouse-Five; or, The Children's Crusade: A Duty-Dance with Death* (1969), Vonnegut is acknowledged as a major voice in modern American literature.

Ernest Hemingway (1899–1961): An American author and veteran of World War I who received the Pulitzer Prize in Literature in 1953 for his novella *The Old Man and the Sea* (1952) and the Nobel Prize in Literature in 1954.

John Steinbeck (1902–1968): A Nobel Prize–winning American author who wrote about the struggles of the working class and is most famous for his Pulitzer Prize–winning novel *The Grapes of Wrath* (1939) and his novella *Of Mice and Men* (1937).

Lyndon B. Johnson (1908–1973): U.S. vice president under John F. Kennedy who succeeded Kennedy as president after the latter's assassination in 1963.

Alfred Hitchcock (1899–1990): A highly influential British American filmmaker who innovated a variety of techniques in thriller genres.

"Slight Rebellion Off Madison," which was later rewritten to become a part of *The Catcher in the Rye*. Salinger quickly became one of the top contributors to the prestigious magazine.

Heated Controversy Provokes Author's Withdrawal After *The Catcher in the Rye* was published in 1951, Salinger found himself at the center of a storm of controversy. The 1950s in the United States were marked by social conservatism, and while his novel was lauded by many, it was condemned by others for its sometimes crude language and social criticism. When it began to find its way onto the recommended reading lists of educational institutions, it became the target of numerous censorship campaigns. Salinger reacted to all the publicity by becoming increasingly reclusive. Still, Robert Coles reflected general critical opinion when he praised Salinger as "an original and gifted writer, a marvelous entertainer, a man free of the slogans and clichés the rest of us fall prey to." Indeed, *The Catcher in the Rye*, now regarded as a classic work of adolescent angst, drew such great attention during the 1950s that those years have been called by some "The Age of Holden Caulfield" in honor of the novel's sensitive, alienated sixteen-year-old protagonist (who, like Salinger, was expelled from a prestigious

boarding school). The 1950s were a time of relative peace and prosperity for many Americans, but they were also marked by what many intellectuals and artists considered moral prudery, ultranationalism, paranoia about the perceived perils of communism, and extreme pressure to conform to social expectations. Holden's (and Salinger's) frank expression of dislike for American culture shocked many readers.

An Interest in Eastern Philosophies The vast appeal of *The Catcher in the Rye* drew many readers to Salinger's subsequent short fiction, collected in *Nine Stories* (1953), *Franny and Zooey* (1955), and *Raise High the Roofbeam, Carpenters; and Seymour: An Introduction* (1963). Most of these stories focused on the fictional Glass family, a group of seven gifted siblings led by Seymour, their seer-artist and elder brother. In all his work, Salinger captured a profound feeling of dissatisfaction with the spiritual emptiness of contemporary American life. Salinger attempt to counter his own feelings of disillusionment with an interest in various religions. He followed certain practices of kriya yoga, an ancient Hindu discipline, starting in 1955. He also explored Dianetics and Christian Science. Salinger's interest in Eastern philosophy was somewhat out of the mainstream at the time, though not entirely unusual. The Beat Generation writers, including novelist Jack Kerouac and poet Allen Ginsberg, also took a keen interest in Zen Buddhism (Kerouac's 1958 novel *The Dharma Bums* shows this influence clearly). In 1951, German writer Hermann Hesse's 1922 novel *Siddhartha* about the life of Gotama Buddha appeared in English translation for the first time, and became extremely popular with the growing countercultural movement, selling fifteen million copies by the early 1970s. Salinger's interest in Eastern philosophies can be seen most clearly in the character of Seymour, who displays familiarity with Zen Buddhism and Hindu sacred texts.

Later Work and Life in Seclusion Salinger's later works were not as well received as *The Catcher in the Rye*. As years passed, and his continuing work on the Glass family saga drew increasing critical attacks from even those corners of the literary establishment that had once accorded him an almost cultlike reverence, he withdrew from publishing and public life altogether. His novella-length story "Hapworth 16, 1924," which once again revolved around an incident in the Glass family, appeared in the *New Yorker* in 1965; it was his last published work. Since the early 1960s, he has lived in seclusion in New Hampshire. He reentered the headlines in the 1990s after two memoirs of people close to him were published: one by Joyce Maynard (a former girlfriend) and one by his daughter Margaret. Reportedly, he continues to write, but only for his own satisfaction; he is said to be completely unconcerned with his standing, or lack of it, in the literary world.

Works in Literary Context

Salinger's reputation derives from his mastery of symbolism, his idiomatic style, and his thoughtful, sympathetic insights into the insecurities that plague both adolescents and adults. The thematic content of his work is said to have been influenced by his own experiences growing up, as well as by published works such as F. Scott Fitzgerald's *The Great Gatsby* (1925).

The Idealist Adrift in a Corrupt World *The Catcher in the Rye* and much of Salinger's shorter fiction share the theme of idealists adrift in a corrupt world. Often, the alienated protagonists are rescued from despair by the innocence and purity of children. One of the author's most highly acclaimed stories, "For Esmé—with Love and Squalor" (collected in *Nine Stories*) concerns an American soldier, also an aspiring writer, who encounters a charming young English girl just before D-Day (the Allied Powers' invasion of Normandy during World War II). Almost a year later, suffering serious psychic damage from his combat experiences, the soldier receives a gift and a letter from the girl. Her unselfish gesture of love heals him, and he is once again able to sleep and write.

In *The Catcher in the Rye*, Holden Caulfield is driven to the brink of a nervous breakdown by his disgust for the "phoniness" of the adult world, which he is about to enter. He finds peace only in the presence of Phoebe, his young sister. Much like Holden, Franny Glass (whose story "Franny" is half of *Franny and Zooey*) undergoes a physical and nervous collapse due to the conflict between her involvement with a crude, insensitive boyfriend and her desire for a pure, spiritual love experience. In the "Zooey" section of *Franny and Zooey*, Franny's older brother attempts to help her resolve her confusion by discussing with her the worldly nature of religious experience. But for some of Salinger's characters, like Seymour Glass, the only relief from the anguish of living in the hellish modern world comes in the form of suicide. In "A Perfect Day for Bananafish" (part of *Nine Stories*), Seymour encounters an innocent young child on the beach and converses with her; later that evening, however, he shoots himself in his hotel room.

Salinger's fiction remains popular today and continues to exert an influential force on its readers. Among the writers who have been influenced by Salinger are John Updike, Philip Roth, Stephen Chbosky, Carl Hiaasen, Susan Minot, Haruki Murakami, Gwendoline Riley, Tom Robbins, Louis Sachar, and Joel Stein.

Works in Critical Context

The Catcher in the Rye Beginning with *The Catcher in the Rye*, Salinger's work has provoked considerable comment and controversy. Critic James Bryan summarized the common psychological reading of the work when he observed:

> The richness of spirit in this novel, especially of the vision, the compassion, and the humor of the narrator reveal a psyche far healthier than that of the boy who endured the events of the narrative. Through the telling of his story, Holden has given shape to, and thus achieved control of, his troubled past.

COMMON HUMAN EXPERIENCE

Foremost among Salinger's themes is the idea that the corrupt world has a harmful influence on the pure. Here are some works that feature idealistic heroes in harsh worlds:

The Book of Exodus (c. 450 BCE), a book of the Torah compiled by various authors. In this book, also incorporated as the Old Testament of the Christian Bible, Moses is faced with the difficulties of leading a community of people corrupted by worldly pleasures.

Don Quixote (1605), a novel by Miguel de Cervantes. In this novel, Alonso Quixano obsesses about books of chivalry, believing them word-for-word, and sets out as a knight-errant only to be mocked by everyone around him. Though ridiculous, he is also somehow more noble and admirable than the world that laughs at his ideals.

Mr. Smith Goes to Washington (1939), a film directed by Frank Capra. Surrounded by corrupt politicians, Mr. Smith proves that it is possible for one individual to make a difference—sort of.

The book has also been praised retrospectively for its author's early depiction of dissatisfaction with the repression and smugness that characterized post–World War II America. William Faulkner once paid Salinger the compliment of calling him the best of "the present generation of writing" because *The Catcher in the Rye* "expresses so completely" what Faulkner himself had tried to say about the tragedy of a youth who found "when he attempted to enter the human race ... there was no human race there." Later, however, Faulkner expressed the reservation that there was only enough material in the book for a short story.

When *The Catcher in the Rye* was published in July 1951, reviews were generally good. Reviewing the book for the *New York Times*, Nash K. Burger called it "an unusually brilliant first novel." It was a main selection of the Book-of-the-Month Club and was on the *Times* bestseller list for seven months, reaching fourth place in October of that year. Yet no reviewer foresaw its becoming the classic novel of a generation. It would be five years before academics began writing about the novel and assigning it to their students. By 1968, however, it was listed as one of the top twenty-five American best sellers since 1895. In the late 1980s it was still selling about a quarter of a million copies per year. *The Catcher in the Rye* has recurrently been banned by public libraries, schools, and bookstores, however, due to its profanity, sexual subject matter, and rejection of "traditional American values."

Other Fiction *Nine Stories* also drew a widely varied response. The volume's first story, "A Perfect Day for Bananafish," has been read alternately as a satire on bourgeois values, a psychological case study, and a morality tale. *Franny and Zooey*, along with several of the pieces in *Nine Stories*, stands as Salinger's most highly acclaimed short fiction. Critics generally applauded the satisfying structure of "Franny," as well as its appealing portrait of its heroine, while "Zooey" was praised for its meticulous detail and psychological insight. *Raise High the Roofbeam, Carpenters; and Seymour: An Introduction* proved less satisfying to literary commentators, who began to find the Glass clan self-centered, smug, perfect beyond belief, and ultimately boring. It was after its publication that the cult of Salinger began to give way to an increasing perception that the author was too absorbed in the Glass saga to maintain the artistic control necessary for literary art. Whatever the flaws detected, however, few deny the immediacy and charm of the Glasses, who are so successfully drawn that numerous people over the years have reportedly claimed to have had personal encounters with relatives of the fictitious family.

Responses to Literature

1. Discuss the word "phony" as it is used in *The Catcher in the Rye*. Look at several specific instances in the text in which Holden uses the word. What does Holden mean when he calls someone "phony"? What is it about phoniness he dislikes? Do you agree with him?

2. Characterize the relationship between Holden and Mr. Spencer in *The Catcher in the Rye*. What is the significance of this relationship to the story as a whole?

3. Why do you think Salinger places so much emphasis on the intellectualism of the Glass family? Do you think there is a connection between the extreme intelligence of the Glasses, particularly Seymour, and the despair they often feel?

4. Why did *The Catcher in the Rye* create so much controversy upon its publication? Write an essay expressing your opinions and emotional reaction to the text in the context of the debates surrounding Salinger's work.

BIBLIOGRAPHY

Books

Alsen, Eberhard. *Salinger's Glass Stories as a Composite Novel.* Troy, N.Y.: Whitston, 1983.

Bloom, Harold, ed. *J. D. Salinger: Modern Critical Views.* New York: Chelsea House, 1987.

French, Warren. *J. D. Salinger.* New York: Twayne, 1963; rev. ed. Boston: Twayne, 1976.

———. *J. D. Salinger Revisited.* Boston: Twayne, 1988.

Grunwald, Henry Anatole, ed. *Salinger: A Critical and Personal Portrait.* New York: Harper, 1963.

Hamilton, Ian. *In Search of J. D. Salinger.* New York: Random House, 1988; London: Heinemann, 1988.

Miller, James E., Jr. *J. D. Salinger.* Minneapolis: University of Minnesota Press, 1965.

Salzberg, Joel. *Critical Essays on Salinger's* The Catcher in the Rye. Boston: G. K. Hall, 1990.

Salzman, Jack. *New Essays on* The Catcher in the Rye. New York & London: Cambridge University Press, 1991.

Sublette, Jack R. *J. D. Salinger: An Annotated Bibliography, 1938–1981.* New York & London: Garland, 1984.

✸ Sonia Sanchez

BORN: *1934, Birmingham, Alabama*

NATIONALITY: *American*

GENRE: *Poetry*

MAJOR WORKS:

We a BaddDDD People (1970)

Ima Talken bout the Nation of Islam (1972)

A Blues Book for Blue Black Magical Women (1973)

homegirls & handgrenades (1984)

Under a Soprano Sky (1987)

Sonia Sanchez   *Christopher Felver / Corbis*

Overview

Sonia Sanchez is often named among the strongest voices in black nationalism, the cultural revolution of the 1960s in which many black Americans sought a new identity distinct from the values of the white establishment. In most of her works, including collections of poetry and stories for children, she presents positive role models and often harshly realistic situations in an effort to inspire her readers to improve their lives. Her use of idiomatic language and obscenities reflects urban, black English and lends a powerful edge to her works. As she developed as a writer, she began to critique, not only the white establishment, but the treatment of African American women by African American men.

Works in Biographical and Historical Context

A Rough Road from Alabama to Harlem   Born in Birmingham, Alabama, Sanchez was a shy child who rarely spoke because of a stutter. Her mother died when Sanchez was only a year old. For a time, Sanchez and her sister were cared for by their paternal grandmother, Elizabeth "Mama" Driver. This beloved grandparent is the "Dear Mama" of Sanchez's poem by the same name in *Under a Soprano Sky* (1987). Mama Driver died when Sanchez was five, and the frail youngster endured a period of family instability, including abuse and neglect by a stepmother and frequent moves from one relative's house to another. The defiant women in her family—one of whom Sanchez watched spit in the face of a driver who asked her to leave a bus because of her race—impressed upon the author at a young age the inner strength of blacks.

In 1943 Sanchez moved with her father, Wilson L. Driver, to Harlem, a neighborhood on New York City's West Side. Black migrants from the South had flocked to Harlem between the world wars. As a result, Harlem had been the center of a flourishing of African American cultural activity in the 1920s and 1930s, a period of time known as the Harlem Renaissance. The art of African American musicians and singers, painters and sculptors, writers and poets had been celebrated there. Driver, a musician, took Sanchez to hear such prominent jazz artists as Billie Holiday, Billy Eckstine, and Art Tatum.

Sanchez reached adulthood in Harlem. She studied political science and poetry at Hunter College and New York University during the 1950s. After graduating from Hunter College, Sanchez studied creative writing under Louise Bogan, whose interest in the young poet encouraged her to pursue a literary career. Along with Haki R. Madhubuti (Don L. Lee) and others, Sanchez established a weekly writers' group that gave public readings. She soon began publishing poetry in small magazines, and later, in black periodicals. She was instrumental in establishing one of the first university-level black studies programs in the United States.

Embracing the Nation of Islam   Committed to the black liberation movement of the 1960s, Sanchez supported the Congress of Racial Equality (CORE). CORE was an interracial organization founded in 1942 to combat racism and discrimination; it used nonviolence and passive resistance techniques to expose white racism and the injustices of discrimination. In the early 1960s, the organization was instrumental in organizing sit-ins and freedom rides in the American South.

By the mid-1960s, Sanchez was a single mother of two sons. At that time, she, like many educated African Americans who enjoyed economic stability, held integrationist ideals such as those held by CORE. But after hearing Malcolm X of the Nation of Islam say that African Americans would never be fully accepted as part of mainstream America despite their professional or economic achievements, she chose to base her identity on her racial heritage. The Nation of Islam, led by Elijah Muhammad, was a branch of Islam founded in the United States that urged African Americans to separate from whites. Sanchez was a member of Elijah Muhammad's Nation of Islam from 1972 to 1975. She stated that she joined the group because she wanted her children to see an "organization that was trying to deal with the concepts of nationhood, morality, small businesses, schools. . . . And these things were very important to me."

A Revolution Within   While a member of the Nation, Sanchez continued to give public readings and voice her opinions about the direction of the organization. Some of her ideas, however, conflicted with those of the organization, which viewed women's roles as secondary to those of men, and Sanchez left the Nation after three years. *A Blues Book for Blue Black Magical Women* (1973), and several poems in *Love Poems* (1973), were composed during this time and reveal a strong commitment to family and support for the African American man.

While her early books speak more directly to widespread social oppression, the plays Sanchez wrote during the 1970s give more attention to the poet's interpersonal battles. For example, *Uh Huh; But How Do It Free Us?* (1974) portrays an African American woman involved in the movement against white oppression who also resists subjection to her abusive husband. The women's liberation movement began in the 1960s, but emerged as a strong force in the early 1970s, in part in response to the unequal treatment that women had received in the civil rights, black power, and antiwar movements. Women not only fought for equal civil rights, but also argued that "the personal is political" and examined inequality in their personal relationships with men. Sanchez became a voice in what Stephen E. Henderson calls "a revolution within the Revolution" that grew as black women in general began to reassess their position, as not only victims of discrimination based on race, but also victims of patriarchy within the black community. This consciousness surfaces in works that treat politics in the context of personal relationships.

LITERARY AND HISTORICAL CONTEMPORARIES

Sanchez's famous contemporaries include:

Martin Luther King, Jr. (1929–1968): An African American minister, Nobel Peace Prize winner, and civil rights leader, King promoted a strategy of nonviolence within the civil rights movement. He was assassinated in 1968.

Gloria Steinem (1934–): A writer and activist, Steinem has been a leader in the late-twentieth century women's liberation movement. She founded *Ms.* magazine, the first national women's magazine run by women.

John Robert Lewis (1940–): A prominent civil rights activist, Lewis participated in sit-ins, freedom rides, and protest marches throughout the South and led the Student Nonviolent Coordinating Committee (SNCC) from 1963–1966. He was elected in 1986 as a representative from Georgia to the U.S. Congress, where he continues to serve.

Maya Angelou (1928–): One of the finest contemporary black authors, Angelou is most famous for her several autobiographical volumes that trace her search for identity and emotional fulfillment during and after her childhood in the rural, segregated American South.

Jimmy Carter (1924–): Born in the rural town of Plains, Georgia, Carter was elected the thirty-ninth president of the United States in 1976 and served one term before being defeated by Ronald Reagan in 1980.

Sanchez's dramas, such as *Sister Son/ji* (1969) and *Uh Huh; But How Do It Free Us?* have been identified as precursors of black feminist awareness.

Much of Sanchez's work can be seen as autobiographical in nature. *A Blues Book for Blue Black Magical Women*, which has been called "a spiritual autobiography," follows the development of one woman's consciousness as she ages and explores her personal and social position within a black Muslim community. The volume reveals what it is like to be female in a society that, according to Sanchez, "does not prepare young black women, or women period, to be women"; it also tells about the author's political involvements before and after her commitment to ethnic pride. Sanchez extends her personal experience to encompass that of all black people. She commented: "We must move past always focusing on the 'personal self' because there's a larger self. There's a 'self' of black people." *Love Poems* contains many of the haiku Sanchez wrote during a particularly stressful period in her life. She embraced haiku as a powerful medium that allowed her to "compress a lot of emotion" into a few lines, as well as to express her increased interest in Eastern cultures.

A Maturing Style Two of Sanchez's later volumes of poetry, the American Book Award winner *homegirls &*

handgrenades (1984) and *Under a Soprano Sky*, received overwhelming praise, with many commentators claiming that the poet had matured personally and stylistically without losing her political fervor. Her focus in many poems turned to drug addiction, homelessness, and loneliness, celebrating, according to Sanchez, "some homegirls and homeboys … who needed to be celebrated but never came through the Harlems of the world."

Sanchez has given presentations at more than five hundred universities and colleges nationwide throughout her career and has traveled around the world reading her poetry. She was the first Presidential Fellow at Temple University in Philadelphia in 1977. She served as the Laura Carnell Chair in English at Temple until she retired in 1999. She continues to live in Philadelphia.

Works in Literary Context

Use of Dialect One aspect of Sanchez's stand against acculturation to white society is a poetic language that does not conform to the dictates of standard English. Haki R. Madhubuti credits her with "legitimizing the use of urban Black English in written form. … She has taken Black speech and put it in the context of world literature." By inserting extra letters in some words and extra space between lines, words, and syllables within a poem, Sanchez provides dramatic accents and other clues that indicate how the poem is to be said aloud. In addition, Sanchez developed techniques for reading her poetry that were unique in using auditory elements, such as traditional chants and differences in volume, which made her a highly sought-after public speaker. According to Kalamu ya Salaam:

> The sound elements, which give a musical quality to the intellectual statements in the poetry, are akin to Western African languages; Sanchez has tried to recapture a style of delivery that she felt had been muted by the experience of slavery. In her successful experimentation with such techniques, she joined … others in being innovative enough to bring black poetry to black people at a level that was accessible to the masses as well as enjoyable for them.

Sanchez was one of the pioneers of the renaissance of African American art in the 1960s that began to use street language and black dialect to convey the black speaking voice. In using black dialect, she was a direct descendant of Paul Laurence Dunbar, one of the first African American poets to become widely recognized and who was best known for his poems in dialect. Sanchez credits Malcolm X with influencing her use of language. Sanchez commented: "A lot of our words and language came from Malcolm. He was always messing with the language and messing with people, and sometimes in a very sly kind of way demanding things of people …" She commented on her decision to write in black dialect: "I decided along with a number of other Black poets to tell the truth in poetry by using the language, dialect, idioms, of the folks we believed our audience to be." Another poet who developed this poetic style was Haki Madhubuti.

Slave-Narrative Tradition Sanchez's emphasis on poetry as a spoken art, or performance, connects Sanchez to the traditions of her African ancestors, an oral tradition preserved in earlier slave narratives and forms of music indigenous to the black experience in America. Her autobiographical writings, which may be called "neo-slave narratives," share a similar purpose to the originals in that genre by pre-Civil War writers such as Frederick Douglass, William Wells Brown, and Harriet Jacobs. In slave narratives, the life of an individual or family was used to comment on the evils of slavery and the necessity of abolition; they ultimately aimed for psychological and physical freedom. Sanchez's overtly political work comments upon the social condition of contemporary Afro-Americans in an effort to accomplish their psychological freedom and, where necessary, their physical freedom. In *homegirls & handgrenades*, she builds the neo-slave narrative to a stunning artistic summit in prose poems that reflect on a lifetime of struggle. This volume contains Sanchez's best-known prose piece, "After Saturday Nite Comes Sunday." Based on her life and delivered in tattered, yet vivid images, the work concentrates upon a woman whose love is being abused by a man strung out on dope. Images of dope—the debilitating drug first noticed in her childhood in a New York tenement—pervade Sanchez's work as a metaphor for ultimate evil; it is a living death, a snuffing out the will to live. From such debilitations, Sanchez would make her people free.

Works in Critical Context

Sonia Sanchez has been recognized as one of the preeminent authors writing about African American equality and black feminist issues. Her writing evolved from a confrontational, brash style during the black power movement to the intimate tone of her later works. She pioneered in using language, both writing in black dialect and her experimentation with dramatic reading styles, to express black power and nationalist ideas. Kamili Anderson writes of her style:

> Sanchez has a penchant for enlisting words to imagery. She can mesmerize with scenarios that require readers to transfuse all of their senses, so much so that the ability to discern whether one is reading with the soul or with the eyes, or listening with the heart or the ears, is lost.

We a BaddDDD People Critics laud Sanchez for reflecting black consciousness in her poetry. Critics argue that her book *We a BaddDDD People* (1970) most exemplified "the ideals and realization of *blackness*," which, wrote Sebastian Clarke, "so profoundly pervades her work." Critics believed the poems in this work signaled her move into "a new life of militancy and social activism." Sanchez's poems, writes Johari Amini in a review in *Black World*, actually "hurt (but doesn't anything that cleans good) and [the] lines are blowgun dartsharp with a wisdom ancient as Kilimanjaro." Haki Madhubuti's essay

COMMON HUMAN EXPERIENCE

Sanchez's work celebrates African American culture. Other works that draw on the history of that culture include:

Sweet Honey In the Rock (1976), an album by Sweet Honey In the Rock. The first album released by this African American women's vocal group incorporated traditional African American rhythms and sounds from blues, spirituals, hymns, rap, reggae, African chants, hip hop, and jazz.

The Weary Blues (1926), a poetry collection by Langston Hughes. In this collection of poems that were modeled on blues and jazz rhythms and sounds, Hughes focuses on the lives of ordinary African American people.

St. Louis Woman (1946), a musical by Harold Arlen and Johnny Mercer. Based on the novel *God Sends Sunday* (1931), by Arna Bontemps, this stage production uses song and folklore to portray the life of the most successful African American jockey in St. Louis, Little Augie.

in *Black Women Writers (1950–1980)* comments on this same effect, first remarking that Sanchez "is forever questioning Black people's commitment to struggle," saying again later that she is "forever disturbing the dust in our acculturated lives." In the volume, writes another critic, "Sanchez is wielding a survival sword that rips away the enemy's disguise" while celebrating "black love, talent, courage, and continuity."

homegirls & handgrenades *Homegirls & handgrenades*, an autobiographical collection of sketches of individuals from Sanchez's past, was widely praised for its depth and honesty, but also for its skill in illustrating "significant truths." Wrote one critic, "From the past, she draws images that explode the autobiographical into universal truths." Critics called the book a "marvelous collage of thirty-two short stories, poems, letters, and sketches that often ring loudly with the truth of an autobiographical fervor." Joyce A. Joyce calls the volume, like its title, "forceful, realistic, and hardhitting." Joyce praises the work for communicating Sanchez's "strong vision of the self and her desire to use that knowledge to awaken the spirit and heighten the political awareness of African-Americans."

Responses to Literature

1. Try your hand at writing a short story using dialogue that reflects how real people actually talk. Model the characters and their styles of speech on people from your own life.

2. Select a poem from one of Sanchez's early works, such as *We a BaddDDD People*, and a selection from

her later, more autobiographical work *homegirls & handgrenades*. Write a paper comparing and contrasting the styles of the two poems.

3. Sanchez credited her unique language, in large part, to the writings of Malcolm X. Read *The Autobiography of Malcolm X* (1965), written by Alex Haley from his interactions with the leader. Can you find examples of the unique language Sanchez refers to?

4. Sanchez's early work championed black separatism, and especially the Nation of Islam. Using your library and the Internet, research the larger black nationalist movement of the early 1970s. In your opinion, what has been the legacy of this movement?

BIBLIOGRAPHY

Books

Basel, Marilyn K. "Sonia Sanchez." *Black Writers*. Detroit: Gale Research, 1989.

Evans, Mari. *Black Women Writers: A Critical Evaluation*. New York: Doubleday, 1984.

Gabbin, Joanne Veal. "The Southern Imagination of Sonia Sanchez." *Southern Women Writers: A New Generation*. Edited by Tonette Bond Inge. Tuscaloosa: University of Alabama Press, 1990.

Joyce, Joyce Ann. *Ijala: Sonia Sanchez and the African Poetic Tradition*. Chicago: Third World Press, 1996.

Tate, Claudia, ed. *Black Women Writers at Work*. New York and London: Continuum, 1983.

Periodicals

Clarke, Sebastian. "Black Magic Woman: Sonia Sanchez and Her Work." *Presence Africaine* vol. 78 (1971): 253–261.

Saunders, James Robert. "Sonia Sanchez's *Homegirls and Handgrenades*: Recalling Toomer's *Cane*." *MELUS* vol. 15 (1988): 73–82.

Web sites

Sonia Sanchez. Academy of American Poets Web site. Retrieved November 15, 2008, from http://www.poets.org/poet.php/prmPID/276.

Sonia Sanchez. Voices from the Gap. Retrieved November 15, 2008, from http://voices.cla.umn.edu/vg/Bios/entries/sanchez_sonia.html.

❋ Carl Sandburg

BORN: *1878, Galesburg, Illinois*

DIED: *1967, Flat Rock, North Carolina*

NATIONALITY: *American*

GENRE: *Poetry, biography*

MAJOR WORKS:

Chicago Poems (1916)

Abraham Lincoln: The Prairie Years (1926)

Carl Sandburg   *Sandburg, Carl, photograph. The Library of Congress.*

Abraham Lincoln: The War Years (1939)

Complete Poems (1950)

Overview

Carl Sandburg became one of the most celebrated poets in America. He used a form of free verse that was sometimes applauded and sometimes panned, but represented Midwestern vernacular. His simple style and realistic depictions of common scenes and ordinary people made his work appeal to a wide variety of people. His works were among the most influential twentieth-century American poetry. His two-volume biography of Abraham Lincoln was monumental.

Works in Biographical and Historical Context

Midwestern Youth Sandburg, the son of Swedish immigrants August and Clara Mathilda Anderson Sandburg, was born in Galesburg, Illinois, on January 6, 1878, and raised there. In the year of his birth, memories of the Civil War were still fresh. As a boy Sandburg met Civil War veterans, as well as old associates of Lincoln, and learned about the Lincoln-Douglas debate that had taken place at Galesburg's Knox College. The youth left school after the eighth grade, took rough odd jobs, and rode boxcars. In 1898, at age twenty, he volunteered for the Spanish-American War and served in Puerto Rico. On his return, he decided to go back to school and in 1899, enrolled in Galesburg's Lombard College, which he left in 1902 before graduating.

After leaving school, Sandburg worked for several newspapers in the Midwest. His first essay on Abraham Lincoln, "The Average Man," which was produced in 1906 or 1907, to some degree reflected his interest in socialism. A member of the Social Democratic Party, Sandburg campaigned with Socialist presidential candidate Eugene V. Debs in Wisconsin in 1908, and then became the private secretary of Milwaukee's Socialist mayor in 1910.

Poetry and Journalism   Sandburg moved to Chicago in 1914, and while writing poetry, gathered information on Lincoln for a biography. Six of his poems were published in *Poetry* magazine in 1914. Sandburg received a certain amount of recognition as a result and came to the attention of Henry Holt and Company, the publisher of his first large volume of poems, *Chicago Poems* (1916). *Chicago Poems* provided what one reviewer called "a stark but idealized view of the working class" in an urban setting. Over the next twenty years, this work and five others made Sandburg a very popular poet. At the same time, Sandburg worked as a reporter and then a columnist for the *Chicago Daily News*. During World War II, he also made radio broadcasts for the U.S. Office of War Information, lectured, recited his poetry, and sang folksongs.

Lincoln: The Work of a Lifetime   Sandburg's two volume account of the life of Abraham Lincoln (*The Prairie Years* (1926) and *The War Years* (1939) was one of the monumental biographical works of the century. Sandburg collected and classified Lincoln material for thirty years, moving himself into a garret, storing his extra material in a barn, and for nearly fifteen years, writing on a cracker-box typewriter. His intent was to separate Lincoln the man from Lincoln the myth, to avoid hero-worship, to relate with graphic detail and humanness the man he so admired.

The two-volume *Abraham Lincoln: The Prairie Years* was published in 1926. *The Prairie Years* covered Lincoln's life before his inauguration in 1861. Sandburg's Lincoln was decidedly folksy and rustic and was widely praised as the "real" Lincoln rather than a cold statue or a Sunday-school model for aspiring youths.

Sandburg, Lincoln, and Roosevelt   By 1928 Sandburg had decided to write a sequel to *The Prairie Years* on the war years. The project occupied the next eleven years of his life, interrupted by his writing other shorter works and by his undertaking cross-country tours on which he lectured, read poetry, and strummed folk songs on a guitar. The two principal influences on his treatment of the war years were his journalistic experience and his changed political views. Having worked for various magazines and Chicago newspapers, Sandburg tended to see histor-

LITERARY AND HISTORICAL CONTEMPORARIES

Carl Sandburg's famous contemporaries include:

Franklin Delano Roosevelt (1882-1945): The thirty-second president of the United States, Roosevelt was elected at the height of the Great Depression. His policies of providing economic relief to Americans were collectively known as the New Deal. He saw the nation through World War II before his death in 1945.

Paul Laurence Dunbar (1872–1906): The son of former slaves, Dunbar's poetry collections were written largely in black American dialect, and reflected the lives of ordinary black folk.

Robert Frost (1874–1963): Major American poet, like Sandburg, a master of the plain vernacular style, and awarded the Pulitzer Prize four times.

Ezra Pound (1885–1972): American-born expatriate poet, a leader in the modernist literary movement in Europe.

Edna St. Vincent Millay (1892–1950): This American lyric poet spoke frankly about social justice and the liberation of women and expressed the emotions of youth during the 1920s.

Luis Munoz Rivera (1859–1916): This Puerto Rican political leader negotiated Puerto Rican autonomy from Spain.

ical events as a newspaperman, as an endless stream of daily dispatches, news stories unconnected by historical threads and measured by their daily impact rather than by their significance in retrospect. In the 1930s, Sandburg became a big admirer of President Franklin Delano Roosevelt and the New Deal. The New Deal was the collective name for programs Roosevelt had put into place upon taking office at the height of the Great Depression to provide Americans relief, including unemployment compensation, jobs programs, and social security. Sandburg's treatment of Lincoln was somewhat influenced by his view of Roosevelt as a similarly heroic politician leading the American people through a dark period.

The War Years   *Abraham Lincoln: The War Years* was published in 1939 in several volumes. Once again Sandburg relied on a massive accumulation of details. The books had no single theme and appeared to most reviewers to give almost a journalistic chronicle of the Lincoln administration. Sandburg again presented the president as a human being, a careworn man facing a crisis of immense proportions. Sandburg managed to show Lincoln as both a stern war leader and a personally forgiving man. *The War Years* was widely acclaimed as a literary masterpiece, and earned Sandburg the Pulitzer Prize for history in 1940.

COMMON HUMAN EXPERIENCE

Sandburg was hardly alone in his fascination with Lincoln. Here are some other biographies of the sixteenth president:

Team of Rivals: The Political Genius of Abraham Lincoln (2005), by Doris Kearns Goodwin, examines how Lincoln brought his opponents together in his cabinet and marshaled their talents to help preserve the Union and win the Civil War.

Lincoln at Gettysburg: The Words That Remade America (1992), by Garry Wills, examines the influences on Lincoln's Gettysburg address. The book won the 1993 Pulitzer Prize.

Lincoln the Man (1931), by Edgar Lee Masters, offered a rare negative portrayal of Lincoln.

Herndon's Lincoln (1889), by William Herndon. One of the most important early biographies of Lincoln, written by a personal friend of the president; the two were partners in a law practice in Springfield, Illinois.

Much of the appeal of the Lincoln biographies was due to the time in which they appeared, particularly *The War Years*, which was released on the brink of the Second World War. As Stephen Vincent Benet noted, *The War Years* was a "good purge for our own troubled time and for its more wild-eyed fears." In his time, nevertheless, Sandburg greatly broadened the audience for books on Lincoln. On February 12, 1959, Sandburg delivered a Lincoln Day address before a joint session of Congress attended by the Supreme Court, the cabinet, and the diplomatic corps.

Sandburg published his *Complete Poems* in 1950, and it won the Pulitzer Prize. At age eighty-five, Sandburg published his last book of poems, *Homey and Salt* (1963), and then retired to his home in North Carolina, where he died in 1967.

Works in Literary Context

Free Verse   Sandburg composed his poetry primarily in free verse, following in the style of Walt Whitman, whom he admired. Concerning rhyme, a predominant feature in traditional poetry, Sandburg once said, "If it jells into free verse, all right. If it jells into rhyme, all right." Free verse poetry is organized to the cadences of speech and image patterns rather than according to a regular metrical scheme. Its proponents argue that free verse eliminates much of the artificiality of poetry and is more suited to a more modern, casual style. The first English-language poets to be influenced by free verse, a movement that originated in France in the 1880s, were T.E. Hulme, F.S. Flint, Richard Aldington, Ezra Pound, and T.S. Eliot. Sandburg dabbled in the techniques of imagism, a move-ment initiated in England in 1912 by Aldington, Pound, Flint, and Hilda Doolittle; according to the imagist manifesto, one of their aims was "to compose in sequence of the musical phrase, not in sequence of the metronome." Carl Sandburg, William Carlos Williams, Marianne Moore, and Wallace Stevens all wrote some variety of free verse.

The Lincoln Biography   Biographies of Lincoln began to appear right after his assassination. Dozens of scholars have written biographies of Lincoln, and Sandburg followed that tradition. One of the most important early biographies of Lincoln appeared before Sandburg's were published, *Herndon's Life of Lincoln* (1889). Sandburg's biographies of Lincoln were probably the most popular. However, because Sandburg's biography of Lincoln was the work of an amateur historian, its influence was somewhat undermined. His books contained both small and large errors. Sandburg's criteria for evidence, especially early on, were more poetical than historical; he liked good stories. He soft-pedaled Lincoln's racial views and failed to comprehend the significance of his long adherence to the Whig party. However, Sandburg's goal was to "take Lincoln away from the religious bigots and the professional politicians and restore him to the common people," and in this he succeeded admirably.

Works in Critical Context

Both Sandburg's poetry and his huge multi-volume biography of Abraham Lincoln met mixed reviews. At best, his poetry was thought to be only at times brilliant, while the harshest critics believed it was not poetry at all. His Lincoln biographies, while painstakingly researched, were also beset with errors. Professional historians sometimes praised and sometimes panned his work. Nevertheless, Sandburg won a Pulitzer Prize both for his *Collected Poems* and *Lincoln: The War Years*.

Chicago Poems   Sandburg's free verse met with mixed reviews. In *Carl Sandburg*, Karl Detzer says that in 1918, "admirers proclaimed him a latter-day Walt Whitman; objectors cried that their six-year-old daughters could write better poetry." *Chicago Poems* provided what one review called "a stark but idealized view of the working class" in an urban setting. Amy Lowell, a poet and literary promoter, called *Chicago Poems* "one of the most original books this age has produced." Lowell's observations were reiterated by columnist H. L. Mencken, who called Sandburg "a true original, his own man." *The New York Times Book Review* praised the work for "pictures of our modern life, short, vivid, conveyed in few and telling words." However, the same reviewer criticized Sandburg for his free verse: "Some of it is poetry, some is decidedly not poetry. It is a pity that so many writers are bent on confusing the terms."

Work on Lincoln   Some reviewers of the biography of Lincoln were uneasy with Sandburg's presentation of Lincoln's life more as a story and less as a historical account. Wrote one reviewer, "There is in it so much of poetry and imagination, so much of tradition mingled with fact, that some may doubt whether it be biography at all. It is clearly not within the canons of historical writing." Nevertheless, maverick historian Charles A. Beard called Sandburg's Lincoln biography "a noble monument of American literature," and praised the work for its detail and thoroughness. Allan Nevins saw it as "homely but beautiful, learned but simple, exhaustively detailed but panoramic ... [occupying] a niche all its own, unlike any other biography or history in the language." The *New York Times Book Review* called Sandburg's work on Lincoln "the fullest, richest, most understanding of all the Lincoln biographies. ... *The War Years* follows *The Prairie Years* into the treasure house which belongs, like Lincoln himself, to the whole human family." The reviewer went on, "Mr. Sandburg's great work is not the story of the one man's life. It is a folk biography. The hopes and apprehensions of millions, their loves and hates, their exultation and despair, were reflected truthfully in the deep waters of Lincoln's being, and so they are reflected truthfully in these volumes." James G. Randal said in 1942 that Sandburg's made all other Lincoln books "dull or stupid by comparison." The Pulitzer Prize committee, prohibited from awarding the biography prize for any work on Washington or Lincoln, circumvented the rules by placing the book in the category of history.

Responses to Literature

1. Find an interesting current event in the newspaper. Rewrite the news article in the style of a short story, using your imagination to insert interesting, realistic-sounding details. What is the difference between the two accounts? Which is more interesting? Which is more believable?

2. Read a short biography of Lincoln and a short biography of Franklin Delano Roosevelt. Why do you think Sandburg admired these two politicians? Do you see any similarities between the two?

3. Read Sandburg's poem "Chicago." Why is this poem considered "free verse"? Write a paper in which you review this poem, including its style and language.

4. Read a section of Sandburg's biographies of Lincoln. Why do you think the biographies were so popular? How do you think his work differs from the work of traditional historians? To extend this activity, read a portion of another modern biography of Lincoln, and write a paper relating what the two works tell you, not just about Lincoln, but about the act of writing history.

BIBLIOGRAPHY

Books

Callahan, North. *Carl Sandburg: Lincoln of Our Literature*. New York: New York University Press, 1970.

Corwin, Norman. *The World of Carl Sandburg: A Stage Presentation*. New York: Harcourt, Brace, 1960.
Detzer, Karl. *Carl Sandburg: A Study in Personality and Background*. New York: Harcourt, Brace, 1941.
Durnell, Hazel. *The America of Carl Sandburg*. Seattle: University of Washington Press, 1965.
Golden, Harry. *Carl Sandburg*. Chicago: World, 1961.
Lowell, Amy. *Tendencies in Modern American Poetry*. New York: Macmillan, 1917.
Monroe, Harriet. *A Poet's Life*. New York: Macmillan, 1938.
Niven, Penelope and Katie Davis. *Carl Sandburg: Adventures of a Poet*. Orlando: Harcourt, 2003.
Untermeyer, Louis. *Modern American Poetry*. New York: Harcourt, Brace, 1936.

Periodicals

Hackett, Francis. "Impressions." *The New Republic* 8 (October 28, 1916), 328–329.
"The Lincoln of Carl Sandburg," *The New York Times Book Review*, (December 3, 1939), 1, 14.
Lowell, Amy, "Poetry and Propaganda." *The New York Times Book Review* (October 24, 1920), 7.
A Review of *Chicago Poems*. *The New York Times Book Review* (June 11, 1916), p. 242.
Woodburn, James A. A review of *Abraham Lincoln: The Prairie Years*. *American Political Science Review* 20 (August 1926), 674–77.

Web sites

CarlSandburg.net. Retrieved November 16, 2008, from http://www.carlsandburg.net/. Last updated on October 18, 2007.

William Saroyan

BORN: *1908, Fresno, California*

DIED: *1981, Fresno, California*

NATIONALITY: *American*

GENRE: *Drama, fiction, nonfiction*

MAJOR WORKS:

The Daring Young Man on the Flying Trapeze and Other Stories (1934)
The Time of Your Life (1939)
My Heart's in the Highlands (1939)
Hello Out There (1941)
Cave Dwellers (1957)

Overview

Saroyan is best known for his plays *The Time of Your Life*, for which he won the Pulitzer Prize in 1940, and *My Heart's in the Highlands*. The son of Armenian immigrants, Saroyan wrote about the lighter side of the immigrant experience in America, with special emphasis on

William Saroyan   *Saroyan, William, photograph. The Library of Congress.*

humor and family life, both of which are central to Armenian culture. Most of his works are set in the United States and reveal his appreciation of the American dream and his awareness of the strengths and weaknesses of American society.

Works in Biographical and Historical Context

Difficult Early Life   Saroyan was born in 1908 in Fresno, California, to Armenian immigrant parents. The instability of his early life is crucial to understanding his autobiographical short fiction. His father died in 1911, and Saroyan spent the next four years in an Oakland orphanage, while his mother worked in San Francisco and visited her children on weekends. In 1915 the children returned to Fresno, where they joined their mother, Takoohi Saroyan, then working as a domestic servant. Saroyan began selling newspapers at the age of eight and worked at various jobs while still in school. He began writing at the age of thirteen. Eventually he landed a job as a messenger boy for a telegraph company, a job that later became one of the major sources for his fiction and drama.

Saroyan left school at the age of fifteen and never graduated, but he did not shirk either his work or his decision to become a writer. His jobs included those in his uncle's law office, the vineyards around Fresno, grocery stores, and a post office. He made good use of the

public library. He boasts that at nineteen he had become the San Francisco Postal Telegraph Company's youngest branch manager. Within a year, he had published his first short story in a San Francisco literary magazine, *Overland Monthly and Outwest Magazine.*

Short Stories   Despite a prolific career, Saroyan's reputation as short-story writer still rests largely on his first collection, *The Daring Young Man on the Flying Trapeze and Other Stories* (1934). When the title piece was published in *Story* magazine in February 1934, the public response was so favorable that in less than a year Random House had compiled the collection. As in many of his stories, Saroyan's narrator in "The Daring Young Man on the Flying Trapeze" is a young writer, a thinly veiled representation of the author himself. The young man tries to find work, gets disgusted with the bureaucracy, stops eating, falls back on literature to sustain him, and finally finds fulfillment only in death. "A Cold Day" takes the form of a letter from Saroyan to an editor of *Story* magazine in which he tells of the hardships of writing in an unheated apartment. Though the idea of this story may seem overly simple, it, perhaps more than any other story in the collection, links Saroyan personally to the concept of the daring young man. These stories establish one of the main themes that permeates almost all of his subsequent writings—the brilliance and importance of life in the face of death.

Saroyan subsequently published seven more volumes of short stories. These early collections project a wide variety of thematic concerns, yet they are united in their portrayal of America between the two world wars. Saroyan's first books reflect the painful realities of the Depression of the 1930s. The young writer without a job in his first famous story "The Daring Young Man on the Flying Trapeze" goes to be interviewed for a position and finds that "already there were two dozen young men in the place." The story "International Harvester" from the 1936 collection *Inhale and Exhale* also gives a bleak vision of complete economic collapse: "Shamefully to the depths fallen: America. In Wall Street they talk as if the end of this country is within sight." Readers clearly saw their troubled lives vividly portrayed in Saroyan's stories; though they depicted the agony of the times, the stories also conveyed great hope and vigorously defiant good spirits.

Playwriting   Between 1939 and 1943, Saroyan published and produced his most famous plays. Such works as *My Heart's in the Highlands* (1939), *The Beautiful People* (1941), and *Across the Board on Tomorrow Morning* (1942) were well received by some critics and audiences; *The Time of Your Life* (1939) won the Pulitzer Prize as the best play of the 1939–1940 season. Saroyan refused the award on the grounds that businessmen should not judge art. Although championed by critics like George Jean Nathan, Saroyan had a strained relationship with the theatrical world. From the time his first play appeared on Broadway, critics called his work surrealistic, sentimental, or difficult to understand. His creation of a fragile, fluid, dramatic universe full of strange, lonely, confused, and gentle people startled theatergoers accustomed to conventional plots and characterization. His instinctive and highly innovative sense of dramatic form was lost on many audiences. These plays were a wonderful amalgam of vaudeville, absurdism, sentiment, spontaneity, reverie, humor, despair, philosophical speculation, and whimsy. They introduced a kind of rambunctious energy into staid American drama. His "absurdity" was directly related to his sorrow at observing the waste of the true, vital impulses of life in the contemporary world.

In 1941, after two active years on Broadway, Saroyan traveled to Hollywood to work on the film version of *The Human Comedy* (1943) for Metro-Goldwyn-Mayer. When the scenario was completed, it was made into a successful motion picture. From the beginning of his career, Saroyan had committed himself to celebrating the brotherhood of man, and in *The Human Comedy* he preached a familiar sermon: love one another, or you shall perish. This portrayal of love's power in small-town America offered consolation to millions ravaged by the suffering and death brought on by World War II.

Nevertheless, before 1942 was over, yet another Saroyan one-act play that had premiered a year earlier in California came to the New York stage. It was *Hello Out There* (1949), a script for two performers. The play, which opened on September 29, 1942, at the Belasco, was a story of a romance between a drifter, brought to jail for his own protection after being falsely accused of rape, and the young girl who cleaned the prison. The story ends tragically when a lynch mob kills the prisoner.

Meanwhile, on January 9, 1943, Saroyan had been elected to the department of art and literature at the National Institute of Arts and Letters. He had reached the peak of his recognition as an American writer. In February 1943 he married Carol Marcus, beginning a period of several tumultuous years. While his fame spread, his personal life seemed to suffer. As his later memoirs illustrated, he was obsessed with gambling and alcohol, even to the extent that he would complete works specifically to pay off gambling debts.

Past His Peak, with Personal Problems Saroyan went on to publish several novels between 1951 and 1964, including: *Rock Wagram* (1951), *The Laughing Matter* (1953), *Boys and Girls Together* (1963), and *One Day in the Afternoon of the World* (1964). Each novel explores in fictional form the troubled years of Saroyan's marriage to Carol Marcus and that marriage's aftermath. These thinly disguised transcriptions of Saroyan's own life might be termed the "fatherhood novels," for they are linked thematically through the author's concern with founding a family. Each Armenian-American protagonist in these novels is searching for (or has already found) a wife and children, his emblems of human community. In the novels, as in the plays and short stories, the family symbolizes humanity in microcosm and localizes the

LITERARY AND HISTORICAL CONTEMPORARIES

Saroyan's famous contemporaries include:

Lillian Hellman (1905–1984): Hellman was an American playwright who explored controversial themes in her work. Her most famous work, *The Children's Hour* (1934), revolved around a child's accusation that two of her teachers were lesbians, which led to one woman's suicide.

Richard J. Daley (1902–1976): Mayor of Chicago for six consecutive terms, Daley headed the Democratic political machine in that city from 1955 until his death. By the 1960s he was one of the most important Democratic politicians in the United States.

Beverly Cleary (1916–): Cleary is the author of the popular children's books in the *Ramona Quimby* series, as well as many other books for children.

Ronald Reagan (1911–2004): Reagan was a Hollywood actor, two-term governor of California, and president of the United States (1981–89). He earned the nickname "The Great Communicator" because of his rapport with the American public.

Clark Gable (1901–1960): Gable was America's top male film star in the 1930s, 1940s, and 1950s. He won an Academy Award for best actor in 1934 for the film *It Happened One Night*.

desire for universal brotherhood that had always marked Saroyan's vision.

During the 1930s and 1940s, Saroyan had reached the peak of his fame; by the time he reached middle age in the 1950s, Saroyan's early success had faded. Many critics cite Saroyan's refusal to adapt his writing to changes in American life as a significant factor in the decline of his literary reputation. Biographers also attribute Saroyan's change in fortune to his excessive drinking and gambling.

Nevertheless, hardly a year goes by in which professional actors somewhere in America do not revive *The Time of Your Life*. *My Heart's in the Highlands* has been made into an opera and televised, and other Saroyan plays are occasionally featured on television. *My Heart's in the Highlands* and *The Time of Your Life* are collected in popular and school anthologies of American drama, and on the basis of those plays, the place of William Saroyan in the history of the American theater still seems as secure as he always told us it would be. Indeed, on November 18, 1979, Saroyan became one of the initial inductees to the Theater Hall of Fame at the Uris Theater in New York City. He died of prostate cancer in Fresno, California, in 1981.

COMMON HUMAN EXPERIENCE

Saroyan's work is largely informed by his experience as a second-generation Armenian immigrant to the United States. Other works that deal with the immigrant experience are:

Bread Givers (1925), a novel by Anzia Yezierska. This work tells the story of young immigrants who struggle to free themselves from orthodox Jewish culture.

The Woman Warrior (1976), a novel by Maxine Hong Kingston, the daughter of Chinese immigrants. The book incorporates stories of five women, including Kingston's aunts, mother, and Kingston herself.

Sari of the Gods (1998), a collection of short stories by G.S. Sharat Chandra. The stories focus on the Indian-American immigrant experience.

The Joy Luck Club (1987), a novel by Amy Tan, the daughter of Chinese immigrants. This work explores the complicated relationship between Chinese immigrant mothers and their American daughters.

Garden of Exile: Poems (1999). A poetry collection by Aleida Rodriguez. The author fled Cuba for the United States when she was nine years old.

Works in Literary Context

Saroyan acknowledged the influence of British playwright George Bernard Shaw, who enjoyed both popular and critical success with plays such as *Androcles and the Lion* (1923) and *Saint Joan* (1923).

Existentialism Saroyan's work can be characterized as existentialist. Existentialism had its roots in the work of philosophers Søren Kierkegaard and Friedrich Nietzsche in the nineteenth century. These philosophers celebrated the living, thinking, feeling individual and regarded traditional philosophy as too removed from human experience. Existentialism was expressed in the work of writers such as Franz Kafka and Fyodor Dostoevsky, whose characters grapple with a feeling of hopelessness and the absurdity of life. However, as critic Maxwell Geismar remarked, "the depression of the 1930s, apparently so destructive and so despairing," was actually a time of "regeneration" for the major writers of the period. Furthermore, "the American writer had gained moral stature, a sense of his own cultural connection, a series of new meanings and new values for his work." The crisis writers were experiencing was, of course, more than merely economic. A deep cultural schism had rocked Europe since Nietzsche's work and affected such American writers as Henry Miller, whose *Tropic of Cancer* (1934) appeared in the same year as Saroyan's first collection of short fiction.

Romanticism Saroyan also often expressed romantic themes. Romanticism places a stress on a character's emo-

tion and experience. Saroyan's early, romantic themes included man's innate goodness, men's dreams as they are changed by the passage of time, and personal isolation as the ultimate tragedy. Death, for him, is as natural as life; in fact, its closeness should lead to an intensified view of the preciousness of life. He followed in the footsteps of American romantic writers such as poet Emily Dickinson and Herman Melville, author of *Moby-Dick* (1851).

Works in Critical Context

Saroyan's work has been widely reviewed, but it has rarely received serious critical analysis. In structure and in philosophy, his writing is simple, an attribute for which he has been both praised and scorned. Many critics contend that Saroyan did not grow as an artist after the 1940s, that his subject matter and outlook were stuck in the Depression and World War II eras, and that he did not challenge himself to vary his proven formulae. Especially in the later years, critics were almost unanimous in calling Saroyan's work overly sentimental. Although many have claimed that his loosely structured, anecdotal stories and memoirs overflow with sentiment and description and lack structure and form, Saroyan's works are still widely read. His special talent lay in his ability to create poetic, humorous characters and situations, and, as one critic said, "to write from joy, which is ... sparse as a tradition in our literature."

The Time of Your Life Critics wondered at the success of *The Time of Your Life*, as it departed from the ordinary rules of playwriting and paid little attention to action and plot. They believed it overly sentimental and romantic. One reviewer wrote, "Saroyan certainly made too little effort to think things through and work things out." One critic wrote, "The bulk of his writing, although vivid, is careless and formless." Reviewers saw some good things in the play, but argued that Saroyan's work was often "shoddy and his idealism fuzzy." However, some critics lauded the play for its social awareness, its humor, and its emphasis on individualism. Wrote one reviewer, "Both the common and the uncommon people of the play were, in one respect or another, marvelously vital, imaginative, or sensitive." The fact that the work did arouse such enthusiasm as well as hostility suggested to some critics that Saroyan "has something important to say."

Responses to Literature

1. Along with a few other students, read and then enact a scene from *The Time of Your Life*. What challenges do you encounter when speaking the words aloud and enacting them that you do not encounter in silent reading?

2. Read the short story "The Daring Young Man on the Flying Trapeze." Research the history of the era in which this story was written. Why do you think this story was so popular in 1939?

3. In an essay, compare and contrast a story from Saroyan's first short story collection, *The Daring Young Man on the Flying Trapeze*, with a story from his later collection *Dear Baby* (1945). Do you feel Saroyan had changed or developed as a writer? In what sense does he seem the same? In what sense does he show development?

BIBLIOGRAPHY

Books

Floan, Howard R. *William Saroyan: A Study of the Short Fiction*. Boston: Twayne, 1966.
Leggett, John. *A Daring Young Man: A Biography of William Saroyan*. New York: Knopf, 2002.

Periodicals

Carpenter, Frederic I. "The Time of William Saroyan's Life." *The Pacific Spectator* (Winter 1947).
Fisher, William J. "What Ever Happened to Saroyan?" *College English* vol. 16 (March 1955).
Mills, John A. "What. What Not: Absurdity in Saroyan's 'The Time of Your Life'." *The Midwest Quarterly* vol. XXVI (Winter 1985).

Web sites

William Saroyan Literary Foundation. Retrieved December 7, 2008, from http://www.william saroyan.org.

❀ Chief Seattle

BORN: *c. 1786, Washington*

DIED: *1866, Washington*

NATIONALITY: *American, Native American*

GENRE: *Nonfiction*

MAJOR WORKS:
"Chief Seattle's 1854 Oration"

Overview

Chief Seattle, leader of the Duwamish and Suquamish people of the Puget Sound area in what is today the state of Washington, was responsible for continued good relations between his people and the new white settlers in the Pacific Northwest. By consistently choosing not to fight the encroaching settlers, his people knew peace throughout the turbulent nineteenth century. Chief Seattle is best known for the farewell speech he delivered before removing his people to a reservation, despite much controversy over the speech's authenticity.

Works in Biographical and Historical Context

Appreciative of Two Worlds Chief Seattle was born around 1786 in the central Puget Sound area in what is

Chief Seattle   *Chief Seattle, photograph. The Library of Congress.*

now Washington State. Schweabe, his father, was a Suquamish chief, while his mother, Scholitza, was the daughter of a Duwamish chief. As a member of a patrilineal society, that is, one in which power was handed down from father to son, Chief Seattle learned his father's Suquamish dialect.

When Chief Seattle was four years old, European settlers arrived in the Puget Sound area. In later years, he said he was present when Captain George Vancouver anchored the British ship H. M. S. *Discovery* off Bainbridge Island on May 20, 1792. Chief Seattle claimed that his lifelong appreciation of Westerners was formed during the explorer's visit.

According to early Seattle historian Clarence Bagley, Chief Seattle was known to be a courageous, daring leader when he was a young warrior. In 1810, a Duwamish alliance with the neighboring Suquamish gave Chief Seattle control of the affiliated tribes, and he continued the amiable relations with white settlers that his father had begun. By the 1840s, Chief Seattle had been converted

LITERARY AND HISTORICAL CONTEMPORARIES

Chief Seattle's famous contemporaries include:

Stephen F. Austin (1793–1836): Austin, known as the "Father of Texas," established the first Anglo-American colony in Tejas, a province of Mexico at the time.

Simón Bolívar (1783–1830): Regarded as the father of Latin American independence, Bolívar and his armies liberated Colombia and Venezuela in 1819.

Sacagawea (c.1788–1812): Sacagawea, daughter of a Shoshone chief, accompanied the Lewis and Clark expedition into the American West as an interpreter.

James Polk (1795–1849): The expansionist policies of President Polk allowed the United States to acquire a vast area of the West.

Sojourner Truth (1797–1883): An advocate for the rights of the disadvantaged, Truth, a former slave, assisted newly freed slaves who gathered in Washington after the Civil War.

Sam Houston (1793–1863): Houston, who ordered the attack at San Jacinto that secured Texas its independence from Mexico, was the first president of the Lone Star Republic.

to Catholicism by French missionaries and was baptized as "Noah." In addition to having his children baptized as well, Chief Seattle instituted morning and evening church services for Native Americans.

Seattle, Washington The California gold rush of 1849 filled the Pacific Northwest with white settlers seeking the natural wealth of the area. Chief Seattle continued to cooperate with the newcomers, and he often spoke out for friendship and open trade with the settlers. Always fascinated by white culture, he became good friends with David "Doc" Maynard. Besides saving Doc when another Native American tried to kill the man, Chief Seattle also helped protect a small group of settlers from Native American attacks. Out of respect for their friend and ally, the whites at Puget Sound named their settlement after him in 1852. Seattle's people, however, believed that frequently mentioning a dead person's name would disturb that person's eternal rest. In order to use his name for their city, the settlers agreed to pay the chief a small tax for the trouble that his spirit would encounter when his name was said.

Losing the Land As settlers continued to pour into the area, the U.S. government pressed the issue of purchasing land from the Native Americans. In December 1854, Chief Seattle met with Washington territorial governor Isaac Stevens to discuss the sale of native lands in exchange for smaller reservations and government money. At that time, he agreed to help the whites and the U.S. government by moving the Puget Sound bands to a reservation. His famous—and controversial—farewell speech at this meeting was purportedly translated into English and transcribed by Dr. Henry Smith, a recent arrival to the area.

In 1855, Chief Seattle signed the Port Elliott treaty between the Puget Sound Native Americans and the United States. Soon after the treaty was signed, however, its terms were broken by whites. This betrayal led to a series of Native American uprisings from 1855 to 1858, including the Yakim War from 1855 to 1856. In accordance with the treaty, Chief Seattle moved his people to the Port Madison reservation, located across Puget Sound from the current city of Seattle, on the east shore of Bainbridge Island. He died on the reservation in 1866 after a brief illness.

Works in Literary Context

Notwithstanding debate over its accuracy, Chief Seattle's oration is well known in American society today. For instance, the text of his speech has been anthologized in American literature books many times. Furthermore, news and television media have frequently quoted his words, and the Smithsonian Institution's "Nations of Nations" exhibit includes an excerpt of Seattle's speech. Probably the most important aspect of Chief Seattle's legacy lies within the role he played in fostering peaceful interactions between whites and Native Americans and contributing to the history of the Pacific Northwest.

The Language of the Earth Linguistic theorists hundreds of years ago, notes linguist Thomas H. Guthrie, speculated that the first languages were purely figurative and poetic; Native American languages are no exception, as they characteristically reduce speech to image. Native Americans, who considered themselves to be children of nature, expressed their humanity using metaphor and imagery reflective of the natural world around them.

In his 1854 oration, Chief Seattle makes a passionate, sorrowful appeal to the settlers, asking that they honor the land as he and his people have done. His intensity was not lost on his listeners, nor has it been lost on generations of readers. "Nineteenth-century writers commonly suggested," states Guthrie, that metaphor and the "rich use of figurative language ... [made Native American] speeches more lofty and impressive." In fact, so powerful is Chief Seattle's choice of words, continues Guthrie, that "we commune with him, listen to his complaints, understand, appreciate, and even feel his injuries."

Works in Critical Context

Chief Seattle's 1854 address to the Washington territorial governor about the status of his people and their future was said to have been moving and expressed very well. Unfortunately, at least four versions of the speech have been printed throughout the years, and no one knows for certain which is the most accurate. Still, even though historians disagree about its different versions, Chief Seattle's famous speech remains an important document for its look at dealings between Native Americans and whites.

Original Version   Academics have long debated which native dialect Chief Seattle would have used, either Suquamish or Duwamish, in his speech. They do agree that no matter what dialect Chief Seattle spoke, his words were translated immediately into Chinook, a Northwest trade language, and then into English for U.S. government representatives. The only surviving transcript was produced from the notes reportedly taken by Dr. Henry Smith as Chief Seattle spoke; however, Dr. Smith waited thirty years before he transcribed his notes. On October 29, 1887, the *Seattle Sunday Star* published what Dr. Smith maintained was the basic substance of Chief Seattle's words. Common criticism of this first version is that Dr. Smith "rendered his memory of Chief Seattle's speech in the rather ornate (to modern ears) English of Victorian oratory," contends scholar Kenneth Greg Watson, leading some readers to believe that Smith made up at least part of the speech that was published.

Environmentalism   The harshest critics of Seattle's speech argue that his words have been used as propaganda to "justify and fortify current attitudes regarding the treatment of the first Americans and the natural environment in the United States," claims academic Jerry A. Clark. According to Watson, Chief Seattle's text was revived in the 1960s by writers who introduced completely new material, and "these fabricated versions became something of a manifesto for human rights and environmental activists." Clark agrees that "the attitudes reflected ... are in harmony with those professed by individuals upset at the damage to the natural environment perpetrated by our industrial society." No matter how embellished Chief Seattle's speech has become over the years, however, "the words themselves," writes Watson, "remain a powerful, bittersweet plea for respect of Native American rights and environmental values."

Responses to Literature

1. The city of Seattle was named after a chief. Other Native American names have been used in more commercial ways, such as the brand of car named after Chief Pontiac, and images of Native Americans have been used as commercial symbols for many different enterprises, most notably sports teams. Do you think this is a way of honoring Native American contributions to American culture or merely an attempt to capitalize on them?

2. Portrait photographer Edward S. Curtis often took pictures of Seattle's daughter, Princess Angeline. His interest in her developed into an interest in other Native Americans, and Curtis spent most of his career photographing Native Americans throughout the country. Locate some of these pictures online. What

---

COMMON HUMAN EXPERIENCE

Chief Seattle shared the values and traditions of his Suquamish and Duwamish followers in a speech that upheld the pride of his tribe. Certainly, the need to protect a people's cultural identity is a fundamental desire of humankind, as evidenced in the works listed below:

The Power of Horses and Other Stories (1990), stories by Elizabeth Cook-Lynn. Born on a reservation in South Dakota, Cook-Lynn, a member of the Crow Creek Sioux tribe, depicts lives held together by tradition amidst violent change in this collection of short stories.

The Scent of the Gods (1991), a novel by Fiona Cheong. Through the voice of an eleven-year-old girl, this novel describes the conflicts of family, heritage, and national identity after Singapore's independence in 1965.

Efuru (1966), a novel by Flora Nwapa. The first nonwhite African woman to be published in Europe, Nwapa explores a tradition in this novel in which spirits are a part of everyday life and representative of the values in a Nigerian village.

Bread Givers (1925), a novel by Anzia Yezierska. With insightful dialogue, Yezierska's novel celebrates the Jewish heritage that has enriched North American language and culture.

---

do you think motivated Curtis to devote his life to photographing Native Americans? What stories do you think his photographs tell about Native Americans?

3. On Native American reservations today, the tribal council, not the local or federal government, has jurisdiction over its land and people. Each reservation has its own system of government, which may or may not be the same as forms of government found outside the reservation. What is your opinion of such autonomy in the United States? Can you find other countries in which a similar situation exists?

4. In addition to his famous speech, Chief Seattle allegedly wrote a letter to President Pierce about the Native Americans' relationship to the Earth and its natural resources. Write your own letter to the current president of the United States in which you express both positive and negative views of how natural resource conservation and economic development have affected various regions of the United States.

BIBLIOGRAPHY

Books

Eckrom, J. A. *Remembered Drums: A History of the Puget Sound Indian War.* Walla Walla, Wash.: Pioneer Press Books, 1989.

Kaiser, Rudolf. "Chief Seattle's Speech(es): American Origins and European Reception," in *Recovering the Word: Essays on Native American Literature*. Berkeley: University of California Press, 1987.

Watt, Roberta Frye. *Four Wagons West*. Portland, Ore.: Binsford & Mort, 1934.

Periodicals

Buerge, David. "Seattle Before Seattle." *Seattle Weekly* (December 17, 1980).

Buerge, David. "Seattle's King Arthur: How Chief Seattle Continues to Inspire His Many Admirers to Put Words in His Mouth." *Seattle Weekly* (July 17, 1991).

Web sites

Chief Seattle Arts. *Chief Seattle, According to an Early Historian*. Retrieved August 25, 2008, from http://www.markhoffman.net/history/chiefseattle/bagley.htm.

Clark, Jerry A. *Thus Spoke Chief Seattle: The Story of an Undocumented Speech*. Retrieved August 25, 2008, from http://www.archives.gov/publications/prologue/1985/spring/chief-seattle.html.

Guthrie, Thomas H. *Good Words: Chief Joseph and the Production of Indian Speech(es), Texts, and Subjects*. Retrieved August 25, 2008, from http://ethnohistory.dukejournals.org/cgi/reprint/54/3/509.pdf.

Watson, Kenneth Greg. *Seattle, Chief Noah (178?–1866)*. Retrieved August 25, 2008, from http://www.historylink.org/essays/output.cfm?file_id=5071.

✸ Alice Sebold

BORN: *1963, Philadelphia, Pennsylvania*

DIED:

NATIONALITY: *American*

GENRE: *Fiction, nonfiction*

MAJOR WORKS:

Lucky (1999)

The Lovely Bones (2002)

The Almost Moon (2007)

Overview

Alice Sebold was launched into the national spotlight when *New York Times* columnist Anna Quindlan appeared on the *Today Show* and declared that Sebold's soon-to-be published book, *The Lovely Bones*, was the one book everyone should read that summer. The response was enormous, leading the publisher to increase the size of the book's first printing from thirty-five thousand to fifty thousand copies. Before the book's official publication date, it was in its sixth printing. Within months, more than two million copies were in print.

Alice Sebold   *Sebold, Alice, photograph. AP Images.*

Works in Biographical and Historical Context

Rape at Syracuse   Sebold grew up in Philadelphia and attended Syracuse University from 1980 to 1984. As an eighteen-year-old freshman, she was beaten and raped in a tunnel leading to an amphitheater on campus. Several months later she recognized her rapist on the streets of Syracuse and played a key role in his arrest and successful prosecution.

After graduation, Sebold entered the M.F.A. program at the University of Houston but did not finish her degree. After leaving the program, she moved to New York City and lived there for ten years. Eventually, she returned to graduate school. She received a master's degree in fine arts from the University of California at Irvine. She met her future husband, Glen David Gold, while in graduate school. They married in 2001.

While in the M.F.A. program at Irvine, Sebold began her memoir, *Lucky*, which took its title from the comments of a police officer at the time of her attack, who told her she was lucky to be alive. The memoir tells the story of her rape, how she coped, the reactions of her friends and family, and her alcohol and drug abuse that resulted from the trauma. Sebold also relates the events that led to the rapist's conviction.

Breakout First Novel   Sebold has stated that she needed to write *Lucky* before she could tell the story of Susie, the fourteen-year-old protagonist in *The Lovely Bones*. She said, "That story was getting in the way of all the other stories that I didn't even know I wanted to tell. I had to get it out before I could move on." In the first chapter of *The Lovely Bones*, Susie is raped and murdered. The rest of the book, told from Susie's perspective in heaven, deals with the impact of Susie's murder on her family and friends.

The Lovely Bones proved immensely popular, changing Sebold's life virtually overnight. The book was made into a movie scheduled to be released in 2009.

Sebold's third book, *The Almost Moon*, was published in 2007. Sebold revisited her themes of violence and trauma in this book, which tells the story of a woman who kills her mother and stores her body in the freezer. The novel opens with the act of violence, much as *The Lovely Bones* did: "When all is said and done, killing my mother came easily." The rest of the novel deals with the repercussions of that act. Critics almost universally dismissed the book.

Works in Literary Context

Memoir Memoir is a subcategory of autobiography. While autobiographies are life stories usually covering all the important events of a person's life in chronological order, memoirs generally focus on one event in life, or an aspect in life, and are primarily concerned with emotion and reflection. Memoir has become a very popular genre in recent years.

While memoirs have a long history, Sebold's *Lucky* represented what Joyce Carol Oates called the "New Memoir." She describes it as "the memoir of sharply focused events, very often traumatic, in distinction to the traditional life-memoir." In these memoirs, the individual, who is often relatively young, writes the story of the traumatic ordeal and the path to coping and recovery. *Lucky* follows in the tradition of *Angela's Ashes* (1996), by Frank McCourt, which tells the story of McCourt's poverty-stricken childhood in Ireland, and *Girl, Interrupted* (1993), by Susanna Kaysen, which relates the story of her two-year stay in a mental institution as a young woman.

Magic Realism Sebold's first novel, *The Lovely Bones*, is narrated by Susie from heaven. The most obvious predecessor for this narrative device was Thornton Wilder's Pulitzer Prize–winning play *Our Town* (1938) in which the main character, Emily, also has omniscient knowledge after her death. Such a device uses elements of magic realism. Magic realism is a mode of fiction in which magical or fantastic elements are included in an otherwise realistic story. Some of the most famous examples of magic realism are the writings of Gabriel García Márquez, such as *One Hundred Years of Solitude* (1967 in Spanish; first English translation, 1970) and Isabel Allende's *Of Love and Shadows* (1985).

Works in Critical Context

Although commentators are divided on the literary merit of Sebold's work, her books have garnered significant interest from critics and readers alike. Sebold has been praised for handling such dark material in honest, provocative, and imaginative ways.

Lucky *Lucky* met with almost universal critical acclaim, although it was not nearly as popular as *The Lovely Bones*, published three years later. Wrote Joyce Carol Oates, "*Lucky* is an utterly realistic, unsparing and distinctly unsugary account of violent rape and its aftermath." She wrote, "Exemplary memoirs like *Lucky* break the formula with their originality of insight and expression." In comparison with Sebold's breakout novel, wrote one author, "*Lucky* is the more integrated and successful book." Andrea Dworkin concurs: "*Lucky* is burdened with facts, more pedestrian, more real. *Lucky* is the more important book."

The Lovely Bones *The Lovely Bones* met mixed reviews. Some reviewers called the book too sentimental and "sugary." They pointed out that the book's extraordinary popularity might be due to the national mood after the

COMMON HUMAN EXPERIENCE

In both Sebold's memoir and her fiction a recurring theme is violence against women and children; however, the characters eventually are able to transcend their status as victims and move on to survival. Here are some other works that focus on violence and survival:

Thicker than Water (1991), a novel by Kathryn Harrison. This novel is about a child raised by her grandparents who is subjected to regular abuse by both her parents. However, her struggles lead to triumph in the end.

I Know Why the Caged Bird Sings (1970), an autobiography by Maya Angelou. This autobiography relates Angelou's childhood in the Deep South. The book recounts Angelou's rape by her mother's boyfriend when she was seven years old and her subsequent refusal to speak for five years.

Eight Bullets: One Woman's Story of Surviving Anti-Gay Violence (1995), a nonfiction work by Claudia Brenner. This book chronicles an attack on two lesbian women that left one dead and the other, Claudia Brenner, critically wounded. Brenner lived to identify her attacker and successfully prosecute him. She became an outspoken advocate of hate crimes legislation.

Bastard out of Carolina (1992), a novel by Dorothy Allison. This novel relates the story of Bone, a young girl living in poverty in the South, who endures abuse and incest but turns her life around in adolescence.

The Burning Bed (1984), a made-for-television film based on a nonfiction book of the same name by Faith McNulty. It tells the story of a battered wife who, after exhausting all other avenues of escape, murders her husband in his sleep after he rapes her one night.

September 11, 2001, terrorist attacks in New York and Washington D.C. "Its goal," writes Joyce Carol Oates, "is to confirm what we wish we could believe and not to unsettle us with harsh, intransigent truths about human cruelty." Noting that the book is much more about tracing the process of healing than it is about confronting horrifying violence head-on, Daniel Mendelsohn criticizes the book for "stitch[ing] improbably neat closure for some very untidy wounds." He goes on to write, "Sebold's novel consistently offers healing with no real mourning, and prefers to offer clichés ... of comfort instead of confrontations with evil, or even with genuinely harrowing grief." Sarah Churchwell concurs, writing, "Those in the mood to believe that suffering guarantees maturity, hard-earned wisdom and the smell of baking downstairs, will love all of *The Lovely Bones.*"

On the other hand, many reviewers praised the work, beginning with Anna Quindlan on the *Today Show. Los Angeles Times* critic Paula L. Woods writes, "With a well-balanced mix of heavenly humor, Earth-bound suspense and keen observation of both sides of Susie's in-between, Sebold teaches us much about living and dying, holding on and letting go ... and has created a novel that is painfully fine and accomplished." Churchwell praises at least the first half of the book as "a wonderfully observed, moving portrait of adolescence as a series of losses and accommodations to the pains of adulthood." Reviewing *The Lovely Bones* in the *New York Times*, Michiko Kakutani gives it high praise. "What might play as a sentimental melodrama in the hands of a lesser writer becomes in this volume a keenly observed portrait of familial love," Kakutani noted, "and how it endures and changes over time." The *Times'* notoriously frank critic did concede that the plot falters toward the end, but "even these lapses do not diminish Ms. Sebold's achievements: her ability to capture both the ordinary and the extraordinary, the banal and the horrific, in lyrical, unsentimental prose; her instinctive understanding of the mathematics of love between parents and children; her gift for making palpable the dreams, regrets, and unstilled hopes of one girl and one family," Kakutani concluded.

Responses to Literature

1. Read *Lucky* and *The Lovely Bones*. Which book did you prefer? Why? Write an essay in which you explain your preference for one book over the other.

2. How do you think the September 11, 2001, terrorist attacks may have contributed to the overwhelming popularity of *The Lovely Bones*?

3. One of the first things a writer of a fictional work must decide is who is going to narrate the story. Write a short story in the first-person voice. It can be based on a real event in your life or completely imaginary. Then recast your story so that it is told by an omniscient narrator. How does the choice of narrators affect the structure and tone of the story? What have you learned from this exercise about the importance of the narrative voice?

4. What is the difference between traditional autobiography and memoir? Create a bibliography of five to eight notable works in each genre, then read at least one book from each list. Which book did you find more compelling, and why?

BIBLIOGRAPHY

Periodicals

Abbott, Charlotte. "How About Them Bones?" *Publishers Weekly*, vol. 249, no. 30 (July 29, 2002): 22–24.

Churchwell, Sarah. "A Neato Heaven." *Times Literary Supplement*, no. 5186 (August 23, 2002): 19.

Dworkin, Andrea. "A Good Rape." *New Statesman*, vol. 132, no. 4644 (June 30, 2003): pp. 51–52.

Eder, Doris L. "The Saving Powers of Memory and Imagination in Alice Sebold's *Lucky* and *The Lovely Bones*." *Contemporary Literary Criticism*, 193 (2004).

Mendelson, Daniel. "Novel of the Year." *New York Review of Books*, vol. 50, no. 1 (January 16, 2003): 4–8.

Oates, Joyce Carol. "Trauma, Coping, Recovery." *Times Literary Supplement*, no. 5229 (June 20, 2003): p. 15.

Siegel, Lee. "Mom's in the Freezer." *New York Times* (October 21, 2007).

Woods, Paula L. "Holding On and Letting Go." *Los Angeles Times Book Review*, July 7, 2002, p. 7.

Web sites

Carter, Imogen. "Howling at the Moon." *The Guardian*. Retrieved November 22, 2008, from http://www.guardian.co.uk/books/2008/oct/12/fiction6.

Weich, Dave. "Interview with Alice Sebold." *The World Meets Alice Sebold*. July 22, 2002. Retrieved November 22, 2008, from http://www.powells.com/authors/sebold.html.

David Sedaris

BORN: *1956, New York, New York*

NATIONALITY: *American*

GENRE: *Fiction, nonfiction*

MAJOR WORKS:

Barrel Fever (1994)

Me Talk Pretty One Day (2000)

Dress Your Family in Corduroy and Denim (2004)

When You Are Engulfed in Flames (2008)

Overview

David Sedaris is an American humorist, radio contributor, and best-selling author. His work became nationally known when National Public Radio broadcast "SantaLand Diaries," his essay about his time working as a Christmas elf at Macy's, in 1992. Several of his autobiographical essay collections have become *New York Times* best sellers.

Works in Biographical and Historical Context

Sedaris, the second of six children, was born in 1956. His family moved to Raleigh, North Carolina, when he was very young, and it was there that he grew up. Sedaris later described his home as fairly chaotic and dysfunctional, and he used these stories in his books of essays about his life. He attended Kent State University for a short time but dropped out in 1977. He attended the Art Institute in Chicago and occasionally read his work on the National Public Radio programs *The Wild Room* and *This American Life*.

David Sedaris   *Sedaris, David, 2004, photograph. Ralph Orlowski / Getty Images.*

After Sedaris moved to New York City in 1991, National Public Radio personality Ira Glass asked him to put together a holiday-themed essay for one of his programs. Sedaris did, and scored his first hit, "Santa-Land Diaries," which aired on December 23, 1992. In this essay, Sedaris recounts his experiences working as Crumpet the Elf in Macy's department store during the holiday shopping season. This story became an instant hit and earned him a monthly spot on NPR's *Morning Edition* and a two-book contract with Little, Brown. Just like "SantaLand Diaries," his monologues drew on his personal experience in the many odd jobs he held to supplement his income, such as cleaning houses.

Sedaris bases his stories on not only his family's quirks but also on his feeling of alienation growing up as a gay man in Southern society. He pokes fun not only at his family and society but at himself.

Sedaris's first book, *Barrel Fever*, was published in 1994. These essays attracted national attention as well when he read them on National Public Radio. His second collection of essays, *Naked* (1997), established Sedaris as a premier essayist. Critics praised not only Sedaris's humor but the emotional range in his essays, which ranged from stories about hitchhiking and his battle with childhood nervous disorders to his stay at a nudist colony.

LITERARY AND HISTORICAL CONTEMPORARIES

Sedaris's famous contemporaries include:

Ellen DeGeneres (1958–): DeGeneres is a comedienne, actress, and talk-show host. She received intense media attention when the character she played on television came out as a lesbian in 1997, the first character to do so on prime-time television.

Al Franken (1952–): Franken is a political humorist and writer for *Saturday Night Live*. Franken's book *Rush Limbaugh Is a Big Fat Idiot and Other Observations* (1996) became a best seller. He ran for a U.S. Senate seat in Minnesota in 2008.

Barack Obama (1961–): Obama is a former senator from Illinois. He won the 2008 election for president of the United States and became the first African American to win that office.

Katie Couric (1957–): Couric worked as the host of the *Today Show*, a morning news program on NBC, for fifteen years before becoming the first female solo anchor for an evening newscast on a major U.S. network in 2006.

Jamaica Kincaid (1949–): Kincaid, who was born in Antigua, gained widespread acclaim for her fiction, autobiographical pieces, and books on gardening.

Sedaris's work took a softer turn with the publication of *Me Talk Pretty One Day*. Sedaris continues to tell stories about his family, about living in New York, and about his life in his new home in Paris with his partner, Hugh Hamrick. His latest book, *When You Are Engulfed in Flames*, was published in 2008.

Works in Literary Context

Sedaris emerged from two traditions: humor writing and gay and lesbian literature. He was one of the first humor writers to speak and write openly about his homosexuality and yet still achieve phenomenal success. Most of his essay collections have become *New York Times* best sellers, highlighting his crossover appeal.

Humor Writing Humor writing has a long history in the United States. Newspapers and magazines in the nineteenth century published many humorous essays. The first American humorist may have been Washington Irving, who published *History of New York … by Diedrich Knickerbocker* (1809) and *The Sketch Book* (1820), both of which include exaggerated tall tales about Northeastern Americans. Mark Twain continued this American tradition of humor in *The Adventures of Tom Sawyer* (1876) and *Adventures of Huckleberry Finn* (1884). In the early twen-

tieth century, humor writing remained largely the domain of newspaper and magazine columnists, with authors like H. L. Mencken and Dorothy Parker achieving success at the *Baltimore Sun* and the *New Yorker*, respectively. By the latter half of the twentieth century, popular writers of American humor included Erma Bombeck and Dave Barry, both nationally syndicated humor columnists.

Gay and Lesbian Literature The visibility of gay and lesbian literature increased in the early twentieth century with the publication of works such as *The Well of Loneliness* (1929) by Radclyffe Hall, which was censored in Britain and nearly banned in the United States because of its lesbian theme. Gay and lesbian pulp fiction proliferated in the 1940s and 1950s, but the Stonewall riots in 1969 in New York City, credited as the beginning of the modern gay rights movement, proved a watershed for gay and lesbian writers. Openly homosexual writers of the twentieth century include Audre Lorde, Augusten Burroughs, Alice Walker, and James Baldwin. In his humorous essays, Sedaris often addresses the issues he encounters as a homosexual and his difficulties adjusting to his environment while growing up. However, he always addresses these issues for humorous effect and in a way that touches upon universal themes, such as awkwardness and the desire to fit in.

Works in Critical Context

David Sedaris has achieved recognition as not just a humorist but as a commentator on family, society, and daily life. Ira Glass was quoted in *People* magazine saying, "People come to his work because he's funny. … But there's a complicated moral vision there." Others agree, noting that beneath Sedaris's humor is often a deeper commentary. A reviewer for *Publishers Weekly* wrote, "Sedaris can hardly be called a humorist in the ordinary sense … Sedaris is instead an essayist who happens to be very funny."

Radio Monologues Sedaris's first big hit was his "SantaLand Diaries," read on the air on National Public Radio. *Booklist* critic Benjamin Segedin calls the piece a "minor classic." John Marchese writes in the *New York Times*, "Mr. Sedaris has shown remarkable skill as a mimic and the ability to mix the sweet and the bitter: to be naïve and vulnerable and at the same time, jaded and wickedly funny." *Newsweek* reviewer Jeff Giles praises Sedaris's delivery, saying his "nicely nerdy, quavering voice" is particularly effective on the radio.

Me Talk Pretty One Day Critics have noted that Sedaris's 2000 book *Me Talk Pretty One Day* is somewhat softer than his earlier work. Ira Glass writes in *Esquire*, "A lot of people think they love David for his acidic tongue … but I think it's … his skill in evoking real affection and sadness in his stories, that from the beginning brought people back for more." Michiko Kakutani also notes that much of his newer work is softer than his previous work, which she praised. "Though he still whips off tart put-downs with practiced ease ... he also shows himself capable, in these pages, of something approaching empathy and introspection." *Entertainment Weekly* writer Lisa Schwarzbaum comments, "These days Sedaris glitters as one of the wittiest writers around."

Responses to Literature

1. Sedaris writes about his own very unique experiences as a gay man growing up in the South and living in New York City. Read one of his essays. How does he relate his experiences to themes that are universal to readers?

2. Write an essay in which you compare and contrast an essay from Sedaris's first essay collection, *Barrel Fever*, and an essay from his most recent collection, *When You Are Engulfed in Flames*. How has his style or subject matter changed, if at all? Be sure to provide specific examples from each work to support your statements.

3. Compare Sedaris's writing to that of another American humorist from a different time period, such as Dorothy Parker or Mark Twain. How do the two writers differ in subject matter and style? In what ways do they cover similar literary territory?

4. Listen to a recording of one of Sedaris's spoken-word pieces, such as "The SantaLand Diaries." Does his reading of the piece add to its emotional impact? Does it make it funnier? Why or why not? How is his work different from that of a typical stand-up comedian?

BIBLIOGRAPHY

Books

"Sedaris, David." *Newsmakers.* Edited by Laura Avery. Detroit: Thomson Gale, 2005.

Periodicals

Carlin, Peter Ames. "Elf-Made Writer: Former Santa's Helper David Sedaris Turns His Odd Life into Literature." *People*, October 20, 1997.

Glass, Ira. Review of *Me Talk Pretty One Day. Esquire*, June 2000.

Kakutani, Michiko. "Books of the Times; The Zeitgeist of Cyberspace Isn't at 59th and Lex." *New York Times*, June 16, 2000.

Marchese, John. "He Does Radio and Windows." *New York Times*, July 4, 1993.

Schwarzbaum, Lisa. Review of *Me Talk Pretty One Day. Entertainment Weekly*, June 2, 2000.

Segedin, Benjamin. Review of *Barrel Fever. Booklist* (June 1, 1994).

COMMON HUMAN EXPERIENCE

Sedaris is the best known of a new generation of gay humorists. Some other similar books include:

The Little Book of Neuroses: Ongoing Trials from My Queer Life (2001), a story collection by Michael Thomas Ford. This is a book of stories in which the author pokes fun at himself and a variety of gay archetypes.

Out, Loud, & Laughing: A Collection of Gay & Lesbian Humor (1995), a collection edited by Charles Flowers. This work offers essays from fifteen contemporary gay and lesbian humorists, including Sedaris.

A Funny Time to Be Gay (1997), a nonfiction book by Ed Karvoski Jr. This book documents the development of gay and lesbian stand-up comedy and includes interviews with thirty-two lesbian and gay comics along with examples of their material.

Do What I Say: Ms. Behavior's Guide to Gay and Lesbian Etiquette (1995), a collection by Meryl Cohn. Cohn, a humor columnist for the Boston publication *Bay Windows*, here compiles her humorous etiquette writing aimed at satirizing both advice columns and the gay lifestyle.

Municipal Bondage: One Man's Anxiety-Producing Adventures (1995), an essay collection by Henry Alford. This book is a mix of original and reprinted essays about a variety of Alford's adventures in odd jobs and other absurdities.

⊛ Maurice Sendak

BORN: *1928, Brooklyn, New York*

NATIONALITY: *American*

GENRE: *Fiction*

MAJOR WORKS:
The Sign on Rosie's Door (1960)
The Nutshell Library (1962)
Where the Wild Things Are (1963)
Outside Over There (1981)
We Are All in the Dumps with Jack and Guy (1983)

Overview

During his distinguished career in children's books, Maurice Bernard Sendak has provided richly varied pictures for more than eighty works. Of this number, nineteen have been stories that the artist himself has written. As might be expected, these works provide telling insights into those qualities of mind and heart that have helped to make Sendak an international figure, possibly

Maurice Sendak   *ARMEN KATCHATURIAN / SAGA / Landov*

the preeminent children's picture-book author/illustrator of our time. Sendak is often credited with being the first author-artist to deal openly with the feelings of young children. Each of Sendak's own stories is characterized by a loving observation of, and familiarity with, the ways of real children. He has also said, "To me, illustrating means having a passionate affair with the words," and this intensity of approach goes far toward explaining his uncanny ability to make palpable the emotional reality in which his tales take place.

Works in Biographical and Historical Context

Sendak's Early Life   Sendak's childhood is especially important to an understanding of his art. He was born on June 10, 1928, in Brooklyn, New York. His parents, Philip and Sarah Schindler Sendak, were both Polish immigrants who had come to New York from small Jewish villages outside Warsaw before World War I. His sister Natalie was nine and his brother Jack was five when he was born.

Undoubtedly one of the major influences that shaped his childhood was the experience of being a first-generation American. The artist has described his childhood as includ-

ing elements from both the Old and New Worlds. On the one hand, he was exposed to the most intoxicating and bustling of modern American cities. Juxtaposed to this experience of modern American culture were his parents' memories of life in the Old Country. Sendak has said that as a child he felt himself to be a part of both his parents' past and modern American life. Both of his parents seemed to have communicated to their children a rather dark, pessimistic view of life, which Sendak appears to have spent much of his adult life trying to overcome.

Although Sendak's family was not particularly religious and usually went to synagogue only on High Holy Days, the artist's Jewish heritage has had a perceptible impact on his work. Some early reviewers of his illustrations felt that the children portrayed looked too European. Sendak affirmed that he had indeed drawn the greenhorn immigrant children he had known in Brooklyn in his youth.

Sendak was a sick child; he had a dangerous case of measles followed by double pneumonia at age two and a half and scarlet fever at age four. Frail and sickly, he remembers being terrified of death as a child. His parents were extremely anxious about his health, and Sendak was an overprotected child. Sendak's childhood was further complicated by his family's frequent moves and by his hatred of school. Perhaps because of his early illnesses and confinements in bed, Sendak developed a talent as a child for observing life. He seems to have known that he was already collecting the raw material he would use for his work.

Sendak's high school years during the 1940s were very anxious ones for the family. When Germany invaded Poland in 1939, Adolf Hitler resolved to exterminate all of the Polish Jews in death camps. By 1941 Jewish newspapers in the United States were publishing reports of Hitler's plan to kill all the Jews of Europe. Sendak's paternal grandfather died in Poland, the news arriving the day of his bar mitzvah. Philip Sendak was unsuccessful in helping any of his brothers and sisters to escape from Poland, and they all perished in the Holocaust. Other tragedies also hit the family; Natalie's fiancé, a soldier, was killed during World War II, and Jack was stationed in the Pacific. During this time, Sendak excelled in art but continued to be uninterested in other classes. He worked on the school yearbook, literary magazine, and newspaper. He also had a job with All-American Comics after school, working on background details for the "Mutt and Jeff" comic strip. During his vacations from high school, Sendak began to teach himself about illustration, and he created original drawings for a number of works including "Peter and the Wolf," "The Happy Prince," and "The Luck of Roaring Camp."

After graduating from high school in 1946, Sendak sought work as an illustrator but finally landed a full-time job in the warehouse of a Manhattan window-display company—a period he remembers as one of the happiest times in his life. Two years later he was promoted to a different department and, unhappy in this new environment, he left in the summer of 1948.

During this period of unemployment, Sendak lived at home with his parents and began seriously to sketch the street life of children he observed out of his window. He also, with his brother and sister, created models for six wooden mechanical toys. The brothers took the prototypes to the toy store F.A.O. Schwarz, where the models were admired; however, the brothers were told that the toys would be too expensive to mass produce. However, Sendak so impressed managers with his artistry that he was offered a job as an assistant in the preparation of the store's window displays. For the next three years Sendak worked at Schwarz during the day and took evening classes at the Art Student's League in oil painting, life drawing, and composition.

Early Work as an Illustrator After studying his work at F.A.O. Schwarz, the distinguished children's book editor, Ursula Nordstrom, offered Sendak the chance to illustrate Marcel Ayme's *The Wonderful Farm* (1951). This proved to be the beginning of an important personal and professional relationship for both parties. Sendak's first big success came with his illustrations for Ruth Krauss's *A Hole Is to Dig* (1952). This "concept book" has no plot; it consists of a group of children's definitions of words, collected by the author. For this book, Sendak used a small format, sepia-tinted paper, and cross-hatched pen-and-ink drawings to create a mid-nineteenth-century look. The work received excellent reviews. Encouraged by the book's success, Sendak gave up his full-time job at F.A.O. Schwarz, moved into an apartment in Greenwich Village, and became a freelance illustrator. Between 1951 and 1982 Sendak illustrated dozens of books and wrote seven of his own.

Begins to Write *Kenny's Window* (1956), the first book that Sendak wrote as well as illustrated, was published when the artist was twenty-seven years old and already an established illustrator. An overly long and diffuse tale about an imaginative child eager to discover more about the world beyond his front door, *Kenny's Window* is a treasure trove of the themes, characters, and psychological excursions that would become the core of Sendak's mature work. Undergoing psychoanalysis at the time, Sendak had become increasingly aware of the wellsprings in childhood of people's deepest fears and desires. To these influences he attributes the discovery of his prototypical child hero—and the subject that has engaged his talent and sensibility from that moment on: children who, in his own words, "are held back by life and, one way or other, manage miraculously to find release from their troubles." More introspective than any of his future heroes, Kenny escapes into dreams and fantasy to discover significant—occasionally even painful—truths about his own life.

In his next book, *Very Far Away* (1957), Sendak tells a modest, affecting story about small Martin, who must come to terms with an unexpectedly painful home truth:

his mother is so busy caring for a new baby that she has no time for him when he most craves her attention. Martin opts to run off "very far away," which, in Sendakian terms, is "many times around the block and two cellar windows from the corner." There, Martin and three new friends—a bird, a horse, and a cat—live together very happily "for an hour and a half." (Clearly the author knows how children reckon endless stretches of time and distance.) At story's end, a less sulky Martin returns home in the hope that his mother may now be free to answer at least a few of his questions.

In *The Sign on Rosie's Door* (1960), Sendak re-created the Brooklyn of his own 1930s childhood. His irrepressible Rosie, based on a real-life child Sendak once spent months observing from his Brooklyn apartment window, is a heroine capable of carrying her less imaginative cronies aloft on flights of therapeutic fancy. In this way they can happily pass summer days otherwise filled with "nothing to do."

Sendak's next work was his still popular *The Nutshell Library* (1962), a medley of four miniature volumes: a reptilian alphabet, *Alligators All Around*; a rhymed romp through the months of the year, *Chicken Soup with Rice*; a forward-backward counting book, *One Was Johnny*; and a contemporary cautionary tale, *Pierre* ("The moral of Pierre is: CARE!"). Revealing the author at his most fanciful, this quartet has been referred to by one critic as a young listener's "Compleat Companion into literacy" and shows just how much a gifted writer could expand upon conventional nursery themes.

COMMON HUMAN EXPERIENCE

A common theme running through Sendak's books is his main character's mastery of strong emotions. In *Outside Over There*, Sendak grapples with the powerful emotions of jealousy between siblings. Other stories that involve sibling rivalry include:

Tales of a Fourth Grade Nothing (1972), novel by Judy Blume. This novel follows the story of Peter and his little brother, Fudge. Peter hates his two-year-old brother, who seems always to get what he wants, even as he misbehaves badly.

The Parent Trap (1961), a film directed by David Swift. This Disney classic tells the story of identical twins who, separated as toddlers when their parents divorced, rediscover one another at summer camp. Once they discover they are sisters, their bitter rivalry disappears as they try to get their parents back together.

Dinner at the Homesick Restaurant (1982), a novel by Anne Tyler. Tyler tells the story of the Tull family of Baltimore. The father deserts his wife and children, and the two brothers develop an intense sibling rivalry when their mother openly favors one of them.

Jacob Have I Loved (1980), a novel by Katherine Paterson. This is a story about twin girls growing up in the 1940s. One twin struggles to gain recognition and a sense of self-worth apart from her prettier and talented sister.

Where the Wild Things Are (1963), which showed a child mastering "the uncontrollable and frightening aspects of his life" through the help of fantasy, won Sendak the Caldecott Medal. The story represented the culmination of his attempts to portray a child mastering frightening things through the help of fantasy. Unlike Sendak's earlier protagonists, who tended to use fantasy and daydreams as escapes from real-world emotional confrontations, the intrepid Max has a temper tantrum when his mother calls him "Wild Thing!" He then sails off to tame Wild Things of his own imagining. When he returns, the supper he didn't expect to get is waiting for him at his bedside. Though countless librarians and educators worried about the book's frightening aspects for young children—raw rage and monstrous fantasy figures—the work was an immediate success. Children seemed to find comfort in a hero who could be angry with his mother and triumph over his own rage. Sendak wrote two more books in what he considered a trilogy of children's mastery of various strong feelings: *In the Night Kitchen* (1970), whose protagonist is an angry boy who is frightened in the night, and *Outside Over There* (1985), a story of jealousy and sibling rivalry.

The intriguing and decidedly American fairytale *Higglety Pigglety Pop! or, There Must Be More to Life* (1967) begins where traditional fairy tales leave off, at "And they lived happily ever after." Jennie, the story's dog heroine, has everything—a loving master, two windows from which to enjoy the view, two pillows (one for upstairs, one for down), and two eating bowls. Yet, she announces at the story's start: "I am discontented. There must be more to life than having everything." Jennie was modeled after the author's beloved pet Sealyham. When he was working on the book, Jennie's health was failing and his own mother was dying; Sendak felt disquieting intimations of mortality, and he wanted to immortalize Jennie, perhaps himself as well. Many of Sendak's admirers feel that this is his most ambitious and poetic work. Certainly, it is the one tale in which the words have as much resonance and power as the pictures.

The artist's picture book *We Are All in the Dumps with Jack & Guy* (1983) is an apocalyptic improvisation on two little-known English nursery rhymes. With the help of an interracial cast of parentless children who live in a haunting city slum, Sendak examines poverty, violence, AIDS, and human indifference. When the book's two heroes, Jack and Guy, manage to rescue a "poor little kid" and a sackful of kittens from the clutches of two unregeneratively evil rats, they affirm their creator's lifelong view that children, with their unblinkingly honest acceptance of harsh realities and their miraculous resilience, still offer humanity's best (and possibly only) hope for redemption.

Sendak continued to publish during the 1990s and into the twenty-first century. He produced his first pop-up book, *Mommy?*, in 2006. He also illustrated *The Happy Rain* (2004), written by Jack Sendak, and *Bears!*, by Ruth Krauss (2005).

Works in Literary Context

Illustrations Drawing on the great tradition of nineteenth-century book illustration, Sendak has forged a unique visual vocabulary and artistic style, at once rooted in the past yet contemporary in spirit and approach. His early work was unusual for the period in that it was more nineteenth-century in spirit than modernist or abstract.

Fantasy Fantasy creates an alternative world for its readers. Many of Sendak's books create such a world, including the fantasy place where Max finds the Wild Things in *Where the Wild Things Are*. In this sense, Sendak can be understood as a successor to children's fantasy writers such as J. R. R. Tolkien (*The Lord of the Rings* [1954–1955]) and C. S. Lewis (*The Chronicles of Narnia* [1950–1956]). His books *Where the Wild Things Are*, *In the Night Kitchen*, and *Outside Over There* all involve the main characters' travels to another world.

Works in Critical Context

Beginning with the appearance in 1963 of Sendak's most famous and popular work, *Where the Wild Things Are*, both critical acclaim and controversy have heralded the publication of almost each new book. Credited by many critics and scholars as being the first artist to deal openly with the emotions of children, "Sendak has forthrightly confronted such sensitive subject matters as childhood anger, sexuality, or the occasionally murderous impulses of raw sibling rivalry," wrote one reviewer of his work. Sendak's honesty has troubled or frightened many who would wish to sentimentalize childhood—to shelter children from their own psychological complexity or to deny that this complexity exists.

Where the Wild Things Are Many critics hailed Sendak's Caldecott-winning book *Where the Wild Things Are* as a new type of children's literature that was not afraid to deal with the strong emotions of childhood. Mary Lystad wrote, "*Where the Wild Things Are* is a warm and witty fantasy. . . . It marks a critical point in American literature for children because it dares to present openly anger, conflict, and rage, and because it resolves these issues satisfactorily for the child." John Cech agreed, writing that the book was "electrifying, controversial, precedent setting" and that it represented "a point of departure from which there could really be no easy return to the same old forms and subjects."

However, praise for the book was not unanimous. Most criticism leveled at *Where the Wild Things Are* revolved around the frightening aspects of the book. Child psychologist Bruno Bettelheim, in *Ladies' Home Journal*, wrote that Sendak "failed to understand . . . the incredible fear it evokes in the child to be sent to bed without supper." Other critics argued that the book was "silly." J. H. Dohm wrote, "Unfortunately, some of us find his Medal winning book the most disappointing and irritating of all—obviously he was due to receive the medal before long . . . but it seemed a pity it should go first to a book of such surpassing silliness."

Responses to Literature

1. Write your own children's story in which a child escapes into a fantasy world and learns to conquer his or her fears.

2. Write an essay in which you compare the illustrations from three of Sendak's books.

3. Sendak's book *In the Night Kitchen* has frequently been challenged or banned from public or school libraries. Read the book and then write a letter to the editor of a school newspaper either in support of or against removing this book from the school library.

4. Write a review of one of the books Sendak both wrote and illustrated. In what ways does the book succeed? Does it have any weak points? Is the story interesting, the characters well developed?

BIBLIOGRAPHY

Books

Cech, John. "Max, Wild Things, and the Shadows of Childhood." In *Angels and Wild Things: The Archetypal Poetics of Maurice Sendak*. University Park: Pennsylvania State University Press, 1995.

Lanes, Selma G. *The Art of Maurice Sendak*. New York: Abrams, 1980.

Periodicals

Bettelheim, Bruno. Review of *Where the Wild Things Are*. *Ladies Home Journal*, March 1969.

Dohm, J. H. "20th Century Illustrators: Maurice Sendak." *The Junior Bookshelf* 30 (April 1966).

Lystad, Mary. "Taming the Wild Things." *Children Today* 18 (March–April 1989).

Web sites

"The Fantasy World of Maurice Sendak." Indianapolis Museum of Art. Retrieved December 5, 2008, from http://www.absolutearts.com/artsnews/1999/10/31/26082.html.

"Wild Things: The Art of Maurice Sendak." Jewish Museum. Retrieved December 5, 2008, from http://www.tfaoi.org/aa/5aa/5aa307.htm.

⊛ Dr. Seuss

BORN: *1904, Springfield, Massachusetts*

DIED: *1991, La Jolla, California*

NATIONALITY: *American*

GENRE: *Fiction*

MAJOR WORKS:
The Cat in the Hat (1957)
How the Grinch Stole Christmas (1957)
Green Eggs and Ham (1960)
The Butter Battle Book (1984)
Oh, The Places You'll Go! (1990)

Overview

Known by the pseudonym Dr. Seuss, Theodor Seuss Geisel distinguished himself as a children's author with his innate understanding of children and a genuine respect for their individuality and imagination. He is recognized for his inventiveness, diversity, humor, and lack of inhibition in the picture books he wrote and illustrated for over fifty years. Many of his works feature characters now accepted as contemporary folklore, including the Cat in the Hat and the Grinch who despises Christmas. In addition, Seuss is credited with initiating a new type of children's literature: pleasure reading for beginning and reluctant readers.

Theodor Geisel, also known as Dr. Seuss *Geisel, Theodor aka Dr. Seuss, photograph. The Library of Congress.*

Works in Biographical and Historical Context

No Talent for Art Born on March 2, 1904, Theodor Seuss Geisel grew up in Springfield, Massachusetts. He was an avid reader and loved to draw, but his childhood dream did not include becoming an author and illustrator of children's books. When Seuss was in high school, an art teacher told him that he would never learn to draw and advised him to skip the class for the rest of the semester. As an adult, Seuss maintained that his lack of formal art lessons only ensured that he would develop a distinctive style of his own.

Cartoons and Advertising After high school, Seuss attended Dartmouth College, where he became the editor of *Jack-o-Lantern*, the school's humor magazine. In the journal, Seuss contributed numerous drawings of bizarre cartoon animals, the very kinds of illustrations that would eventually appear in his children's books. With the intent of becoming an English professor, Seuss enrolled at Oxford University for graduate school, but he abandoned his literature studies when Helen Palmer, a fellow student who had watched him doodle in class, encouraged him to pursue cartooning. In addition to taking her advice, Seuss

made her his chief advisor and manager, and the two married in 1927.

The couple returned to the United States, and soon Seuss was marketing drawings and prose pieces for such magazines as *Life* and *Vanity Fair*. When one of his cartoons caught the attention of the Standard Oil Company, Seuss was contracted to illustrate billboard advertisements. Although his advertising work became famous, he still had other ambitions, which included writing serious fiction and humor for adults; however, his contract with Standard Oil prohibited outside writing except for children's books.

The Dr. Seuss Persona Is Born After writing and illustrating an ABC book, which contained all sorts of fantastic animals, Seuss could not find a publisher for it, and he did not try another children's book for four years. Written in verse inspired by the rhythm of ship engines on a transatlantic voyage, *And to Think I Saw It on Mulberry Street* (1937) introduces Seuss's fascination with the potential of a child's imagination. As with his ABC book, however, Seuss had difficulty in finding a publisher until a former Dartmouth classmate, whom he had encountered by chance, accepted the work for Vanguard Press. At this time, Seuss decided to use his middle name for his children's books, saving his last name for more serious writing. He added "Dr." as a flippant reference to the doctorate he never finished at Oxford.

War in Hollywood The outbreak of World War II forced Seuss to give up writing for children and devote his talents to the war effort. Working with the Information and Education Division of the U.S. Army in Hollywood, he made documentary films for American soldiers. One of these Army films, "Hitler Lives," won an Academy Award, a feat Seuss repeated with "Design for Death," a documentary about the Japanese war effort, and the cartoon "Gerald McBoing-Boing," featuring a little boy who can speak only in sound effects. Because filmmaking involves coordination between words and pictures, Seuss credited his experiences in Hollywood during these years as invaluable to his development as a children's book author.

Bright and Early Books In a mid-1950s article entitled "Why Johnny Can't Read," John Hersey claimed that beginning primers, such as the *Dick and Jane* series, were dull and unimaginative and made children view reading as a job rather than a pleasure. Hersey suggested that fanciful writers be recruited to create more interesting books that would still stimulate a child's vocabulary. In response, Seuss published *The Cat in the Hat*, regarded as a revolutionary work because it demonstrates that books for beginning readers can entertain children as well as teach them to read. Because of its success, Seuss founded Beginner Books, a publishing company that was later acquired by Random House with Seuss as its president. Seuss continued to publish books for the fledgling reader; by the late 1960s he was writing and illustrating "Bright and Early Books for Beginning Readers," a series for preschoolers, which emphasizes simple language and sentence structure and focuses on subject matter engaging to very young readers.

Seuss and Beginner Books created many modern classics for children, from *Green Eggs and Ham* (1960), about the need to try new experiences, to *Fox in Socks* (1965), a series of boisterous tongue-twisters, to *The Lorax* (1971), a comment on environmental preservation. In 1986, Seuss published *You're Only Old Once*, a very different kind of book that follows an elderly gentleman's examination at The Golden Age Clinic on Century Square, where he is subjected to pointless tests by merciless physicians and grim nurses. According to Seuss, who was eighty-two at the time, this story is much more autobiographical than anything else he had written. Although Theodor Geisel died on September 24, 1991, Dr. Seuss lives on, inspiring generations of children of all ages to explore the joys of reading.

Works in Literary Context

According to scholar Heinz Insu Fenkl, "Seuss was always quite honest about his rhetorical intentions. He referred directly to the influence of writers like Belloc, Swift, and Voltaire, and did not hesitate to refer to his own radical and revolutionary ideas." His literary tools include rhyme, rhythm, onomatopoeia, and the invention of words, all of which influenced such children's writers as Jack Prelutsky and Shel Silverstein.

Positive Messages for Children   Even at his most extravagant, Seuss centered his works around positive values. Many of his books contain veiled moral statements that balance the zaniness of his characters and situations. Concerned thematically with creativity, tenacity, loyalty, and self-confidence, Seuss also explores political and social issues such as racial and religious prejudice, conservation, and the nuclear arms race. Seuss typically leaves his readers with a lighthearted optimism. In both *The Cat in the Hat* and *Green Eggs and Ham*, for example, Seuss pushes the limits of good behavior and common sense, permits the chaotic consequences, then careens back to a safe and familiar world. However, his satire on the possibility of nuclear war, *The Butter Battle Book* (1984), deviates from this lighthearted approach in its ethical lesson. A thinly disguised portrayal of the United States and Russia, the work presents readers with an open ending: two characters from opposing countries stand poised on a dividing wall, each figure holding a bomb. Seuss said that the ending of *The Butter Battle Book* is up to the adults of the world, a philosophy that generated much controversy but did not affect the book's popularity.

Works in Critical Context

Critics admire Seuss's works for their remarkable ingenuity, as well as their brilliant integration of text and illustration. Praised as an outstanding nonsense poet and storyteller whose books are ideal for reading aloud, he is also considered a moralist who offers children a positive and enthusiastic view of life. While some critics view Seuss's

---

LITERARY AND HISTORICAL CONTEMPORARIES

Dr. Seuss's famous contemporaries include:

P. D. Eastman (1909–1986): Known for such children's books as *Are You My Mother?* (1960) and *Go Dog. Go!* (1961), Eastman was a leading writer for the Dr. Seuss Beginner Books line.

Benjamin Spock (1903–1998): Spock was a U.S. physician who published *The Common Sense Book of Baby and Childcare* (1946), which encourages parents to be gentle and affectionate with their children.

Charles M. Schulz (1922–2000): This American cartoonist is best known for his *Peanuts* comic strip, featuring the characters Charlie Brown and Snoopy.

Kornei Chukovsky (1901–1969): Because of its simplicity, playfulness, and mischief that appeals to children, the work of this Russian children's book author has been compared to that of Dr. Seuss.

Louis Armstrong (1901–1971): This musician pioneered a new style of jazz called scat singing, which consists of vocal improvisation that imitates the sounds of instruments.

---

involvement with beginning readers as a limit to his creativity, most academics agree with journalist Miles Corwin, who says, "[Seuss] has had a tremendous impact on children's reading habits and the way reading is taught and approached in the school system." Although some critics disapprove of his unconventional English and unschooled art, most praise Seuss as an imaginative genius.

The Butter Battle Book   Accustomed to the light-hearted, whimsical side of Seuss, the public was shocked by 1984's *The Butter Battle Book*, which introduces children to the Cold War and the nuclear arms race. Focusing primarily on the book's content and not on its literary merit, critics and parents alike have questioned the appropriateness of Seuss's topic for a children's book. Such concern is reflected in the comments of reviewer Anne L. Okie: "The language of the story rhymes and amuses in customary Seuss fashion … one wonders, however, if a book for young children is a suitable vehicle for such an accurate and uncloaked description of the current stalemate in nuclear disarmament." Particularly disturbing to readers is the ending because it offers no resolution, an issue that incited the ire of reviewer David R. Bechtel: "I was … angry at Dr. Seuss, the storyteller, for tricking me." Indeed, the man who shows children how to escape reality by the power of their creative imagination in so many other books appears to see no creative antidote for the modern threat of nuclear war.

Despite concerns from critics and the general public, *The Butter Battle Book* was overwhelmingly successful,

COMMON HUMAN EXPERIENCE

Writing in a variety of forms, Seuss often narrates his works in rhythmic, repetitious verse that includes many examples of wordplay and word invention. Here are some works by other writers who are known for their linguistic play:

"Jabberwocky" (1871), a poem by Lewis Carroll. Considered by many to be the greatest nonsense poem in English, "Jabberwocky" introduced such invented words as "chortled" into the English language.

The Book of Nonsense (1846), verse by Edward Lear. Popularizing the limerick form, this collection features fantastical poems reflecting the poet's delight in the sounds of both real and imaginary words.

Where the Sidewalk Ends (1974), poetry by Shel Silverstein. This humorous—yet profound—collection of poems, all illustrated by Silverstein, introduces readers to preposterous situations, including a boy who turns into a television and a crocodile that goes to the dentist.

and Seuss won a Pulitzer Prize the year it was published. Admirers of the book point out that Seuss had always been a moralist, taking stands against prejudice, tyranny, ecological abuse, and other flaws in human beings. In *The Butter Battle Book*, they contend, Seuss takes a tough moral stand in showing children that their elders have been foolish and that their foolishness threatens the survival of the world. As John Garvey notes, "The book's description of the illogical nature of the arms race is uncomfortably true: there really is something crazy about what we have done and continue to do."

Responses to Literature

1. *The Lorax* carries within it a powerful message about protecting the environment. How does the situation depicted in the book relate to the environmental situation in modern society? How do you think cultural attitudes toward protecting the environment have changed since the book was first written?

2. Read *Green Eggs and Ham*. What techniques does Seuss use to encourage young readers to expand their horizons beyond things with which they are already familiar?

3. Early in his career, Seuss made a name for himself for creating advertising slogans and illustrations. Choose an item in your backpack—a pencil, a ruler, paper, a book, etc.—and create a billboard for that item using your own original slogan and illustrations.

4. Investigate the Cold War and the nuclear arms race. Based on your findings, why do you think *The Butter Battle Book* stirred such controversy? In your opinion, is the topic appropriate for a children's book? Do you believe the book would evoke the same reaction today? Find examples of children's books published within the past ten years that have tackled controversial topics, and compare them to the reception of *The Butter Battle Book*.

BIBLIOGRAPHY

Books

Bader, Barbara. *American Picturebooks from Noah's Ark to the Beast Within*. New York: Macmillan, 1976.

Greene, Carol. *Dr. Seuss: Writer and Artist for Children*. Chicago: Children's Press, 1993.

Lystad, Mary. *From Dr. Mather to Dr. Seuss: 200 Years of American Books for Children*. Boston: G. K. Hall, 1980.

MacCann, Donnaroe, and Olga Richard. *The Child's First Books*. New York: Wilson, 1973.

MacDonald, Ruth K. *Dr. Seuss*. Boston: Twayne, 1988.

White, Mary Lou. *Children's Literature: Criticism and Response*. Columbus, Ohio: Merrill, 1976.

Periodicals

Bechtel, Daniel R. "Dr. Seuss, Prophet to Giant-Killers." *The Christian Century* vol. 101, no. 12 (April 11, 1984): 359.

Garvey, John. "Guns & Butter: Dr. Seuss's Liberal Sentimentality." *Commonweal* vol. CXI, no. 14 (August 10, 1984): 423–424.

Okie, Anne L. "*The Butter Battle Book* (book review)." *School Library Journal* (May 1984): 24.

Web sites

Fenkl, Heinz Insu. *The Secret Alchemy of Dr. Seuss*. Retrieved October 8, 2008, from http://www.endicott-studio.com/rdrm/forseus.html.

◉ Anne Sexton

BORN: *1928, Newton, Massachusetts*

DIED: *1974, Weston, Massachusetts*

NATIONALITY: *American*

GENRE: *Poetry*

MAJOR WORKS:

To Bedlam and Part Way Back (1960)
All My Pretty Ones (1962)
Love Poems (1969)
Transformations (1971)
The Death Notebooks (1974)

Anne Sexton   *Sexton, Anne, 1962, photograph. AP Images.*

Overview

Anne Sexton began writing poetry at age twenty-eight as a form of psychotherapy; by the time of her suicide at age forty-five she had become a major figure in postwar American poetry. Her work was intimate, confessional, comic, formally complex, and psychologically acute; her popular public readings were spectacles of performance art. Admired by peers for her technical skill and compelling imagery, Sexton won most of the prizes available to American poets. She also gained, for a poet, an exceptionally wide audience of readers. Her poetry was distinctive in its straightforward treatment of mental illness and prosperous suburban life in the era of the Vietnam War and the sexual revolution in America.

Works in Biographical and Historical Context

Poetry as Therapy   Sexton was born Anne Gray Harvey on November 9, 1928, in Newton, Massachusetts. She was educated in a variety of schools, both public and private, including a finishing school in Boston. She left after her first year to elope with Alfred Muller "Kayo" Sexton II, in 1948. After their marriage, Kayo Sexton joined Anne's father's wool business as a salesman, and the Sextons made their home in Newton Lower Falls and in Weston, Massachusetts. They had two daughters, Linda, born 1953, and Joyce, born 1956.

Shortly after the birth of her second child, Sexton began psychiatric treatment for what was initially diagnosed as postpartum depression. She became dangerously suicidal and was hospitalized, and her children were removed from her care. Her psychiatrist encouraged her to take up writing as a way of strengthening self–esteem. Sexton found writing poetry and engaging in psychotherapy to be oddly similar activities, each requiring a fine sensitivity to the ways language works, and the multiple meanings behind words. Writing, she later explained in a lecture, "is like lying on the analyst's couch, re-enacting a private terror, and the creative mind is the analyst who gives pattern and meaning to what the persona sees as only incoherent experience."

Developing Her Talent   Having little background in literature and little training as a writer, Sexton enrolled in a night–school course at the Boston Center for Adult Education in 1957, where she met the poets Maxine Kumin, George Starbuck, and John Clellon Holmes. The four of them met regularly in an informal workshop after the course at the Boston Center ended; Sexton's emerging talent flourished in the environment of their praise and criticism. She called her newfound purpose in life "a kind of rebirth at twenty–nine."

Sexton's development as an artist got its first major push when she received a scholarship to the Antioch Writers' Conference in the summer of 1958. There she studied with the poet W. D. Snodgrass, whose enthusiastic recommendation helped Sexton gain admission that fall to Robert Lowell's writing seminar at Boston University. The poet, Sylvia Plath, also joined Lowell's seminar that year, and she and Sexton became friends. Observing the positive impact that Plath's suicide in 1963 had on her reputation as an artist, Sexton felt cheated that Plath got there first, telling her doctor, "that death was mine!"

Lowell's influence on Sexton's career continued, as he helped her select the contents of her first volume, *To Bedlam and Part Way Back* (1960) and get it published. The Boston publishing house of Houghton Mifflin accepted the book just as Lowell's seminar was ending in May 1959, and he remained her American publisher throughout her career. Lowell's blurb on the cover helped bring the book to national attention; the poems that spoke frankly and eloquently of mental illness, such as "You, Dr. Martin" and "Music Swims Back to Me," were particularly singled out. Most of the reviews were respectful, and *To Bedlam and Part Way Back* was nominated for the prestigious National Book Award that year. Sexton had soared from complete obscurity to major recognition, a mere three and a half years after writing her first poems in therapy.

Expanding Beyond Home   Sexton's career passed another significant milestone with her appointment in 1961 as a scholar of the Radcliffe Institute, founded that year to encourage college–educated housewives to reenter the intellectual labor force. Sexton was something of a "maverick" among the Radcliffe scholars: she had no college education and had received her artistic training

LITERARY AND HISTORICAL CONTEMPORARIES

Sexton's famous contemporaries include:

Sylvia Plath (1932–1963): American poet. Like Sexton, Plath struggled with mental illness and alluded to depression in her writing. Although she is primarily known as a poet, her semi-autobiographical novel, *The Bell Jar* (1963), is probably her most famous work.

Robert Lowell (1917–1977): American poet. A mentor to Sexton, Lowell, a founder of "confessional poetry," was one of the most important American poets of the twentieth century. Like his mentee, he suffered from alcoholism and depression.

Betty Friedan (1921–2006): American feminist and writer. With the publication of *The Feminine Mystique* in 1963, Friedan helped launch the modern feminist movement. Friedan later cofounded the National Organization for Women, a group dedicated to achieving equality for men and women in all aspects of society.

Oliver Sachs (1933–): British neurologist. Sachs writes about serious brain illnesses in an engaging style that has brought him popular and critical acclaim. The most famous of his books is *Awakenings* (1973), a chronicle of his work with patients suffering from Encephalitis lethargica.

Jack Kevorkian (1928–): American pathologist. Kevorkian challenged medical ethics by providing assisted suicides to some 130 patients with terminal illnesses. Kevorkian was convicted of first–degree homicide in 1999, but was released after eight years in prison.

on the job. The two years Sexton spent as a fellow of the Radcliffe Institute provided her with the collegiality of a variety of other professional women and her first contact with feminist thought, which was undergoing a renaissance in the early 1960s. Under the influence of Olsen, Sexton discovered Virginia Woolf's *A Room of One's Own* (1929), a feminist classic whose imagined idea of Shakespeare's sister wondered whether, had Shakespeare been born a woman, the world would now have her poems and plays. Sexton also encountered Betty Friedan's newly published book *The Feminine Mystique* (1963), which became a major topic of debate among the scholars.

Sexton's next book, *All My Pretty Ones* (1962), strengthened her national reputation and garnered international attention as well. Despite her impressive achievements, Sexton continued to suffer from debilitating bouts of depression. Her condition had worsened in 1960 after the deaths of both her parents within a few months of one another; she was now seeing her psychiatrist three times a week. He began taping their sessions and required her to replay them and take notes. The years of taping (1961 to

1964) were to have a profound effect on Sexton's writing, which became looser, more shaped by the rhythms of speech than by metrical norms. She also became interested in writing for the theater, an interest that resulted in three plays, all versions of the same story, in which a young woman, Daisy, seeks out refuge from her suicidal despair, first in religion, and then in psychotherapy.

Though only the third version of the play, *Mercy Street* (1969), was produced, and never published, dramatic writing would shape the rest of Sexton's career. More and more, Sexton wrote poems that were dramatic monologues intended for performance—her own. Her third volume of poems, *Live or Die* (1966), contained a mixture of formal verse and a more rambling, associational mode of free verse that many critics saw as undisciplined. Poems that seemed shapeless on the page could be animated by a live reading, and the active poetry circuit of the time was lucrative for a poet who could please a crowd. Sexton, an exceptionally effective reader, had become, by the mid-1960s, a well–paid act. At rallies organized to protest the war in Vietnam, Sexton always read a poem celebrating the puberty of her elder daughter, Linda ("Little Girl, My Stringbean, My Lovely Woman"), which often seemed more to the point than work in a didactic or angry mode. By 1968, Sexton had added music to her performances. Traveling with a "chamber rock" group christened "Anne Sexton and Her Kind," Sexton, dressed in a glamorous evening dress, chanted her poetry in well–rehearsed collaboration with five musicians playing flute, keyboards, guitar, bass, and drums. The group disbanded in 1971 after a handful of concerts, largely because Sexton found travel disorienting and fatiguing.

In Her Prime In 1967 *Live or Die* was awarded the Pulitzer Prize for poetry. Sexton, at thirty–eight, was in her prime. During the next three years she wrote the books that remain her best sellers: *Love Poems* (1969) and *Transformations* (1971). *Love Poems* gave American literature its first fully sexual heroine; its poems tell the story of an affluent wife and mother emboldened by the sexual revolution in the wake of the Kennedy assassination. *Love Poems's* significance comes not just from the theme of adultery, but from its female point of view, which upends the tradition of women being punished for their adultery in literature, rather than empowered by it.

Sexton's second most popular book was *Transformations*, which consists of seventeen narrative poems based on the Grimm brothers' fairy tales. A work of black humor narrated by "a middle–aged witch, me," it draws on Sexton's years of psychotherapy in retelling the stories of such stories as "Briar Rose" (which explains a daughter's fear of going to bed), "Rapunzel" (which accounts for a girl's willing entrapment by a seductive older woman), and "Snow White" (in which a cold, neglectful mother is punished). *Transformations* was a popular success, even if it received little critical attention and represented a departure from Sexton's usual style: it contained no evidently "confessional" poetry.

A number of teaching experiences—from public schools to a mental institution—led Sexton to take a position teaching creative writing at Boston University in 1970. By 1972, after receiving a number of honorary doctorates, Sexton was promoted to full professor. The following year she was appointed to a prestigious chair of poetry at Colgate University, which she held during the spring of 1972. But by the early 1970s, Sexton's mental health, never secure, had begun deteriorating noticeably under the influence of alcohol and pills. The divorce from her husband of twenty–four years and a deepening sense of isolation only made things worse, and she began organizing her literary estate. She felt her death was imminent, but still had a few more books to complete. *The Book of Folly* (1972), with its surreal poems of the unconscious, is a foray into experimental form. *The Death Notebooks* (1974) investigates Sexton's lifelong fixation on death. Her last book, *The Awful Rowing Toward God* (1975), was completed in a month–long whirlwind of writing; she finished correcting the proofs on October 4, 1974. That same afternoon she committed suicide by parking her car in her garage and letting it idle.

Works in Literary Context

"Confessional" Poetry   Though poetry had long revolved around personal themes—love, mourning, etcetera—the 1950s ushered in a new kind of personal writing dubbed "confessional" poetry. Pioneered by such poets as W.D. Snodgrass and Robert Lowell, both of whom served as teachers and mentors to Sexton, the genre allowed for a new honesty and directness, exploring and exposing the rawest, and at times, ugliest of emotional experiences. While confessional poetry allowed for a refreshing authenticity that could be just as cathartic for readers as it was for the poets, the confessional mode was not without its critics. Some thought it was undisciplined, with form and decorum seemingly thrown to the wind. Poets like Sylvia Plath and Allen Ginsberg managed to fit their deeply autobiographical writing into traditional forms, and others, including Sexton, helped to redefine rhythm in the cadences of spoken language, and shifted new emphasis onto the sounds and suggestiveness of the words themselves.

Works in Critical Context

All My Pretty Ones   *All My Pretty Ones*, completed during Sexton's term at Radcliffe, is often judged to be her best book, winning gratifying praise from many poets: Sylvia Plath wrote in a personal letter that it was "womanly in the greatest sense," and Elizabeth Bishop wrote in another letter that it was "harrowing, awful, very real—and very good." However, the book was savaged in *Poetry* by James Dickey for "dwell[ing] ... insistently on the pathetic and disgusting aspects of bodily experience." Sexton's art was always going to be judged more on content than on form.

COMMON HUMAN EXPERIENCE

Sexton's struggle with suicidal depression was what prompted her to write, and it formed the subject matter of much of her poetry. Here are some other works that explore mental illness:

The Bell Jar (1963), a novel by Sylvia Plath. Plath, Sexton's friend and fellow poet, chronicles her harrowing experience with mental illness, early suicide attempts, and a stay in a mental hospital in this semi-autobiographical novel. It was not published in her name until three years after her 1963 suicide.

Hamlet (c. 1600), a play by William Shakespeare. The sanity or insanity of the title character of *Hamlet*, perhaps Shakespeare's best–known work, is one of the play's central mysteries. Ghost sightings, paranoid thoughts, erratic behavior, and contemplations of suicide: is Hamlet mad, or is his response to extreme circumstances the only sane choice?

One Flew Over the Cuckoo's Nest (1962), a novel by Ken Kesey, made into an Academy Award–winning film by Milos Forman and starring Jack Nicholson (1975). Set in a mental hospital, Kesey's novel investigates the heavy-handed approach to treating mental illness that dominated the field in the 1950s, and the effects of such therapies as electroshock treatment and tranquilizers on patients, while exploring the interrelation of authority and mental health.

A Beautiful Mind (2001), a film directed by Ron Howard. *A Beautiful Mind* is based on the true story of John Forbes Nash, a brilliant mathematician whose personal life was severely compromised by the paranoid schizophrenia he developed in adulthood. Refusing to be treated with drugs, Nash eventually found a way to live with his illness, and bounced back enough to earn a Nobel Prize in Economics.

Live or Die   Dissent among the reviewers continued with the appearance of *Live or Die*, Sexton's best-known book. *A Virginia Quarterly Review* critic believed that Sexton was "a very talented poet" who was perhaps too honest:

Confession, while good for the soul, may become tiresome for the reader if not accompanied by the suggestion that something is being held back. ... In [*Live or Die*] Miss Sexton's toughness approaches affectation. Like a drunk at a party who corners us with the story of his life, ... the performance is less interesting the third time, despite the poet's high level of technical competence.

Joel Conarroe, however, had a more positive view of Sexton's candor.

Miss Sexton is an interior voyager, describing in sharp images the difficult discovered landmarks of her own inner landscape. . . . Poem after poem focuses on the nightmare obsessions of the damned: suicide, crucifixion, the death of others. . . . It is, though, through facing up to the reality (and implications) of these things that the poet, with her tough honesty, is able to gain a series of victories over them. . . . All in all, this is a fierce, terrible, beautiful book, well deserving its Pulitzer award.

Responses to Literature

1. Sexton often dramatized her poetry at popular live performances; listen to the audiobook *Anne Sexton Reads* (1999), recorded shortly before her death, after you have read the poems. Listen for emphasis, pronunciation, and rhythm, and write a short paper in which you discuss the poet's approach to the reading. How are the poems different on the page than on the tape?

2. Sexton's first book of poems, *To Bedlam and Part Way Back* (1960), was praised for its evocation of mental illness. How do the poems manage to do this? Read the poems carefully and write an essay, using specific examples, on the book's portrait of mental illness.

3. By committing suicide, Sexton joined a long line of artists who secured their own legacy with one fatal gesture, from Thomas Chatterton in 1770 to David Foster Wallace in 2008. Using your library and the Internet, research suicide among literary figures, and write a paper. Why do they do it? What is the effect of their deaths on the popular and critical reputation of their work?

BIBLIOGRAPHY

Books

Bixler, Frances, ed. *Original Essays on the Poetry of Anne Sexton*. Conway: University of Central Arkansas Press, 1988.

Conarroe, Joel. *Eight American Poets: An Anthology*. New York: Random House, 1994.

George, Diana Hume. *Oedipus Anne: The Poetry of Anne Sexton*. Urbana: University of Illinois Press, 1986.

Hall, Caroline King Barnard. *Anne Sexton*. Boston: Twayne, 1989.

McClatchy, J. D., ed. *Anne Sexton: The Artist and Her Critics*. Bloomington: Indiana University Press, 1978.

Middlebrook, Diane Wood. *Anne Sexton: A Biography*. Boston: Houghton Mifflin, 1991.

Sexton, Linda Gray. *Searching for Mercy Street: My Journey Back to My Mother, Anne Sexton*. New York: Little, Brown, 1994.

Wagner–Martin, Linda, ed. *Critical Essays on Anne Sexton*. Boston: G. K. Hall, 1989.

Periodicals

Poulin, A. Jr. "A Memorial for Anne Sexton." *American Poetry Review*, May/June 1975.

Review of *Live or Die*. *Virginia Quarterly Review*, Winter 1967.

Ntozake Shange

BORN: *1948, Trenton, New Jersey*

NATIONALITY: *American*

GENRE: *Drama, fiction, poetry*

MAJOR WORKS:

For Colored Girls Who Have Considered Suicide/ When the Rainbow Is Enuf (1978)
nappy edges (1978)
Three Pieces (1981)
Betsey Brown: A Novel (1985)

Overview

Ntozake Shange is an influential African American playwright, poet, and novelist who created a new theatrical

Ntozake Shange   *Shange, Ntozake, 1976, photograph. AP Images.*

form that she named the "choreopoem": a merging of poetry, prose, song, dance, and music that grew out of her experiences as an African American woman. In the years since her first choreopoem, the award-winning *For Colored Girls Who Have Considered Suicide/When the Rainbow Is Enuf* (1978), was produced in New York, Shange has contributed her writing, directing, performing, and teaching talents to theaters and universities around the country, and she has created a distinguished and substantial body of dramatic work.

Works in Biographical and Historical Context

A Young Life of Adversity and Inspiration   Shange was born Paulette Williams on October 18, 1948, in Trenton, New Jersey, to surgeon Paul T. Williams (for whom she was named) and Eloise Williams, a psychiatric social worker and educator. Shange, the oldest of four children, had a middle-class upbringing that was marked by educational opportunities and important cultural influences. Her family's affluence did not shield her from experiencing racism as a child, however. When Shange was eight years old, her family moved to St. Louis, Missouri, where they lived for five years. Although St. Louis offered Shange the things that she liked best, such as opera, music, dance, literature, and art, she experienced much disappointment as she struggled against rejection and abuse in the then-segregated city. Until the landmark 1954 *Brown versus the Board of Education of Topeka* court decision, Shange and other African American children attended different schools than white students. That ruling desegregated schools, and instituted programs to bus African American students to formerly all-white schools. As a result, the eight-year-old Shange was transferred to a German American school where blatant racism abounded. There, Shange was forced to struggle with bigotry at a young age, including a teacher's denouncement of the work of influential African American poets Langston Hughes and Paul Lawrence Dunbar.

Shange adjusted and even formed tenacious bonds to St. Louis. She also had a rich intellectual and family life to fall back on. Always an avid reader, Shange's earliest favorite authors were Mark Twain, Herman Melville, Simone de Beauvoir, and Jean Genet, as well as Harlem Renaissance writers including Hughes and Countee Cullen. In addition to her exposure to literary giants, Shange also came in contact with the thriving African American cultural community. She met musicians and singers like Dizzy Gillespie, Chuck Berry, Charlie Parker, Miles Davis, and Josephine Baker, all of whom were friends of her parents. W. E. B. DuBois was also a family visitor.

After five years in St. Louis, the family returned to New Jersey, where Shange completed high school and went on to attend Barnard College, graduating with honors and a bachelor's degree in American studies in 1970. She enrolled at the University of Southern California in

Los Angeles and was awarded a master's degree in American studies in 1973. Despite her academic success, these years were marked by depression, a failed first marriage, and several suicide attempts that were partly a result of her struggle with feelings of rage against a society that devalued women and people of color.

Finding Strength and Solidarity on Stage   An important turning point in her life came in 1971, when she changed her name from Paulette Williams to Ntozake Shange (pronounced en-toh-ZAHK-kay SHONG-gay). Adopted from the Xhosa language, the name demonstrates a commitment to her African heritage and her resolution to build for herself a new and stronger identity: Ntozake means "she who comes with her own things" and Shange means "one who walks like a lion." Shange's name change was a way of redefining herself apart from the European and patriarchal cultures that she felt were oppressing her. After her name change, Shange moved to the San Francisco Bay area to seek out other women with whom she could share her experiences and her artistic vision. During this time, the Black Arts movement was gaining momentum and impacting American culture. The movement was an offshoot of the civil rights and Black Power movements, and emphasized an embracing of African cultural heritage.

Shange taught humanities, women's studies, and ethnic studies at several colleges from 1972 to 1975. She pursued the study of women's mythology, women's literature, and women's language. She danced and recited poetry in several African American dance companies, and was inspired to start her own company called For Colored Girls Who Have Considered Suicide. In the summer of 1974, Shange began to work on a series of seven poems to give voice to seven nameless women whose stories would represent a range of emotions and experiences. These poems eventually become Shange's first and best-known choreopoem, *For Colored Girls Who Have Considered Suicide/When the Rainbow Is Enuf* (1975). Shange transformed the poetry collage into a theatrical work that was performed at various venues in California before she and choreographer Paula Moss moved to New York and produced the show in an off-Broadway theater in July of 1975. The work continued to transform as it moved to Broadway in 1976, where it played for two years. After the Broadway show closed, touring companies took the production around the United States, Canada, and the Caribbean. Shange's choreopoem had a total of 867 New York performances, 747 of which were on Broadway.

Stories of Living and Surviving   In *For Colored Girls Who Have Considered Suicide*, seven women designated only by the colors (brown, yellow, orange, red, purple, blue, and green) take turns telling stories that reveal the pain and complexity of "bein alive & bein a woman & bein colored." In their stories, the women communicate the pain of living along with the triumph of surviving. Shange earned several awards for *For Colored Girls Who Have Considered Suicide*, including an Obie Award, the Outer

LITERARY AND HISTORICAL CONTEMPORARIES

Shange's famous contemporaries include:

Sonia Sanchez (1934–): American poet, playwright, essayist, and professor, Sanchez has published more than a dozen books of poetry as well as numerous plays, children's books, and anthologies.

Amiri Baraka (1934–): An American poet, playwright, and essayist, Baraka is the founder of the American Black Arts movement.

Sam Shepard (1934–): Shepard is an American playwright, actor, and screenwriter. Shepard is a key figure in twentieth-century theater, and he has also written and acted in numerous films.

Wendy Wasserstein (1950–): American playwright Wasserstein has won the Tony Award and Pulitzer Prize for her plays that deal with the complexities of gender, race, and class.

August Wilson (1945–2005): A Pulitzer Prize winner, playwright Wilson is well known for his sophisticated, engaging dramas about African American life.

Critics Circle Award for drama, an Audelco Award, and the Mademoiselle Award. The work also received Tony, Grammy, and Emmy nominations. Although the play enjoyed critical and commercial success, some unfavorable reviews questioned Shange's technique, noting the lack of traditional character development and linear plot structure. Many critics also challenged Shange's negative depiction of black men and relationships in the play. Shange has depicted many varieties of male and female characters and relationships in subsequent works.

Shange was uncomfortable with the public sensation created by the show, and resisted the fame it brought her. She continued to pursue her writing career and married for a second time, to musician David Murray in 1977. The couple had a daughter, Savannah, but the marriage was later dissolved. In the wake of the success of *For Colored Girls Who Have Considered Suicide*, Shange published poetry and fiction while continuing to write pieces for the theater. In 1976, she published *Sassafrass: A Novella*, followed by a volume of poetry titled *nappy edges* in 1978. *Sassafrass* was expanded and republished in 1982 as *Sassafrass, Cypress & Indigo: A Novel*. Shange also became an outspoken black feminist, appearing in newspapers and magazines that included *The Detroit Free Press*, *Black American Literature Forum*, and *Ms*.

Decades of Creative and Challenging Work

Throughout the 1980s, Shange produced a wide range of work. Her 1980 adaptation of Bertolt Brecht's play *Mother Courage and Her Children* (1941) earned Shange a second Obie Award. She set her version in post–Civil War America, recasting Mother Courage as an emancipated slave. In 1981, she published the poetry collection *Three Pieces* and won the *Los Angeles Times* Book Prize for poetry. In 1985, Shange published her second novel, *Betsey Brown*, a coming-of-age tale that is her most traditional text.

In the past two decades, Shange has applied her enormous imagination and energy to the production of works in every major genre, including children's literature. *Whitewash* (1997) tells the story of a young girl, Helene-Angel, who is assaulted with white paint by a group of boys. The story is based on two separate real-life incidents in which children in New York City were accosted by gang members and spray-painted white. Her other children's books include *Daddy Says* (2003) and *Ellington Was Not a Street* (2004). In 1994, she published her third novel *Liliane: Resurrection of the Daughter*, that was later adapted for the stage.

She explored yet another genre with her 1998 cookbook, *If I Can Cook/You Know God Can*. The volume is filled with recipes she collected from black cultures of North and South America and the Caribbean, blended with a discussion of history, literature, vernacular, culture, and philosophy. Her effort to convey to readers the connections among the varied cultures that make up the African Diaspora is rooted in the same impulse that led her to combine diverse artistic media in most, if not all, of her works. Her creative efforts continued to earn her national recognition: she was the recipient of the Lila Wallace-Reader's Digest Writers Award from 1992 to 1995, and held the Heavyweight Poetry Champion of the World title, awarded at the Taos Poetry Circus poetry festival, from 1991 to 1993.

From the beginning of her writing career, Shange has determined her artistic course by reflecting on her experience as a black woman in America. Although *For Colored Girls Who Have Considered Suicide/When the Rainbow Is Enuf* remains her most successful and most often revived work, Shange has proved to be a prolific and versatile writer. Her work defies generic categorization; her proven ability to traverse the boundaries of poetry, playwriting, dance, and music is her greatest legacy. Her theatrical experimentation has enlarged the American dramatic canon and has encouraged other writers to take up their places in a theatrical tradition enriched and expanded by the perspectives that Shange has spent her career exploring.

Works in Literary Context

A New Theatrical Paradigm With *For Colored Girls Who Have Considered Suicide/When the Rainbow Is Enuf*, Shange created a new type of theatrical form, the choreopoem, which combined poetry, drama, dance, and improvisation. Shange deliberately created the choreopoem to break away from Western theatrical traditions, including naturalism and linear plot structures. Shange's innovations can be regarded in the larger category of experimental theater, but it differs from many products of experimental theater in that it is a deliberate attempt to create a form to capture the distinctive voice and experiences of women of color.

Works in Critical Context

Shange's works present a contradiction to critics. She set out to be something other than a playwright, denying her connection to that term and the limitations that a European dramatic tradition imposes on those who choose to work in it. Yet, many critics insist on evaluating her work according to that tradition and have consequently found her work lacking in dramatic form. Despite that criticism, Shange has remained true to her vision of what black theater is and has concentrated on creating her own unique dramatic form. As a result, the critical consensus is that Shange has expanded the definition of American drama. As critic Barbara Frey concludes, "These linguistic and generic innovations of Shange, then, resist the 'anxiety of influence' of white/male and even black/male literary texts, enabling her to write of black women's experiences freshly and empathetically."

For Colored Girls Who Have Considered Suicide/ When the Rainbow Is Enuf Shange's choreopoem is powerful and provocative in many respects and has been highly praised by numerous critics, yet it shows weaknesses in terms of depth of content and character development. The critical divide is as much about Shange's vision and articulation of what theater, especially black theater, should do. Shange replaces the emphasis on individuated, realistic characters of Western drama with a more fluid design in keeping with the dance, music, and poetry of the piece. Critic Neal Lester sums up much critical analysis about the unconventional nature of the play, arguing that, with "minimal attention to traditional plot development, Shange focuses instead on the discussions, attitudes, and behaviors of these black individuals, particularly as they recognize and acknowledge their sexuality as essential parts of their identities."

Liliane: A Resurrection of the Daughter Shange's third novel is a portrait of an African American artist who explores her cultural and sexual identity. The novel combines traditional narrative with multiple points of view, as well as dialogue between the title character and her therapist. Critics have praised Shange for her structural and literary innovations in the novel to discuss complex social, historical, and personal influences on relationships and identity. Critic Deirdre Nelson writes, "Not a polemic, the novel nevertheless is political as well as poetic: *Liliane* joyfully celebrates the complexity of sexual relationships, the dynamics of family and friendship, and the emerging multicultural ethos that is America."

Responses to Literature

1. What role does language play in the development of character and identity in *For Colored Girls Who Have Considered Suicide/When the Rainbow Is Enuf?*

COMMON HUMAN EXPERIENCE

In Shange's work, she explores the meaning, experience, and complexities of being both an African American and a woman. Here are some other works that focus on the interrelationship of race and gender in African American women's experiences:

Annie Allen (1949), a poetry collection by Gwendolyn Brooks. This Pulitzer Prize–winning volume is a series of individual poems telling the story of an African American girl's journey into womanhood.

The Color Purple (1982), a novel by Alice Walker. This novel that self-consciously explores the life of several black women in America won the National Book Award and the Pulitzer Prize for fiction.

Praisesong for the Widow (1983), a novel by Paule Marshall. This novel focuses on a widow's journey through the Caribbean to explore her cultural identity.

Fires in the Mirror (1993), a play by Anna Deavere Smith. Smith used a documentary style of theater to dramatize the 1991 Crown Heights Riot in New York. She modeled characters from interviews with real people and inhabited them on stage to explore the intersections of race, class, gender, and religion.

---

2. In *Liliane*, Shange tells the story from multiple points of view. What impact does this type of storytelling have on your understanding of the character? How does your perception or viewpoint change as you read the novel?

3. Dance is a recurring motif throughout many of Shange's plays, poems, and novels. Find examples of her use of dance in non-stage works such as poems and novels. What do you think is the meaning and importance of dance as a mode of expression in Shange's works?

BIBLIOGRAPHY

Books

Geis, Deborah R. "Distraught Laughter: Monologue in Ntozake Shange's Theater Pieces." *Feminine Focus: The New Women Playwrights*. New York and Oxford: Oxford University Press, 1989.

Lester, Neal A. *Ntozake Shange: A Critical Study of the Plays*. New York and London: Garland, 1995.

Tate, Claudia, ed. *Black Women Writers at Work*. New York: Continuum, 1983.

Periodicals

Brown-Guillory, Elizabeth. "Black Women Playwrights: Exorcising Myths." *PHYLON* 48 (Fall 1987): 229–239.

Waxman, Barbara Frey. "Dancing Out of Form, Dancing into Self: Genre and Metaphor in Marshall, Shange, and Walker." *MELUS* 19 (Fall 1994): 91–106.

Gillespie, Marcia Ann. "Ntozake Shange Talks with Marcia Ann Gillespie." *Essence* (May 1985): 122–123.

Neilen, Deirdre. "A Review of *Liliane*." *World Literature Review Today* 69 (1995): 584.

Stevens, Andrea. "*For Colored Girls* May Be for the Ages." *New York Times* (September 3, 1995): H5.

✸ Sam Shepard

BORN: *1943, Fort Sheridan, Illinois*

NATIONALITY: *American*

GENRE: *Drama*

MAJOR WORKS:

The Tooth of Crime (1972)

Buried Child (1978)

True West (1980)

Paris, Texas (1984)

Overview

Sam Shepard is widely acknowledged among contemporary scholars and critics as one of the major playwrights of the second half of the twentieth century—particularly of the late 1970s and 1980s. He has been awarded eleven Obies (being the first American playwright to win three Obies in one year) and a Pulitzer Prize, and his screenplays have been shown at both the Sundance and Cannes Film Festivals, with *Paris, Texas* winning the *Palme d'Or* in 1984. His works continue to be produced around the world.

Works in Biographical and Historical Context

Growing Up Western Sam Shepard was born on November 5, 1943, in Fort Sheridan, Illinois. He was given the name Samuel Shepard Rogers, which his forefathers used for six generations, and nicknamed Steve, as were

Sam Shepard   *Shepard, Sam, 1996, photograph. AP Images.*

the six preceding "Sams." He later dropped the nickname and family surname, becoming Sam Shepard. His father served in the Army Air Corps in World War II, and the family spent time on army bases in South Dakota, Utah, Florida, and Guam. Retiring from the service in 1949, Shepard's father settled the family first in South Pasadena, California, and then in 1955, on a ranch in Duarte, California. Shepard developed a lifelong interest in the land and animals, especially horses, working in his teens as a ranch stable hand. He also developed an interest in music, initially from his father, who played drums with a semi-professional band and enjoyed Dixieland jazz.

Shepard spent only a year at a local community college, where he pursued agricultural science, hoping to work with animals, and got involved with the theater. He soon found a ticket out of his small community by joining a touring theater group; he left the troupe in 1963 to remain in New York City. Through his job at a jazz club, he met Ralph Cook, founder of the group Theatre Genesis. Cook encouraged Shepard to write, and by late 1964 had produced Shepard's first two one-act plays, *Cowboys* and *Rock Garden*. Shepard quickly developed a following in what became known as the Off-Off-Broadway movement, which had sprung up as a reaction against the commercialism of Broadway and even Off-Broadway, and against theatrical realism. This reaction spurred a new wave of theatrical experimentation and encouraged a host of unknown playwrights, inspired not by literary tradition, but by aspects of pop culture, including comic strips, commercials, movies, and the worlds of music and drugs.

Becoming a Playwright Shepard's first two one-acts played to small audiences for a few weeks, garnering poor reviews from mainstream theater critics, until a review in New York's influential alternative weekly newspaper *The Village Voice* suddenly brought him a large audience. From then on, Shepard wrote and was produced frequently, with his plays recognized by the likes of Edward Albee, performed on programs at major theaters in New York and Chicago, and winning a number of Obie awards.

By the mid-sixties, Shepard was living with the actress Joyce Allen, who acted in a number of his plays. A trip they took together to Mexico in 1965 was the inspiration for Shepard's first full-length (two-act) play, *La Turista* (1967), which further developed his favored cowboy theme. It was the first Shepard play produced in an established venue outside Greenwich Village and ran for two weeks, garnering Shepard his fourth Obie and a glowing review in *The New York Review of Books*, an intellectual beacon.

The 1960s also saw Shepherd's increased involvement in music: he joined two bands and incorporated their music into his plays. He also made his first forays into the movies, cowriting several films including 1969's *Zabriskie Point* with renowned filmmaker Michelangelo Antonioni. National recognition also increased with Shepard's various successes: he received a Rockefeller grant, university fellowships, two more Obies, and, in 1968, a

prestigious Guggenheim fellowship. In 1969 he married the actress O-Lan Johnson (aka O-Lan Jones), and in 1970 their son Jesse was born. They were divorced in 1986 after numerous separations and reconciliations.

In 1970 Shepard met the rock poet Patti Smith and moved with her to the Chelsea Hotel, a temporary home and gathering place for many of the most famous writers, musicians, and visual artists of the 1960s and 1970s, from Bob Dylan to Jack Kerouac. Patti Smith inspired Shepard to write prose poems, several of which were published in *Hawk Moon* (1973), dedicated to Smith. She also collaborated with him on *The Cowboy Mouth* (1971), one of the most popular short plays in Shepard's canon.

Escape from the New York Theater Scene In 1971 Shepard and Johnson reconciled and moved to England to escape the stifling New York theater scene. His work proved popular in theater-savvy London, and the Shepard family stayed for three years. There, he wrote *The Tooth of*

COMMON HUMAN EXPERIENCE

Much of Shepard's work involves the search for identity—particularly an identity that has been lost and needs to be recovered. Here are some other works that feature characters in search of their identities:

Six Characters in Search of an Author (1921), a play by Luigi Pirandello. In Pirandello's theatrical experiment, six strangers appear in the middle of a play rehearsal, indicating that they are characters waiting for an author to complete their stories. The subsequent interactions between them and the people whose lives they are supposed to be acting out, shed copious light on the construction of identity.

Being John Malkovich (1999), a film written by Charlie Kaufman and directed by Spike Jonze. In *Being John Malkovich* two office workers discover a portal into the mind of the enigmatic real-life actor John Malkovich, and begin charging thrill seekers for a trip inside the actor's mind. As the main characters begin spending more and more time inside Malkovich's mind, the boundaries between their identities and his become blurred to the point of chaos.

A Portrait of the Artist as a Young Man (1916), a novel by James Joyce. Joyce's semi-autobiographical novel follows the artistic and intellectual awakening of Stephen Dedalus, a young Irishman whose assumption of his identity as a literary artist involves questioning the religion in which he was raised, and leaving his homeland behind for the brighter lights of Paris.

Memento (2000), a film directed by Christopher Nolan. Guy Pearce plays a man who, owing to severe head trauma, can remember nothing more than five minutes old, but nevertheless, has a mystery to solve: the murder of his wife. He records what he can in notes, photographs, and tattoos to help him in his continual reconstruction of events. The audience is made to share in the character's loss of memory—and thus identity—as the scenes are shown in reverse chronological order.

Crime (1972), one of his most popular plays. Set in a post-apocalyptic, Western-tinged future world, *The Tooth of Crime* displayed a new theatrical complexity and has proved difficult for later directors to produce, mostly owing to Shepard's use of music in the staging.

After leaving England, Shepard and his family eventually settled on a horse farm in Northern California. He soon became a fixture of the San Francisco theater scene and found it offered him a freedom that the New York and London scenes lacked. One of Shepard's plays from this period, *Buried Child* (1978), won the Pulitzer Prize as well as another Obie, garnered him unanimously good reviews and went quickly to production Off-Broadway. That same year, Shepard made his first featured appearance as a movie actor in *Days of Heaven*. He has since acted in more than twenty domestic and foreign movies and movies made for television, earning an Oscar nomination for his portrayal of Chuck Yeager in *The Right Stuff* in 1983.

In the summer of 1980, one of Shepard's most popular and frequently produced plays—and by far the most accessible to mainstream audiences—*True West*—had its premiere. A production the following fall attracted negative reviews and closed after an eight-week run. The play's original director resigned, and Shepard issued a public statement essentially disavowing his involvement. The play was redeemed, however, by the highly successful Steppenwolf Theater production in Chicago.

In 1982 Shepard met actress Jessica Lange on the set of *Frances*, in which they costarred. After Shepard's divorce from Johnson, they moved in together and have been a couple ever since; they have two children: Hannah (born 1985) and Walker (born 1987). Soon after, Shepard wrote the screenplay for *Paris, Texas* (1984), which won the *Palme d'Or* at the Cannes Film Festival. The movie, directed by Wim Wenders, builds on the themes of the search for identity and the idea of the West that Shepard's plays had long explored.

While Shepard's dramatic output has decreased since 1990, he remains one of the most produced playwrights in America. His literary canon is diverse, including plays, screenplays, and radio plays, prose, and poetry. He has also appeared regularly as an actor, on both stage and in film, both in his own work and in that of others. In his dual status as a highly lauded playwright and popular celebrity, Shepard holds a distinguished place among American dramatists.

Works in Literary Context

The Western Although Shepard's plays are infused with the sights and sounds of music and popular culture, they are also guided by the themes of the Western, in more or less explicit ways. The notion of the West has evolved over time in literature and film: in the nineteenth century it stood for freedom, opportunity, and challenge as settlers from the crowded cities of the eastern United States took their dreams westward. As the West proved difficult to govern, the idea of the Wild West came to dominate the popular imagination, inspiring such works as Owen Wister's classic *The Virginian* (1902), which dramatizes what was known as "plains justice": the people taking the law into their own hands. Real-life outlaws such as Jesse James (1947–1882), whose mythology grew larger than life after their deaths, helped keep the fantasy of the Wild West alive. With the advent of film, and as the lawlessness of the West was fading into memory, a number of themes crystallized into cinematic formulas: the sheriff vs. the outlaw (*Gunfight at the O.K. Corral* (1957) and many others), the good-hearted drifter (as in 1953's *Shane*), and of course, the outlaw gang (see 1969's *The Wild Bunch*). Shepard began writing his Western-themed plays in the mid-1960s, when the Western had already begun to be appropriated by other movie genres, at times being used as a parable of the present day, at other times substituting unlikely characters, such as Hippies, for the classic cowboys, outlaws, lawmen, ranchers, and Indians. Shepard was thus freed to use Western themes to explore identity, family, and America, while employing characters, images, and scenarios that would be quite familiar to audiences from their long history with the Western.

Works in Critical Context

The critical response to Shepard's work is often holistic, in that critics view the dozens of plays as one long theatrical fantasia as much as individual works. Speaking of Shepard's work as a whole, Richard Eder wrote in the *New York Times* that it is marked by "a spirit of comedy that tosses and turns in a bed of revulsion." Critics have noted that malicious mischief and comic mayhem intensify Shepard's tragic vision; in many of his plays, inventive dialogue supplements vigorous action. As David Richards wrote in the *Washington Post*, actors and directors "respond to the slam-bang potential in [Shepard's] scripts, which allows them to go for broke, trash the furniture, and generally shred the scenery. Whatever else you've got, you've got a wild and wooly fight on your hands." The theatrical fisticuffs, sometimes physical, sometimes verbal, is set to American musical rhythms, as *New York Times* theater critic Clive Barnes noted: "Mr. Shepard writes mythic plays in American jazz-poetry. ... He is trying to express truths wrapped up in legends and with the kind of symbolism you often find nowadays in pop music." Sidney Homan makes a similar point in *Critical Quarterly*: "Shepard's vivid use of language and flair for fantasy have suggested something less like drama and more like poetry in some unfamiliar oral tradition."

Buried Child In *Buried Child*, Richards wrote in the *Washington Post*, Shepard "delivers a requiem for America, land of the surreal and home of the crazed. ... Beyond the white frame farmhouse that contains the evening's action, the amber waves of grain mask a dark secret. The fruited plain is rotting and the purple mountain's majesty is like a bad bruise on the landscape." Richard Christiansen, in the *Chicago Tribune*, called the Pulitzer Prize–winning play "a Norman Rockwell portrait created for *Mad Magazine*, a scene from America's heartland that reeks with 'the stench of sin.'"

Responses to Literature

1. Read one of Shepard's explicitly Western-themed plays, such as *The Cowboy Mouth* or *True West*, and compare it to a more traditional Western (there are any number of films to choose from). What about Shepard's work is classically western, and what represents a departure from the genre? Write a paper in which you discuss what "Western" seems to mean to Shepard.

2. Shepard is known for incorporating music into his plays; *Paris, Texas*, for which he wrote the screenplay, is also noted for its distinctive and haunting soundtrack by Ry Cooder. Watch the film, paying particular attention to the music. How does the score enhance the viewing experience? Does it work differently than traditional movie scores with their emotional cues? Write a short paper evaluating the effect of the music in, and on, *Paris, Texas*.

3. Shepard's plays often require a high degree of physicality from the performers: they have to dance, fight, and destroy things with equal vigor. Stage a reading of one of Shepard's plays that strikes you as particularly physical, and discuss the play's demands with your actors. How far are they prepared to go? What sort of preparation is required of them? What sort of precautions do you have to take as director? How does this kind of performing differ from simply reading the lines?

BIBLIOGRAPHY

Books

Bottoms, Stephen J. *The Theatre of Sam Shepard: States of Crisis*. New York: Cambridge University Press, 1998.

Roudané, Matthew, ed. *The Cambridge Companion to Sam Shepard*. New York: Cambridge University Press, 2002.

Shewey, Don. *Sam Shepard*. New York: Da Capo, 1997.

Wade, Leslie A. *Sam Shepard and the American Theatre*. Westport, Conn.: Greenwood Press, 1997.

Periodicals

Barnes, Clive. "What's Opened in the Theater?" *The New York Times*, March 25, 1973.

Christiansen, Richard. "Shepard's Play Chills to Marrow." *Chicago Tribune*, December 6, 1979.

Eder, Richard. "Theater Review: Buried Child." *The New York Times*, November 7, 1978.

Hardwick, Elizabeth. "Word of Mouth." *New York Review of Books*, April 6, 1967.

Homan, Sidney. "American Playwrights in the 1970's: Rabe and Shepard." *Critical Quarterly*, Spring 1982.

Richards, David. "America the Depraved." *The Washington Post*, April 22, 1983.

✸ Leslie Marmon Silko

BORN: *1948, Albuquerque, New Mexico*

NATIONALITY: *American*

GENRE: *Fiction*

MAJOR WORKS:

Ceremony (1977)

Storyteller (1981)

Almanac of the Dead (1991)

Leslie Marmon Silko   © *Christopher Felver / Corbis*

Overview

Leslie Marmon Silko is one of the most important writers to emerge from the Native American Renaissance, a period of intense literary productivity that began in the late 1960s and brought a long-marginalized segment of American writing into the mainstream of literature. The variety and breadth of Silko's writing have established her as one of the most creative and versatile of living American writers. Her work is widely known and respected in Europe as well, where she is considered a major U.S. author, rather than an ethnic writer.

Works in Biographical and Historical Context

Growing Up Amid the Mesas   Leslie Marmon was born on March 5, 1948, in Albuquerque, New Mexico, of mixed European, Mexican, and Laguna ancestry. She grew up at Old Laguna, a Pueblo Indian reservation west of Albuquerque on the Rio Grande plateau, a high-desert area that has been inhabited by the Laguna people for at least a thousand years. Silko was raised next door to her great-grandfather Robert's second wife, Marie Anaya, the Grandmother A'mooh of *Storyteller* (1981). She, along with Silko's great-aunt Susie and paternal grandmother Lillie, filled Silko's youth with ancient Laguna stories and encouraged

her to keep the stories alive, a responsibility that later became an impetus and foundation of her writing. The old stories also helped to shape Silko's identity, providing context for her relationships within the community and with the community of Laguna itself, which she came to know intimately through a childhood spent wandering on foot and horseback through its sand hills and mesas.

After a childhood in both Native American and Catholic schools, Silko graduated Phi Beta Kappa from the University of New Mexico with a degree in English. That same year, 1969, her first important publication, the short story "The Man to Send Rain Clouds," appeared in *New Mexico Quarterly*. Then, inspired by her father's role in helping Laguna win back a piece of land from the state in the 1950s, Silko entered the Fellowship Program in American Indian Law at the University of New Mexico. In 1971 she received a National Endowment for the Arts Discover Grant. Frustrated by a legal system she had come to feel would never achieve justice for Native Americans, Silko dropped out of law school and began to think of herself as a writer. She entered a graduate program in English at the University of New Mexico but left to teach at Navajo Community College.

Writing to Live   In 1973 Silko moved to Ketchikan, Alaska, where she wrote *Ceremony* (1977), the novel that was to secure her place in what later became known as the Native American Renaissance. Isolated in an unfamiliar place and dealing with a troubled marriage—to her second husband, John Silko—as well as physical illness and the unfamiliar, depressing spectacle of continuous rainfall, Silko wrote to reconstruct the desert landscape of her home and to save her own sanity. The novel is at once a healing ceremony and an analysis of the effects of colonialism and world war on contemporary Native Americans. Above all, the novel is about the power of stories both to wound and to heal.

After the publication of *Ceremony* in 1977, Silko received greater recognition for her earlier short stories. Among her most noteworthy stories were "Lullaby," "Yellow Woman," and "Tony's Story." "Lullaby" is an old woman's recollection of how her children were once taken away for education and how they returned to a culture that no longer seemed familiar or comfortable. "Yellow Woman" concerns a Navajo woman who is abducted by a cattle ranger; she begins to believe that she is simultaneously herself and the mythical Yellow Woman. "Tony's Story" is about an Indian who kills a vicious policeman and equates the murder with the Pueblo exorcism ritual, enacted as a way of dealing with external forces outside human control. Some of Silko's stories were included in the anthology *The Man to Send Rainclouds* (1974), which derives its title from Silko's humorous tale of conflict between a Catholic priest and Pueblo Indians during a Native American funeral. Silko also included some of her early stories in her 1981 collection *Storyteller*, which features her poetry as well.

Storyteller brings many of her previously published stories and poems together with accounts of family history and photographs (many taken by her father, Lee Marmon, a professional photographer), carefully arranged to create a coherent whole. Originally termed a "collection," *Storyteller* is now more often considered autobiography. The relationships of materials in the book emphasize the continuity of oral and literary traditions and the power of story to shape experience, while the photographs evoke a sense of place that helps readers imagine themselves inside the stories.

Major Successes Silko returned to New Mexico in 1976, but left again to teach at the University of Arizona, in Tucson, in 1978. She earned a reprieve from the demands of teaching in 1981, when she was awarded a prestigious MacArthur Foundation "genius grant" for her small but influential body of work. The award—at the time worth $176,000—was particularly appreciated by Silko, who had produced most of her writing while also working as an English professor. Acknowledging her cash prize, she told *Time* that she was now "a little less beholden to the everyday world." Indeed, Silko used that money to work on an epic novel, *Almanac of the Dead* (1991), which ultimately took ten years to complete and whose unconventionality raised more than a few eyebrows. More than seven hundred pages long, *Almanac of the Dead* weaves history, myth, prophecy, cultural analysis, and political diatribe with several strands of narrative involving more than seventy primary characters in an intricate web. It is epic in scope, taking in hundreds of years of conflict between Native Americans and European settlers, and following one mixed-race family on their far-flung voyages.

Silko's third novel, *Gardens in the Dunes* (1999), counters the destruction portrayed in *Almanac of the Dead* by restoring bonds and drawing parallels between Native American and European experience, and exploring ways humans can restore their contiguity with the world and participate in the recovery of Earth from the devastation of colonial and capitalist greed.

Married and divorced twice, Silko has two sons, Robert William Chapman, born in 1966, and Cazimir Silko, born in 1972. Silko still lives in Tucson, in the desert landscape that first inspired her to write.

Works in Literary Context

The Native American Renaissance While Native Americans have oral and storytelling traditions that predate what we now think of as American culture, their myths and folktales remained something separate until 1968, when N. Scott Momaday's novel *House Made of Dawn* won the Pulitzer Prize. This achievement ushered in a phase of literary productivity by Native Americans, as well as writers of mixed Native and European ancestry, dubbed the "Native American Renaissance" by literary critic Kenneth Lincoln in his 1983 book of the same

---

LITERARY AND HISTORICAL CONTEMPORARIES

Silko's famous contemporaries include:

Louise Erdrich (1954–): Erdrich uses her mixed Native American and European ancestry as material for exploring questions of cultural identity. Many of her poems and stories are set among Native American communities in the Upper Midwest.

Maxine Hong Kingston (1940–): The child of working-class Chinese immigrants, Kingston has written about the complexities of immigrant life in California. Her most famous work is the literary autobiography *The Woman Warrior* (1975).

Barbara Kingsolver (1955–): An American novelist and journalist, Kingsolver started her writing career by publishing work on environmental issues and later branched out into fiction. Like Silko, Kingsolver focuses on social and political problems in her writing and has established an award for "literature of social change," the Bellwether Prize.

Sam Shepard (1943–): Shepard is an American actor and playwright whose works often involve an exploration of the changing mythology of the American West, as in his screenplay for the movie *Paris, Texas* (1984). Shepard's career has also crossed over into acting and music.

Leonard Peltier (1944–): A member of the American Indian Movement (A.I.M.) in South Dakota, Peltier was involved in a 1975 gun battle on the Pine Ridge Indian Reservation. He was convicted of murdering two FBI agents on the reservation, although the fairness of the trial has been challenged by many groups, including Amnesty International.

---

name. Such writers as Louise Erdrich and Sherman Alexie blended a rich sense of Native American identity with unmistakably modern stories. But Leslie Marmon Silko's writing has not just helped to shepherd this movement; it has added another dimension as well: nature writing. Native American writers are just beginning to make their way into studies of this genre, which until recently was the purview of European and American male writers in the tradition of Henry David Thoreau and John Muir. Ecocritics see Silko as bringing a particularly rich voice to the genre. Silko's biographer Gregory Salyer observes that with her work "comes a new chapter in the imagination of land in American literature."

Works in Critical Context

Ceremony With its depiction of life on the Indian reservation and its exploration of philosophical issues, *Ceremony* established Silko as an important Native American writer

COMMON HUMAN EXPERIENCE

In Silko's writing, the act of storytelling serves a number of functions: healing, uniting past and present, and explaining the mysteries of action and existence. Here are some other works that see storytelling as a path to a kind of salvation:

The Arabian Nights (c. 800–1400 CE), originally known as *The Book of One Thousand and One Nights*, a collection of stories developed over many centuries and in many countries and many languages. The tales that make up *The Arabian Nights* are told by Scheherazade, apparently destined to be the latest in a long line of royal brides killed by their husband, the king, after spending one night with him. Scheherazade lights on the idea of telling the king a story each night, but breaks off at dawn before she reaches the end. In this way, she keeps the king interested from night to night. Using this clever strategem, she survives.

The Canterbury Tales (c. late fourteenth century CE), a collection of stories in verse by Geoffrey Chaucer. The tales of the title are told by a group of pilgrims journeying to the English town of Canterbury; they take turns entertaining the group with their stories. Some of the stories are personal histories, others are bawdy fictions designed for laughs, while others are parables intended to warn, educate, or possibly even save the souls of the listeners.

The Liars' Club (1995), a memoir by Mary Karr. The title of Karr's memoir comes from a group of her father's friends who, to pass the time after a long day's work, told each other fantastic stories. The young Karr absorbed this lesson, and was eventually able to transmute her own wretched childhood experiences into moving, powerful, and often funny stories.

and marked her as the first Native American woman novelist. Charles R. Larson, writing in *Washington Post Book World*, calls *Ceremony* a novel "powerfully conceived" and attributed much of the book's success to Silko's incorporation of Native American elements. "Tayo's experiences may suggest that *Ceremony* falls nicely within the realm of American fiction about World War II," Larson writes. "Yet Silko's novel is also strongly rooted within the author's own tribal background and that is what I find especially valuable here." Similarly, Frank MacShane writes in the *New York Times Book Review* that Silko skillfully incorporates aspects of Native American storytelling techniques into *Ceremony*. "She has used animal stories and legends to give a fabulous dimension to her novel," he declares. MacShane adds that Silko is "without question ... the most accomplished Indian writer of her generation." Some critics also considered *Ceremony* a powerful confirmation of cosmic order.

Elaine Jahner, who reviewed the novel for *Prairie Schooner Review*, writes that the book "is about the power of timeless, primal forms of seeing and knowing and relating to all of life." She observes that the Native American storytelling tradition provides the novel with both theme and structure and adds that the main character, Tayo, eventually "perceives something of his responsibilities in shaping the story of what human beings mean to each other." Peter G. Beidler focuses on the importance of storytelling in *Ceremony* by writing in *American Indian Quarterly* that the novel is both "the story of a life [and] the life of a story." Beidler calls *Ceremony* "a magnificent novel" that "brings life to human beings and makes readers care about them."

Responses to Literature

1. Leslie Marmon Silko's work often focuses on the mystical aspects of Native American culture. Using your library and the Internet, research Native American spirituality, in history or as it exists today, for a specific tribe. How is devotion to the divine expressed? What sorts of rituals play a part? Write a paper summarizing your findings.

2. *Storyteller* has been considered to be both a collection of pieces in different media (prose, poetry, photography, etc.) and a cohesive autobiography. Read Silko's book and start a discussion about genre. Why would the book be considered a collection, and how might it also be considered a cohesive whole? What are the standards for calling it one genre or another? Can you think of other works (in literature, visual art, or film) that similarly blur the border between genres?

3. If Silko is the representative Native American author of her generation, Sherman Alexie—born in 1966—could be said to be the representative Native American author of his. Read a few of Silko's famous short stories, and compare them to some of Alexie's stories, such as those in *The Toughest Indian in the World* (2000). What are the similarities and differences between the ways the two authors handle Native American issues? How do they represent their cultures (whether they seem to do so on purpose or not)? Do gender, generational differences, or the more recent inclusion of Native American writing into the mainstream seem to account for any of the differences? Write a paper comparing the two authors' work.

BIBLIOGRAPHY

Books

Arnold, Ellen L., ed. *Conversations with Leslie Marmon Silko*. Jackson, Miss.: University of Mississippi Press, 2000.

Lincoln, Kenneth. *Native American Renaissance*. Berkeley, Calif.: University of California Press, 1983.

Nelson, Robert M. *Place and Vision: The Function of Landscape in Native American Fiction.* New York: Peter Lang, 1993.

Salyer, Gregory. *Leslie Marmon Silko.* New York: Twayne, 1997.

Periodicals

Allen, Paula Gunn. "The Psychological Landscape of *Ceremony.*" *American Indian Quarterly,* no.1 (1979).

Beidler, Peter G. Review of *Ceremony. American Indian Quarterly* (Winter 1977–1978).

Jahner, Elaine. Review of *Ceremony. Prairie Schooner Review* (Winter 1977–1978).

Larson, Charles R. Review of *Ceremony. Washington Post Book World* (April 24, 1977).

MacShane, Frank. Review of *Ceremony. The New York Times Book Review* (June 12, 1977).

Pierce, Kenneth M. "The Most Happy Fellows." *Time* (August 8, 1983).

◉ Shel Silverstein

BORN: *1932, Chicago, Illinois*

DIED: *1999, Key West, Florida*

NATIONALITY: *American*

GENRE: *Fiction*

MAJOR WORKS:

The Giving Tree (1964)

Where the Sidewalk Ends: The Poems and Drawings of Shel Silverstein (1974)

A Light in the Attic (1981)

Shel Silverstein   © *Jeff Albertson / Corbis*

Overview

Shel Silverstein, best known for his books of children's poetry that also contain his idiosyncratic illustrations, spread his creative energies in surprisingly diverse directions. In addition to his work for youngsters, he composed songs recorded by famous people, wrote well-received plays for adults and collaborated with major figures of the American stage, and drew cartoons for decidedly adult publications. Such diversity makes Silverstein hard to pigeonhole.

Works in Biographical and Historical Context

Cartooning for Children, and for Grown-ups, Too Born in Chicago on September 25, 1932, Silverstein began his long and diverse career in the arts as a cartoonist for the Pacific edition of the military newspaper *Stars and Stripes.* Silverstein, a child of the Great Depression, came of age during the morally unambiguous days of World War II, when young men willingly volunteered to fight in Europe, North Africa, and Asia against the Axis Powers of Germany, Italy, and Japan. In his own early adulthood, Silverstein joined the U.S. military, and was stationed in Japan and Korea. After leaving the military, Silverstein became a cartoonist for the men's magazine *Playboy* in 1956.

Silverstein's career as a children's author began in 1963, with the publication of *Uncle Shelby's Story of Lafcadio, the Lion Who Shot Back,* a tale about a lion who acquires a hunter's gun and practices until he is good enough to join the circus. Silverstein later confessed that he had never intended to write or draw for children, until a friend convinced him that he should. Although *Lafcadio* and its follow-up, *Uncle Shelby's Giraffe and a Half* (1964), met with moderate success, it was not until the publication of *The Giving Tree* (1964) that Silverstein first achieved widespread fame as a children's writer. The story of a tree that sacrifices its shade, fruit, branches, and finally its trunk to a little boy in order to make him happy, *The Giving Tree* experienced slow sales at first, but its readership steadily grew. In fact, it found a broader audience; the tree seemed to many readers to embody an altruistic, spiritual ideal, and the book was cited in religious services and Sunday schools.

In the early 1970s, Silverstein began to develop the style he is best remembered for: his self-illustrated children's poetry. In 1974 he published the best-selling

LITERARY AND HISTORICAL CONTEMPORARIES

Silverstein's famous contemporaries include:

Johnny Cash (1932–2003): Often labeled as a Country musician, Cash was, in reality, a singer whose unique baritone voice defied narrow categories. Cash recorded traditional ballads, gospel music, rock and roll, and the most famous version of Silverstein's humorous song, "A Boy Named Sue," in 1969.

Leonard Cohen (1934–): The Canadian musician and poet Cohen is both a songwriter and poet whose work is beloved outside normal poetry circles. Cohen's work, however, is darker and more melancholic than Silverstein's.

Dick Gregory (1932–): Gregory was one of the first African American comedians able to play to both white and black audiences in the 1960s. His humor was politically charged by the Civil Rights and anti-Vietnam War movements.

Hunter S. Thompson (1937–2005): The American journalist Thompson defied the conventions of American reporting with his "Gonzo journalism." Often inserting his own drug-inspired experiences into his reporting, Thompson gained a cult following in the 1970s with such works as *Fear and Loathing in Las Vegas* (1972).

collection of poems titled *Where the Sidewalk Ends*. The book earned him favorable comparisons to Dr. Seuss and Edward Lear. The poems in *Where the Sidewalk Ends* can be witty, humorous, and profound, and they often conceal, in the guise of silliness and whimsicality, important observations about childhood fantasies and realities. This is especially true in such poems as "Sarah Cynthia Sylvia Stout Would Not Take the Garbage Out" and "The Gypsies Are Coming." The collection and its 1981 successor, *A Light in the Attic*, continue to be popular with both children and adults.

Developing Other Passions Beginning in 1981, Silverstein embarked on yet another aspect of his creative career by writing plays for adults. One of his best-known works in this form, *The Lady or the Tiger Show* (1981), has been performed on its own and with other one-act works collectively entitled *Wild Life*. Updating a short story by American novelist and fiction writer Frank Stockton, *The Lady or the Tiger Show* features a game-show producer willing to go to extreme lengths to achieve high ratings. Placed in a life-or-death situation, the contestant on the show is forced to choose between two doors. Behind one door lies a ferocious tiger, while the girl of his dreams is concealed behind the other; the result is a satire of show business and media hype.

The 1980s also saw a number of collaborations with one of the American theater's most respected figures: David Mamet, the playwright, scriptwriter, director, and novelist. Mamet, whose work is characterized by complicated plots and fast-talking, foulmouthed characters, would not seem to be a natural partner for the kid-friendly Silverstein, but their collaboration proved fruitful. The two cowrote the screenplay for Mamet's 1988 film *Things Change*, which starred Joe Mantegna and Don Ameche, and two of Silverstein and Mamet's plays, *The Devil and Billy Markham* and *Bobby Gould in Hell* (1989), have been published and produced together under the collective title *Oh, Hell*. Performed as a monologue, Silverstein's *The Devil and Billy Markham* relates a series of bets made between Satan and a Nashville songwriter and singer. The play allowed Silverstein to integrate theater with yet another of his creative pursuits: music. Over the years, Silverstein had been a working songwriter, composing music and penning lyrics for many of Country and pop music's famous names. For example, he wrote the Grammy-winning "A Boy Named Sue" (1969), which has since become one of the legendary Johnny Cash's most popular recordings.

With *Falling Up* (1996), Silverstein returned after a fifteen-year break to poetry—which, like his earlier work, was ostensibly for children but which contained much to appeal to adults. This collection of 140 poems and drawings ranges in subject matter "from tattoos to sun hats to God to—no kidding—a garden of noses," wrote Susan Stark in the *Detroit News*.

Though Silverstein refused to grant interviews later in life, his successes in multiple genres served him well: he maintained homes on the island of Martha's Vineyard, Massachusetts, in Manhattan's Greenwich Village, in Key West, Florida, and in Sausalito, California. On May 10, 1999, Silverstein suffered a heart attack and was later found dead, in his Key West home. He had two children: Shoshanna, born in 1970, who died of a cerebral aneurysm at the age of eleven, and Matthew, born in 1983.

Works in Literary Context

Children's Literature The genre for which Silverstein is mostly remembered, children's poetry, has its origins in the mid-nineteenth century, when the concept of childhood as a special time devoted to growth, imagination, and learning took hold. No longer seeing children as miniature adults, British and American culture began to recognize a potential market for literature that would appeal directly to the imaginations of children. The boundary between popular literature and literature meant specifically for children was at first blurred. For example, Charles Dickens's Christmas Books—most notably *A Christmas Carol* (1843)—were not directly marketed for children, but are now primarily placed in that genre. But with Lewis Carroll's works of fantasy, especially his *Alice's Adventures in Wonderland* (1865), and with the nonsense poetry of Edward Lear, a new age of inventive children's literature was born. Carroll and Lear's direct descendants in delightfully silly literature include Dr. Seuss and Roald Dahl. Though Shel Silverstein's illustrated poems have not spawned the immense sales accorded Dr. Seuss, they too have found a permanent place in the library of childhood classics.

Works in Critical Context

The Giving Tree Although chiefly known as a poet, Silverstein's most popular work has proven to be his illustrated prose book *The Giving Tree*. Beloved by millions of readers for its simple tale of unconditional love, the work has also been criticized by those searching for other, deeper meanings. William Cole, writing for *The New York Times Book Review*, concedes that the book "touches a sensitive point clearly and swiftly," but offers a more skeptical view of the message: "My interpretation is that that was one dum-dum of a tree, giving everything and getting nothing in return." Jean Marie Heisberger and Pat McLaughlin, in a review for *New Catholic World*, also point out that the tree "seems to be rewarding ... selfishness in a kind of masochistic way." Barbara A. Schram, writing in *Interracial Books for Children*, finds an even more ominous message: by categorizing the tree as "she," Schram argues, "it is clear that the author did indeed have a prototypical master/slave relationship in mind."

The Missing Piece In 1976 Silverstein published *The Missing Piece*, which, in common with *The Giving Tree*, has been the subject of varying interpretations. This volume chronicles the adventures of a circle who, lacking a piece of itself, goes along singing and searching for its missing part. But after the circle finds a wedge, he decides he was happier searching without the missing wedge than he is with it. As Anne Roiphe explains in *The New York Times Book Review*, *The Missing Piece* can be read in the same way as

> the fellow at the singles bar explaining why life is better if you don't commit yourself to anyone for too long—the line goes that too much togetherness turns people into bores—that creativity is preserved by freedom to explore from one relationship to another. ... This fable can also be interpreted to mean that no one should try to find all the answers, no one should hope to fill all the holes in themselves, achieve total transcendental harmony or psychic order because a person without a search, loose ends, internal conflicts and external goals becomes too smooth to enjoy or know what's going on. Too much satisfaction blocks exchange with the outside.

Responses to Literature

1. *The Giving Tree*, while treasured by millions of readers worldwide, has been criticized for its depiction of human selfishness and the tree's refusal to stand up for itself. Do you agree with these criticisms? Do you think young readers absorb these deeper meanings, or are these criticisms an example

---

COMMON HUMAN EXPERIENCE

Many of Silverstein's poems play on the gulf between parents and children. Here are some other works that explore the communication and understanding gap between adults and children:

Matilda (1988), a children's novel by Roald Dahl. Unappreciated by her dullard parents, the title character of Dahl's novel discovers that her brainpower is strong enough to move objects, and she implements a plan to help her supportive teacher while she teaches her parents a lesson.

Jude the Obscure (1895), a novel by Thomas Hardy. In this work, the title character's previously unknown, eight-year-old son arrives in his life. The boy has such a sad and wise demeanor that his father and stepmother dub him "Father Time." The boy lives up to his name in a startlingly tragic way.

The Polar Express (2004), a film directed by Robert Zemeckis. Inspired by the Chris Van Allsburg book of the same name, this Christmas tale focuses on the willingness to believe in the fantastic that separates children from adults. A boy who is beginning to doubt the existence of Santa Claus is whisked away to the North Pole on a magical train.

---

of the gap between how children and adults view the world differently?

2. Like many children's authors, Silverstein illustrated his own poems and stories. In fact, in many of the poems the drawings are inseparable from the text. Unity of text and image is not limited to children's literature, however: authors from William Makepeace Thackeray in the mid-nineteenth century to W. G. Sebald in the late twentieth century used their own images to enhance their stories. Compare the work of one of these authors—or of another of your choice—to a self-illustrating children's author such as Silverstein or Dr. Seuss. Then write a paper in which you explore the various ways authors use images to illuminate their words.

3. Get to know the other, less well-known aspects of Shel Silverstein. Explore his music—you might start with his soundtracks to the films *Ned Kelly* (1970) and *Postcards from the Edge* (1990), or his 1965 album *I'm So Good That I Don't Have to Brag*—and his dramatic work, some of which was published in 2003 as *An Adult Evening of Shel Silverstein*. What do these works in other genres have in common with his more famous works for children? Do you see the same creative mind at work?

BIBLIOGRAPHY

Books

MacDonald, Ruth K. *Shel Silverstein*. New York: Twayne, 1997.

Rogak, Lisa. *A Boy Named Shel: The Life & Times of Shel Silverstein*. New York: Thomas Dunne Books, 2007.

Periodicals

Cole, William. "About Alice, a Rabbit, a Tree …" *The New York Times Book Review* (September 9, 1973): 8.

Heisberger, Jean Marie and Pat McLaughlin. Review of *The Giving Tree. New Catholic World* vol. 222, no. 1328 (March–April 1979): 92.

Honan, William H. "Shel Silverstein, Zany Writer and Cartoonist, Dies at 67." *The New York Times* (May 11, 1999).

MacDonald, Ruth K. "The Weirdness of Shel Silverstein." *Studies in American Humor* (Winter 1986–1987).

Mercier, Jean F. "Shel Silverstein." *Publishers Weekly* (February 24, 1975).

Review of *A Light in the Attic. Publishers Weekly* (September 18, 1981).

Review of *Falling Up. Publishers Weekly* (April 29, 1996).

Roiphe, Anne. Review of *The Missing Piece. The New York Times Book Review* (May 2, 1976).

Schram, Barbara A. "Misgivings about 'The Giving Tree.'" *Interracial Books for Children* vol. 5, no. 5 (1974): 1, 8.

Stark, Susan. Review of *Falling Up. Detroit News* (May 1, 1996).

Charles Simic   *AP Images*

✹ Charles Simic

BORN: *1938, Belgrade, Yugoslavia*

NATIONALITY: *American*

GENRE: *Poetry, nonfiction*

MAJOR WORKS:

Dismantling the Silence (1971)

The World Doesn't End: Prose Poems (1990)

Walking the Black Cat (1996)

Jackstraws (1999)

Overview

Charles Simic, the fifteenth poet laureate of the United States, is a native of Yugoslavia who immigrated to the United States during his teens, and has become a pillar of poetry in his adopted homeland. Simic's poetry has won numerous prestigious awards, among them the 1990 Pulitzer Prize and the coveted MacArthur Foundation "genius grant." Although he writes in English, Simic draws upon his own experiences of war-torn Belgrade to compose strikingly original poems about the physical and spiritual poverty of modern life.

Works in Biographical and Historical Context

A Turbulent Youth Charles Simic was born in Belgrade, Yugoslavia, on May 9, 1938. His early childhood coincided with World War II, during which Yugoslavia was occupied by the Axis Powers (Nazi Germany and its allies). During the war, his family had to evacuate their home several times to escape indiscriminate bombing. After the war ended in 1945, the atmosphere of violence and desperation continued, and Simic recalls that the years from 1945 to 1948 were marked by hunger and deprivation. During this time, Simic's father left the country for work in Italy, and his mother tried several times to follow, only to be turned back by authorities. In the meantime, young Simic was growing up in Belgrade, where he was considered a below-average student and a minor troublemaker.

When Simic was fifteen, his mother finally arranged for the family to travel to Paris. After a year spent studying English in night school and attending French public schools during the day, Simic sailed for America. He moved with his family to Chicago, where he enrolled in high school. In that environment—a suburban school with caring teachers and motivated students—Simic began to take new interest in his courses, especially literature. The young Simic discovered jazz, as well as American poetry and folklore, and underwent a transformation in outlook that led to him becoming an international poet and a gifted multicultural spokesman.

Simic's first poems were published in 1959, when he was twenty-one. Between that year and 1961, when he entered the U.S. Army, he wrote a number of poems, most of which he has since destroyed. He served in the U.S. Army until 1963, then pursued a college education at New York University, where he received his B.A. in 1966. Between 1966 and 1973, he worked as an editorial assistant for the photography magazine *Aperture*. Simic married Helene Dubin, a fashion designer, in 1965. In 1974, Simic began teaching at the University of New Hampshire, where he has been a professor of English for over thirty years.

Finding a Poetic Voice Simic's first full-length collection of poems, *What the Grass Says*, was published in 1967. In a very short time, Simic's work—original poetry in English and translations of important Yugoslavian poets—began to attract critical attention. This first collection, as well as his other early works, including *Somewhere Among Us a Stone Is Taking Notes* (1969), *Dismantling the Silence* (1971), and *Return to a Place Lit by a Glass of Milk* (1974), feature a number of "object" short poems such as "Watch Repair," "Fork," and "Spoon", which focus on everyday objects or images. In these works, Simic challenges the dividing line between the ordinary and extraordinary by giving life to inanimate objects, meditating upon their strangeness. In doing so, Simic associates many of these objects with war, violence, and tragedy, and their surrealism takes on a dark, bizarre edge. Although the poems were intensely surrealistic, they were nonetheless engaging to readers and critics alike.

Starting in the mid-1970s, Simic's work moved in a new direction, focusing on a more complete consideration of self and the contradictory nature of modern life. His subjects began to break away from objects to more thorough considerations of people and urban life in the Harriet Monroe Prize for Poetry–winning collection *Classic Ballroom Dances* (1980), as well as *Weather Forecast for Utopia and Vicinity* (1983), *Unending Blues* (1986), and *The Book of Gods and Devils* (1990). Simic's 1989 collection, *The World Doesn't End: Prose Poems*, won the Pulitzer Prize for its series of prose poems that present a struggle with the idea of personal and political history. In one poem of the collection, a child is stolen by gypsies, is taken right back by his parents, is stolen again by the gypsies, and so on until his head swims and he can no longer tell the difference between his two sets of mothers and fathers. In another, a family is so poor that the child must take the place of the bait in the mousetrap; in a third, the last Napoleonic soldier is still retreating from Moscow two hundred years after the French invasion in 1812, and passes German soldiers on

LITERARY AND HISTORICAL CONTEMPORARIES

Charles Simic's famous contemporaries include:

Harry S. Truman (1884–1972): President of the United States after World War II, from 1945 to 1953, Truman was a major influence on twentieth-century international politics.

W. S. Merwin (1927–): American poet. A Pulitzer Prize winner, Merwin is a poet whose work is marked by a unique evolution throughout his career.

Ishmael Reed (1938–): American poet, novelist, and essayist. A controversial, but critically acclaimed African American author, Reed is known for satires of oppressive political and social structures.

James Tate (1943–): American poet. Winner of both the Pulitzer Prize and a National Book Award for Poetry, Tate is a noted contemporary surrealist poet.

Andrei Codrescu (1946–): Romanian-born American poet, novelist, and essayist. A prolific surrealist poet in both English and Romanian, Codrescu emigrated to the United States in the mid-1960s.

Slobodan Milosevic (1941–2006): Milosevic was president of Serbia from 1989 to 1997. He was considered responsible for stirring up Serbian nationalism that led to wars in the former Yugoslavia during the 1990s. In 2001, he was indicted for crimes against humanity by the International Criminal Tribunal for the former Yugoslavia. He died of a heart attack in 2006, before a verdict could be reached.

their way to the Russian front in World War II. The poems employ a wide range of historical and political allusions, as well as Simic's trademark combination of ironic humor and dark subject matter. Childhood experiences of war, poverty, and hunger lie behind a number of these poems, and echo a concern that Simic's work, throughout his career, has shared: the impact of war.

Poetic Prominence After earning the Pulitzer Prize, Simic continued to gain prominence in the literary community. Simic published several more books of poetry in the 1990s, including *Hotel Insomnia* (1992), *A Wedding in Hell* (1994), and *Walking the Black Cat* (1996), which was a finalist for the National Book Award for Poetry. In 1999, Simic's collection, *Jackstraws*, was named a Notable Book of the Year by the *New York Times*. He has continued to write and publish poetry, and was awarded the esteemed Griffin Poetry Prize in 2005 for his 2004 collection, *Selected Poems: 1963–2003*. In August 2007, Simic, a naturalized citizen, was appointed to the distinguished position of poet laureate of the United States. Simic's influence has been felt beyond poetry, as well. In

COMMON HUMAN EXPERIENCE

Central to Simic's poetry is an exploration of historical and contemporary militarism, which is a principle that asserts that a government or nation should maintain a strong military presence and stay prepared to use it aggressively. Here are some other literary works that explore the concept and impact of militarism:

Three Soldiers (1920), a novel by John Dos Passos. The novel is a strikingly realistic portrayal of World War I that contemplates the political repercussions of the war.

"Roosters" (1969), a poem by Elizabeth Bishop. Bishop imagines war as a barnyard battle in order to investigate the impact of aggression and nationalism.

"Nuremburg U.S.A." (1968), a poem by Bill Knot. In this Vietnam-era poem, Knott compares war and human love to critique militarism.

Austerlitz (2001), a novel by W. G. Sebald. A significant German novel, *Austerlitz* is an attempt to reconcile the German history of nationalism with contemporary international policy and the real life and cultural identities of modern Germans.

addition to the publication of his memoirs, *A Fly in the Soup* (2000), Simic has published critical essays and translations of poetry from a number of different languages.

Works in Literary Context

Blending Realism with Surrealism Simic's work is difficult to categorize in terms of a single genre or literary tradition. He is often labeled a "surrealist" or "imagist" poet, but Simic's self-exploration and his emphasis on real-world situations and issues challenges that categorization. Instead, one of the keys to Simic's unique appeal is his ability to blend surrealist techniques with realist subjects. Surrealism was a twentieth-century cultural movement and response to rationalism. Surrealists believed in using the unconscious to produce art and literature that was more "real" than work produced self-consciously. Surrealist poetry is often characterized by the juxtaposition of unexpected images and dreamlike language. Simic drew upon the literary techniques of surrealism, including abstract language and images, surprising comparisons (often blending "light" images with dark and morbid associations), and absurdity to create his poetry. Yet, his subject matter—beyond his "object" poems—rarely conforms to surrealism. His enduring concern with historical and human issues resonates with the tradition of literary realism, which seeks to dramatize contemporary life in a real and authentic manner. Simic's ability to draw upon these two literary

traditions makes his work uniquely challenging, as well as singularly compelling.

Works in Critical Context

Simic is widely regarded as one of the most skillful poets of the twentieth century for both his technical abilities and the depth of his subjects. Critics also find Simic's style particularly accessible, a substantial achievement for an author for whom English is a second language. Simic's personal history and his displacement from his native country also enable him to approach his subjects and themes with a unique and enriching sensibility. As critic Brian C. Avery wrote, "Despite the inescapable tragedy of our age, Simic has also discovered the value of the familiar to raise us above the incessant suffering inherent to any age."

Dismantling the Silence Simic's 1971 collection was lauded by critics for its technical mastery and its innovative approach to the everyday. Critic Victor Contoski applauded the work and highlighted Simic's simplistic style and masterful use of silence instead of sound. He wrote, "[Simic] is a listener rather than a speaker, and a listener to the tiny voices of things." Contoski further elaborated on the complexity of Simic's approach to poetry, which resonates with the type of contradictions that make Simic one of the most unique poets of his time: "Coupled with Simic's simplicity is, paradoxically, a kind of aristocratic attitude toward his art, a combination that makes his work unique indeed."

The World Doesn't End: Prose Poems Winner of the Pulitzer Prize for Poetry, Simic's collection, *The World Doesn't End: Prose Poems*, was not without controversy. Several critics and prominent members of the literary community felt that Simic's choice to use the prose structure put the collection at odds with the poetry community that was honoring it. Yet, the majority of critics felt that the prose poem form was the most suitable for Simic's subject matter. Critic Christopher Buckley defends the choice, writing, "Simic chooses the prose poem for this book, as it best provides a form for the voice and material that go back to his essential poetic roots—the European or Eastern European folk tale."

Responses to Literature

1. In the poem "Stone," Simic writes that he is "happy to be a stone." What does this say about Simic's approach to poetry and life?

2. How does Simic depict poverty in the prose poem "We were so Poor"?

3. Read Simic's poems "Watch Repair," "Fork," and "Spoon," in his collection, *Return to a Place Lit by a Glass of Milk*. How does the poet make you see familiar objects in unfamiliar ways? What is the overall effect of these short poems?

4. Select two or three poems from Simic's *The Voice at 3:00 A.M.: Selected Late and New Poems* (2003) and show how Simic creates his effects through surreal, dreamlike images. What are some of his typical images?

BIBLIOGRAPHY

Books

Avery, Brian C. "Unconcealed Truth: Charles Simic's *Unending Blues.*" *Charles Simic: Essays on the Poetry.* Ed. Bruce Weigl. Ann Arbor: University of Michigan Press, 1996, pp. 73–95.

Buckley, Christopher. "Sounds That Could Have Been Singing: Charles Simic's *The World Doesn't End.*" *Charles Simic: Essays on the Poetry.* Ed. Bruce Weigl. Ann Arbor: University of Michigan Press, 1996, pp. 96–113.

Lysaker, John T. *You Must Change Your Life: Poetry, Philosophy, and the Birth of Sense.* University Park, Pa: Pennsylvania State University Press, 2002.

Periodicals

Bond, Bruce. "Immanent Distance: Silence and the Poetry of Charles Simic." *Mid-American Review* 8, no. 1 (1988): 89–96.

Contoski, Victor. "At the Stone's Heart: Charles Simic's *Dismantling the Silence.*" *Modern Poetry Studies* 2, no. 5 (1971): 236–40.

Corbet, William. "Charles Simic." *Poets & Writers Magazine* 24. no. 3 (May–June 1996): 30(6).

Hart, Henry. "Charles Simic's Dark Nights of the Soul." *Kenyon Review* 27.3 (Summer 2005): 124(24).

Heaney, Seamus. "Shorts for Simic." *Harvard Review* no. 13 (Fall 1997): 14–20.

Reynolds, Susan Salter. "A New Chapter in Verse." *Los Angeles Times* (August 26, 2007): 12.

Vendler, Helen. "Totemic Sifting." *Parnassus: Poetry in Review* 18/19, nos. 1 and 2 (1993): 86–99.

✸ Neil Simon

BORN: *1927, Bronx, New York*

NATIONALITY: *American*

GENRE: *Drama*

MAJOR WORKS:

Barefoot in the Park (1963)

The Odd Couple (1965)

Sweet Charity (1966)

Brighton Beach Memoirs (1984)

Lost in Yonkers (1991)

Overview

Neil Simon is a master of comedy and one of the most popular dramatists in the history of the American theater. His plays, which range from light romantic comedy and farce to drama, have entertained Broadway audiences for almost five decades and have also been a mainstay for regional and amateur theater companies. Active as a writer for the screen as well as the stage, Simon has

Neil Simon Simon, (Marvin) Neil, photograph. AP Images.

adapted more plays to movies than any other American dramatist and has written ten original screenplays.

Works in Biographical and Historical Context

From the Army to Showbiz Marvin Neil Simon was born in the Bronx, New York, on July 4, 1927, and grew up in the Manhattan neighborhood of Washington Heights during the Great Depression. His parents had a stormy marriage; his father, a garment salesman, abandoned the family frequently during Simon's boyhood, causing serious financial strain as well as emotional turmoil. "I think part of what has made me a comedy writer," Simon told Richard Meryman in 1971, "is the blocking out of some of the really ugly, painful things in my childhood and covering it up with a humorous attitude."

After graduating high school at sixteen, Simon enlisted in the Army Air Force Reserve training program at New York University. In 1945 he was assigned to Lowry Field, Colorado, where he attended the University of Denver and worked—as did many creative types who were swept up in World War II—for a military publication, serving as sports editor for *Rev-Meter.* Simon later used his experience in the army as material for *Biloxi Blues* (1985), the second play in his semiautobiographical Brighton Beach trilogy.

After his discharge as a corporal in 1946, Simon launched his career in show business with his brother, Danny, writing comedy for CBS. For the next decade the Simon brothers collaborated in writing comedy sketches for radio and for television series, such as Sid Caesar's *Your Show of Shows*. Simon continued to write comedy for television until the opening of his first Broadway play, *Come Blow Your Horn*, in 1961, to which he brought a gift for writing gags and one-liners and an instinctive knowledge of what would make an audience laugh. Recounting Simon's first experience of living on his own, *Come Blow Your Horn* focuses on the theme of coming of age and follows the experiences of two brothers living as roommates, Simon's first stab at the notion of the "odd couple." Critics found Simon's first play slender in plot and overly dependent on stock characters, but they were uniformly impressed by Simon's gift for witty dialogue. Running for 677 performances, *Come Blow Your Horn* marked an auspicious beginning to Simon's theatrical career.

Finding a Voice in the Theater   Simon continued his autobiographical approach to playwriting in the romantic comedy *Barefoot in the Park* (1963), in which he affectionately recalled the early days of his marriage to his wife, Joan. (They married in 1953.) Rather than adopting the traditional "boy-meets-girl" framework of romantic comedy, Simon employed his favorite variation of that story line: the "problem marriage" plot. The newlyweds portrayed in the play are deeply in love but of opposite temperament and have to learn the delicate art of compromise. *Barefoot in the Park* was a major critical and commercial hit, running on Broadway for 1,532 performances.

Simon's next big hit, *The Odd Couple* (1965), was a natural outgrowth of *Barefoot in the Park*, since it, too, focused on the theme of incompatibility. Simon employed the same "problem marriage" setup as in his previous comedy, but he altered it to depict a pair of heterosexual men, Felix and Oscar, who have separated from their spouses and now share an apartment. While Oscar is sloppy, irresponsible, and carefree, Felix is compulsively neat, fussy, and high-strung. The characters, and the notion of the "odd couple," have since transcended the play itself and become stock characters in television and big-screen comedy.

Keeping Up with the Times   Though Simon had established himself by riffing on domesticity, a sensibility that was shaped by the cultural values of the 1950s, he was attuned to the culture changing around him. Simon's 1969 play *Last of the Red Hot Lovers*, a popular success, was inspired by the sexual revolution of the 1960s and focuses on the midlife crisis of Barney Cashman, whose anxiety at his disappearing youth leads him to attempt an affair. Barney proves to be a clumsy ladies' man, however, and his three seduction attempts all end in failure.

In the early 1970s, as Simon was rounding the corner into middle age, he brought out *The Sunshine Boys* (1972), an ostensible tribute to the bygone art of vaudeville, focusing on two old comedians who reunite in an effort to revive their classic comedy act for television. But the play is also a sensitive look at old age, with the characters suffering not just the physical effects of time but also the dismaying loss of dignity that accompanies it. The play was both a popular and critical success, not just for subject matter Simon's audiences could relate to, but because the jokes and one-liners he was known for worked particularly well in a play about comedians.

Loss and Rebirth   In July of 1973 Simon's first wife, Joan, died of cancer at the age of thirty-nine. She and Simon had been married for nearly twenty years and were raising two daughters, Ellen and Nancy. (Simon later adopted Bryn, the daughter of his third wife, Diane Lander.) Devastated by grief, Simon wrote *God's Favorite* (1974), a comic retelling of the biblical story of Job. As Simon explained in a 1991 interview, "I could not understand the absurdity of a thirty-nine-year-old beautiful, energetic woman dying so young." The play was Simon's "railing at God to explain to me why He did this thing." Despite its heartfelt origins, however, the play was neither a popular nor a critical success.

Simon bounced back professionally, with a new collection of playlets, the crowd-pleasing *California Suite* (1976), and personally, with his marriage to actress Marsha Mason (b. 1942). Mason starred in a number of films based on Simon's plays and screenplays, most notably 1977's *The Goodbye Girl*, which was written for the screen. Simon's next theatrical offering, *Chapter Two* (1977), is an autobiographical work dealing with Simon's sorrow over Joan's death and his mixture of joy and guilt about his remarriage a few months later. The play remains a romantic comedy despite its realistic portrayal of bereavement, ably blending the humorous with the poignant.

With 1983's *Brighton Beach Memoirs*, Simon returned to his life story as a dramatic source, warmly recalling his boyhood in New York City during the Depression. Played by Matthew Broderick in the Broadway premiere, the adolescent Eugene Jerome, who hopes to become a writer someday, speaks directly to the audience, revealing his family's assorted financial and health problems. The play offers substantial hope that the family will nevertheless survive; according to Simon himself, it is the idealization of the family that has made *Brighton Beach Memoirs* one of his most widely performed plays. Simon turned *Brighton Beach Memoirs* into a trilogy with two subsequent plays: *Biloxi Blues* (1985), inspired by Simon's time in the military, and *Broadway Bound* (1986), which follows the protagonist into his comedy-writing career. The most serious of the three plays, it inspired *New York Newsday*'s critic to write that *Broadway Bound* seemed "as though a familiar Simon comedy were intertwined with an Arthur Miller play."

The Many Sources of Laughter   After an attempt at farce with *Rumors* (1988), which was a popular if not a critical success, Simon returned to form with his Pulitzer Prize–winning *Lost in Yonkers* (1991). Set in 1942, *Lost in*

Yonkers is one of Simon's darkest comedies, focusing on a dysfunctional Jewish family helmed by a stern, intimidating grandmother and populated by a variety of other eccentric characters. Less sentimental than the Brighton Beach trilogy and resonating with audiences as painfully true to life, *Lost in Yonkers* had a long run on Broadway and was soon after made into a feature film (1993).

In 1993 Simon found another rich source from his past to mine: his days as a comedy writer, in particular for Sid Caesar's *Your Show of Shows*, which formed the foundation for that year's *Laughter on the 23rd Floor*, a fond look back at the Golden Age of comedy. Since then Simon has continued to turn out plays and scripts, his most recent work being the stage production *Rose's Dilemma* (2003). In addition to his marriage to Mason, which ended in 1981, Simon was twice married to Diane Lander and is currently married to actress Elaine Joyce (b. 1950).

Works in Literary Context

Theatrical Comedy When Simon created his play *The Sunshine Boys* (1972), about two vaudeville comedians, he wasn't just picking the perfect subject matter for his favorite kind of joke—the one-liner. He was also paying homage to the long theatrical tradition that laid the groundwork for his own brand of theater. A peculiarly American format, vaudeville rose up in the late nineteenth century and featured a series of unrelated acts ranging from musical performance to dramatic readings to family skits. While by the 1930s vaudeville was mostly a thing of the past, two types of stage acts transcended the genre and went on to provide the basis for new kinds of shows: burlesque or striptease, and comedy. With the rise of radio and then television, comedy—in the form of sketches or one-liner-filled monologues—had found a new medium, and many of the early writers and performers were veterans of the vaudeville circuit. Sid Caesar, the impresario of classic TV comedy whose *Your Show of Shows* was one of Simon's early employers, got his training by performing on the resort circuit, whose variety-show format borrowed much from classic vaudeville.

Works in Critical Context

The Brighton Beach Trilogy While for most of Simon's theatrical career critics had trouble seeing past his one-liners, the 1980s brought consistently positive reviews with the autobiographical trilogy of *Brighton Beach Memoirs*, *Biloxi Blues*, and *Broadway Bound*. Speaking of the critical reception of *Brighton Beach Memoirs*, David Richards, who reviewed many of Simon's plays, explained that "the critics, who have sometimes begrudged the playwright his ability to coin more funny lines per minute than seems humanly possible, have now decided that he has a very warm heart."

Brighton Beach Memoirs earned Simon some of the best reviews of his career. One critic wrote that *Brighton*

LITERARY AND HISTORICAL CONTEMPORARIES

Simon's famous contemporaries include:

Woody Allen (1935–): Allen is an American director and writer. Like Simon's work in drama, Allen's work in film has ranged from lighthearted comedy to serious family drama. Allen started his career as a comedy writer but has also been highly influenced by the work of the Swedish director Ingmar Bergman, whose name is synonymous with highbrow European filmmaking.

Sid Caesar (1922–): Caesar is an American comedian and writer. A pioneer of television comedy, Caesar served as host of *Your Show of Shows* during the 1950s, a late-night variety program and a forerunner of *Saturday Night Live*.

Burt Bacharach (1928–): Bacharach is an American pianist and composer. A composer of many 1960s pop tunes that have become jazz standards, Bacharach's work has been featured in many TV shows and films, including the 1967 James Bond film *Casino Royale*.

Edward Albee (1928–): Albee is an American dramatist. Albee earned a controversial Pulitzer Prize in 1963 for his play *Who's Afraid of Virginia Woolf?*, which was one of the first plays in American theater to use profanity and deal with sexual themes in an unflinching manner. Albee has also been noted for "Americanizing" the European school of "theater of the absurd."

Mel Brooks (1926–): Brooks is an American director, producer, and actor. Brooks is most famous for screwball parodies such as *Blazing Saddles* (1974) and *Young Frankenstein* (1974), but he has also written darker comedies such as *The Producers* (1968), which continues to be a source of controversy over its comedic treatment of Adolf Hitler.

Beach Memoirs has "plenty of laughs," but "Simon avoids the glib, tenderly probing the often-awkward moments where confused emotions cause unconscious hurts. ... Simon's at his best, finding the natural wit, wisecracking and hyperbole in the words and wisdom of everyday people."

Biloxi Blues was less of a smash than its predecessor, but garnered critical respect nonetheless. "For all the familiarity of its set pieces," Dan Sullivan of the *Los Angeles Times* wrote, "it feels like life, not 'Gomer Pyle.'" Critics have also been impressed with how Simon subordinates the play's humor to its more serious concerns. David Richards claimed that *Biloxi Blues* "may be the most touching play ever written about the rigors of basic training."

Critics were also impressed by the sensitive portrayal of the hero's mother in the final installment of the trilogy, *Broadway Bound*, as well as its insight into family life.

COMMON HUMAN EXPERIENCE

One of Simon's standbys—a theme he returned to again and again—was the humor and pathos of family life. Here are some other great family stories:

Anna Karenina (1877), a novel by Leo Tolstoy. Tolstoy's novel has one of the most famous opening lines in all of literature: "All happy families are alike; every unhappy family is unhappy in its own way." Thus begins the great Russian tale of courtship, marriage, adultery, and tragedy.

The Royal Tenenbaums (2001), a film directed and co-written by Wes Anderson. Set in a fictionalized New York City, Anderson's dark comedy focuses on the lives of a family of child prodigies who are now grown up. Each eccentric member of the Tenenbaum family, including the parents, harbors his own secrets and obsessions.

Radio Days (1987), a film written and directed by Woody Allen. With a tone very much like Simon's *Brighton Beach Memoirs*, Allen's film is a warm look back at his childhood amid a noisy and loving extended family in 1940s New York.

The Corrections (2001), a novel by Jonathan Franzen. Franzen's novel, the winner of multiple awards, including the National Book Award, is a modern family drama constructed around a set of parents and their three adult children, all five of whom make questionable choices in their efforts to make it through life in one piece.

Frank Rich, writing in the *New York Times*, remarked that the play "contains some of its author's most accomplished writing to date—passages that dramatize the timeless, unresolvable bloodlettings of familial existence as well as the humorous conflicts one expects."

Lost in Yonkers Simon received further critical recognition of his status as one of America's major playwrights in 1991, when his play *Lost in Yonkers* won both a Pulitzer Prize for Drama and a Tony Award for best drama. The play, which tells the story of a dysfunctional Jewish American family during World War II, is "closer to pure surrealism than anything Mr. Simon has hitherto produced," writes David Richards in the *New York Times*, "and take[s] him several bold steps beyond the autobiographical traumas he recorded in *Brighton Beach Memoirs* and *Broadway Bound*." The critic continues,

No longer content to dramatize divisive arguments around the family table, he has pulled the family itself out of shape and turned it into a grotesque version of itself. These characters are not oddballs, they're deeply disturbed creatures. Were it not for his ready wit and his appreciation for life's incongruities, *Lost in Yonkers* could pass for a nightmare.

Responses to Literature

1. Many of Simon's plays revolve around the lives of Jewish families and make use of Jewish humor. Watch the film version of one of Simon's Jewish-themed plays, such as *Brighton Beach Memoirs* (1986) or *Lost in Yonkers* (1993). What, exactly, gets the "Jewishness" of the characters and scenarios across? Is it the way the characters speak, their history, their cultural references? Write a paper in which you explain why Simon is often discussed as a Jewish playwright.

2. One of Simon's theatrical standbys was the "problem marriage" plot. Two of its variations appear in *Barefoot in the Park* and *The Odd Couple*. In the former, there is literally a marriage; in the latter, the friendship between the two roommates functions like a marriage. Watch the film versions of the two plays and compare the handling of the "problem marriage." When is the relationship a source of humor, and when is it handled seriously? Are the two variations of a similar plot ultimately more similar or more dissimilar? Write a short paper comparing the two stories.

3. Pick a Simon play that's particularly full of one-liners—*Laughter on the 23rd Floor* or *The Sunshine Boys* might be a good choice—and stage a reading. If your goal is to get the audience to laugh, what will you need to focus on? What does it take to get the jokes across? Is the humor in the writing, the delivery, or the timing (or all three)?

BIBLIOGRAPHY

Books

Koprince, Susan. *Understanding Neil Simon*. Columbia: University of South Carolina Press, 2002.

Schiff, Ellen. "Funny, He *Does* Look Jewish." In *Neil Simon: A Casebook*, edited by Gary Konas. New York: Garland, 1997.

Simon, Neil. *Rewrites: A Memoir*. New York: Simon & Schuster, 1996.

Walden, Daniel. "Neil Simon's Jewish-Style Comedies." In *From Hester Street to Hollywood: The Jewish-American Stage and Screen*, edited by Sarah Blacher Cohen. Bloomington: Indiana University Press, 1983.

Periodicals

Bryer, Jackson R. "An Interview with Neil Simon." *Studies in American Drama: 1945–Present* (1991).

Meryman, Richard. "When the Funniest Writer in America Tried to Be Serious." *Life*, May 7, 1961.

Rich, Frank. Review of *Broadway Bound*. *New York Times*, December 5, 1986.

Richards, David. "The Last of the Red Hot Playwrights." *New York Times Magazine*, February 17, 1991.

Sullivan, Dan. Review of *Biloxi Blues*. *Los Angeles Times*, December 15, 1984.

Wallach, Allan. Review of *Broadway Bound*. *New York Newsday* (December 5, 1986).

✳ Upton Sinclair

BORN: *1878, Baltimore, Maryland*

DIED: *1968, Bound Brook, New Jersey*

NATIONALITY: *American*

GENRE: *Fiction*

MAJOR WORKS:

The Jungle (1906)

Overview

Upton Sinclair was a writer whose main concerns were politics and economics, and whose ideas about literature were inseparable from his dreams of social justice. Since the essential purpose of literature, for Sinclair, was the betterment of human conditions, he was a "muckraker," a propagandist, an interpreter of socialism and a critic of capitalism, a novelist more concerned with content than form, a journalistic chronicler of his times rather than an enduring artist. Since World War II, his literary reputation has declined, yet *The Jungle* (1906) is one of the best known and most historically significant of American novels, and Sinclair himself remains an important figure in American political and cultural history.

Works in Biographical and Historical Context

Becoming a "Real" Writer Upton Beall Sinclair Jr. was born in Baltimore, Maryland, on September 20,

Upton Sinclair   *Sinclair, Upton, 1942, photograph. AP Images.*

1878, into an aristocratic, but impoverished, Southern family whose financial difficulties dated back to the Civil War era. His father, a traveling salesman who turned to alcohol to cope with the unaccustomed pressures of having to work for a living, rarely made enough money to provide Upton and his mother Priscilla with some measure of comfort. This life of genteel hardship contrasted sharply with that of Priscilla Sinclair's wealthy Baltimore relatives; it was a difference that disturbed young Sinclair, who could not understand why some people were rich and others poor. Many years later, at the age of eighty-five, he remarked at a gathering held in his honor that he still did not understand.

A sickly but precocious child, Sinclair entered New York's City College at the age of fourteen. Determined to become financially independent from his unreliable father, he immediately began submitting jokes, riddles, poems, and short stories to popular magazines; by the time he graduated, Sinclair was selling full-length adventure novels (which appeared under various pseudonyms) to Street Smith, one of the day's foremost publishers of pulp fiction. During this period, the teenager learned to write quickly, prolifically, and with a minimum of effort, turning out an average of six to eight thousand words per day, seven days per week.

After receiving his degree, Sinclair went on to graduate school at Columbia University, where he was attracted to the romantic poets and their belief in the power of literature to make an appreciable difference in the world. To this end, he decided to give up hack writing and concentrate on "real" writing instead. The next few years were filled with nothing but misery for Sinclair, his wife Meta (whom he married in 1900), and their infant son David as they watched his first three novels fade into oblivion soon after being published. His next novel, however, *Manassas* (1904), proved to be the turning point in his career. With its theme of a rich young Southerner who rejects plantation life to join the abolitionist movement, *Manassas* demonstrated the author's growing interest in radical politics. The book eventually brought him to the attention of the American Socialists, a movement that had origins in the revolutionary activity in Europe in the mid-nineteenth century as well as the women's rights, abolition, and utopian movements at the same period in America.

Into The Jungle Once in contact with members of the socialist movement, Sinclair began studying philosophy and was soon invited to contribute articles to major socialist publications. In late 1904 Sinclair was encouraged to write about the "wage slaves" of industry in the same way he had written about the "chattel slaves" on the Southern plantations in *Manassas*. Sinclair took as his starting point an article he had recently worked on dealing with an unsuccessful strike in the Chicago meat-packing

LITERARY AND HISTORICAL CONTEMPORARIES

Sinclair's famous contemporaries include:

John D. Rockefeller Jr. (1874–1960): American businessman and philanthropist. Rockefeller was the only son of billionaire industrialist John D. Rockefeller Sr., the founder of Standard Oil. Rockefeller Jr. oversaw the breakup of the oil monopoly but expanded his father's work in philanthropy and the arts.

H. L. Mencken (1880–1956): American journalist and essayist. Mencken was at once a satirist and an observer of American cultural and political life. As a critic, he championed the works of Joseph Conrad and Friedrich Nietzsche; as a journalist, he lampooned religious zealotry and hypocrisy. Mencken's unpredictable tastes are often described as "elitist."

Fiorello LaGuardia (1882–1947): American politician. As mayor of New York City during the Great Depression, LaGuardia was a major figure in the implementation of New Deal public works projects and in weeding out corruption.

Carl Sandburg (1878–1967): American poet and writer. As a young journalist in Chicago, Sandburg became interested in the poetic possibilities of the booming Midwestern city. His poem "Chicago" (1918) is a classic, celebrating the city as the "Hog Butcher for the World / Tool Maker, Stacker of Wheat." Like Sinclair, Sandburg was also a socialist.

Eleanor Roosevelt (1884–1962): American activist and humanitarian. During Franklin Delano Roosevelt's four terms as president, Eleanor became a pioneering First Lady, writing newspaper columns, working for civil rights, and promoting her husband's New Deal policies. After Franklin's death in 1945, she continued advocating for women's rights and civil rights.

industry. Having received an advance for his novel-to-be, Sinclair moved his family to a farm in New Jersey and set out for Chicago in November 1904, promising to "shake the popular heart and blow the roof off of the industrial tea-kettle." It was, notes William A. Bloodworth in his study *Upton Sinclair*, a trip that "made a traumatic, life-long impression on him." Explains the critic,

> What World War I meant to Ernest Hemingway, what the experiences of poverty and crime meant to Jack London, the combination of visible oppression and underlying corruption in Chicago in 1904 meant to Upton Sinclair. This kind of evidence, this kind of commitment to social justice became the primal experience of his fiction. For at least the next

four decades, . . . Sinclair would continually retell the story of what happened to him in Chicago.

Sinclair's investigative work for his novel, *The Jungle*, took seven weeks, during which time he talked with workers and visited meat-packing plants, both on an official basis and undercover. "I sat at night in the homes of the workers, foreign-born and native, and they told me their stories, one after one, and I made notes of everything," he recalled. Sinclair fashioned the resulting story around the experiences of a fictional Lithuanian immigrant who arrives in Chicago fully expecting a piece of the American dream; instead, he is confronted with the reality of poverty, back-breaking labor, and death. As Bloodworth writes, he is "brutalized by working conditions in the Chicago packing houses and exploited by corrupt politics." To dramatize his story of pain and oppression, Sinclair included some unpleasant passages on the meat-packing process itself, focusing on the diseased and chemically tainted condition of the products manufacturers were offering to the American public.

Because Sinclair had a political purpose in writing his novel, he was left with the problem of ending *The Jungle* on a note of socialist hope. His hero, too beaten down to lead the revolution, instead stumbles into a political meeting and undergoes what most critics call a "religious conversion" to socialism. Sinclair completed *The Jungle* in late 1905; balking at the subject matter, his publisher rejected it. It took four more tries—and the house of Doubleday's fact-checking trip to Chicago—to get the novel published.

Though *The Jungle* was written as a socialist novel, it was promoted as an exposé of the food industry, which was an issue that easily stirred up outcry at the turn of the century. *The Jungle* shocked and infuriated Americans; it was, in fact, this widespread revulsion that made the book a best seller and its author a world-famous writer. But never again did Sinclair write a novel with quite the impact of *The Jungle*.

The Next Acts Between 1906 and 1914, Sinclair's career took several directions. He organized a communal living experiment in New Jersey only to see the building burn down in March 1907. Continuing to write novels about socialism, and seeking answers to personal problems, especially the breakup of his marriage, Sinclair made several attempts at utopian communal living. He also wrote about diet and health; about the corrupt worlds of the wealthy and of high finance; about feminism and the modern marriage; and about sexually transmitted disease.

Around 1914 Sinclair found his footing again, beginning a successful second marriage (to Mary Craig Kimbrough) and relocating to southern California. There he wrote *King Coal* (1917), a *Jungle*–esque look at the lives of miners in Colorado. It was less successful than the earlier venture, however, as it was released at the dawn of World War I when Americans were far more interested in submarines than they were in coal or labor.

It was not until the end of the 1920s that Sinclair had another major novelistic success, and that was with a pair of novels again dealing with current events, *Oil!* (1927) and *Boston* (1928). *Oil!* is a long, expansive novel based loosely on the oil scandals of the Harding administration (1921–23) and revolves around the son of a prosperous oilman who finds himself torn between loyalty to his father and the radical politics he has come to believe in. *Boston* is a fictional account of the Sacco-Vanzetti case, in which two Italian American anarchists were arrested, tried, and then executed for murder in 1927; it is widely believed that the men's political beliefs—including confidence in violence against the government as a solution—were used to convict them unfairly. The novel represents Sinclair's best effort at using his medium as a means to publicize and interpret contemporary events.

Sinclair did not just write about politics in novel form, but actually attempted to influence them. In 1934 he ran, unsuccessfully, for governor of California on an antipoverty platform; his experience is reflected in his novel *Co-Op* (1936). By the end of the 1930s, however, with the world on the brink of yet another World War, Sinclair turned his attentions to writing historical novels, detailing the major, world-changing events in history from 1913 to 1950 as told through the experiences of one character, Lanny Budd. His writing career wound down in the 1950s. When Sinclair died in 1968 most of the obituaries were generous in their praise. Some of them noted one of the main ironies of his career: that such an essentially gentle person could have written some of the most socially combative works in American fiction.

Works in Literary Context

Muckraking While the novels of Sinclair—in particular *The Jungle*—have become classic examples of "muckraking," the term covers much more than just the politically motivated novel. It primarily refers to a type of investigative journalism that aims to expose large-scale, widespread fraud and corruption by governments and institutions, as well as the appalling social conditions of workers and slum-dwellers. Muckraking was a popular journalistic practice in the late nineteenth and early twentieth centuries, but its appeal—both for writers and readers—has persisted, with many writers willing to hold the powerful accountable even if nobody else will. Often, muckraking succeeds in bringing about change: Ralph Nader's *Unsafe at Any Speed* (1962) led to major safety regulations in the auto industry. At other times, muckraking makes for a powerfully good read, when such literary talents as Jessica Mitford feel called to investigate: Mitford's *The American Way of Death* (1963), an exposé of the funeral industry, remains a classic of literary journalism.

Works in Critical Context

The Jungle Writing about the nature of *The Jungle*'s phenomenal success, Alfred Kazin observes, in his book *On Native Grounds,*

COMMON HUMAN EXPERIENCE

Sinclair was not the first writer, or the last, to decry the exploitation of workers. Here are some other works that illuminate the plight of the "wage slave":

Sibyl, or The Two Nations (1845), a novel by Benjamin Disraeli. Like Sinclair, Disraeli worked out his social philosophy through literature (though Disraeli was also a successful politician). His novel *Sibyl* dramatizes the severe contrast between rich and poor and details the dire economic straits of the textile worker in England.

"The Chimney Sweeper" (1789), a poem by William Blake, from *Songs of Innocence*. Written in the voice of a small child who was sent off to do the dangerous, life-shortening work of cleaning chimneys, Blake's poem suggests the nightmare of the chimney sweep's life by describing the boy's unattainable fantasy of a different life.

Matewan (1987), a film directed by John Sayles. Based on a true story, *Matewan* recounts a 1920 coal-miners' strike in West Virginia after the workers' attempt to unionize is quashed.

The Grapes of Wrath (1939), a novel by John Steinbeck. In Steinbeck's Depression classic, the Joad family is forced to leave their farm in Oklahoma and, with thousands of others, migrate west in search of a better life. What they find is too few jobs for too many workers, and industrial farms in collusion to keep wages down. Consequently, the dreamed-of future never arrives.

Maria Full of Grace (2004), a film written and directed by Joshua Marston. The heroine is caught between two forms of economic exploitation: her job in Colombia at a sweat shop, and the dangerous decision she makes to work as a "mule" smuggling drugs into the United States.

The Jungle attracted attention because it was obviously the most authentic and most powerful of the muckraking novels. The romantic indignation of the book gave it its fierce honesty, but the facts in it gave Sinclair his reputation, for he had suddenly given an unprecedented social importance to muckraking. ... No one could doubt it, the evidence was overwhelming: here in *The Jungle* was the great news story of a decade written out in letters of fire.

But while few critics discount *The Jungle*'s importance, many maintain that the novel isn't great literature. Its plot and characterization have come under particularly heavy fire, with *Bookman*'s Edward Clark Marsh, for instance, arguing that "we do not need to be told that thievery, and prostitution, and political jobbery, and economic slavery exist in Chicago. So long as these truths are before us only as abstractions they are meaningless." As for its characters, Marsh found them underformed, while

Walter Rideout, writing in *The Radical Novel in the United States*, saw the protagonist as a composite of many of the people Sinclair would have met in Chicago. While this is still a kind of flawed characterization, Rideout writes that the characters' "mere capacities for infinite suffering … finally do come to stand for the masses themselves." Many reviewers were also disappointed with the book's ending, especially the abrupt switch from fiction to political rhetoric that occurs when the protagonist is "converted" to socialism. Writing in *The Strenuous Age in American Literature*, Grant C. Knight observes that the final section "is uplifting but it is also artificial, an arbitrary re-channelling of the narrative flow, a piece of rhetoric instead of a logical continuation of story."

Responses to Literature

1. The horrors of the meat-packing industry Sinclair wrote about in *The Jungle* may be a thing of the past, but the working life is far from easy. Read about the modern-day struggles of the working poor in Barbara Ehrenreich's *Nickel and Dimed: On (Not) Getting By in America* (2001). What has changed? What remains the same about the lives described in the two books?

2. One of Sinclair's more successful novels, *Boston*, is about a controversial real-life event. Using your library and the Internet, research the trial and execution of Sacco and Vanzetti, and write a paper in which you put forward your own theory of why the men were condemned.

3. Upton Sinclair is one of those novelists whose body of work is forever overshadowed by one novel, in his case *The Jungle*. Why is this? Read *The Jungle* and another of Sinclair's novels, and write an essay in which you speculate on the justice or injustice of this reputation. Be sure to consider the literary "quality" of the novels, as well as the historical circumstances that might determine public interest.

BIBLIOGRAPHY

Books

Bloodworth, William A., Jr. *Upton Sinclair*. Boston: Twayne, 1977.

Dell, Floyd. *Upton Sinclair: A Study in Social Protest*. New York: Doran, 1927.

Karsner, David. *Sixteen Authors to One: Intimate Sketches of Leading American Story Tellers*. New York: Copeland, 1928.

Kazin, Alfred. *On Native Grounds: An Interpretation of Modern American Prose Literature*. New York: Harcourt, 1942.

Knight, Grant C. *The Strenuous Age in American Literature*. Chapel Hill: University of North Carolina Press, 1954.

Mookerjee, Rabindra Nath. *Art for Social Justice: The Major Novels of Upton Sinclair*. Metuchen, N.J.: Scarecrow Press, 1988.

Rideout, Walter. *The Radical Novel in the United States 1900–1954: Some Interrelations of Literature and Society*. Cambridge: Harvard University Press, 1956.

Scott, Ivan. *Upton Sinclair: The Forgotten Socialist*. Lanham, Md.: University Press of America, 1996.

Sinclair, Upton. *The Autobiography of Upton Sinclair*. New York: Harcourt, Brace and World, 1962.

Periodicals

Marsh, Edward Clark. Review of *The Jungle*. *Bookman* (April 1906).

◉ Isaac Bashevis Singer

BORN: *1904, Leoncin, Poland*

DIED: *1988, Surfside, Florida*

NATIONALITY: *American*

GENRE: *Fiction*

MAJOR WORKS:
Satan in Goray (1943)
The Family Moskat (1950)

Isaac Bashevis Singer *Singer, Isaac Bashevis, photograph.* © *Jerry Bauer. Reproduced by permission.*

Gimpel the Fool and Other Stories (1957)

Shosha (1978)

Yentl, the Yeshiva Boy (1986)

Overview

Isaac Bashevis Singer, the only writer in Yiddish ever to be awarded the Nobel Prize in Literature, was among the most popular and widely read authors of the twentieth century. Singer's extensive body of work expresses his preoccupation with the destruction of the lost Orthodox Jewish world of Eastern Europe. The tension in Singer's fiction is generated by the conflict between faith and rationalism. His typical protagonist is a man like himself who abandons the regimen of strict, devout Orthodox Jewish observance in which he was raised and embraces the secular, modern world but is unable to find contentment there.

Works in Biographical and Historical Context

Early Life and Education The son and grandson of rabbis on both sides of his family, Singer was born Icek-Hersz Zynger, the second son of strictly observant Orthodox Jewish parents, on July 14, 1904, in the village of Leoncin, a provincial town northeast of Warsaw in Poland, where his father, Pinkhos-Menakhem Zynger, was the resident rabbi. Singer's father was a learned and devout follower of Hasidism, a movement that developed among East European Jews in the eighteenth century. Singer's father's strong emotional bent was sharply counterbalanced by the uncompromising rationalism of his wife, the practical and studious Basheve. She and her family were *misnagdim*, unbending opponents of Hasidism and its ecstatic, mystical, and hierarchical traditions. Both were apparently gifted storytellers, but their opposed conceptions of how the physical world operated, aggravated by the family's bitter poverty, led to conflicts.

When Isaac was four years old, the family had moved to Warsaw, where his father established his rabbinical court. In 1914, at the outbreak of World War I, Singer's mother sought safety for Isaac and his younger brother Moshe (both his mother and Moshe would later perish in a Soviet work camp during World War II) by returning to her birthplace, the Polish village of Bilgoray, where her father ruled his strictly observant community uncompromisingly—barring all manifestations of modernity. Bilgoray was a town with a long-established scholarly reputation, and there Singer acquired an intimate knowledge of the minutest observances of Jewish Orthodoxy, of ancient Jewish folk customs and superstitions, and of a rich range of Yiddish—his native language and the language he would write in—idioms. Yiddish is the thousand-year-old form of German developed by Jews, using the Hebrew alphabet and incorporating ancient Hebrew and Aramaic words. Its vocabulary expanded by adapting words from European languages with which Jews had contact, including Russian and English. Dur-

ing the Middle Ages, it became the language for daily speech among Jews, especially in Eastern Europe.

Like all Orthodox Jewish boys of his time, Singer received his early education in traditional religious schools. His older brother (by eleven years), Israel Joshua—who also became a highly respected writer and intellectual—had a profound impact on Isaac's education, supplying him with secular books and Yiddish translations of popular literature. Israel Joshua's devotion to rationalism would essentially divorce him from all religious beliefs, and he would later challenge Isaac to take the same steps, though Isaac would never fully disavow religion.

Since his parents expected him to enter the rabbinate, at the age of seventeen, Singer enrolled in the Tachkemoni Rabbinical Seminary in Warsaw. However, he remained a student for only one year, between 1921 and 1922. Following his unhappy stint in seminary, Singer taught Hebrew for a short while before deciding he would try to devote himself fully to writing.

Israel Joshua had established a growing reputation as a journalist, and in the summer of 1923, he introduced his brother to the Warsaw Yiddish Writers' Club, where Isaac would find an artistic home but feel permanently ill-at-ease with the favor, which would contribute to a guilty, yet intense, sibling rivalry he maintained with Israel Joshua. Like his brother, Singer worked as a proofreader for the distinguished Warsaw Yiddish journal *Literarishe bleter* (*Literary Pages*) between 1923 and 1933, and supplemented his meager income by translating several mainstream European novels into Yiddish, including *Di vogler* (*The Wanderers*) and *Viktoria*, by Knut Hamsun, a Norwegian writer whose novel *Hunger* had sustained Singer in the dark days of his rabbinical studies. Hamsun's novel dealt with a desperate, nameless hero estranged from Christiania (Oslo) society; the hero, nevertheless, is deeply, if invisibly, rooted in the life and culture of Norway. This theme of simultaneous separation and connectedness would echo through Singer's own body of work.

Identity and Early Successes Singer began work on his own writing in Yiddish, which appeared in Warsaw to some acclaim. In 1925, his first published work of fiction, a short story titled "Oyf der elter" ("In Old Age"), won a high-status prize offered by *Literarishe bleter*. This debut story was also the first to be signed Yitskhok Bashevis, the pseudonym by which Singer elected to be known to his Yiddish readers. This name had several intentions; he was dissociating himself from the family name under which his brother had become famous and admired, partly in an attempt to cut himself free from the debts owed to Isaac Joshua's influence and generosity. Moreover, the name he chose publicly declared his intellectual kinship with his rationalistic mother. In Yiddish usage, the name Bashevis is the possessive form of the name Basheve, so Singer became, "the one belonging to Basheve." He used this name exclusively for his fiction in Yiddish.

LITERARY AND HISTORICAL CONTEMPORARIES

Singer's famous contemporaries include:

Irène Némirovsky (1903–1942): Jewish author who resided in Paris during the Nazi Occupation. Her extraordinary novelistic account of this time, *Suite Francaise*, was discovered by her daughter and published to great acclaim in 2006. Despite having converted to Catholicism, Némirovsky was arrested and died at Auschwitz.

Langston Hughes (1902–1967): American poet, novelist, and playwright, he was one of the most well known and influential figures of the Harlem Renaissance, the eruption of creativity and transformative art produced by African Americans in the 1920s and 1930s in the New York neighborhood of Harlem.

John Steinbeck (1902–1968): An American Pulitzer and Nobel Prize–winning author, his novels chronicled the plight of Depression-era families and individuals struggling to maintain their dignity in the face of abject poverty and hardship.

Menachem Begin (1913–1992): A former prime minister of Israel and Siberian Exile, Begin won the Nobel Peace Prize after signing a peace treaty with Egypt in 1979.

Bernard Malamud (1914–1986): The son of Russian Jewish immigrants, Malamud was one of the most prominent of twentieth-century Jewish American authors. His novel, *The Fixer* (1967), was awarded the Pulitzer Prize.

The various ways he chose to sign different genres of his writing remained a matter of great importance to him throughout his creative life. To distance himself further from his brother, he became a regular visitor in the home of Hillel Tseytlin, the conservative leader of Warsaw's intellectual religious community, where he formed a lifelong friendship with his son, Arn, with whom he would found the Yiddish literary journal *Globus*. Singer would serialize his first novel, *Satan in Goray*, in *Globus*. The connection with Tseyltin put distance between him and his brother, who was antireligious at this point. Between 1926 and 1935, Singer lived with, but never married, Rohkyl Shapira, by whom he had one son, Israel Zamir, born in 1929.

Immigration and the Progress of Translation The complications of Singer's personal life had merged with the deepening crisis in world affairs. His father had died in 1929; the mother of his son was a fervent Communist, an ideology Singer detested; Hitler's rise to power in Germany had led to an intensification of Jew hatred in Poland. Israel Joshua had immigrated to the United States in 1934. There his reputation and ability had established him as a senior member of the staff of the leading Yiddish daily, *Forverts* (*Jewish Daily Forward*). With Israel Joshua's help, Isaac Bashevis immigrated, alone, to the United States in 1935 and settled in New York. His son and Shapira settled in then-Palestine. In 1940, Singer married Alma Wassermann, a German Jewish immigrant, and became a naturalized United States citizen in 1943. His beloved brother Israel Joseph passed away in 1944, and shortly thereafter, Singer became a columnist at *Forverts*. He would remain loyal to the newspaper for the rest of his life; in it he published the greatest part of all his work in Yiddish.

Singer called Yiddish "my mother language and the language of the people I wanted to write about," but soon after his arrival in America, he realized that he would have a limited future if his work were only published in a language with a steadily diminishing readership. Determined to follow the example of Sholem Asch, the first Yiddish writer to gain international recognition and a mass readership in English translation, he began to translate his work, consciously addressing two differing sets of readerships. It was these translations that catapulted his celebrity, though massive amounts of it remain untranslated to this day.

After his immigration, Singer wrote fervently about the horrors of the Holocaust and the issues concerning the fate of Yiddish. He condemned all attempts in Yiddish to create modern literature, arguing instead for a return to the "hidden treasures" of the age-old Jewish folk culture. He argued that, since in America the Yiddish language had become obsolete, it could no longer realistically depict contemporary American life, but should instead renounce the present in favor of the past by recording and preserving the destroyed world of Eastern Europe. He began work on his long saga novel, *The Family Moskat*, which aimed to depict, through the fortunes of one family, the decline and fall of twentieth-century Polish Jewry. He dedicated the English translation to Israel Joshua.

Short Stories and Serializations During the 1950s, and until the end of his life, Singer found his short stories in great demand; they appeared prominently in such high-profile magazines as *The New Yorker*, *Harper's*, and *Esquire*. In 1966, Singer produced *Zlateh the Goat and Other Stories*, the first of his many books for children and based it, in part, upon old Jewish folktales. Wittily illustrated by Maurice Sendak, this book was well received and won Singer his first Newberry Honor Book Award.

Singer would eventually publish, in English, ten collections of short stories. His novels typically began their life in Yiddish, in *Forverts*, where they would take on a unique structure—smaller, plot-driven scenes that would play well in serializations. These short stories and novels would be a forum for Singer to work on, and work out, his demons. Directly exposed for the first thirty years of his own life to those twentieth-century intellectual, political, and social upheavals that radically undermined traditional Jewish identity, Singer set out to weigh what the Jewish people had gained against what they had lost by surrendering the traditional observances of their faith. By shifting the settings of his fictions over a period of nearly four centuries, Singer forced his readers to recognize the value of what had been lost, but also compelled them to question whether its recovery was either possible or desirable.

Final Years In 1978, Singer won the Nobel Prize for Literature, and accepted it, seemingly, on behalf of Yiddish itself. This appalled the majority of native speakers of Yiddish, among them his fellow Yiddish writers and poets. They objected to the fact that Singer had become known exclusively through English translation and had, therefore, done nothing to promote Yiddish itself. They argued that his subject matter—particularly his use of demons and sexuality—was unwholesome and designed to cater to predominantly non-Jewish mass tastes and that Singer had no respect for the Yiddish literary tradition, which he denigrated, together with its leading practitioners, at every opportunity. Singer changed little about the way he wrote following the criticism.

In 1989, the American Academy of Arts presented Singer with its highest honor, a Gold Medal, and a year later, he was elected as a member of the academy, the first American author who did not write exclusively in English to be so honored. Director Paul Mazursky's 1989 movie adaptation of *Enemies, A Love Story* became the first of Singer's works adapted for the big screen to please the critics: the movie received two Academy Award nominations. By the turn of the decade, Singer was seriously ill with Alzheimer's disease, and it is unlikely that he played any active role in the translation and publication of *Scum*, the last of his novels published in his lifetime, which appeared in 1991. As he had aged, Singer spent more and more time with the Jewish community in Miami. He eventually moved there and died following a series of strokes in 1991.

Works in Literary Context

Jewish Literature Singer remains among the most influential Jewish writers of the twentieth century. His enormous popularity enabled him to bring to vivid life, and to international attention, the destroyed world of the shtetl. His novels and stories made non-Jewish readers aware of the spiritual depths of the Jewish faith, and of the irreplaceable loss of the Jews of Eastern Europe. For Jewish readers, his primary importance lies in his confrontation with the need to seek a meaningful identity in a secular world far removed from traditional Orthodox observance. For the literary world at large, not least among Singer's achievements, has been his influence in calling to general attention the valuable body of modern Yiddish literature from which he himself drew so deeply, and to which he contributed so significantly. The writers whom he has most influenced have taken their cues from his longing for the shtetl and his poignant separation

---

COMMON HUMAN EXPERIENCE

In *Yentl, the Yeshiva Boy*, among other stories, Singer explores both the power and helplessness of sexual identity in Judaism. Here are other works in which Jewish characters try to escape or confront their issues of gender identity or sexual preference.

The Amazing Adventures of Kavalier and Clay (2000), a novel by Michael Chabon. Sam Klayman, a comic book writer, creates a character called the Escapist, who helps him wrestle with his homosexuality during the post–World War II era. He eventually settles into a heterosexual marriage and fatherhood that brings contentment and community in place of romantic passion.

Angels in America (1993), a play by Tony Kushner. The character, based on deeply closeted Roy Cohn, a real-life McCarthy-era attorney who played a significant role in the capital convictions of Julius and Ethel Rosenberg in 1951, utilizes a questionable loophole to deny his gay identity. He eventually succumbs to AIDS, haunted by the ghost of Ethel Rosenberg, as he lies dying.

Torch Song Trilogy (1982), a play by, and starring, Harvey Fierstein. The play centers on the trials and search for acceptance of a Jewish New York City drag queen, Arnold Beckhoff, his lovers, and his gay son.

---

from it. Jonathan Safran Foer's *Everything Is Illuminated* (2002), pays a tremendous debt to Singer, as does the work of Cynthia Ozick—another writer with ties to the Yiddish language and an unfailing belief in the art form as the most sensible forum for moral discussion.

Works in Critical Context

By the turn of the millennium, some critical consensus about Singer's work had emerged. Widely accepted as self-evident is Alfred Kazin's 1962 contention that "Singer's work does stem from the Jewish village, the Jewish seminary, the compact (not closed) Jewish society of Eastern Europe. ... For Singer, it is not only his materials that are 'Jewish'; the world is so. Yet, within this world he has found emancipation and universality—through his faith in imagination." Earlier critical disputes about whether Singer was a modernist or an existentialist have largely been laid to rest. Singer is clearly not modernist in his techniques, and his putative "existentialism" is now viewed as deeply personal misery about the human condition. In a 1992 article for *Judaism*, Dan Miron succinctly summed up Singer's worldview: "He approached the act of literary creation with a base-experience of underlying awareness that falls under the sign of fatalism and nihilism."

Gimpel the Fool The work that brought Singer to the forefront of American literary critical attention was

"Gimpel the Fool," sensitively translated by Saul Bellow and published in *Partisan Review* in May 1953. This short story was the piece by which Singer became best known, and in December 1955 it was hailed by the *Saturday Review* as "a classic of Yiddish literature." Its central character, the seemingly naive water carrier, Gimpel, is among the most vividly drawn of a long line of saintly innocents who appear throughout Yiddish literature. Through his subtly nuanced re-creation of the archetypal Jewish folk figure of the schlemiel, or bumbling, unworldly incompetent, Singer poses profound questions about the nature of truth and lies, through which he points to the difference between this world and the world to come. One critic for *The New York Times Book Review* declared that, with this volume, "Singer takes his place with the epic storytellers, transcending geographical and chronological boundaries."

Shosha 1978, the year Singer won the Nobel Prize, also saw the English translation of *Shosha*. Set in the years immediately preceding Hitler's invasion of Poland, *Shosha* marks the debut of Aaron Greidinger, Singer's fictional alter ego. This writer and unapologetic lover of women decides to marry his childhood sweetheart, the titular Shosha, a mentally retarded woman. The scenes of their youth in Warsaw set a tender tone, one that is torn away in the latter part of the book, as the Holocaust approaches.

Shosha suggests that the impotent thoughts and doings that preoccupy the characters of prewar Warsaw is the spiritual dead end into which worldly secularization has led, a familiar Singer theme. The fatalism with which these Jews await extirpation at Nazi hands is presented as a collective death wish, as much as a passive acceptance of political events outside their personal control. Like Singer, the narrator of *Shosha* was able to escape Warsaw, but his luck, by comparison with the millions who were unable to flee, obviously remained deeply rooted in his psyche. Hence, Aaron Greidinger attempts to memorize every one of Warsaw's sights and sounds in the hope that by recording them in writing, he will miraculously be able to bring the destroyed world of Jewish Warsaw back to life.

Shosha met with an openly hostile reception from Leon Wieseltier in the *New York Review of Books*, who dismissed it as "a stunted novel about stunted lives." Alan Lelchuk, however, writing in the *New York Times Book Review*, pointed out Singer's unwillingness to confront a true dramatic dilemma, but praised the work as a whole for its entertainment value. "The author permits [Greidinger] to exit quietly from Poland and eventually take up life anew in America, while an external madness (Nazism) has obliterated the other characters ... [But] The way out for Singer is the dream, the fantasy, the mythic, not the real ... Singer's aim is to entertain, and by this standard he fully succeeds in *Shosha*."

Responses to Literature

1. Read Singer's *Gimpel the Fool and Other Stories*. What sort of characters are featured most frequently as the protagonists of these stories? Do the stories present a pessimistic or an optimistic vision of human life? How do his main characters cope with suffering?

2. Isaac Singer was forced to bear witness to the steady decline and near-loss of Yiddish—his first, much beloved language. As the pace of globalization quickens, more and more languages are threatened with extinction. Research two or three dead or dying languages and the people who spoke them. Write a paper in which you explore the conditions that led to their demise, the rise of any possible replacements and what the consequences might mean for any surviving speakers.

3. Singer was able to escape Warsaw and immigrate to the United States, even as his mother and brother died in a Soviet work camp. Subsequently, his art would reflect the nature of his simultaneous guilt and gratitude. Read the work of other Jewish writers who remained, and perished, in Europe at the hands of the Nazis, and discuss the differences in tone and style you perceive that can be attributable to that difference.

4. "Yentl, the Yeshiva Boy," was made into both a successful Broadway play (1975), and a hit film starring Barbra Streisand (1983). Singer, however, was outspoken in his disdain for the treatment his story received when it became the Streisand musical. Read the story and then watch the film version. Write a paper in which you defend or repudiate the adaptation, based on its artistic merit.

BIBLIOGRAPHY

Books

Allentuck, Marcia. *The Achievement of Isaac Bashevis Singer*. Carbondale: Southern Illinois University Press, 1969.

Hadda, Janet. *Isaac Bashevis Singer: A Life*. New York: Oxford University Press, 1997.

Irving, Malin. *Isaac Bashevis Singer*. New York: Unger, 1972.

Sanders, Ronald. *The Americanization of Isaac Bashevis Singer*. Syracuse, N.Y.: Syracuse University Press, 1989.

Siegel, Ben. *Isaac Bashevis Singer*. Minneapolis: University of Minnesota Press, 1969.

Tuszyńska, Agata. *Lost Landscapes: in Search of Isaac Bashevis Singer and the Jews of Poland*. New York: Morrow, 1998.

Periodicals

"Isaac Bashevis Singer, Nobel Laureate for His Yiddish Stories, Is Dead at 87" *New York Times* (July 26, 1991).

Lelchuk, Alan. "Sex, Torah, Revolution" *New York Times* (July 23, 1978).

Gussow, Mel. "Theater: Fierstein's 'Torch Song'" *New York Times* (November 1, 1981).

Pinsker, Sanford. "Cynthia Ozick, Aesthete." *Partisan Review* 2 (2002): vol. 69.

New York Review of Books (December 7, 1978).

Web sites

IBDB: The Official Source for Broadway Information. Retrieved November 21, 2008, from http://www.ibdb.com/show.php?id=1596.

✪ Jane Smiley

BORN: *1949, Los Angeles, California*

NATIONALITY: *American*

GENRE: *Fiction*

MAJOR WORKS:

A Thousand Acres (1991)

Moo (1995)

Thirteen Ways of Looking at the Novel (2005)

Overview

Jane Smiley is an acclaimed novelist and short-fiction writer who won the Pulitzer Prize for *A Thousand Acres* (1991), her reworking of William Shakespeare's play *King Lear* (c. 1603). Smiley writes about the complex, often secret, emotional dynamics that underlie ordinary human relationships. At the heart of Smiley's fiction is her belief that there

are answers—sometimes bitter, even traumatic—to the questions that afflict human beings.

Works in Biographical and Historical Context

Turbulent Family, Political Times Smiley was born on September 26, 1949, in Los Angeles. By the time Smiley was four years old, her parents had divorced, and Smiley moved with her mother to St. Louis, Missouri. In 1960, Smiley's mother remarried, to a man who had two children of his own. Throughout her youth, Smiley lived in close contact with a large extended family, a fact that influenced the many fictional families she placed at the center of her novels and short stories.

Smiley came of age during the 1960s, one of the most turbulent periods in American history. America's involvement in the Vietnam War was met with growing opposition throughout the United States. The result was a deep divide between war supporters and the antiwar movement. Yet, this was also a time of incredible social progress. The civil rights movement made significant achievements over the course of the decade, and feminism and the environmental movements also came to the fore. Against this backdrop, Smiley graduated from high school and enrolled

Jane Smiley *Smiley, Jane, photograph. AP Images.*

LITERARY AND HISTORICAL CONTEMPORARIES

Smiley's famous contemporaries include:

Lyndon B. Johnson (1908–1973): President of the United States from 1963–1969, Johnson presided over much of the turbulent decade of the 1960s.

Cormac McCarthy (1933–): McCarthy is a Pulitzer Prize–winning author of novels, plays, and screenplays in many genres, though he is best known for his violent Western novel *Blood Meridian* (1985).

Joyce Carol Oates (1938–): One of the most prolific contemporary American authors, Oates's works are heavily influenced by cultural and historical events since the 1960s.

Judy Chicago (1939–): Chicago is a feminist artist who began making art during the 1960s; she is most famous for her work *The Dinner Party* (1979).

Amy Tan (1952–): A Chinese-American fiction writer widely recognized for her novel *The Joy Luck Club* (1989), Tan often writes about the complexities of mother-daughter relationships.

in Vassar College, in Poughkeepsie, New York. During the summer of 1970, Smiley lived with John B. Whiston in a commune in New Haven, Connecticut. In September of that year, the two were married.

Shortly after they were married, Smiley and Whiston moved to Iowa City, Iowa. Smiley worked in a factory while Whiston pursued graduate work in history. In 1972, she was accepted into the doctoral program at the University of Iowa. She was interested in writing as well as studying literature, and she participated in the Iowa Writers' Workshop in 1974 even as she continued to work on her master's degree. In 1975, she and Whiston divorced. With the aid of a Fulbright-Hays grant, Smiley spent the academic year of 1976–1977 in Iceland, researching Icelandic sagas for her doctoral dissertation. During this same year she also received her MFA from the Iowa Writers' Workshop. In 1978, Smiley completed her PhD and began her second marriage, to editor William Silag. 1982, Smiley took a position with Iowa State University, where she taught courses on literature and creative writing until 1997.

Professional Success, Personal Difficulties Shortly after she completed her PhD, Smiley began publishing short fiction in various journals and finished two novels, *Barn Blind* (1980) and *At Paradise Gate* (1981). The latter won the Friends of American Writers Prize that year. *Barn Blind* chronicles the life of Kate Karlson, a domineering mother of four teenage children. In *At Paradise Gate*, the impending death of Ike Robinson provides an opportunity for his wife and her three daughters to revisit the family's shared

regrets, sorrows, and personal victories. In these first novels, Smiley began the exploration of family dynamics that she continued to refine throughout much of her work. Smiley's skill as a short-story writer also became evident during this time, and in 1982, she was awarded an O. Henry Award for "The Pleasure of Her Company," originally published in *Mademoiselle* (1981).

In the summer of 1984, Smiley traveled to England, Denmark, and Greenland, and began work on the novel *The Greenlanders* (1988). The following year, her status as a preeminent author of short fiction was solidified when her story "Lily" (1984) shared first prize in the O. Henry Awards. With "Lily," which was originally published in *The Atlantic* and later collected in *The Age of Grief* (1987), Smiley introduces a character whose obsession with order prevents her from comprehending the complexities of intimacy. Lily underestimates the diverse, often contradictory, impulses underlying motivation and desire. In "Lily," Smiley reflects on how important it is to recognize the truth of the heart's complexity, a theme that is present in many of her works.

Smiley's personal life also shared some of the relationship tensions she wrote about in her novels and fiction. In 1986, she and Silag were divorced, and she married screenwriter Stephen Mortensen the following year. During that same year she published *The Age of Grief*, which received a Book Critics Circle Award nomination. The title novella, composed during her breakup with Silag, provides an intimate portrait of marriage, parenthood, and the emotional trauma of infidelity. *The Age of Grief* also includes the story "Long Distance," which became Smiley's third story to win an O. Henry Award for short fiction. In 1988, she published the novel *The Greenlanders* and a volume comprising her two novellas, *Ordinary Love & Good Will*. In 1990, Smiley published *The Life of the Body: A Story*, a limited-edition volume. After being reprinted in *Antaeus*, the story won Smiley her fourth O. Henry Award in 1996. "The Life of the Body" is often recognized as Smiley's most poignant short story. It also speaks to the complexities of intimacy, the secrets that bind families together, and the mysterious potency of people's inner lives, themes that feature heavily in her most widely recognized work, *A Thousand Acres*.

Creating a Modern Masterpiece from a Classic Play
In 1991, Smiley published *A Thousand Acres*, a feminist reimagining of William Shakespeare's *King Lear*, which won her the Pulitzer Prize, the National Book Critics Circle Award, and the Heartland Award. *A Thousand Acres* tells the story of the Cooks, a Midwestern farming family devastated by both incest and the technological changes in American agriculture. When Ginny Cook, the eldest daughter, remembers the sexual abuse she suffered at her father's hands, she begins to question the familial and communal foundations of her reality. The novel earned

Smiley critical acclaim, vastly expanded her readership, and was adapted in a feature film of the same title in 1997.

A Busy Writing and Teaching Life After the publication of *A Thousand Acres*, Smiley continued writing and teaching. In 1995, Smiley published her sixth novel, *Moo*, which received a Book Critics Circle Award nomination. The novel is a comedy set in a college located in a small Midwestern town that satirizes the petty politics of the university. *Moo* is undoubtedly influenced by Smiley's own experience as a professor at the Iowa State University, where she taught until moving to California in 1997. In 1998, she published *The All-True Travels and Adventures of Lidie Newton*, a historical novel set in the mid–nineteenth century in America's Midwest, a region divided by the issue of slavery. Smiley drew upon her many years of teaching and writing for her nonfiction exploration of the history and craft of the novel, *Thirteen Ways of Looking at the Novel* (2005). Her latest work, *Ten Days in the Hills* (2007), focuses on a group of ultrarich and powerful Hollywood friends and acquaintances who shut themselves off from the outside world at the beginning of the Iraq War in 2003.

Works in Literary Context

Although her novels and short stories belong to a number of different genres, Smiley's work is firmly grounded in realism. The movement of literary realism began in nineteenth-century fiction and extended well into the twentieth century. Realism is concerned with dramatizing an authentic representation of contemporary, everyday life. Smiley is a notable American realist similar to Edith Wharton, Theodore Dreiser, and Joyce Carol Oates, all of whom use the style to engage in subtle critiques of the social issues that influence their characters.

Domestic Fiction Because of Smiley's emphasis on family life and her focus on exploring relationships, she can be regarded as a modern author of domestic fiction. Principally regarded as a nineteenth-century genre, domestic fiction (sometimes referred to as "sentimental fiction") is a category of novel that depicts family life and the relationships of a heroine. Smiley's work is both influenced by domestic fiction and responding to it: she shares many of the concerns of traditional domestic fiction, but her works often depict home and family as a place of instability, rather than stability.

Comic Novels Many of Smiley's later works are comic novels of social observation, including *Moo*, which satirizes the university system; *Good Faith* (2003), a comical examination of the financial boom of the mid-1980s; and *Ten Days in the Hills*, a biting Hollywood satire. While the chief concern of comic novels is to amuse their readers, Smiley joins many American authors—including Tom Wolfe, Carl Hiaasen, and John Kennedy Toole—in using the form to explore and critique social issues.

COMMON HUMAN EXPERIENCE

In *A Thousand Acres*, Smiley reworks *King Lear* to examine patriarchal family systems and their impact on women. Here are some other novels that rework classic texts in order to explore ideas, concepts, and literary genres:

Wide Sargasso Sea (1966), a novel by Jean Rhys. Rhys reimagines the characters and relationship of Charlotte Brontë's *Jane Eyre* (1847) with a focus on the "madwoman" in the attic in order to explore postcolonialism.
Grendel (1971), a novel by John Gardner. This novel is a retelling of the epic poem *Beowulf* (ca. 1000 C.E.) from the perspective of the monster Grendel, in order to interrogate ideas of good and evil.
Mary Reilly (1990), a novel by Valerie Martin. Reilly reworks Robert Louis Stevenson's *Strange Case of Dr. Jekyll and Mr. Hyde* (1886) from the point of view of a young woman.
H.: The Story of Heathcliff's Journey Back to Wuthering Heights (1992), a novel by Lin Haire-Sargeant. Haire-Sargeant reimagines the plot of Emily Brontë's *Wuthering Heights* (1847) to explore Gothic fiction.

Works in Critical Context

Jane Smiley is widely acclaimed for her ability to craft novels and short fiction about the families and the complexities of family relationships. She is also notable for her ability to effectively use a wide range of settings in her fiction. Many critics have also commended the political aspects of her work, including what many perceive as her feminist point of view in *A Thousand Acres*. Most, however, agree with critic Suzanne MacLachlan, who concludes, "Smiley writes as if she were sitting at the kitchen table telling a story to a friend. Her style is simple, yet she never misses a detail."

A Thousand Acres The Pulitzer Prize–winning *A Thousand Acres* reworks Shakespeare's *King Lear* as a subtle account of a Midwestern farm family's disintegration. Critic Mary Paniccia Garden summarizes critical assessment of Smiley's intent, writing that Smiley focuses "on the cultural mechanisms that define and delimit a woman's place as her father's daughter." Some critics felt that the novel was overly melodramatic, while others felt it was too transparently a feminist critique of male-dominated families. Yet, the vast majority of critics recognize the novel as a modern achievement. As Rupert Christiansen writes in a review for *Spectator*, "*A Thousand Acres* has a moral weight, a technical accomplishment and a sheer eloquence that demands some special recognition."

The Greenlanders A historical novel set in fourteenth-century Greenland, *The Greenlanders* also focuses on family relations, tracing the effects of a curse on several generations of a single family. Critics applauded the manner in which Smiley conveyed the landscape and culture of Greenland, with critic Melissa Pressley concluding in her review for *Christian Science Monitor*, "Smiley conveys the emotional starkness of the Greenlanders' lives. Her voice is the voice of a people numbed by years of the monotony of survival, a people inured by hopelessness into tacit acceptance of the harshest of fates." Critic Niel Nakadate also recognizes a crucial personal dimension to the work that is shared with many members of Smiley's generation. He writes:

> Smiley's preoccupation with explaining Greenland's collective, catastrophic death seems to have had a nagging analog in her personal life: an extraordinary preoccupation with fear—of accidents, of random violence, of nuclear annihilation—and therefore an almost overpowering sense of mortality.

Responses to Literature

1. How does the family of Shakespeare's *King Lear* compare to the family in *A Thousand Acres*? In what ways are they similar? In what ways are they different?

2. With its focus on university life, *Moo* appears to be very different from Smiley's other novels. Yet this novel, also, is about a set of relationships. How do the relationships of the university community in *Moo* compare to the family relationships in Smiley's other works?

3. Secrets are at the center of both the story "The Life of the Body" and the novel *A Thousand Acres*. Compare the way that secrets affect the characters of each. In what ways are they similar? How are they different?

BIBLIOGRAPHY

Books

Nakadate, Neil. *Understanding Jane Smiley*. Columbia: University of South Carolina Press, 1999.

Pearlman, Mickey. "Jane Smiley." *Listen to Their Voices: Twenty Interviews with Women Who Write*. New York: Norton, 1993.

Periodicals

Bakerman, Jane S. "'The Gleaming Obsidian Shard': Jane Smiley's *A Thousand Acres*." *Midamerica* XIX (1992): 127–137.

Carden, Mary Paniccia. "Remembering/Engendering the Heartland: Sexed Language, Embodied Space, and America's Foundational Fictions in Jane Smiley's *A Thousand Acres*." *Frontiers* 18, no. 2 (1997): 181–201.

Christiansen, Rupert. "Speaking Less than She Knowest." *Spectator* vol. 269 (October 10, 1992): 38.

MacLachlan, Suzanne. "Kitchen-Table Tales of Desire and Will." *Christian Science Monitor* vol. 81, 234 (October 30, 1989): 13.

Pressley, Melissa. "A Stark Saga of an Icy Island Settlement in the Dark Ages." *Christian Science Monitor* vol. 80, 196 (September 7, 1988): 18.

Keppel, Tim. "Goneril's Vision: *A Thousand Acres* and *King Lear*." *South Dakota Review* vol. 33 (Summer 1995): 105–117.

Schiff, James A. "Contemporary Retellings: *A Thousand Acres* as the Latest *Lear*." *Critique* 39, no. 4 (Summer 1998): 367–381.

⊛ Anna Deavere Smith

BORN: *1950, Baltimore, Maryland*

NATIONALITY: *American*

GENRE: *Fiction, nonfiction, drama*

MAJOR WORKS:

Fires in the Mirror: Crown Heights, Brooklyn, and Other Identities (1992)

Twilight: Los Angeles, 1992 (1993)

Talk to Me: Listening Between the Lines (2000)

House Arrest: A Search for American Character in and Around the White House, Past and Present, and Piano: Two Plays (2004)

Letters to a Young Artist (2006)

Overview

In the early 1990s, playwright and actress Anna Deavere Smith reclaimed the American theater as a forum for a vital political and social discourse about the issues of race, class, gender, and violence. Her mission was to give voice to people who had never been heard from before and to reach audiences that had never come to the theater.

Biographical and Historical Context

Early Life and Exploration Born September 18, 1950, in Baltimore, Maryland, Smith grew up in a middle-class black family, the eldest of five children. Smith's father ran a small tea and coffee business. Her mother, an educator who taught in the public school system, became an elementary school principal. Smith, who claims she was shy as a child, grew up in a segregated Baltimore. *Brown v. Board of Education* was decided in 1954, but it wasn't until she was a teenager and sent to a predominantly Jewish middle school that she had contact with an integrated community.

In 1967, Smith entered Beaver College outside of Philadelphia. The institution, which was then predominantly white and all female, failed to shelter her from the turbulence of the late 1960s. In 1968, her sophomore year, Martin Luther King Jr. was assassinated. That seminal event, and the subsequent assassination in June 1968 of Bobby Kennedy, the protests against the Vietnam War, the women's movement, the civil rights and black liberation movements, all prompted in her an uneasy social awareness. After graduation, she moved to California and

Anna Deveare Smith   *Robert Pitts / Landov*

began taking acting classes at the American Conservatory Theater in San Francisco.

Epiphanies of Language and Identity   Two events occurred when Smith was in her twenties that were to permanently inform her writing. They both dealt with language and identity. The first was the consequence of an assignment in a Shakespeare class at the American Conservatory. Her instructor, Juanita Rice, assigned an exercise—students were to pick fourteen lines of Shakespeare, at random, and recite them aloud until the words revealed a deeper level of meaning. Smith randomly choose Queen Margaret's blistering words to the mother of Richard III (Richard III 4.4.47–54).

Late one night she repeated Queen Margaret's speech over and over. Smith recounts that a fully formed vision of Queen Margaret appeared in her room, conjured only by those powerful words and the potency of her own imagination. In that instant, language took on the characteristics of a mystical phenomenon; she understood that an individual's words would be her key to understanding. She came to the realization that if she were able to interview and record a person's voice, and then listen to his or her words over and

over again on a tape recorder, she might, in fact, be able to embody that person, physically and vocally, on stage.

Smith completed her master's degree at the American Conservatory Theater at the age of twenty-seven. Casting directors and agents informed Smith, somewhat unkindly, that it would be difficult for her to land roles because she looked neither white nor black. So Smith began a teaching stint at Carnegie Mellon University, but she soon gave up her tenure-track job to face the daunting odds of looking for work as an actor in New York City. She held a series of temporary jobs, had a brief flurry of success getting cast in plays, but was soon unemployed again. Her second major artistic epiphany came in 1981, while working a secretarial job in the complaint department of the airline KLM. It was during this time that Smith first conceived of creating her own performance pieces, a notion that occurred after a tremendous amount of time spent reading wide-ranging complaint letters. Once she got beyond the menial task, suddenly people's individuated words and stories began to resonate with her, and she found herself envisioning a theater project. She wanted to know what the relationship of character was to language. As she put it, "What does language, the way we render language, tell us about who we are?"

The same year, she had a chance meeting at a party with a linguist with whom she discussed her work at the complaint department and also talked about her frustrations with method-based acting. Smith articulated her craving to get people engaged in a genuine conversation. To find her own artistic voice, Smith intuitively knew that she had to develop her ability to listen. The linguist suggested a series of questions that might get people to open up and let down their guard: "Have you ever come close to death? Do you know the circumstances of your birth? Have you been accused of something you did not do?" For the next few years Smith carried a tape recorder and those three questions with her at all times. She would walk up to people and say "If you give me an hour of your time, I'll invite you to see yourself performed."

Moving Toward a New Theatrical Expression   Feeling constrained by traditional forms of drama, Smith realized that she had been influenced by other forms of media, particularly popular television talk shows and celebrity interviews. She was interested in moving past the artifice inherent in the staged interview. When she began doing her own interviews, stripped of the distractions and diversions provided by laugh-tracks and commercial breaks, she was able to begin to pinpoint, and, later, mimic, the intricacies of her subjects' language—which, for Smith, meant getting ever-closer to understanding their true identities.

Smith soon found that in order to bring to the stage the real people that she was interviewing, she needed to create, not only her own method of recording and writing, but also her own approach to the process of acting itself. She began shaping the interviews into an ongoing series of solo performances, a sound financial decision in addition to an artistic one. The first of these "On the

Road: The Search for American Character" pieces was performed at A Clear Space in New York City in 1982. In subsequent years, she performed a new piece almost every year.

The Theater as Documentary   In December of 1991, Smith premiered a ground-breaking piece that would later be expanded into *Fires in the Mirror: Crown Heights, Brooklyn, and Other Identities* (1992). It was inspired by the eruption of racially charged urban violence that took place in August of that year in Crown Heights—the diverse neighborhood fifteen minutes from downtown Brooklyn. There had been tensions between the settled Caribbean Americans and the more recently arrived Lubavitchers, a sect of Hasidic Jews. These tensions spiraled into four days of riots after a seven-year-old Guyanese child was killed when a car from the police-escorted motorcade of Grand Rebee Menachem Scheerson, the leader of the Lubavitchers, spun out of control. A rabbinical student visiting from Australia was stabbed to death three hours later in what appeared to be retaliation.

Disturbed by these events, Smith took a short leave from her one-year fellowship at Radcliffe's Bunting Institute and traveled to New York. Over a period of eight days in the fall of 1991, she interviewed people connected to the events in Crown Heights. She spoke with leaders from both the black and the Lubavitch communities, local residents, New York activists, scholars, and with family members of both of the victims. Her purpose was not to conduct a journalistic investigation of the facts of the riots, but rather, to document what she referred to as the "how" rather than the "why" of their speech. The dramatic piece she subsequently wrote begins with the poet Ntozake Shange discussing the word "identity," how people define it and how it defines them, a theme that runs through all of Smith's work. By taking on and performing twenty-six different identities herself, she was able to bring about a sense of connection between the most disparate of characters.

The final preview of *Fires in the Mirror* (performances of a new play are given for critics before opening to the general public), scheduled for April 29, 1992, was cancelled after rioting broke out in Los Angeles. The play opened the following night to an ecstatic reception from critics, and Smith went on to win several important prizes for the work, including a nomination for the Pulitzer Prize.

Immediately after *Fires in the Mirror* closed in New York, Smith was on her way to Los Angeles to plunge headlong into the aftermath of the devastating riots following the Rodney King verdict. Gordon Davidson, the artistic director/producer of the Mark Taper Forum in Los Angeles, commissioned Smith to create a piece about the event, which was spurred by an unexpected acquittal by an all-white jury of four white police officers, whose brutal beating of King, a black man, had been captured on videotape. Fifty-one people were killed in the riots that followed, the violence crossing both racial and ethnic boundaries. Smith found herself immersed in an even

more extensive research process than she had undergone for *Fires in the Mirror*.

To create *Twilight: Los Angeles, 1992*, Smith interviewed some two hundred people over a period of several months, from the former Los Angeles police commissioner to former gang members, people who witnessed the events, King's aunt, scholars, artists, and Korean community members. *Twilight: Los Angeles, 1992* was given rapturous receptions in Los Angeles, New York, and on Broadway.

Political Writing   For her next project, Smith traveled to Washington, D.C., in 1995 to begin what would be a five-year investigation into politics, the presidency, and the press. In another departure from her previous work, Smith, after interviewing hundreds of Washington politicians, reporters, historians, and social pundits, chose not to perform her own material but scripted her first play for other actors. She was also hired by *Newsweek* as a special correspondent, and she covered both the Democratic and Republican national conventions during the 1996 election campaign.

In 1997, Smith premiered *House Arrest—First Edition*, a play that explored the moral foibles of American presidents and the growing power of the press. After the Monica Lewinsky scandal in 1998, in which President Bill Clinton's affair with a White House intern led to his impeachment by the House of Representatives and subsequent acquittal by the Senate, Smith expanded her play to include a part on various presidential infidelities. Another section of the show focused on the assassinations of Abraham Lincoln and John F. Kennedy, and another on the trials that women in high-powered jobs have faced. The original version showcased a troupe of actors, but Smith would later stage a version where she played all the roles.

During this time, Smith also completed a memoir, *Talk to Me: Listening Between the Lines* (2000), that splices together her memories of growing up in segregated Baltimore with her thoughts on playwriting, the creative process, and the development of her own political consciousness. Smith's interviews with an array of Washington personalities are interspersed throughout the book, written as if they were lines of verse.

Acting and Academia   Smith taught at the American Conservatory Theater, Carnegie Mellon, University of Southern California, Yale, and Stanford, before joining the faculty at New York University, where she holds a joint appointment as university professor in the Performance Studies Department at the Tisch School for the Arts, and in the Department of Art and Public Policy at the New York University School of Law. She is the founder of the Institute on the Arts and Civic Dialogue at Harvard, which has returned after several years in hiatus.

Smith worked steadily as an actress in both television and the movies beginning in the early 1990s, notably in a recurring role as National Security Advisor Nancy McNally on NBC's *The West Wing* and as a supporting actor in films *The American President* and *The Human Stain*.

In 2006, her acting and educational impulses met in her book *Letters to a Young Artist: Straight-up Advice on Making a Life in the Arts—For Actors, Performers, Writers, and Artists of Every Kind*, which offers practical suggestions for those who wish to enter the arts.

Works in Literary Context

Activism For all her efforts on behalf of encouraging a dialogue about racial issues in America, Smith does not consider herself a social activist. It is impossible, however, to distance her work from the tradition of activism in art that is very much a part of her generation. In 1998, Smith founded the Institute on the Arts and Civic Dialogue at Harvard. For three years the institute brought artists, scholars, and other professionals together to explore ways in which the arts could be more directly engaged in vital social issues and impact a wider and more diverse audience. In 2008, the institute will once again gather artists from around the world to advance that cause. Previous participants have included artists, architects, and musicians.

The Oral Tradition Smith's most famous and beloved works are those she transcribed and performed—an almost exclusively oral expression. Her respect and even reverence for an individual's idiomatic use of language is evident in the care and effort she puts into translating those words and ideas onto the stage. A generation of spoken word poets, and even the gifted mimics of sketch comedy, have given her a tradition to build upon.

Documentary Theater Documentary theater uses factually based material to dramatize and comment on social issues, usually from a leftist or liberal perspective. This type of theater was associated in the early twentieth century with the names Bertolt Brecht (1898–1956), a German dramatist, and Erwin Piscator (1893–1966), a German director. Documentary theater may use a variety of nonfiction materials, including interviews, court transcripts, speeches, and other public documents. Its aim is to get the audience to think seriously about matters such as social injustice, political corruption, or issues related to class, race, gender, or sexual orientation. A contemporary example of documentary theater is *The Exonerated* (2002), a play by Jessica Blank and Erik Jensen, which examines the injustices that result from the use of the death penalty in the United States. The dramatists constructed their play entirely from interviews, court documents, and case files concerning six people who were sentenced to death for crimes they did not commit. Another example is the play *The Laramie Project*, created by the Tectonic Theater Project, which used interviews to create the text for the play, which was based on the murder of a gay man, Matthew Shepard, in Laramie, Wyoming, in 1998. In addition to Smith, other contemporary American dramatists who write documentary the-

ater include Mark Wolf, Emily Mann, Eve Ensler, and Sarah Jones.

Works in Critical Context

Fires in the Mirror and Twilight: Los Angeles, 1992 Critical reception of these two bookended pieces was almost universally positive and contributed to Smith being awarded a MacArthur Fellowship, frequently known as the "Genius Grant." Of *Fires in the Mirror* Frank Rich in the *New York Times* wrote, "Quite simply the most compelling and sophisticated view of urban racial and class conflict that one could hope to encounter. ... Ingenious in concept."

In *The New Yorker*, John Lahr wrote that "*Twilight* goes some way toward reclaiming for the stage its crucial role as a leader in defining and acting out that experiment called the United States." Smith garnered several Obie and New York Drama Critics Circle awards for these works.

House Arrest: A Search for American Character in and Around the White House, Past and Present In stark contrast to the reception of Smith's earlier work documenting racial strife, the Los Angeles premiere of

COMMON HUMAN EXPERIENCE

Before her work became synonymous with racial turmoil, Smith had planned to follow the advice of Walt Whitman and "absorb America." Her initial intention was to interview subjects all across the country, from every socioeconomic background and at every age. She has been able to come closer to that vision lately, interviewing and performing as a young rodeo rider, among other individuals. This is a list of works in which the authors have interacted with and documented the lives of people quite different from themselves.

The Mole People: Life in the Tunnels Beneath New York City (1993), by Jennifer Toth. This is a work of nonfiction that grew out of an article Toth wrote for the Raleigh *News and Observer*. Toth explored the infamous abandoned subway tracks and tunnels deep under Manhattan, home to a semi-permanent gang of addicts and other lost souls. Toth interviewed and befriended the motley misfits that made the dark, fearsome tunnels their home.

In Cold Blood (1966), Truman Capote's narrative non-fiction account of the aftermath of a brutal small town murder. Capote and his cousin, author Harper Lee, conducted extensive interviews, honing their technique and producing reams of the source material used to create this chilling, true-crime volume.

Anthony Bourdain: No Reservations (2005–), an Emmy-nominated television show that follows chef and writer Anthony Bourdain as he travels all over the world—including some rather inhospitable regions—to try as many cuisines and drink the regional brew with as many locals as he can manage in each one-hour episode.

her politically driven play *House Arrest: A Search for American Character in and Around the White House, Past and Present*, was met with boredom, confusion, and in some cases, disdain. The original staging called for actors, a departure for Smith, to play the roles of the famous individuals from the political past and present. When this was changed for the New York debut, critical reception did not improve. Ben Brantley of the *New York Times* commented, "You have the definite impression that Ms. Smith, confronted with the vastness of her subject, has lost control of her material. ... As is, she emerges as a wanderer in an immense forest of facts and ideas who, somewhere along the way lost her compass"

Responses to Literature

1. In producing *Fires in the Mirror*, Anna Deavere Smith utilized several dramaturgies from different backgrounds and perspectives to ensure that the story expanded beyond the racial makeup of the riot participants. Using the Internet or your library, research the history and function of a dramaturg (someone who adapts a work for the stage), and discuss the importance or significance of that task.

2. Smith underwent a transformation in her thinking after an assignment to read and reread lines of Shakespeare. Replicate the exercise: pick fourteen lines at random, and say them to yourself until you have uncovered a deeper layer of meaning. Write a brief essay in which you describe the process and any benefits you may have obtained from it.

3. Record an interview with a friend or family member and attempt to internalize the interviewee's personality. Perform a short piece based on the interview for your class.

4. Watch a video of Anna Deavere Smith performing one of her signature documentary-style pieces, and then read a printed version of the same work. Write a paper in which you compare the experience of watching Smith embody her characters with the experience of reading it in silence. What is gained? What is lost? Which do you prefer?

BIBLIOGRAPHY

Books

Eisler, Garrett, ed. *Dictionary of Literary Biography*, Vol. 341, *Twentieth-Century American Dramatists, Fifth Series*. Dearborn, Mich: Gale, 2008.

Smith, Anna Deavere. *Letters to a Young Artist: Straight-up Advice on Making a Life in the Arts—For Actors, Performers, Writers, and Artists of Every Kind*. New York: Vintage, 2006.

Tharp, Twyla. *Push Comes to Shove*. New York: Bantam, 1992.

Periodicals

Brantley, Ben. Review of *House Arrest*. *New York Times* (March 27, 2000).

Lahr, John. "Under the Skin." *The New Yorker* (June 28, 1993).

Rich, Frank. "Diversity of America in One-Person Shows." *New York Times* (May 5, 1992).

Web Sites

Aaron Sorkin. Retrieved November 22, 2008, from http://www.nndb.com/people/519/000022453.

Errol Morris Biography. Retrieved November 22, 2008, from http://www.errolmorris.com/biography.htm.

IBDB: The Official Source for Broadway Information. Retrieved November 21, 2008, from http://www.ibdb.com/show.php?id=1596.

IMDB: The Internet Movie Database. Retrieved November 22, 2008, from http://www.imdb.com/name/nm0258127.

⚙ Gary Snyder

BORN: *1930, San Francisco*

NATIONALITY: *American*

GENRE: *Poetry, nonfiction*

MAJOR WORKS:
Riprap (1959)
Myths & Texts (1960)
Earth House Hold (1969)
Turtle Island (1974)
Mountains and Rivers Without End (1996)

Overview

Gary Snyder is one of the most important American poets of the second half of the twentieth century. A translator and essayist as well, he has written with eloquence and grandeur in celebration and defense of the natural world. Winner of the 1975 Pulitzer Prize for poetry, his intelligent and provocative poetry and essays have contributed to a greater knowledge of, and greater respect for, the natural world and its inhabitants.

Works in Biographical and Historical Context

Early Life and Education Gary Sherman Snyder was born to Harold and Lois Wilkey Snyder on May 8, 1930,

Gary Snyder *Snyder, Gary, photograph. AP Images.*

in San Francisco. Roughly a year and a half after Snyder's birth, his family moved to a farm north of Seattle. The Depression-era work ethic of Snyder's family and the local foresters would have a permanent impact on his writings.

Snyder acquired an early love of reading, in part through the influence of his mother, also a writer, and his weekly visits to the library. His teenage years were marked by reading the works of John Muir and Robinson Jeffers, two environmental writers to whom critics have pointed as Snyder's literary progenitors. However, Snyder's early reading habits were almost as widely defined as those of his adult years, ranging from literary to anthropological readings, from essays to poetry, from both Anglo-American and Native American traditions.

In 1942, the Snyder family moved to a low-income housing facility in Portland, Oregon. His parents' marriage ended shortly thereafter, and Snyder and his younger sister, Anthea, stayed with their mother. During his high-school years, Snyder worked at a camp on Spirit Lake in Washington, and in 1945, he climbed Mount St. Helens with a climbing party from the local YMCA. He later joined a mountaineering club and spent much of his free time exploring. Mountains would become a recurring theme in much of his writing, including his magnum opus *Mountains and Rivers Without End* (1996).

Higher Education and Life as Japhy Ryder In 1947, Snyder entered Reed College, in Oregon, on a scholarship. He published his first poems in its student publications, and he commenced his lifelong friendship with fellow poets Lew Welch and Philip Whalen. Snyder also became seriously involved with anthropological and archaeological work, and in 1950, he worked on his first archaeological site at Fort Vancouver.

After spending the summer following his graduation working as a member of an Oregon logging operation, he hitchhiked to Indiana University to begin his graduate study in anthropology. In 1952, Snyder left graduate school and divorced his wife, whom he had married the previous year. Soon after, he moved to San Francisco, where he lived with his college friend, Whalen. He returned to graduate school in 1953, enrolling at the University of California at Berkeley to study Asian languages.

In California, Snyder met the poet Kenneth Rexroth, the elder statesman who served as mentor for writers who were known later as "The San Francisco Renaissance," a group including Snyder, Michael McClure, and City Lights publisher, Lawrence Ferlinghetti. In the fall of 1955, Snyder met and became close with Allen Ginsberg. Through Ginsberg, Snyder met and befriended Jack Kerouac. In his novel of Zen philosophy and mountain-climbing experiences, *The Dharma Bums* (1958), Kerouac immortalizes Snyder as "really sharp ... Japhy Ryder is a great new hero of American culture." This association led to Snyder's somewhat mistaken grouping with the Beats—although he shared many of the principles of Beat

LITERARY AND HISTORICAL CONTEMPORARIES

Snyder's famous contemporaries include:

Allen Ginsberg (1926–1997): Ginsberg was an American poet, activist, and essayist. Ginsberg was a legendary figurehead of the Beat Generation; his seminal work, the long poem *Howl* (1956), is a classic of counterculture literature.

Lawrence Ferlinghetti (1919–): Ferlinghetti is an American poet, who helped to spark the San Francisco literary renaissance of the 1950s and the subsequent Beat movement in American literature. Ferlinghetti's most important contribution to American literature may have been the bookstore he founded, City Lights Books, still a fixture of San Francisco.

John F. Kennedy (1917–1963): Kennedy was the president of the United States from 1961–63. He was also the author of the Pulitzer Prize–winning *Profiles in Courage* (1955).

Margaret Atwood (1939–): Atwood is a Canadian author and environmentalist. She is the Booker Prize–winning author of *The Handmaid's Tale* (1985).

Denise Levertov (1923–1997): Levertov was a British-born poet who became an American citizen in 1955. Her poetry is notable, among other things, for its exploration of the spiritual dimensions of the natural world.

poetry, his own poetry was less concerned with the urban world of social ills than with an attention to nature and the political significance of man's interactions with it.

Zen and Nature as Touchstones Although affiliated with, and working in, San Francisco, Snyder had been able to leave the city every summer and work in the forests of the Pacific Slope. His time as a fire lookout became important in both his spiritual and stylistic development, as did his work as a member of a trail crew in Yosemite. In many examples from "Lookout's Journal" (an account of his outdoor summer work), one can see the use of prose and poetry simultaneously—one of the first signs that Snyder would become a major prose stylist. This selection also shows evidence of the Eastern thought that infuses much of his later work after his study of Zen Buddhism. Zen complements his poetic practice in two important ways: sparse description and direct capture of the natural world.

In the beginning of 1956, Snyder lived with Kerouac in a shack on a hillside in Marin County, California. He soon left for Japan, where he entered a Buddhist monastery in Kyoto and practiced Zen meditation. Although he left the school shortly thereafter, he never abandoned his Zen practice; the philosophy is evident in many of his

subsequent works. What emerged from those studies is a poetry that is deceptively simple, rather than superficially simplistic. In accordance with the teachings of Zen, Snyder envisions the world as a network of relationships unapproachable by traditional Western logic, rather than as a conglomeration of things that can be identified, codified, and rationalized. Snyder would remain in Asia, on and off, for over a decade.

Snyder published his first volume of poetry, *Riprap*, in 1959. It is a collection of poems about his experiences in the backwoods of the American Far West and on his early experiences in Japan. He defines "riprap" at the start of his collection as "a cobble of stone laid on steep, slick rock to make a trail for horses in the mountains." Accordingly, Snyder traces a trail for his readers to follow, providing the necessary footing for his audience. The volume contains some of his best and strongest poems, among them "Riprap," "A Stone Garden," and "Praise for Sick Women." The last poem is particularly important to an understanding of Snyder's view of women in general—that they remain closely bound to the earth, both in poetic image and in his own regard.

Gary Snyder was an unabashed lover of women, and while abroad, he married his second wife, Joanne Kyger, whom he would divorce five years later. His next spouse, Masa Uehara, would remain so for twenty years, and they would have two children together: Kai and Gen. This nuclear family life figured prominently in Snyder's work. After his divorce from Uehara, Snyder wed Carole Koda, to whom he was married until her death in 2006.

Prolific Years in Poetry and Prose While in Asia, Snyder published a steady stream of poetry and prose including *Myths & Texts*, a long poetic sequence that Snyder composed between 1952 and 1956 and was published in 1960; *Six Sections from Mountains & Rivers without End*, and a new edition of *Riprap*, which included his translations of the "Cold Mountain Poems" of the ancient Chinese poet Han Shan, in 1965.

Environmentalism and Education Upon his return to California in 1968, Snyder built a sustainable, self-sufficient home on land he had purchased with Ginsberg and others in Sierra Nevada foothills. Snyder, his family, and some like-minded neighbors sought a way of life that honored the nonhuman world. As he and his wife raised their two sons, family life found its way into Snyder's art, notably in *Regarding Wave* and *Turtle Island*.

While *Turtle Island* won him a Pulitzer in 1975, for Snyder, the 1970s and the 1980s were a time for publishing more prose and essay pieces—mainly focused on environmentalism—and less poetry (though he would be the recipient of a number of poetry prizes during this period). He would also begin his career as an English professor at the University of California at Davis.

In his 1995 collection, *A Place in Space: Ethics, Aesthetics, and Watersheds: New and Selected Prose*, Snyder offers an optimistic reflection: "The need for ecological literacy, the sense of home watershed, and a better understanding of our stake in public lands are beginning to permeate the consciousness of the larger society." His calls for sustainable living scenarios and respect for the environment have found new relevance in recent years.

No other contemporary poet has been quite so successful at blending Eastern and Western poetic traditions. Much of Snyder's poetry is based on the Japanese haiku—sharp, uncomplicated images that, like many Asian paintings, form sketches that the reader's imagination must fill in. But Snyder also acknowledges his debt to D. H. Lawrence, Kenneth Rexroth, Robinson Jeffers, William Butler Yeats, and Ezra Pound.

Works in Literary Context

Myth   Snyder had a penchant for myth since childhood, especially the creation myths of the Native Americans he read about in books. After his extensive study of Buddhism and Asian texts and languages, Snyder drew a clear point of congruence between the East and West in the American Indian and in the myths he created to explain his universe. In its nonlinear progression and abundance of allusion, most notably to Buddhist and Native American sources, his collection of poems entitled *Myths & Texts* presents challenges to the reader akin to those found in modernist epics such as T. S. Eliot's *The Waste Land* and Ezra Pound's *Cantos*. In the final poem of the work, he pits myth—the invented, sacred story—and text—historical and realistic—against one another, and ultimately reconciles the two.

It is interesting to note that Snyder, mythologized as Japhy Ryder, was a character in a book before he wrote one himself. It is even more amusing to read Kerouac's passages and realize they are only modestly fictionalized, so in thrall was Kerouac to Snyder.

Eastern Expression   Snyder's pull toward Eastern religion, language, and literature would be another distinguishing characteristic that set him apart from his Beat Generation contemporaries. Indeed, for the majority of the sixties, when the counterculture was making its mark, Snyder was studying and traveling in Japan, India, and other parts of Asia, meditating on Zen Buddhism and writing poetry that had little to do with the urban-centered art his friends were creating. He was also honing his skills as a translator, working on an English version of the work of Chinese poet Han Shan. Han Shan, "a mountain madman" and poet of the T'ang dynasty (618–906), along with his constant companion, Shih-te, became models for Snyder, exemplars of a common character in Chinese literature—the wise fool. Arthur Sze (1950–), a Chinese American poet, can be seen as a natural heir to Snyder. Sze's poetry touches on the interconnectedness of humans and nature, Zen Buddhism, and a commitment to exploring environmental issues.

COMMON HUMAN EXPERIENCE

In stark opposition to his friends, Kerouac and Ginsberg, Snyder was seemingly low on self-destructive tendencies and was addicted to nothing so innocuous as fresh air. His high came from simplicity of living, nature, and the contemplation of his place in it. Here is a sampling of the works of other artists who came to profound insight outside the city limits.

Walden (1854), a nonfiction book by Henry David Thoreau. This seminal American work, a two-year experiment in uncluttered, near-hermetic living, was undertaken by Thoreau in an effort to ensure he would not come to die only to discover '[he] had not lived.'

Summer Days (1936), one of the most famous paintings by American artist Georgia O'Keeffe. O'Keeffe was endlessly moved by the landscape of the New Mexico desert, and this particular piece highlights objects—a skull, the desert background—that are iconic of the setting in which she painted.

Monolith, the Face of Half Dome (1927), the iconic black-and-white image by American photographer and noted environmentalist Ansel Adams. Adams took this photograph in Yosemite National Park when he was twenty-five years old.

Works in Critical Context

Riprap   Critics in the late sixties and seventies posited that the simplicity and cleanness of the language in Snyder's poetry has made it accessible to youthful audiences that often distrust more complex lyricism. Poet and critic G. S. Fraser wrote in the *Partisan Review* that Snyder "is one of the poets whom the young enormously overrate, perhaps because they fear complexity." A similar sentiment is expressed by Robert Boyers, also writing in the *Partisan Review*, Snyder's poetry is "monotonous, flat and superficial, and probably for those reasons is much esteemed by a variety of people, most of them young." Nevertheless, the voices of Fraser and Boyers form a minority dissent. Thomas Parkinson wrote that Snyder is "a skillful poet, and his work develops steadily toward more thorough and profound insight."

Turtle Island   Snyder used an old Seneca word for North America when he titled his Pulitzer Prize–winning work, *Turtle Island* (1974). He made light of the fact that he wished to be a spokesman for nature in the work, and one section was devoted to essays on ecology. The critical response to *Turtle Island* was mostly positive, and some, like Katsunori Yamazato, praised Snyder's cross-cultural vision and sensitivity to the progression of his understanding of the natural world and his place in it. "Snyder believes that, in its anthropocentric view of the world, modern industrial civilization—East and West—has tended to ignore the lives of other beings that coexist with humanity. From this general tendency, it has earned the ecological crisis that we witness today. *Turtle Island* offers the reader not only a sense of 'how to be' in a world with just such an ecological crisis but also, in Charles Molesworth's words, 'a new sense of what it means to be human.'"

However, some critics and readers felt that its ecopolitics and polemicism—heavy-handed arguments—detracted from the work. Writing in the *New York Review of Books* Herbert Leibowitz commented that, "[Snyder] is on the side of the gods. But as [the poet] remarks, 'Poetry is the vehicle of the mystery of voice,' and the voice of *Turtle Island*, for all its sincerity and moral urgency, lacks that mystery and 'inspired use of language' we call style."

Responses to Literature

1. When Snyder finally published *Mountains and Rivers Without End* in 1996, he had been at work on it—in some form or another—for approximately four decades. It is widely regarded as his magnum opus—his masterpiece. Research other magnum opi in literature, film, visual art, and music, and write a paper exploring the nature of a masterpiece. What are the qualities a work must have to be considered a masterpiece? Does every artist have one? Who is the final arbiter of the decision to name a work that artist's masterpiece?

2. At the core of Snyder's *Myths & Texts* is the notion that the texts of civilized society, when held up against the myths of primitive cultures, are found wanting. Discuss other examples of individuals or communities who have shared the opinion that there is little in modernity that improves upon what came before. How do they attempt to reconcile the time in which they live with their preferred values or art forms from the past?

3. The artists of the Beat Generation and the San Francisco Renaissance responded to American politics and culture in a way that had not been seen before. Read some of the critical articles on the movement and the counterculture, and then discuss what in particular may have triggered the generation's unique style.

4. Write a paper in which you compare one of Gary Snyder's poems to a poem by his contemporary and friend, Allen Ginsberg (e.g., compare Snyder's *Riprap* to Ginsberg's *Howl*). Stylistically, do they belong in the same genre? Which poet most fully realizes his intent? Which do you prefer and why?

BIBLIOGRAPHY

Books

Charters, Anne, ed. *Dictionary of Literary Biography*, Vol. 16, *The Beats: Literary Bohemians in Post-War America*. Dearborn, Mich.: Gale Research, 1983.

Halper, John, ed. *Gary Snyder: Dimensions of a Life*. San Francisco: Sierra Club Books, 1991.

Kerouac, Jack. *The Dharma Bums*. New York: Viking, 1958.

Yamazato, Katsunori. "How to Be in This Crisis: Gary Snyder's Cross-Cultural Vision." In *Critical Essays on Gary Snyder*, ed. Patrick D. Murphy. Boston: G. K. Hall & Co., 1991. pp. 230–247.

Zhou, Xiaojing. "'The Redshifting Web': Arthur Sze's Ecopoetics." In *Ecological Poetry: A Critical Introduction*, ed. J. Scott Bryson. Salt Lake City: University of Utah Press, 2001, pp. 179–194.

Periodicals

Boyers, Robert. "Mixed Bag." *Partisan Review* (Summer 1969): vol. 36, 306–315.

Fraser, G. S. "The Magicians." *Partisan Review* (Winter 1971–1972): vol. 36, 469–478.

Lebowitz, Herbert. "Ecologies of the Finite and the Infinite." *New York Review of Books* 2 (March 23, 1975): vol. 69.

Parkinson, Thomas. "The Poetry of Gary Snyder." *Southern Review* 2 (1968): vol. 69, 616–632.

Web Sites

Ansel Adams. Retrieved November 24, 2008, from http://www.anseladams.com.

Department of English, UC Davis. *Gary Snyder*. Retrieved November 24, 2008, from http://english.ucdavis.edu/people/directory/fzsnyder.

⊛ Susan Sontag

BORN: *1933, New York, New York*

DIED: *2004, New York, New York*

NATIONALITY: *American*

GENRE: *Fiction, nonfiction*

MAJOR WORKS:
"Notes on 'Camp'" (1964)
Styles of Radical Will (1969)
On Photography (1977)
Illness as Metaphor (1978)

Overview

Labeled a radical, an intellectual, and a postmodernist, Susan Sontag spanned across writing genres both to compose and to question art. Known primarily for her essays and reviews, Sontag also authored three novels, wrote and directed four feature-length films, composed numerous

California at Berkeley for one year before transferring to the University of Chicago.

At seventeen, following a ten-day courtship, Sontag married the sociologist Philip Rieff in 1950. After obtaining her B.A. in philosophy from the University of Chicago in 1951, Sontag moved to Boston with Rieff where she earned masters degrees in both English and philosophy at Harvard University and completed all but her dissertation for a doctoral degree. While she was a graduate student at Harvard, Sontag taught philosophy there and English at the University of Connecticut, Storrs. During this time, Sontag also studied abroad at Cambridge University and the University of Paris. Following her return from Europe, Sontag divorced her husband and moved with her son, David, who was born in 1952, to New York City to begin her career as a freelance writer and novelist. Between 1959 and 1960 she taught philosophy courses at the City College of New York and Sarah Lawrence College, and from 1960 to 1964 she was an instructor in the religion department at Columbia University. She has also been a writer in residence at Rutgers University, New Brunswick (1964–1965).

Exploring the Intellect Sontag's first novel, *The Benefactor*, was published with acclaim in 1963. Set in Paris, it follows two protagonists, Hippolyte, a sixty-one-year-old dreamer, and Jean-Jacques, a professional boxer, novelist, and prostitute, and is said to be modeled after the French writers Antonin Artaud and Jean Genet. Ambitious and experimental, *The Benefactor* is reminiscent of the plays and novels of Samuel Beckett, a writer whose work Sontag characterized as "delicate dramas of the withdrawn consciousness—pared down to essentials."

While *The Benefactor* was well received critically, Sontag first attracted national attention with her essay "Notes on 'Camp,'" written in 1964 for the *Partisan Review*. Here Sontag delineates the phenomenon of "camp" sensibility, a sensibility that celebrates the artifice of art with irony and whimsy. "Notes on 'Camp'" marked Sontag as an intellectual who understood the bizarre and the forbidden in modern culture. This essay was republished in 1966 in Sontag's first collection of essays *Against Interpretation*. The groundbreaking title essay and its companion piece, "On Style," set up the intellectual perimeters for the essays in *Against Interpretation*, which includes writings on philosophers Albert Camus, Michel Leiris, Georg Lukacs, Jean-Paul Sartre, Nathalie Sarraute, and Norman O. Brown among others. These essays read as manifestos for change as Sontag critiqued the way Americans reviewed literature and art in the early and mid-1960s. It was in this time that Sontag wrote, "What is important now is to recover our senses. We must learn to see more, to hear more, to feel more."

As the 1960s advanced, so did the counterculture of the predominantly young, white middle-class men and women who rebelled against capitalism and conformity. As part of this rebellion, Sontag demonstrated in anti-war

Susan Sontag   *Sontag, Susan, photograph. AP Images.*

short stories, and penned several plays. With an existential view she often questioned the position of art and the role of the artist in a world she perceived as declining and deranged. Her continual analysis expounded both a political and philosophical voice that influenced society for more than four decades.

Works in Biographical and Historical Context

The Young Academic Born in New York City in 1933, Sontag (whose birth name remains a mystery, although it may have been Jacobson) was raised by relatives while her parents worked in the fur trade in Tianjin, China. Upon the death of Sontag's father in China from tuberculosis, Sontag's mother returned from abroad and took Sontag and her younger sister to live in Arizona. In 1945, Sontag's mother married a Captain Sontag whose surname Sontag adopted. The family then moved to Los Angeles suburb Canoga Park where Sontag described her years as ones of intellectual exile. A precocious student, Sontag graduated from North Hollywood High School at the age of fifteen and attended the University of

LITERARY AND HISTORICAL CONTEMPORARIES

Sontag's contemporaries include:

Annie Leibovitz (1949–): Leibovitz is a world-renowned American photographer known for her collaborative work with her subjects. She has had her photographs published in a variety of publications, including *Rolling Stone* and *Vanity Fair*. She and Sontag were romantic partners for over a decade.

Jackson Pollock (1912–1956): Pollock was an American painter who defined the Abstract Expressionist movement with his large, "paint-splattered" style of painting covering the entire canvas and avoiding identifiable images.

Woody Allen (1935–): Jewish-American dramatist Allen has written movies that were parodies of existentialism, acting and directing in his New York-focused comedies. *Annie Hall* (1977), *Stardust Memories* (1980), and *Crimes and Misdemeanors* (1989) are among his films.

protests and challenged the traditional way of looking at culture. Sontag's challenges to societal conventions appear in her collections of essays, *Styles of Radical Will* (1969), *On Photography* (1977), and *Under the Sign of Saturn* (1980). She criticizes racism in America, United States foreign policy, and especially the war in Vietnam. In her essay "What's Happening in America?" Sontag asserts that nothing can "redeem what this particular civilization has wrought upon the world." Although her political positions shifted over the years, from enthusiastic support for the Communist cultural revolution in China led by Mao Zedong in the 1960s to a controversial repudiation of all forms of Communist governments in 1982 during a rally at the Town Hall in New York City, Sontag consistently critiqued the status quo and argued in defense of the disenfranchised and the politically oppressed.

Life Imitating Art When Sontag was diagnosed with breast cancer, her experience with the disease led her to write the acclaimed *Illness as Metaphor* (1978). As she discusses the metaphors used to describe illness, particularly tuberculosis, cancer, and insanity, she argues that such metaphors distort the event of the illness and involve the patient in a system of symbolic meaning that goes beyond the disease itself. At this time, breast cancer was often a taboo topic, and it had yet to receive adequate funding for research. Sontag's exploration of the illness and perceptions of it prove her position as a revolutionary writer. A decade later, Sontag revised and expanded this work into *AIDS and Its Metaphors*. When Acquired Immune Deficiency Syndrome (AIDS) was first identified and began to spread in the 1980s, victims were often

shunned. Though the blood-borne disease can afflict anyone, homosexuals and intravenous drug users were more likely to contract it, and for a time mainstream society associated the disease with what they considered morally reprehensible behavior. In *AIDS and Its Metaphors* Sontag extended her reflection on the persistent, and often harmful, metaphors used by Western culture to think about disease. In particular, she condemned the view that those who suffered from AIDS were being punished for their sexuality or addiction.

A Woman Who Defied Definition Although Sontag acquired much of her fame from nonfiction prose, she is also admired for her novels, short stories, screenplays, and plays. In one interview Sontag asserted herself primarily a creative writer. Sontag's three novels, *The Benefactor*, *Death Kit* (1967), and *The Volcano Lover: A Romance* (1992), have been highly lauded, but it is her short stories that have garnered the most critical enthusiasm. Published in various periodicals including *The New Yorker* and the *Partisan Review*, Sontag gathered eight of her stories for her collection *I, etcetera* (1978). For the screen, Sontag's work includes *Duet for Cannibals* (1969) and *Brother Carl* (1971) while the stage has seen the well-received *Alice in Bed: A Play in Eight Scenes* (1993).

After the World Trade Center tragedy of September 11, 2001, Sontag made controversial statements criticizing American military intelligence, policies in the Middle East, and the reaction of President George W. Bush, political officials, and the media. She stated that the government was trying to convince a naïve public of the country's strength rather than confront the underlying issues of the attack. One of her last essays, "Regarding the Torture of Others," published in *The New York Times Magazine* in 2004, discussed American soldiers' torture of Iraqi prisoners. She died of leukemia in 2004.

Works in Literary Context

Existentialism A literary and philosophical movement of the post–World War II years, existentialism stresses that people are entirely free and thus responsible for the consequences of their own actions. A sense of isolation in an indifferent world characterizes the thought. The idea that life is without objective meaning generalizes the movement. Sontag's essays discuss proponents of this thinking as well as capture its essence in her own writing. In this vein, Sontag expounds the idea of art for art's sake. Rather than impose meaning on art, Sontag argues that art is created for the sake of itself. Its value is its transparency. There is a similarity between Sontag's focus on the artwork itself rather than on its interpretations and the insistence of New Criticism of the mid-twentieth century that art should "not mean, but be."

Continental Influence One of Sontag's key functions as an American critic has been to introduce American readers to European literature. Through her essays, editing, and book reviews, Sontag has brought her audience's attention to, and clarified for them, the works of such authors as Nathalie Sarraute, Antonin Artaud, Walter Benjamin, Jean-Paul Sartre, Roland Barthes, Alain Robbe-Grillet, and Maurice Blanchot—not in the 1980s, when these names have become critical and academic anchors, but in the early 1960s, when the works of most of these writers were yet to be translated and unfamiliar to more than a small segment of her American audience. Many American readers approached these writers through Sontag, borrowing her insights into and her preference for modern European literature. Displaying an adept understanding of the philosophical and critical bases of Continental European thought, Sontag has made available not only these works but keys to understanding them as well.

Works in Critical Context

Regarded as a preeminent social critic of her time, Sontag was both revered and rejected for her views. Although Sontag has been criticized for being too trendy and too inclined to favor modernism at all costs, even at the expense of critical judgment, she has also been heralded as a vital influence of the intellectual elite.

Against Interpretation   Her compilation of critical essays that appeared in literary magazines in the early 1960s, *Against Interpretation* received much attention. The premise of her writings rejects the tendency to find meaning in art. Instead, Sontag directs observers to experience art sensually. In defense of "lobotomizing" art, Sontag calls her approach "aesthetic experience." Critic Elmer Borklund explains how Sontag valued the "transparency" of art, what Sontag described as "the luminousness of the thing in itself, of things being what they are." Borklund further explains that "Interpretation, which seeks to replace the work with something else—usually historical, ethical or psychological" reduces art. It is in the gaps of interpretation that silence exists, allowing a reader or viewer to experience an art form. As critic Jeffords stated, "Ordinary language does not acknowledge the wedge silence drives into meaning." Ironically, Sontag's silence would have prevented much questioning and understanding, which Robert Hughes captured in *Time*, when he wrote that "there are perhaps half a dozen critics in America whose silence would be a loss to writing itself, and Sontag is one of them."

Illness as Metaphor   As a cancer patient herself, Sontag was able to experience disease, and her analysis of it brought about *Illness as Metaphor*. Discussing how disease gets turned into a stigma or symbol, she explains how metaphors allow people to view disease from a safe distance. As critic David Gates explains, "Sontag believes that how we speak of a given illness often betrays fears and fantasies that have little to do with the disease itself." The general reaction to this book was favorable. A *Newsweek* reviewer described it as "one of the most liberating books of our time." *AIDS as Metaphor*, according to

---

COMMON HUMAN EXPERIENCE

In Sontag's *The Benefactor*, her character Hippolyte lives between a dream state and reality. Here are other works in which the theme of illusion versus reality appear:

A Midsummer Night's Dream (1594–1596), a play by William Shakespeare. Little is as it seems to be in this comedy that details two couples getting lost in a forest fantasy world.

Death of a Salesman (1949), a play by Arthur Miller. The protagonist, traveling salesman Willy Loman, wavers between his real life of unfulfilled achievement and his imagined life of success and popularity. Many scenes of the play take place in Willy's daydreams.

A Streetcar Named Desire (1951), a play by Tennessee Williams. As Southern belle Blanche Dubois visits her sister and abusive brother-in-law, she experiences a conflict between her actual life of promiscuity and alcoholism and her ideal life of virtue and culture.

Don Quixote (1614), a novel by Miguel de Cervantes. In his mind, Alonso Quixano is the courageous knight Don Quixote who views the prostitute Aldonza as his honorable princess Dulcinea. Throughout the story, the protagonist undergoes challenges that display unclear distinctions between illusion and reality.

Gates, was less successful because "Sontag's adversaries [were] less formidable and their ideas less seductive."

Responses to Literature

1. Sontag wrote about the importance of avoiding interpretation when considering art. How does this approach to art affect one's experience with it? Find an image of a work of art that was created during Sontag's life and in a short essay respond to it emotionally and aesthetically, rather than intellectually.

2. Søren Kierkegaard is the nineteenth-century Danish philosopher said to have founded modern existentialism. Read some of his work and select a few key aspects that appear in any of Sontag's writing. Compare these two writers of different genders and eras to find common thinking.

3. Think of an illness or disease and describe the metaphors that are typically associated with it. Discuss how such symbols of the disease influence perception of those who suffer from such illnesses. Explain why people might choose to view disease more symbolically than realistically.

4. As a political writer of the turbulent 1960s, Sontag challenged American government, particularly the

country's involvement in the Vietnam war. Read her nonfiction work *Trip to Hanoi* (1969). What, if any, of her arguments are relevant today? How might her rationale be viewed by a contemporary audience?

BIBLIOGRAPHY

Books

Borklund, Elmer. "Susan Sontag: Overview." *Contemporary Novelists.* Edited by Susan Windisch Brown. Sixth ed. New York: St. James Press, 1996.

Clark, Judith F. "Sontag, Susan (1933–)." *Encyclopedia of World Biography.* Edited by Suzanne M. Bourgoin. Second ed. Detroit: Gale Research, 1998.

Pague, Leland, ed. *Conversations with Susan Sontag.* Jackson, Miss.: University Press of Mississippi, 1995.

Sayres, Sohnya. *Susan Sontag: The Elegaic Modernist.* New York: Routledge, 1990.

Walker, Susan. "Susan Sontag." *American Novelists Since World War II: First Series.* Edited by Jeffrey Helterman and Richard Layman. Detroit: Gale Research, 1978.

Periodicals

Capouya, Emile. "The Age of Allegiance." *Saturday Review* 52 (May 3, 1969): 29.

DeMott, Benjamin. "Lady on the Scene." *New York Times Book Review* (January 23, 1966).

Gates, David. "Now, Metaphor as Illness." *Newsweek* Vol. CXIII, No. 5 (January 30, 1989): 79.

"Women, the Arts and the Politics of Culture: An Interview with Susan Sontag." *Salmagundi* 31–32 (1975): 29–48.

Web sites

"The Talk of the Town." *The New Yorker* Online Archive.. Accessed November 11, 2008, from http://www.newyorker.com/archive/2001/09/24/010924ta_talk_wtc. Originally published September 24, 2001.

✸ Gary Soto

BORN: *1952, Fresno, California*

NATIONALITY: *American*

GENRE: *Poetry, essays, fiction*

MAJOR WORKS:
The Elements of San Joaquin (1977)
The Tale of Sunlight (1978)
Living Up the Street (1985)
New and Selected Poems (1995)

Overview

Widely regarded as one of the foremost living Chicano writers, Gary Soto has expressed himself successfully in a number of genres, most notably poetry and the essay. His

Gary Soto   *Soto, Gary, photograph by Carolyn Soto. Reproduced by permission of Gary Soto.*

writing uses distinct details and concrete imagery to evoke emotions that are universally felt and understood. Though essentially Chicano, his writing has overcome the boundaries of cultural classification and earned a place for itself in the American literary canon.

Biographical and Historical Context

Mexican American Identity in California   The son of American-born parents of Mexican background, Soto was born on April 12, 1952, in Fresno, California. He grew up in the broad, flat San Joaquin Valley in Central California, one of the nation's most productive agricultural regions and the site of the 1933 cotton strike, which according to historian Ramón Chacón, "paralyzed cotton farming operations … and threatened to destroy the state's cotton crop valued at more than $50,000,000." Seventy-five percent of the striking workers in 1933 were Mexican, part of an extensive Chicano community into which Soto was born almost twenty years later.

Soto was also born only nine years after a key turning point in the history of Mexicans and people of Mexican descent in the U.S.: the Zoot Suit Riots, in which young Mexican Americans living in Los Angeles rioted to demonstrate their power and their independence as a social group. The culture in which Soto was raised had a newfound sense of itself, a unique identity that would come, in the 1960s, to be known as Chicano.

Although he grew up in a Spanish-speaking community, Soto was never formally taught Spanish and has suggested in interviews that the language was not the most important aspect of the San Joaquin laborer culture he inherited. "Assimilation was looked upon as something for kids to go through," he says, pointing to the fact that much of the culture he grew up in he was expected to forget. What impressed him most deeply, however, and what has since found expression in his writing, was "the culture of poverty" through which he developed an essential understanding of people and their relations.

"A Human Pain" In 1970, Soto began attending Fresno City College, where he majored in geography "for no articulate reason except that I liked maps," he has stated. He soon gave up geography, however, and decided to pursue poetry instead, moved by the poem "Unwanted" by Edward Field. In Field's poem, Soto saw his own alienation from society described and saw that a sense of alienation was not unique to him, but rather that "it was ... a human pain." This sense of universality—the concept that all people, regardless of their ethnicity, suffer similar emotions—would become a key component of Soto's own writing.

The Power of the Written Word In 1972 and 1973, at California State University, Fresno, Soto studied with poet Philip Levine, under whose guidance Soto learned the concrete linguistic tools for shaping language into poetry. Levine, whose poetry often illuminates the lives of the working class, became a mentor to Soto and provided him with an example of a man who had made poetry his career.

In 1974, Soto graduated *magna cum laude* from California State University. He married Carolyn Oda on May 24, 1975. In 1976, he earned an MFA in creative writing from the University of California, Irvine, spending that year as a visiting writer at San Diego State University. In 1977, he began teaching at the University of California, Berkeley, where he remained as an associate professor in both the English and Chicano studies departments until 1993.

Discovering the power of the written word and disciplining his talents and energy have allowed Soto to accomplish much in a short span of time. Since his first poetry publication in 1977, *The Elements of San Joaquin,* Soto has kept up a steady stream of publications. His attention to craft and subject matter has taken his poetry into the pages of such well-known periodicals and journals as the *Paris Review,* the *Nation, American Poetry Review,* and *The New Yorker.*

Testing Himself Beginning in 1985, after earning considerable acclaim for his poetry, Soto composed and published three autobiographical prose works: *Living Up the Street: Narrative Recollections* (1985), *Small Faces* (1986) and *Lesser Evils: Ten Quartets* (1988). When asked to speak

LITERARY AND HISTORICAL CONTEMPORARIES

Soto's famous contemporaries include:

Philip Levine (1928–): Levine is an introspective American poet known for poetry grounded in the harsh reality of contemporary urban life. Levine was a teacher and mentor to Soto.

Estela Portillo Trambley (1936–): Trambley was the first woman to receive the Premio Quinto Sol, the prestigious national award for Chicano literature, and to publish successfully in the male-dominated field of Chicano literature. Her work centers largely around strong female protagonists who must overcome great obstacles to achieve peace and freedom.

Luis Omar Salinas (1937–): Salinas is a Chicano poet known for his surrealistic imagery in the discussion of such themes as alienation, loneliness, death, and honor.

César Chávez (1927–1993): A Mexican American agricultural labor leader, Chávez founded the National Farm Workers Association to protect laborers' rights and was a strong proponent of using nonviolent means to achieve social change.

Dolores Huerta (1930–): Co-founder with César Chávez of the United Farm Workers, Huerta broke with societal traditions to become one of the most powerful labor leaders of the twentieth century. She raised eleven children while working as an organizer for the labor movement.

about what prompted the move from poetry to prose, Soto replied in an unpublished 1988 interview that his motivation was curiosity: "I was testing myself." In a lecture at a University of New Mexico symposium, "Reconstructing The Canon: Chicano Writers and Critics," Soto argued that essayists leave behind poetic license and in "plain, direct, unadorned" style construct scenes that are exciting to read.

This emphasis on plainness and directness has been a tenet both of Soto's poetry and of his prose work throughout his career. Speaking of his prose, he states, "I made a conscious effort not to tell anything but just present the stories ... just show not tell." *Living Up the Street* was a critical success, earning Soto the American Book Award in 1985.

A New Focus Soto has turned his talents to several other genres as well, most notably children's and young adult literature, which he continues to compose today. His popular works for young adults include the short story collections *Petty Crimes* (1998), *Help Wanted* (2005), and *Facts of Life* (2008), which feature Hispanic

COMMON HUMAN EXPERIENCE

A common theme in much of Soto's work is that of alienation. Here are some other famous works that explore similar ideas:

The Stranger (1952), a novel by Albert Camus. Camus' best-known work, this novel explores the author's philosophy that death is random and inevitable and that the meaning of life is entirely personal and subjective.

Native Son (1940), a novel by Richard Wright. This work explores the themes of alienation and violence through the chilling exploits of its protagonist Bigger Thomas. Contracted as a chauffeur by a wealthy white man, Bigger accidentally murders the man's daughter and goes on the run to escape persecution.

Snow (2005), by Orhan Pamuk. In this Nobel Prize–winning novel, a poet returns to Turkey, the country of his birth, after a long absence and discovers that the revolution he once promoted is now burning in the hands of radical Muslims. The protagonist tries to find a place for himself amid the violence, but feels increasingly baffled and alone in the place he wished to call home again.

Edward Scissorhands (1990), a film by Tim Burton. In this modern fairy tale starring Johnny Depp, an orphaned young man with scissors for hands tries to fit in with his suburban neighbors after living for years in isolation.

adolescents coping with typical teen struggles. Perhaps this emphasis on young readers is his way of addressing many of the injustices he experienced in his youth: on his personal Web site, Soto urges young people "to build our intellectual capital ... [to] put down our electronic toys and read."

Works in Literary Context

Chicano Literature Soto is one of America's most honored writers of Chicano poetry, or poetry written by the American-born or early-immigrated children of Latin American parents. The definition of the term Chicano has changed over generations, and today it is largely a political term, suggesting that Chicano writers work not only with poetry, but also with politics. One of the difficulties some Chicano artists face is learning how to integrate the two—art and politics—without allowing one to overwhelm the other.

Chicano literature has evolved due to a need for the expression of ideas and perspectives that had not previously appeared in American literature. The literary movement has sometimes been criticized for, as Jose Antonio Villarreal puts it, its willingness "to settle for anything" as its participants rush to commit to paper the ideas and emotions that were long suppressed. Recent Chicano critics, however,

have striven to create a set of standards by which the artistic merits of Chicano literary work can be measured.

Soto's work is notable for its ability to transcend social barriers. For example, though the characters in his short stories for young adults are primarily Hispanic, they often deal with the same sorts of problems as any other kids, such as the loss of a parent to cancer. While thoroughly Chicano, his writing has gone beyond the limits of the political movement to create art that is universally felt and acknowledged.

Works in Critical Context

Soto has earned the respect of critics and reviewers of his work because he represents his experience in a manner that, through simple and direct diction, contains glimpses of the universal. From the well-crafted and gritty lines of *The Elements of San Joaquin*, to the direct prose style and ironic humor of *Lesser Evils*, Soto, in the words of Ramírez, "portrays his characters and their patterns of behavior in such a vivid, concrete, sensorial, convincing manner that the Chicano condition becomes one of the forms of the human condition."

Living Up the Street Soto's *Living Up the Street* is filled with stories of mischief from childhood, adventures of adolescence, and the trials of adulthood, all represented in Soto's manner of "show not tell." The book has been widely acclaimed, winning a Before Columbus Book Award. Geoffrey Dunn, writing in the *San Francisco Review of Books*, states: "Soto's poetic prose goes right to the core of Chicano experience." A reviewer for *Booklist* declares, "Poet Gary Soto's first prose work is a pleasure to read."

Some critics of his autobiographical works, however, expressed concern that Soto's wife, Carolyn, did not appear as any more than a conventional figure; typical was Paredes, who states in the *Rocky Mountain Review of Language and Literature*:

> As he depicts them, the roles are wholly conventional. ... It is perhaps too much to say that Soto's portrayals of his wife and daughter are offensive but it is significant that his imagination, so finely tuned in other circumstances to the diversity and nuance of behavior, should perform unremarkably here.

The Elements of San Joaquin Soto's first book of poetry, *The Elements of San Joaquin*, was widely praised for its particular portrayals of disintegration and decay that led to universal meaning. Writing in *Discurso Literario*, Patricia de la Fuente notes: "[The] gradual erosion of energy is most consistently revealed on the intimate, individual level, where the very essence of the human condition is undergoing a pervasive disintegration." De la Fuente is also referring to the decay of the "elements" referenced in the book's title, which Julian Olivares has called "icons that refer to his own cultural context." As Olivares remarks in his 1990 essay in *Latin American Literary Review*, "With regard to his personal vision, Soto often selects from his view of the street negative signs. ... Gutters, sewers, cans and broken bottles ... the world of the outsider." These elements are necessary guideposts to all who come to Soto's poetry without a full understanding of the culture it represents, and their presence in his writing has made it successful among a diverse audience.

Responses to Literature

1. Using your library and the Internet, read three examples of Chicano poetry from Soto and other authors. How does the Chicano perspective differ from what you have read in other American poetry? How is it similar?

2. Soto often uses simple, concrete images—blood, earth, sweat, stone—to achieve certain effects in his writing. Read his poem "Mission Tire Factory," 1969, and identify several images in the poem, explaining how Soto's use of imagery contributes to the overall effect of the poem.

3. Watch the film *The Fight in the Fields*, which portrays César Chávez' struggle for farm workers' rights. In what ways does the film help you better understand Soto's poetry? What parallels can you draw between the events of those times and events occurring in the immigrant community today?

4. While primarily known as a poet, Soto has also written a good deal of fiction for children and young adults. Read one of his stories in *Facts of Life* and discuss how the writing style compares to his poetry. What do you think he means by "Just show, not tell"? Find some examples of how he shows but does not tell the reader what is happening in the story.

BIBLIOGRAPHY

Books

Chacón, Ramón. "Labor Unrest and Industrialized Agriculture in California: The Case of the 1933 San Joaquin Valley Cotton Strike." *En Aquel Entonces: Readings in Mexican-American History.* Edited by Manuel G. Gonzales and Cynthia M. Gonzales. Bloomington, Ind.: Indiana University Press, 2000.

Kanellos, Nicolás. "Chicano Literature." *Hispanic American Almanac.* Edited by Sonia G. Benson. Third ed. Detroit: Gale, 2003.

"Soto, Gary (1952–)." *Hispanic American Almanac.* Edited by Sonia G. Benson. Third ed. Detroit: Gale, 2003.

Periodicals

Bradley, Jerry. "Review of *The Elements of San Joaquin.*" *Western American Literature* (Spring 1979): 92–93.

De la Fuentes, Patricia. "Entropy in the Poetry of Gary Soto: The Dialectics of Violence." *Discurso Literario*, Vol. 5, No. 1 (Autumn 1987): 111–120.

Dunn, Geoffrey. "A Review of Living Up the Street: Narrative Recollections." *San Francisco Review of Books* (Summer 1986): 11.

Olivares, Julian. "The Streets of Gary Soto." *Latin American Literary Review*, Vol. XVIII, No. 35 (January–June 1990): 32–49.

Paredes, Raymund A. "Recent Chicano Fiction." *Rocky Mountain Review* Vol. 41, no. 1–2 (1987) 126–128.

Web sites

"Dolores Huerta." *National Women's Hall of Fame: Women of the Hall.* Accessed November 11, 2008, from http://www.greatwomen.org/women.php?action=viewone&id=81.

The Official Gary Soto Web Site. Accessed November 11, 2008, from http://www.garysoto.com/index.html.

✺ Nicholas Sparks

BORN: *1965, Omaha, Nebraska*

NATIONALITY: *American*

GENRE: *Fiction*

MAJOR WORKS:
The Notebook (1996)
Message in a Bottle (1998)
A Walk to Remember (1999)

Nicholas Sparks   Sparks, Nicholas, photograph. © by Jerry Bauer. Reproduced by permission.

Overview

A best-selling American novelist for over a decade, Nicholas Sparks is a writer of dramatic fiction, or literary fiction with elements of romance. Three of his novels have been *New York Times* number-one best sellers, and several have been made into films. Though they often center around romance, his novels explore deeper themes of hope and sacrifice with which millions of readers worldwide avidly identify.

Works in Biographical and Historical Context

On Track for Success   Born on New Year's Eve in the snowy plains city of Omaha, Nebraska, Nicholas Sparks grew up as one of three children to Patrick Michael and Jill Emma Marie Sparks. Following his father, who was still involved in graduate studies, his family moved from Nebraska to Minnesota, then to Los Angeles, California, back to Nebraska, and then back to California. Sparks, whose father was a professor, graduated valedictorian from his high school in Fair Oaks, California, and went on a full track scholarship to study at Notre Dame.

Running was not only Sparks's passion—he also excelled at it. In 1985, as a freshman at Notre Dame, he broke a school record as part of a relay team. Only an injury

prevented him from continuing to devote himself to track: he spent the summer recovering and writing his first (never published) novel. Sparks went on to graduate with high honors in business finance, and he eventually went back to running, but of these activities, it would turn out to be writing at which he excelled most.

Sparks had a considerable distance to go, however. He wrote his second novel after marrying in 1989, but again the novel was not published, and he took on a variety of jobs over the next few years to make ends meet. After working as a real estate appraiser, a server and a dental supply salesperson, he finally broke into publishing by a collaborative book with his longtime friend, Olympic gold medalist Billy Mills, entitled *Wokini: A Lakota Journey to Happiness and Self-Understanding* (1990). The book sold well and provided Sparks with a certain amount of experience with which to pursue his writing career.

A String of Hits   Sparks's first published novel, *The Notebook* (1996), was a resounding success, one of only three novels in recent history to spend more than a year on the hardback best-seller list. The story of a World War II couple's romance, as told through the notebook of an elderly man, *The Notebook* was bought in 1995 on a seven-figure advance by Warner Books, thereby securing Sparks's reputation as a novelist.

Over the next decade, Sparks followed up his initial success with ten more novels, all of which earned a place on the best-seller list. *Message in a Bottle* (1998), *A Walk to Remember* (1999), *The Notebook*, and *Nights in Rodanthe* (2002) have all been made into films, and the film rights have been purchased for several of his other novels.

Sparks continues to write and to be involved in his community. Following the American tradition of giving back to the organizations that gave to him, Sparks provides scholarships, internships, and fellowships to writers in the creative writing MFA program at Notre Dame. He lives in North Carolina with his wife, Catherine, and their five children.

Works in Literary Context

Romance and Dramatic Fiction   Romance fiction is a genre, or type, of fiction that, according to *Twentieth-Century Literary Criticism* (2008), "traces the developing romantic relationship between two people, chronicles the obstacles the couple must endure to be together, and concludes with a declaration of love and likely marriage." Although Sparks's work contains some elements of romance, his novels differ from romances in a number of significant ways. First, they tend to not to end "happily ever after"; Sparks's couples often learn that hope ends in disappointment. Second, they present a wider variety of more carefully drawn characters than often appear in romance novels—realistic characters who have to deal with real-life situations.

Nicholas Sparks's novels have been considered "dramatic fiction," a type of fiction that employs dramatic elements to create a more exciting effect than that of traditional literary fiction. His novels deal with topics more serious than those generally addressed in the romance genre—Alzheimer's, loss of family members, infertility—and, though they tend to focus on romance, are better classified in this subgenre of literary fiction. The term could be used to apply to the works of such writers as Michael Ondaatje, Mitch Albom, and Ian McEwan.

Works in Critical Context

One of the top-selling American novelists of the past decade, Nicholas Sparks has impressed critics with his tender, yet natural, narration of love stories. Though his work is sometimes criticized as being unrealistic or overly sentimental, readers seem to identify easily with his characters and themes, and his novels' constant presence on best-seller lists qualifies his work as overwhelmingly successful.

The Notebook   Sparks's first published novel, *The Notebook*, is a frame narrative in which an elderly man recounts the romance with his wife that began nearly sixty years before. It was both a popular and a critical success, with *Reviewer's Bookwatch* critic Marty Duncan writing, "Read this book. Be prepared to shed a tear or three. Be prepared for visions of two lovers holding hands with tenderness. Be prepared to feel sad for them both."

Perhaps one reason for the book's popularity was readers' ability to find consolation in that sadness. The notebook referred to in the book's title is the notebook from which the protagonist retells the story of their romance to his wife, who is afflicted with Alzheimer's. As Martha Whitmore Hickman postulates, "Is it possible that, despite the medical prognosis, love can redeem some hours for those afflicted with Alzheimer's?"

A Walk to Remember   Another of Sparks's best sellers, *A Walk to Remember*, is generally considered in the same vein as his earlier novels. Patty Engelmann writes in *Booklist*, "Sparks ... proves once again to be a master of pulling heartstrings and bringing a tear to his readers' eyes."

Some critics fault the work for this very fact, complaining that Sparks is merely following the same pattern by which he has established past success. A *Publishers Weekly* reviewer states, "This is the author's most simple, formulaic, and blatantly melodramatic package to date." Other reviewers, while not as harsh, admit that many of the narrative devices in this novel, such as flashbacks, secrets, and monumental decisions, have been seen in Sparks's work before.

Responses to Literature

1. Read Emily Brontè's novel *Wuthering Heights* and write an essay in which you compare this classic work to Sparks's contemporary novel *The Notebook*. What similar themes do you see in each? Do you think that

COMMON HUMAN EXPERIENCE

A common theme in much of Sparks's work is love that ends tragically. Here are some other famous works that explore similar ideas:

Romeo and Juliet (1562), a play by William Shakespeare. In this classic tragedy, teenage lovers Romeo and Juliet are prohibited from marrying by a family feud. After wedding in secret, their escape plans are ironically miscarried, and in the resultant confusion, both characters take their own lives.

Anna Karenina (1877), a novel by Leo Tolstoy. A focal work of Russian literature, this novel tells the story of the wife of a high bureaucrat who falls in love with a rich army officer, leaves husband and child for her paramour, and, driven to despair, commits suicide.

A Farewell to Arms (1929), a novel by Ernest Hemingway. One of Hemingway's best-known works, this novel was originally banned in the United States for explicit sexual content. It tells the story of Frederic Henry, an American serving in the Italian army, whose lover, Catherine Barkley, dies of complications due to a failed pregnancy.

Love Story (1970), a film directed by Arthur Hiller. This film shows the tragic story of Oliver and Jenny, who marry despite the disapproval of Oliver's father. After trying to have a child, they discover that Jenny is terminally ill. Her death brings about the reconciliation of father and son.

Sparks's novel might someday be considered classic literature? Why or why not?

2. It is sometimes considered a sign of weakness for a man to show his feelings, especially feelings of pain or love. Yet the male characters in Sparks's novels are often noted for showing their emotions. Find several examples in Sparks's work of men behaving in ways that would not traditionally be considered "macho." Is the portrayal positive or negative?

3. Watch the film version of *The Notebook*, and discuss how major themes from the novel are treated in the movie. Can you identify elements left out of the film, and if so, why do you think they were cut? Are there any ways in which the film is more successful than the novel?

4. A number of Sparks's novels are written in "frame narrative" structure. Using your library and the Internet, find a definition of frame narrative. Write an essay in which you discuss how the technique is used in two of Sparks's novels.

5. Write a short story in which two characters experience a tragic ending to their romance. Focus on making the characters believable and sympathetic to your reader.

BIBLIOGRAPHY

Books

"Romance Fiction in the Twentieth Century."
Twentieth-Century Literary Criticism, Vol. 198.
Detroit: Gale, 2008, pp. 236–342.

Periodicals

Review of *A Walk to Remember. Publishers Weekly* 246,
Issue 34 (August 23, 1999): 42.
Hickman, Martha Whitmore. Review of *The Notebook.*
Christian Century (December 17, 1997): 1201.
Monaghan, Pat. Review of *Wokini: A Lakota Journey to
Happiness and Self-Understanding. Booklist* (April 1,
1994): 1407.
Paul, Nancy. Review of *A Walk to Remember. Booklist*
(May 15, 2000): 144.
Smith, Sarah Harrison. Review of *Message in a Bottle.*
New York Times Book Review (June 14, 1998): 21.
Steffens, Daneet. Review of *Message in a Bottle.*
Entertainment Weekly (April 24, 1998): 75.
Wilkinson, Joanne. Review of *The Notebook. Booklist*
(August 1996): 1856.

Web sites

*Nicholas Sparks, Author of "Nights in Rodanthe" and "The
Notebook"* (online chat). *The Washington Post* online
edition. Accessed November 12, 2008, from http://
www.washingtonpost.com/wp-dyn/content/
discussion/2008/09/12/DI2008091202569.html.
Last updated on November 15, 2008.
Nicholas Sparks: Formal Biography. The Official Nicholas
Sparks Web site. Accessed November 12, 2008, from
http://www.nicholassparks.com/ShortBio.html.
Last updated in 2005.
Profiles: Billy Mills. Running Past Web site. Accessed
from http://www.runningpast.com/billy_mills.
htm. Last updated in 2008.

◉ Art Spiegelman

BORN: *1948, Stockholm, Sweden*

NATIONALITY: *American*

GENRE: *Fiction*

MAJOR WORKS:
Maus: A Survivor's Tale (1986, 1991)

Overview

Art Spiegelman, the son of Holocaust survivors, is one of
the most prominent "second-generation" creators of
depictions of the Holocaust and an important contemporary American sequential artist. Since the 1970s he has
produced intellectually intriguing comics and illustrations, some of which are considered controversial, for
numerous highly regarded publications. His major Hol-

Art Spiegelman   *Spiegelman, Art, photograph. Henny Ray Abrams /
Reuters / Landov.*

ocaust work, *Maus: A Survivor's Tale* (1986, 1991), is a
graphic novel, an extended comic book that treats serious
subjects in greater depth and with a wider variety of
techniques than is possible in the popular comic book.
Despite its designation as a "novel," *Maus* is not exclusively limited to fiction but often includes autobiography,
biography, and other forms of nonfiction narrative.
Nevertheless, it is considered a masterpiece of the graphic
novel genre.

Works in Biographical and Historical Context

A Commitment to Artistic Integrity Spiegelman
was born in Stockholm, Sweden, on February 15, 1948,
to refugees Vladek and Anja Spiegelman. His father was a
businessman, and his mother was a housewife. Arthur
immigrated with them to the United States in 1951.
They settled in the Rego Park area of Queens, New York
City, a neighborhood heavily populated by Jews. Spiegelman began creating comics and cartoons at the age of
thirteen, when he drew for his junior-high-school newspaper. While still attending the High School of Art and
Design, he was given an opportunity to join a commercial
comics syndicate, but he refused because joining would
have required him to conform his art to syndicate rules.
Then as now, Spiegelman maintained his independence

and defended the integrity of the comics form. He has also refused to adapt his comics for motion pictures, which would involve group production.

Heading Underground Spiegelman attended Harpur College (now part of Binghamton University) in upstate New York from 1965 to 1968. He dropped out before completing a bachelor's degree and, in 1968, suffered a nervous breakdown. He spent one month in a mental hospital, as recorded in the "Prisoner on the Hell Planet" comic strip (first published in *Short Order Comix* (1973) and later included in the first volume of *Maus*). As that strip also reports, his mother committed suicide soon afterward, possibly influenced by the death of her brother in an auto accident.

Clearly it was a difficult period for Spiegelman. His psychological troubles may have been compounded by the fact that, at that time, his chosen art and mode of expression were not socially accepted. The mid-1950s had seen a sharp decrease in the number of comics being created and sold in America, due to a strident campaign that blamed comics for the moral degradation of teenage boys. The result: comics were redrafted to flatter establishment ideals (introducing, for example, the Justice League of America), and their survival depended on how successfully they achieved this goal. Many comics artists and publishers, including the future publisher of *Mad* magazine, lost their jobs or even their careers because they refused to conform.

Such a publishing atmosphere did not offer much freedom of creativity for a mind like Spiegelman's. His only choice was to work independently, and in 1966 he began to do so, creating underground comics that defied the status quo. In 1971 he moved to San Francisco, which was flowering as a center for countercultural arts. There, under pseudonyms such as Joe Cutrate and Skeeter Grant, he published a series of original comics, one of which portrayed Jewish Holocaust victims as mice. He returned to New York in 1975, and in 1977 he married Françoise Mouly, with whom he founded the influential avant-garde comics anthology *Raw* in 1980. As early as 1978, Spiegelman initiated the research that led to *Maus*, which included trips to Auschwitz first in 1978 and again in 1986, the year the first volume of the graphic novel was published. In 1991, thirteen years after he began his project, the second and final volume of *Maus* appeared.

Maus and Man Many have speculated on where Spiegelman might have garnered inspiration for the depiction of his characters in his widely acclaimed graphic novel. Jewish sources were especially prominent. Spiegelman was working under the influence of William Gaines and Harvey Kurtzman's satirical *Mad* magazine, in which the frequent appearance of Yiddish betrayed the presence on its staff of several Holocaust survivors. Speaking at a Jewish writers' conference in 2001, he stated, "I read *Mad* and read words like *fershlugginer* and had a clue they came from my neighborhood."

More tellingly, Spiegelman has likened his creation of *Maus* to his coming out of an assimilationist, or conformist, closet to reveal the Jewish element in himself. This concept of embracing one's cultural roots matches the post-1960s context of the civil rights and sexual liberation movements, including ethnic identification and self-confession. In fact, Spiegelman has told interviewers that he got the immediate idea for *Maus* from a college film course in which the instructor showed cartoons of cat-and-mouse chases along with racist movies in order to demonstrate the similarity between the depictions of mice and minorities in those genres.

In 1986, after the first volume of *Maus* appeared, it garnered the Present Tense/Joel M. Cavior Award for Jewish Writing, and after the second volume was published in 1991, the work received a Pulitzer Prize as well as a National Book Critics Circle Award, a Los Angeles Times Award, an American Book Award, and the Before Columbus Foundation Award (all in 1992). *Maus* is now taught in high school and college courses in Jewish studies, American literature, philosophy, and European history throughout the United States.

COMMON HUMAN EXPERIENCE

A common theme in Spiegelman's work is the conflict of identity. Here are some other famous works that explore similar ideas:

Hamlet (1602), a play by William Shakespeare. Often considered Shakespeare's masterpiece, *Hamlet* explores the inner conflict of Prince Hamlet of Denmark, whose identity as his father's son urges him to take revenge on his father's murderer—who, incidentally, has become his stepfather.

Portrait of a Lady (1881), a novel by Henry James. This novel tells the story of Isabel Archer, a young, single American woman who inherits some money while traveling in Europe. Though she wishes to remain independent, her identity as a woman practically requires her to marry. She expresses her independence by choosing the suitor her society considers her worst choice.

"Yentl the Yeshiva Boy" (c. 1960), a short story by Isaac Bashevis Singer. A short story that was made into a play and a film starring Barbara Streisand, "Yentl" tells of a young Jewish girl who disguises herself as a boy to pursue her studies. Conflict arises when she falls in love with her roommate, who believes she is a man.

Bless Me, Ultima (1972), a novel by Rudolfo A. Anaya. In this novel, set in New Mexico after World War II, protagonist Antonio finds himself forced to choose between his mother's family and his father's, amid personal doubts and a crisis of faith.

Persepolis (2007), a film by Vincent Paronnaud and Marjane Satrapi. Named after the ancient capital of Persia (now Iran), this film is a biographical account of an outspoken Iranian girl who comes of age during the Islamic revolution that would result in women losing many of their rights and freedoms.

Over the two decades since the release of *Maus*, Spiegelman has continued to work in the comics genre and as a graphic artist. He co-edited several volumes of the *Little Lit* series, sophisticated children's stories told in comic-art style. At least one of the stories in this series, contributed by Spiegelman himself, is based on a Hasidic, or traditional Jewish, tale. Spiegelman remains close to his ethnic origins, and a generation of overtly Jewish comic artists has followed in his path. His work and influence have undeniably enriched the American graphic novel, American art and literature, and most of all, the unsettling art of Holocaust remembrance.

Works in Literary Context

Spiegelman's work has included comics, critical essays, and illustrations, some of which have been considered controversial. His most important work, however—*Maus: A Survivor's Tale*—is also the hardest to classify. It has been called a graphic novel for the sake of convenience, but in fact, *Maus* contains elements of several genres, including autobiography, biography, epic, and fiction.

Graphic Novel The term *graphic novel* has a number of definitions, among them "adult comic" and "sequential art narrative" according to George Dardess. Possibly due in part to the reputation of its predecessor in print—the comic book—what to call the genre has arisen as an important question. The word *graphic* seems to imply violence, while the term *adult* suggests that the works contain lewdness. Generally speaking, however, a graphic novel is a written work that combines comics-style illustrations with extended stories, often on controversial subjects.

Spiegelman's *Maus* has traditionally been classified as a graphic novel. But it departs from the definition of the fictional novel in that it includes certain factual elements. The characters bear the same names as their real-life counterparts, for example, and many actual events related to the Holocaust are incorporated into the story. For convenience, however, the work continues to be included in the graphic novel genre.

Postmodern Art Spiegelman's mix of narrative types is characteristic of what has been called postmodernism, "a style of thought which is suspicious of classical notions of truth, reason, identity, and objectivity," according to Terry Eagleton. Essentially, postmodernists believe that nothing can be known absolutely; their art, therefore, often incorporates a variety of techniques to view its subjects from numerous perspectives.

Spiegelman's use of so many literary resources to portray the tortured history of his family suggests that he believed one genre would be inadequate to capture it all. The enormity of the Holocaust makes its representation in any format difficult. And because of the great exposure the Holocaust has received over the past half century, many worthy representations fail to impress as deeply as they should. Spiegelman's serious literary adaptation of the allegedly frivolous comic-book format shocked many readers into seeing the Holocaust in a new way.

Works in Critical Context

Maus: A Survivor's Tale Critical reaction to *Maus* has been largely positive, with reviewers praising Spiegelman's use of dialect and imagery and his parallel exploration of the Holocaust and his relationship with his father. Michael Staub has called the work "much more accessible to a general audience than many other accounts, because it is particularly effective at inviting emotional involvement."

Some critics, however, disagree, claiming that the subject of the Holocaust is too solemn to address in the graphic novel format. Critic Sheng Mei-Ma states that "[Spiegelman] verges on irreverence by coupling the genre with Shoah [Holocaust] in *Maus*." The central question seems to be whether the graphic novel genre is as worthy of respect as genres such as poetry or the novel. This question goes back to original arguments over the social value of comics and has not yet been resolved.

Regardless, with the publication of *Maus*, Spiegelman undoubtedly made an impact, not only on the graphic novel genre, but also on American literature as a whole. As critic Lawrence L. Langer has stated: "Perhaps no Holocaust narrative will ever contain the whole experience. But Art Spiegelman has found an original and authentic form to draw us closer to its bleak heart."

Responses to Literature

1. The argument over whether comics and graphic novels have any lasting value has been going on for almost a century. What do you think? Why do you think some people believe that a graphic novel should not treat serious subjects? What benefits did Spiegelman gain by presenting his ideas in this genre?

2. The Holocaust is considered perhaps the darkest period in modern human history. Using your library and the Internet, research three or four more portrayals of the Holocaust, either in literature or in film. What are some of the different ways artists tell their stories? Which portrayals do you think are most effective, and why?

3. Watch the film *Persepolis*, based on the graphic novel of the same name. Why do you think the writers chose to present the story in illustrations, rather than in actual images? In what ways do you think your reaction to the story would change if it were filmed with human actors?

4. Create your own short comic based on a passage from a work of literature you have studied in class. Focus on making sure the story comes out both in images and in text. Share the comic with your classmates and ask them to compare it to the original text.

5. Using your library and the Internet, research the history of comics in the United States. Pay special attention to the ways in which comics have been perceived by the public. Discuss how certain public perceptions of the genre have changed, and how some remain the same today.

BIBLIOGRAPHY

Books

Eagleton, Terry. *The Illusions of Postmodernism*. Malden, Mass.: Blackwell, 1996.

Periodicals

Dardess, George. "Bringing Comic Books to Class." *College English* 57, no. 2 (February 1995): 213–222.

Ma, Sheng-Mei. "Mourning with the (as a) Jew: Metaphor, Ethnicity, and the Holocaust in Art Spiegelman's Maus." *Studies in American Jewish Literature* 16 (1997): 115–129.

Staub, Michael. "The Shoah Goes On and On: Remembrance and Representation in Art Spiegelman's Maus." *MELUS* 20, no. 3 (Fall 1995): 33–46.

Web sites

"Comic Creator: Harvey Kurtzman." *Lambiek*. Accessed November 15, 2008, from http://lambiek.net/artists/k/kurtzman.htm. Last updated on December 14, 2007.

"The History of Comics." *Comic Art and Graffix Gallery*. Accessed November 15, 2008, from http://www.comic-art.com/history.htm. Last updated in 2006.

"Joseph Raymond McCarthy, U.S. Senator." *CNN Interactive*. Accessed November 15, 2008, from http://www.cnn.com/SPECIALS/cold.war/kbank/profiles/mccarthy/. Last updated in 1999.

Devlin, Desmond. "The Untold History of *Mad* Magazine." *DC Universe*. Accessed November 15, 2008, from http://www.dccomics.com/mad/?action=about.

❀ Jerry Spinelli

BORN: *1941, Norristown, Pennsylvania*

NATIONALITY: *American*

GENRE: *Fiction*

MAJOR WORKS:
Space Station Seventh Grade (1982)
Maniac Magee (1990)
Wringer (1997)

Overview

Author of the Newbery Award–winning book *Maniac Magee* (1990), Jerry Spinelli is known for his ability to write humorous, engaging stories that are meaningful to his young-adult audience. His novels address topics sometimes considered by parents to be too controversial for young readers—topics such as racism, sex, homelessness, and illiteracy—but he enjoys immense popularity with young audiences.

Works in Biographical and Historical Context

Becoming a Writer Spinelli was born and raised in Norristown, Pennsylvania, just outside the city limits of Philadelphia. For a little while he wanted to be a cowboy when he grew up; then he changed his mind and decided to become a baseball player. When a junior in high school, however, Spinelli got his first taste of literary success when a poem he had written was published in the hometown newspaper. With that, as Spinelli states on his Web site, "I traded in my baseball bat for a pencil and became a writer."

Jerry Spinelli   *Spinelli, Jerry, photograph. Reproduced by permission.*

Spinelli attended Gettysburg College, where he served as editor of the college literary journal and tried his hand at writing short stories. After college he got a job as an editor for a department store magazine and worked on a novel during his lunch breaks, after dinner, and on weekends. The novel was never published, nor were any of the three that came after it. It was not until marrying fellow writer Eileen Spinelli, and simultaneously becoming father to her five children, that he found the inspiration his writing needed.

Finding Inspiration in Youth   Though he used every means available to drown out the sound of his noisy new family—cotton, earplugs, closed doors—Spinelli soon found that the bickering and chaos brought back memories of his own childhood. These memories, apparently, were just what he needed to energize his imagination. He later told an interviewer of an incident in which one of the children "swiped" the chicken he had been saving for his own lunch. "When I discovered that the chicken was gone," he said, "I wrote about it." This theft-inspired tale became the groundwork for his first published novel, *Space Station Seventh Grade* (1982).

The novel, which was a success, launched Spinelli's writing career with the story of Jason Herkimer, a thirteen-year-old boy who girl-watches, marvels over his (sometimes repulsive) maturing body, and works on a model space station in his spare time. Spinelli went on to tell more of Jason's exploits in a sequel, *Jason and Marceline* (1986), in which Jason repels his crush Marceline by his macho attitude until at last he saves a classmate and engages in the utterly un-macho behavior of accepting the boy's appreciative hug.

Spinelli's most acclaimed book to date, *Maniac Magee* (1990), was largely inspired by events he experienced in his own childhood. Jeffrey Lionel Magee, an orphan nicknamed 'Maniac' on account of his hyperactive speed, was inspired by a black friend Spinelli remembered from his youth. As Spinelli recalled in his Newbery Medal acceptance speech, the friend had tried to enter a public pool with several other kids one summer but was refused admittance because of the color of his skin.

To date, Spinelli has published twenty-five books. His once raucous children have grown up and had more than a dozen children of their own. While Spinelli continues to live in Pennsylvania and write, he also maintains the curiosity and adventurousness common to many of his characters that allow him room to explore.

Works in Literary Context

Spinelli writes primarily in the genre of the young adult fiction—that is, fiction written for people between the ages of about eleven and seventeen. Karen Coats has written that "One of the key features of the young adult genre is its currency, its absolute synchronicity with the concerns of the audience to whom it is marketed." In other words, young adult fiction often is not 'timeless' in the same way as works of literature for adults; its success depends on its ability to communicate with readers about the issues they face in the moment in which they read it.

Young Adult Novel   Young adult novels are lengthy works of fiction written for people who are just beginning to deal with the more serious issues of adulthood. They are differentiated from children's books by their subject matter, which usually relates to the lives of older readers, and by the more honest, complex treatment of issues generally considered too sensitive to discuss with children. Many of Spinelli's books address difficult subjects with which today's young people must deal at an early age. In *Space Station Seventh Grade*, one of the protagonist's friends is a Korean American who deals with subtle racism. Several of Spinelli's female characters struggle with, and ultimately defy, traditional gender roles.

Some scholars argue that young adult novels seem to have less success when they avoid controversial subjects, or when their writers—adults—use them as a medium through which to return to "something innocent and precious which we have destroyed," as Patricia Head has suggested. The fact seems to be that young adult readers gravitate toward books that communicate with them on a more mature level.

Works in Critical Context

Jerry Spinelli is considered "a master of those embarrassing, gloppy, painful and suddenly wonderful things that happen on the razor's edge between childhood and full-fledged adolescence," according to Deborah Churchman in the *Washington Post Book World*. Although some reviewers have considered his work too risqué or even unrealistic, by and large the response to his work has been very positive.

Maniac Magee   *Maniac Magee* has been considered a "quest" novel in which the protagonist, Maniac, who gets his nickname from his speed and hyperactivity, tries to find his way to a safe home. The novel is considered unusual among works for young adults in that it deals openly with the subject of racism—and according to most critics, does so successfully. Catherine Camper writes in her 1990 review of the novel, "Spinelli writes humorously and bravely about a subject that most children's authors and publishers try to avoid." Although she notes that Spinelli's view of racism, "though politically correct, is still white," Camper nevertheless commends him for the honesty of his efforts to portray it, as do most critics.

While Dirk Mattson has criticized the novel for being "exaggerated" and "full of repetition" Mary Voors suggests that these qualities become part of its folkloric style. "Just as you start to think this is a realistic portrayal of the contemporary problems of racism and homelessness," she writes in *Voice of Youth Advocates*, "Spinelli suddenly tilts the focus so it becomes an imaginative folktale of racial prejudice in America."

Space Station Seventh Grade   "There is no doubt that this [novel] holds a realistic mirror up to early teenage life," writes Ilene Cooper in her *Booklist* review of *Space Station Seventh Grade*. Most critics seem to agree. Though the humorous, episodic novel about Jason Herkimer has been faulted for its characters seeming "a little bit cartoonish," the book has been widely praised by readers and critics alike for its portrayal of adolescence.

Responses to Literature

1. Read Spinelli's novel *Wringer*. What part does peer pressure play in the main character's dilemma over becoming a wringer during the Pigeon Day shoot? How does Spinelli show the effects of these pressures?

2. Read Spinelli's *Maniac Magee*. What are some of the subjects it addresses that you think most parents prefer not to discuss with their kids? Do you think it deals with these subjects maturely and honestly? Why or why not?

3. In Spinelli's novel *There's a Girl in My Hammerlock*, a controversy arises regarding whether girls should be allowed to participate on the wrestling team.

LITERARY AND HISTORICAL CONTEMPORARIES

Spinelli's famous contemporaries include:

Martin Luther King Jr. (1929–1968): A Baptist pastor in the 1950s, King became the central spokesperson for the civil rights movement of the 1960s that would break down racial barriers that had segregated the country for centuries. He was assassinated in 1968.

Neil Armstrong (1930–): Astronaut Armstrong became the first human being ever to set foot on the moon in 1969.

Lois Lowry (1937–): A widely acclaimed author of children's books, including the Newbery Award–winning *Number the Stars* (1989), Lowry often writes about the fear of being weird.

J.K. Rowling (1964–): World-renowned British author of the *Harry Potter* fantasy series for young adults, Rowling is ranked one of the wealthiest authors of all time.

Write a letter to the editor of your school newspaper discussing why you think girls should or should not be allowed to play football. Use examples from *There's a Girl in My Hammerlock* or other books or films you have discussed in class.

BIBLIOGRAPHY

Periodicals

Camper, Catherine A. "Review of *Maniac Magee*." *Five Owls* 4 (July 1990): 108.

Churchman, Deborah. "Tales of the Awkward Age." *Washington Post Book World* (January 13, 1985): 8.

Coats, Karen. "Abjection and Adolescent Fiction." *Journal for the Psychoanalysis of Culture & Society* vol. 5, no. 2 (Fall 2000): 290.

Cooper, Ilene. "Review of *Space Station Seventh Grade*." *Booklist* 79, no. 12 (15 February 1983): 780.

Gormley, Emma. "Name and Identity in Spinelli's *Stargirl* and *Loser*." *Bookbird* 44, no. 2 (2006): 14–21.

Head, Patricia. "Robert Cormier and the Postmodernist Possibilities of Young Adult Fiction." *Children's Literature Association Quarterly* 21.1 (Spring 1996): 28–33.

Jameyson, Karen. Review of *Who Put That Hair in My Toothbrush?* *Horn Book* (June 1984): 343–344.

Karrenbrock, Marilyn H. Review of *Space Station Seventh Grade*. *ALAN Review* (Winter 1985): 35.

Knorr, Susan. Review of *There's a Girl in My Hammerlock*. *School Library Journal* (September 1991): 260.

Keller, John. "Jerry Spinelli." *Horn Book* (July/August 1991): 433–436.

Mattson, Dirk P. "Finding Your Way Home: Orphan Stories in Young Adult Literature." *ALAN Review* 24, no. 3 (Spring 1997): 17–21.

Voors, Mary R. Review of *Maniac Magee*. *Voice of Youth Advocates* 13, no.5 (December 1990) 290.

Web sites

The John Newbery Medal. American Library Association Web site. Accessed November 13, 2008, from http://www.ala.org/ala/mgrps/divs/alsc/awardsgrants/bookmedia/newberymedal/aboutnewbery/aboutnewbery.cfm. Last updated in 2008.

Spinelli Interview. Jerry Spinelli Official Web site. Accessed November 13, 2008, from http://www.jerryspinelli.com/newbery_008.htm. Last updated in 2007.

❀ William Stafford

BORN: *1914, Hutchinson, Kansas*

DIED: *1993, Lake Oswego, Oregon*

NATIONALITY: *American*

GENRE: *Poetry*

MAJOR WORKS:
Traveling Through the Dark (1962)
Allegiances (1970)
Someday, Maybe (1973)
A Glass Face in the Rain (1982)

Overview

One of America's most prolific poets, William Stafford is generally considered a regional poet and one of the foremost practitioners of plain style, a kind of writing that uses simple language and concrete imagery to evoke a powerful response. Though his poetry has not always received the highest praise—and in fact, has elicited extensive criticism—the overall body of Stafford's work has classified him as a poet worthy of study and placement in the American literary canon.

Works in Biographical and Historical Context

Adventures in Learning   Stafford was born in Hutchinson, Kansas, a small town on the Arkansas River, a few years before the start of World War I. His parents maintained a liberal and nonconformist household, attending church regularly, for example, but never formally joining any of the congregations, so important to the social life of their town. Stafford's father, who appears regularly as a persona representing justice and tolerance in his son's poems, encouraged his son's reading habits and demonstrated the values of personal responsibility and hard work. Forced to travel to Wichita, Liberal, Garden City, and El Dorado to find work in the 1930s, during the Great Depression, Earl Stafford subjected his family to the rigorous life of the working poor.

When recalling his youth, however, Stafford does not focus on the hardship his family endured—the fact, for instance, that he had to supplement the family income as a child by working in the fields and raising vegetables to sell. Instead, he recalls his childhood as a period of intellectual freedom and adventure, with the town's library as a central element in his explorations. This attraction to learning remained with Stafford throughout his life: He went on to study at the University of Kansas, earning Bachelor's and Master's degrees there, and the University of Iowa, where he was awarded a Ph.D. in 1955.

A Conscientious Objector   Stafford was drafted during World War II and chose to join alternative civilian service as a conscientious objector, or a person who refuses to

William Stafford   *AP Images*

participate in the war for ethical or moral reasons. Though anti-war protesters are somewhat common in America today, objectors to the 1940s war against Germany and Japan were scarce. They were viewed as cowardly and un-American; in reality, however, it required a great deal of moral strength to voice objection to America's participation in the war. This moral strength would become a notable quality of Stafford's work two decades later.

Early Career   The four years Stafford spent working in civilian public service camps—mostly in forestry and soil preservation—served as both inspiration and preparation for his writing career. During that period he formed the habit of rising very early in the morning to write, a habit which he would maintain throughout his life, for he found those still hours most conducive to receiving and following the lead of the impressions that evolve into poems. His first book, however, was not poetry, but a fictionalized account of the years he spent working in the camps, *Down in My Heart* (1947).

In 1944, the year before the war ended, Stafford married Dorothy Hope Frantz, a teacher and the daughter of a minister in the pacifist Church of the Brethren. The couple eventually had two sons and two daughters. After the war ended, Stafford began a teaching career with Lewis and Clark College, where he would remain for almost thirty years, until his retirement in 1978. His only absence from Lewis and Clark came when he attended the University of Iowa to pursue his doctorate degree.

"First Sustained Relation to Other Writers"   As Stafford related in *Contemporary Authors Autobiography Series*, the experience at the University of Iowa provided his "first sustained relation to other writers." He has also stated that "those two years remain the principal reference point I have for the literary life as lived by others." This is particularly significant in view of the fact that Stafford has never been influenced by anyone else's concept of "the literary life," nor the critical and commercial expectations that often beset it.

Indeed, individualism would become a key tenet in Stafford's work. The theme, along with many other of his favorites, became apparent in his first collection of poetry, *West of Your City* (1960). This volume included poems on the American Midwest and West of the poet's birth, childhood, and mature life; history and tradition; home and family; the Native Americans who share the West; the natural elements and animal life from which he derives inspiration; memory and the perspective it provides on experience; and—always essential to his creative process—exploration, the undistracted awareness that leads into "new territory" in which Stafford finds his poems.

Stafford's strong adherence to a moral code also became one of the more remarkable aspects of his poetry. In the 1960s, while much of American literary culture was trumpeting individual freedom and universal acceptance, Stafford insisted on a qualification: individual freedom and universal acceptance, but only when they came with moral responsibility. His belief in strictly defined categories of good and evil made him something of an anomaly among his fellow writers, but for a man who had long been an outcast, this was nothing new.

Lasting Recognition   Despite the tentative reception his works often received at first, Stafford soon came to be recognized as one of the foremost poets of his generation. His use of concrete imagery and plain language meshed well with his boldly colored view of the world and gained him a reputation as a "plain-style" poet. Not all of his poetry was successful: Stafford published only a fraction of what he wrote, and some critics felt that even that fraction was too much. Stafford, however, was not bothered by their opinions. "A writer must write bad poems," he wrote. "Finicky ways can dry up sources."

In 1992, just months before his death of myocardial arrhythmia, Stafford responded to a call from the U.S. Forest Service to write a series of poems to appear on signs at scenic turnouts on the highway that twists through the 8,000-foot peaks rising from the Methow Valley in northern Washington state. Stafford's willingness to participate in such a democratic poetic project and the scenario itself—juxtaposing nature and poetry and the modern highway—serve as the perfect symbol for all his work. Starting with *Down in My Heart* and continuing through more than 3,000 published poems and many prose pieces, this prolific writer grappled with his ambivalence about the blessings of modern technology and industry and the disappearing wilderness of the American West.

LITERARY AND HISTORICAL CONTEMPORARIES

Stafford's famous contemporaries include:

T. S. Eliot (1888–1965): Eliot was an American modernist whose writing had a tremendous influence on the style and diction of poets who followed him. In his most famous work, *The Waste Land* (1922), the narrators include a tarot-card reader and a person who walks with the spirits of the dead.

John Berryman (1914–1972): Another innovative American poet, Berryman is best known as the author of *The Dream Songs* (1969), an unconventional poem sequence praised for its magnitude and uniquely American voice.

Robert Lowell (1917–1977): A well known confessional poet of the mid- to late-twentieth century, Lowell's work is remarkably idiosyncratic and difficult to summarize.

Allen Ginsberg (1926–1997): Infamous leading member of the Beat Generation and author of the chaotically original poem, *Howl*, Ginsberg is now considered one of the most popular American poets of all time.

Franklin Delano Roosevelt (1882–1945): The thirty-second president of the United States, Franklin Roosevelt led the nation through the Great Depression of the early 1930s until nearly the end of World War II. After his death, Congress moved to limit presidential reelection to a single four-year term.

Works in Literary Context

Stafford's poetry and essays have often been compared to the writings of American authors Walt Whitman and Ralph Waldo Emerson, both of whom stressed the wonder of nature and the power of the individual in their works. Whitman and Emerson are both identified with the romantic symbolism movement that arose in America in the mid-nineteenth century.

Romantic Symbolism Romantic symbolism was a movement in America in the middle of the nineteenth century in which the details of the natural world and the actions of people were used to suggest abstract ideas. For example, the changing of leaves in the fall may be referenced in a poem to symbolize change or death. Both Emerson and Whitman, considered two of the first and foremost wholly American poetic geniuses, used romantic symbolism extensively in their poetry and essays. Stafford followed in their footsteps by focusing on nature and simple human acts in his poetry as a means of addressing larger, more universal ideas.

Plain Style Unlike Emerson, however, and to a great extent more than Whitman, Stafford eschewed an elegant, artificial style and instead, crafted his poems around plain language, concrete imagery, and simple structure. This style of writing, which has been called plain style, gains much of its impact from its simplicity and accessibility to a broad audience. It has also been considered distinctly American in that it reflects the country's democratic nature and individualistic spirit.

Works in Critical Context

While critics through the years have not been unanimous in ranking Stafford as a major poet, they concur that he is one of the most esteemed. His work has been praised for its attention to craft, the ways in which his plain style illuminates complex subjects, and his focus on a purer kind of life in which, by the time his poems began to be published in the 1960s, few Americans seemed to believe anymore. Nevertheless, many critics have been reluctant to consider Stafford a master poet because of the unevenness and repetitiveness of his work. There is a question of quantity versus quality which seems, in the minds of many critics, to have damaged Stafford's overall reputation. As Judith Kitchen has mentioned, "Stafford's refusal to edit his own work and to limit the amount he publishes has caused critics to take him less seriously than they should."

Opinion has been divided on the moral stance Stafford takes in his poetry, an approach that was not fashionable in the 1960s, when his work began to be read widely. Overwhelmingly, however, he is applauded for his straightforward style, his allegiance to nature and simple values, his ability to make contact with his readers, and his worldview. As George S. Lensing and Ronald Moran state in *Four Poets and the Emotive Imagination*, the life Stafford depicts is "a richly attractive alternative to contemporary society ... a mechanical existence that divorces the individual from authentic human values."

Traveling through the Dark Stafford's poetry collection *Traveling through the Dark* (1962), which became his best known collection, won high acclaim for its elegance, style, and breadth of perception. Writing in 1989, Henry Taylor stated, "*Traveling through the Dark* immediately established Stanford as a poet of rare gifts and unusual productivity." The judges for the National Book Award for Poetry, which Stafford won for the volume, stated, "William Stafford's poems are clean, direct, and whole. They are both tough and gentle; their music knows the value of silence."

Some critics, however, fault the collection for including not only Stafford's best work, but a number of lesser poems as well. Peter Davison wrote in the *Atlantic Monthly* in 1962, "In the less good poems you tend to be aware of a bustle of preparation, but the lesser poems are simply a little less intense, less striking." Davison expresses what seems to be the general opinion of Stafford's contemporary critics, however, when he goes on to write, "If William Stafford can discipline himself to publish only the best of his poems, watch out. He is a poet with something to say."

Responses to Literature

1. The conflict between nature and civilization has been a major theme of writers from around the world for thousands of years. Why do you think the subject interests writers so much? Using your library and the Internet, find three or four modern examples of books, films, or songs based on the same theme.

2. Many people think that poetry must use fancy or artificial language. Do you agree? Why or why not? Using your library and the Internet, find two or three examples of famous poems and discuss how they support your argument.

3. Read Stafford's poem "Traveling Through the Dark" and Robert Frost's poem "Stopping By Woods on a Snowy Evening" (1923). Both poems concern the experiences, thoughts, and decisions of lone travelers at night. What is similar about these two travelers? What is different?

4. Stafford was a conscientious objector during World War II and writes of his feelings in the poem "Objector." Read the poem and discuss the concept of conscientious objection. Is it cowardly? Brave? Right? Wrong? Using your library or the Internet, research the life of another famous American conscientious objector and write a short biographical essay on that person.

BIBLIOGRAPHY

Books

Cuddon, J. A., ed. *The Penguin Dictionary of Literary Terms and Literary Theory*, Third Ed. New York: Penguin, 1992.

Stitt, Peter. *The World's Hieroglyphic Beauty: Five American Poets*. Athens: University of Georgia Press, 1985.

Taylor, Henry. "'Thinking for Berky': Millions of Intricate Moves." *On William Stafford: The Worth of Local Things*. Edited by Tom Andrews. Ann Arbor: University of Michigan Press, 1993. 221–232.

Periodicals

Bentley, Beth. "An Interview with William Stafford." *Madrona* 2, No. 5 (1972): 5–18.

Bradley, Sam. "Reciprocity vs. Suicide: An Interview with William Stafford." *Trace* 46 (Summer 1962): 223–226.

Davison, Peter. "William Stafford." *The Atlantic Monthly* (November 1962): 88.

Roberts, J. Russell, Sr. "Listening to the Wilderness with William Stafford." *Western American Literature* 3 (Fall 1968): 217–226.

COMMON HUMAN EXPERIENCE

A common theme in Stafford's work is the conflict between civilization and the wilderness. Here are some other famous works with similar themes:

Gilgamesh (unknown; transcribed c. 2000 BCE), an epic poem of unknown authorship. In this epic poem, Gilgamesh, a mythological king, leaves his throne, which is representative to civilization, to seek out adventure in the wilderness with his friend Enkidu.

The Jungle Book (1894), a story collection by Rudyard Kipling. This collection of tales about Mowgli, an Indian boy who was abandoned in the jungle and raised by wolves, has inspired several films.

The Sea-Wolf (1904), a novel by Jack London. Written by the author of *The Call of the Wild* (1903), this novel pits the educated, refined Humphrey Van Weyden against the raw and brutal Wolf Larsen. Their struggle for mastery represents the struggle between nature and civilization.

O Pioneers! (1913), a novel by Willa Cather. This novel tells the story of Swedish immigrants in Nebraska whose lives are shaped by their struggle to tame the land.

"William (Edgar) Stafford (1914–1993)." *Contemporary Authors Online*. Online ed. Detroit: Gale, 2004.

"William Stafford (1914–1993)." *Poetry Criticism*. Ed. Michelle Lee. Vol. 71. Online ed. Detroit: Thompson Gale, 2006.

Web sites

"The Good War and Those Who Refused to Fight It: World War II Pacifists." *PBS Online*. Accessed November 18, 2008, from http://www.pbs.org/itvs/thegoodwar/ww2pacifists.html. Last updated in 2008.

✸ Danielle Steel

BORN: *1947, New York City*

NATIONALITY: *American*

GENRE: *Fiction*

MAJOR WORKS:
The Promise (1978)
The Long Road Home (1998)
The House on Hope Street (2000)
Answered Prayers (2002)
Ransom (2004)

Danielle Steel *Sylvain Gaboury / FilmMagic / Getty Images*

Overview

Danielle Steel is an internationally best-selling author of over thirty romance novels. Since publishing her first book in 1973, Steel has acquired an enormous following of loyal, avid readers. In 1986, she was recognized by the *Guinness Book of World Records* for having at least one of her books on the *New York Times* best-seller list for two hundred and twenty-five consecutive weeks. Most of Steel's novels feature rich, beautiful, and talented women who have to overcome setbacks before realizing their dreams. Many of her heroines face the modern dilemma of choosing between a satisfying career or love and family. Usually, like Steel herself, they succeed in achieving both.

Works in Biographical and Historical Context

A Daughter of Fortune Steel was born in New York City, the only child of John Schuelein-Steel, a member of Munich's wealthy Lowenbrau beer family, and Norma Schuelein-Steel, an international beauty from Portugal. Steel's parents divorced when she was seven or eight years old. Afterward, she was raised by relatives and servants in Paris and New York. She graduated from the Lycée Français, a private high school in New York where instruction is conducted in French, when she was not quite fifteen. In 1963, she entered New York's Parsons School of Design. However, she soon abandoned her dream of becoming "the new Chanel" when the pressure to succeed caused her to develop a stomach ulcer. She then enrolled at New York University, where she studied until 1967.

When Steel was only eighteen, she married her first husband, a French banker with homes in New York, San Francisco, and Paris. The jet-setting lifestyle he had to offer soon bored her, but it would become a source of inspiration almost two decades later when Steel began to write romance novels. Within a few years, Steel decided—against her husband's wishes—to find a job. In 1968, she was hired as vice president of public relations and new business for Supergirls, a Manhattan public relations and advertising agency. A few years later, the five-woman firm began to falter, and Steel began looking to the future.

A New Career About the time Steel began looking for a new occupation, one of her clients, then the editor of *Ladies' Home Journal*, suggested she try writing. Steel took her up on the idea, isolated herself at her home in San Francisco for several months, and produced her first book, *Going Home*. Published by Dell paperbacks in 1973, the novel had moderate sales.

Around the same time, Steel's marriage broke up. She soon turned to writing in earnest, composing five more novels that were rejected before *Passion's Promise* was published by Dell in 1977. During these years, she also wrote advertising copy as well as poems about love and motherhood that appeared in women's magazines. Some of these poems were included in the later abridged edition of her only volume of poetry, *Love Poems: Danielle Steel* (1981).

After *Passion's Promise*, Dell published three more of Steel's romances: *The Promise* (1978), a novelization of a screenplay by Garry Michael White, *Now and Forever* (1978), which was adapted for a film released in 1983, and *Season of Passion* (1979). Sales of *The Promise*, Steel's first big success, reached two million copies in 1979, and in the same year, she signed a six-figure contract with Dell.

Balancing Work and Family Steel set a grueling pace for herself, composing two to three novels a year, and in the early 1980s, several more best-selling paperbacks appeared. Despite such a full schedule, however, Steel has always tailored her work habits to meet family considerations. In 1981, she married John Traina, a shipping executive who, like herself, had two children. The couple had five children together. To spend time with her family and help protect them from the chaos of fame, Steel shies away from the limelight, refusing to do promotional tours and living a relatively quiet life. She works in concentrated marathon sessions, up to eighteen hours a day, which affords her blocks of time that she can devote to her large family.

Today there are more than 570 million copies of her books in print in forty-seven countries and twenty-eight languages. She has written more than seventy best-selling novels, including twenty-one that have been adapted for television. Since 1989, she has produced a number of books for children, including the "Max and Martha" series and the "Freddie" series. Despite her work ethic and tremendous success, Steel continues to maintain a balance between work and family, dividing her time between San Francisco and Paris, France.

Works in Literary Context

Steel's romances feature both contemporary and historical settings, and their exotic and exciting locales offer readers fast-paced escape from the routine of daily life. They typically focus on a glamorous, well-to-do heroine who proves that women can "have it all"—love, family, and career. However, Steel's characters are beset by obstacles on their road to fulfillment; often they are confronted with the task of rebuilding their life after an emotionally crippling tragedy. Sometimes Steel's heroines have one or more unlucky romances before they find lasting love, but all their relationships with men lead them to increased self-awareness, which, in many cases, helps them to establish successful careers.

Romance Novels The romance novel comes from a tradition of writing that stretches back several centuries. The word 'romance' comes from the Old French words *romaunt* and *roman*, which mean "courtly romance in verse" or "a popular book." Primarily written for entertainment, a romance novel usually includes elements of fantasy, such as exotic locations, wild adventures, attractive characters, and the life of luxury.

Although Steel has written in other genres, such as poetry and children's books, she is primarily known as a romance writer, and the majority of her books follow the general definition of the genre. In a typical Steel novel, the story is dominated by the presence of a single character, usually a rich and glamorous heroine who has everything but still feels unfulfilled. In contrast to some romance novels, however, her protagonists' journeys usually do not end in love; love is rather the path they take to reach a better understanding of themselves. The outcome in most of Steel's stories is the emergence of a more resolute and strengthened being.

Works in Critical Context

While Steel can lay claim to one of the largest readerships in popular fiction, she is anything but a favorite among critics. Even when reviewers acknowledge that Steel is a commercial writer who does not pretend to write serious literature, they seem compelled to point out what they see as major weaknesses in her novels: bad writing, shallow characterization, preposterous plot twists, unconvincing dialogue, and rigid adherence to the "poor little rich girl" formula. Her novels are also faulted as being

---

LITERARY AND HISTORICAL CONTEMPORARIES

Steel's famous contemporaries include:

Martha Stewart (1941–): Through her television program, magazine, and a number of books, Stewart has become famous for her creative cooking and decorating skills, which promote an exceptionally high standard of in-home elegance.

Nora Roberts (1950–): Another highly prolific and successful romance writer, Roberts, writing under her own name and under the pseudonym J.D. Robb, has published over one hundred and forty novels since 1981.

Oprah Winfrey (1954–): World-renowned host of *The Oprah Winfrey Show*, Oprah has been named one of the one hundred most influential people of the twentieth century.

Princess Diana (1961–1997): Born Lady Frances Spencer, Princess Diana (or Princess Di) was perhaps the most beloved royal personage of the twentieth century. Known for her charity work and physical beauty, the princess died in a car accident in 1997 and was mourned throughout the world.

J.K. Rowling (1964–): Famed British author of the *Harry Potter* series for young adults, Rowling is ranked as one of the wealthiest authors of all time.

---

unrealistic because they focus on the lives of the wealthy and privileged.

Critics reserve their harshest comments for Steel's prose style, which is generally considered to be sloppy and careless. A number of critics have expressed amazement that Steel's books do not undergo more extensive editing, and some have appeared to take delight in pointing out her run-on sentences, non sequiturs, and frequent repetition of certain words and phrases. In a review of *Daddy*, for example, Edna Stumpf remarks:

> Ms. Steel plays with the themes of love and work like a child with a Barbie doll. She strips a life down, only to dress it up in billows of her famous free-associative prose, as scattered with commas as a Bob Mackie gown is with bugle beads.

Nevertheless, while some critics might prefer to dismiss Steel without comment, her enormous popularity makes her impossible to ignore. Beginning with her third hardcover, *Crossings* (1982), all of Steel's novels have received coverage in the *New York Times Book Review*. Despite their low appraisals of Steel's talents as a writer, critics concede that her tear-jerking tragedies and happy endings meet some need in her millions of readers, be it a desire for satisfying diversion or for emotional catharsis.

COMMON HUMAN EXPERIENCE

A common theme in Steel's work is finding a balance between career and family. Here are some other famous works that explore similar ideas:

Bridget Jones's Diary (1996), a novel by Helen Fielding. In this bastion of "chick lit"—novels written to appeal to young, unmarried career women—Bridget Jones relates her struggles with men and work in a humorous, yet poignant, tone. The book has sold over two million copies.

White Oleander (1999), a novel by Janet Fitch. This novel tells about the coming of age of Astrid, a girl estranged from her brilliant poet mother, who must find her way in life without the supportive foundation of a loving family.

The Queen (2006), a film directed by Stephen Frears. A candidate for several Academy awards, including Best Picture, this film tells the story of Queen Elizabeth of England, and how focusing on family after Princess Diana's death caused many of her subjects to lose faith in her.

The Women (2008), a film directed by Diane English. In this film starring Meg Ryan, Annette Bening, Eva Mendes, Debra Messing, and Jada Pinkett Smith, the powerful but jaded female protagonists reflect on the choice they feel they must make between having a happy family and pursuing their careers.

Responses to Literature

1. Romance novels are often criticized for being superficial and unrealistic. In what ways can these characteristics provide pleasure to readers? In what ways might they be detrimental to readers? Using your library or the Internet, find a work of literature with a plot or theme similar to one of Steel's novels. Discuss which treatment you feel is more successful and why.

2. Many popular writers are disparaged, or criticized, by literary critics. Why do you think critics respond differently to some works than the general reading public? What kinds of things might a critic be looking for in a work? What might the average reader want from a book instead?

3. Join Oprah's Book Club and read one of the books she recommends. Then use the Internet to connect with other readers and find out what they think about the book. How does your opinion differ from some of theirs? How is it similar?

4. Write a short romance story and share it with your classmates. Discuss what makes a romance interesting or uninteresting to read. What elements do most romance stories seem to have in common?

5. Using your library and the Internet, research the history of romance writing. Write a report on how the genre originated and how it has developed into the modern romance novel.

BIBLIOGRAPHY

Books

Cuddon, J. A., ed. *The Penguin Dictionary of Literary Terms and Literary Theory*. Third Ed. New York: Penguin, 1992.

Bane, Vicki L., and Lorenzo Benet. *The Lives of Danielle Steel*. New York: St. Martin's Press, 1994.

Contemporary Popular Writers. Farmington Hills, Mich.: St. James Press, 1997.

Web sites

"About Danielle." *Danielle Steel: The Official Website*. Accessed November 17, 2008, from http://www.randomhouse.com/features/steel/meet_about.html. Last updated in 2008.

✺ Wallace Stegner

BORN: *1909, Lake Mills, Iowa*

DIED: *1993, Santa Fe, New Mexico*

NATIONALITY: *American*

GENRE: *Fiction, nonfiction*

MAJOR WORKS:
The Big Rock Candy Mountain (1943)
Wilderness Letter (1960)
Angle of Repose (1971)
The Spectator Bird (1976)
Where the Bluebird Sings to the Lemonade Springs, Living and Writing in the West (1992)

Overview

Whether writing about the American West directly in his nonfiction or indirectly in his novels and short stories, Wallace Stegner explored such themes as the effect of the past on the present and the importance of place and history in defining cultural origins. Concerned with questions of personal identity and how one achieves stability amid the impermanence and dislocation of the modern world, Stegner's writing is grounded in a realism that connects readers to the land. An environmentalist whose works were influential in wildlife preservation legislation, Stegner emphatically voiced his belief that the land must be respected if humanity is to have any hope of surviving on it.

Works in Biographical and Historical Context

A Nomadic Childhood Wallace Earle Stegner was born in the rural community of Lake Mills, Iowa, on February 18, 1909. He spent most of his childhood moving from

Wallace Stegner   *Paul Conklin / Pix Inc. / Time Life Pictures / Getty Images*

place to place—Utah, North Dakota, Washington, Montana, Wyoming—while his father searched for the perfect get-rich-quick scheme in areas that had only recently been frontier lands. After living in East End, Saskatchewan, Canada, for six years, Stegner's family moved to Salt Lake City, Utah, a town that provided the twelve-year-old Stegner with the social, cultural, and intellectual stimulus denied him by his father's wanderings. For Stegner, his father became a role model for many characters in his books: characters who relentlessly seek personal gain without any consideration for whom or what they destroy in the process.

A Writer's Education   Stegner attended the University of Utah, where he served as editor and contributor to the university's literary magazine. He was also hired as a freelance writer for the *Salt Lake Telegram*. After graduating with a bachelor's degree in 1930, Stegner accepted a teaching assistantship from the University of Iowa and entered a graduate program in creative writing. Stegner earned a master's degree in 1932, remaining at the university for doctoral work. His mother's death in 1933 after a lengthy struggle with cancer affected him greatly, as she provided her family some sense of cohesion as Stegner's father moved them across prairies and mountains. In the months before she died, she continued to show the strength and determination that Stegner later recalled through many of his female characters, especially in his portrait of Elsa in *The Big Rock Candy Mountain* (1943).

Writing Success   In 1934 Stegner married Mary Stuart Page, a graduate student he had met at the University of Iowa. After earning his doctorate from Iowa in 1935, he began teaching at the University of Utah and publishing short stories in various journals. A book contest sponsored by the publishing house Little, Brown first prompted Stegner to try his hand at writing a novel. His entry, *Remembering Laughter* (1937), won the top prize of $2,500. The book became a literary and financial success and helped gain Stegner a position as an instructor at Harvard University, where he taught composition from 1939 to 1945.

Over the next five years, Stegner published several short novels exploring the relationships between individuals and their communities, as well as a nonfiction account of the Mormon culture. None of his early books achieved the success of his first novel until *The Big Rock Candy Mountain* appeared in 1943. Largely autobiographical, this novel tells the story of a family's travels over the American and Canadian West as the father, obviously based on Stegner's own, endlessly searches for the opportunity that will make him a quick, easy fortune.

Environmentalism   At the end of World War II, Stegner returned to the West and became a professor of English at Stanford University in California. At Stanford, he instituted what would become one of the most prestigious writing programs in the country, serving as its director until 1971 and establishing himself as his generation's most outstanding writing instructor. After publishing the nonfiction work *One Nation* (1945), an award-winning book criticizing the racial and religious lines that were being drawn in the United States at the time, Stegner was convinced by a friend who was an editor at *Harper's* magazine to write an article about the environmental threats to U.S. public lands. The following year, Stegner published a biography of John Wesley Powell, a Colorado River explorer. The book gained the attention of David Brower, who asked Stegner to help write and edit *This Is Dinosaur: Echo Park Country and Its Magic Rivers* (1955) for the Sierra Club. Sent to members of Congress, the book revealed the natural beauty of Dinosaur National Monument between Colorado and Utah and succeeded in thwarting plans to build dams that would have destroyed it.

In 1960 Stegner wrote his famous *Wilderness Letter*, originally delivered as a speech to the University of California's Wildlands Research Center, which was conducting a national wilderness inventory for a presidential commission. Stegner's message became a mission statement hailed by conservationists around the world, and it was used to introduce the bill that established the National Wilderness Preservation System in 1964. Stegner's involvement in environmental causes increased when he served as an assistant to the Secretary of the Interior, Stewart Udall, in 1961. In 1962 Udall appointed Stegner to the National Parks Advisory Board. This was followed by a three-year term on the board of directors of the Sierra Club, an

LITERARY AND HISTORICAL CONTEMPORARIES

Stegner's famous contemporaries include:

A.B. Guthrie (1901–1991): Guthrie was an American novelist and historian who won the 1950 Pulitzer Prize for *The Way West* (1949), a fictional work about a leader of a wagon train heading from Missouri to Oregon.

W.O. Mitchell (1914–1998): Mitchell was a Canadian writer who was often called the Mark Twain of Canada. Mitchell depicts the adventures of boys growing up on the Canadian prairies.

Rachel Carson (1907–1964): Carson was an American biologist and nature writer whose book *Silent Spring* (1962), a warning about the ecological effects of pesticides such as DDT, is a founding text of the modern environmental movement.

John Wayne (1907–1979): Wayne was a film actor and icon of American Westerns and war movies. Wayne was also known for his conservative political views.

Ansel Adams (1902–1984): Adams was an environmentalist and world-famous photographer. He is best known for his black-and-white photographs of the American West.

Richard Nixon (1913–1994): Nixon was president of the United States from 1969 to 1974. Nixon is recognized as one of the country's most environmentally conscious presidents in history.

organization Stegner profoundly affected during his forty-year association with its causes. The environmental movement gained momentum a few years later, with the creation of the Environmental Protection Agency in 1969 and the passage of the Clean Air Act the following year. Stegner became one of the movement's leading literary figures.

Always a Writer   Despite great efforts in the conservation movement, Stegner considered himself first and foremost a writer. In 1972 he won the Pulitzer Prize for his novel *Angle of Repose*, a work that tells the story of a retired history professor in California who is editing the papers of his grandmother, a writer and illustrator of the nineteenth century. This blending of past and present is vital to Stegner's major works and was apparent again in *The Spectator Bird* (1976), which won the 1977 National Book Award for Fiction. Stegner continued to write both fiction and nonfiction until his death on April 13, 1993, from injuries received in a car accident in Santa Fe, New Mexico.

Works in Literary Context

Stegner's childhood experiences traveling around the West and the respect he developed for the wilderness while living in Saskatchewan had an immense influence on his literary involvement in environmental and social issues. However, he was more than a writer and an environmentalist; he was perhaps the most highly regarded writing instructor of his time. In addition to owning his body of work, Stegner's legacy is remembered in the works of other writers whom he instructed at Stanford, a list that includes Larry McMurtry, Ken Kesey, Wendell Berry, Ernest Gaines, and Robert Hass.

Setting   The settings of Stegner's works are of utmost importance, for they illustrate the connections between people and the land. In *Second Growth* (1947), for instance, Stegner's descriptive talent delivers the beauty of the New England countryside with the same precision and realistic detail seen in his Western settings. In doing so, Stegner develops a sharp contrast between the wildness of the natural environment and the social restrictions found in New England village life, as the young people in Stegner's town find little room for cultural or spiritual growth independent of their natural surroundings. In "Goin' to Town" (1940), one of the many stories acknowledging one's relation to the earth as a healthy antidote to the daily disorder that separates people from place, Stegner frames the story's increasingly chaotic set of events between a boy's peaceful connections to the earth. The boy starts the morning by tracking across the damp ground of his yard, noticing how smoothly his foot fits into the earth. After a tumultuous chain of events throughout the day, the boy finds his morning footprint and realigns his foot within its outline, and Stegner leaves him intimately bound to the earth.

In delivering a solid experience of place, Stegner portrays the earth as a force to be respected and admired. The conception of nature as a central force is especially apparent in Stegner's later fiction, which reflects the same environmental concerns addressed in his nonfiction. Although *A Shooting Star* (1961) focuses on the relationship between a mother and daughter as they confront their personal weaknesses, what offers the mother the most hope is her growing awareness of the environmental necessity to preserve and protect land from commercial exploitation. In many ways, she fictionally argues the case Stegner was making more overtly through his nonfiction publications. More complex than *A Shooting Star* is Stegner's *Wolf Willow: A History, a Story, and a Memory of the Last Plains Frontier* (1962), a work that integrates both real and fictionalized personal recollections with geographical and historical facts to reconstruct the Saskatchewan region Stegner knew as a boy. Most importantly, the work makes a case for knowing as well as preserving the environment.

Works in Critical Context

"Stegner is a regional writer in the richest sense of that word," maintains reviewer James D. Houston, "one who manages to dig through the surface and plumb a region's deepest implications, tapping into profound matters of how a place or a piece of territory can shape life, character, actions, dreams." While many would agree with critic

Daniel King who says that Stegner is "the greatest writer of the West," others assert that he is much more than that. Indeed, Richard H. Simpson (quoted on the Web site bookrags.com) contends that Stegner's "main region is the human spirit" and that each one of Stegner's novels "explores a question central in Stegner's life and in American culture: How does one achieve a sense of identity, permanence, and civilization—a sense of home—in a place where rootlessness and discontinuity dominate?" Stegner scholars Merrill and Lorene Lewis agree: "The central theme of all his work is the quest for identity, personal and regional, artistic and cultural."

The Big Rock Candy Mountain With the publication of *The Big Rock Candy Mountain* in 1942, Stegner achieved his first popular and critical success and established himself on the literary scene. More fully developed than its predecessors, the novel chronicles the lives of a family that continuously travels across the American and Canadian West as the father, convinced he will find a place where opportunity awaits him, seeks to make his fortune. According to Merrill and Lorene Lewis, *The Big Rock Candy Mountain* is "more than the dream of ... Success. It is the 'dream of taking from life exactly what you wanted,' and the quest for the Promised Land."

Overall, *The Big Rock Candy Mountain* was a critical and popular success. Reviewer Orville Prescott concludes that the novel "is a sound, solid, intelligent, interesting novel, a good story and an excellent interpretation of an important phase of American life," while Robert Canzoneri deems *The Big Rock Candy Mountain* "a once-in-a-lifetime book." Critics have particularly praised Stegner's handling of character. Reviewer Milton Rugoff, for example, observes that through the character of Bo Mason, "Wallace Stegner conveys to us a vividness and a fullness hardly less than that with which we know our own fathers."

Responses to Literature

1. Stegner's novels are known for the strength of their settings. Select one of his novels. What role does the land have in that work? Would you consider the land to be a character in the novel? Can you describe it in human terms?

2. Research Frederick Jackson Turner and his writings about the importance of the frontier in American life and culture. What evidence of Turner's ideas can you find in Stegner's works?

3. To many, Stegner is a hero to the wilderness movement in America, yet he is not a household name. Why do you think this is so? What has overshadowed or downplayed his importance to the movement?

4. What separates Stegner's fiction from most Western fiction, which romanticizes heroes, villains, and the West? Can his novels be called "Westerns"? Discuss Stegner's role in the literary tradition of American realism.

COMMON HUMAN EXPERIENCE

Regionalism is a term applied to literature that emphasizes a specific geographical setting, focusing on the history, habits, speech, and beliefs of that area. Although readers recognize the universal themes of such works as *Wolf Willow*—the search for one's identity, for instance—Stegner is most often described as a regional writer. Listed below are works by other authors considered examples of regionalism:

Peace Like a River (2002), a novel by Leif Enger. This story, set in the Minnesota countryside and North Dakota Badlands during the early 1960s, relates an asthmatic boy's search for his brother, an escaped convict.

Housekeeping (1980), a novel by Marilynne Robinson. Set in a remote town in Idaho, this work tells the story of two girls who are brought up by a succession of relatives.

Desert Solitaire (1968), nonfiction by Edward Abbey. Based on Abbey's experiences as a park ranger in Arches National Park near Moab, Utah, this book is often compared to Henry David Thoreau's *Walden* (1854). Abbey was a former student of Stegner's at Stanford.

Man with a Bull-Tongue Plow (1943), a book of poems by Jesse Stuart. This collection of more than 700 sonnets creates a mythic portrait of the Appalachian Mountain region.

BIBLIOGRAPHY

Books

Arthur, Anthony, ed. *Critical Essays on Wallace Stegner*. Boston: G. K. Hall, 1982.

Lewis, Merrill, and Lorene Lewis. *Wallace Stegner*. Boise, Idaho: Boise State College, 1972.

Robinson, Forrest G., and Margaret G. Robinson. *Wallace Stegner*. New York: Twayne, 1977.

Periodicals

Canzoneri, Robert. "Wallace Stegner: Trial by Existence." *Southern Review* 9 (October 1973): 796–827.

Eisinger, Chester E. "Twenty Years of Wallace Stegner." *College English* 20 (December 1958): 110–116.

Houston, James D. "Wallace Stegner." *Los Angeles Times Book Review* (March 7, 1993): 12.

King, Daniel. "Wallace Stegner: His Life and Work." *World Literature Today* (Winter 1998): 22–23.

Peterson, Audrey C. "Narrative Voice in Stegner's *Angle of Repose*." *Western American Literature* 10 (Summer 1975): 125–133.

Prescott, Orville. "Review of *The Big Rock Candy Mountain*." *Yale Review* (Winter 1944): 189.

Web sites

Bookrags Staff. *Wallace (Earle) Stegner*. Retrieved December 3, 2008, from http://www.book rags.com/biography/wallace-earle-stegner-dlb/. Last updated in 2005.

John Steinbeck

BORN: *1902, Salinas, California*

DIED: *1968, New York City*

NATIONALITY: *American*

GENRE: *Fiction*

MAJOR WORKS:
Of Mice and Men (1937)
The Grapes of Wrath (1939)
East of Eden (1952)

Overview

One of America's most treasured novelists, John Steinbeck confused many critics during his lifetime by the broad variation of topics, themes and styles in his writing. His widely acknowledged masterpiece, *The Grapes of Wrath* (1939), appeared early in his career, and many critics believe he never repeated the success. Through his active role in politics and his efforts in fiction, essay, and screen-writing, however, Steinbeck continued to have an impact on readers until his death in 1968. Today, he is considered one of the foremost American novelists of all time.

John Steinbeck   *Steinbeck, John, photograph. The Library of Congress.*

Works in Biographical and Historical Context

A California Native   John Ernst Steinbeck was born in Salinas, California, on February 27, 1902. He was the third child born to John Ernst Steinbeck and Olive Hamilton Steinbeck. Olive had been a schoolteacher, and John Ernst senior, after weathering a period of economic reversals beginning in 1910, served as Treasurer of Monterey County until 1935. After a bookish, but rambunctious, childhood as the only brother of three sisters, Steinbeck entered Stanford University in 1919. His older sisters Beth and Esther had graduated from Mills College, but Mary, three years younger than he, followed him to Stanford a few years later. A serious student of writing, literature, and marine biology, Steinbeck attended Stanford sporadically, regularly taking time off to earn money as a laborer. He left the university for good in 1925, never having made any attempt to fashion a program that would lead to a degree.

While working at a fish hatchery in the summer of 1928, Steinbeck met Carol Henning (later, Brown) who would be his first wife, in-house editor, intellectual sounding board, typist, and greatest early supporter. They were married on January 14, 1930. Later that year, Steinbeck first met Edward "Doc" Ricketts, a marine biologist with whom he formed what was to become the closest, and the most intellectually vital friendship of his life. During the first years of the Steinbecks' marriage, they lived primarily in his parents' summer cottage in Pacific Grove and subsisted on Carol's paychecks from a variety of jobs, a twenty-five-dollar-a-month allowance from Steinbeck's father, and the harvest from their garden and the nearby Monterey Bay.

It is still a matter of debate among critics as to how much of Steinbeck's philosophy can be directly attributed to Ricketts's influence. Ricketts was a brilliant marine biologist of wide-ranging interests whose *Between Pacific Tides* (1938) would prove instrumental in shifting the focus of marine biology from taxonomy to ecology, but Steinbeck's study of marine biology and his interest in animals—including people—in their environments predated his acquaintance with Ricketts. What is clear is that the friends shared a number of concerns and interests that helped to shape Steinbeck's writing in significant ways. Steinbeck brought the eye of a modern ecological biologist to the study of people. His characters have instinctual needs, and they exist and compete and sometimes cooperate with each other in specific—primarily Californian—environments.

Tough Times and Eventual Success   Steinbeck published his first novel, *Cup of Gold*, in 1929. It was dismissed by critics; even Steinbeck himself concluded that the novel was "on the whole, utterly worthless." Making a living as a writer proved difficult, especially with the onset of the Great Depression, a worldwide economic slowdown that began with substantial losses in the American stock market at the end of 1929. Businesses failed, families were forced from their homes, and the added burden of poor agricultural production during the Dust Bowl—a series of dust storms during the 1930s exacerbated by drought and overfarming—left millions of Americans without a means of support. At the height of the Depression, one in four able-bodied workers could not find a job.

Steinbeck continued writing, though his following two novels sold poorly. Yet, he had a few fans. One day in 1934, as Steinbeck was actively looking for a new publisher, Pat Covici of the publishing firm Covici-Friede, overheard a Chicago bookseller berating a customer because he had not heard of John Steinbeck. Covici had never heard of him either, and Abramson pressed on him copies of Steinbeck's first two books. Covici was impressed enough to sign Steinbeck to the first of what was to be a series of contracts over the remaining thirty-four years of Steinbeck's life.

Fortunately for both men, the first book Steinbeck wrote for Covici-Friede, *Tortilla Flat* (1935), also turned out to be his first success. The novel—a darkly mock-Arthurian and often comic tale of *paisanos* struggling for food, wine, women, and community—became a best-seller, and won a gold medal award for fiction from the Commonwealth Club of California.

Creating a Classic Steinbeck's appreciation of his new-found success was limited. He had always been wary of what fame did to writers, and his natural shyness only made the experience that much more uncomfortable when fame first descended upon him. Also, the two years before the book's publication had been personally painful. Steinbeck's mother had died in February 1934, after a long illness during which both Steinbeck and his wife had, for pro-longed periods, helped care for her. Steinbeck's father never recovered from the loss, and he died a year later.

Personal tragedy, however, did not diminish Stein-beck's dedication to his craft. In 1936 he published *In Dubious Battle*, a brutal strike novel and a far cry from the comic *Tortilla Flat*. *In Dubious Battle* was the first book in a trilogy of migrant farmworker novels Steinbeck produced in the 1930s. The second, *Of Mice and Men*, appeared in 1937. The story of two hoboes who travel together and dream of owning a farm, *Of Mice and Men* took the themes Steinbeck had worked out on a societal level in his previous novel and brought them down to the personal level with his protagonists Lenny and George. He wrote it both in nov-ella and in play form in order to reach the widest audience possible, and both versions were successful.

Steinbeck's success with these novels led to his being increasingly identified with the cause of migrant workers and, in turn, to his greater involvement with that cause. In the summer of 1936, *The San Francisco News* commis-sioned Steinbeck to do investigative reporting on the living conditions of the recently arrived refugees from the Dust Bowl. With that seven-part series—titled, "The Harvest Gypsies," in the *News* and later collected as *Their Blood Is Strong* (1938)—Steinbeck began his research for what would become *The Grapes of Wrath*.

Steinbeck became a national figure in 1939 with the publication of *The Grapes of Wrath*. This final novel in his migrant-worker trilogy, and the top-selling book of the year, won Steinbeck the Pulitzer Prize—the highest national award in the United States for writers. It tells the story of migrant workers during the Dust Bowl. Unable to eke a living out of their own land, many Americans were forced to sell their farms and move to California in hopes of earning a living as migrant farmers.

The publication of *Grapes of Wrath* changed both Steinbeck's writing career and his personal life forever. He thought he had taken the novel as far as it could go and began working in other genres. His increasing fame put further strain on his already tumultuous marriage. Around 1940, he began having an affair with the young Gwendolyn "Gwyn" Conger, whom he married almost immediately after Carol sued him for divorce in 1942. Despite their mutual attraction, Steinbeck and Conger's marriage was never a happy one.

The War and After The years of World War II—a global conflict that had begun in 1939, but which the United States entered at the end of 1941 after the Japanese attack on Pearl Harbor—were hectic for Steinbeck, who had taken advantage of his growing fame to become some-thing of a moral and political counselor for many govern-ment officials, including President Franklin Roosevelt. Gwyn wanted a settled life; but, they moved from home to home and were constantly apart while Steinbeck was doing a variety of jobs for various branches of the govern-ment. Despite his new marriage and occupations, however, he continued to write, producing the nonfiction work *Bombs Away: The Story of a Bomber Team* (1942) and the novel *The Moon Is Down* (1942), which tells the story of the conquest and occupation of a Scandinavian town by a brutal enemy. He also produced numerous newspaper articles, which were published as a collection entitled *Once There Was a War* in 1958.

In response to soldiers telling him they wanted to read something funny that didn't remind them of the war, Steinbeck wrote *Cannery Row*, his first work that could be called fully postmodern. It is a comic work, full of rowdy fun and goodwill. Nevertheless, Cannery Row is a profoundly lonely place in which relations between men and women tend to be short-lived, based on money and biology, or bitter failures. Its protagonist, Doc, considered to be Steinbeck's best drawn character, was inspired by his friend Ricketts.

After the war, Steinbeck and his wife moved to New York, where he continued to write and to be involved in political activities. He wrote *A Russian Journal* (1948) after a trip to the Soviet Union in 1947 during which he gained access to certain parts of the country that were

LITERARY AND HISTORICAL CONTEMPORARIES

Steinbeck's famous contemporaries include:

Franklin Delano Roosevelt (1882–1945): The thirty-second president of the United States, Roosevelt led the nation through the Great Depression of the early 1930s until nearly the end of the second World War. After his death, Congress moved to limit presidential reelection to a single four-year term.

F. Scott Fitzgerald (1896–1940): Fitzgerald was an American novelist and short story writer best known for his novel*The Great Gatsby* (1925), which has been considered by some the "perfect" American novel.

Edward Ricketts (1897–1948): Steinbeck's best friend and closest intellectual companion, Ricketts was also a well-known marine biologist and the co-author of an important book of marine biology entitled *Between Pacific Tides* (1939).

William Faulkner (1897–1962): One of the most important American modernists, Faulkner was a novelist and screenwriter whose portrayals of the post–Civil War South are considered among the best ever written.

Ernest Hemingway (1899–1961): Hemingway was one of the most widely acclaimed American novelists and a member of the "Lost Generation," a group of expatriate writers and artists who gathered in Paris, France after the first World War. Hemingway is famous for his spare style and his depictions of men in battle.

John F. Kennedy (1917–1963): The thirty-fifth president of the United States, Kennedy, also referred to as JFK, represented new hope to Americans tired of political corruption. However, he, too, fell into scandal with the Cuban Missile Crisis of 1962 and was assassinated on November 22, 1963.

typically closed to visitors from the West. Soviet authorities, however, kept Steinbeck constantly moving and plied with vodka, and the result was a fairly superficial account of life in the country that would soon become America's most frustratingly unknown foe.

Steinbeck's homecoming was not a happy one. On May 7, 1948, Steinbeck's friend, Ricketts, drove his car around a blind turn and into the path of an oncoming train. On Steinbeck's return to New York, Gwyn, who had grown increasingly irritated that she was raising their two children while her husband traveled around the world, demanded a divorce. Steinbeck moved back to California that September, and in December he was elected to the American Academy of Arts and Letters.

A Culmination of All His Work   In late May 1949, Steinbeck met Elaine Anderson Scott, a former Broadway stage manager and native Texan. They married on December 28, 1950, in a union that would last for the rest of Steinbeck's life. Elaine became his traveling partner and confidante, and the two of them traveled extensively around the world, often on political errands. Meanwhile Steinbeck continued to work. In 1948 he had begun research in the morgue of the *Salinas-Californian* newspaper for his next book, which was to be the culmination of everything he had ever done. *East of Eden* (1952), a narrative consisting of two interwoven stories: the story of the fictional Trask family and the history in the Salinas Valley of Steinbeck's mother's family, the Hamiltons. The book was dedicated to Pat Covici with the statement: "[H]ere's your box. Nearly everything I have is in it."

Despite what was perhaps his intention to give up writing fiction, Steinbeck continued to write long after *East of Eden* was published. *Sweet Thursday*, the sequel to *Cannery Row*, appeared in 1954; the satirical *The Short Reign of Pippin IV*, based on his experiences in Paris, in 1957; and his last novel, *The Winter of Our Discontent*, in 1961.

In 1960, despite his increasingly poor health, Steinbeck took a journey across America and back with his poodle, Charley. His goal was to escape his own fame and to reacquaint himself with his country and the people, so he tried to avoid the interstate highways. The trip did not go well. California depressed him, because he no longer belonged there. The cheerleaders who led crowds in taunting young African American students at a newly desegregated school in New Orleans sickened him. One white hitchhiker's belligerent racism caused Steinbeck to toss him out of the truck. Nevertheless, the book that came from the trip was a success: *Travels with Charley* (1962) includes sections of vintage Steinbeck reportage, and sales began at a better rate than for any of his previous works.

Taking the Prize   One morning in 1962, Steinbeck turned on the television expecting to see some news about the Cuban Missile Crisis and instead saw a report that he himself had just won the Nobel Prize in Literature. Steinbeck was stunned. His great pride in being chosen for the award was nearly overcome by worries that he might not be able to continue as a working writer, due to official responsibilities and the complacency of fame. His declining health and increasing public persona were more powerful than his determination to beat what he thought of as the Nobel's curse. After two more mildly successful publications, Steinbeck died of emphysema and blockages of the coronary arteries on December 20, 1968.

Works in Literary Context

Steinbeck often puzzled critics during his lifetime because early in his career his style and subject matter seemed to change with each new story, and after World War II, there was a generally acknowledged, but inexplicable decline, in his artistic powers. Now, however, Steinbeck's work can be seen as a consistently developing vision of man's relation to his environment. His work forms a bridge between the social realism popular in American writing during the early 1900s, and postmodernism, with environmental themes apparent throughout.

This consistent interest in the environment also helps explain why Steinbeck has been considered a regional writer, or a writer whose works tend to relate only to a particular region. Sometimes used pejoratively, the term does not adequately describe the scope of Steinbeck's writings, which ranged in setting from the American Midwest to the West to marine environments and even foreign countries.

Social Realism   Popular in the United States during the early half of the twentieth century, social realism focused on ordinary people, rather than on aristocrats or heroes, and their relations with society through their daily existence. It brought attention to widespread social issues such as segregation and poverty, and illuminated the day-to-day life of average Americans. Steinbeck's Pulitzer Prize–winning *The Grapes of Wrath* is often considered to be social realism, since the novel focuses on a lower-middle-class family as it struggles with poverty, the journey west, and the almost insurmountable difficulties of starting a new life. However, *The Grapes of Wrath* also contains elements of mysticism, the idea that humankind's connection to the land is not only pragmatic but spiritual, in addition to the highly modernist characteristic of irony.

Postmodernism   Postmodernism has been defined by Terry Eagleton as "a style of thought which is suspicious of classical notions of truth, reason, identity, and objectivity." Essentially, postmodernists believe that nothing can be known absolutely; their art, therefore, often incorporates a variety of techniques to view its subjects from numerous perspectives. *Cannery Row* is considered the first of Steinbeck's novels that can be placed decisively in the postmodernist era. An extended play on the ways in which language and narrative shape experience, it is both a collection of episodes and a coherent novel. Postmodernist works like this novel can often be compared to a collage, in which many pictures or pieces of pictures are glued together to create a larger effect.

Works in Critical Context

Throughout most of his career, Steinbeck's work was problematic to critics who could not keep up with his frequent changes in subject matter and tone, and therefore, could not classify his work as belonging to a particular movement or group. Because many of his works were political, their reception often hinged on whether critics agreed with him politically. Even after being awarded the Nobel Prize in 1962, Steinbeck was criticized by many who thought he did not deserve the prize—particularly since his best work had been written more than twenty years before. The *New York Times* editorial headline read, "Does a Moral Vision of the Thirties Deserve the Nobel Prize?" and Steinbeck him-

---

COMMON HUMAN EXPERIENCE

A common theme in Steinbeck's work is the connection of people to the land. Here are some other famous works with similar themes:

> *O Pioneers!* (1913), a novel by Willa Cather. This novel tells the story of Swedish immigrants in Nebraska, whose lives are shaped by their struggle to tame the land.
> *As I Lay Dying* (1930), a novel by William Faulkner. One of this Nobel laureate's best-known novels, this book tells the story of the Bundren family as they take the body of Addie, the matriarch, across the state to be buried in the land where she was born.
> *The Field* (1990), a film directed by Jim Sheridan. Based on the famous Irish play by John B. Keane, this film tells the story of Bull McCabe, a poor farmer who works in a rented field and, because the field has been watered with his blood and sweat, feels that it should belong to him.

---

self fueled criticism by admitting in a press conference that he felt he did not.

The Grapes of Wrath   Despite mixed reactions to his work during his lifetime, *The Grapes of Wrath* has been almost universally acclaimed as a masterful work. In a review for *New Republic*, Malcolm Cowley writes that the book "has the force of the headlong anger that drives ahead from the first chapter to the last, as if the whole six hundred pages were written without stopping." Cowley places the book "very high in the category of the great angry books like *Uncle Tom's Cabin* that have roused a people to fight against intolerable wrongs." In a contemporary review of the novel, critic and novelist Christopher Isherwood calls Steinbeck "a master of realistic writing" and states, "a writer of Mr. Steinbeck's caliber can only be insulted by mere praise; for his defects are as interesting as his merits." Isherwood's statements suggest that by this time Steinbeck's reputation as a great writer could be taken for granted, as indeed it was at certain times during his career and has certainly become today.

Responses to Literature

1. The public's reaction to John Steinbeck's work often depended on whether people agreed with the political opinions portrayed in it. Do you think it is sensible to judge a work based on whether or not you agree with the author? Why or why not? Cite some examples of works you have either liked or disliked because you disagreed with the author.

2. The connection between people and the land has been a frequent theme in literature for thousands of

---

years. Using your library and the Internet, find three examples of current films or books that use the theme. Is the theme addressed differently today than it was in Steinbeck's time?

3. Read a few pages of Faulkner's *Absalom, Absalom!* (1936) and compare the style to that of Steinbeck's *The Grapes of Wrath*. Which is easier to read? What might it mean that two such different books, both considered great literary works, were composed at about the same time?

BIBLIOGRAPHY

Books

Astro, Richard. "John Steinbeck: A Biographical Portrait." *John Steinbeck: A Dictionary of His Fictional Characters*, edited by Tetsumaro Hayashi. Metuchen, N.J.: Scarecrow Press, 1973, pp. 1–24.

Benson, Jackson L. *The True Adventures of John Steinbeck, Writer: A Biography*. New York: Viking, 1984.

Eagleton, Terry. *The Illusions of Postmodernism*. Malden, Mass.: Blackwell, 1996.

Fensch, Thomas. *Steinbeck and Covici: The Story of Friendship*. Middlebury, Vt.: Erikson, 1979.

Farrell, Keith. *John Steinbeck, the Voice of the Land*. New York: M. Evans, 1986.

Hughes, R. S. *John Steinbeck: A Study of the Short Fiction*. Boston: Twayne, 1989.

Kiernan, Thomas. *The Intricate Music: A Biography of John Steinbeck*. Boston: Atlantic/Little, Brown, 1979.

O'Connor, Richard. *John Steinbeck*. New York: McGraw-Hill, 1970.

Parini, Jay. *John Steinbeck: A Biography*. New York: Holt, 1995.

Simmonds, Roy S. *John Steinbeck: The War Years, 1939–1945*. Lewisburg, Penn.: Bucknell University Press, 1996.

Valjean, Nelson. *John Steinbeck: The Errant Knight*. San Francisco: Chronicle Books, 1975.

Periodicals

Isherwood, Christopher. "The Tragedy of Eldorado." *Kenyon Review* 1, no.4 (Autumn 1939): 450–453.

✸ Wallace Stevens

BORN: *1879, Reading, Pennsylvania*

DIED: *1955, Hartford, Connecticut*

NATIONALITY: *American*

GENRE: *Poetry*

MAJOR WORKS:
Harmonium (1923)
Ideas of Order (1935)
Parts of a World (1942)
Collected Poems (1954)

Wallace Stevens   *Stevens, Wallace, photograph. The Library of Congress.*

Overview

Wallace Stevens is one of the main pillars in twentieth-century American poetry, notable for his meditative poems that engage with the natural world in order to explore and express personal meaning. Stevens balanced his writing life with a successful career in law and business, earning widespread literary recognition late in life.

Works in Biographical and Historical Context

Early Aspiration and Inspiration Wallace Stevens was born in Reading, Pennsylvania, on October 2, 1879. He was close to his mother, a former schoolteacher, but his father, a prominent attorney in Reading, was a dominant force in the shaping of his personality and career. Stevens was deeply private, yet driven to succeed.

Stevens was a reporter for the student newspaper of his high school, and his interest in journalism led him to enroll at Harvard University in 1897. At Harvard, Stevens began keeping a journal full of lush descriptions of the natural world. He also began to write poetry seriously, publishing numerous poems in the *Harvard Advocate* and the *Harvard Monthly*. He joined the staff of the *Harvard Advocate* in the spring of 1899, and soon thereafter he was named as a member of the editorial board.

Stevens left Harvard in June 1900 without earning a degree to pursue a career in journalism. He moved to New York City, which was quickly becoming the most important commercial hub of the United States after it consolidated its five boroughs in 1898. Stevens landed a position at the *New York Tribune*. During his time as a reporter, he kept a journal to catalogue his explorations of New York, and many of his entries reflect a tension between the natural world and the urban landscape of New York, which was full of industry and teeming with new immigrants. Despite his interest in writing, Stevens soon began to grow dissatisfied with journalism. During a visit home in 1901, his father urged him to start a career in law.

A Career in Law and Business, a Passion for Poetry
Although he had always had a longing for a literary career, Stevens was drawn to the stability of law. He took his father's advice and enrolled at the New York Law School. He graduated in 1903, and began practicing in New York after he was admitted to the New York State bar in 1904. In 1904, he also met his future wife, Elsie Viola Kachel. They were married on September 21, 1909, in Reading. Stevens diligently pursued his legal career and was soon offered a prestigious position with the Hartford Accident and Indemnity Company. He moved to Hartford, Connecticut, in 1916. His new position required a great deal of travel, including many trips to Florida, which became a central landscape for many of his most brilliant poetic works. Stevens's professional success was sullied only by the death of his father on July 14, 1911.

Despite his flourishing professional career, Stevens still devoted time to his writing and poetry. He found time to compose and publish "Cannet de Voyage," a set of eight poems, in *The Trend* in 1914. These were the first poems Stevens had published since his days at Harvard. The same year as his appointment to Hartford Accident and Indemnity Company, Stevens's play "Three Travelers Watch a Sunrise" won a prize offered by the Players' Producing Company of Chicago. One of the judges was Harriet Monroe, the longtime editor of *Poetry* magazine. Stevens began a long-standing and beneficial association with Monroe, and *Poetry* became a regular publisher of Stevens's poems throughout his life. From 1915 onward, Stevens gained substantial momentum as a writer, even as his career as a lawyer and businessman was also gaining substantial speed.

In 1915, Stevens published two significant early poems, "Peter Quince at the Clavier" and "Sunday Morning." During the period from 1913 to 1920, Stevens was loosely associated with a group of poets named "Imagists" after poet Ezra Pound's 1913 anthology *Des Imagistes*. Imagism was a movement that focused on clear expression through the use of the most precise images and language. Imagist poets included Ezra Pound, William Carlos Williams, Amy Lowell, and H.D. The impact of imagism is evident in many of Stevens's early poems, including "Thirteen Ways of Looking at a Blackbird."

LITERARY AND HISTORICAL CONTEMPORARIES

Stevens's famous contemporaries include:

William Carlos Williams (1893–1963): American poet, novelist, playwright, essayist, and medical doctor. His work, in all genres, is characterized by a direct treatment of reality, creating an artistry of immediacy and freshness.

T.S. Eliot (1888–1965): The winner of the 1948 Nobel Prize in Literature, Eliot wrote one of the most famous and influential poems of the twentieth century, *The Waste Land* (1922).

James Joyce (1882–1941): Irish novelist and fiction writer. The author of *A Portrait of the Artist as a Young Man* (1916) and *Ulysses* (1922), Joyce is widely recognized for creating new literary forms and using stream of consciousness techniques to depict human nature.

Pablo Picasso (1881–1973): Spanish artist. A pivotal painter, sculptor, and artist, Picasso is best known as the founder of the Cubist movement, although he was influential in nearly every art movement of the twentieth century.

Franklin D. Roosevelt (1882–1945): President of the United States during the Great Depression and World War II, 1933–1945.

Although Imagism was an influence on his work, Stevens recognized the poetic limitations of imagism and soon parted ways with this group of modernist poets. From 1916 to 1917, Stevens published nearly a poem a month in various literary magazines, and by 1923 he had gained enough momentum to publish his first collection, *Harmonium* (1923). Unfortunately, Stevens's literary experimentation and abstract approach in *Harmonium* was greeted with less than wild enthusiasm from critics. Discouraged by this lukewarm reception, Stevens shifted focus to his new daughter and his business career from 1924 until 1930.

Literary Success Late in Life
In 1931 *Harmonium* was republished with the addition of fourteen new poems. In 1935, Stevens published *Ideas of Order*, a collection that includes "The Idea of Order at Key West," a poem that focuses on the question of representation and the relationship of art and the world. The poem is a milestone in Stevens's career and a strong articulation about poetry and philosophy that is central to most of his writing from 1935 until his death. Stevens's critical reception also increased after the release of *Ideas of Order*. In 1936, his poem "The Men That Are Falling" was awarded the poetry prize from *The Nation*. The 1940s were an even more prolific period for Stevens, beginning with the publication

COMMON HUMAN EXPERIENCE

In Stevens's poetry, nature is the central site for exploring the relationship between human life and the world. Here are some other works that focus on the interrelation of nature and the imagination:

"Lines Composed a Few Miles above Tintern Abbey on Revisiting the Banks of the Wye during a Tour, July 13, 1798" (commonly titled "Tintern Abbey") (1798), William Wordswith. This romantic poem explores the idea of memory and imagination with the relationship between nature and humanity.

Walden (1854), Henry David Thoreau. In his famous essay, Thoreau relates his attempt to achieve transcendence through his experiences with nature.

"The Map" (1955), Elizabeth Bishop. In this poem, Bishop considers the difference between reality and the imagination of reality through the exploration of a land map.

"Mind" (1980), Jorie Graham. In this poem, Graham compares natural processes to the ways that the human mind creates meaning.

of the collection *Parts of a World* (1942), which includes his classic "Of Modern Poetry." His readership continued to grow as well, and he garnered numerous accolades, including induction into the National Institute of Arts and Letters in 1946 and the Bollinger Prize in poetry in 1949. In 1951, he was awarded the Gold Medal of the Poetry Society of America, and the National Book Award for Poetry. In 1954, in honor of his seventy-fifth birthday, Alfred A. Knopf published *The Collected Poems of Wallace Stevens*, which included his final twenty-five poems. In 1955, his collected poems received the National Book Award, and he was awarded the Pulitzer Prize in poetry. Stevens died later that year of stomach cancer. Many of his last poems are retrospective and affirm the importance of poetry and the power of the imagination.

Works in Literary Context

Modernism Modernism was a cultural movement that emerged at the beginning of the twentieth century in Europe and America, and included art, architecture, philosophy, and literature. Modernist writers are chiefly distinguished by their desire to break from the past and experiment with literary forms and styles. Modernist poetry was often characterized by discarding traditional meter and rhyme for free verse. In addition to Stevens, poets who are commonly recognized as modernist include Ezra Pound, William Carlos Williams, Amy Lowell, H.D., and Marianne Moore.

The Power of the Poetic Imagination At the heart of Stevens's poetry is a bold assertion about the power of the imagination and how it can help people to live and to experience a sense of fullness. Stevens's poems are characterized by wordplay, rich imagery, and thoughtful meditation. One of his greatest contributions to poetry is his reinforcement of its importance. To Stevens, poetry infused life with meaning by maintaining the balance of the real and the imaginative, as well as the harmony between the individual and the natural world.

Works in Critical Context

Now revered as a master of poetic language, as well as a profound philosophical thinker, Stevens did not achieve widespread critical recognition until shortly before his death. Many critics of his early works felt that his abstract language and approach to poetry was impersonal and obscure. By the latter half of the twentieth century, critics began to applaud both his form and themes, widely agreeing with the literary critic Harold Bloom, who hails Stevens as "the best and most representative American poet of our time."

"Sunday Morning" An early work, "Sunday Morning" has been singled out by critics because of its eloquent, bold assertion that poetry should be regarded as the supreme religion in the twentieth century. The poem focuses on a woman's contemplation of Christianity and spirituality, and concludes with a celebration of poetry as engaging and interrogating the individual place in the world. Critical appraisal has centered on Stevens's articulation of the relationship between poetry and the natural world. Critic J. Hillis Miller concludes:

> "Sunday Morning" is Stevens' most eloquent description of the moment when the gods dissolve. Bereft of the supernatural, man does not lie down paralyzed in despair. He sings the creative hymns of a new culture.

"The Idea of Order at Key West" "The Idea of Order at Key West" is one of Stevens's most complex, challenging, and popular works. Early critics tended to view the poem as a discourse on just the creative process, but today's critics regard it as a demonstration of the vitality of poetry and power of the poetic imagination. Richard Gray discusses the power of the poem by emphasizing "the poet as maker, inventing a world rather than simply reporting one," noting that in doing so, Steven is "uncovering a possibility available to everyone." The essence of "The Idea of Order at Key West" examines the issue of human and natural order, as well as the vitality of the creative process and artistic representation.

Responses to Literature

1. "Thirteen Ways of Looking at a Blackbird" is composed of thirteen short poems about blackbirds. What does the poem imply about perception? How does your perception or viewpoint change as you read it?

2. In "Sunday Morning" Stevens writes, "Death is the mother of beauty." What do you think this means? How is it related to the concepts of imagination and the natural world?

3. "The Idea of Order at Key West" features two poetic voices: the female singer and the poem's speaker. Compare these two voices and their relationship to the imagination. In what ways are they similar? In what ways are they different?

BIBLIOGRAPHY

Books

Beckett, Lucy. *Wallace Stevens.* Cambridge, M.A.: Cambridge University Press, 1974.

Bloom, Harold. *Wallace Stevens: The Poems of Our Climate.* Ithaca, N.Y.: Cornell University Press, 1977.

Borroff, Marie, ed. *Wallace Stevens: A Collection of Critical Essays.* Englewood Cliffs, N.J.: Prentice-Hall, 1963.

Miller, J. Hillis. *Poets of Reality: Six Twentieth-Century Writers.* Cambridge, M.A.: Harvard University Press, 1966.

Kermode, Frank. *Wallace Stevens.* London: Oliver & Boyd, 1960.

Kessler, Edward. *Images of Wallace Stevens.* New Brunswick, N.J.: Rutgers University Press, 1972.

Pearce, Roy Harvey and J. Hillis Miller, eds. *The Act of the Mind: Essays on the Poetry of Wallace Stevens.* Baltimore: Johns Hopkins University Press, 1965.

Periodicals

Eberhart, Richard. "Emerson and Wallace Stevens," *Literary Review*, 7 (1963): 51–71.

Gray, Richard. "Poetry and the Subject of the Poem: Wallace Stevens." *Modern American Poetry*, (1984): 41–57.

McFadden, George. "Poet, Nature, and Society in Wallace Stevens." *Modern Language Quarterly*, 23 (1962): 263–271.

✷ R. L. Stine

BORN: *1943, Columbus, Ohio*

NATIONALITY: *American*

GENRE: *Fiction*

MAJOR WORKS:

The Baby-Sitter (1989)

The *Fear Street* series (1989–1997)

The *Goosebumps* series (1992–1997)

Overview

R. L. Stine has more than three hundred million books in print, yet at the height of his popularity in the early

R. L. Stine *AP Wide World Photos*

1990s, most adults were not even familiar with his name. This best-selling author's success is based on his popularity among children and teens, who, in the mid-1980s, and through the 1990s, purchased the titles in his "Fear Street" and "Goosebumps" horror series at a rate of more than one million copies each month. During that period, a new book in each series was released every month, making Stine one of the most prolific authors of all time. His success did not please all critics, some of whom dismissed his work as insignificant. But teachers, librarians, and parents reported that many youngsters who were previously uninterested in books turned into avid readers after becoming hooked on Stine's works.

Works in Biographical and Historical Context

A Life's Ambition Robert Lewis Stine was born October 8, 1943, in Columbus, Ohio, son of Lewis Stine, a retired shipping manager, and Anne Stine. Growing up, Stine never wanted to be anything but a writer, and by the age of nine, he was creating his own magazines filled with short stories and jokes. He attended Ohio State

LITERARY AND HISTORICAL CONTEMPORARIES

Stine's famous contemporaries include:

Richard Robinson (1937–): Son of Robbie Robinson, founder of Scholastic Corporation, Richard Robinson is the current CEO of the company. Scholastic is the world's largest distributor and publisher of children's books.

Bill Clinton (1946–): The forty-second president of the United States, Bill Clinton served from 1992 until 2000. Clinton was the second president ever to be impeached; however, he was found not guilty of the charges brought against him.

Stephen King (1947–): Probably the best-known horror writer of all time, King has over three hundred million books currently in print. His most widely praised work is the apocalyptic novel *The Stand* (1978).

Clive Barker (1952–): A well-known writer of dark fantasy and horror, Barker is the author of works such as *The Thief of Always* (1992) and *Weaveworld* (1987).

Christopher Pike (1954–): Pike is the pseudonym of Kevin McFadden, a best-selling author of young adult thrillers. One of his best-known works is *Slumber Party* (1985), his first novel that became a best-seller.

University, where he earned a B.A. degree in 1965 and worked as editor of the campus humor magazine for three years. After graduating, he taught social studies at a junior high school for one year and then set out for New York City in search of a job in magazine publishing.

In 1968, Stine began a sixteen-year stint as an editor for Scholastic Inc., which publishes many classroom magazines and children's books. Stine worked on several titles before finally becoming editor of *Bananas*, a humor magazine for children aged twelve and older. He was thirty-two at the time and felt that he had achieved his life's ambition.

His Own First Book   Greater success than Stine had ever dreamed of was still in store for him. For all his work in publishing, Stine had never published a book. His work on *Bananas* impressed an editor at Dutton, who asked him to create a humor book for children. Thus, Stine's first book, *How to Be Funny: An Extremely Silly Guidebook*, was published in 1978. The book was successful and led to a long string of funny books, many of which were published under the name "Jovial Bob Stine."

In 1985, due to financial difficulties, Stine was let go from Scholastic. Stine stepped up his career as a book author, turning out action-adventure and "twist-a-plot" stories (which allowed the readers to direct the action) in addition to his humorous story and joke books. Only a

year later, the editorial director at Scholastic asked him to try writing a horror novel for young adults. She gave him a title to work with: *Blind Date* (1986). The result was his first young adult horror novel, a pleasantly surprising success.

Even Greater Success   During this time, young-adult horror was a fast-growing genre, and Stine proved he could duplicate the appeal of *Blind Date* with two subsequent scary tales, *Twisted* (1987) and *The Baby-Sitter* (1989). Stine's wife Jane, who is also involved in the publishing industry, suggested that he try to come up with an idea for a series. Thus, "Fear Street," a horror series designed for readers aged nine to fourteen, was born. Fear Street is a place where terrible things happen and where "your worst nightmares live," according to copy on the covers of the early titles. The main characters change from one book to the next, but all attend Shadyside High—a fictional school with an appalling frequency of murder.

After "Fear Street" came the idea for "Goosebumps," a less gory, but still spooky, series for eight- to eleven-year-old readers. Both series rely on cliffhanger endings in each chapter to keep readers turning the pages. Stine focused on making his fictional characters speak and act like real, modern kids in order to connect with his audience. In addition to listening to his teenage son Matt for inspiration, Stine also read young adult magazines and watched MTV. In a *Time* magazine article by Paul Gray, Stine freely admitted to using "cheap thrills" and "disgusting, gross things" to pump up the appeal of his stories.

Between 1988 and 1993, Stine had over fifty books published under his name, most of them in the teen thriller genre. In 1995, he took another big step in his career: publishing his first novel for adults, a horror story called *Superstitious*. Contrasting the book with Stine's young-adult offerings, a *Publishers Weekly* reviewer commented that in the new novel, "several characters ... curse, enjoy X-rated sex and die gruesomely detailed deaths."

Current Endeavors   By the end of the 1990s, Stine's publishing career seemed to be slowing down. The popularity of young adult horror, particularly the formulaic brand of which Stine had been one of the most popular and prolific authors, was waning. Nevertheless, he has continued to write and to be known as one of the most popular children's book authors of all time. Stine's latest innovation is a series of twelve books entitled "Goosebumps Horrorland." Each book in the series contains two stories, the first of which stands alone, and the second of which is part of a longer story that is carried out over all twelve books in the series. His film *Mostly Ghostly*, written in part by his son Matt Stine, appeared in October 2008 on DVD.

Works in Literary Context

Stine began writing young adult horror novels largely in response to the genre's growing popularity in the 1980s. Somewhat comparable to today's magic- and fantasy-related novels for young people, horror and thriller novels were exceedingly popular from the mid-1980s through the mid-1990s, with authors such as Stine selling millions of books, often with similar characters and structures.

Young Adult Thriller   The young adult thriller is a branch of young adult fantasy, or writing that involves characters or events that could not or probably would not happen in "real life." As opposed to realism, it aims to excite the reader through suspense, and to entertain by providing an escape from everyday life.

Stine's novels have been called "formulaic" for their reliance on typical young adult horror plots and stock characters. He has also admitted that he is not above mentioning something disgusting or grotesque just to increase the horror value of his stories. However, Stine's books are unique in that they have a comic edge—something that many novels in the genre lack. Many of his books are filled with characters playing practical jokes which, more than often, backfire or have unexpected tragic results. In this sense, they can be viewed as offering a message to young readers about the dangers of misbehaving.

Works in Critical Context

Stine's work has not been a favorite among critics, yet because of his novels' overwhelming success among young people, many have turned to them again to find out why. Some critics are willing to offer begrudging praise. Patrick Jones has noted, "Some [Stine novels], of course, are better than others, but considering they are chucked out almost once a month, the actual quality of them is quite surprisingly good." Nevertheless, the overall consensus among critics seems to be that Stine's work, though at times fun to read, has little to no literary merit. Roderick McGillis stated: "I think of Stine's books as camp because they are so artificial, so formulaic, so predictable, so repetitive, so bad."

Blind Date   When *Blind Date*, Stine's first horror novel, was published in 1986, reviewers not yet jaded by the coming deluge of young-adult horror accepted it for what it was: a book that should be seen "as entertainment only," as a reviewer for *Kliatt Young Adult Paperback Book Guide* puts it. Stephanie Zviria, in a review for *Booklist*, states, "Not for the squeamish and riddled with contrivances, the story is well paced and has a TV-ish flair that is likely to appeal to teens." In her review for *Voice of Youth Advocates*, Mary I. Purucker writes, "The unsophisticated will like this for its dark twists and turns, but mystery buffs will recognize the hoary and convoluted had-I-but-known style." Judie Porter sums up critical opinion of this and most other Stine works in her review for *School Library Journal*: "It's mindless entertainment."

Responses to Literature

1. The horror in Stine's books has been considered "safe horror" in that its intention is to entertain, not really to frighten readers. Do you think this is an

---

COMMON HUMAN EXPERIENCE

A common theme in Stine's work is fear of the unknown. Here are some other famous works with similar themes:

"The Tell-Tale Heart" (1843), a short story by Edgar Allan Poe. This well-known short horror story is told from the first person by a mad narrator who murders an old man and then discovers that the sound haunting him from under the floorboards is the old man's heart.

Moby-Dick, or The Whale (1851), a novel by Herman Melville. Often considered one of the greatest American novels ever written, *Moby-Dick* tells of a hunt for a mysterious white whale that ultimately ends in the deaths of all but one sailor on the ship.

House of Leaves (2000), a novel by Mark Danielewski. One of this novel's multiple story lines follows a group of explorers as they plumb the depths of a house that consists of infinite doors and passageways completely devoid of light.

---

ideal choice for Stine's intended audience? Why or why not?

2. Read the short story "The Tell-Tale Heart" by Edgar Allan Poe. What is it about the story that makes it suspenseful? What techniques does Poe use that you have also seen in Stine's work?

3. Write a horror story and share it with your classmates. Ask your classmates at what point in the story they felt frightened and why.

BIBLIOGRAPHY

Books

"Fantasy in Contemporary Literature." *Contemporary Literature Criticism*. Ed. Tom Burns and Jeffery W. Hunter. Vol. 193. Detroit: Thomson Gale, 2005, pp. 137–250.

Periodicals

Porter, Judie. Review of *Blind Date*. *School Library Journal* vol. 33, no. 3 (November 1986): 108–109.

Purucker, Mary I. Review of *Blind Date*. *Voice of Youth Advocates* vol. 10, no. 1 (April 1987): 33–34.

Review of *Blind Date*. *Kliatt Young Adult Paperback Book Guide* vol. XX, no. 6 (September 1986): 18.

Zviria, Stephanie. Review of *Blind Date*. *Booklist* vol. 83, no. 2 (September 15, 1986): 121.

Web sites

"About Scholastic: People and History." Scholastic Online. Accessed November 19, 2008, from http://www.scholastic.com/aboutscholastic/people/index.htm. Last updated in 2008.

"Elements of Horror." Notes from Noel Carroll's *Philosophy of Horror*, Dark Cloud Press Online. Accessed November 19, 2008, from http://www. darkcloudpress.com/blog_files/horror.pdf. Last updated in 2008.

"News." R. L. Stine: The Official Website. Accessed November 19, 2008, from http://www.rlstine. com/#nav/news. Last updated in 2008.

✸ Harriet Beecher Stowe

BORN: *1811, Litchfield, Connecticut*

DIED: *1896, Hartford, Connecticut*

NATIONALITY: *American*

GENRE: *Fiction*

MAJOR WORKS:

Uncle Tom's Cabin; or, Life among the Lowly (1852)

Oldtown Folks (1869)

Oldtown Fireside Stories (1871)

Harriet Beecher Stowe   *Stowe, Harriet Beecher, photograph. National Archives & Records Administration.*

Overview

Author of the best-selling novel of the nineteenth century, and among the best-paid writers of her day, Harriet Beecher Stowe has been designated a leading creator of what might be called "the New England myth." Her idealistic vision of Yankee village life charmed a readership growing uneasily conscious of industrialization after the Civil War. Despite her idealism, however, Stowe is best known for her antislavery novel *Uncle Tom's Cabin; or, Life among the Lowly* (1852), a novel that, it is sometimes suggested, pushed the nation over the brink of the Civil War.

Biographical and Historical Context

Born in Litchfield, Connecticut, on June 14, 1811, to well-known Presbyterian minister Lyman Beecher and his wife Roxana (Foote) Beecher, Harriet Elizabeth Beecher was raised in an atmosphere of stern Calvinist piety. As a teenager, she read widely and was commended for her outstanding memory. Her father saw her special qualities, but he had trouble appreciating them in a daughter. "Harriet is a great genius," he wrote in a private letter. "I would give a hundred dollars if she was a boy." Genius or not, Harriet's learning depended almost entirely on her sister Catharine's attention to her gifts. As headmistress of the Hartford Female Seminary, Catharine set her sister a rigorous study schedule; it suited Harriet well and even left time for her to edit the *School Gazette*.

First Literary Earnings   After moving to Cincinnati, Ohio, with her father in 1831, Harriet began to devote herself to writing. In 1833, she published her first book, *Primary Geography for Children, on an Improved Plan*, under Catharine's name. Other literary efforts of this period included a character essay that Stowe based on Lyman Beecher's stories about his adoptive father: "A New England Sketch" (April 1834; later "Uncle Tim"). This sketch won a local literary prize and an honorarium of fifty dollars.

On January 6, 1836, Harriet married Calvin Stowe, a childless widower who was a Bible scholar in her father's school. As his wife, she would give birth to seven children in fifteen years. To help out with the finances, she continued to write optimistic New England sketches to publish in such magazines as *Godey's Lady's Book*. In 1843, she collected the best of her work in *The Mayflower; or, Sketches of Scenes and Characters among the Descendants of the Pilgrims*.

Stowe's husband took a position at Bowdoin College in Maine in 1850. Having returned to the New England life she loved, Stowe was again inspired to write, and by spring 1851, she had begun working on the novel that would bring her widespread fame and financial success. *Uncle Tom's Cabin*, which Stowe claimed was written by "the Lord Himself," appeared in 1852 to outstanding acclaim, selling ten thousand copies in the first week after its publication.

Uncle Tom and Civil War Legend has it that President Abraham Lincoln, upon meeting the author of *Uncle Tom's Cabin*, said, "So this is the little lady who made this big war." While most historians agree that the president probably did not say this, the story illustrates the devastating impact of the novel on a nation already leaning toward war.

The novel's success brought Stowe international fame. She began traveling extensively in Europe, forming friendships with well-known writers Elizabeth Barrett Browning and George Eliot. Her travels inspired two more books, *Sunny Memories of Foreign Lands* (1854) and *Dred: A Tale of the Great Dismal Swamp* (1856). Neither was as critically acclaimed as *Uncle Tom's Cabin*. Her next slave novel, *The Minister's Wooing* (1859), however, was better written and helped maintain her status as a gifted writer.

Civil war broke out in 1861 and lasted until the Confederacy, or the union of southern states, surrendered in 1865. Interestingly, despite her renown as an antislavery writer, Stowe's literary efforts returned to focus on domestic matters during the war—possibly due to the fact that one of her sons was fighting in it. Family concerns took up much of her attention throughout the following decade, during which time she is generally considered not to have written anything of lasting significance.

A Success-driven Downfall Stowe's postbellum writings—that is, books she wrote after the war—are considerably more polished, as a whole, than her earlier works. *Oldtown Folks* appeared in 1869 and was followed by *Oldtown Fireside Stories* (1871), both of which sold extremely well. Many modern readers consider these New England stories her best-imagined and most realistic work.

Confident of her standing in the wake of this popular and critical success, Stowe embarked on the publication that led to scandal. In the course of her travels, she had befriended Lady Byron, wife of the immensely famous English poet George Gordon, Lord Byron. As Stowe felt compelled to reveal in "The True Story of Lady Byron's Life," published in *Atlantic Monthly*, Lord Byron had left his wife and embarked on an incestuous affair with his half sister Augusta Leigh.

The results of publicizing this affair, which at the time was shocking to the point of disbelief, were disastrous for Stowe. She fell from grace among the literary community, most of the members of which considered her choice to publish the essay extremely indecent. Although she would continue to write, and even to publish, Stowe never regained her former esteem among the public in her lifetime. She died in the care of a home nurse on July 1, 1896.

Works in Literary Context

Stowe's work is often classified as regionalism, or literature that emphasizes the landscape, dialect, customs, and folklore of a particular geographic region. She is considered a primary architect of the "New England myth" and is sometimes referred to as a sentimentalist—a pejorative

---

LITERARY AND HISTORICAL CONTEMPORARIES

Stowe's famous contemporaries include:

George Gordon, Lord Byron (1788–1824): English Romantic poet best known for his extended satiric poem *Don Juan* (1819–1824). Lord Byron left his wife and engaged in an affair with his half sister Augusta Leigh, as Stowe reported in "Lady Byron Vindicated."

George Eliot (1819–1880): George Eliot was the pen name of Mary Anne Evans, one of the most brilliant novelists ever to write in the English language. Some of her best-known works include *Middlemarch* (1869) and *Silas Marner* (1861).

Elizabeth Barrett Browning (1806–1861): English Romantic poet best known today for her *Sonnets from the Portuguese* (1850), one of which begins, "How do I love thee? Let me count the ways."

Abraham Lincoln (1809–1865): Sixteenth president of the United States, Lincoln served from 1861 to 1865, during the years of the American Civil War. He was assassinated by John Wilkes Booth in 1865.

Frederick Douglass (1818–1895): Brilliant African American leader of the abolitionist movement in the nineteenth century. Douglass taught himself to read before escaping from slavery. He went on to become a nationally renowned public speaker, author, abolitionist, and women's rights advocate.

---

term describing writers who tend to idealize characters and events instead of creating a more complete, realistic picture. Her major antislavery works, however, transcend both regionalism and sentimentalism and are sometimes placed alongside other major abolitionist works of the mid-nineteenth century, such as Frederick Douglass's *Narrative of the Life of Frederick Douglass* (1845).

Regionalism Regionalism is an American literary movement of the late nineteenth century that is characterized by the realistic depiction of small town and rural life. The movement, which was an early stage in the development of American realistic writing, assisted in the development of distinct identities among certain regions like New England, the South, and the West. One of the period's most famous writers was Mark Twain.

Many of Harriet Beecher Stowe's novels and sketches, sometimes considered forerunners of Twain's, represent key works of New England regionalism. *Oldtown Folks* and *Oldtown Fireside Stories*, often considered to be her best written works, consist of numerous detailed, intimate sketches of New England and the people who lived there. Stowe was explicit in her desire to capture real moments of New England life: when she revised *The Mayflower* years

COMMON HUMAN EXPERIENCE

A common theme in Stowe's work is the evil of slavery. Here are some other famous works with similar themes:

Oroonoko, or the Royal Slave (1668), a novel by Aphra Behn. This short novel about a slave uprising in Surinam, a Dutch colony in South America, has been considered the first English work to portray blacks sympathetically.

The Tragedy of Pudd'nhead Wilson (1894), a novel by Mark Twain. This bitter satire tells the story of how Roxy, a fair-skinned woman designated as a slave by her tiny fraction of African blood, switches her baby with the master's shortly after their births so that her son will not grow up a slave.

Narrative of the Life of Frederick Douglass (1845), an autobiography by Frederick Douglass. The autobiography of a former slave, this book is considered one of the foremost works of abolitionist literature. It became a bestseller on two continents and was translated into French and German.

Amazing Grace (2007), a film directed by Michael Apted. This film tells the story of William Wilberforce, leader of the British antislavery movement in the eighteenth century.

after its publication, she asked readers to recall "the good old catechizing, churchgoing, school going, orderly times" of the New England past.

Works in Critical Context

Despite its popular success during her lifetime, Stowe's work has become controversial due to its depiction of blacks. The sentimentalism derided by early critics is now largely overlooked, while its particular focus on nineteenth century New England often is not. Her better known works, *Uncle Tom's Cabin* and *Oldtown Folks*, overcome this drawback, breaking away from merely regional concerns to address the universal; however, the former is not as widely praised now for its universality as it once was.

Uncle Tom's Cabin   This novel brought Stowe widespread fame during her lifetime and was widely praised by critics and the public alike. Mark Twain, a brilliant satirist and contemporary of Stowe's, called it "a drama which will live as long as the English tongue shall live." Even the renowned British novelist Charles Dickens wrote to Stowe to express his approval of the novel: "I have read it with the deepest interest and sympathy, and admire, more than I can express to you, the generous feeling which inspired it, and the admirable power with which it is executed."

Many modern readers, however, have criticized the novel for its portrayal of blacks, who must be submissive

in order to be saved. Author James Baldwin stated in his well-known essay "Everybody's Protest Novel," "[I]f, being mindful of the necessity of good works, [Stowe] could not cast out the blacks ... she could not embrace them either without purifying them of sin." Noted author Charles Johnson states in his introduction to the 150th anniversary edition of the novel that it presents, "a portrait of black people that, from a twenty-first-century perspective, is ineluctably racist."

Oldtown Folks   Like many of Stowe's works, *Oldtown Folks* has been faulted for its attention to the particular, idealized world of mid-nineteenth century New England, along with certain literary defects with which her work was often plagued. Nineteenth century critic J. R. Dennett remarked that willing critics "will discover matter for fault-finding throughout the book. There is none of Mrs. Stowe's books ... in which she has not failed as completely in the creation of a character as she has succeeded in the depiction of [New England] character[s]."

Dennett's remarks, however, point to what has indeed been considered great about Stowe's work: her characterization of New Englanders. In a 1927 essay, Constance Mayfield Rourke said of *Oldtown Folks* that it was "Filled to the brim with lively notations of people and places ... the richest and raciest of Mrs. Stowe's novels." Many modern critics have agreed. Writing in 1974, John R. Adams remarked, "When completed [*Oldtown Folks*] was acclaimed ... as her major work and still holds that position."

Responses to Literature

1. George Orwell, a well known English political writer and author of such books as *Animal Farm* (1945), and *1984* (1949), once wrote: "In a peaceful age I might have written ornate or merely descriptive books, and might have remained almost unaware of my political loyalties." How might this statement relate to Stowe's career?

2. Read *Uncle Tom' Cabin*, keeping in mind what critics have said about Stowe's "sentimentalism." Write an essay in which you argue that the novel either does or does not display this characteristic.

3. Read Abraham Lincoln's First Inaugural Address, made in 1861. What do you think the political climate in America was like at the time he gave it? Discuss how some of the major concerns he addresses in his speech are also addressed in *Uncle Tom's Cabin*.

4. Watch the film *Amazing Grace* (2007). How does the antislavery movement in England compare to the movement in the United States, as it is portrayed in Stowe's work?

5. Read Stowe's *Oldtown Folks* and choose two of its characters to compare in an essay. Show how Stowe uses details to make these characters seem complete and realistic.

BIBLIOGRAPHY

Books

Gienapp, William E. *Abraham Lincoln and Civil War America: A Biography.* New York: Oxford University Press, 2002.

Rourke, Constance Mayfield. *Trumpets of Jubilee.* New York: Harcourt Brace Jovanovich, 1927, pp. 87–148.

Periodicals

"Review of *Oldtown Folks.*" *American Literature* Vol. 69, No. 1 (March 1997): 39.

Adams, John R. "Structure and Theme in the Novels of Harriet Beecher Stowe." *American Transcendental Quarterly*, No. 24, Part 1 (Fall 1974): 50–55.

Baldwin, James. "Everybody's Protest Novel." *Partisan Review*, Vol. 16, No. 6 (June 1949): 578–585.

Bornstein, George. "Best Bad Book: Black Notes and White Notes to the Tale of Uncle Tom." *Times Literary Supplement* I. 5426 (March 30, 2007): 3–4.

Randall, Ericka. "Review of *Uncle Tom's Cabin.*" *Women's Studies* Vol. 36, I. 3 (April–May 2007): 221.

Web sites

"The Life and Work of Lord Byron 1788–1824." *English History.* Accessed November 21, 2008, from http://englishhistory.net/byron.html.

"Prose Fiction." *Antislavery Literature.* Accessed November 20, 2008, from http://antislavery.eserver.org/prose.

"A Short Biography of Frederick Douglass." *Frederick Douglass Comes to Life.* Accessed November 21, 2008, from http://www.frederickdouglass.org/douglass_bio.html.

Metcalf, Stephen. "Uncle Tom's Children: Why Has *Uncle Tom's Cabin* Survived—and Thrived?" *Slate.* Accessed November 28, 2008, from http://www.slate.com/id/2118927.

✹ William Styron

BORN: *1925, Newport News, Virginia*

DIED: *2006, Martha's Vineyard, Massachusetts*

NATIONALITY: *American*

GENRE: *Fiction*

MAJOR WORKS:

Lie Down in Darkness (1951)

The Confessions of Nat Turner (1967)

Sophie's Choice (1979)

This Quiet Dust, and Other Writings (1982)

Darkness Visible (1990)

William Styron   *photograph by A. Blakelee Hine. The Library of Congress.*

Overview

William Styron was a prominent twentieth-century American novelist noted for tackling some difficult moral questions in his fiction. A Southerner by birth, Styron is often associated with the Southern Gothic tradition in literature, along with prominent writers William Faulkner, Flannery O'Connor, and Carson McCullers. His most famous novels, *The Confessions of Nat Turner* (1967) and *Sophie's Choice* (1979), tackle such difficult subject matter as slavery and the Holocaust.

Works in Biographical and Historical Context

Southern Upbringing and World War II William Styron was born in Newport News, Virginia, in 1925. His father, William Clark Styron, was a shipyard engineer who battled clinical depression, and his mother was Pauline Styron, a native of Pennsylvania whose father had served as a Confederate officer during the Civil War. His paternal grandparents had owned slaves, but his parents were liberal and discussed race relations in the home. The subject matter would later find its way into his writing.

Styron's mother died from a long battle with cancer when the writer was thirteen. Styron was a rebellious child, and because of this, his father moved him from Hilton Elementary School to Christchurch School, an Episcopal preparatory school located in the Tidewater area of Virginia. He then went on to Davidson College, where he enrolled in the Marines' reserve officer training program. He soon transferred to Duke University, only to be called into active duty in 1944. World War II had begun in 1939, with Germany invading Poland, and the United States had entered the conflict in 1941, following Japan's bombing of Pearl Harbor. Because Japan and Germany were allies, this put the United States in the difficult position of engaging in large-scale warfare on two fronts: in the Pacific and in Europe. Styron trained for a year, became a second lieutenant, and was assigned to aid in the planned invasion of Japan. Later, the United States dropped atomic bombs on the Japanese cities of Hiroshima and Nagasaki. The attacks destroyed the cities and killed tens of thousands of civilians instantly. Japan surrendered, and Styron was discharged before he had the chance to engage in combat. He later earned his Bachelor of Arts degree in English from Duke.

Following graduation, he worked as an associate editor for McGraw-Hill in New York City. During this time, he began work on his first novel, *Lie Down in Darkness* (1951). This first novel is set in Virginia and focuses on a Southern girl's suicide, as it is viewed by her friends and family members during the funeral. Using flashbacks to explain the events leading up to Peyton Loftis's death, Styron exposes a dysfunctional family, full of secrets and tragedies. The atomic bomb is a major metaphor in the novel: Peyton's suicide coincides with the dropping of the bomb. The novel's focus on a deeply troubled Southern family and Styron's lyrical language, prompted critics to compare him to such Southern Gothic writers as William Faulkner and Flannery O'Connor.

The Civil Rights Movement and His Confession
In 1967, Styron published *The Confessions of Nat Turner*, a novel that revisited the story of a notorious rebellion led by the slave, Nat Turner, in 1831, in which fifty-five white people were killed. The timing of the novel helped it as much as its story: the movement for African American civil rights was reaching its zenith in the late 1960s. Many of the major milestones of the civil rights movement had already occurred. The Reverend Martin Luther King Jr., had led his 1963 March on Washington for Jobs and Freedom and had given his famous "I Have a Dream" speech. The Civil Rights Act of 1964 was signed into law by President Lyndon Johnson. This Act outlawed racial segregation in schools, in the workplace, and in public places. The National Voting Rights Act of 1965 ended many of the discriminatory practices that had prevented African Americans from voting in the United States. This act made it illegal to require voters to pass a literacy test as a prerequisite for voting, something that

specifically targeted potential African American voters. It was a time of great change in the United States, and Styron's novel, which offered a somewhat sympathetic picture of Nat Turner, sparked many discussions about race, the history of slavery, and the role of literature in activism and history. The novel won the 1968 Pulitzer Prize for fiction, among many other awards.

Morality and Sophie's Choice
Styron's next novel was the equally provocative *Sophie's Choice* (1979). Much had been written about the atrocities of World War II, especially the torture and murder of Jews, gays, and other groups of people in Nazi-run concentration camps. Styron's novel was different because it focused on the things people had to do to stay alive while in such camps, and the aftermath of such difficult decisions. The book won the 1980 American Book Award. The 1982 film adaptation of the book was nominated for multiple Academy Awards. Actress Meryl Streep won a Best Actress Oscar for her acclaimed performance as the title character, Sophie, a beautiful Polish immigrant to the United States, haunted by memories of her fight to survive the war.

Depression and the Last Years
In 1985, at the age of sixty, Styron quit drinking alcohol. The following year, he was hospitalized for depression. His 1990 memoir, *Darkness Visible: A Memoir of Madness*, would recount his bouts with serious and sometimes debilitating depression. With an increased interest in mental health that was emerging in the 1990s, and an increased diagnosis and medication for illness, his memoir was timely. He described his battle with depression as "despair beyond despair."

Depression plagued Styron for many years. He was hospitalized a number of times following the publication of his memoir and stories. Styron would continue to receive awards and attention until his death, in 2006, of pneumonia while in Martha's Vineyard. He was eighty-one years old.

Works in Literary Context

Styron's work is as famous for its subject matter as it is its rich, lyrical language. An important member of the post–World War II generation of writers, he tackled issues of race, class, and ethnicity in his many novels. His work is highly regarded for not only its strong characters and Southern Gothic influences, but also for its willingness to address the complexities of moral dualities such as good and evil. Throughout his lifetime, Styron was influenced by such writers as William Faulkner, James Baldwin, and James Jones, among others.

Southern Gothic
William Styron is considered one of the great American writers writing in the Southern Gothic tradition. This literary style is focused around the culture and issues specific to the southern regions of the United States. Much Southern Gothic work is critical of Southern society, and tragedies are used as a means of social critique.

Southern Gothic works generally focus on someone ostracized or isolated due to societal expectations. Tennessee Williams's *A Streetcar Named Desire* (1948), for example, suggests that behind the Southern belle stereotype lies vanity and mental instability.

Many of Styron's characters in *Lie Down in Darkness* and *The Confessions of Nat Turner* are Southern. Additionally, the story of Nat Turner is told in the context of the South and is meant to break down stereotypes of slaves. However, Styron's work is more about the individual dealing with internal struggles rather than with society and its effects. Styron himself did not think his work fit into the Southern Gothic genre, despite critical claims. He responded in *The Paris Review* in the spring of 1953 by stating:

> I don't consider myself in the Southern school, whatever that is. Only certain things in the book are particularly Southern ... [Peyton] didn't have to come from Virginia. She would have wound up jumping from a window no matter where she came from.

Slave Narratives The slave narrative is a literary form inspired and influenced by the experiences of enslaved Africans. Many former slaves in the United States, Canada, and other countries told accounts of their life during slavery during the eighteenth and nineteenth centuries. These first-person slave narratives were distributed by abolitionists in an effort to show both the cruelty with which slaves were subjected, and the eloquence with which slaves could express themselves. Eventually, the narratives became more and more popular and sold in the tens of thousands. Frederick Douglass, Booker T. Washington, and Harriet Jacobs were three of the most popular figures in the slave narrative tradition. They focused their writings on how African Americans rebelled and survived during slavery and focused on the pursuit of freedom.

Styron's work, along with that of Toni Morrison and Sherley Anne Williams, helped to popularize the neo-slave narrative. These pieces of fiction are inspired by the slave narratives of the past. They use existing documents, such as the slave narratives and court documents, along with oral histories, to craft works that seek to give former slaves a voice across time.

Works in Critical Context

During his lifetime, Styron was both praised and criticized for taking on such controversial subject matter as slavery, the Holocaust, and mental illness. His work was praised for its lyrical language and criticized for its wordiness. Often, because of the narrators and subject matter of his stories, critics wondered whether Styron had the experience and authority to tell the stories he told.

The Confessions of Nat Turner Many critics of Styron's *The Confessions of Nat Turner* worried that Styron was rehashing stereotypes of both blacks and whites, and that the book was more destructive than it was educa-

---

LITERARY AND HISTORICAL CONTEMPORARIES

Styron's famous contemporaries include:

William Faulkner (1897–1962): Faulkner was an American author best known for his novels and short stories. He is widely considered one of the greatest American writers of the South. He is best known for his novels, which include *The Sound and the Fury* (1929) and *As I Lay Dying* (1930).

James Baldwin (1924–1987): Baldwin is an American novelist, poet, and activist whose work is well known for exploring race, sexuality, and issues regarding identity. He is best known for the novels *Go Tell It on the Mountain* (1953) and *Giovanni's Room* (1956).

Gore Vidal (1925–): Vidal is an American novelist, essayist, and politician whose novel *The City and the Pillar* (1948) is considered to be the first major American novel to include blatant homosexuality.

Norman Mailer (1923–2007): Mailer was an American novelist, essayist, and activist; he won two Pulitzer Prizes for his books *Armies of the Night* (1968) and *The Executioner's Song* (1979).

James Jones (1921–1977): Jones is an American author best known for examining World War II and its effects through works such as *From Here to Eternity* (1951).

Flannery O'Connor (1925–1965): O'Connor was an American novelist and short story writer famous for her contributions to the Southern Gothic style and for such works as the short story collection *Everything That Rises Must Converge* (1965).

---

tional. A critic from *Negro Digest* criticizes Styron's discussion of Turner's sexuality by writing:

> In the name of fiction, Mr. Styron can do whatever he likes with History. When his interpretation, however, duplicates what is white America's favorite fantasy (i.e., every black male—especially the leader—is motivated by a latent (?) desire to sleep with the Great White Woman), he is obligated to explain (in the structure of the novel, of course) this coincidental duplication—or to be criticized accordingly.

Still, his work had many defenders. George Steiner once commented about Styron's relevance as a writer by stating in *The New Yorker*, "The crisis of civil rights, the new relationships to each other and to their own individual sensibilities that this crisis has forced on both whites and Negroes ... give Mr. Styron's fable [*The Confessions of Nat Turner*] a special relevance." Styron's friend, the writer James Baldwin, praised the novel, saying it had "begun to write the common history—ours."

COMMON HUMAN EXPERIENCE

Suicide is a major theme in Styron's work. Other works that deal with this theme include:

The Awakening (1891), a novella by Kate Chopin. While on a vacation, the book's protagonist breaks free of her confining social roles, only to ultimately find happiness more elusive than she first thought.

Mrs. Dalloway (1925), a novel by Virginia Woolf. This novel concerns a wealthy woman's preparations for a party, and includes her thoughts upon hearing of a former soldier's suicide.

The Bell Jar (1961), a novel by Sylvia Plath. This book chronicles the main character's descent into mental illness brought on by her inability to fulfill the societal roles expected of her.

Better Off Dead (1985), a film by Savage Steve Holland. In this teen comedy, John Cusack plays a heartbroken loser who tries to end it all until a beautiful foreign exchange student shows him that life is worth living.

Sophie's Choice Styron was criticized for his treatment of the African American experience in *The Confessions of Nat Turner*, with critics questioning whether a white man could ever do such a subject justice. Similar criticism was launched at Styron after the publication of *Sophie's Choice*, which focused on the life of a Polish Catholic victim of the Nazi regime. Alvin Rosenfeld criticized Styron for trivializing the Holocaust by including elements of sexuality and sensationalism in the novel's plot. He argues that the novel is not about the Holocaust, but is more concerned with the characters' sexuality and the narrator's growth as an artist.

Most critics, however, had high praise for the novel. In the *New Statesman*, David Caute comments on the influences present in the book by writing that "neo-Biblical cadences of Southern prose, of [Thomas] Wolfe and Faulkner, jostle with the cosmopolitan sensibility of an F. Scott Fitzgerald."

Responses to Literature

1. What role does suicide play in Styron's novels? Why do you think it is a major component of much of his work? What does suicide symbolize in *Lie Down in Darkness*?

2. What is the Southern Gothic writing style? How do Styron's novels fit this writing style? Think about whether or not a novel has to be set in the South in order to fit this subgenre of the Gothic style. Explain how Styron's work both fits and does not fit into this category.

3. Read *The Confessions of Nat Turner* and discuss the role of the Bible in this work. How does this faith influence Turner, his relationships, and his decisions?

4. What was the decision Sophie had to make in Styron's novel, *Sophie's Choice*? What would you have done in her situation? Why?

BIBLIOGRAPHY

Books

Casciato, Arthur D., and James L. W. West III, eds. *Critical Essays on William Styron*. Boston: G. K. Hall, 1982.

Clark, John H., ed. *William Styron's Nat Turner: Ten Black Writers Respond*. Boston: Beacon, 1968.

Coale, Samuel. *William Styron Revisited*. Boston: Twayne, 1991.

Cologne-Brookes, Gavin. *The Novels of William Styron: From Harmony to History*. Baton Rouge: Louisiana State University Press, 1995.

Davis, Robert Gorham. "The American Individualist Tradition: Bellow and Styron." *The Creative Present: Notes on Contemporary Fiction*. Edited by Nona Balakian and Charles Simmons. Garden City, N.Y.: Doubleday, 1963, pp. 111–114.

Finkelstein, Sidney. "Cold War, Religious Revival, and Family Alienation: William Styron, J. D. Salinger, and Edward Albee." *Existentialism and Alienation in American Literature*. New York: International Publishers, 1965.

Fossum, Robert H. *William Styron: A Critical Essay*. Grand Rapids, Mich.: Eerdmans, 1968.

Friedman, Melvin J. *William Styron*. Bowling Green, Ohio: Bowling Green University Press, 1974.

Periodicals

"The Holocaust According to William Styron." *Midstream* vol. 25 (10) (December 1979): 43–49.

Web Sites

Lehmann-Haupt, Christopher. "William Styron, Novelist, Dies at 81." Retrieved November 8, 2008, from http://www.nytimes.com/2006/11/02/books/02styron.html. Last updated on November 4, 2006.

Row, Jess. "Styron's Choice." Retrieved November 8, 2008, from http://www.nytimes.com/2008/09/07/books/review/Row-t.html. Last updated on September 5, 2008.

"William Styron." Retrieved November 8, 2008, from http://www.pbs.org/wnet/americanmasters/database/styron_w.html/. Last updated on November 1, 2006.

✳ May Swenson

BORN: *1919, Logan, Utah*

DIED: *1989, Ocean View, Delaware*

NATIONALITY: *American*

GENRE: *Poetry*

MAJOR WORKS:
Iconographs (1970)
Nature: Poems Old and New (1993)

Overview

Best known for her shape poems, which she called "iconographs," and her work incorporating riddles and wordplay, May Swenson was considered one of the most imaginative and innovative contemporary American poets. Though she was often compared to Emily Dickinson, her subject matter was unique and ranged from the ordinary to the metaphysical. As Priscilla Long comments in *The Women's Review of Books*, "Swenson was a visionary poet, a prodigious observer of the fragile and miraculous natural world."

May Swenson © *Oscar White / Corbis*

Biographical and Historical Context

Swedish Heritage   May Swenson was born in Logan, Utah, on May 28, 1913. Her full name, Anna Thilda May Swenson, gives some indication of her Swedish heritage; her father, a professor of mechanical engineering at Utah State University, and her mother immigrated from Sweden. They spoke Swedish at home, and, therefore, English became May Swenson's second language. She demonstrated the habits of a writer at an early age, keeping a journal in which she wrote in multiple genres.

Swenson attended Utah State University and received a bachelor's degree in 1934. Upon graduation, Swenson went to work as a reporter in Salt Lake City. After only one year, she relocated to New York City, where she would live for most of the remainder of her life. She held various jobs—including working as a stenographer, ghostwriter, secretary, and manuscript reader—to support herself while she wrote poetry and worked toward publication.

Early Acclaim   Swenson's first volume of poetry, *Another Animal*, was published by Scribner in 1954 to widespread acclaim. Her poetry was admired for its "adventurous word play and erotic exuberance" and came to be compared to the writings of Emily Dickinson, E. E. Cummings, Gertrude Stein, and Elizabeth Bishop. With this first volume, however, she had not yet delved into the experimental forms that would mark her later work.

Swenson's second volume, *A Cage of Spines*, appeared in 1958. The following year she took a job as an editor for New Directions Press. However, her success as a poet was exceptional, and seven years later she was able to leave the job in order to fully devote her time to writing. Over the following two decades she served as poet-in-residence at several colleges and universities in the United States and Canada, including Bryn Mawr, Purdue University, the University of North Carolina at Greensboro, and her alma mater, Utah State University. Swenson also received numerous awards and grants for her writing during this time, including a Guggenheim Fellowship and a Rockefeller Foundation grant, and in 1970, was elected to membership in the National Institute of Arts and Letters.

Experimentation   Swenson's best-known and most experimental volume of poetry, *Iconographs*, appeared in 1970. It was considered an experimental masterpiece, successful in that her experimentation—in language and subject, but most importantly in form—was not an end in itself but instead a useful means of discovering something new. Coming out of the 1960s, a decade during which experimentation had come to be known as valuable in itself, Swenson's work demonstrated that the purpose of experimenting was to create results that could not be reached by any other means.

LITERARY AND HISTORICAL CONTEMPORARIES

Swenson's famous contemporaries include:

Gertrude Stein (1874–1946): An American fiction writer and poet to whom Swenson is sometimes compared. Stein is best known for her memoir, *The Autobiography of Alice B. Toklas* (1933), and for her prominence in the Parisian community of American expatriates during the first decades of the twentieth century.

Carl Sandburg (1878–1967): An American poet and winner of two Pulitzer prizes, Sandburg composed some shape poems. His best known shape poem is entitled "Fog".

T. S. Eliot (1888–1965): An American modernist who later became a naturalized British citizen. Eliot's writing had a tremendous influence on the style and diction of poets who followed him. In his most famous work, *The Waste Land* (1922), the narrators include a tarot-card reader and a person who walks with the spirits of the dead.

Elizabeth Bishop (1911–1979): Bishop was a widely acclaimed poet and friend of Swenson's who, by the time of her death, had won every major poetry award in the United States.

Gloria Steinem (1934–1961): A leading American feminist, Steinem was the founder in 1971 of the pioneering feminist *Ms.* magazine.

After the resounding success of *Iconographs*, Swenson went on to produce several more volumes of poetry, including a number of collections for young adults and a translation of Tomas Tranströmer's work entitled *Windows and Stones: Selected Poems of Tomas Tranströmer*. In 1980, she was chosen as chancellor of the American Academy of Poets, a position she filled until her death in 1989.

In the last decade of her life, Swenson lived in Sea Cliff, New York, on the north shore of Long Island. She was a frequent contributor to *The New Yorker* magazine, and many of her poems published therein were included in the collection *New and Selected Things Taking Place* (1978). With this volume, Swenson retreated a few steps from her earlier experimentalism and devoted her energies instead to more in-depth, personal reflection. Some critics found that this and the last collection published in her lifetime, *In Other Words* (1988), lacked the exuberance of her earlier, more experimental works; others found the poems contained therein to be the ruminations of a woman who has explored her outer limits and is now reaching towards her core. She died in Ocean View, Delaware in 1989.

Works in Literary Context

Swenson is often compared to Emily Dickinson, not only for her irregular typesetting, but also for her interest in

the subject of death. However, her shape poems, for which she is best known, recall the art and craft of English seventeenth-century poet George Herbert: both she and Herbert are equally concerned about making the shape a functional and essential feature of a poem's sense. Swenson is also noted for her use of wordplay and riddles in her poetry.

Shape Poems Swenson's shape poems, "iconographs," were crafted in a particular shape that somehow related to its subject. One of the most famous examples of a shape poem is George Herbert's "Easter Wings" (1633), which is shaped like a pair of butterfly wings and addresses the subject of rebirth. The twentieth-century American poet Carl Sandburg is another noted author of shape poems.

Riddles The use of riddles, or puzzle questions, in literature is ancient and universal to all cultures. Their use in poetry, however, has been limited to mystic poets who wish to suggest links with ancient prophecies or mysteries. As a woman riddler, Swenson follows in the tradition of the sibyls, female prophets in Greek and Roman mythology, whose prophecies were riddles that had to be interpreted by priests. The use of riddles in her poetry lends it a sense of mysticism akin to that of modernist poets T. S. Eliot and William Butler Yeats.

Works in Critical Context

Often experimental in both form and appearance, Swenson's poetry has earned widespread critical acclaim. As Priscilla Long comments in *The Women's Review of Books*, "Swenson was a visionary poet, a prodigious observer of the fragile and miraculous natural world." Renowned poet Ann Stanford has called Swenson "the poet of the perceptible" and stated, "No writer employs with greater care the organs of sense to apprehend and record the surfaces of the world."

Iconographs *Iconographs* is Swenson's most experimental volume in terms of typography. In it she explores to the fullest extent the uses of shape poetry, from icons to irony. Sven Birkerts stated in *The Electric Life: Essays on Modern Poetry*, "By insisting that the poem function visually, [Swenson] drew the elastic to its limit." In other words, she took the concept of image and text as far as it could go.

Not all critics are pleased with the result. Dave Smith has complained that the wit so often praised in her poetry feels artificial: "For me [Swenson] has too strong a willingness to keep work marked by visual puns … work less felt and sustaining than contrived and biodegradable." Indeed, puns and play form such an integral part of Swenson's poetry that the ability to enjoy them may be necessary to the appreciation of her work.

Nature: Poems Old and New This posthumous collection of Swenson's work is almost universally praised for its lyricism, imagery, and wit. Priscilla Long, writing for *The Women's Review of Books*, remarks, "Swenson was an unrelentingly lyrical poet, a master of the poetic line in which similar sounds accumulate and resonate so that the poem exists, beyond its meanings, as a rattle or a music box or, in moments of greatness, a symphony." Such glowing descriptions are common among criticism of the work: Donna Seaman called it "a dazzling posthumous collection of nature poems by a poet who epitomized the art of awareness." Widely acclaimed in her lifetime, Swenson appears only to have grown in reputation since her death.

Responses to Literature

1. Read several of Swenson's poems and identify the objects she references in each. Discuss how pairing two of the objects together can illustrate different aspects of each that might not otherwise have been apparent.

2. Swenson uses numerous scientific terms in her poetry. Do you feel that science and poetry are compatible subjects? Why or why not? How might the study of poetry help you better understand science?

3. Read George Orwell's *Animal Farm* (1945) and discuss how human nature is portrayed through the animal characters. Do you think the novel would have been as effective if it had been written with human characters? Why or why not?

4. Using your library and the Internet, research three women poets who wrote during the twentieth century. Read some of their work and write an essay comparing it to Swenson's.

5. Compose a shape poem on a subject of interest to you. Discuss how arranging the poem in the shape of its subject or theme affects one's reading of the poem.

BIBLIOGRAPHY

Periodicals

Review of *Nature: Old Poems and New. Publishers Weekly*, Vol. 241, No. 22 (May 30, 1994): 46.

Clarence, Judy. Review of *Nature: Poems Old and New. Library Journal* (June 15, 1994): 72.

Long, Priscilla. Review of *Nature: Poems Old and New. Women's Review of Books*, Vol. 12, no. 4 (January 1995): 8–10.

Salter, Mary Jo. Review of *In Other Words. New Republic* (March 7, 1988): 40.

Seaman, Donna. Review of *Nature: Poems Old and New. Booklist*, Vol. 90, no. 19–20 (June 1, 1994): 1763.

Smith, Dave. "Perpetual Worlds Taking Place." *Poetry*, Vol. CXXXV, no. 5 (February 1980): 291–6.

Wiman, Christian. Review of *Nature. Poetry* (November 2001): 97.

Zona, Kirstin Hotelling. "A 'Dangerous Game of Change': Images of Desire in the Love Poems of May Swenson." *Twentieth Century Literature* (Summer 1998): 219.

Web sites

"Famous Women Poets and Poetry." *Famous Poets and Poems.* Accessed November 24, 2008, from http://famouspoetsandpoems.com/poets_women.html.

"May Swenson." *Poets: From the Academy of American Poets.* Accessed November 21, 2008, from http://www.poets.org/poet.php/prmPID/168.

"Women in Education." *Women's Issues Then and Now: A Feminist Overview of the Past Two Centuries.* Accessed November 21, 2008, from http://www.cwrl.utexas.edu/~ulrich/femhist/education.shtml#history.

COMMON HUMAN EXPERIENCE

A common theme in Swenson's work is the animal nature of human beings. Here are some other famous works with similar themes:

On the Origin of the Species (1859), a scientific treatise by Charles Darwin. This revolutionary work introduced the concept of evolution and the idea that humans were not hand-crafted by God, but evolved from lower primate species.

Animal Farm (1945), a novel by George Orwell. This fable about an animal takeover of the farm where they work is not intended to show the human nature of animals, as it may at first seem, but to decry the bestial nature of humans.

Lord of the Flies (1954), a novel by William Fielding. This novel by the NobelPrize-winning author tells of a troop of young boys left to fend for themselves on a desert island after a plane crash. Left to their own devices, the boys become savages.

Of Love and Other Demons (1995), a novel by Gabriel García Márquez. In this novel, written in the style of magic realism, a young girl in a Latin American port town raised by African slaves is feared for her breeding and characteristics that remind the Spanish occupiers of animal behavior.

T-Z

Mary TallMountain

BORN: *1918, Nulato, Alaska*

DIED: *1994*

NATIONALITY: *American*

GENRE: *Poetry, fiction*

MAJOR WORKS:

There Is No Word for Goodbye (1980)
The Light on the Tent Wall: A Bridging (1990)
A Quick Brush of Wings (1991)

Overview

When Mary TallMountain died in September 1994 at the age of seventy-six, she had been seriously writing and publishing poetry and fiction for a little more than twenty-five years. Although her work never attracted the notice given to some Native American Renaissance women writers, it has attracted a large and loyal following. Many of her readers are teachers who find that the spiritual quality of her work and her awareness of being a survivor (and more) often moves their students to tears. Her stories and poetry illuminate the experiences of a lifetime committed to bringing all her various worlds—Athabascan, Russian, Irish-American, pagan, Catholic, agnostic, tribal, and middle-class Anglo—together in one body.

Biographical and Historical Context

Adoption from an Athabascan Village Mary Tall-Mountain was born Mary Demoski on June 19, 1918, in the tiny Koyukon village of Nulato, Alaska, just west of Fairbanks. TallMountain's mother, Mary Joe Demoski, was of mixed heritage, Russian and Athabascan; Athabascans are the native inhabitants of modern-day central Alaska who, most scientists believe, are descended from people who migrated from Asia over 35,000 years ago. Her father, Clem Stroupe, was an American soldier of Irish and Scottish descent who was stationed with the U.S. Army at Nulato.

Like many native Athabascans at that time, Tall-Mountain's mother was stricken with tuberculosis even before Mary TallMountain was born. When TallMountain was six and her brother Billy was four, Mary Joe Demoski, knowing that she would not live, made the decision to give up her two children for adoption to the Randles, the white government doctor and his wife. She hoped that, by doing so, the children would receive the education and advantages she had longed for and, most important, that they would be saved from inevitably contracting tuberculosis themselves. Because of the decision of the village council, the little boy stayed, and Mary was sent away with the Randles.

A Silent and Self-Destructive Rage Although Tall-Mountain was saved from dying of tuberculosis, she came close to losing her life anyway through the toll of the move on her spirit and emotions. In Oregon, she was exposed to the ridicule of white schoolchildren, an experience she recounts in her poem, "Indian blood," in *The Light on the Tent Wall: A Bridging* (1990). Forbidden to speak her native tongue by the Randles, she also began to be molested by her new stepfather. The molestation continued for years and would lead TallMountain to alcoholism as an adult.

TallMountain's adolescent and early adult years were marked by tragedy. Because of financial troubles during the Great Depression of the 1930s, her family became migrant workers, finally ending up in Portland, Oregon. Her adoptive father died of heart failure just after she graduated from high school, and her husband, Dal Roberts, whom she married at the age of nineteen, died after only three years of marriage. TallMountain's adoptive mother committed suicide in 1945 because she was dying of Parkinson's disease and diabetes. Alone, TallMountain left Portland for Reno, where she would train as a legal secretary.

Mary TallMountain   *Lance Woodruff*

Struggles with Alcoholism and Cancer   From Reno, TallMountain moved to San Francisco, where she continued working as a legal secretary. The pain of her past drove her to secret drinking, and she continued to drink and live in what she described as a "grey world" into her forties. Eventually she realized the toll that alcoholism was taking on her body and her life, and she decided to stop drinking completely. TallMountain then set up her own stenography business and, for a while, enjoyed a new feeling of being her own boss. She was diagnosed with cancer in 1968. She fought and overcame it, but in the process, she lost her business and her apartment and had to move to the Tenderloin, a poorer part of San Francisco to which many of the elderly poor, the homeless, prostitutes, and drug addicts gravitate.

Taking Up Her Journals Once More   It was in the Tenderloin that she took up the journals that her adoptive mother, Agnes, had taught her to keep as a child. TallMountain's illnesses eventually resulted in her inability to work and finally, in her receiving a disability pension; the small income enabled her to spend her later years writing, teaching, giving readings, and getting published. Circumstances that might have thrown a less committed person into the street and destitution offered TallMountain the opportunity to dedicate herself to what she came to see as her life's work.

TallMountain began writing poetry in the mid-1960s, and Simon Scanlon, the editor of *The Way of St. Francis*, encouraged her. In 1977, after TallMountain's second bout with cancer, Scanlon published *Nine Poems*, TallMountain's first chapbook, through Friars Press in San Francisco. She was fifty-nine years old. The following year, *Good Grease* was published by Strawberry Press in New York.

Shortly after the second cancer went into remission, TallMountain followed a rumor of her birth father's whereabouts and was able to locate him in Phoenix, Arizona. He, too, had been diagnosed with cancer, and TallMountain moved to Phoenix to spend the last two years of his life with him. After his death in 1978, she began work on the poetry that would become her first volume of clearly Native American poetry, *There Is No Word for Goodbye* (1980).

Discovered by Alaskan poet Geary Hobson and provided with a grant to travel and teach in local schools, TallMountain returned to Alaska after her father's death. In subsequent years, she regularly traveled north to read poetry and teach in community centers, schools, and prisons. In 1987, she founded the Tenderloin Women Writers Workshop, a support group where local women could share written expression of their lives. In 1990, *The Light on the Tent Wall* was published, and in the following year, Freedom Voices Publications, an associate of the Tenderloin Reflection and Meditation Center, published *A Quick Brush of Wings*.

Only after a stroke left her with aphasia in 1992 did TallMountain begin to turn down the many requests to read that still flowed to her at her apartment in Petaluma, California, where she had moved that year. She continued to write until her death in 1994.

Works in Literary Context

Although her earlier work is difficult to classify, TallMountain was known primarily as a writer of Native American poetry. She was the best-known poet from the Athabascan region in central Alaska, and many of the poems in her collections *There Is No Word for Goodbye* and *The Light on the Tent Wall* evoke some aspect of Athabascan culture. However, she was most widely known for her poetry's continual struggle to overcome the sense of alienation that may result from a mixed ethnic and cultural heritage and unite various aspects of her being.

Native American Poetry   Native American poetry typically finds its inspiration either from specific tribal traditions or from the sense of collective Native American identity, which sees the fact of being Native American as an experience that is shared among all tribes and cultures. Like many forms of minority writing, Native American poetry seeks to illuminate experiences that have been either misinterpreted by mainstream culture or ignored. Some of its unique characteristics is its tendency to blend nature with spirituality, and to incorporate elements of the oral storytelling tradition.

TallMountain is ranked among scholars with other Native American poets such as Joy Harjo, Linda Hogan, and Wendy Rose. Like theirs, TallMountain's poetry makes extensive use of natural imagery. Her work also often recalls a sense of alienation and displacement in modern mainstream society.

Works in Critical Context

Despite her presence in anthologies and journals, TallMountain's work has attracted little in the way of critical reviews. She was, nonetheless, recognized as one of the foremost poets and fiction writers of the Native American Renaissance. Many public figures have rated her work among that of such acclaimed Native American poets as Joy Harjo, Leslie Silko, Linda Hogan, and Wendy Rose. Those who have commented on her work—largely her peers—agree that TallMountain's poetry deserves far greater critical coverage than it has received.

Rayna Green, in *That's What She Said: Contemporary Poetry and Fiction by Native American Women*, comments on the critical status of Native American women writers in general: "In spite of inclusion...in anthologies, prizes, awards, fellowships, and readings throughout the country, [Native American women writers] find appreciation primarily among a specialized audience—Indian, feminist, politically attuned."

Very little academic criticism of TallMountain's writings is available except in Paula Gunn Allen's volume *The Sacred Hoop*, published in 1986, well before the appearance of *The Light on the Tent Wall*. In *The Sacred Hoop*, Allen describes TallMountain's work as revealing "a deeply spiritualized sensibility." She claims to be disturbed, however, by the "difficult and uneasy alliance" that she perceives between TallMountain's "pagan awareness...and the less earthy, more judgmental view of medieval Christianity."

Light on the Tent Wall   The foreword, written by Allen for *Light on the Tent Wall*, indicates she had come to understand, by the time of its publication, that TallMountain was fully capable of embracing both beliefs—pagan and Christian—and making her home within the transformation. Rather than a source of disjunction, Allen finds that the apparent contradiction in TallMountain's beliefs can become a source of unity and universality: "In telling her life and the life of her far away people, she tells all our stories; she tells our lives. And in so doing not only affirms life, but re-creates it."

Responses to Literature

1. In much of TallMountain's poetry there is a sense of alienation in mainstream culture. Why do you think this might be? Using your library and the Internet, find three more poems written by Native Americans in which alienation is a major theme.

2. Using your library and the Internet, research the history of the Athabascan people and their culture. Based on what you learn, analyze one of TallMountain's poems and show how her Athabascan heritage has influenced her writing.

3. Based on what you have learned in this article, why do you think Mary TallMountain's work has not received much attention from critics? What do you think is the purpose of literary criticism? How might a lack of attention from critics have affected the impact of TallMountain's work?

4. Using your library and the Internet, find an article on a current event that demonstrates the destructive power of technology on the environment. Discuss how the article relates to TallMountain's work.

LITERARY AND HISTORICAL CONTEMPORARIES

TallMountain's famous contemporaries include:

Austin E. "Cap" Lathrop (1865–1950): For a time, Alaska's wealthiest resident, Lathrop benefited greatly from Alaska's low-tax natural resources and argued against changing its legal status from that of a territory to that of a state.

Ernest Gruening (1887–1974): An Alaskan senator from 1959, the first year of Alaska's statehood, to 1969, Gruening is considered "the father of Alaskan statehood." His address at the 1955 Alaskan Constitutional Convention was entitled "Let Us End American Colonialism."

Paula Gunn Allen (1939–): A well-known Native American critic, essayist and poet, Allen greatly admires TallMountain's work and has done much to promote the publication and study of Native American literature.

Joy Harjo (1951–): A well-known Creek poet and musician, Harjo's poetry is often linked to the land of Oklahoma, site of a Creek reservation since the 1800s.

Wanda Coleman (1946–): Wanda Coleman, an African American performance poet, worked with writers Charles Bukowski and Diane Wakoski to create an alternative literary scene in Los Angeles in the 1970s and 1980s. Her urban-naturalist poetry has yet to be fully recognized by the commercial publishing establishment.

Linda Hogan (1947–): A Native American Chickasaw poet and fiction writer committed to environmental preservation, Hogan writes in celebration of the natural world and dismay at those who scar it.

COMMON HUMAN EXPERIENCE

A common theme in TallMountain's work is the destructive force of modern technology. Here are some other famous works with similar themes:

Frankenstein (1818), a novel by Mary Shelley, was a warning, at the time of the Industrial Revolution, against the misuse of science. Victor Frankenstein, a scientist succeeds in creating life, but his creation is a monster that turns against him.

Brave New World (1932), a dystopian novel by English writer Aldous Huxley, set in the distant future. The novel satirizes the idea of progress through science (especially biology) and technology, Everyone is happy in the World State Huxley depicts, but only because they are manipulated by their rulers.

Les Rougon-Macquart (1871–93), a series of twenty novels by the foremost French naturalist, Émile Zola. This series, which took the author nearly twenty-five years to complete, narrates the birth of modern mass civilization as it struggles with the forces of nature.

Anna Karenina (1877), a novel by Leo Tolstoy. Through the story of Levin, a landed Russian nobleman dissatisfied with urban society, Tolstoy explores the conflict between nature and modern society.

I, Robot (2004), a film adapted from the science fiction novel by Isaac Asimov. This film starring Will Smith tells the story of how robots, created by human technology, develop the capacity to disobey orders and set about destroying humankind.

BIBLIOGRAPHY

Books

Gunn, Paula Allen. *The Sacred Hoop: Recovering the Feminine in American Indian Traditions.* Boston: Beacon Press, 1992.

Periodicals

Review of *The Light on the Tent Wall. Ms.* Vol. 3 (September 1992): 62.

Review of *The Light on the Tent Wall. Western American Literature* Vol. 27 (Spring 1992): 91.

Czapla, Cathy. "And a Deer's Ear, Eagle's Song and Bear's Grace: Animals and Women." *The Animals' Agenda* Vol. 11, no. 8 (October 1991): 49.

Tucker, Debbie. Review of *Raven Tells Stories: An Anthology of Alaskan Native Writing, Library Journal* Vol. 116, no. 13 (August 1991): 102.

Welford, Gabrielle. "Mary TallMountain's Writing: Healing the Heart—Going Home." *Ariel* Vol. 25, no. 1 (January 1994): 136(19).

Web sites

Gislason, Eric. "A Brief History of Alaska Statehood." *American Studies at the University of Virginia.* Accessed November 25, 2008, from http://xroads.virginia.edu/~cap/BARTLETT/49state.html.

Partnow, Patricia. "Athabascans of Interior Alaska." *Alaska Native Knowledge Network.* Accessed November 25, 2008, from http://www.ankn.uaf.edu/Curriculum/Athabascan/Athabascans/alaskanathabascans.html.

✸ Amy Tan

BORN: *1952, Oakland, California*

NATIONALITY: *American*

GENRE: *Fiction*

MAJOR WORKS:
The Joy Luck Club (1989)
The Kitchen God's Wife (1991)
The Hundred Secret Senses (1996)

Overview

Amy Tan is one of the most significant contemporary Asian American women writers. Her novels have received both critical praise and popular success, and she is among

Amy Tan   *Tan, Amy, 1993, photograph. AP Images.*

the first women writers to bring Asian-American culture and experiences to a broad mainstream audience. Tan's works, which focus on Chinese people who have immigrated to the United States, illustrate the difficulties of maintaining a dual cultural identity. Many of the conflicts her characters experience, however, transcend cultural differences and speak to the universal struggles of a broad and varied audience.

Biographical and Historical Context

Daughter of Chinese Immigrants The second of three children, Amy Ruth Tan, whose Chinese name is An-mei (Blessing from America), was born on February 19, 1952, in Oakland, California. Her father, John Yuehhan Tan, an electrical engineer and Baptist minister, had emigrated to the United States in 1947; her mother, Daisy Tu Ching Tan, a vocational nurse, arrived in 1949. The family moved frequently among various California cities, eventually settling in Santa Clara. Like many of the mothers and daughters in Tan's novels, Tan and her mother had a strained relationship. Tan's mother had high expectations for her, and Tan felt pressured to excel. Also, her mother's attire and accent embarrassed Tan as a child and adolescent.

When Tan was fifteen, both her older brother, Peter, and her father died of brain cancer. Her mother, believing the house occupied with evil spirits, took Tan and her brother John to New York, Washington, and Florida and finally to Europe. After Tan graduated from high school in Montreux, Switzerland, the family returned to the United States and settled in the San Francisco area. Tan switched from a premed major to English at Linfield College, a Baptist school in Oregon. After meeting Lou DiMattei on a blind date, eighteen-year-old Amy transferred to San Jose State University, where DiMattei was a law student, and put herself through college with the help of a scholarship and income from a job in a pizza parlor. She earned a BA in English and linguistics in 1973 and a master's degree in linguistics in 1974.

In the spring of that same year, Tan married DiMattei. She began work on a doctorate at the University of California, Berkeley, but left the university in 1976 to take a position as a language-development specialist for disabled children. Frustrated with the administrative aspects of the job, in 1981 she became a reporter for the journal *Emergency Room Reports*, rising to managing editor and associate publisher in a matter of a few years. In 1983 she became a freelance technical writer and began producing pamphlets and other documents for corporations.

Although highly successful in her field, Tan began to feel that she had become addicted to work—she spent an average of ninety hours a week on the job. In her late thirties she underwent counseling to remedy the problem. When that counseling failed, Tan began her own program, which consisted of learning to play jazz piano and reading and writing fiction. Her first short story, "The Rules of the Game," earned her admission to the Squaw Valley

---

LITERARY AND HISTORICAL CONTEMPORARIES

Tan's famous contemporaries include:

Elaine Chao (1953–): Chao is the first Chinese American to serve in a president's cabinet. She was appointed U.S. Secretary of Labor in 2001, in the administration of George W. Bush.

Toni Morrison (1931–): The first black woman to receive the Nobel Prize in literature, Morrison was born Chloe Wofford. She is known for her portrayals of African American women and the explorations of race, class, and sex in her novels.

Maxine Hong Kingston (1940–): Considered the most influential Chinese-American writer of the twentieth century, Kingston wrote *The Woman Warrior* (1976), a collection of mythical and historical stories that presents a feminist view of Chinese heritage.

Sue Monk Kidd (1948–): Author of the best-selling novel *The Secret Life of Bees* (2002), Kidd focuses on the stories of women, often of mothers and daughters, in her novels.

Matt Groening (1954–): Best known as the creator of the *Simpsons* television series, Groening has won eleven Primetime Emmys for his work. One *Simpsons* episode featured Tan, whose voice she provided herself.

Community of Writers, directed by novelist Oakley Hall. That experience became part of the groundwork for her novel *The Joy Luck Club*, which was published in 1989.

An Instant Success *The Joy Luck Club* was an instant success among both critics and readers. It remained on the *New York Times* best-seller list for nine months. It also won the 1989 Bay Area Book Reviewer Award for Best Fiction and the Best Book for Young Adults Award from the American Library Association. In 1993, the novel was adapted into a critically acclaimed motion picture with Tan coauthoring the screenplay.

Tan continued her therapeutic exploration of mother-daughter relationships in her second novel, *The Kitchen God's Wife* (1991). The plot is a fictionalized version of the life of Daisy Tan, Amy's mother. Having been asked by many of her friends whether she was the inspiration for the mother character in *The Joy Luck Club*, Daisy complained to her daughter that she wanted her real story told. Amy videotaped her mother telling her own life story and transformed it into her second novel. The final message of the novel is one of forgiveness and hope.

The success of her first two novels ensured Tan a loyal readership, and despite the fact that few of her subsequent novels or children's books have received the critical acclaim of the first two, they have still been extremely popular

COMMON HUMAN EXPERIENCE

A common theme in Tan's work is the relationship between mothers and daughters. Here are some other famous works with similar themes:

Little Women (1869), a novel by Louisa May Alcott. This novel, a best-seller in its time, tells of four sisters who decide to take a journey to overcome their deepest character flaws and along the way must come to terms with their relationships with their mother.

East Wind: West Wind (1930), a novel by Pearl S. Buck. This novel tells the story of Kwei-Lan, a young Chinese woman who marries a man educated in America. Through her relationship with him, she comes to confront and finally to understand her mother in a way she could not when they lived in the same home.

Terms of Endearment (1983), a film directed by James L. Brooks. Based on the novel by Larry McMurtry, this film follows a mother and daughter through several years after the daughter's marriage as they struggle to understand one another and search for meaning in their lives.

The Secret Life of Bees (2002), a novel by Sue Monk Kidd. This novel tells the story of a nurse who, ordered by a doctor to take his own baby girl to an institution for children with Down Syndrome, chooses to keep the girl instead and becomes her mother.

among readers. Her work has been translated into thirty-five languages, and several of her novels have been designated Notable Books by the *New York Times*.

Today, Tan continues to write and to pursue interests outside her work. She sings with the Rock Bottom Remainders, an authors' rock-and-roll band that also includes Stephen King, Dave Barry, and Matt Groening, creator of the animated television series *The Simpsons* (beginning 1989). The group gives concerts across the United States and donates the proceeds to various charities. Tan also recently produced a libretto version of her novel *The Bonesetter's Daughter* (2001), which was performed by the San Francisco Opera in 2008. She and her husband have homes in San Francisco and New York City.

Works in Literary Context

Tan's novels belong to the subgenre of Chinese-American literature. Some major themes include alienation, the conflict of multiple identities, cultural differences, and generational differences. This last is particularly marked in many Chinese-American works, due to the immense cultural differences between China and the United States during the period in which the writers' parents immigrated.

Chinese-American Literature The subgenre is distinguished from mainstream writing primarily by its focus on Chinese traditions and the struggles of Chinese-Americans to come to terms with a multicultural identity. Maxine Hong Kingston, considered the most influential Chinese-American writer of the twentieth century, created a style consisting of an amalgamation of oral histories, family stories, myths, and fictionalizations, and it is this style against which many writers in this subgenre, such as Tan, continue to be compared.

While Tan's work resembles Kingston's in its tendency to blend family stories and myths with pure fiction, it is distinct in its fixation on and portrayal of mother-daughter relationships. Tan uses the techniques common to much Chinese-American fiction in order to explore a reality that is both specific to her culture and universal to all women.

Works in Critical Context

Critical reception of Tan's work has been generally positive, though it has become less so throughout her career. Many critics, while praising Tan's renditions of Chinese-American culture and mother-daughter relationships, have noted that she seems to be telling the same story over and over again. The fact that most of her novels become best-sellers despite their repetitive elements has been dubbed "the Amy Tan phenomenon" and described by critic Sau-ling Wong as "naïve voyeurism" on the part of "nonintellectual consumer[s] of Orientalism." Nevertheless, most critics agree that Tan's writing has real significance in both the sphere of feminist and of Chinese-American writing.

The Joy Luck Club Tan's first novel, *The Joy Luck Club*, received almost unanimously favorable reviews. It won many awards and was on the *New York Times* hardcover best-seller list for nine months—longer than any other book that year. In addition to being extremely popular among readers, the novel also impressed critics with its portrayal of mother-daughter relationships and generational differences among immigrants and their children.

In her 1993 essay on matrilineage and mother/daughter texts, Marina Heung praised the novel for "foregrounding the voices of mothers as well as daughters," addressing what some critics saw as a flaw in novels exploring the same theme at that time. Marianne Hirsch had envisioned a work "written in the voice of mothers, as well as those of daughters . . . [that] in combining both voices [finds] a double voice that would yield a multiple female consciousness." That consciousness was present, perhaps for the first time, in Tan's first novel.

The Kitchen God's Wife Tan's second novel also garnered appreciative reviews. Elgy Gillespie in *San Francisco Review of Books* wrote, "If anything, *The Kitchen God's Wife* is a more satisfying book than its predecessor. It deals with the same themes, but more profoundly and sensitively, and its linear structure allows puzzle to be unraveled and truths to unfurl along the way." Helen Yglesias, in *Women's Review of Books*, took a similar view, writing that anyone who enjoyed *The Joy Luck Club* would also enjoy its successor, "since both tell the same story—and this time around Tan has executed the work better in conception, in design, in detail, and in sheer pleasure for the reader."

The Hundred Secret Senses With her third novel, *The Hundred Secret Senses,* Tan began to lose some of her status with critics. Because the novel's themes are strikingly similar to those of her first two, Tan has been accused of merely trying to capitalize on her former successes. Pin-chia Feng stated that Tan's "portrayal of China [in this novel] is at its most questionable," largely due to the dependence of the plot on the concept of reincarnation. Feng writes: "Instead of the revisionist mythmaking in her first two novels, Tan takes a step toward 'Chinese superstitions' to embrace the concept of reincarnation. The result, if sensational, is also unbelievable and disappointing."

Many other critics expressed similar thoughts on her third novel. Nevertheless, *The Hundred Secret Senses* was popular among readers, as her successive works have continually proven to be as well.

Responses to Literature

1. Tan is noted for her portrayals of mother-daughter relationships. How do these relationships differ from those between fathers and sons? Using your library and the Internet, find three examples of books or films that explore father-son relationships.

2. Using your library and the Internet, research the treatment of Chinese immigrants to the United States during the nineteenth and twentieth centuries. How might this treatment have affected the perceptions of recent Chinese immigrants? How might their American children have felt differently—or the same?

3. In Kingston's influential work *The Woman Warrior* (1976), women of Chinese heritage are presented as warriors—but not always in the ways we might expect. How do the women in Tan's works present the image of female warriors? What kinds of wars do they wage?

4. Watch the 1994 film version of *Little Women.* Discuss how the sisters' relationship to their mother compares to the relationships of the women in *The Joy Luck Club* to their mothers.

BIBLIOGRAPHY

Books

Feng, Pin-Chia. "Amy Tan." *Reference Guide to American Literature.* 3rd ed.Ed. Jim Kamp. Detroit: St. James Press, 1994.

Ling, Amy. *Between Worlds: Women Writers of Chinese Ancestry.* New York: Pergamon, 1990.

Sau-Ling, Cynthia Wong. *Reading Asian American Literatures: From Necessity to Extravagance* Princeton, N.J.: Princeton University Press, 1993.

Periodicals

Gillespie, Elgy. "Amy, Angst, and the Second Novel." *San Francisco Review of Books* (Summer 1991): 33–34.

Heung, Maria. "Daughter-Text/Mother-Text: Matrilineage in Amy Tan's *Joy Luck Club.*" *Feminist Studies,* Vol. 19, No. 3 (Fall 1993): 597–616.

Lelyveld, Nita. "Mother As Muse: Amy Tan Had to Unravel the Mystery of Li Bingzi, Who Had Become the Voice of Her Novels." *Philadelphia Inquirer Sunday Magazine* (February 28, 2001).

Mones, Nicole. "China Syndrome." *Washington Post Book World* (February 11, 2001): 4.

Reese, Jennifer. "Review of *Saving Fish from Drowning.*" *Entertainment Weekly* (October 21, 2005): 78.

Solomon, Charles. "A Review of The Kitchen God's Wife." *Los Angeles Times Book Review* (July 5, 1992): 10.

Wang, Dorothy. "A Review of The Joy Luck Club." *Newsweek,* Vol. 113, no. 16 (April 17, 1989): 69.

Yglesias, Helen. "The Second Time Around." *Women's Review of Books* (September 1991): 1. 3.

Zipp, Yvonne. "A Life Recalled from China: A Daughter Struggles for Assimilation, while Mother Clings to Their Culture." *Christian Science Monitor* (February 15, 2001): 20.

Web sites

"Amy Tan." *Amy Tan Home Page.* Accessed November 25, 2008, from http://www.amytan.net.

⊛ Ida Tarbell

BORN: *1857, Erie County, Pennsylvania*

DIED: *1944, Bridgeport, Connecticut*

NATIONALITY: *American*

GENRE: *Nonfiction*

MAJOR WORKS:

The Life of Abraham Lincoln, Drawn from Original Sources and Containing Many Speeches, Letters, and Telegrams Hitherto Unpublished (1900)

The History of the Standard Oil Company (1904)

The Tariff in Our Times (1911)

Overview

Ida Minerva Tarbell is recalled as the writer who blew the whistle on the first and most powerful trust in America. *The History of the Standard Oil Company,* her most important work, was published in 1904 and immediately convinced the public that the Standard Oil Company and its imitators in other industries threatened the underpinning of democracy—equal opportunity. The Supreme Court of the United States eventually concurred; in a 1911 decision the Court decreed the breakup of Standard Oil. Tarbell became known as the Joan of Arc of the oil

Ida Tarbell   *Louis Van Oeyen / Western Reserve Historical Society / Getty Images*

regions, a historian who not only recorded history but also helped powerfully to shape it.

Works in Biographical and Historical Context

Born of Pioneers   Ida Tarbell was born in 1857 on the Erie County, Pennsylvania, farm of her maternal grandparents, known to history only as the McCulloughs. She came from a long line of Scottish and English ancestors who had first arrived on the continent in the seventeenth century and had continued ever since to push west. At the time of her birth, her mother, Esther Ann Tarbell, was staying with her parents while her husband Franklin sought new farmland in Iowa. Two years after Ida's birth, the discovery of oil about forty miles south of the McCullough farm sent Franklin Tarbell on a new quest and launched the family into the oil age. He built a shanty in a settlement near the oil fields, where he would become a successful prospector and driller.

The Standard Oil Takeover   During Tarbell's high school days, John D. Rockefeller and his associates in the Standard Oil Company swiftly completed a takeover of the Pennsylvania oil regions. Although many able independent drillers joined Standard, Tarbell refused. He was outraged by the South Improvement Company, a scheme through which Standard meant to ruin competitors by high freight

rates arrived at in collusion with the railroad companies, while at the same time receiving from the railroads secret rebates from their own and their rivals' shipments. This particular scheme was discovered in time to prevent its implementation, but Tarbell and his daughter remained convinced that Standard gained control of the oil industry through such unfair and illegal means.

Pursuing a Career   Despite her father's troubles in the oil industry, Tarbell went on to attend Allegheny College in Meadville, Pennsylvania, where she was the only female member of her freshman class. Her college years were rewarding; she profited from her academic program, majored in biology, and managed to avoid what she considered the pitfall of marriage. She graduated in 1880, aware that her desire to continue her studies in biology at the graduate level would remain a dream.

Nevertheless, Tarbell continued to refuse to marry and focused instead on pursuing a career. After two unhappy years as a teacher, she took an unofficial job as managing editor of a Meadville-based magazine, *Chatauquan.* Though she was never officially recognized for her work, she developed a passion for writing, along with an interest in prominent women during the French Revolution that would lead her to study historiography, at age thirty-three, in Paris, France.

While in France, Tarbell supported herself as a freelance writer of articles on Parisian life. Her work caught the eye of Samuel McClure, founder of *McClure's Magazine,* who commissioned her to write a serialized biography of Napoleon Bonaparte for his magazine. The articles, which were extremely popular among the magazine's readership, were published as Tarbell's first book-length work, *A Short Life of Napoleon Bonaparte,* in 1895.

Encouraged by the success of Tarbell's Napoleon biography, Scribners published *Madame Roland: A Biographical Study* in 1896. The book did not sell well, but it is a benchmark in Tarbell's development as a historian/biographer. Her next assignment, a biography of Abraham Lincoln, brought her more fame and the magazine more fortune.

Muckraking: A New Direction in Journalism
Around 1900 McClure and his staff, which included Ray Stannard Baker and Lincoln Steffens, became restless. They were seeking originality, a new direction in journalism that would attract readers. They decided on muckraking, the practice of digging up dirt on people, businesses, and institutions to reveal their flaws to the public. McClure assigned Tarbell to cover the history of Standard Oil, Baker to probe the practices of labor unions, and Steffens to sniff out municipal corruption. From 1902 to 1904 these writers revealed to eager readers the injustices and corruption that permeated big business, labor, and politics, and lambasted the sleazy morality that tolerated them.

The History of the Standard Oil Company, published in 1904, marks the high point of Tarbell's achievement and probably that of muckraking journalism. Seven years after its publication, the Supreme Court ruled to dissolve Standard Oil's holding company. The connection between her work and the Supreme Court decision was pointed out by American historian Charles D. Hazen: "Miss Tarbell is the only historian I have ever heard of whose findings were corroborated by the Supreme Court of the United States."

In 1906, after a policy dispute with the tempestuous and erratic McClure, most of his staff, including editor John S. Phillips, Tarbell, Baker, and Steffens, quit. They bought the *American* magazine from Frederick L. Colver and started production of a magazine that imitated the one they had helped bring to great popularity and influence. Capitalizing on her success with Standard Oil, Tarbell ran a series titled *The Tariff in Our Times* from 1906 to 1911, the year it was published in book form.

The Woman Question From 1909 through 1913 Tarbell wrote three series of articles on women. Despite her belief in equal opportunity in business, and despite her own status as a woman, she argued against women's suffrage, or right to vote—a question that was being much debated at the time. Historians have struggled to reconcile these two seemingly contradictory opinions. A recent feminist theory holds that Tarbell accepted the fact of male dominance as a necessary norm, believing that women were not up to full equality. Others believe that Tarbell, an advocate of gradual change, saw the suffrage movement as revolutionary and therefore damaging to society as a whole. The question, however, has never been satisfactorily resolved.

The End of Muckraking After World War I, Tarbell became once again a freelance writer and lecturer. She did not, however, return to her previous successes for inspiration; she felt that muckraking journalism had served its purpose and that big business practices had changed. Her laudatory biography *The Life of Elbert H. Gary: The Story of Steel* appeared in 1925 and was considered by many critics a betrayal of her earlier views. But, she maintained she had not changed; business had.

Final Works Tarbell's last major history of business was published in 1936, when she was seventy-nine years old. It was *The Nationalizing of Business, 1878–1898*, volume 9 of the distinguished *A History of American Life* series edited by Arthur M. Schlesinger Sr. and Dixon Ryan Fox. The fact that Tarbell was invited to contribute to this series is ample evidence of respect for her among academic historians, who by 1936 were largely predominant in the field of history.

All in the Day's Work, Tarbell's autobiography, was published in 1939 near the end of her long and productive life. Self-revelation was not easy for Tarbell, and her care to observe the proprieties results in lack of color. In the latter part of the autobiography, however, a chronicle of her many activities as a writer and public figure demonstrates a love of work and a zest for the life she chose.

LITERARY AND HISTORICAL CONTEMPORARIES

Tarbell's famous contemporaries include:

Susan B. Anthony (1820–1906): Anthony was one of the most prominent advocates for women's rights. She campaigned relentlessly for almost forty years to establish women's right to vote.

John Sherman (1823–1900): Sherman was a U.S. senator for whom the Sherman Antitrust Act was named. Sherman was instrumental in creating much of the post–Civil War nation's financial system and in preventing the domination of big business.

John D. Rockefeller (1839–1937): Rockefeller was a cofounder with Samuel Andrews of Standard Oil. Rockefeller's attempts to control the oil industry throughout the United States made him America's first billionaire.

Samuel McClure (1857–1949): McClure established one of the first newspaper syndicates in the world, along with *McClure's Magazine*, which pioneered the journalistic style of muckraking.

Theodore Roosevelt (1858–1919): Roosevelt was the twenty-sixth president of the United States. He became known as the "trust-buster" for his opposition to trust monopolies, such as Standard Oil.

Jack London (1876–1916): London was a well-known American author of novels, including *The Call of the Wild* (1903) and *The Sea-Wolf* (1904). London also wrote much fiction for serial publications, such as *McClure's Magazine*.

Tarbell died of pneumonia at the age of eighty-six in a Bridgeport, Connecticut, hospital near her home. She was returned to Titusville to rest in Woodlawn Cemetery among kinfolk and neighbors whose rights she had so valiantly defended.

Works in Literary Context

Tarbell is best known for her biographies and her history of the Standard Oil Company. The latter was one of the first book-length works ever published that could be considered muckraking, and it became one of the most influential books of the age.

Biography Biography, according to seventeenth-century British dramatist John Dryden, is "history of particular men's lives." Like the definition itself, the authorship of biography has been historically dominated by men. Tarbell's contribution to the genre, however, was exceptional not only in the fact that she was a woman, but also in that, at the time of its publication, Tarbell's *Life of Abraham Lincoln* was the most extensively detailed and accurate biography of Lincoln ever written. It remained a standard

COMMON HUMAN EXPERIENCE

A common theme in Tarbell's work is the danger of big business. Here are some other famous works with similar themes:

The Jungle (1906), a novel by Upton Sinclair that depicts in disturbing detail the damaging effects of corruption in the meat-packing industry. Public reaction to the novel instigated the passage of the Meat Inspection Act and the Pure Food and Drug Act of 1906.

The Turn of the Balance (1907), a novel by Brand Whitlock, is a study in contrasts between the rich and the poor, the just and the unjust, the compassionate and the merciless. It presents observations on the nature of modern urban industrial society.

Super Size Me (2004), a film documentary by Morgan Spurlock. This documentary exposes the dangers of the commercial food industry as Spurlock undergoes a thirty-day fast-food diet.

Iron Man (2008), a film directed by Jon Favreau. When the protagonist of this film, weapons manufacturing mogul Tony Stark, is captured by terrorists, he discovers how his weapons are being used to spread terror throughout the world.

work of study until 1947, when the Lincoln papers to which she had been forbidden access were finally released to scholars.

Muckraking Muckraking, a style of journalism pioneered by Tarbell and her fellow writers at *McClure's Magazine*, was heralded in January 1903 with the appearance of several articles on municipal government, labor, and trusts, written by Tarbell, Steffens, and Baker. The movement as such largely disappeared between 1910 and 1912. Among the novels produced by muckrakers were Upton Sinclair's *The Jungle* (1906), about the meat-packing industry in Chicago, and Brand Whitlock's *The Turn of the Balance* (1907), which opposed capital punishment.

Tarbell is considered a pioneer of the muckraking movement, as her articles on Standard Oil were some of the first ever to be published in the movement. She herself, however, saw the movement not as a permanent shift in journalistic style, but as a response to a need for societal change. Tarbell's biography *The Life of Elbert H. Gary: The Story of Steel*, published fourteen years after her last great muckraking work, demonstrates through its laudatory depiction of its subject that she felt muckraking had served its purpose.

Works in Critical Context

In both biography and journalism, Tarbell was widely acclaimed during her lifetime by critics and readers. Her work had a profound influence on the politics of business during the early twentieth century, and her biographies of Abraham Lincoln and Napoleon were considered authoritative for several decades after their publication. Today, due to later biographies that have displaced hers in the literary canon, Tarbell is remembered almost solely for her great contribution to muckraking journalism and to American business ethics: *The History of the Standard Oil Company*.

The History of the Standard Oil Company The *History of the Standard Oil Company*, though actually written at a turning point in Tarbell's career, is generally acknowledged as her most important work. Writing just after its publication in 1904, George Alger stated: "It is impossible for us to read this story and miss its meaning. ... The enormous evil which finds graphic illustration in her book is the power which the transportation companies have been given over the accumulation and distribution of wealth in this country." Though the problem to which Alger referred had been felt by American citizens for many years, it had not been successfully articulated until the appearance of Tarbell's book.

Modern critics continue to point to the immense importance of this work. Though Mary Tomkins states in her 1974 essay that "all the other productions of [Tarbell's] variegated career are forgotten"—a statement that is no longer true— she also remarks, "The historic encounter between Ida Tarbell and the forces represented by the Standard Oil Company lives on in the public's memory ... [because] the issues she raised ... have continued to be of vital ongoing concern for the nation."

Responses to Literature

1. Since its decline in the late 1910s, muckraking has taken on a negative connotation in the world of journalism. Using your library and the Internet, research the muckraking movement, including Tarbell's involvement, and write a report to show how reporting styles have changed over time.

2. Watch the documentary *Super Size Me*, paying special attention to the qualities it shares with muckraking journalism. Discuss how Spurlock's style of reporting compares with Tarbell's in *A History of the Standard Oil Company*.

3. Based on what you have learned in this article, why do you think Tarbell might have opposed women's suffrage? Using your library and the Internet, research the women's suffrage movement in America and discuss how it does or does not fit in with Tarbell's philosophies.

4. Using Tarbell's work as a model, write a muckraking article regarding a current issue with which you are familiar. Pay special attention to the methods Tarbell uses to avoid unfairly attacking her opponents and try to incorporate the same methods into your work.

BIBLIOGRAPHY

Books

Brady, Kathleen. *Ida Tarbell: Portrait of a Muckraker.* New York: Seaview/Putnam's, 1984.

Marzolf, Marion. *Civilizing Voices: American Press Criticism, 1880–1950.* New York: Longman, 1991.

Schudson, Michael. *Discovering the News: A Social History of American Newspapers.* New York: Basic Books, 1978.

Tarbell, Ida. *All in the Day's Work.* Champaign: University of Illinois Press, 2003.

Tomkins, Mary E. *Ida M. Tarbell.* Boston: Twayne Publishers, 1974.

Periodicals

Alger, George. "Miss Tarbell's 'History of the Standard Oil Company': How the Railroad Makes the Trust." *McClure's Magazine* 24, no. 2 (Christmas 1904): 217–223.

Reitman, Janet. "The Muckraker vs. the Millionaire." *Scholastic Update,* Teachers' Edition, 131 (November 1988).

Web sites

"The Dismantling of the Standard Oil Trust." *The Linux Information Project.* Accessed November 25, 2008, from http://www.bellevuelinux.org/standardoil.html.

"People and Events: Ida Tarbell, 1857–1944." *The Rockefellers: A Family of Wealth and Power.* Accessed November 25, 2008, from http://www.pbs.org/wgbh/amex/rockefellers/index.html.

"Trusts [and] Monopolies." *1896: The Presidential Campaign.* Accessed November 25, 2008, from http://projects.vassar.edu/1896/trusts.html.

✸ Sara Teasdale

BORN: *1884, St. Louis, Missouri*

DIED: *1933, New York, New York*

NATIONALITY: *American*

GENRE: *Poetry*

MAJOR WORKS:
Love Songs (1917)
The Collected Poems (1937)

Overview

Sara Teasdale was one of the most popular poets in America from the years of World War I through the 1920s. Her new work, appearing almost monthly in the major national magazines, was read aloud before large groups, quoted and occasionally parodied in the press, and frequently set to music.

Works in Biographical and Historical Context

A Pampered Childhood Sara Teasdale was the late-arriving and youngest child of John Warren Teasdale, a

Sara Teasdale   *The Library of Congress*

prosperous St. Louis wholesaler of dried fruits and nuts, and a pious mother, Mary Elizabeth Willard Teasdale, who strove for perfect middle-class rectitude. Teasdale was sheltered, pampered, educated in private schools, and led to believe that she was frail, chronically ill, and in constant need of protective care.

At twenty she joined a group of local young women in an amateur artists' club called the Potters. For several years they published a hand-printed and illustrated magazine, the *Potter's Wheel* in which Teasdale's earliest work appeared.

In 1907 Teasdale, at the age of twenty-three, put together a collection of twenty-nine poems in a volume she titled *Sonnets to Duse and Other Poems.* Her parents gave her $290 for a printing of a thousand copies by the Poet Lore Company of Boston.

Entering a Literary Life Teasdale was ready with a second volume of poems in 1910, but she circulated the manuscript for nearly a year in both England and America before G. P. Putnam's Sons accepted it in 1911, publishing it as *Helen of Troy and Other Poems. Helen of Troy and Other Poems* is most noteworthy for a single poem, "Union Square." Teasdale had spent several weeks in New York in the early spring of 1911, attending some of the first meetings of the newly formed Poetry Society of America. Seeing the sights with two St. Louis friends, she composed a series of poems depicting imaginary love relationships in various appropriate locales in the city and added them to the manuscript of her book before it was accepted by Putnam's. In "Union Square" she yearns to express an unspoken love for a man who is unaware of it, and she envies the prostitutes who can take the initiative and ask for love shamelessly. Reviewers pounced on the poem, startled that a decent woman might harbor thoughts of sexual aggressiveness.

After 1911 and a taste of New York literary life, Teasdale was never again satisfied to remain in the Midwest. She had made many new friends, including poet and journalist Jessie Rittenhouse, who had advised her that "Union Square" was a strong poem and ought to be published. She returned eagerly to New York the next winter for the Poetry Society meetings, developing a warm friendship with Jean and Louis Untermeyer and arranging to go on a trip to Europe the following summer with Jessie Rittenhouse. But, at the age of twenty-six, she was still dependent on her parents, needing their permission for every trip away from home, unprepared to make a living for herself, and writing poem after poem filled with desperate longing for a love relationship that she believed would set her free.

A Period of Expansive Freedom

Teasdale dreaded becoming an "old maid." Following her trip to Europe in 1912, she initiated several romances and began to distance herself from the oppressiveness of her St. Louis Baptist background and gain a measure of mature self-assurance, even though St. Louis had to remain for a while her home base. The period from 1912 to 1914 was one of a rapid unfolding of her talent and her emotional life, the most voluminously productive period of her life, and probably the only period in which she was ever to feel expansive and free.

This time coincided with a national poetry renaissance. In 1912 Harriet Monroe launched *Poetry* magazine in Chicago; William Stanley Braithwaite started the *Poetry Journal* in Boston; and the Poetry Society of America adopted publicizing poetry as a cause. Critics have since designated this time as the birth date of modernism. But, the wave of energy was much broader and deeper and carried T. S. Eliot, Ezra Pound, and Wallace Stevens into being along with countless poets still writing in traditional modes.

In 1913 Teasdale met Harriet Monroe, who became another close friend and useful critic, publishing her work frequently in *Poetry*. Teasdale spent ten days in Chicago, guided by Eunice Tietjens, Monroe's assistant, into an acquaintance with Floyd Dell and the bohemian crowd. The new sexuality, which she witnessed for the first time, shocked and fascinated her. Later in the summer of 1913 Vachel Lindsay, on Harriet Monroe's suggestion, initiated a correspondence with Teasdale that led to another intimate friendship, one that lasted to his death in 1932.

Choosing a Husband

Teasdale returned to New York in the fall of 1913 with the manuscript of her third volume of poems in preparation and with the private intention of inducing John Hall Wheelock to marry her; however, Wheelock was in love with someone else and failed to respond. After nearly a year of futile effort, Teasdale weighed the alternatives: Vachel Lindsay, a penniless small-town eccentric who by now had decided he was in love with her and wanted to keep her for his permanent inspiration; and Ernst Filsinger, a St. Louis businessman introduced to her recently by Eunice Tietjens and also worshipful of her. She had them both come to New York in the summer of 1914, first Lindsay and then Filsinger, in a sort of trial of her affections and to be introduced to her friends. The competition ended predictably as Teasdale selected Filsinger—a choice of middle-class propriety and security and of a man acceptable to her parents. They were married in a private ceremony at her parents' home on December 19, 1914.

Success

Teasdale reached a pinnacle of success in the late 1910s, first with the publication of the enormously popular *Rivers to the Sea* (1915) and then with *Love Songs* (1917). In spite of these successes, Teasdale had drifted into morbid depression of the kind that would periodically afflict her with increasing intensity until her suicide in 1933.

World War I was deeply troubling to her; she felt that the nation had gone mad. She and her husband took a pacifist position during most of the war, influenced in part by his background in the liberal German community of St. Louis. At the end of the war, Ernst Filsinger began a series of lengthy business trips abroad. Over the next decade he went to Europe, South America, and the Near East. Teasdale was left alone for many months at a time, gradually becoming more reclusive and self-absorbed. With her fame secure, and her youthful romanticism waning, she became an ironic and truthful observer of her own states of mind and emotion.

A major shift in her work was under way when she published *Flame and Shadow* (1920), her fifth book in thirteen years. Most of the ninety-two new poems in the book had been written in the troubled time since 1917. Her notebooks from this period show repeated attempts to come to terms with her complex emotional disturbance. She was trying to make the best of a marriage from which she was gradually withdrawing to fight her battle with herself, the conflict between her self-determination as a woman and the grip of the forces of patriarchy.

Declining Productivity

Through the early 1920s Teasdale's productivity began to decline. She fled more and more frequently to country inns in New Jersey or New England for lengthy "rests," and Filsinger was often away on business trips. In 1921 the death of her father, with whom she had always had an adoring attachment, left her feeling depressed and vulnerable for a long time. Becoming fastidious and sensitive to an extreme and more filled than ever with indefinable ailments, she rarely went out and saw few friends. She continued to wear clothing in the styles popular before World War I. Suffering from insomnia, she spent nights working on her poems and rose late. Sometime in the early 1920s she had begun taking Veronal, a sedative, regularly.

Longer and longer gaps began to occur between her periods of creativity as she wondered whether she would ever again have enough poems for another volume. By 1926 she was able to gather fifty-nine poems for a new book, *Dark of the Moon*. Also in 1926, a young college student named Margaret Conklin wrote Teasdale a charming letter, which, contrary to her custom, she answered. On meeting, Teasdale was startled to find someone who, she felt, was herself all over again. At a time in life when she felt herself sinking under a weight of hopelessness, she revived, as if an infusion of youth could restore her to the time before everything began to go wrong. She took Margaret on a ten-week trip to England in 1927, trying to repeat the happy summer she had spent in Europe with Jessie Rittenhouse fifteen years earlier in her own youth. She told friends that Margaret was the daughter she had always wanted to have. From then until Teasdale's death, Margaret Conklin was her closest friend and afterward became her literary executor.

By 1928 Teasdale had decided to get out of her marriage, which seemed to stand in the way of her finding herself again. Instead of finding release and freedom following her divorce, Teasdale lapsed further into loneliness and inactivity, refusing to discuss her problems with her friends and writing almost nothing for two years. But in 1931, when her increasing morbidity began to frighten even herself, she turned to her despair as a subject and began to write again. Over the next two years she produced around fifteen moving and skilled lyrics, recovering her voice as she yielded to the dark side she had not been able to prevail against. Vachel Lindsay's suicide in December 1931, following a mental breakdown, shattered Teasdale's self-control, partly because she had often entertained the thought of suicide herself.

In search of a project, she had signed a contract with Macmillan in 1931 to edit and prepare an introduction for a collection of love poems by Christina Rossetti. The research seemed endless and took her to England in the summer of 1931 and again in 1932. She completed about eleven thousand words before being stricken with pneumonia in both lungs in England in August 1932. Teasdale then returned to New York, ill and severely depressed; her state of mind was alarming to her friends. She recovered enough physically to spend two weeks in Florida in early January 1933 with Jessie Rittenhouse, who urged her to seek psychiatric care. In her apartment at 1 Fifth Avenue in New York, in the early morning hours of Sunday, January 29, 1933, she took an overdose of sleeping pills and lay down in a bathtub filled with warm water. Her body was found the next morning by her nurse.

Works in Literary Context

Teasdale had a relatively brief but shining period of success. This success arose from two essential features in her work: her technical mastery of the brief lyric in simple, sometimes ironic language—she called her poems "songs"—and the fact that she typically wrote of love from a woman's point of view.

LITERARY AND HISTORICAL CONTEMPORARIES

Teasdale's famous contemporaries include:

Rainer Maria Rilke (1875–1926): Rilke was an Austrian poet widely considered one of the greatest German-language poets of the twentieth century.
Hermann Hesse (1877–1962): Hesse was a German Swiss writer whose best-known works explore the individual search for spirituality; he was awarded the 1946 Nobel Prize in Literature.
James Joyce (1882–1941): Joyce was an Irish writer who is widely considered one of the literary giants of the twentieth century, particularly because of his masterwork, *Ulysses* (1922).
Sinclair Lewis (1885–1951): Lewis was an American author who, in 1930, became the first American to win the Nobel Prize in Literature.
T.S. Eliot (1888–1965): Eliot was an American-born poet and dramatist who became a British citizen at the age of thirty-nine. He won the Nobel Prize in Literature in 1948.
Edna St. Vincent Millay (1892–1950): Millay was an American poet whose popular verses captured the rebellious mood of post–World War I youth.
E. E. Cummings (1894–1962) Cummings was one of the most popular American poets of the twentieth century; he was known for his avant-garde style and surrealism.

Probably no other figure, except Sappho, whom Teasdale revered, is so closely identified with feminine love poetry. In her later years, however, and in her best work, she extended her range in philosophical depth and self-examination.

Painfully Outgrowing Victorian Attitudes Although Teasdale thought of her poetry as continuing in a tradition of nineteenth-century women's verse, particularly that of Christina Rossetti and Elizabeth Barrett Browning, she outgrew the conventional Victorian attitudes of her early work to probe in maturity the personal conflicts she experienced as revolutionary changes swept twentieth-century society. Women were thrown to the forefront of those changes, with both greater freedom and the heavier, sometimes confusing, demands placed upon them. Teasdale's venture into independent professionalism, like those of the new female journalists and scientists, was a departure typical of a new generation. She sensed that the freedom of action she sought also had its corollary in sexual freedom; yet, she was too heavily burdened with the inhibitions and submissiveness of her Victorian middle-class upbringing to follow her more rebellious instincts. The result was a troubled ambivalence, a constant wavering between daring and guilt, desire and fear,

COMMON HUMAN EXPERIENCE

One of the major themes in Teasdale's poetry was the beauty of nature. Here are some other works with similar themes:

Elephant Rocks (1997), poems by Kay Ryan. This book of poems combines observations about quirky aspects of the natural world with meditations on the ideas inspired by nature's beauties and oddities.

Conamara Blues (2004), poems by John O'Donohue. This collection of poems focuses on the author's native region to generate a sense of intimacy with the natural world.

Why I Wake Early (2005), poems by Mary Oliver. This collection of poems about birds communicates the beauty the author finds in the world.

assertiveness and retreat, that, to paraphrase her own imagery, was an inner wound bleeding ceaselessly. Teasdale ended up not so much a heroine of the new age as much as a victim, and her later work reflects the cost exacted by disillusion in romantic love, a failed marriage, divorce, striving for professional prominence, and eventual loneliness and suicide.

Taking Sides in the Great Poetry Debates The post–World War I years were an explosive time for poetry. What began as simply a popular groundswell of interest had broken up into quarrelsome "schools," competing theories, and competing personalities. Temperamentally, Teasdale reacted with distaste to the new modernist productions of T. S. Eliot, Wallace Stevens, and James Joyce. While indifferent to, and unchallenged by, modernist experimentation, Teasdale felt a greater impact from poets in the familiar lyric tradition, particularly Robert Frost and William Butler Yeats. Frost's tough-mindedness and colloquial realism, much admired by her husband, were influential in the direction her own work took.

Two of the major controversies of the war years, free verse and imagism versus the traditional forms, engaged her briefly. Ultimately she felt that both of the new movements were essentially trivial, though she tried her hand at a few freeform pieces, concluding that formal restraints, like social conventions, produced more forceful poems. She already shared with the imagists a taste for the pictorial and for succinct, self-contained imagery.

Works in Critical Context

Fluctuating Critical Attention Teasdale was one of America's most popular poets during World War I and the 1920s. Her work appeared frequently in major national magazines and was widely anthologized. After her death in 1933, however, Teasdale's work gradually disappeared from anthologies and textbooks, and her critical reputation declined as the fortunes of modernist poets rose in the 1940s and 1950s.

Despite her decline in critical attention, Teasdale's popularity with nonacademic readers nevertheless continued. *The Collected Poems* (1937) went through more than twenty printings before being republished in paperback in 1966. With the rise of women's studies and feminist criticism in the 1970s, Teasdale's work emerged in a new light. John Hall Wheelock considered her "one of the great lyric poets of the English language." Her struggle with her identity and conventional role as a woman has emerged as an important concern in the work of recent critics. While critical estimation of her work is still being formed, there is no doubt that Teasdale's popularity with readers has remained surprisingly constant since she first came to public notice in the early decades of the century. During World War II a Liberty ship was named after her. When *Love Songs* was republished by Macmillan in 1975, 2,760 copies were sold the first year. *The Collected Poems* has remained continuously in print since 1937.

Rivers to the Sea Teasdale's third volume of poetry was as well received by critics as it was popular with readers. For Joyce Kilmer, writing in the *Bookman*, the book "is full of poetry more finely wrought than any she has written before, and, furthermore, it has the virtues of variety in form and thought, and of a wholesome and joyous inspiration." O. W. Firkins, in the *Nation*, expressed a similarly positive view. Rating Teasdale very highly among contemporary American poets, he commented, "The passion which these lyrics embody is a strong, but also an unhurried, unimpetuous, clear-sighted, and self-guiding passion.... Hence the rare combination of fervor with a high, serene discretion, a poised and steadfast art, which makes the expression of feeling in these compact poems half-ardent, half-austere." In the view of William Stanley Braithwaite, "There is in Miss Teasdale's art the purest song quality in American poetry. Her poems are brief, alluring and simple in expression. No mystery, no symbol, no inexplicable allusions, are woven into them. They are swift like swallows, with emotions; glittering and sparkling with the sunlight of love, on which an occasional shadow falls.... Love is her great theme."

Responses to Literature

1. Teasdale was a product of a strict Victorian upbringing, and in her own life, she was unable to experience the passion that she expressed in her poetry. In what ways was her poetry a form of liberation for her, and in what ways did her Victorian upbringing and values inhibit her poetry from being truly freeing?

2. Teasdale was afraid of becoming an "old maid," but she ended up making a choice that led to an unhappy marriage and eventually divorce. In what way was Teasdale's poetry after her marriage a reflection of the emotions that were spawned by her marital

problems? Would she have written the same kind of poetry if she had had a happier marriage?

3. Teasdale took a stand against modernist experimentation during the post–World War I years, and she remained outwardly committed to the familiar lyric traditions of poetry. Write an essay that analyzes the effects of modernism on Teasdale's poetry. Be sure to look at ways that she was influenced by modernist productions despite her own commitments and also to look at ways that her reaction against modernism affected her stylistic and thematic choices.

4. Teasdale's critical acclaim waned in the 1930s, when modernist poetry became more popular and critically respected, but Teasdale has remained popular throughout the ensuing decades, and critics have been reexamining her importance and impact. Choose a modernist poet from the 1930s or 1940s and write an essay comparing his or her lasting impact with Teasdale's lasting impact. Be sure to discuss which of them seems to have more relevance today.

BIBLIOGRAPHY

Books

Braithwaite, William Stanley. "The Best Poetry of 1915." *Anthology of Magazine Verse for 1915 and Year Book of American Poetry.* New York: Gomme & Marshall, 1915, pp. 223–255.

Carpenter, Margaret Haley. *Sara Teasdale, A Biography.* New York: Schulte, 1960.

Drake, William. *Sara Teasdale: Woman and Poet.* San Francisco: Harper & Row, 1979.

Rittenhouse, Jessie. *My House of Life.* Boston & New York: Houghton Mifflin, 1934.

Schoen, Carol. *Sara Teasdale.* Boston: Twayne, 1986.

Untermeyer, Jean Starr. *Private Collection.* New York: Knopf, 1965.

Walker, Cheryl. *Masks Outrageous and Austere: American Culture's Legacy to Modern Women Poets.* Bloomington: Indiana University Press, 1991.

Periodicals

Firkin. O. W. *Nation* 102, no. 2636 (January 6, 1916): 12–14.

Kilmer, Joyce. "This Autumn's Poetry." *Bookman* 42, no. 4 (December 1915): 457–462.

◉ Studs Terkel

BORN: *1912, New York, New York*

DIED: *2008, Chicago, Illinois*

NATIONALITY: *American*

GENRE: *Nonfiction*

MAJOR WORKS:

Division Street: America (1966)

Studs Terkel   *Terkel, Studs, 1992, photograph. AP Images.*

Working: People Talk about What They Do All Day and How They Feel about What They Do (1974)

"The Good War": An Oral History of World War II (1985)

Overview

One of the best-known popular chroniclers of twentieth-century American culture, Louis "Studs" Terkel is best known for his adaptation of oral history to print. His best work, *"The Good War": An Oral History of World War II*, for which he won a Pulitzer Prize in 1985, succeeded in presenting through oral history various perspectives and ideas about World War II that, despite the extensive attention that it had already received from historians and academics, had never before been seen. As an interviewer Terkel probed average Americans concerning their jobs, their dreams, their prejudices, and their memories. Today, he is largely credited with transforming oral history from a culture-specific tradition into a universal art form.

Works in Biographical and Historical Context

Poverty and Entrepreneurship Terkel was born in the Bronx borough of New York City on May 16, 1912. His parents, Samuel and Anna Terkel, were recent Jewish

LITERARY AND HISTORICAL CONTEMPORARIES

Terkel's famous contemporaries include:

Dwight Eisenhower (1890–1969): Eisenhower was the thirty-fourth president of the United States and served during the height of McCarthyism, a period of intense fear of communism during which many public figures were blacklisted for their political views.

Joseph McCarthy (1909–1957): McCarthy was a Republican senator from Wisconsin who instigated an anticommunist campaign to eradicate those with even slightly communist sympathies from public life. Those he accused, including many artists and political activists, often saw their careers compromised or ruined.

Truman Capote (1924–1984): Capote was an American writer and one of the foremost practitioners of New Journalism, a style of journalism developed by Tom Wolfe. Capote is best known for his "nonfiction novel" *In Cold Blood*, which transforms extensive interviews and research into a nonfiction narrative.

Anthony Mazzocchi (1926–2002): Mazzocchi was a well-known labor leader and organizer who was black-listed in the 1950s, founded America's Labor Party and argued for national health insurance, free college tuition, and changes in various labor laws.

Jan Myrdal (1927–): Myrdal is a Swedish political writer and journalist best known for his journalistic reports on impoverished or developing countries, such as Afghanistan.

immigrants from the Russian-Polish border, where poverty was rife and political contentions would soon turn the area into the main fighting ground of World War I. In the United States, Terkel's parents worked in the garment industry and managed to save enough for a move to Chicago in 1921. There they ran a series of rooming houses, through which they began to prosper. However, with the advent of the Great Depression in 1929, their earning power was greatly reduced.

Terkel attended the University of Chicago, graduating in 1932. At the height of the Great Depression, with few job prospects, Terkel elected to remain in school. He graduated with a JD from the University of Chicago in 1934 and, after one failed attempt, passed the bar examination. However, he never practiced law. Instead he took a number of short-term jobs, including a position with the Works Project Administration writing scripts. From this he developed an interest in acting and became involved in radio drama. It was while working as an actor during this period that he earned his nickname "Studs."

"Long Live the Blacklist" In 1945 Terkel launched a radio program called *Wax Museum*, which consisted of music and interviews with musicians. The program was successful and brought him enough acclaim that by 1950 he was hosting his own television program, "Studs' Place." Terkel had always been a vocal supporter of liberal causes, such as workers' rights and civil rights, and these political views caused NBC to cancel his show during the anticommunist Red Scare. Terkel was informed that he could redeem himself by claiming that he had been "duped" into signing liberal petitions. He refused. As a result, he was blacklisted—his name put on a list of people who were not to be hired because of their political beliefs.

Rather than blaming the anticommunists for destroying his career, however, Terkel wryly credited his blacklisting with saving him from a career of popular but banal television work. In an interview conducted several years later, Terkel cheered, "Long live the blacklist!" and stated that without it, he never would have returned to his real interest: "the little FM station playing classical music." That station, WFMT in Chicago, would provide him with a platform from which to launch the "Studs Terkel Show" in 1958—a show that he would continue to host for forty-five years.

National Recognition Building on his loyal Chicago fan base, Terkel's show was eventually nationally syndicated, earning Terkel a national reputation as a radio commentator and personality. In the 1960s, after the appearance of his first book, *Giants of Jazz* (1957), Terkel was commissioned by André Schiffrin, publisher of Pantheon Books, to write an account of the lives of ordinary Americans similar in style to Jan Myrdal's *Report from a Chinese Village*. The result, *Division Street*, the first in his series of sociological, popular history books based on his interviews with average Americans, appeared in 1967.

Division Street combined Terkel's experience as a radio interviewer with his editing and compilation skills to create what was widely considered a work of journalistic art. Consisting only of the transcripts of seventy conversations with Chicago residents from myriad backgrounds, the book was received with great acclaim by critics. Peter Lyon, writing for the *New York Times Book Review*, called the compilation "a modern morality play, a drama with as many conflicts as life itself."

Terkel garnered increasing attention for his later books, three of which focused on events significant to his own life: *Hard Times* (1970), a look at the Depression; *"The Good War": An Oral History of World War II*, for which he was awarded a Pulitzer Prize; and *Coming of Age: The Story of Our Century by Those Who've Lived It* (1995), a compilation of Terkel's conversations with around seventy men and women, ages seventy and older. These books were followed by two memoir volumes, *Touch and Go* (2007) and *P.S.: Further Thoughts from a Lifetime of Listening*, which appeared in November 2008, just after Terkel's death.

Throughout his ninety-six-year life, Terkel never seemed to slow down. He claimed in interviews that the force that drove him was curiosity. Interviewers and critics have hailed him as perpetually energetic, actively involved with the issues that, for nearly a century, profoundly touched American lives.

Works in Literary Context

Terkel used the method of interviewing to discover how average Americans feel about contemporary issues or to define historic events. He was known to travel across the country interviewing hundreds of people from all races, backgrounds, geographic locations, and classes, posing the same questions and recording their replies. He would then edit what he deemed to be the best of these replies into seamless chapter-length accounts, which he prefaced with biographical information about the source.

Though his techniques might be comparable to those of New Journalists Truman Capote and Tom Wolfe, Terkel's goal ultimately is different: He strives to present the words of Americans exactly as they are, with little or no authorial interference. It is for this reason that his work has been compared with the works of Sherwood Anderson, James Agee, Erskine Caldwell, and Edmund Wilson.

Oral History   Oral history—history that is composed of stories, poetry, or songs transmitted from speaker to listener, rather than writer to reader—has been a part of human tradition for thousands of years. Some of the earliest known oral histories are the (semi-historical) accounts of the Trojan War attributed to the Greek poet Homer, the *Iliad* and the *Odyssey*, around 900 to 800 B.C.E. Oral history thrived in America among the Native American and African cultures from 1600 onward; among the literary establishment however, it began to be considered less reliable than written accounts and fell out of favor in the late eighteenth century.

Terkel became known as the man who validated oral history among the establishment and the general public. His works, though sometimes criticized for their lack of fact checking and their reliance on fallible human memory, have been widely praised as providing perspectives on history that might otherwise never have been seen. As an oral historian he has been widely imitated over the past several decades, but he continues to be considered one of the foremost authors of the genre.

Works in Critical Context

Terkel's books have been enthusiastically received by both the public and critics. Critics praise him for continuing in the long American tradition of seeking the voice of the common person and recording it so that it might resonate for others, particularly future generations. However, some critics fault Terkel, claiming that he does not offer enough insight into the interview process and the questions he asks.

"The Good War": An Oral History of World War II   *"The Good War": An Oral History of World War II*, for which Terkel was awarded a Pulitzer Prize in 1967, was widely praised for its portrayal of World War II through the stories of myriad people who had experi-

---

COMMON HUMAN EXPERIENCE

A common theme in Terkel's work is disillusionment with the American dream. Here are some other famous works with similar themes:

The Great Gatsby (1925), a novel by F. Scott Fitzgerald. This novel, which has been considered the best American novel ever written, follows the trials of Gatsby as he embraces the American dream of financial success, yet fails to reach his goal of marrying the woman he loves.
Death of a Salesman (1949), a play by Arthur Miller. When the protagonist of this play, Willy Loman, finds he can no longer support his family, he becomes obsessed with his own interpretation of the American dream that leads to his suicide.
Fear and Loathing in Las Vegas (1972), a nonfiction book by Hunter Thompson. This book, the first example of what came to be known as gonzo journalism, expresses Thompson's disgust with the moral decay of the American dream.
Foreign Brides (1999), a collection of stories by Elena Lappin. These stories about women from around the world who leave their countries to marry American men portrays their disillusionment with the reality they find once they reach their destination.

---

enced it. Loudon Wainwright nodded to the book's lasting impact on history and the world of journalism when he wrote:

> Mr. Terkel, who in six books over the past 15 years has turned oral history into a popular art form, has captured an especially broad and impressive chorus of voices on his tape recorder this time. The result, whatever its limitations, is a portrait of a national experience drawn in the words of the men and women who lived it.

The book was not, however, an unqualified success. Many critics noted the deficiency of the interview method, pointing out that it presented the decades-old memories of hand-picked respondents as if they were fact. Jonathan Yardley, while commending Terkel for his ability to bring out "the deepest thoughts and recollections of other people", also remarked: "The chief shortcoming of *The Good War* is that the viewpoints expressed in it ... seem largely to be Terkel's own.... [T]he result is a book that, however fascinating, does not give the whole story."

Division Street: America   Terkel's first collection of interviews, *Division Street* was widely praised by critics for the skillful way in which it rendered the particular world of seventy-two Chicago residents universal. Martin Marty stated in his 1967 review: "[T]he title of this book ... refers to nothing more than Chicago and 72 of its people. In the hands of interviewer-author Terkel, however, it takes on macrocosmic dimensions and serves . . . as a comment on the Human Condition." Though some critics preferred to think of *Division Street* as simply a collection of interviews, most nevertheless agreed that Terkel, for his role as an interviewer, editor, and arranger of the work, deserved high praise.

Responses to Literature

1. Although oral history such as that practiced by Terkel has been part of human tradition for thousands of years, sometimes it is not considered to be as reliable or factual as written history. Why do you think this is? Using your library and the Internet, find two examples of published oral history and compare them to one of Terkel's works.

2. Terkel has denied in interviews the existence of objectivity, claiming "there ain't no such animal." What do you think he means by this? Using your library and the Internet, research the practice of objectivity in journalism and write a paper in which you either support or argue against Terkel's remark.

3. Read Truman Capote's *In Cold Blood*, another famous nonfiction work that relies extensively on the information gathered from interviews, and compare it to Terkel's *"The Good War": An Oral History of World War II*. What techniques does each author use to turn his interviews into a story?

4. Interview several of your classmates about an issue taking place in your school that is of interest to you. Record your conversations, and when you are finished, transcribe the interviews and arrange them, together with biographical information about each interviewee, in an order that creates a story.

BIBLIOGRAPHY

Books

Terkel, Studs. *Talking to Myself: A Memoir of My Times.* New York: Pantheon, 1977.
———. *Touch and Go: A Memoir.* New York: New Press, 2007.

Periodicals

Gewen, Barry. "Facts Are Not Enough." *New Leader* 67, no. 20 (November 12, 1984): 12–13.
Grimes, William. "Studs Terkel, Listener to Americans, Dies at 96." *New York Times*, October 31, 2008.
Marty, Martin E. "Chicago: The Divided City." *Book Week—World Journal Tribune* (January 15, 1967): 1–2.
Snowden, Audry. Review of *P.S.: Further Thoughts from a Lifetime of Listening. Library Journal* 133, no.17 (October 15, 2008): 70.

Review of *Touch and Go: A Memoir. Publishers Weekly* 254, no. 34 (August 27, 2007): 70.
Wainwright, Loudon. "'I Can Remember Every Hour.'" *New York Times Book Review* (October 7, 1984): 7, 9.
Yardley, Jonathan. "World War II: The Best Years of Their Lives." *Book World—Washington Post* (September 30, 1984): 3, 9.

Web sites

Corley, Cheryl. "Studs Terkel, Oral Historian and Radio Legend, 96." *NPR: All Things Considered*. Accessed November 30, 2008, from http://www.npr.org/templates/story/story.php?storyId=94573985.
"Studs Terkel: Conversations with America." *Chicago Historical Society*. Accessed November 30, 2008, from http://www.studsterkel.org.

⊕ Ernest Lawrence Thayer

BORN: *1863, Lawrence, Massachusetts*

DIED: *1940, Santa Barbara, California*

NATIONALITY: *American*

GENRE: *Poetry*

MAJOR WORKS:
"Casey at the Bat" (1905)

Overview

Best remembered for his lengthy comic poem "Casey at the Bat," Ernest Lawrence Thayer was also a writer for the *San Francisco Examiner*. Though most of his writing has been lost over time, "Casey at the Bat" has won a place in the American literary canon and is considered one of the best-loved American poems of all time.

Biographical and Historical Context

Working as a Humorist Born in Lawrence, Massachusetts, on August 14, 1863, Ernest Lawrence Thayer was the son of Edward Davis and Ellen Darling Thayer. His father was a moderately prosperous textiles manufacturer, and as a result of his family's prestige and his own intelligence, Thayer was admitted to Harvard University in 1881. He studied philosophy and worked on the school humor publication, the Harvard *Lampoon*. Future newspaper tycoon William Randolph Hearst worked as business manager of the publication, and the two met during their Harvard years.

After graduating from Harvard, Thayer took a tour of Europe that lasted several months. Meanwhile, his friend Hearst took over the *San Francisco Examiner*, and he offered Thayer a job writing a humor column. Thayer accepted the position, and for the next year and a half he contributed editorials, obituaries, and poems to the paper, often using the pseudonym "Phin."

A Final Contribution In the winter of 1887, Thayer's health began to fail. He returned home to rest and began working for the family business, but he continued to send a few pieces to the paper. As one of his final contributions, he composed "Casey at the Bat" in May of 1888. It appeared in the June 3 edition of the paper and received as much attention as any of the other comic ballads he had written—which is to say, almost none. Like the paper in which it was published, the poem might have been lost in time, if it had not happened to fit the theme at Wallack's Theater in New York City one night in the late 1880s: baseball.

Saved from Obscurity De Wolf Hopper, a well-known actor of the period, was to perform at Wallack's, and he wanted to do something special. A friend had read Thayer's poem in the paper and clipped it to pass on to Hopper. After some misgivings over whether he could memorize such a lengthy work, Hopper decided to do it, and in August 1888 he performed the poem at Wallack's Theater. The performance was an extraordinary success and undoubtedly saved the poem from obscurity, as did the resultant controversy over its authorship. For several years, investigations sought the author of the poem, and Thayer's authorship was not fully established and recognized until around 1910.

"Casey at the Bat" went on to be known, by the time of Thayer's death, as a masterpiece. Thayer himself thought little of the poem: in an interview for *Something about the Author* he said, "During my brief connection with the *Examiner*, I put out large quantities of nonsense.... In general quality 'Casey' (at least in my judgment) is neither better nor worse than much of the other stuff."

Perhaps this nonchalant attitude towards his writing helps explain why, despite the success eventually gained by his baseball ballad, Thayer wrote little more in his lifetime. He contributed a few poems to newspapers, which were soon forgotten. Otherwise, he focused on his family's mills until he retired in 1912. He died of a brain hemorrhage in Santa Barbara, California, on August 21, 1940.

Works in Literary Context

According to his own statement, Thayer wrote much "nonsense" in his career, and "Casey at the Bat" was intended as more of the same. The poem, however, can be considered both a ballad and a mock epic, two genres that merit greater respect than Thayer gave his own work.

Ballad "Casey at the Bat" is written in the form of a ballad, or a poem that tells a story. Its singsong rhythm renders it easily adaptable to oral performance, and indeed, the original ballads were songs. Perhaps it is for this reason that the poem only seemed to acquire half its meaning through print; the other half, which Hopper contributed in his oral performance of the work, was necessary to give the poem its full, striking effect.

LITERARY AND HISTORICAL CONTEMPORARIES

Thayer's famous contemporaries included:

William Randolph Hearst (1863–1951): Hearst was an immensely successful newspaper publisher who owned over thirty newspapers across the United States at the height of his career.

De Wolf Hopper (1858–1935): A well-known actor around the turn of the century, Hopper made Thayer's poem famous. Upon retiring, he claimed to have performed it ten thousand times throughout his career.

Mike Kelly (1857–1894): One of the first superstars of baseball, Kelly is supposed to have been the model for Thayer's mighty Casey.

Henry James (1843–1916): James was an American-born novelist best known for *The Ambassadors* (1903) and *The Turn of the Screw* (1898). James was also brother to William James, one of Thayer's best friends at Harvard.

George Santayana (1863–1952): Santayana was a Spanish poet and philosopher who worked on the Harvard *Lampoon* with Thayer and greatly praised his wit.

Other well-known ballads written in the English language include Samuel Taylor Coleridge's "Rime of the Ancient Mariner," (1798), John Keats's "La Belle Dame Sans Merci," (1819), and Oscar Wilde's *The Ballad of Reading Gaol* (1898). Thayer's work differs from these examples, however, in that it is meant to be comic, whereas the most famous English ballads are tragic.

Mock Epic A mock epic takes a relatively trivial subject, such as a baseball game, and applies to it the poetic techniques used in an epic—a long narrative poem that generally tells the story of warriors and heroes. The result is comic, at the expense both of its subject and of epic ideals.

"Casey at the Bat" belongs in this genre alongside Alexander Pope's masterpiece *The Rape of the Lock* (first version, 1712; expanded version, 1714) and Clive James's more recent *Peregrine Prykke's Pilgrimage Through The London Literary World* (1974). Some modern satires, while they do not technically belong to the genre, share similar characteristics.

Works in Critical Context

Most of Thayer's writing, which was done for newspapers and mostly, by his own account, for money, has been forgotten over the years. The merit in his one enduring work is obvious from the fact that the public has continued to enjoy it, and critics to discuss it, for more than a hundred years after he himself dismissed it as "nonsense." Today it is considered, together with such works as Mark

COMMON HUMAN EXPERIENCE

A common theme in Thayer's work is the relationship between society and the hero. Here are some other famous works with similar themes:

Don Quixote (part 1, 1605; part 2, 1615), a two-volume comic novel by Miguel Cervantes. Don Quixote, an aging gentleman, dubs himself a knight and travels across the countryside imagining a world of chivalry and enchantment out of peasants and mundane objects.

The Great Gatsby (1925), a novel by F. Scott Fitzgerald. This novel, which has been considered by some to be the best American novel ever written, demonstrates a hero's lack of attachment to his public, as Gatsby allows people to overrun his home, but is rarely present among them.

Monty Python and the Holy Grail (1975), a film directed by Terry Gilliam and Terry Jones. This British comedy lampoons the legend of King Arthur and his knights, taking Arthur through numerous obstacles posed by his often less-than-adoring subjects.

Brilliant Creatures (1983), a novel by Clive James. The protagonist of this novel, Lancelot Windhover, suffers panic attacks and depression because he is no longer considered a hero in the public eye.

Twain's novel *Huckleberry Finn* (1884), and Tennessee Williams' play *A Streetcar Named Desire* (1947), a piece of literary Americana.

"Casey at the Bat" When it appeared in the *San Francisco Examiner* in 1888, "Casey at the Bat" aroused little attention. It was not until after the poem's oral performance that the public, as well as critics, began to recognize its value. William Lyon Phelps hailed the work, stating, "The psychology of the hero and the psychology of the crowd leave nothing to be desired. There is more knowledge of human nature in this poem than in many of the works of the psychiatrist." The poem is beloved, not only because of its psychology, but also because of the story it tells and the way in which it is told. According to a New York *World* article on the day following its first performance, "The audience literally went wild. Men got up in their seats and cheered . . . it was one of the wildest scenes ever seen in a theatre."

Responses to Literature

1. Thayer often referred to his writing as "nonsense." What do you think he meant? Do you agree with his opinion? Why or why not?
2. Read *Casey at the Bat* silently to yourself. Then listen as your teacher reads the poem aloud. Discuss how the poem's impact changes when it is performed orally.
3. "Casey at the Bat" is considered a mock epic in that it mocks, or makes fun of, epic traditions such as that of the conquering hero. Watch the film *Star Wars* (1977) and discuss how its hero, Luke Skywalker, is portrayed. Is he a traditional hero or are there elements of mock epic in the film?

BIBLIOGRAPHY

Books

Moore, Jim, and Natalie Vermilyea. *Ernest Thayer's "Casey at the Bat": Background and Characters of Baseball's Most Famous Poem.* New York: McFarland and Co., 1994.

Neiman, LeRoy, and Ernest L. Thayer. *Casey at the Bat.* New York: Ecco, 2002.

Phelps, William Lyon. *What I Like in Poetry.* New York: Scribner, 1934.

Periodicals

"Casey at the Bat." *San Francisco Examiner* (June 3, 1888).

Croy, Homer. "Casey at the Bat." *Baseball* (October 1908).

Web sites

"'Casey at the Bat' by Ernest Thayer." *Baseball Almanac.* Accessed November 30, 2008, from http://www.baseball-almanac.com/poetry/po_case.shtml. Last updated in 2008.

"Ernest Lawrence Thayer and 'Casey at the Bat'." *Joslin Hall Rare Books.* Accessed November 30, 2008, from http://www.joslinhall.com/casey_at_the_bat.htm.

"From the Page to the Stage: Ernest Lawrence Thayer." *Speaking of Stories.* Accessed November 30, 2008, from http://www.speakingofstories.org/Author%20Bios/ernest_lawrence_thayer.htm.

❁ Hunter S. Thompson

BORN: *1939, Louisville, Kentucky*

DIED: *2005, Aspen, Colorado*

NATIONALITY: *American*

GENRE: *Nonfiction, fiction*

MAJOR WORKS:

Hell's Angels: A Strange and Terrible Saga (1966)

Fear and Loathing in Las Vegas: A Savage Journey to the Heart of the American Dream (1972)

Fear and Loathing on the Campaign Trail '72 (1973)

The Curse of Lono (1983)

Generation of Swine: Tales of Shame and Degradation in the '80s; Gonzo Papers, Volume Two (1988)

Hunter S. Thompson   *Thompson, Hunter S., 1990, photograph. AP Images.*

Overview

Hunter S. Thompson is one of the original and best known practitioners of New Journalism, a style of reporting that evolved in the United States in the 1960s and combines the techniques of fiction with traditional reportage. Thompson, who has called his brand of reporting "Gonzo journalism," was perhaps the most visible—and harshest—of the New Journalism writers, a group that included Tom Wolfe and Gay Talese, among others. As national affairs editor for *Rolling Stone*, freelance writer, and author of widely read books, including *Hell's Angels: A Strange and Terrible Saga* (1966), *Fear and Loathing in Las Vegas: A Savage Journey to the Heart of the American Dream* (1972), and *Fear and Loathing on the Campaign Trail '72* (1973), Thompson recorded the disillusionment and the delirium of a volatile era. He pioneered a new approach to reporting, allowing the story of covering an event to become the central story itself.

Biographical and Historical Context

Hunter S. Thompson (also known as Hunter Stockton Thompson) was born July 18, 1939, in Louisville, Kentucky, one of three sons to insurance salesman Jack R. Thompson and his wife Virginia, who would go on to struggle with alcoholism. Hunter attended public schools in Louisville, where he gained a reputation as an intelligent but unmanageable rascal. In the spring of his senior year, he was arrested for vandalism during the middle of the school day and taken to a juvenile detention center. According to friends, Thompson enjoyed the trip. Eleven days before graduation he was arrested again with two friends and charged with armed robbery. An attorney persuaded the judge to release Thompson after thirty days with the expectation that he enlist in the United States Air Force.

"Totally Unclassifiable" A week after his release from jail, Hunter Thompson arrived drunk at Randolph Air Force Base near San Antonio, Texas, for basic training. In December 1955, he was assigned to electronics school at Scott Air Force base in southern Illinois. Six months later he was sent to Eglin Air Force Base at Pensacola, Florida, where he quickly became a staff writer and sports editor for the base newspaper. He also moonlighted as a sports columnist for the *Playground News* in nearby Fort Walton Beach, writing under the byline "Thorne Stockton." A fictitious news release on Air Proving Ground Command stationery secured Thompson's early discharge in late 1958. Thompson was "totally unclassifiable," the release said, quoting an Air Force classification officer. "I almost had a stroke yesterday when I heard he was being given an honorable discharge. It's terrifying—simply terrifying."

Soon after his release from the Air Force, Thompson moved to New York City, where he landed an eighty-five-dollar-a-week job as a copyboy for *Time* magazine. There he met Sandra Dawn Conklin, a Goucher College graduate and businessman's daughter who would eventually become his wife. Unsuccessful in his bids to become a foreign correspondent for *Time*, Thompson eventually landed a job as a reporter for *El Sportivo* in San Juan, Puerto Rico. Conklin joined him in Puerto Rico, where he survived by earning extra income as a stringer for the *New York Herald Tribune* and by writing tourist brochures.

Thompson and Conklin returned to the continental United States in 1960 and were eventually lured to California's Big Sur, a long-fabled artists' and writers' colony. Thompson worked as a caretaker in exchange for the rent on a dilapidated cottage. In a July 1961 article, "Big Sur: The Tropic of Henry Miller," Thompson wrote: "This place is a real menagerie.... There are two legitimate wives on the property; the other females are either mistresses, 'companions,' or hopeless losers." The owner of the property—Bunny Murphy, grandmother of best-selling novelist Dennis Murphy—was furious and evicted him and Conklin within twenty-four hours.

Now homeless and broke, Sandy Conklin went back to New York, and Thompson retreated to live with his mother in Louisville and to continue freelancing. During the next few years, he wrote numerous articles for the *Louisville Courier-Journal*, the *Chicago Tribune*, and the *National Observer*. The last of these publications sent him to cover South America in Colombia, Ecuador, Peru, and finally, Brazil, where Conklin joined him again. When the pair returned home, Thompson was treated by the *Observer* "as a man who'd been a star." He and Conklin headed back to California, stopping in Jeffersonville, Indiana, to wed. The couple settled in San Francisco, where a social revolution was underway.

A "Great Rumbling": The Countercultural Movement in America

"There was a great rumbling—you could feel it everywhere," Thompson recalled, referring to the growing unrest that would result in the formation of a new counterculture and a nationwide social revolution during the 1960s. This revolution, which included the civil rights movement, the antiwar movement, the Free Speech Movement, and a general defiance of established authority, appealed to Thompson's rebellious nature and was a great influence on his future anti-establishment writings.

Like the revolution itself, Thompson's writings were, in large part, a reaction to what he saw as the hypocrisy and decadence of American life. As early as his high school days, and perhaps even earlier, Thompson had learned, according to a classmate, that "the people who were in the establishment, the power structure, were not all that impressive." This concept developed into a loathing of the establishment itself, societal structures and beliefs that had given rise to the American dream which, in Thompson's view, boiled down to "a license to steal."

While many adherents of the 1960s social revolution expressed themselves with sex, drugs, and rock 'n' roll, Thompson channeled his disillusionment into a revolutionary style of writing: Gonzo journalism.

Gonzo Journalism

In 1964, Thompson was commissioned by the editor of the *Nation* to write a story on Hell's Angels, a motorcycle gang accused of viciously raping two teenage girls during a Labor Day rally. The resultant article grabbed the attention of publishers, who sent letters with offers to pay Thompson to write a book. *Hell's Angels: The Strange and Terrible Saga of the Outlaw Motorcycle Gangs* was published in March 1967, selling about 40,000 copies; the paperback followed in 1968. Reviews of the book show that it broke away from familiar, objective reporting methods, and demonstrated Thompson's entry into the realm of what he would call Gonzo.

Gonzo journalism was an offshoot of a more broad-scoped journalistic movement: the New Journalism movement, of which Thompson is also considered a member. New Journalism applied certain techniques of fiction writing such as stream-of-consciousness, extended dialogue, and detailed characterization to traditional reportage. An outgrowth of the 1960s belief that everything was relative, this more objective style of reporting changed American journalism forever. As with most things, however, Thompson took New Journalism further. He experimented with more modern fiction techniques, such as stream-of-consciousness, collage, and exploded syntax, to create a style of writing that few or none have ever been able to imitate.

Hell's Angels, the first example of this kind of writing, brought the twenty-six-year-old Thompson a degree of notoriety—and a steady stream of writing offers. In 1968, *Pageant* magazine sent him to the New Hampshire primary to write about the political comeback of former vice president Richard Milhous Nixon, then a candidate for the Republican presidential nomination. In "Presenting: The Richard Nixon Doll (Overhauled 1968 Model)," published in July, Thompson called Nixon "a foul caricature of himself, a man with no soul, no inner convictions, with the integrity of a hyena and the style of a poison toad."

A Home Base in Colorado

In 1967, Thompson, Sandy, and their three-year-old son Juan moved to Aspen, Colorado, where Thompson bought a house and approximately 120 acres for $75,000. "Owl Farm" at Woody Creek, five miles northeast of Aspen, became the base for his freelance forays and retreat for the next 30 years.

Soon after settling in Aspen, Thompson was assigned a freelance article about the Kentucky Derby for *Scanlan's Monthly*. Thompson's article, "The Kentucky Derby Is Decadent and Depraved" (June 1970) unleashed his pent-up rage at the bigoted, chauvinistic, and caste-bound culture of his hometown. A few days after the story appeared, Thompson began getting phone calls and letters from around the country calling the article a journalistic breakthrough.

During the following decades, Thompson contributed over 30 articles to the fledgling *Rolling Stone* magazine, including an article investigating the 1970 death of Chicano journalist Reuben Salazar, which would ultimately lead to the Vegas getaways that inspired his hilarious and widely acclaimed masterpiece, *Fear and Loathing in Las Vegas: A Savage Journey to the Heart of the American Dream.*

Thompson's next book-length treatise of Gonzo journalism, *Fear and Loathing: On the Campaign Trail '72*, appeared only one year later and gave the writer an opportunity to vent his disgust with the establishment against the man who had been in charge of it for the past four years: President Richard Nixon. His goal of preventing Nixon's reelection was not a success, but the book was. By 1974 Thompson had gained a measure of celebrity status.

Columns and Collections Sandra Conklin Thompson and Hunter S. Thompson filed for divorce in February 1979; the divorce became final in 1981. Thompson's *The Curse of Lono* was published in 1983. The book, dedicated to Thompson's mother, Virginia Ray Thompson, sold 200,000 copies in ten years.

Over the next few years, publishers, such as William Randolph Hearst III, commissioned Thompson to write columns in an effort to boost circulation. *Generation of Swine: Tales of Shame and Degradation in the '80s* (1988) collects the columns published between December 1985 and March 1988. In many of the articles, he attacked politicians for their deception and betrayal with a parody of biblical prophecy.

Another anthology, *Songs of the Doomed: More Notes on the Death of the American Dream; Gonzo Papers, Volume Three* (1990), collected excerpts from his unpublished novels *Prince Jellyfish* and *The Rum Diary* and previously published articles interspersed with autobiographical commentaries on incidents in his career. The book concludes with a twenty-five-page section, "Welcome the Nineties: Welcome to Jail," that describes his arrest and indictment in 1990 for third-degree sexual assault and possession of controlled substances (LSD, cocaine, and marijuana) and incendiary devices (blasting caps and dynamite).

Winding Down In the 1990s, Thompson's writing career seemed to be winding down. *Better than Sex: Confessions of a Political Junkie; Gonzo Papers, Volume Four* (1993) was "his final book on politics," its dust-jacket copy stated. *Newsweek* proclaimed him "the wise old hipster" who had become "officially respected—if not quite respectable" with the publication of a Modern Library edition of his *Fear and Loathing in Las Vegas*, which ranks among the classics of the American literary canon.

Acceptance by the establishment, however, whether in publishing or politics, was never what Thompson had sought. After publishing his "long lost novel" *The Rum Diary* in 1998 and two collections in the new millennium, he took his own life at his home in Aspen, Colorado, on February 22, 2005.

LITERARY AND HISTORICAL CONTEMPORARIES

Thompson's famous contemporaries include:

William Burroughs (1914–1997): An American writer known for his semi-autobiographical accounts of his struggles with heroin addiction. His best known work, *Naked Lunch*, is a series of fantastic episodes arranged in collage form, the whole being held together by a manic and comic narrative voice that turns matters inevitably to the theme of human control.

Truman Capote (1924–1984): One of the foremost practitioners of New Journalism, a style of journalism developed by Tom Wolfe. Obsessive and eccentric, he is best known for his "nonfiction novel" *In Cold Blood*, which recounts the murders of Kansas farmer Herbert Clutter and his family in chilling detail.

Tom Wolfe (1930–): Considered one of the most original prose writers in American literature, Tom Wolfe is credited with developing New Journalism, a form of journalism that unites traditional reporting with fictional techniques such as stream-of-consciousness, shifting points of view, extended dialog, character description, and detailed scene-setting.

Richard Nixon (1913–1994): Thirty-seventh president of the United States, Nixon resigned from office in 1974 under threat of impeachment due to the Watergate scandal.

Ken Kesey (1935–2001): A major figure in the countercultural movement of the 1960s and author of *One Flew Over the Cuckoo's Nest* (1962).

Grace Slick (1939–): Lead singer of the 1960s rock band Jefferson Airplane. Jefferson Airplane's song "White Rabbit" (1967) is featured in a memorable scene in Thompson's *Fear and Loathing in Las Vegas*.

Works in Literary Context

Rising to prominence in the mid-1960s as one of the creators of New Journalism, Hunter Thompson went beyond the boundaries of the genre and developed a style of writing that he called "Gonzo journalism." He combined the techniques of both traditional and contemporary fiction with reporting techniques, exploding the conventional belief that a reporter should be neutral. Also, unlike the more mannered writings of his contemporaries Tom Wolfe and Truman Capote, Thompson's Gonzo writings rely on vituperation, or sustained and bitter condemnation, to parody current events and satirize American culture.

New Journalism While Thompson is credited with developing a style of journalism all his own, its roots belong to the New Journalism movement that arose in the United States in the 1960s. In New Journalism, much of the

COMMON HUMAN EXPERIENCE

A common theme in much of Thompson's work is that of alienation within one's own society. Here are some other famous works that explore similar ideas:

Fahrenheit 451 (1953) by Ray Bradbury. A dystopian science fiction set at an unspecified future time, this novel tells of the disillusioned "fireman," or book-burner, Guy Montag, who rebels against his society's anti-intellectualism by stealing a book. The story presents books as an antidote to apathy, passivity, and alienation.

The Old Man and the Sea (1952) by Ernest Hemingway. One of Hemingway's most famous works, this novella tells the story of an old Cuban man, Santiago's heroic struggle to bring down a marlin. Though Santiago lives in a society of fishermen, he is ostracized by his age, poverty, and bad luck and therefore, must battle the fish alone.

The Color Purple (1982), a novel by Alice Walker. Walker, one of the best known and most acclaimed African American women writers of our time, explores the position of African American women in 1930s society through the novel's protagonist Celie. Celie battles violent physical, sexual, and emotional abuse due to the social position into which she was born to become an independent businesswoman.

objectivity and impersonality of standard journalism is abandoned; the voice of the author is clearly heard, and sometimes the author even becomes a character in the article or book (as, for example, does Thompson in *Fear and Loathing in Las Vegas*). Since many authors of this style also write fictional works, they often employ numerous literary devices in their journalistic efforts, such as flashbacks and the invention of imaginary characters.

Gonzo Journalism Thompson's colleagues in New Journalism essentially revolutionized journalism by applying the literary conventions of the eighteenth century to modern reportage. The movement's founder, Tom Wolfe, believed that more modern fiction techniques had no place in journalism. Thompson disagreed. He applied innovative methods such as stream-of-consciousness, exploded syntax, and collage to create one of the most unique American prose styles ever written. Thompson's writings have been classified both as journalism and as fiction. This incongruity has created much critical controversy, and has occasionally served to discredit the authenticity of Thompson's insights. Nevertheless, most critics consider Thompson's work original and perceptive.

Works in Critical Context

Thompson is generally regarded as a highly original writer whose often-imitated style and viewpoint have earned their place in the American literary canon. His use of literary

devices usually reserved for black-humor fictions creates a result that critic John Hellman has called "journalism which reads as a savage cartoon." The word "savage" appears frequently both in Thompson's work and in critiques of it, as if the word somehow expressed the essence of Thompson himself—and no wonder, since his work dissolves the boundaries between fiction and nonfiction, biography and autobiography.

The Fear and Loathing Books His best known and probably most accomplished works, *Fear and Loathing in Las Vegas* and *Fear and Loathing on the Campaign Trail* display the techniques Thompson employed to create Gonzo journalism. To overcome the tension between his own background and that of the subjects he wishes to explore, Thompson develops a persona to serve as both narrator and protagonist. According to Hellman, "The persona is a paradox of compulsive violence and outraged innocence, an emblem of the author's schizophrenic view of America." It allows the narrator to parody America's impulses to violence and paranoia while remaining untainted by them.

While the device may have enabled Thompson to develop an entirely new perspective on American life, some critics believe that it obstructs the writer's message. It sets up an "us-versus-them" mentality that forces the reader either to accept Thompson's thesis completely or to side with the people he attacks. "The thesis of *Loathing* is that Hunter Thompson is interesting," states critic Wayne Booth in his comparison of Thompson's *Fear and Loathing on the Campaign Trail* and Theodore White's *The Making of the President*. "At his best, he can cover a lot of ground fast, and he can be both vivid and very funny. . . . At his worst, Thompson reads like a bad parody of himself."

Responses to Literature

1. Why do you think a person might feel alienated in his or her society? How can alienation affect a person, and what are some ways in which he or she might react to it? Using your library and the Internet, find two or three more examples of alienated figures, either in real life or in literature, and discuss how the sense of alienation affects their lives.

2. Americans love a rebel. Yet some forms of rebellion are more appreciated than others. Why do you think some rebels are eventually accepted by mainstream society? What effect does this have on their rebellion? Using your library and the Internet, research a few examples of rebels in literature. Discuss how they express their rebellion, paying attention to the parallels between their actions and those of rebels with whom you are familiar in popular culture.

3. Watch the film version of *Fear and Loathing in Las Vegas*. How does Thompson's unique style emerge in the film? What parallels do you see between the

protagonist in the film and Hunter Thompson the man? In what ways do his major themes emerge?

4. Thompson wrote extensively on President Richard Nixon, calling him "a man with no soul, no inner convictions, with the integrity of a hyena." Find out more about President Nixon by reading *The Final Days* (1976) by Bob Woodward and Carl Bernstein, an account of the months leading up to Nixon's resignation. Both authors worked to expose the Watergate scandal and have a unique, insider's perspective on the dramatic events surrounding Nixon's last days.

5. Write a paper in which you compare one of Hunter Thompson's novels to one of Truman Capote's (for example, compare Capote's *In Cold Blood*, 1966, to Thompson's *Hell's Angels*). What part does the narrator play in each of their works? What stylistic differences do you see? In what ways do they change your reading of the stories?

BIBLIOGRAPHY

Periodicals

Klein, Joe. "Forever Weird." *The New York Times*, November 18, 2007.

Web Sites

"New Journalism." *DISCovering Authors*. Online ed. Detroit: Gale, 2003. *Discovering Collection*. Gale. K12 Trial Site. Retrieved Nov. 8, 2008 from http://galegroup.com

"Overview of Hunter S(tockton) Thompson." *DISCovering Authors*. Online ed. Detroit: Gale, 2003. *Discovering Collection*. Gale. K12 Trial Site. Retrieved Nov. 6, 2008 from http://galegroup.com

"Thompson, Hunter S(tockton) (1939-)." *DISCovering Authors*. Online ed. Detroit: Gale, 2003. *Discovering Collection*. Gale. K12 Trial Site. Retrieved Nov. 6, 2008 from http://find.galegroup.com/

Booth, Wayne C. "Loathing and Ignorance on the Campaign Trail: 1972." *DISCovering Authors*. Online ed. Detroit: Gale, 2003. *Discovering Collection*. Gale. K12 Trial Site. Retrieved Nov. 6, 2008 from http://galegroup.com

Hellman, John. "Journalism and Parody: The Bestial Comedies of Hunter S. Thompson." *DISCovering Authors*. Online ed. Detroit: Gale, 2003. *Discovering Collection*. Gale. K12 Trial Site. Retrieved Nov. 6, 2008 from http://galegroup.com

Hicks, Jack. "William S. Burroughs." *DISCovering Authors*. Online ed. Detroit: Gale, 2003. *Discovering Collection*. Gale. K12 Trial Site. Retrieved Nov. 6, 2008 from http://galegroup.com

Klinkowitz, Jerome. "Hunter S. Thompson." *DISCovering Authors*. Online ed. Detroit: Gale, 2003. *Discovering Collection*. Gale. K12 Trial Site. Retrieved November 6, 2008, from http://galegroup.com

⊛ Henry David Thoreau

BORN: *1817, Concord, Massachusetts*

DIED: *1862, Concord, Massachusetts*

NATIONALITY: *American*

GENRE: *Nonfiction*

MAJOR WORKS:

"Civil Disobedience" (1849)

Walden, or a Life in the Woods (1854)

Overview

Henry David Thoreau is one of the key figures of the American Transcendentalist movement. His works embody the tenets of American Transcendentalism as articulated by Ralph Waldo Emerson and others. His aphoristic, yet lyrical, prose style and intense moral and political convictions have secured his place beside Emerson as the most representative and influential of the New England Transcendentalists. He is considered, along with such figures as Emerson, Nathaniel Hawthorne, and Herman Melville, as a major nineteenth-century American author.

Henry David Thoreau   *Thoreau, Henry, David, 1856, photograph. Hulton Archive / Getty Images.*

LITERARY AND HISTORICAL CONTEMPORARIES

Thoreau's famous contemporaries include:

Margaret Fuller (1810–1850): Fuller was an American journalist and women's rights activist whose book, *Women in the Nineteenth Century* (1845), was one of the first feminist works written in the United States.

P. T. Barnum (1810–1891): Barnum was an American showman and entrepreneur who founded a circus that he called the "Greatest Show on Earth."

Edgar Allan Poe (1809–1849): Poe was an American writer best known for his macabre poems and short stories.

Karl Marx (1818–1883): Marx was a German philosopher and social critic who was one of the founders of the modern Communist movement.

Herman Melville (1819–1891): Melville was an American novelist best known for his metaphysical whaling novel, *Moby-Dick* (1851), which is widely considered one of the best American novels of all time.

Fyodor Dostoyevski (1821–1881): Dostoyevski was a Russian writer whose novels explored human psychology and universal philosophical questions.

Works in Biographical and Historical Context

Thoreau was born in Concord, Massachusetts, on July 12, 1817. He grew up in an atmosphere of genteel poverty. Although his father, a businessman with a history of failure, ultimately succeeded in pencil manufacturing, Thoreau's mother kept a boarding house to supplement the family's income. The only child in the family to receive a college education, Thoreau graduated in 1837 from Harvard, where he became interested in natural history, religious studies, the classics, and English, French, and German literature.

Two important influences at Harvard were the famous naturalist, Louis Agassiz, and the rhetorics professor, Edward Tyrrel Channing. Following his commencement, Thoreau taught at the Concord Academy but was soon dismissed because of his opposition to corporal punishment. He and his brother, John, founded their own school in 1838, and became renowned for utilizing the progressive educational methods of the American Transcendentalist Amos Bronson Alcott.

Living with Emerson   Thoreau aspired to be a poet, and when Ralph Waldo Emerson invited him in 1841 to live with him and his family in Concord, where he could write and earn his keep by acting as a general handyman, he accepted. The Concord community, already scandalized by Thoreau's unconventional way of life, ridiculed his lack of ambition and material success. However, Thoreau flourished with Emerson as his mentor. He kept an extensive journal and became an avid reader of Hindu scripture. He had ample time after his chores to write and think, and in Emerson's home he met many of the greatest figures of American Transcendentalism, including Sarah Margaret Fuller and George Ripley.

Emerson and Fuller had recently founded a journal, the *Dial*, as the literary organ of the New England Transcendentalists, and there they published Thoreau's first efforts in prose and poetry. Thoreau also worked as an assistant on the *Dial* and regularly lectured at the Concord Lyceum during this period. He briefly lived in New York during 1843 and 1844 as a tutor to Emerson's brother's children. When he returned to Concord, he supported himself by working as a surveyor, managing his father's pencil factory, and securing odd jobs around town. Thoreau and Emerson had grown distant due to differences of opinion and temperament and were no longer on close terms.

Walden and Political Activism   On July 4, 1845, Thoreau moved to Walden Pond, located on Emerson's property, where he remained for almost two years. Though he was actually near Concord and had many visitors daily, Thoreau was regarded as a hermit, mystic, and eccentric, an image that was enhanced by a night he spent in jail in Concord in 1846. Thoreau was incarcerated for refusing to pay taxes to the commonwealth of Massachusetts because of its endorsements of slavery and the Mexican War; Thoreau was morally opposed to both. In his later political essays, he explored the individual's right to dissent from a government's policies in accordance with his or her own conscience and also treated the issue of slavery.

Thoreau was an active abolitionist in his later years, and he lectured widely and publicly spoke against the Fugitive Slave Law of 1850. In keeping with his interest in naturalism, much of his writing and lecturing in the 1850s also concerned the conservation of natural resources. In 1854, he published *Walden, or a Life in the Woods*, an account of his two years living at Walden Pond.

Thoreau had suffered from poor health most of his life and was stricken in 1860 with tuberculosis, from which he never recovered. Thoreau died in 1862, in Concord, Massachusetts. Although he was considered cold, misanthropic, and disagreeable by some, he was much respected and admired by his circle of friends.

Works in Literary Context

Thoreau's writings can be generally divided into two groups—travel essays and political essays. His travel narratives—most of which were published after his death—combine perceptive observations about flora and fauna with Thoreau's philosophical musings. The political essays—"Resistance to Civil Government," later published as "Civil Disobedience," "Slavery in Massachusetts," "A Plea for Captain John

Brown," and "Life without Principle"—are impassioned rhetorical essays laying out Thoreau's fundamental beliefs; these were written in response to important political issues of the time, but they are widely regarded as universal statements about individual choice and responsibility. Thoreau's poems, mostly celebrations of nature, are most often considered banal, whereas his prose is usually seen by critics to be especially poetic. His *Journal*, because of its completeness and intensity, is sometimes named as his greatest literary achievement.

A Transcendental Philosopher   Though not a professional philosopher, Thoreau is recognized as an important contributor to the American literary and philosophical movement known as New England Transcendentalism. His essays, books, and poems weave together two central themes over the course of his intellectual career: nature and the conduct of life. In his moral and political work, Thoreau aligned himself with the post-Socratic schools of Greek philosophy—in particular, the Cynics and Stoics—that used philosophy as a means of addressing ordinary human experience.

Thoreau's importance as a philosophical writer was little appreciated during his lifetime, but his *Walden, or a Life in the Woods* and "Civil Disobedience" gradually developed a following and by the latter half of the twentieth century had become classic texts in American thought. "Civil Disobedience," which works out Thoreau's conception of the self-reliant individual's relationship to the state and suggests that one can resist a government without resorting to violence, has influenced such diverse writers and leaders as Leo Tolstoy, Martin Luther King, Jr., Jack Kerouac, Mohandas Gandhi, and Allen Ginsberg. *Walden, or a Life in the Woods*, the work of a man who spent almost his entire life in his native town of Concord, has been translated into virtually every modern language and is today known all over the world.

Not only have these texts been used widely to address issues in political philosophy, moral theory, and, more recently, environmentalism, but they have also been of central importance to those who see philosophy as an engagement with ordinary experience and not as an abstract deductive exercise. In this vein, Thoreau's work has been recognized as having foreshadowed central insights of later philosophical movements such as existentialism and pragmatism.

Nature and Self-Sufficiency   Thoreau's naturalistic writing integrated straightforward observation and cataloguing with Transcendentalist interpretations of nature and the wilderness. In many of his works, Thoreau brought these interpretations of nature to bear on how people live or ought to live. In *Walden, or a Life in the Woods*, Thoreau makes a record of two years that he spent living alone in the woods near Concord, Massachusetts. Part autobiography, part fiction, part social criticism, *Walden, or a Life in the Woods* advocates a simple, self-sufficient way of life in order to free the individual from

COMMON HUMAN EXPERIENCE

Thoreau's philosophy of life centers around the idea of retreating from civilization for the purposes of contemplation. Here are some other works that promote a similar philosophy:

"Self-Reliance" (1841), an essay by Ralph Waldo Emerson. In this essay, Emerson argues that individuals must avoid conformity and follow their own instincts and ideas, even if this takes them away from so-called civilized norms.

Desolation Angels (1965), a novel by Jack Kerouac. This semi-autobiographical novel covers the author's life during, and just after, the period when he was a solitary fire lookout in the remote mountains of Washington State.

Into the Wild (1996), a book by Jon Krakauer. This book tells the story of a young man who goes alone into Alaska's wilderness to pursue an ascetic lifestyle.

A Book of Silence (2008), by Sara Maitland. This book, which tells of the author's experience spending periods of silence in the Sinai desert, the Australian bush, and a remote cottage on the Isle of Skye, combines memoir with history, mythology, psychoanalysis, and discussions of philosophy and religion.

self-imposed social and financial obligations. Thoreau pleads for a more intimate relationship between human beings and nature as an antidote to the deadening influence of an increasingly industrialized society.

Toward the end of his life, Thoreau's naturalistic interests took a more scientific turn; he pursued a close examination of local fauna and kept detailed records of his observations. Nevertheless, he kept one eye on the moral and political developments of his time, often expressing his positions with rhetorical fire as in his "A Plea for Captain John Brown" (1860). He achieved an elegant integration of his naturalism and his moral interests in several late essays that were published posthumously, among them "Walking" and "Wild Apples" (both in 1862).

Works in Critical Context

During the nineteenth century, Thoreau was generally considered an obscure, second-rate imitator of Emerson. Though Thoreau was not well known during his lifetime outside the circle of New England Transcendentalists, his reputation has gradually grown. Assessment of his literary merits was long hampered by James Russell Lowell's disparagement of his early work. An extremely influential critic, Lowell accused Thoreau of being an imitator of Emerson and attacked what he saw as his egocentrism and lack of humor. Robert Louis Stevenson deemed

Thoreau a "prig," a "skulker," and an idler, but he valued his "singularly eccentric and independent mind." Ironically, Emerson's funeral elegy on Thoreau served to reinforce the image of Thoreau as a cold, reclusive man. Thoreau's admirers, however, came to his defense: John Burroughs praised his dedication as a naturalist and Amos Bronson Alcott and Ellery Channing offered testimonials to his personal warmth and charm.

There had been a Thoreau critical revival at the hundredth anniversary of his birth, but Thoreau's critical reputation did not really blossom until the 1930s when the depressed American economy imposed a radically frugal, Thoreauvian lifestyle on many people. At that time, Thoreau's ideas about individual freedom and responsibility stood out in stark relief against the growing threat of fascism. In the 1940s, encouraged by F. O. Matthiessen's landmark study of sense imagery in *Walden, or a Life in the Woods*, scholars turned their attention to more particular matters of Thoreau's style and diction. Critics now almost universally admire Thoreau's prose style for its directness, pithiness, and variety. Though Lowell termed his poetry "worsification," modern critics praise Thoreau's vivid use of imagery and irregular rhythms and suggest that his poetry anticipated the experimental verse of the twentieth century. Many of the most recent studies of Thoreau, aided by closer examination of his journals and letters, are psychological in approach. There is now no dispute that Thoreau ranks as one of the greatest figures in American literature.

Walden, or a Life in the Woods *Walden, or a Life in the Woods*, regarded by most critics as Thoreau's masterpiece, comprises a group of loosely connected essays that are organized in a seasonal sequence so that the narrative concludes in spring, a time of spiritual as well as natural rebirth. Thoreau telescoped his two years' experience at Walden Pond into the span of one year in order to fit his essays into his chosen time frame. Contemporary critics who had greeted his earlier work with mixed reviews reacted to *Walden, or a Life in the Woods* with measured praise and also some cries of "humbug." Modern critics especially praise his playful, witty prose style in *Walden, or a Life in the Woods*, as well as the sense of humor manifested in his use of paradox, puns, and satire. Critics also appreciate the philosophic depth of *Walden, or a Life in the Woods*. As Perry Miller puts it, the book "tells us of some Eden of the soul in which at least one American held off the pressures of materiality and mediocrity. The more harrassing these confinements became … the more Thoreau's report takes on qualities of a symbolic eternity."

Responses to Literature

1. Commentators have admired Thoreau for both his moral and political ideas as well as his poetic prose style. In what ways are his ideas and style connected? Would Thoreau's ideas have been as influential if he had employed a more traditional philosophical style? Did his poetic prose style have an influence on the kinds of moral and political ideas he expressed in his writing?

2. During his lifetime, Thoreau was not much respected as a philosopher in his own right; commentators at the time saw him as essentially an eloquent adherent to Ralph Waldo Emerson's philosophies. In what ways was Thoreau merely an advocate of Emerson's ideas, and in what ways did Thoreau extend and change Emerson's ideas? Which of the two seems like the more relevant philosopher today?

3. Thoreau's "Civil Disobedience" was an argument about his decision to avoid paying taxes to support a government committed to what he thought was an unjust position—the Mexican-American War and the extension of slavery. Write your own essay arguing your opinion on the legitimacy of avoiding paying taxes to the government today if that government were supporting something that you opposed.

4. Thoreau has been credited with influencing a number of important literary and political figures, from Leo Tolstoy and Mohandas Gandi to Allen Ginsberg, Jack Kerouac, and Martin Luther King, Jr. Choose a writer or political activist who was influenced by Thoreau, and write an essay that traces these influences to specific works of Thoreau's.

5. Thoreau's *Walden, or a Life in the Woods* argues for people living a simple, self-sufficient life, free from self-imposed social and financial obligations. Write an argumentative essay that either supports or opposes Thoreau's position.

BIBLIOGRAPHY

Books

Adams, Stephen, and Donald Ross Jr. *Revising Mythologies: The Composition of Thoreau's Major Works.* Charlottesville: University Press of Virginia, 1988.

Atkinson, Brooks. *Henry Thoreau: The Cosmic Yankee.* New York: Knopf, 1927.

Borst, Raymond R. *The Thoreau Log: A Documentary Life of Henry David Thoreau, 1817–1862.* New York: Macmillan, 1992.

Buell, Lawrence. *The Environmental Imagination: Thoreau, Nature Writing, and the Formation of American Culture.* Cambridge, Mass.: Harvard University Press, 1995.

Cain, William, ed. *The Oxford Guide to Henry David Thoreau.* Oxford: Oxford University Press, 2000.

Emerson, Edward. *Henry Thoreau as Remembered by a Young Friend.* Boston: Houghton Mifflin, 1917.

Harding, Walter. *The Days of Henry David Thoreau.* New York: Knopf, 1965.

Lebeaux, Richard. *Thoreau's Seasons.* Amherst: University of Massachusetts Press, 1984.

McGregor, Robert Kuhn. *A Wider View of the Universe: Henry Thoreau's Study of Nature*. Urbana: University of Illinois Press, 1997.

Meltzer, Milton and Walter Harding. *A Thoreau Profile*. New York: Crowell, 1962.

Miller, Perry. "Afterword." *Walden or Life in the Woods* and "On the Duty of Civil Disobedience" by Henry David Thoreau. New York: New American Library, 1980.

Richardson, Robert D., Jr. *Henry Thoreau: A Life of the Mind*. Berkeley: University of California Press, 1986.

Salt, Henry S. *The Life of Henry David Thoreau*. London: Bentley, 1890.

Sanborn, Franklin Benjamin. *The Life of Henry David Thoreau*. Boston: Houghton Mifflin, 1917.

Scharnhorst, Gary. *Henry David Thoreau: A Case Study in Canonization*. Columbia, S.C.: Camden House, 1993.

✸ James Thurber

BORN: *1894, Columbus, Ohio*

DIED: *1961, New York, New York*

NATIONALITY: *American*

GENRE: *Fiction, nonfiction, drama*

MAJOR WORKS:

Is Sex Necessary? (with E.B. White) (1929)

My Life and Hard Times (1933)

My World—and Welcome to It (1942)

Many Moons (1943)

The Wonderful O (1957)

James Thurber   *Thurber, James, 1954, photograph by Fred Palumbo. NYWTS / The Library of Congress.*

Overview

Though an Ohioan at heart, James Grover Thurber made his name as one of the earliest contributors to *The New Yorker* magazine. Hired by founder Harold Ross in 1927, Thurber wrote humor and satirical pieces, and created cartoons that became one of the magazine's best-known features. He straddled several genres during his three-decade career, dipping joyfully into autobiography, fable writing, children's literature, acting, and playwriting. Thurber was also a prolific correspondent; his witty and warm letters for family and famous friends—E.B. White and Dorothy Parker among them—have been anthologized in several volumes. Thurber's most famous creation is the dreamy, eponymous hero of the short story, "The Secret Life of Walter Mitty," first published in *The New Yorker* in 1939. An increasingly prominent theme in his later writing was a deep concern for language and usage.

Works in Biographical and Historical Context

A Midwestern Beginning   Born in Columbus, Ohio, on December 8, 1894, James Grover Thurber was Charles and Mary Fisher Thurber's second son. Charles Thurber

had hoped to be an actor or a lawyer, but instead he spent his life in various politically appointed positions, forever miscast and ill at ease. Mame, as Mary Thurber was nicknamed, was from an influential Ohio family, and she ordered the lives of those around her. Thurber recalled her as a gifted and fearless comedienne and prankster. Both parents would serve as prototypes for their son's famous gender archetypes—the models he would use to create his distinct characters.

In the summer of 1901, the three Thurber boys were playing "William Tell"—a game mimicking the legendary Swiss hero known for expertly shooting an arrow straight through an apple perched atop his son's head. Tragically, eldest brother William missed, and pierced one of James's eyes. There was considerable delay in removing the damaged eye, a circumstance that probably led to Thurber's total blindness by 1951, and the long series of operations and illnesses that accompanied that decline.

Early on, affected but not devastated by his injury, Thurber began his writing career by working on the high-school newspaper. After entering Ohio State University in 1913, he worked on the university's literary and humor magazines. His writing was influenced by the popular culture of his day, which included comic strips, movies, and dime novels. He also enjoyed the work of short-story master O. Henry. In college he read the works of Willa Cather, Joseph Conrad, and a new favorite and lifelong influence, Henry James. He also befriended Elliott Nugent, with whom he would later coauthor the popular Broadway play *The Male Animal* (1940).

An International Reporter In 1917, the United States entered World War I, which had raged across Europe since 1914. Thurber was eager to join the military, but his damaged eyesight barred him from service. Instead, from November 1918 until March 1920, Thurber served as a code clerk for the State Department in Paris. His letters of the period to Nugent reveal Thurber as a Midwestern innocent, both enticed and offended by provocative postwar Paris. He returned to Ohio in the spring of 1920 and reported for the *Columbus Evening Dispatch*. In 1922 he married Althea Adams by most accounts, an attractive and strong-willed woman.

After a stint in New York City, and another in Ohio, the Thurbers headed back to France, and arrived in Normandy in 1925. Thurber worked on a novel, later jettisoned, before they relocated to the French capital, where he was hired at the *Paris Tribune*. It was there he began to display his particular writing genius.

Thurber transformed the skeletal details of sporting events and political speeches into epic stories—a flirtation with fabulist tendencies that would define his writing style over the course of his career. The most significant of his freelance publications at this time was the short story "A Sock on the Jaw—French Style," published in 1926. It humorously contrasts French and American modes of disagreement and celebrates the elaborate chaos resulting from the French method. Notably, Thurber did not socialize with local expatriates Ernest Hemingway, F. Scott Fitzgerald, or Gertrude Stein, who also lived in Paris at the time, though he knew their work. By 1931, he still regarded himself an amateur writer, and so departed for New York to make a serious effort at professional writing.

A Niche at The New Yorker After showering him with rejection slips, the fledgling magazine *The New Yorker* finally accepted three of Thurber's pieces. In February 1927 Harold Ross hired Thurber as an editor, but he was much better suited to his next title—staff writer. Thurber's office mate at the magazine was writer E. B. White, who greatly influenced Thurber's prose style and enthusiastically promoted his drawings. At White's insistence, Thurber's illustrations appeared in their coauthored satirical book, *Is Sex Necessary?* (1929). The book was a humorous reaction to the growing popularity of and popular misconceptions concerning psychologist Sigmund Freud, credited with being the father of modern psychoanalysis. Freud was particularly renowned for his theories regarding sex, development, and gender identity.

Thurber became one of the most prolific and best known of *The New Yorker* writers. He embraced what has come to be called the "New Yorker style," which features correct, clean, urbane, and witty prose. As an editor he helped impose this style on other contributors—writers and cartoonists alike.

Thurber was encouraged to write humor about the line of tension where order and chaos meet. Writing in these early years, he established several of his most important subjects. One was the perpetual battle between dominant, unimaginative women and neurotic, fantasy-embracing men. Another was the constant conflict between man and machinery. He also focused on the general superiority, in character and good sense, of animals over humans, and the bewildering but liberating powers of chaos, idiosyncrasy, and imagination. Thurber's classic and oft-anthologized short story "The Secret Life of Walter Mitty" (first published in *The New Yorker* in 1939) featured perhaps the best example of the dreamy "Thurber man," while the shrewish and domineering wife in "The Unicorn in the Garden" typifies the "Thurber woman."

Thurber resigned from his staff position at *The New Yorker* on the heels of his divorce from Althea in 1935 (they had one child, Rosemary, born in 1931). He then married a former magazine editor, Helen Wismer, (whom he later labeled his "seeing eye wife.") just one month later. Thurber remained a regular contributor to *The New Yorker* for many years, and always maintained a fondness for the magazine. The relationship between Thurber and the magazine is best summarized by the author's contention, stated in a letter to Ross: "*The New Yorker* is the only magazine for which a man can write with dignity and tranquility."

After his departure, Thurber once again found himself in France. It was 1937, and he and Althea enjoyed good social contact with Hemingway, Dorothy Parker, and Lillian Hellman, among others. Much of the conversation of those gatherings focused on the Spanish Civil War, in which many American writers and artists had become actively involved on the Loyalist side. Thurber, however, opposed his friends' political fervor, arguing that writers should simply write and not allow themselves to be caught up in war and factionalism. His views on this seem to have changed in later years, as his fables became starker, gloomier, and more pointedly in opposition to the disturbing events and such figures as Adolf Hitler, who led Nazi Germany into World War II, and U.S. Senator Joseph McCarthy, who accused thousands of Americans of being Communist sympathizers in the 1950s.

Fables and Fairytales as Blindness Descends Thurber's increasing interest in fables and fairytales (of which he eventually produced seven volumes), began with the onset of his blindness, as did the increased emphasis upon word-game comedy and conversation pieces. Thurber once explained his attraction to fables in the following way: "Every writer is fascinated by the fable form; it's short, concise, and can say a great deal about human life." Among Thurber's fables is an updated version of "Little Red Riding Hood," in which Little Red, rather than be fooled by the wolf's disguise, "took an automatic pistol out of her basket and shot the wolf dead."

By the time he became effectively blind, his famously savant-like memory was so accurate that he could compose a two-thousand-word story in his mind at night and then edit it as he dictated it next morning. Thurber's outlook during this period became darker and more cynical. Only *The Years With Ross* (1959) and the montage play, *A Thurber Carnival* (1960)—both of which drew upon earlier experiences and materials—broke the pattern of ever-increasing pessimism that characterized the works of Thurber's later period, such as *Further Fables for Our Time* (1956) and *Lanterns and Lances* (1961). In these bitter volumes, chaos—whether social, political, cultural, or linguistic—is neither funny nor liberating, as it once seemed to Thurber, but is instead the mark of a terrible decline in the modern world. Thurber, too, would suffer a swift and terrible decline. After attending a party for actor and playwright Noel Coward in October of 1961, Thurber endured a massive stroke that kept him hospitalized in a state of semiconsciousness until November 2, 1961, when he died of pneumonia.

Works in Literary Context

Semi-Autobiography   Thurber was a master at mining his own life for humorous material, starting, naturally, with his childhood and family—a wickedly funny mother, a middle-America setting. David Sedaris, with his witty and humorous autobiographical essays and *The New Yorker* connection, is among those in debt to Thurber's signature blend of fact and fiction. The radio storyteller Garrison Keillor, himself an editor of a Thurber anthology, and famous for his tales of Lake Woebegone on *A Prairie Home Companion*, makes similar use of his experiences.

Fantasy   It is often said that the fantasy genre must be as accommodatingly immense as the imaginations of the writers whose work comprises it. Though Thurber's style of fantasy, which became more and more prevalent as his eyesight deteriorated, wasn't reminiscent of the genre's standard-bearers like J. R. R. Tolkien and C.S. Lewis, he shared with those writers the idea of the noble quest. His heroes were men of imagination, shapers who ordered the meaningless jumble and made sense out of them. These fantasists succeed where more practical men—represented by mathematicians, physicians, lawyers, and experts of every type—fail. In fact, the playful yet biting modern fiction of both George Saunders and Kurt Vonnegut owes a debt to Thurber's fantasy-tinged humor and satire pieces.

Works in Critical Context

The Secret Life of Walter Mitty   This story is unquestionably Thurber's most famous; published first in March of 1939 in the *New Yorker* and later collected in *My World—and Welcome to It*, the story has been frequently reprinted and anthologized. In addition to being renown, Mitty is a truly beloved character, one to whom many can relate. There isn't anyone who hasn't been wrenched out of a

dream—asleep or awake—and not experienced the acute longing to return to the comfort of sleep or the quiet of one's own thoughts. He is a hero who does not prevail, yet finds joy and solace within himself, just as everyone must do.

Carl Linder, writing in the *Georgia Review*, writes "As a result of being perpetually interrupted at crucial moments in these fantasies, it seems only proper that Mitty's final role should be that of the condemned man about to be executed by a faceless firing squad for reasons not explicitly given. This vision is a marvelously telling projection of Mitty's place in the world as he feels it."

The Thurber Carnival   The publication in 1945 of *The Thurber Carnival*, a collection of past hits and new material, was proof that Thurber had arrived as an important figure in American letters. The critical reception was extravagant and wide, and for the first time a Thurber book found a truly mass audience, and set the stage for all that would follow.

Between 1939 and 1957, Thurber wrote one self-illustrated parable, two collections of fables, and five fairytales. What critics observe most frequently about these works is, as Richard Tobias remarked, that "although the stories seem to be written for children, they are more rich for an adult mind that catches and enjoys the outrageous tricks played in them upon experience and time."

COMMON HUMAN EXPERIENCE

Like Walter Mitty, some of Thurber's most memorable characters are individuals with a penchant for the fantastic, though they may be mired in the mundane. Here is a selection of works that feature individuals using their imaginations to escape or cope with an unsatisfying reality:

> *Don Quixote* (1605), a novel by Miguel de Cervantes. One of the most celebrated works of literature in history, *Don Quixote* tells the story of a gentleman so infatuated with the exaggerated tales of chivalry in books that he decides to reinvent himself and the pedestrian world around him in the name of honor and adventure.
>
> *Alice's Adventures in Wonderland* (1865), a novel by Lewis Carroll. A mainstay of both children's literature and cherished adult works, *Alice's Adventures in Wonderland* is a celebration of the extraordinary—and possibly dangerous—powers of imagination, and an endorsement for the willful disregard of rote tasks.
>
> *Who's Afraid of Virginia Woolf?* (1962), originally a play by Edward Albee, later turned into a film released in 1966. The story follows two highly dysfunctional couples over the course of one drunken evening. The hosts, George and Martha, rely on a fragile domestic fantasy they have concocted to sustain their relationship. When that fantasy begins to unravel, it sets into motion a series of increasingly cruel mind games.

Responses to Literature

1. An artist's physical impairment can have an enormous impact on the work he produces. James Thurber pushed further into fantasy as his eyesight deteriorated. Using your library and the Internet, research artists who have either overcome or succumbed to their debilitations or addictions, and analyze how these obstacles affected the art they created.

2. Thurber flourished in an age that predated the onslaught of television and the Internet. Write a paper in which you imagine how Thurber's humor would be received if he were just beginning to write and submit for publication today. Would it be easier or more difficult for him to find readers? In your opinion, what are the criteria an artist must meet if their work is to stand the test of time?

3. Write a paper in which you compare Thurber's *New Yorker* cartoons to the contemporary cartoons featured in the magazine today. What are the major similarities and differences between Thurber and modern artists such as Roz Chast?

What do you believe are the key elements to achieving humor in an art form like a *New Yorker* cartoon?

BIBLIOGRAPHY

Books

Bernstein, Burton. *Thurber*. New York: Dodd, Mead, and Company, 1975.

Black, Steven A. *James Thurber: His Masquerades*. The Hague: Mouton, 1970.

Holmes, Charles S., ed. *Thurber: A Collection of Critical Essays*. Englewood Cliffs, N.J.: Prentice-Hall, 1974.

Tobias, Richard C. *The Art of James Thurber*. Athens: Ohio University Press, 1969.

White, E.B. *The Letters of E.B. White: Revised Edition*. New York: HarperCollins, 2006.

Periodicals

Gottlieb, Robert. "The Years with Thurber." *The New Yorker* (September 8, 2003).

Maslin, Janet. A Mailbag of Thurber, From Fond to Scathing, *The New York Times* (July 31, 2003).

Lindner, C. "Thurber's Walter Mitty: The Underground American Hero." *Georgia Review Review* (2001): Summer, 1974, p. 283–289.

Web Sites

Wilhelm Tell Festival-New Glarus Wisconsin. Retrieved November 9, 2008 from http://www.wilhelmtell.org/about/.

IBDB: The Official Source for Broadway Information. Retrieved November 17, 2008 from http://www.ibdb.com/show.php?id=9341.

✸ Jean Toomer

BORN: *1894, Washington, D.C.*

DIED: *1967, Doylestown, Pennsylvania*

NATIONALITY: *American*

GENRE: *Fiction, poetry*

MAJOR WORKS:
Cane (1923)
Essentials (1931)
"As the Eagle Soars" (1932)
"The Blue Meridian" (1936)

Overview

The literary reputation of Jean Toomer is based primarily on *Cane*, a collection of poems, impressionistic prose sketches, and stories on Afro-American topics. He published other poems, stories, and dramas, as well as some essays and book reviews, in various periodicals, but none of them equaled his achievement in *Cane*. Though an influence on black writers of the Harlem Renaissance, he

Jean Toomer   © *Bettmann / Corbis.*

did not identify himself closely with them, preferring instead to think of himself as a new kind of man, a blending of races, an American. He was, as he said, of the human race.

Works in Biographical and Historical Context

A Childhood of Turbulence and Tranquility

Toomer was born in Washington, D.C., on December 26, 1894. As a boy, a strong influence on Toomer was his grandfather P. B. S. Pinchback, an important Louisiana politician of the Reconstruction Era—the era of rebuilding the devastated South after its defeat in the American Civil War. Toomer spent much of his childhood in the home of his grandfather, who was living in Washington, D.C., by the time Toomer was born. Pinchback dominated his family, including his daughter Nina, Toomer's mother, who remained most of her life a member of her parents' household. Pinchback opposed her marriage to Nathan Toomer, a Georgia planter, who deserted his wife after about a year. Without resources, Nina moved with her newborn child back to her father's home. The child was christened Eugene Nathan Toomer, but was known by the surname Pinchback through much of his childhood. Later in life he shortened Eugene to Jean.

In "On Being an American," one of his autobiographical writings, Toomer later described his racial heredity as "Scotch, Welsh, German, English, French, Dutch, Spanish, with some dark blood." His grandfather's home on Bacon Street was not in a black neighborhood, and he remembered it as free of racial prejudice.

When Toomer was eleven, his mother married a second time. This marriage also failed, but it initiated a new phase in Toomer's life, which was marked by frequent changes of residence, a gradual decline in his grandfather's finances, and an increasing racial awareness. The unsettled nature of his life became even more evident when he entered college and tried to decide on a profession. Incapable of sustained effort, he skipped from one interest to another, one institution to the next: the University of Wisconsin in 1914, the Massachusetts College of Agriculture in 1915, both the American College of Physical Training and the University of Chicago in 1916, and the City College of New York in 1917. He retreated after each failure to his grandfather's home, only to be faced there by increasing irritation and disenchantment. He tried different kinds of work: directing physical education, working in a shipyard, selling cars, working in a store. None of it gave him much satisfaction.

In the midst of this meandering activity he began to write. He also read constantly, and sought authors with whom he felt empathy or in whose work he found useful models. Victor Hugo stirred his sense of social justice. George Bernard Shaw exemplified to him the virtues of candor and independence. Walt Whitman, he thought, had something to teach him about the American experience. Johann Wolfgang von Goethe, in his creation of the character of Wilhelm Meister, gave him a model he could follow. He read Robert Frost, Sherwood Anderson, and books by social reformers. Finally, in 1919 in New York, he began to meet a number of authors with whom he could discuss his interests and compare his abilities. The most important of these new acquaintances was Waldo Frank who, during those years in which *Cane* was created, remained his closest literary associate.

In the summer of 1920 Toomer returned to Washington to live with his grandparents. While there, he wrote enough manuscripts to fill a trunk—essays, fiction, poetry, drama—but he thought none of it good enough to publish. Yet, his confidence in his ability grew, until finally, as he described it in his "Outline of an Autobiography," "I was *inside, I knew literature!* And what was my joy!"

A Literary Breakthrough and a Spiritual Search

In the fall of 1921, Toomer was asked by the head of a black school in Sparta, Georgia, to serve as his replacement during his temporary absence. Toomer jumped at the opportunity to see that part of the South from which the black part of his heritage had come. Though this visit lasted only a few weeks, it became the impetus for *Cane*. What Toomer found was a dying culture, beautiful and sad, and the book he wrote was a farewell to that culture, arranged in a format intended to unify the rural southern and urban northern black experiences. He sent part of the

LITERARY AND HISTORICAL CONTEMPORARIES

Toomer's famous contemporaries include:

Sigmund Freud (1856–1939): The Austrian psychiatrist Freud was one of the most influential thinkers of his age. He is the founder of modern psychology, the science of the human mind and its processes, and of the practice of psychoanalysis, the procedure of treating psychological problems by investigating unconscious mental processes. Jean Toomer was an avid reader of Freud's writings.

George Bernard Shaw (1856–1950): Shaw, an Irish playwright, is famous for his insights into social problems, and his comedic approach to dealing with these problems. Jean Toomer read Shaw's work while in college.

George Ivanovich Gurdjieff (c. 1866–1949): G. I. Gurdjieff was a charismatic Greek-Armenian storyteller who viewed himself as a spiritual leader and accumulated a number of followers, including Toomer, following World War I. Gurdjieff preached a self-improvement technique he described as "the Work," which involved exercises designed to develop the body, mind, and emotions.

Virginia Woolf (1882–1941): The English novelist Virginia Woolf is one of the most important writers of the twentieth century literary movement called modernism. Her novel *To the Lighthouse* (1927) is considered to be one of the most important modernist works and is held up as an exemplar of "high modernism," a movement that also included Toomer's *Cane*.

James Joyce (1882–1941): Joyce is renowned for his extremely complex and experimental high modernist novels *Ulysses* (1922) and *Finnegan's Wake* (1939).

Pablo Picasso (1895–1972): One of the most influential and celebrated painters, sculptors, and personalities of the twentieth century, Spanish-born Pablo Picasso is most recognized as one of the founders of the Cubist art movement.

manuscript to Waldo Frank, who found a publisher for it. In his foreword to *Cane* Frank praised the book but made more of a point of the author's black heritage than Toomer wanted. For his publicity, Liveright, the publisher, wanted to stress the same racial element, which upset Toomer even more. *Cane* became a critical but not a popular success. The reviewers described it as the beginning of a new era and praised its fidelity and truthfulness. One of the ironies of his life, Toomer thought, was that his readers expected him to write more books like *Cane*, when for him, that book was a conclusion. That phase of his life was ended.

Cane can be read as one episode in its author's search for self-identity, and the book ends inconclusively. The search led him next to George Gurdjieff, a Russian mystic, whose magnetic personality attracted many disciples in Europe and the United States. Toomer spent the summer of 1924 at the Gurdjieff Institute in Fontainebleu, France, became Gurdjieff's disciple, and spent many years explaining and adapting what he learned from him. For example, he led Gurdjieff groups in Harlem and Chicago.

At this time, Toomer developed the belief that modern man had insulated himself from nature, and that to achieve wholeness he must attempt to reunite himself with this larger whole, even though the forces of modern society worked against him. He believed that behind the visible world was something even more essential that humanity, in this life, is "out of." Life, then, became an effort at integration and establishing contacts with essentials.

An Unconventional Poet   In 1931 Toomer married Margery Latimer, who died giving birth to their child, Margery. In 1934 he married Marjorie Content and lived the remainder of his life with her in Pennsylvania, where he became a Quaker, a member of a Christian group that most values simplicity in worship and daily life. Toomer wrote poetry intermittently in the years after *Cane* appeared, but he failed to get much of it published. Most of these poems he collected in a volume titled "The Wayward and the Seeking." A few of these poems are published by Turner in his edition of selected works by Toomer, for which he appropriated the title Toomer had given his book of poems. The most important poem Toomer succeeded in publishing is "The Blue Meridian," a long poem different in style and content from his earlier work. He spent much time and effort on it, writing and revising, letting an extract from it, "Brown River, Smile," appear in 1932 before he succeeded in getting the whole poem published in *The New Caravan* (1936). The poem displays an urgency lacking in his earlier poetry, a desire to enlighten and persuade quite different from the nostalgia that pervades the poems in *Cane*. "The Blue Meridian" is an amazing statement to come from one contemporary with the members of the literary group known as the Lost Generation, whose "visions" were more characteristically of wastelands, lonely streets, and sterile relationships. That Toomer was so at odds with the dominant sensibility of his times could help explain why he had such difficulty finding a publisher for "The Blue Meridian."

In 1967, Toomer died with the realization that he failed to accomplish much of what he had dreamed of achieving. He felt isolated and frustrated, sensing within himself some obstacle that prevented him from expressing his thoughts freely. Though the poetry he did publish is not extensive, it displays a variety and richness of expression that makes him a distinctive voice both among the poets of the Harlem Renaissance and among the poets who were developing an American version of symbolism. Poetry, though, is only one aspect of Toomer's literary achievement. It is perhaps best read not by itself, but as part of a unified whole, as but one form in which Toomer chose to describe his quest for identity.

Works in Literary Context

High Modernism   The cultural movement known as "High Modernism" is a development and perfection of the late nineteenth century–early twentieth century movement called "Modernism." Modernism is essentially characterized by its fragmented, experimental approach to literature, music, and the visual arts. The movement was intended to reflect a move away from previously held concepts of societal norms and attempts at capturing realism in the arts. High Modernism designated those modernist works that best define the modernist movement. These are the works that are most consistently modernist in approach and execution. In literature, works of high modernism were most pervasive in the period between World War I and World War II. Among the definitive works of high modernism are James Joyce's *Ulysses* (1922), Jean Toomer's *Cane* (1923), Virginia Woolf's *To the Lighthouse* (1927), and William Faulkner's *The Sound and the Fury* (1929).

Cubism   Cubism is a highly influential artistic movement of the twentieth century generally applied to the visual arts. The definitive characteristic of cubism is the artist's deconstruction of objects and people into an abstract assemblage of geometric shapes. In cubist art, depth is removed and the basic elements of a form are reconfigured at strange angles. For example, a portrait might feature a face with both eyes on one side of its nose, or a figure with both arms jutting from one side of its torso. A 1983 article in *Black American Literature Forum* argues that Jean Toomer's poems "Nullo" and "Storm Ending" are examples of "cubist poetry" because they display the same compression of "many images into one moment" and abandonment of "the conventional beginning-and-end or cause-and-effect scheme" characteristic of cubist art.

Works in Critical Context

Cane   Consistently regarded as a major African American writer of the first half of the twentieth century, Toomer remains best known for his debut novel *Cane.* The novel is comprised of a series of brief scenes that vary in structure from poetry to prose to script form, an experimental approach that thrilled readers at the time of its publication (in 1923, Toomer's colleague Waldo Frank proclaimed, "This book is the South"). Many critics also credited the book with beginning the African American art movement known as the Harlem Renaissance. The book continues to impress critics today. In 2006, Dan Schneider wrote on Hackwriters.com, "the whole book is a tangle of imagery, feeling, and song, and the book seems to flow from harmony, unity, and an almost mythic idyll in part one to almost bleak nihilism in part three." More succinctly, Kenneth J. Whisenton, in a biographical essay on Toomer, declares, "*Cane* shows the strength and beauty of African American culture."

COMMON HUMAN EXPERIENCE

In his most influential work, *Cane*, Toomer focuses in on the African American inhabitants of rural America. Other works of literature focused on rural African-American culture include:

"We Wear the Mask" (1896), a poem by Paul Laurence Dunbar. This poem by revered poet Dunbar is a brief but tremendously powerful examination of the pain behind the seemingly easygoing facades of many rural African-Americans at the end of the nineteenth century.

Sanctified Church (1981), a nonfiction collection by Zora Neale Hurston. *Sanctified Church* collects a number of Hurston's essays on African American folklore and mythology. The book is a means of preserving rural African American customs and music, proving rich examples of the particular speech patterns of that culture.

The Color Purple (1982), a novel by Alice Walker. Walker's best-selling novel tells the story of Celie, a poor African American woman living in the rural South who seeks to escape the cruel treatment she suffers at the hands of men. The novel is mainly composed of letters written by the nearly illiterate Celie.

Beloved (1987), a novel by Toni Morrison. Morrison's novel is both an unflinching depiction of slavery and a suspenseful ghost story. Sethe is an escaped slave now living in Ohio, but she is perpetually haunted by the torments she suffered as a slave.

The Collected Poems of Jean Toomer   While critical assessment of Toomer's *Cane* is almost overwhelmingly positive, not all of his work is as highly regarded as his debut novel. The publication of *The Collected Poems of Jean Toomer* was greeted with mixed responses from some critics who deemed the collection inconsistent. In a review in *The American Book Review*, Alvin Aubert saves his praise for the earlier poems in the collection, which he considers to be the "most aesthetically viable, most acceptable to our contemporary sensibility in their concreteness and existentiality." However, Aubert criticizes the later poems in the collection for their abstract vagueness, even commenting that certain poems in the book "self-destruct."

Responses to Literature

1. Toomer's novel *Cane* is told using a variety of structures: prose, poetry, and playlike dialogue. Read *Cane*, then explain which of these three storytelling approaches most effectively conveys the novel's story and themes. Compose your response in an essay.

2. Although he is often categorized as an important African American writer, Toomer did not want to be categorized by his race. Read *Cane*, then explain

whether or not you think a proper assessment of the book can be made without acknowledging Toomer's African American heritage. Support your response with details from the book.

3. Although the artistic term "cubism" is usually applied to the visual arts (painting, sculpture, etc.), Jean Toomer has been described as a cubist poet. Read Toomer's poem "Storm Ending," then research and view some of Pablo Picasso's cubist paintings. In an essay, explain which qualities Toomer's poem and Picasso's paintings share.

BIBLIOGRAPHY

Books

Benson, Joseph Bryan and Mabel Mayle Dillard. *Jean Toomer*. Boston: Twayne, 1980.

Locke, Alain. *Four Negro Poets*. New York: Simon & Schuster, 1927.

———. *Four Negro Poets*. New York: Simon & Schuster, 1927.

Rosenfeld, Paul. *Men Seen*. New York: Dial, 1967, pp. 227–245.

Turner, Darwin T. *In a Minor Chord*. Carbondale, Ill.: Southern Illinois University Press, 1971, pp. 1–59.

Periodicals

Aubert, Alvin. "Archetypal Victim." *The American Book Review* vol. 10, no. 6 (January–February 1989): 12, 21.

Bush, Ann Marie and Louis D. Mitchell. "Jean Toomer: A Cubist Poet." *Black American Literature Forum* vol. 17, no. 3 (Fall 1983): 106–108.

Holmes, Eugene. "Jean Toomer—Apostle of Beauty." *Opportunity* 10 (August 1932): 252–254, 260.

Kraft, James. "Jean Toomer's *Cane*." *Markham Review* 2 (October 1970): 61–63.

Lieber, Todd. "Design and Movement in *Cane*." *CLA Journal* 13 (September 1969): 35–50.

Mason, Clifford. "Jean Toomer's Authenticity." *Black World* 20 (January 1971): 70–76.

Turner, Darwin T. "Jean Toomer's *Cane*; Critical Analysis." *Negro Digest* 18 (January 1969): 54–61.

Web Sites

Hackwriters.com. *Cane, by Jean Toomer*. Accessed November 21, 2008, from http://www.hackwriters.com/Cane.htm.

District of Columbia Public Library Online. *Jean Toomer*. Accessed November 21, 2008, from http://029c28c.netsolhost.com/blkren/bios/toomerj.html.

■ **William Trogden**

SEE *William Least Heat-Moon*

⚛ Sojourner Truth

BORN: *1797, Ulster County, New York*

DIED: *1883, Battle Creek, Michigan*

NATIONALITY: *American*

GENRE: *Nonfiction*

MAJOR WORKS:
Narrative of Sojourner Truth (1850)

Overview

Sojourner Truth was a former black slave who traveled widely throughout the United States, and advocated the abolition of slavery and the emancipation of women. Along with her historic work for human rights, Truth was a powerful public speaker and the author of the strikingly complex classic autobiography *Narrative of Sojourner Truth* (1850).

Works in Biographical and Historical Context

Years of Bondage At some point in 1797, a black slave girl was born in Ulster County, New York. Her

Sojourner Truth   *AP Images*

father James, who was nicknamed "Baumfree," and her mother Elizabeth, affectionately known as "Mau-Mau Bett," called their daughter Isabella. However, she is known today by the name she chose for herself, many years later: Sojourner Truth. Isabella spent her early childhood on an estate owned by Dutch settlers; accordingly, her first spoken language was Low Dutch. When her owner died in 1806, she was part of his property that was put up for auction. As the slave population of New York and New Jersey at this time was over 36,000, Isabella was only one of many slave children who were separated from their parents at an early age.

In 1810, after having had several owners, thirteen-year-old Isabella was bought by John Dumont of New Paltz Landing, with whom she lived for seventeen years. She worked hard for Dumont, who was impressed by her great physical strength. In 1817, the New York State Legislature passed a law granting eventual emancipation to slaves born before July 4, 1799. The legislation stipulated that Isabella and others in her situation would have to wait ten years for their freedom. So she did not become a free woman until July 4, 1827.

Seeking Justice through the Law

During those ten years, Dumont chose a slave named Thomas as a husband for Isabella, and she had five children with him, four of whom survived. As the date for her emancipation drew closer, she realized that Dumont did not intend to set her free. Instead, he wanted her to make up the work time that she had lost during an earlier illness. Showing what her biographer Victoria Ortiz has described as "a strength and independence of spirit," Isabella left Dumont in 1826, one year earlier than she was permitted.

Her goal was to retrieve her son Peter. Even though slaves were not allowed to be sold outside of the state, Peter had passed through the hands of several owners until he was sold to a Southern plantation owner in Alabama. Believing in the justice of the law, Isabella was determined to free her son, and spent the next year and a half working with a lawyer in Kingston. Remarkably, in 1828 she became the first black woman in American history to take a white man to court and win.

Adopting a New Name

Later, after living in New York and spending some time with a religious organization that turned out to be corrupt, she decided to leave New York and preach the word of God to the people. In 1843, she also decided to change her name to Sojourner Truth. In her autobiography, she explains:

> My name was Isabella; but when I left the house of bondage, I left everything behind. . . . I went to the Lord and asked him to give me a new name. And the Lord gave me Sojourner, because I was to travel up and down the land, showing the people their sins, and being a sign unto them.

The forty-six-year-old preacher began to travel widely, attending prayer meetings and calling her own meetings. An effective public speaker, Truth enjoyed being the center of attention. Supporting herself with odd jobs, she lived for several years with the Northampton Association of Education and Industry, a utopian community that had settled in Massachusetts. There she met women and men who were active in the abolitionist movement, including Frederick Douglass and William Lloyd Garrison, and she made it her mission to work for the liberation of slaves.

In the country at large, the issue of slavery was becoming increasingly divisive. In 1850, Congress passed the Fugitive Slave Law, which held that runaway slaves were to be arrested without a warrant, denied trial by jury, and not allowed to testify in court in their own defense. The new law led many abolitionists to advocate violence as a means of achieving their goals. After the Supreme Court ruled that Dred Scott, a slave from Missouri, was not a citizen and could not therefore bring a legal action to court, the stage was set for increasing tensions between pro- and antislavery forces.

During the 1850s, in spite of an increasingly volatile situation, Truth began a public lecture tour, and visited twenty-two states. She displayed great determination and confidence in her abilities to speak to people, and she was never intimidated even while standing in front of hostile crowds. Her lectures were usually unrehearsed and dealt with her own personal experiences as a slave. Ortiz has noted that "while Frederick Douglass and Harriet Tubman did the vital job of working with their own people . . . Sojourner was one of the few black people of that period who spoke almost exclusively to whites."

Speaking for the Rights of Women and Blacks

In 1853, Truth met Harriet Beecher Stowe, author of *Uncle Tom's Cabin* (1852), while on her travels. She also came to realize that although women were some of the most important members of the abolitionist movement, they were not allowed to vote or hold public office. As a black woman, Truth realized that she was doubly discriminated against. As a result, she became an outspoken supporter of women's emancipation and lectured on both women's rights and black freedom. In 1854, she gave one of her most famous speeches at the Women's Rights Convention in Akron, Ohio. After listening to several clergymen of various persuasions who declared that women were inferior to men and that God had not meant for women to have rights, Truth spoke:

> That man over there says that women need to be helped into carriages, and lifted over ditches, and to have the best place everywhere. Nobody ever helps me into carriages, or over mud puddles, or gives me any best place, and ain't I a woman? . . . I have plowed, and planted, and gathered into barns, and no man could head me—and ain't I a woman? I could work as much and eat as much as a man (when I could get it), and bear the lash as well—and ain't I a woman? I have borne five children and seen most all sold off into slavery and when I cried out with a mother's grief, none but Jesus heard—and ain't I a woman?

LITERARY AND HISTORICAL CONTEMPORARIES

Sojourner Truth's famous contemporaries include:

Dred Scott (1795–1858): Scott is best known for his role in the famous Supreme Court case *Dred Scott v. Sanford* (1857), in which he, a slave living in a state where slavery was illegal, sued his owner for his freedom and lost—an event that help to precipitate the American Civil War.

George Thompson (1804–1878): A tireless British abolitionist who staged a series of antislavery lectures in both Great Britain and the United States. In 1851, Sojourner Truth joined Thompson to lecture in New York.

William Lloyd Garrison (1805–1879): Garrison was the editor of *The Liberator*, an unapologetically radical antislavery publication, and a cofounder of the American Anti-Slavery Society, a group devoted to the emancipation of slaves.

Abraham Lincoln (1809–1865): The sixteenth president of the United States, Lincoln led the country during one of its most terrible periods, the bloody American Civil War (1861–1865). Lincoln played a crucial role in the abolition of slavery when he issued his Emancipation Proclamation (1863).

Harriet Tubman (1820–1913): A former slave who devoted herself to humanitarian causes and fighting for the abolition of slavery after she escaped from her captors. Tubman also worked as a spy for the Union during the American Civil War, and famously assisted the escape of other slaves with her Underground Railroad.

Ulysses S. Grant (1822–1885): Grant, the eighteenth president of the United States, had previously served as the general who ultimately led the North to victory in the Civil War.

In addition to public speaking, Truth produced her autobiography, *Narrative of Sojourner Truth*, which was first published in 1850 and which went through six subsequent editions. Because she was illiterate, Truth was assisted in the writing by Olive Gilbert, whom she had met during her time with the Northampton Association. With the money she received from the sales of her book, Truth bought land and a house in Michigan, near the town of Battle Creek.

Not content to remain in one place for any length of time, Truth resumed her travels and spoke in Ohio, Indiana, Iowa, Illinois, and Wisconsin. Her words became even more poignant when the American Civil War had broken out in 1861, and after Abraham Lincoln had taken office as president of the United States on March 4th of that year. Although in her sixties, Truth displayed the energy and determination that was inherent in her character when she visited and gave words of encouragement to the black Union troops stationed at Detroit.

The height of her involvement in the war effort came when she met Lincoln on October 29, 1864. She described him as a "great and good man…[who treated her] with great kindness and cordiality." Two months later, the National Freedman's Relief Association appointed her to work as a counselor to freed slaves in Virginia. She returned to Washington within five months, and worked in a hospital there. She also filed a suit to affirm that black people had the same legal rights as white people to ride on public transport. Her court case was won, but only after she had her arm dislocated by a conductor who refused to let her board a streetcar.

After the war was over, Truth continued to work with and visit freed slaves. Realizing that many of these women and men were unable to return to their homes and were now living in poverty, she battled to secure land for them. In 1870, at the age of seventy-three, she gave public lectures and circulated petitions that requested that land in the American West be set aside for freed blacks. In the same year, she met President Ulysses S. Grant and paid a visit to the U.S. Senate, where she received a standing ovation from the members.

For the remaining years of her life, and in spite of her failing health, Truth continued to champion the rights of blacks and of women. She also lectured for the temperance movement, which preached moderation in alcohol consumption. By 1883, however, she was confined to her bed as ulcers on her legs became increasingly painful. Without exhibiting any fear, and surrounded by many adoring friends, she died on November 26, 1883, at the age of eighty-six.

Works in Literary Context

Abolitionist Literature   In the nineteenth century, members of the abolitionist movement made a considerable cultural, political, and social impact through the literature it published. Abolitionist literature included poetry, autobiographies, literary fiction, and essays. While this literary movement achieved prominence during the nineteenth century, its roots can be traced back to the previous century and the Age of Enlightenment, an era in which similar human-rights issues arose. The seeds of antislavery sentiment can be found sporadically in certain examples of English poetry and literature of the late 1700s, including Thomas Chatterton's poems the *African Eclogues* (1770). However, the most memorable, influential, and focused examples of abolitionist literature would arise during the nineteenth century in America, as such former slaves as Harriet Tubman, Frederick Douglass, Booker T. Washington, and Sojourner Truth provided harrowing first-person accounts of their own experiences. These works were used to successfully argue the case against slavery in the court of public opinion, especially in the North.

Spiritual Conversion Themes of spiritual conversion have long held a place in both literary fiction and in autobiographies and memoirs. The path one takes from either disbelief (or seemingly misguided beliefs) to an ultimate, satisfying relationship with spirituality can be a dramatic one, ripe for literary exploration. In fiction, spiritual conversion has played a significant role in such novels as Charles Dickens's *A Christmas Carol* (1843) and Lew Wallace's *Ben-Hur: A Tale of Christ* (1880). In the realm of nonfiction, Sojourner Truth describes her own spiritual journey in her autobiography *Narrative of Sojourner Truth*. Following the loss of her son, Truth sought comfort in Christianity, and with just twenty-five cents in her pocket, she began traveling and preaching God's word.

Works in Critical Context

Narrative of Sojourner Truth Original critical assessments dating from the publication of Truth's autobiography are difficult to find, but the book has long been considered one of the classics of nineteenth-century literature. Still, it has not been immune to criticism. In 2000, *The New York Times* described the *Narrative of Sojourner Truth* as "groundbreaking" and "detailed" but "fairly dry, as was the style of the time" and burdened by its "highly religious" nature. However, the general consensus is that the book is, as the *Library Journal* describes it, "a powerful rendering of bondage, denial, and loss transcended by genius, family, and a spiritual base."

Responses to Literature

1. Because Truth was illiterate, she had to narrate her autobiography to writer Olive Gilbert. Read *Narrative of Sojourner Truth* and explain whether or not you think the book was significantly affected by the fact it was narrated, as opposed to being personally written, by Truth. How might Gilbert's perspective and biases have influenced the final work? Support your response with details from the book.

2. The work Truth performed during her lifetime paved the way for significant changes in society that still resonate today. Can you identify any individuals who might be considered modern-day parallels to Truth? Are the issues they focus on similar to the issues Truth dealt with?

3. Truth suffered many hardships during her life, yet she persisted in her fight against slavery. Find examples in her narrative that illustrate her persistence in the face of adversity.

4. The issue of the emancipation of slaves became one of the main causes of the American Civil War. Using your library or the Internet, research the Dred Scott Case. What were the arguments offered by each side? Why did the judges rule the way they did? How did this decision affect the abolition movement?

COMMON HUMAN EXPERIENCE

In her autobiography, Truth describes her years as a slave, as well as her work as an abolitionist and her spiritual beliefs. Other literary works that provide accounts of African American slaves include:

Narrative of the Life of Frederick Douglass, an American Slave (1845), a nonfiction work by Frederick Douglass. Both an account of the trials he suffered as a slave and a dissertation calling for the abolition of slavery, Douglass' book is one of the most famous books written by a former slave. The book is credited for helping to inspire the abolitionist movement to end slavery.

Uncle Tom's Cabin (1853), a novel by Harriet Beecher Stowe. Stowe's antislavery novel is the story of Uncle Tom, a long-suffering black slave who ultimately learns to disobey his white owners. While the novel was composed as an abolitionist message, it has often been accused of establishing certain black stereotypes, and "Uncle Tom" has since come to be used as a term for a black man who allows himself to be subservient to a white.

Incidents in the Life of a Slave Girl (1861), a nonfiction work by Harriet Jacobs. Jacobs's book is distinguished from other slave memoirs by its unflinching look at the tortures female slaves suffered at the hands of their owners. The book includes some disturbing accounts of sexual abuse and was considered to be very shocking in its time.

Up from Slavery (1901), an autobiography by Booker T. Washington. *Up from Slavery* tracks Washington's development from a child slave to a prominent and respected teacher, lecturer, author, and black community leader. The autobiography includes educational and humanitarian philosophies that caused some controversy among critics, who felt Washington was trying too thoroughly to appeal to white readers.

BIBLIOGRAPHY

Books

Mabee, Carleton, with Susan Mabee Newhouse. *Sojourner Truth: Slave, Prophet, Legend*. New York: New York University Press, 1993.

Ortiz, Victoria. *Sojourner Truth, A Self-Made Woman*. Philadelphia: Lippincott, 1974.

Painter, Nell Irvin. *Sojourner Truth: A Life, a Symbol*. New York: Norton, 1996.

Pauli, Hertha. *Her Name Was Sojourner Truth*. New York: Camelot/Avon, 1962.

Stewart, Jeffrey C. Introduction to *Narrative of Sojourner Truth, A Bondswoman of Olden Time, With a History of Her Labors and Correspondence Drawn from her "Book of Life."* New York: Oxford University Press, 1991.

Washington, Margaret. Introduction to *Narrative of Sojourner Truth*. New York: Vintage Classics, 1993.

Periodicals

Collins, Kathleen. "Shadow and Substance: Sojourner Truth." *History of Photography* 7 (July–September 1983).

Villarosa, C. "Children's Books; Serving No Master but the Truth." *The New York Times* (November 19, 2000).

Web Sites

The Black Collegian Online. *Super Hero: Sojourner Truth.* Accessed November 24, 2008, from http://www.black-collegian.com/issues/35thAnn/truth.shtml.

✸ Mark Twain

BORN: *1835, Florida, Missouri*

DIED: *1910, Redding, Connecticut*

NATIONALITY: *American*

GENRE: *Fiction, nonfiction, drama*

MAJOR WORKS:

Roughing It (1872)

The Adventures of Tom Sawyer (1876)

Life on the Mississippi (1883)

Adventures of Huckleberry Finn (1884)

A Connecticut Yankee in King Arthur's Court (1889)

Mark Twain   *The Library of Congress*

Overview

Mark Twain is considered the father of modern American literature and is known in particular for his beloved novel *The Adventures of Huckleberry Finn* (1884). Twain developed a lively, homespun narrative style that liberated American prose from the rigid conventions of the mid-nineteenth century. His specialty was satire that exposed human folly and social injustice. During his lifetime, his writing was often denounced as coarse and improper; subsequently, readers and critics have come to regard Twain's works as the foremost literary expression of the American spirit of pragmatism, egalitarianism, and honesty. Ernest Hemingway wrote: "All modern American literature comes from one book by Mark Twain called *Huckleberry Finn*.... There was nothing before. There has been nothing as good since."

Works in Biographical and Historical Context

Cub Reporter and Steamboat Cub   Mark Twain was born Samuel Langhorne Clemens in Florida, Missouri, on November 30, 1835. In 1839, the family moved thirty miles away to Hannibal, Missouri. As a youth, he frequented the banks of the Mississippi River, and he often traveled in makeshift rafts or cavorted in swimming holes. His formal education lasted only until 1847, when his father died. At that point, he quit school and became a printer's apprentice. By age seventeen, he was also writing stories and sketches for the newspapers he helped print.

Eventually, he began to work for his brother, Orion Clemens, who owned several newspapers. The brothers suffered a series of business failings, whereupon Twain departed for the open road. Throughout the next three years, he wandered from the Midwest to the East Coast, supporting himself by publishing his observations in various newspapers still managed by his brother. He rejoined Orion for two years in Keokuk, Iowa, then left in 1857, intending to sail down the Mississippi to New Orleans and on to South America where he would make his fortune. That spring, he met a veteran steamboat captain named Horace Bixby. Twain was greatly intrigued by the captain and for the next two years served as Bixby's "cub," or apprentice, sailing with him down the Mississippi and enjoying many adventures.

Becoming Mark Twain   Twain obtained his own pilot's license in 1859 and spent more time up and down the Mississippi. His exploits in this period eventually served as material for some of his most inspired writing. The pseudonym he adopted, Mark Twain, is an expression used by riverboat crews to indicate that the water at a given spot is two fathoms deep and thus easily navigable.

After the American Civil War broke out in 1861, Union troops used the Mississippi as an invasion route, effectively closing business travel along the river. Twain joined an irregular band of Confederate sympathizers and briefly experienced combat, then deserted and traveled west with Orion to the Nevada territory. For a year, he tried to cash in on the speculation fever by panning for gold and silver. As a prospector, Twain failed miserably, but he sent some humorous writing to the *Virginia City Territorial Enterprise* for comic relief and joined the staff of that paper in August 1862.

As a journalist, he assumed the Mark Twain pseudonym, alternating straight reporting with Far West humor and wild hoaxes. When he went too far, and a rival journalist challenged him to a duel, Twain fled to San Francisco and wrote for newspapers there. Mixed with his humor was enough righteous indignation that Twain became known as the "Moralist of the Pacific Slope." Again, his writing gave offense, this time to the San Francisco Police Department, and again he departed hurriedly.

Reaching a National Audience When he got back, Twain learned that the prominent humorist Artemus Ward had asked him to write a piece for a forthcoming anthology. The tale Twain contributed arrived too late for inclusion in Ward's volume but was pirated by the *New York Saturday Press* in November 1865, where it won great acclaim. It was eventually copied in newspapers across the country and became the title story of Twain's first book, *The Celebrated Jumping Frog of Calaveras County, and Other Sketches* (1867).

For the rest of the decade, Twain traveled widely and contributed his observations to various West Coast publications. In 1867, the author boarded the ship *Quaker City* for a five-month cruise to Europe and the Middle East and was accompanied by some wealthy and solemnly pious New York socialites. Twain mocked his fellow travelers and called the journey "a funeral excursion without a corpse." The satirical letters he wrote during this voyage were a sensation and established his fame on both coasts. The book Twain fashioned from these pieces, *The Innocents Abroad; or, The New Pilgrim's Progress* (1869), became the most commercially successful publication of his career and one of the most popular books of the mid-nineteenth century.

Twain's talents were well suited to popular travel writing, and throughout his career the genre served him well financially. His wanderlust also reflected the mood of his times. Americans were on the move, with tourism becoming for the first time a common middle-class leisure activity. With broad, satirical humor, Twain's travelogues debunked the pretensions of Europe, declaring cultural independence from the Old World, and it was a message American readers loved. The success of *The Innocents Abroad*, along with his prowess as a public lecturer, established Twain as the leading American humorist.

Twain Takes to Novels While visiting a friend from the *Quaker City* cruise, Charles Langdon—the son of the coal merchant Jervis Langdon of Elmira, New York—Twain fell in love with Langdon's sister, Olivia. Jervis Langdon gave permission for the two to marry, which they did in 1870, and his new father-in-law furnished Twain with part ownership of a newspaper in Buffalo. The couple stayed there only briefly, however, settling instead in Hartford, Connecticut. Here, Twain completed work on a memoir of his experiences out west, *Roughing It* (1872). The book was another major success and remains prominent in the Twain canon.

Twain and his wife lived in Hartford for twenty years, mostly residing in a unique mansion designed by Twain himself. Nearby lived other writers, including Harriet Beecher Stowe and the editor of the *Atlantic Monthly*, William Dean Howells, who became a literary adviser to Twain. In 1874, Twain published his first novel, *The Gilded Age*, cowritten with his neighbor Charles Dudley Warner. This was one of the earliest political satires in American fiction; it exposed corruption and greed using thinly disguised portraits of well-known politicians from Congress and the administration of President Ulysses S. Grant.

Two years later came *The Adventures of Tom Sawyer* (1876), a novel about an enterprising young boy living near the Mississippi River. The story's combination of gentle satire, broad comedy, and adventure gained wide acclaim among readers of all ages. *Tom Sawyer* features some of Twain's most memorable feats of storytelling, including the trial of Injun Joe, the funeral of the missing boys (which is interrupted by the boys' reappearance), and Tom and Becky's dramatic escapades in the cave.

Life on the Mississippi Twain immediately began work on a follow-up novel about Tom Sawyer's friend, the young vagrant Huckleberry Finn. This work took seven years to complete, during which time Twain journeyed through Europe again, producing another travelogue that sold well. In 1881 Twain published *The Prince and the Pauper*, a straightforward novel set in sixteenth-century England, concerning two boys from different stations in life who decide to exchange identities. The book won acclaim as a compelling tale of historical England, but it proved a debacle for its author; Twain had published the book himself and agreed to pay royalties to the publishing company, leaving him with a disturbing financial setback.

In April 1882, Twain decided to go home. The result was *Life on the Mississippi* (1883), in which Twain combines reminiscences of his younger days (originally published in the *Atlantic Monthly* as "Old Times on the Mississippi") with notes upon revisiting his old haunts. Unlike his other travel books, *Life on the Mississippi* is filled with respect and love for his subject: it renders the Mississippi River as an ever-mysterious, unfathomable force.

Huck, Jim, and the River The Mississippi is featured prominently in *The Adventures of Huckleberry Finn*, which Twain finally completed in 1884. Racial animosity was at a fever pitch while Twain was writing *Huckleberry Finn*, with memories of the Civil War still fresh. The novel, set in the antebellum South, directly confronts the inhumanity of slavery and racial prejudice. Huck's tale begins where *Tom Sawyer* left off, Huck having been adopted by Widow Douglas. On a winter day, Huck discovers that his alcoholic father, whom he had not seen for a year, has returned home. Huck's father then appears, takes Huck into the woods and starves and beats him. Huck manages to escape and stages his own death. He flees to an island, where he discovers a fugitive slave, Jim. Back on the mainland, Huck learns that his own death has been attributed to Jim. Jim determines to head north through the slave states to freedom, and Huck decides to join him, heedless of the danger to himself if he were to be caught aiding a runaway slave.

From that point forward, as they embark by raft, Huck and Jim's search for freedom becomes increasingly somber and ominous as they head helplessly in the opposite direction from their goal, controlled by the southward flow of the mighty Mississippi. Moving deeper and deeper into slave territory, they are separated and reunited several times and encounter violence and treachery. The characters and situations Huck and Jim encounter allow Twain to unleash the stinging satire against the South that he avoided using in *Life on the Mississippi*. Nevertheless, the narrative focuses on Huck's developing moral independence from the teachings of his society. Although many of Twain's contemporaries objected to the novel's vernacular dialogue, coarse subject matter, and forthright social criticism, *Huckleberry Finn* was a great popular success and is now considered one of the great American novels.

A Connecticut Yankee and the Perils of Technology

In his next novel, *A Connecticut Yankee in King Arthur's Court* (1889), Twain produced a harsh depiction of life in sixth-century England; he likened its repressive, anti-democratic society to that of post-Civil War America. His protagonist is Hank Morgan, a foreman in a firearms factory, who suffers a blow to the head and wakes up in medieval England. With his practical knowledge and inventiveness, he sets out to enlighten the kingdom and its superstitious courtiers. Hank strings telephone lines (which were being established in the United States as Twain was writing), prints a newspaper, uses gunpowder and other modern "miracles," but these gifts from the future prove destructive. At the end of the book, Hank and fifty-two boys destroy 25,000 knights with dynamite, electrified barbed wire, and a brand-new weapon, the Gatling gun. This grotesque fantasy presciently envisions how mechanization would turn combat into slaughter, most famously in World War I.

With *A Connecticut Yankee*, Twain's fiction veered from lighthearted burlesque to venomous satire. The book's acid humor charmed few readers accustomed to the delights of Tom Sawyer and Huckleberry Finn; many critics, notably in England, condemned the novel as tasteless. In subsequent decades, though, the novel gained recognition as an example of Twain's social criticism. On the surface, Hank is Twain's spokesman for democracy over monarchy, freedom in preference to servitude. Beneath that stance is a bleak depiction of human progress, particularly of technology out of human control.

In real life, technology would also cause Twain trouble. In the 1880s, Twain became almost obsessively concerned with speculation in a typesetting machine, an invention in which he invested hundreds of thousands of dollars. The device malfunctioned frequently and failed commercially, and in the financial panic of 1893 and 1894, Twain was forced to declare bankruptcy. Sixty years old and ailing, Twain made frenzied and futile trips across the ocean to bolster his failing financial situation. He had just one possible source of new revenue: a new manuscript.

Tragedy and Misanthropy

In his novel, *The Tragedy of Pudd'nhead Wilson* (1894), Twain returned to the antebellum Southern setting and to the subject of slavery. The novel tells the tale of two children switched at birth by a mulatto slave, Roxana, who hopes to spare her own child the indignities of slavery. The slave owner's real son is eventually sold into slavery, and Roxana's son, though reared with all social advantages, nonetheless grows up a rogue and a criminal, who sells his own mother "down the river" for cash. The son, Tom, eventually commits murder, for which two Italian immigrant twins are held responsible. In the climactic trial scene, the eccentric lawyer Pudd'nhead Wilson reveals the true killer's identity by using a prized collection of fingerprints. At the time this book was written, fingerprinting had recently been discovered as a means of identification.

Sales of *Pudd'nhead Wilson*, published together with *The Comedy of Those Extraordinary Twins*, helped Twain recover from his financial woes. However, his favorite daughter Susy died in 1896, at age twenty-four, while Twain was in London on a world tour. Another daughter was diagnosed with epilepsy that same year, and Olivia Clemens fell into physical and emotional distress that took her life several years later. For the rest of his life, Twain's natural pessimism deepened into a fatalistic despair, and his work grew increasingly bitter and misanthropic.

In his final years, Twain lived in New York City, where he became a social butterfly and political gadfly, speaking out frequently against a variety of injustices at the height of the Progressive Era. Many of his last published works are polemics, such as the essay *What Is Man?* (1906), which depicts humanity as inherently foolish and self-destructive. He suffered from poor health for several years, before his death on April 21, 1910. Many of his writings—letters, speeches, sketches, stories, an autobiography, and a novella, *The Mysterious Stranger* (1916)—were published posthumously, helping to sustain the Mark Twain legend deep into the twentieth century.

Works in Literary Context

Twain was a true original. His sense of humor, use of vernacular language, and moral sensibility each made a deep impression upon American culture. He was certainly influenced by the popular literature available in his time, such as the novels of Charles Dickens. He cited Miguel de Cervantes' masterpiece *Don Quixote* as a work that helped shape his thinking, and scholars have detected its structural influence on *Huckleberry Finn*. The humorist Artemus Ward helped Twain find his comic voice early on. Other vital influences are less well known: for example, that of his brother Orion, and the newspaper business that was such an important part of his youth, which sharpened his powers of observation and narrative logic.

Twain's Humor A gifted storyteller and raconteur, Twain perfected in written form a kind of folk humor that was all around him as an oral art, in stories, tall tales, and jests. For example, his first successful story, "Jim Smiley and his Jumping Frog," derived from a yarn he heard while camping in the Sierra mountains of California. His early writing features a wild, extravagant, masculine humor typical of the western frontier. Many of his travel sketches feature dialogues between the characters of "Mark Twain," a sentimental idealist, and Mr. Brown, a vulgar realist who inevitably undercuts the other man's rapture with cutting remarks. Out of this comic formula developed the more sophisticated, realistic satire that became Twain's trademark. While his satire could be merciless in its mockery of pretense and pomposity, it was always intended to reveal the foibles and follies of human nature and the human tendency to mistreat one another. Toward the end of his career, the humor grew several shades darker, but just as funny. Consider the dry wit of this aphorism from the calendar of Pudd'nhead Wilson: "If you pick up a starving dog and make him prosperous, he will not bite you. This is the principal difference between a dog and a man."

Outsiders and Misfits Twain adapted the Mark Twain/Mr. Brown dichotomy in *Roughing It* by presenting the narrator as a childish naif who gradually loses his illusions and becomes a wise realist as the book progresses. That education process served Twain in most of his later fiction: the cub pilot of "Old Times on the Mississippi," Tom Sawyer, Huck Finn, David "Pudd'nhead" Wilson, and other characters in shorter works all begin as outsiders and attempt, with varying degrees of success, to come to terms with society. Tom Sawyer represents one kind of misfit, a conniving prankster who gradually moves into society rather than out of it. Tom's rebellions from conformity, however, have none of the subversive quality that Huckleberry Finn would show just a few years later. Beneath the surface conflicts of freedom versus slavery, *Huckleberry Finn* explores whether any human being can transcend his (or her) upbringing, can violate his indoctrination into society's flawed moral code. In his later years, Twain decided firmly that this

LITERARY AND HISTORICAL CONTEMPORARIES

Twain's famous contemporaries include:

Leo Tolstoy (1828–1910): Tolstoy was a renowned Russian novelist whose *War and Peace* and *Anna Karenina* are considered among the finest novels of all time.

Jules Verne (1828–1905): Verne was a French author who was a prominent author of science fiction and is best known for his novel *Twenty Thousand Leagues Under the Sea*.

Henrik Ibsen (1828–1906): Ibsen was Norway's most famous playwright and became a leading figure in European drama. He is best known for his play *A Doll's House*.

Emile Zola (1840–1902): Zola was a French author and outspoken intellectual who became a proponent of "naturalism."

Henry James (1843–1916): James was an American author and novelist whose well-known works include *The Ambassadors* and *Washington Square*.

was impossible. In *Huckleberry Finn*, the issue is more complex. After wrestling with his conscience several times, Huck decides he will "go to hell" rather than turn Jim in. The reader supports Huck's ability to loose the shackles of convention and conformity.

Comedy and Tragedy Scholars recognize in Twain a man divided between a comic and a tragic outlook on life. Throughout his career he looked back nostalgically to his youth on the shores of the Mississippi, finding inspiration in his memories. At the same time, he was skeptical, or cynical, about the wisdom of humanity and the possibility of social progress. His works convey a longing for an idyllic past, as a haven from a hostile present. However, Twain also believed that humanity had been give a chance to remedy its situation in America, where egalitarianism could replace the superstitions and false hierarchies of Europe. In *Huckleberry Finn*, for example, the frontier (in the form of the Mississippi River) allows Huck to escape the clutches of civilization and gain awareness of the importance of courage, honesty, and common sense. Yet, as his career wore on, Twain lost his faith in humanity and free will. His final position coincided with that of literary naturalists Stephen Crane and Theodore Dreiser, who believed that human behavior was determined by environment, breeding, and other social forces.

Folk Idiom One of Twain's greatest contributions to American literature is his brilliant use of ordinary, colloquial language. The style of his early, journalism-based work emulates the rhythms and speech patterns of folk

COMMON HUMAN EXPERIENCE

The Adventures of Huckleberry Finn and *Life on the Mississippi* give the Mississippi River a near-mythic stature in American literature. Rivers are a perennial and potent literary theme, suggesting the flow of time and the wisdom of nature. The following works make intriguing use of this theme.

"The Negro Speaks of Rivers" (1921), a poem by Langston Hughes. This signature poem of the Harlem Renaissance powerfully connects the black experience from ancient history through the present: "my soul has grown deep like the rivers."

"Big Two-Hearted River" (1925), a story by Ernest Hemingway. Nick Adams goes fishing and starts to recover from his shellshock in this story from Hemingway's collection *In Our Time*.

Aguirre, the Wrath of God (1972), a film written and directed by Werner Herzog. A Spanish soldier leads a doomed expedition on the Amazon in search of El Dorado in this acclaimed independent film.

Pilgrim at Tinker Creek (1974), a nonfiction work by Annie Dillard. A unique book of essays that uses the natural environment of a creek as a jumping-off point for meditations on spirituality.

storytelling, as characters relate tall tales and humorous incidents. In *Huckleberry Finn*, Twain raises the rendition of native dialect and idiom, among both whites and blacks, to a high art. Twain's style ranged far from the tidy prose of more conventional realists, such as William Dean Howells, not to mention the erudite expression of a Henry James. But, the language struck audiences as fresh, original, and authentically American.

Father of American Literature Twain's influence has been felt in every succeeding generation of American literature. By breaking from inherited European conventions, Twain helped America develop its own unique, democratic culture and transmit that culture to a mass audience. Many of his characters and scenes are indelibly imprinted upon the American imagination, none more so than the image of Huck and Jim rafting down the river. *Huckleberry Finn* is considered by many to be the greatest work of fiction produced by an American. Twain's gift for transmitting common speech to the page, his wry and pungent maxims, his irreverence, his outspoken political advocacy, and his astringent view of human nature are all living legacies. No less an authority than William Faulkner referred to Twain as "the father of American literature."

Works in Critical Context

Twain reached the heights of literary celebrity early in his career. Readers in the late nineteenth century knew him first and loved him best as a travel writer rather than a novelist. *The Innocents Abroad* and *Roughing It* were widely acclaimed and established their author's rapport with his readers. Twain's novels, on the other hand, met an uneven reception upon their publication. *Tom Sawyer* and *The Prince and the Pauper* were critical and commercial successes, but *Huckleberry Finn* at first repelled many reviewers, who found the characters and situations uncouth and the subject matter not appropriate for young readers. *A Connecticut Yankee* and *Pudd'nhead Wilson* each sold relatively well, but initial critical reaction was generally unfavorable. Perhaps these novels were ahead of their time, for as the decades have passed, their stature has steadily grown.

Contemporary Debates Today, Twain remains one of the most widely read and admired authors in American literature. He is central to the American canon; he captured, with remarkable fidelity, essential aspects of the American experience and national character. While his fiction, especially *Huckleberry Finn*, is frequently assigned in schools, it is also among the most frequently challenged, according to the American Library Association. Because of the cultural importance and literary virtuosity of Twain's prose, it remains the subject of voluminous and lively debate. Twain's detractors have attacked his work for ideologically varied reasons, accusing it of profanity, misanthropy, and, more recently in the case of *Huckleberry Finn*, racism in its characterization of Jim.

Huckleberry Finn Despite meager and almost entirely negative attention at first, *Huckleberry Finn* soon became prized for its recreation of the antebellum South, its insights into slavery, its depiction of adolescent life, and its irreverence. Prominent men of letters, such as H. L. Mencken and Ernest Hemingway, have named it among the world's greatest masterpieces. The book's final chapters, however, seem anticlimactic to many. Even Hemingway, in *The Green Hills of Africa* (1935), advised that "If you read it you must stop where . . . Jim is stolen from the boys. That is the real end. The rest is just cheating."

The question of race hovers over modern scholarship on *Huckleberry Finn*. Jim is treated sympathetically, and the book calls into question the social system predicated on racism. On the other hand, the portrayal of Jim does fall back on some stereotypical notions. For these reasons, some Twain critics cannot go along with the liberal interpretation of *Huckleberry Finn* as an indictment of slavery and racism. Stephen Railton, in "Jim and Mark Twain: What Do Dey Stan' For?," argues that Twain ultimately fails to challenge his readers' stereotypical frame of reference.

Pudd'nhead Wilson Much scholarly attention has recently gone to *Pudd'nhead Wilson*, a work not previously ranked among Twain's greatest. Its melodrama of the changelings brings into relief the moral ambiguities surrounding race in America. It makes a worthy companion piece to *Huckleberry Finn*, published a decade earlier. In *Huckleberry Finn*, the river acts as a state of nature in which the authority of society's ethical codes can be loosened; while in *Pudd'nhead*, the stifling small-town atmosphere of Dawson's Landing magnifies the contradictions of racism. In *Mark Twain: The Development of a Writer*, Henry Nash Smith notes, "The society of Dawson's Landing imposes upon slaves and masters alike the fictions which sustain the institution of slavery. The training corrupts both: the slave by destroying his human dignity, by educating him to consider himself inferior . . . the master by encouraging cruelty toward the human beings he is taught to regard as animals." Thus, while *Pudd'nhead*'s plot and characterizations leave something to be desired, it effectively conveys the essence of Mark Twain's moral concern.

Responses to Literature

1. Mark Twain himself was unsure whether he intended *Tom Sawyer* and *Huckleberry Finn* for a juvenile or adult audience. Do you think they are appropriate for young readers? Why or why not?

2. Noting the historical context, do you think *The Adventures of Huckleberry Finn* challenges or confirms racial stereotypes?

3. Choose any Mark Twain novel and carefully analyze its overall perspective on human character.

4. In his lifetime, Twain's greatest literary successes were his travel books, such as *The Innocents Abroad*. What are the special qualities of his work in this genre?

BIBLIOGRAPHY

Books

Branch, Edgar M. *The Literary Apprenticeship of Mark Twain*. Urbana: University of Illinois Press, 1950.

Carrington, George C. *The Dramatic Unity of Huckleberry Finn*. Columbus: Ohio State University Press, 1976.

Devoto, Bernard. *Mark Twain's America*. Boston: Little, Brown, 1932.

Ferguson, DeLancey. *Mark Twain: Man and Legend*. New York: Bobbs-Merrill, 1943.

Fishkin, Shelley Fisher. *Lighting out for the Territory: Reflections on Mark Twain and American Culture*. New York: Oxford University Press, 1997.

Hill, Hamlin. *Mark Twain: God's Fool*. New York: Harper & Row, 1973.

Howells, William Dean. *My Mark Twain*. New York: Harper, 1910.

Kaplan, Justin. *Mr. Clemens and Mark Twain*. New York: Simon & Schuster, 1966.

Paine, Albert Bigelow. *Mark Twain, A Biography*. 3 vols. New York: Harper, 1912.

Petit, Arthur G. *Mark Twain and the South*. Lexington: University Press of Kentucky, 1974.

Powers, Ron. *Mark Twain: A Life*. New York: Random House, 2005.

Sloane, David E. E. *Mark Twain as a Literary Comedian*. Baton Rouge: Louisiana State University Press, 1979.

Smith, Henry Nash. *Mark Twain: The Development of a Writer*. Cambridge, Mass.: Belknap, 1962.

Wecter, Dixon. *Sam Clemens of Hannibal*. Boston: Houghton Mifflin, 1952.

Periodicals

Railton, Stephen. "Jim and Mark Twain: What Do Dey Stan' For?" *Virginia Quarterly Review*: 63 (1987).

✸ Anne Tyler

BORN: *1941, Minneapolis, Minnesota*

NATIONALITY: *American*

GENRE: *Fiction*

MAJOR WORKS:

Dinner at the Homesick Restaurant (1982)

The Accidental Tourist (1985)

Breathing Lessons (1988)

Overview

For decades, Anne Tyler's best-selling contemporary fiction has focused on the influence and centrality of family, relationship, and place. Tyler gained national fame when her novel *The Accidental Tourist* (1985) was produced as a major film. Her prominence was heightened when she was awarded the Pulitzer Prize for *Breathing Lessons* (1988). Tyler's construction of character and setting, along with her notable themes of family, identity, and love situate her fiction within the literary traditions of realism and Southern regional literature.

Anne Tyler   *Tyler, Anne, photograph. AP Images.*

Works in Biographical and Historical Context

Growing Up on Quaker Communes Tyler was born in Minneapolis, Minnesota, on October 25, 1941, to Lloyd Parry Tyler, a chemist, and Phyllis Mahon Tyler, a social worker. As members of the Society of Friends, her family moved frequently, often living in Quaker communities in the Midwest and South, before settling in North Carolina. Tyler's childhood was marked by her parents' hunt for a commune where they could observe their faith through a life of noncompetitive simplicity. In the Celo commune, one of the longer-lived of utopian experimental communities located in the Blue Ridge Mountains of North Carolina, Anne and her siblings learned of nature, folkways, literature, and other subjects as they were home-schooled. The Tyler children attended public school when the family moved to Raleigh, North Carolina, in 1952. Anne proved to be an excellent student who enjoyed art. She often painted families with a keen eye for detail, foreshadowing her future of creating pictures with words. Tyler attributes being raised in a series of communes as an experience that made her look "at the normal world with a certain amount of distance and surprise, which can sometimes be helpful to a writer."

Tyler finished her college undergraduate work (in three years) at Duke University, during which time she was the student of Reynolds Price, who himself would become a major novelist and longtime friend. After receiving her BA from Duke University in 1961, Tyler attended Columbia University where she completed her doctoral course work (but not the dissertation) in Russian and then worked as a Russian bibliographer at Duke.

Early Married Life and "Southern" Books In 1963 Tyler married Iranian-born child psychologist (and novelist) Taghi Mohammed Modaressi. She and her husband moved to Montreal, where he completed his residency while she served as assistant to the librarian at McGill University from 1964 to 1965. During her time in Montreal she published her first novels, *If Morning Ever Comes* (1964) and *The Tin Can Tree* (1965), and gave birth to her daughters—Tezh in 1965 and Mitra in 1967. The family then moved to Baltimore, where Tyler raised her daughters and polished her prose. Writing before the women's-rights movement expanded careers for women outside the home, Tyler focused on her family. Her prolific output is due to her ability to maintain the division between her private and public life.

Having grown up in North Carolina, Tyler initially considered herself a Southern writer. Her first three novels—*If Morning Ever Comes* (1964), *The Tin Can Tree* (1965), and *A Slipping-Down Life* (1970)—were set in North Carolina and bear, in their focus on the eccentricities of family life and the strong influence of the past upon the present, a resemblance to the Southern Gothic tradition of

William Faulkner, Carson McCullers, and especially Eudora Welty, whom Tyler later met and befriended.

Breakthrough Novels in Baltimore *The Clock Winder* (1972) marked two important changes in Tyler's career and foreshadowed the great success she was to enjoy beginning in 1982 with *Dinner at the Homesick Restaurant* (1982). The first is that, though eccentric, characters remain her hallmark, as in *The Clock Winder*; they are part of or connected to families rather than merely lone individuals seeking whatever fate may afford them. The second adjustment is that in *The Clock Winder* she found Baltimore the proper backdrop for her fiction. Far more often than not, it has been her setting since.

With the publication of *A Slipping-Down Life* and *The Clock Winder*, Tyler began to receive more serious and positive critical attention, but only in the mid-seventies, when such writers as Gail Godwin and John Updike called attention to her, did her novels benefit from widespread recognition. Tyler's stature as an important literary figure was confirmed by the success of *Morgan's Passing* (1980), which was nominated for the National Book Critics Circle award and received the Janet Heidinger Kafka Prize.

The Pulitzer Prize and Hollywood Tyler addresses more complex domestic-psychological issues in her later works. *Dinner at the Homesick Restaurant*, finalist for the 1983 Pulitzer Prize, is the chronicle of a dysfunctional family whose children keep returning to the site of their childhood abuse. Although *Dinner at the Homesick Restaurant* traces the evolution of the fictional Tull family from roughly 1925 to 1979, its theme of child abuse is particularly relevant to the 1980s, the decade in which the novel was published. The first national studies to determine the prevalence of child abuse were conducted in 1974; five years later, the federal Child Abuse Prevention and Treatment Act mandated periodic National Incidence Reports. The 1988 Study of National Incidence and Prevalence of Child Abuse and Neglect arrived at a total of 1.5 million abused or neglected children, and their report broke down the statistics into three categories of abuse—physical, sexual, and emotional.

Tyler's *The Accidental Tourist* was awarded the National Book Critics Award in 1985 and subsequently became a film featuring William Hurt and Geena Davis. The film version of *The Accidental Tourist*, which increased Tyler's fame, deals with the grief of Macon Leary, whose marriage collapses after the murder of his son. Critics find Tyler at the height of her powers of observation in *Breathing Lessons*, honored with a Pulitzer Prize in 1986. The novel presents a poignant portrait of a beleaguered marriage.

Family Life with Diversity Tyler remains concentrated on the family with insight, humor, and hope. Her 2001 novel *Back When We Were Grownups* was written in reaction to her husband's death in 1997 and focuses on a widow trying to reconnect with her own identity. A television movie adaptation of the book was released in 2004. Tyler's 2006 novel *Digging to America* takes up the issue of international adoptions—specifically the adoption of Asian children by American families. Tyler's focus reflects a growing trend in the United States: in 1999, the U.S. State Department statistics indicate that half of the 17,000 adoptions of children from foreign countries by American parents were from Asian countries, such as China, India, Vietnam, and Korea. Many adoptive parents struggle with the issue of how or whether to teach these adopted children about the cultures of their birth countries. This struggle is the subject of *Digging to America*, in which two couples adopting Korean daughters make very different parenting decisions.

Tyler continues to live and work in Baltimore.

Works in Literary Context

Tyler's works reveal familiarity with an extended literary tradition, with influences ranging from Ralph Waldo Emerson and Henry David Thoreau to William Faulkner and Eudora Welty. The narratives of Tyler, brimming with an amiable realism and vulnerable idiosyncrasy, come to life in characters invested with what is distinctive and grand about humanity.

Southern Literary Tradition   The connection between family, place, and identity in Tyler's novels is a recurring topic of critical discussion. She is often placed within the context of the Southern literary tradition, and her work is frequently associated with the key figures of that movement. Her early years in the South formed the background for Tyler's Southern literary flavor. Tyler was particularly inspired by two Southern literary regionalists, Eudora Welty and Reynolds Price. From a 1980 interview with Welty, Tyler mirrors what critics have written of her, portraying Welty as "pleased by words, by ways of saying things, snatches of dialogue overheard, objects' names discovered and properly applied." Tyler's storytelling reflects a like attention to idiom and detail as well as the influence of the Southern allegiance to setting as integral to character and destiny.

American Realists and Experimentation   Following World War II, American writers began to create innovative and self-aware works shaped by popular culture. Tyler's fiction, according to Sanjukta Dasgupta in *Indian Journal of American Studies*, reflects the postmodern "fusion of social and individual consciousness with an emphasis on the latter." From chronicling the elite classes of society, writers increasingly experimented with influences of media and commonplace language. Tyler's narratives and characters echo this realism in the terrain of their everyday life. Employing language and place of ordinary people navigating everyday existence, Tyler and other American realists, as Alfred Kazin describes, "evidence our writers' absorption in every last detail of this American world, together with a subtle alienation from it."

LITERARY AND HISTORICAL CONTEMPORARIES

Tyler's famous contemporaries include:

Eudora Welty (1909–2001): An American novelist and short story writer, Welty was the winner of the 1973 Pulitzer Prize for fiction for her novel *The Optimist's Daughter* (1972).

Saul Bellow (1915–2005): Bellow was an American novelist and Nobel Prize winner best known for works such as *The Adventures of Augie March* (1953) and *Humboldt's Gift* (1975).

John Updike (1932–2009): Updike is an American novelist who was awarded the Pulitzer Prize for *Rabbit Is Rich* (1981) and another for *Rabbit at Rest* (1990).

Nora Ephron (1941–): An American film producer, screenwriter, novelist, and journalist Ephron has earned three Academy Award nominations for screenwriting on films such as *Silkwood* (1983), *When Harry Met Sally* (1989), and *Sleepless in Seattle* (1993).

Gail Godwin (1937–): Godwin is a best-selling Southern fiction writer whose novels include *The Odd Woman* (1974) and *A Mother and Two Daughters* (1982).

Works in Critical Context

Tyler's canon has a good deal of consistency: a tone of amused detachment, an interest in domestic life, and a sympathetic portrayal of eccentric characters uncannily similar to many readers' relatives. Her work is as remarkable for its originality of plot as for its ingeniously conceived characters and polished prose.

The Accidental Tourist   *The Accidental Tourist* was Tyler's tenth novel, and by the time it was published in 1985, critics had grown to expect a certain type of work from the author. Most critics agreed that while the work was distinctly Tyler, it was also her most accessible and successful novel. Author Larry McMurtry, writing in *The New York Times Book Review*, notes a couple of shortcomings—such as the imperfect handling of two intriguing characters—but ranks it as one of Tyler's best books. Jonathan Yardley, in his review for the *Washington Post Book World*, declares, "With each new novel...it becomes ever more clear that the fiction of Anne Tyler is something both unique and extraordinary in contemporary American literature." Yardley calls it "a beautiful, incandescent, heartbreaking, exhilarating book," and concludes, "Words fail me: one cannot reasonably expect fiction to be much better than this." Other critics, such as Rhoda Koenig, were complimentary but not overwhelmed. In her review for *New York Magazine*, she applauds the author's way with words but not her overly cute treatment of the banal, noting that the book "is pleasant enough to read, but irritating when you stop."

COMMON HUMAN EXPERIENCE

Tyler chronicles ordinary situations and eccentric characters with wry humor and keen insight. Here are some other works that involve individuals in everyday adventures:

"Death of a Traveling Salesman" (1936), a short story by Eudora Welty. This tale chronicles a business trip where the protagonist discovers that freedom from family is not necessarily something to relish.

Howl (1956), a poem by Allen Ginsberg. The fundamental text of the Beat Generation is Ginsberg's long-line rant about outcasts in a nightmarish America.

Lives of Girls and Women (1971), a short story collection by Alice Munro. This fiction, set in southwestern Ontario, recalls seemingly insignificant events of a girl's passage from youth to maturity.

American Pastoral (1997), a novel by Philip Roth. This Pulitzer Prize–winning novel traces the life of a conventional Jewish-American businessman, whose life is devastated by political tumult in the 1960s.

Breathing Lessons   *Breathing Lessons*, Tyler's eleventh novel, represented a subtle but discernible shift in tone that, as the novel presents a journey of marriage—Ira and Maggie's—as a very rocky road, so the most faithful of readers may find it a similar trip. "Tyler's strongest card," notes critic Robert McPhilips in *The Nation*, "is her ability to orchestrate brilliantly funny set pieces and to create exasperating but sympathetic characters." McPhilips observes, "In the past, Tyler has used her magic to illuminate seemingly drab lives. Here, she forces one to confront directly lives that even willful magic can't fully alleviate.rdquo; Hilma Wolitzer, in her review for the *Chicago Tribune*, calls it "Anne Tyler's gentlest and most charming novel and a paean to what is fast becoming a phenomenon—lasting marriage." Wolitzer compliments the author's eye for detail and notes that the book contains "scenes of wonderful tenderness and humor." Similarly, Richard Eder, writing for the *Los Angeles Times Book Review*, notes that while the book might not be her best, "it may be her funniest," and also observes that the book contains moments "more powerful and moving, I think, than anything she has done."

Responses to Literature

1. The city of Baltimore, Maryland, is the setting for most of Tyler's fiction. It is an American city with a rich history that has attracted numerous famous writers. To find out more about Baltimore, read Madison Smartt Bell's *Charm City: A Walk Through Baltimore* (2007) or famed Baltimore journalist H. L. Mencken's autobiography *Happy Days* (1940).

2. *Dinner At The Homesick Restaurant* focuses on how the same experiences can be viewed and absorbed differently by different people. Write a short story in which three characters all share a single experience, but in which each character has a radically different view of the events and how those events affect them.

3. In *Breathing Lessons*, read the scene that occurs at the abortion clinic. What are the points of view expressed in the scene?

4. View the film version of Tyler's *The Accidental Tourist* directed by Lawrence Kasdan and compare it to the original novel. What elements of Tyler's style come through most clearly in the film? Are there elements that appear to work better on the page than on the screen, or vice versa?

5. Read *Digging to America*. In your opinion, which of the families presented in the novel takes the "right" approach to raising an adopted baby from another culture? Why?

BIBLIOGRAPHY

Books

Bail, Paul. *Anne Tyler: A Critical Companion*. Westport, Conn.: Greenwood Press, 1998.

Croft, Robert W. *An Anne Tyler Companion*. Westport, Conn.: Greenwood Press, 1998.

Grove, James. "Anne Tyler: Wrestling with the Lowlier Angel." *Southern Writers at Century's End*. Ed. Jeffrey J. Folks and James A. Perkins. Lexington, Ky.: University Press of Kentucky, 1997.

Voelker, Joseph C. *Art and the Accidental in Anne Tyler*. Columbia, Mo.: University of Missouri Press, 1989.

Periodicals

Brookner, Anita. "A Disturbing Absence of Disturbance." *Spectator* 294 (January 3, 2004): 29–30.

Dasgupta, Sanjukta. "Towards Harmony: Social Concern in Anne Tyler's Fiction." *Indian Journal of American Studies* 27 (Winter 1997): 71–75.

Eder, Richard. "Crazy for Sighing and Crazy for Loving You." *Los Angeles Times Book Review* (September 11, 1988): 3.

Gibson, Mary Ellis. "Family as Fate: The Novels of Anne Tyler." *Southern Literary Journal* 16 (Fall 1983): 47–58.

Jacobs, Rita. "Review of Back When We Were Grownups, by Anne Tyler." *World Literature Today* 76 (spring 2002): 154.

Koenig, Rhoda. "Back in Your Own Backyard." *New York Magazine* vol. 18, no. 34 (September 2, 1985): 59–60.

Mathewson, Joseph. "Taking the Ann Tyler Tour." *Horizon: The Magazine of the Arts* 28 (September 1985): 14.

McMurtry, Larry. "Life Is a Foreign Country." *The New York Times Book Review* (September 8, 1985): 1, 36.

McPhilips, Robert. "The Baltimore Chop." *The Nation* 247 (November 7, 1988): 464–466.

Stephens, Ralph. "Welty, Tyler, and Traveling Salesmen: The Wandering Hero Unhorsed." *The Fiction of Anne Tyler* (1990): 110–118.

Wolitzer, Hilma. "'Breathing Lessons': Anne Tyler's Tender Ode to Married Life." *Chicago Tribune* (August 28, 1988): 1, 9.

Yardley, Jonathan. "Anne Tyler's Family Circles." *Washington Post Book World* (August 25, 1985): 3.

⊛ Yoshiko Uchida

BORN: *1921, Alameda, California*

DIED: *1992, Berkeley, California*

NATIONALITY: *American*

GENRE: *Nonfiction, fiction*

MAJOR WORKS:

Desert Exile: The Uprooting of a Japanese-American Family (1982)

Picture Bride: A Novel (1987)

The Invisible Thread (1992)

Yoshiko Uchida   *Yoshiko Uchida, photograph by Deborah Storms. The Bancroft Library. Courtesy of The Bancroft Library, University of California, Berkeley.*

Overview

Yoshiko Uchida was known for her work documenting the hardships of Japanese-American life during World War II and in the postwar era. Over the course of her career, Uchida published more than thirty books, including nonfiction for adults and fiction for children and teenagers, but her reputation in critical circles largely rests upon her autobiographical story *Desert Exile: The Uprooting of a Japanese-American Family* (1982).

Works in Biographical and Historical Context

A Disrupted Life   The daughter of Japanese immigrants, Yoshiko Uchida was born in Alameda, California, in 1921. Uchida's father had a secure job with an international trading company, and her parents provided their two daughters with financial security and a rich education. Uchida traveled to Japan when she was twelve, but she found that she felt little connection with her ancestral land, especially since she could not read the language. The struggle of living with conflicting ethnic identities, however, became a prevalent theme in her writing. Uchida's high-school experience included her first encounter with institutionalized racism: she found that Japanese American pupils were routinely excluded from school activities and social functions. Uchida worked hard in

high school and graduated early, which enabled her to enroll at the University of California, Berkeley, at the age of sixteen.

Everything changed, though, during World War II, when Uchida and her family and thousands of other Japanese Americans were sent to internment camps. On December 7, 1941, Japan bombed Pearl Harbor, Hawaii, bringing the United States into World War II. That day, Uchida's father was taken away for questioning by the FBI. She and her family were initially sent to a detention center at Tanforan racetrack in California, where they were forced to live in horse stables. They were later transferred to Topaz Detention Center in the Utah desert. Conditions there were even worse than at the racetrack. Nevertheless, the Topaz Detention Center became "home" for three long years.

From Internment to Literary Success   In 1943 Uchida was allowed to leave the camp in order to study for a master's degree in education at Smith College, in Massachusetts. She became a teacher and later took various office jobs before becoming a writer in New York. In 1952 Uchida received a fellowship to go to Japan to collect folktales, a trip that resulted in the publication of several collections of stories. Unlike her earlier trip to Japan, this one

LITERARY AND HISTORICAL CONTEMPORARIES

Uchida's famous contemporaries include:

Jeanne Wakatsuki Houston (1911–2004): Houston was a Japanese-American writer who is best known as the author of *Farewell to Manzanar* (1972), an account of her time in an internment camp during World War II.

Roald Dahl (1916–1990): Although he did produce many literary works for an adult audience, British writer Dahl is most beloved for his enduring catalog of classic children's books, which include *James and the Giant Peach* (1961), *Charlie and the Chocolate Factory* (1964), and *The Witches* (1983).

Monica Itoi Sone (1919–): Sone is a Japanese-American writer and the author of *Nisei Daughter* (1953), an account of her experiences in Japanese-American internment camps during World War II.

Daniel Inouye (1924–): Inouye is an American senator from Hawaii of Japanese descent. The Democratic senator is the first Japanese American to serve in the U.S. House of Representatives.

George Takei (1937–): The Japanese-American actor George Takei became a television star during the 1960s when he played Mr. Sulu on the popular science-fiction series *Star Trek*.

made her keenly aware of her connection with her ancestral culture. That connection is abundantly evident in her autobiographical *Desert Exile, Journey to Topaz: A Story of the Japanese-American Evacuations* (1971).

Uchida devotes the early part of her story to establishing her family's relatively harmonious life in America. At this time Uchida sees little conflict within her hyphenated identity, which does not become achingly apparent until the third chapter, which addresses Pearl Harbor and its immediate effects. The harmonious family life Uchida establishes at the beginning of the book is shattered by the abrupt internment of the family. At this point, Uchida emphasizes the loyalty she and other Japanese Americans felt to the United States, which serves to question the need for internment.

Fiction for Children and Adults Although *Desert Exile* is undoubtedly the most famous of Uchida's books, her 1987 novel, *Picture Bride*, has also received significant critical attention, and it has become widely taught in high schools. *Picture Bride* takes place between 1917 and 1943, encompassing World War I, the Great Depression, and World War II. Uchida's narrative emphasizes the racism endured by Japanese Americans during these years. The novel opens with the young female protagonist, a twenty-one-year-old Japanese woman named Hana

Omiya, who is a "picture bride," a woman who was contracted to marry a Japanese American man after the exchange of pictures. Through Hana's story, Uchida skillfully documents the history of Japanese Americans in the harsh environment of mid-twentieth-century America.

Along with her adult fiction and nonfiction, Uchida was an accomplished writer of children's stories. Two of her many children's works bear particular mention for giving voice to aspects of the Asian American experience. *A Jar of Dreams* (1981) was written for older children or young adults, and it relates the story of an eleven-year-old girl, Rinko, the daughter of a Japanese barber living in California during the Great Depression. Rinko and the rest of her family witness and experience the racist abuse of her father by white Californians, who feel that, as a Japanese immigrant, he is taking much needed jobs and resources away from them. Uchida comes to explore the problems Japanese immigrants face integrating into the majority culture and the conflicting demands placed upon people of "hyphenated" ethnicity. Told from an adolescent viewpoint, the story is able to introduce these issues in ways that are appropriate for a young readership.

Uchida's *The Bracelet* (1993), written for children up to eight years of age, takes up similar racial themes. This story addresses the experience of internment from the perspective of a Japanese American child named Emi. When the United States goes to war with Japan, Emi and her family are forced to live in a detention camp. Consequently, Emi is separated from her best friend, Laurie. When the time comes to say good-bye, Laurie gives Emi a bracelet as a symbol of their lasting friendship. Emi soon experiences all of the harshness and deprivation of the detention camp, where her family is forced to live in a stable. Then, while Emi is trying to adjust to her new existence, she discovers that her bracelet is missing. Although she is initially upset, Emi soon realizes that the bracelet is immaterial, as her relationship with Laurie will endure.

Uchida made it her life's work to demonstrate the injustice of the internment of Japanese Americans during World War II. Through her writing for adults and children, she described the experience from a variety of perspectives, both autobiographical and fictional, making her position clear. Yet, the internment issue also formed part of a larger message. Particularly telling in this regard is Uchida's description of her mission as a writer of children's stories:

> I try to stress the positive aspects of life that I want children to value and cherish. I hope they can be caring human beings who don't think in terms of labels—foreigners or Asians or whatever—but think of people as human beings. If that comes across, then I've accomplished my purpose.

During her life, Uchida was immensely prolific. Her bibliography consists of more than forty books ranging from the autobiographical to the fictional. Toward the end of her life, illness curtailed that productivity, but she still continued to publish until her death in 1992.

Works in Literary Context

Japanese Folk Tales The ancient tradition of Japanese folk tales reaches back some twenty centuries. The tales are generally rooted in the country's chief religion, Shinto, as well as the philosophical schools of Buddhism and Taoism. Indian and Chinese literature had a significant influence on the earliest examples of Japan folklore, but as Japan grew increasingly politically isolated, such outside influences became less prominent. Japanese folk tales are abundant in strange situations; colorful arrays of ghosts, gods, and demons; and odd humor. There is also a streak of detachment and a tendency for the hero to emerge unsuccessful in the tales. In her book, *Dancing Kettle and Other Japanese Folk Tales* (1949), Uchida revisited some of her favorite folk tales and rewrote them for a young audience.

The Japanese-American Experience Uchida's works reflect her attempts to document the Japanese-American experience, incorporating both her own firsthand experiences and those of other immigrants. Most notably, she has written of her experiences in an internment camp during World War II; this has formed the core of her work, just as it has become the single most significant event in the cultural history of all Japanese Americans. In addition, Uchida has focused on the experiences of picture-brides—another defining element of early Japanese-American culture, due to restrictive immigration laws—as well as traditional Japanese folktales that function to preserve an element of Japanese identity for a group that would have been otherwise cut off from their native culture.

Works in Critical Context

The Happiest Ending Uchida enjoyed enthusiastically positive responses from critics to both her adult literature and her books for children. *The Happiest Ending* (1986), a story about an arranged marriage, was hailed by *The New York Times* for being "filled in richly with details of Japanese-American life in the 30's: the furniture, clothes, food, social patterns and manners of a culture balanced between two identities." Uchida herself was praised for her "gift for humorous twists and vigorous narrative." However, a reviewer for the *School Library Journal* suggests, "Young readers may be confused by the attitudes expressed and the vocational and educational restrictions imposed upon the Japanese-Americans, for the fact that the story takes place in 1936 is not well integrated into the story." The review concludes on a positive note by stating that "this is a good, comforting rite-of-passage story."

COMMON HUMAN EXPERIENCE

In her book *Desert Exile, Journey to Topaz: A Story of the Japanese-American Evacuations*, Uchida describes her experiences in an internment camp for Japanese-Americans during World War II. Other works written by Japanese-Americans about the internment camp experience include:

Citizen 13660 (1946), a nonfiction book by Miné Okubo. Artist/writer Miné Okubo's account of her own imprisonment in an internment camp during World War II is notable for its absence of anger and bitterness regarding her horrible situation. Instead, she approaches her internment with mild humor and reserved dignity. The text is accompanied by Okubo's own illustrations.

Nisei Daughter (1953), a nonfiction book by Monica Sone. Sone's story of her internment experience is highly personal, examining her feelings as she struggles to find herself amidst the indignities of camp life.

Farewell to Manzanar (1973), a novel by Jeanne Wakatsuki Houston. Houston's autobiographical novel finds her as a seven-year-old girl suddenly placed in the Manzanar internment camp, a surreal environment complete with baton twirling contests, dances, and a house band called the Jive Bombers.

When the Emperor Was Divine (2002), a novel by Julie Otsuka. This story of a family's dehumanizing experiences in an internment camp is divided into five chapters, each chapter told from a different narrative point of view.

The Invisible Thread The last book Uchida published before her death in 1992 was *The Invisible Thread*, an autobiography intended for teenage readers. Like so much of Uchida's work, the book was favorably reviewed. A reviewer for *Booklist* states of the book, "Uchida writes movingly of her family's hardships during World War II" and that it might prove to be "fascinating reading for history students, Japanese Americans, and fans of Uchida's books." A reviewer for *School Library Journal* commends the author, who "tells her story without bitterness or anger, and relays the joy she felt upon achieving her dream of becoming a teacher and author."

Responses to Literature

1. Uchida has retold her life story in a number of different ways. Her *Desert Exile: The Uprooting of a Japanese-American Family* was intended to be read by adults, while *The Invisible Thread* was aimed at teenagers. Read both books, and explain how Uchida alters her storytelling styles to appeal to each book's intended audience.

2. Uchida spent a period of her life in an internment camp during World War II. Research Japanese-American internment and argue whether or not it was necessary to imprison Japanese Americans during wartime. Be sure to support your statement with reasons, facts, and examples.

3. Uchida often based her books on Japanese folktales. Try taking your favorite folktale and rewriting it in your own style.

4. Uchida once said, "I try to stress the positive aspects of life that I want children to value and cherish," even though she wrote about events in American history that many consider shameful and unjust. Read *A Jar of Dreams* and then explain how Uchida manages to stress positive aspects in this story. Support your response with specific details from the book.

BIBLIOGRAPHY

Books

Davis, Rocío G. "Itineraries of Submission: Picture Brides in Recent Japanese American Narratives," in *Asian American Studies: Identity, Images, and Issues Past and Present*, edited by Esther Mikyung Ghymn. New York: Peter Lang, 2000.

Sinnott, Susan. *Extraordinary Asian Americans and Pacific Islanders*. New York: Children's Press, 2003.

Wong, Sau-ling Cynthia. *Reading Asian American Literature: From Necessity to Extravagance*. Princeton, N.J.: Princeton University Press, 1993.

Periodicals

Campbell, Patty. "Children's Books." *The New York Times* (February 9, 1986).

Harada, Violet. "Caught Between Two Worlds: Themes of Family, Community, and Ethnic Identity in Yoshiko Uchida's Work for Children." *Children's Literature in Education* 29, no. 1 (1998): 19–30.

McDiffett, Danton. "Prejudice and Pride: Japanese Americans in the Young Adult Novels of Yoshiko Uchida." *Studies in Culture and the Humanities* 3 (1994): 1–22.

"Yoshiko Uchida, 70, A Children's Author" (obituary). *The New York Times* (June 24, 1992).

Fazoli, Carol. "Autobiographies—The Stories Behind the Stories." *School Library Journal* (November 1, 2003).

Usui, Masami. "Regaining Lost Privacy: Yoshiko Uchida's Storytelling as a Nisei Woman Writer." *English Journal* 90, no. 3 (2001): 60–65.

Web Sites

Online Archive of California. *Finding Aid to the Yoshiko Uchida papers, 1903–1994 (bulk 1942–1992)*. Accessed November 25, 2008, from http://content.cdlib.org/view?docId=tf0c600134&chunk.id=bioghist-1.3.4.

❀ John Updike

BORN: *1932, Reading, Pennsylvania*

DIED: *2009, Beverly Farms, Massachusetts*

NATIONALITY: *American*

GENRE: *Fiction, poetry*

MAJOR WORKS:

Rabbit, Run (1960)
Rabbit Is Rich (1981)
The Witches of Eastwick (1984)
Rabbit at Rest (1991)

Overview

A major contemporary American author, Updike is noted for the subtle complexity of his fiction, verse, and criticism. His values derive from myth and Christianity and are evidenced in his work by his emphasis upon morality. Updike's major subject since the mid-1960s has been the domestic life of the American middle class and its attendant rituals: marriage, sex, and divorce. Against the mundane setting of American suburbia, Updike presents average people—usually men—searching for aesthetic or religious meaning in the secular awareness of their own mortality.

John Updike   *Updike, John, 1990, photograph. AP Images.*

Works in Biographical and Historical Context

Beginnings of a Literary Life John Updike was born on March 18, 1932, in Shillington, Pennsylvania. His father, Wesley, was a high school mathematics teacher, and because Updike's mother, Linda Grace Hoyer Updike, nurtured literary aspirations of her own, books were a large part of the boy's early life. This fertile environment prepared the way for a prolific career that began in earnest at the age of twenty-two, upon the publication of his first story, "Friends from Philadelphia," in *The New Yorker* in 1954.

Updike majored in English at Harvard where he developed his skills as a graphic artist and cartoonist for the *Lampoon*, the college's humor magazine. In 1953, his junior year at Harvard, he married Mary Pennington. Upon his graduation the following year, Updike and his bride went to London where he had won a Knox fellowship for study at the Ruskin School of Drawing and Fine Art in Oxford.

In 1954, Updike graduated from Harvard University. He soon began contributing stories, poems, and criticism to *The New Yorker* and served as a reporter for the magazine's "Talk of the Town" column from 1955 to 1957. Although Updike left *The New Yorker* to pursue his literary career, he has regularly published fiction, verse, and criticism in the magazine.

Prolific and Successful in the 1950s and 1960s Updike's first major work, *The Carpentered Hen, and Other Tame Creatures* (1958), contains poems that whimsically attack such topics as modern values, sports, and journalism. Updike published his first novel, *Poorhouse Fair*, in 1959. His second novel, *Rabbit, Run*, his best-known work, established him as a major novelist. His third novel, *The Centaur* (1963), won a National Book Award in 1963.

Updike's early short fiction, collected in *The Same Door* (1959), also earned him a reputation as a leading practitioner of the short story form. Most of Updike's early stories are set in the fictional town of Olinger, which he modeled after his hometown of Shillington, Pennsylvania. Small-town concerns are the subject of Updike's second short-story collection, *Pigeon Feathers* (1962), which addresses adolescent anxieties regarding love, marriage, and children. Further tales of small-town life are collected in *Olinger Stories* (1964). In the mid-1960s, the fictional Boston suburb of Tarbox largely replaced Olinger as Updike's setting, reflecting his actual move from New York City to Ipswich, Massachusetts, in 1957. The stories set in Tarbox feature sophisticated, urbanized individuals whose marital problems and quests for identity mirror the social anxieties of their times. Tarbox is the setting of *Bech: A Book* (1970), in which Updike introduces his alter ego, Henry Bech. A Jewish bachelor and writer who fears the commitments of marriage and success, Bech aims in these stories to "confess sterility"—to

---

LITERARY AND HISTORICAL CONTEMPORARIES

Updike's famous contemporaries include:

Saul Bellow (1915–2005): One of the foremost American writers of the twentieth century, Bellow was the author of seventeen novels and short story collections, and he won the Nobel Prize in Literature in 1976.

Norman Mailer (1923–2007): Mailer was a novelist, short story writer, essayist, poet, and playwright who was twice awarded the Pulitzer Prize. One of his most famous novels is his first, *The Naked and the Dead* (1948).

Philip Roth (1933–): Roth has been producing fiction of the highest quality for nearly five decades, since the success of his first short story collection, *Goodbye, Columbus*, in 1959.

Gore Vidal (1925–): Vidal is an American novelist, short story writer, playwright, and screenwriter. He is most highly regarded today as an essayist.

Jackson Pollock (1912–1956): Pollock was a prominent American painter and a leader in the abstract expressionist movement. Updike drew on Pollock's life for many of the details in his novel *Seek My Face* (2002).

---

demonstrate how authors betray their integrity for monetary or fashionable reasons

The "Rabbit" Books Though *The Centaur* won him the National Book Award, it was *Rabbit, Run* that most intrigued critics and readers alike. This book explores the prolonged adolescence of an inarticulate working-class father named Harry Angstrom (nicknamed "Rabbit"), who misses the excitement of his high school years as a basketball star. Updike wrote three sequels to *Rabbit, Run*, each reflecting a new decade in Rabbit's life. *Rabbit Redux* (1971) mirrors the unrest of the late 1960s, this time centering on the threat posed to Rabbit's marriage when he brings home a young drug addict and a black revolutionary. The novel begins on the day of the moon shot in 1969. The optimism of American technology is countered by the despair of race riots, anti-Vietnam War protests, and the drug culture. Rabbit is nostalgic for the secure serenity of the 1950s. Critical reaction to the book was largely negative, but reviewers were nearly unanimous in their praise of *Rabbit Is Rich* (1981), for which Updike received the National Book Critics Circle Award, the American Book Award, and the Pulitzer Prize. A quiet tone of acceptance permeates this work, in which Rabbit, middle-aged and basically content with his marriage, must resolve his feelings regarding his daughter's death and his own mortality. The novel also evokes one major crisis of the time: the gasoline shortage in 1979.

The final book of the Rabbit tetralogy, *Rabbit at Rest* (1991), also won the Pulitzer Prize and the National

Book Critics Circle Award. *Rabbit at Rest* brings Rabbit into the 1980s to confront an even grimmer set of problems: AIDS, cocaine addiction, and terrorism. Much of this work focuses on Rabbit's physical deterioration—his overeating, diminished libido, and two heart attacks, the last one of which kills him. Several critics have viewed Rabbit's fate as representative of the United States' decline over four decades.

Later Novels   Updike's novel, *The Witches of Eastwick* (1984), centers on three divorced women who acquire the powers of witches, casting evil spells and pursuing unhappily married men in their suburban community until the arrival of a demonic stranger throws them into competition. The novel received mixed reviews, as did *Roger's Version* (1986), which centers on a divinity school professor's dualistic feelings regarding a student's proposal to prove the existence of God by computer.

Updike has continued to be prolific in his literary output. During the 1990s he wrote the novels *Brazil* (1993), a reworking of the legend of Tristan and Isolde, and *In the Beauty of the Lilies* (1996), which chronicled the lives of an American family over four generations. In Updike's fifth decade of publication, he offered *Gertrude and Claudius* (2000), a prequel to William Shakespeare's *Hamlet* (c. 1600). Other novels followed: *Rabbit Remembered* (2001), *Seek My Face* (2002), *Villages* (2004), *Terrorist* (2006), and *The Widows of Eastwick* (2008).

Updike died in January 2009 from lung cancer.

Works in Literary Context

The Suburban American Experience   Updike has been described as the chronicler of suburban America, of ordinary people living ordinary lives. His typical concerns are with family relationships, sex, marriage and divorce, religion, and aging. He explores the spiritual condition of people's lives from the perspective of Christian theology influenced by his study of the theologian Karl Barth. Updike has said that the central theme of each of his novels is "meant to be a moral dilemma," and that his books are intended as "moral debates with the reader." The tension in his work is often the result of the struggles of his characters to deal with these apparently insoluble dilemmas and determine what is morally right in a constantly changing world. Tempted to act selfishly, they also are aware of the need for self-restraint.

Updike's focus on the complex implications of his characters' moral decisions is sharp, so that the issues are always clear and the consequences of each decision fully developed. While Updike's characters are quick to judge each other, their creator refuses either to bless or to condemn; and each novel clearly demonstrates that the specific moral problem it treats is irresolvable. The world Updike creates in his fiction is morally ambiguous. He himself has said, "My subject is the American Protestant small town middle class. I like middles. It is in middles that extremes clash, where ambiguity restlessly rules."

Works in Critical Context

Hailed by critics and readers for his breadth of knowledge and mastery of presentation, Updike is one of America's great novelists; he is considered a premier chronicler of middle America in all its mundane glory. However, the true merit of his work is subject to fierce debate. Most critics familiar with Updike have strong opinions about the author's work. As Joseph Kanon explains in *Saturday Review*: "The debate . . . has long since divided itself into two pretty firmly entrenched camps: those who admire the work consider him one of the keepers of the language; those who don't say he writes beautifully about nothing very much." In the former category is John Cheever, who deems Updike "the most brilliant and versatile writer of his generation." On the other side of the debate are such literary figures as Norman Mailer and John W. Aldridge, who regard Updike's style as superficial, masking a lack of statement or substance.

Couples   *Couples* met with a generally negative critical response, although this did little to tone down public enthusiasm for the work; it was on the *Publishers Weekly* best-seller list for thirty-six weeks. One of the critics who had harsh words for *Couples* was Elizabeth Dalton. In her *Partisan Review* commentary she asserts: "In its delicacy and fullness Updike's style seems to register a flow of fragments almost perfectly toned. And yet, after pages and pages of his minutely detailed impressions, the accumulated effect is one of waste." Charles Thomas Samuels, in *John Updike*, offers the view that although there is in the novel "a great deal of talk about God and sin," there is very little action to illustrate it. Robert Detweiler, while acknowledging the negative character of many reviews, is of the view that the novel deserves better. He describes it as a "big novel about love and death, free-flowing and clever . . . and socially significant enough to inspire a *Time* cover story on American morals."

The Rabbit Tetralogy By general consent, it was Updike's second novel, *Rabbit, Run*, that established his reputation as a major novelist. Reviewing the novel in the *Times Literary Supplement*, Sir Thomas Wiles Chitty comments, "Updike has written a small-town tragedy and has succeeded in making it convincing, vivid, and awful." However, *Rabbit, Run* was not without its critics. Some reviewers professed shock at the sexual explicitness of the language and situations. "Looking back," writes Eliot Fremont-Smith in the *Village Voice*, "it must have been the sexuality that so upset the respectable critics of *Rabbit, Run* in 1960. Their consternation had to do with what seemed a great divide between John Updike's exquisite command of prose . . . and the apparent no-good vulgar nothing he expended it on."

Rabbit Redux, the second volume in the trilogy, was generally not so well received. Christopher Ricks, in the *New York Review of Books* argues that "[t]he book is cleverer than a barrel full of monkeys, and about as odd in its relation of form to content . . . ; its existence is likely to do retrospective damage to that better book, *Rabbit Run*." The book was not without its defenders. In *Yale Review*, Michael Cooke describes it as "vintage Updike. The prose is swift and sinuous, though the action is somewhat slow and wanting in momentum."

After the comparative failure of *Rabbit Redux*, critical assessment of *Rabbit Is Rich* was, on the whole, laudatory. For Gene Lyons, writing in *The Nation*, it was Updike's "best work in many years. It is beautifully written, compassionate, knowing and wise novel." In the *New York Review of Books*, Alfred Kazin calls the novel "a brilliant performance," observing that Updike "revels in his great gifts of style and social—I mean domestic—observation." Roger Sales in the *New York Times Book Review* believes the book to be far superior to its predecessor in the trilogy.

The publication of *Rabbit at Rest* in 1990 completed the *Rabbit* tetralogy. Many critics regarded the final novel as Updike's masterpiece. For Jonathan Rabin in the *Washington Post*, "From now on it is going to be hard to read John Updike without seeing all his earlier work as a long rehearsal for this book." In the *New York Times*, Michiko Kakutani asserts, the novel "should be read . . . by anyone interested in the vicissitudes of middle-class life in America today."

Responses to Literature

1. Read *The Witches of Eastwick* (1984) and then read the sequel that followed nearly twenty-five years later, *The Widows of Eastwick* (2008). Which novel do you prefer, and why? How has time changed the beliefs, attitudes, and lifestyles of the women depicted in the novels? How has Updike's writing style and choice of subject matter changed in the intervening years?

2. Updike's novel *Couples* (1968) was a best-seller, but some people at the time were shocked by the explicit language and the detailed examination of the sex lives of middle-class couples. Research the changing attitudes to sex that marked the 1960s and note how that is reflected in the novel. As you read the novel forty years after publication, does it seem so shocking now? Have social attitudes to such matters changed over the past forty years? If so, in what ways?

3. Updike is usually admired for his style, but some critics claim that his work lacks depth. Select one novel or short story by Updike. In an essay, describe his style and also agree or disagree with the negative judgment of his work by some. What are the themes of the work under consideration? Are they superficial, or do they leave you pondering some of the deeper meanings in life?

4. Read Updike's novel *Gertrude and Claudius* (2000). How does the novel enrich or alter your understanding of Shakespeare's *Hamlet*? In what ways is this novel different from Updike's usual settings and concerns, and in what sense might it be thought of as similar to his other novels?

BIBLIOGRAPHY

Books

Bloom, Harold, ed. *John Updike: Modern Critical Views.* New York: Chelsea House, 1987.

Burchard, Rachael C. *John Updike: Yea Sayings.* Carbondale, Ill.: Southern Illinois University Press, 1971.

Broer, Lawrence R. *Rabbit Tales: Poetry and Politics in John Updike's Rabbit Novels.* Tuscaloosa, Ala.: University of Alabama Press, 1998.

De Bellis, Jack, ed. *John Updike: the Critical Responses to the "Rabbit" Saga.* Westport, Conn.: Praeger, 2005.

Detweiler, Robert. *John Updike.* Boston: Twayne, 1984.

Hamilton, Alice and Kenneth. *The Elements of John Updike.* Grand Rapids, Mich.: Eerdmans, 1970.

Hunt, George. *John Updike and the Three Great Secret Things: Sex, Religion, and Art.* Grand Rapids, Mich.: Eerdmans, 1980.

Karl, Frederick R. *American Fictions, 1940/1980: A Comprehensive History and Critical Evaluation.* New York: Harper & Row, 1983, pp. 276–383.

Luscher, Robert M. *John Updike: A Study of the Short Fiction.* New York: Twayne, 1993.

Markle, Joyce B. *Fighters and Lovers: Theme in the Novels of John Updike.* New York: New York University Press, 1973.

Newman, Judie. *John Updike.* New York: St. Martin's Press, 1988.

Olster, Stacey. *The Cambridge Companion to John Updike.* New York: Cambridge University Press, 2006.

Pritchard, William H. *Updike: America's Man of Letters*. South Royalton, Vt.: Steerforth Press, 2000.

Ristoff, Dilvo I. *Updike's America: The Presence of Contemporary American History in John Updike's Rabbit Trilogy*. New York: Peter Lang, 1988.

Samuels, Charles Thomas. *John Updike*. University of Minnesota Pamphlets on American Writers, no. 79. Minneapolis: University of Minnesota, 1969.

Schiff, James A. *John Updike Revisited*. New York: Twayne Publishers, 1998.

Uphaus, Suzanne Henning. *John Updike*. New York: Ungar, 1980.

Periodicals

Chitty, Sir Thomas Willes. "Enemies of Promise." *Times Literary Supplement* (September 29, 1961): 648.

Cooke, Michael. Review of *Rabbit Reddux*. *Yale Review* (Summer 1972): 606.

Detweiler, Robert. "Updike's Couples Eros Demythologized." *Twentieth Century Literature* (October 1971): 235–46.

Fremont-Smith, Eliot. "Rabbit Ruts." *Village Voice* (September 30–October 6, 1981): 35, 55.

Kakutani, Michiko. "Just 30 Years Later, Updike Has a Quartet." *New York Times* (September 25, 1990): C13, C17.

Leonard, John. Review of *Rabbit Is Rich*. *New York Times* (September 22, 1981).

Lyons, Gene. *Rabbit Is Rich*. *The Nation* (November 7, 1981): 477–79.

Rabin, Jonathan. "Rabbit's Last Run." *Washington Post Book World* (September 30, 1990): 1, 15.

Ricks, Christopher. "Flopsy Bunny." *New York Review of Books* (December 16, 1971): 7–9.

✸ Jean Valentine

BORN: *1934, Chicago, Illinois*

NATIONALITY: *American*

GENRE: *Poetry*

MAJOR WORKS:

Dream Barker (1965)

Home Deep Blue: New and Selected Poems (1989)

The River at Wolf (1992)

Door in the Mountain: New and Collected Poems 1965–2003 (2004)

Overview

The poetry of Jean Valentine is as thematically diverse as it is stylistically unpredictable. Valentine conjures dream-like images and ethereal rhythms whether she is exploring the most seemingly mundane subject matter, such as a young girl spilling milk on the floor, or life's most pro-

Jean Valentine   *AP Images*

found turning points. Her concise, but thrillingly evocative work has earned her the Maurice English Poetry Award (1991) and the National Book Award (2004). In 2008 she was named the State Poet of New York.

Works in Biographical and Historical Context

A Childhood of Yearning   Jean Valentine was born on April 27, 1934, in Chicago, Illinois. As a child, Valentine held an intense spiritual curiosity. In an interview with Poetry Society.org, Valentine said of this interest in religion, "It wasn't particularly in my family. Maybe one has a guardian angel. It's really a mystery where that comes from. Here, in America, you would never presume that the person next to you would share your religious feelings." This kinship between religion and mystery would often work its way into the poetry she would compose as an adult.

When she was a young girl, Valentine and her parents (John and Jean Purcell Valentine) moved to Massachusetts. There Valentine attended Milton Academy Girls' School. After turning eighteen in 1952, she enrolled at Radcliffe College in Cambridge where she majored in

English. During her time at school, she developed a love of writing that resulted in her first published piece. The poem, simply titled "Poem," appeared in the Harvard University publication *The Harvard Crimson* in 1955. The following year, Valentine graduated from Radcliffe with dreams of continuing upon her poetic path.

Struggling for Success Establishing herself in the world of poetry was not as easy as Valentine had hoped. The following decade found her settling into domesticity in New York while struggling to get further work published. In 1957, she wed her first husband, the late historian James Chase, with whom she would have two daughters, Sarah, in 1958 and Rebecca, in 1960. Meanwhile, she received rejection letter after rejection letter from publications to which she submitted her poems. Perhaps it was the sparkling originality of her work that caused poetry journals to turn away, but Valentine was unwilling to alter her vision even as she longed for acceptance. "I had no choice," she told Poetry Society.org. "It was just the only thing I could do. I did often wish I could do something more popular, but I can't. It would be fun to be having people love your work."

Valentine's earliest poems are more formal than the work for which she would later become most renowned. Her poems were more likely to consist of regular metric and rhymes schemes. She would often tender allusions to the Bible and classical literature in order to lend depth and weight to her work. Her concerns often swirled in the realm of womanhood: romance, marriage, home life, motherhood, feminism, as well as the more personal issues of her struggles with alcohol and depression. Yet, she also relied heavily on fantastic imagery, which leant an aura of mystery and obscurity to her work. The intensity and elusiveness of her imagery proved a stumbling block to some readers, but it also distinguished her as a writer with a singular, startlingly original vision. As she would continue to create, she would continue to develop this style and expand her worldview.

The Breakthrough In 1964, Valentine experienced a career breakthrough when a collection of her poems beat three hundred other entries to win the Yale Series of Younger Poets Award. The following year the collection was published as *Dream Barker and Other Poems*, thus beginning her highly successful and prolific career as a publishing poet and leading her to seek a life away from traditional family life. Valentine and Chace were divorced in 1968. The following year she published her second collection titled *Pilgrims*.

During the 1970s, Valentine released two more collections, *Ordinary Things* in 1974 and *The Messenger* in 1979. Her next anthology, *Home Deep Blue: New and Selected Poems*, would not appear until 1989, when she left the United States to live with painter Barrie Cooke in Ireland. During her time in Ireland (1989–1996), Valentine's poetry reached full maturity, becoming more encompassing in subject matter and distinctive in approach. Stylistically, her work always tended toward the brief and the

LITERARY AND HISTORICAL CONTEMPORARIES

Valentine's famous contemporaries include:

James Chace (1931–2004): Chace was an American historian who wrote twelve books during his lifetime and was celebrated for his elegantly phrased examinations of American history. His writing has had a notable influence on U.S. policy, and his phrase "America, the indispensable nation" was often used by former secretary of state Madeline Albright. From 1957 to 1968, Chace was married to Jean Valentine, with whom he had two daughters.

Mahmoud Darwish (1941–2008): Darwish was a Palestinian poet and author who won a number of awards for his work, which often focused on his homeland of Palestine. Darwish wrote over thirty poetry collections during his lifetime. Jean Valentine has referred to Darwish as an inspiration.

Fanny Howe (1940–): Howe is a multiple award-winning American writer and a highly influential and widely read experimental poet. She has also published numerous novels, short stories, and essays. Valentine is an admirer of Howe's work.

Billy Collins (1941–): Collins was the U.S. poet laureate from 2001 to 2003 and was further honored when he was named New York State Poet in 2004. Collins is beloved for his simple, humorous, and accessible poetry.

Barack Obama (1961–): Obama is a former senator from Illinois. He made history when he became the first African American elected to be president of the United States in 2008.

dreamily evocative, yet her way with rhythm, rhyme, and meter had now grown increasingly free, verging on the experimental. The issues she now tackled in her work were legion, ranging from politics and social issues to the most ordinary daily activities. No matter what a particular poem might be about, Valentine would fashion it with trademark fearlessness and honesty, even when evoking surrealistic, dreamlike images. Unlike her earlier works, which often found the poet focusing her gaze at herself, her more recent poems often zeroed in on characters notable for the down-to-earth way Valentine portrayed them. Even at her most obscure, Valentine displayed a true gift for making her characters seem like living, breathing humans. Her personal feelings of empathy and sympathy for those working across life's myriad obstacle courses are consistently palpable in her work.

Honoring an Original Poet As well as publishing, Valentine has also worked as a poetry teacher at a number of institutions, including City University of New York, Columbia University, Hunter College, Pierson College at

COMMON HUMAN EXPERIENCE

In her poem "Seeing You," Valentine expresses her feminist ideals. Other works of feminist poetry and literature include:

"The Yellow Wallpaper" (1892), a short story by Charlotte Perkins Gilman. Gilman's story finds a woman confined in her bedroom after a male doctor diagnoses her as suffering from a "temporary nervous depression." The doctor's misguided diagnosis results in the woman's full-fledged psychosis as she begins to see strange shapes swimming beneath the yellow wallpaper covering her room. The story is a potent criticism of the flippant medical treatment many women received during the nineteenth century.

Helen in Egypt (1954), an epic poem by H. D. (Hilda Doolittle) in which she provides a feminist take on the epic poetry of Homer (*The Iliad*). H. D. views the events of the Trojan War via the female point of view of Helen of Troy and reflects her annoyance with the decidedly male perspective of male-centric epic poetry.

"Still I Rise" (1978), a poem by Maya Angelou. Angelou's poem is a powerful statement of the perseverance and fortitude of women who refuse to be ground down by controlling men. "Still I Rise" is a celebration of female power and feminine sexuality, as well as a statement on the rise of African Americans from slavery, and is as inspiring as it is unapologetic.

The Color Purple (1982), a novel by Alice Walker. Walker tells the story of Celie, a poor African American woman living in the rural South who seeks to escape the conscienceless treatment she suffers at the hands of men. The novel, an example of both feminist and African American literature, is mainly composed of letters written by the nearly illiterate Celie.

Yale University, Sarah Lawrence College, Swarthmore College, the University of Pittsburgh, and the 92nd Street Young Men's Hebrew Association. No longer able to think of herself as an "unpopular poet," Valentine has received multiple honors, including the Guggenheim Foundation Fellowship, the National Book Award for Poetry (2004) for her collection *Door in the Mountain* and the Jean Kennedy Smith New York University Creative Writing Award of Distinction (2005). In 2008 Valentine received one of the highest honors an American poet can receive when she was named poet laureate of New York State, a title she will hold until 2010.

Works in Literary Context

Imagism The poetry movement called imagism dates back to the early 1910s when poets like Ezra Pound and Amy Lowell used vivid, precisely described visual images to bring their poems to life. They composed concise, clear verses focused on a specific visual image. Early imagists rejected the romanticism and sentimentality of the Victorian poetry of the mid- to late nineteenth century. While the movement only lasted a few years, its influence has continued to spread throughout the years, seeping into the objectivist poetry of the 1930s (which treated poems as objects) and the Beat poetry of the 1950s (which rejected traditional American values in favor of drug and sex experimentation and Eastern spirituality). Imagism has also greatly influenced the work of Valentine, who excels at creating specific, visual images the imagists revered.

Feminist poetry The feminist movement developed over the course of the twentieth century with the intent of providing women with all the civil, human, personal, and legal rights afforded to men in the United States and Britain. The feminist movement was integral in winning women the right to vote in the late 1910s, the legalization of abortion in 1973, and numerous workplace rights, such as maternity leave, protection against sexual harassment, and equal pay. Feminism birthed a movement in poetry that not only championed feminist ideals but distinguished itself through experimentation with style and form. Free verse, rather than formally metered and rhymed verse, was prominent in feminist poetry. Valentine's "Seeing You" is considered to be a prime example of feminist poetry.

Works in Critical Context

In 1992, poet Seamus Heaney remarked, "Jean Valentine opens a path to a mature place where there is 'no inside wall': rapturous, risky, shy of words but desperately true to them, these are poems that only she could write." Other critics of Valentine's poetry have echoed Heaney's sentiment and praised Valentine's uniqueness even further. Poet Adrienne Rich once said,

> Looking into a Jean Valentine poem is like looking into a lake: you can see your own outline, and the shapes of the upper world, reflected among rocks, underwater life, glint of lost bottles, drifted leaves. The known and familiar become one with the mysterious and half-wild, at the place where consciousness and the subliminal meet. This is a poetry of the highest order, because it lets us into spaces and meanings we couldn't approach in any other way.

Indeed, Jean Valentine's poetry is often described as a place where unlike things meet: the mundane and the intense, the dream-like and the real, the fragmented and the full. Valentine's adeptness at making the simplest ideas and images complex fosters a certain kind of trust within a reader; once grounded in the recognizable, the reader will take risks in following the poet into the unexpected. David Rivard, who reviewed Valentine's work for *Ploughshares*, a literary journal, finds "[t]his intimacy is both unsettling and comforting." With the release of Valentine's career-spanning *Door in the Mountain*, *Library*

Journal called Valentine "one of the best [poets] at work in America today."

Growing Darkness, Growing Light Valentine's dreamlike images may seem inaccessible to some readers, but she has long found favor in the critical world. Her 1997 collection *Growing Darkness, Growing Light* inspired *Praxis* to applaud Valentine for her ability to express "an empathy toward her subjects and a desire to convey their struggles, their attitudes and their feelings" while the book caused *Publishers Weekly* to declare Valentine "a commanding poet" and the book "one of [her] best collections." Carol Muske of *The Nation* described Valentine as "a writer of deep-image, projective verse" before stating that "the poems in [*Growing Darkness, Growing Light*] are indeed dreams, but precise dreams of waking: startling junctures of the abstract and the carnal."

Door in the Mountain: New and Collected Poems 1965–2003 Valentine's relatively recent collection *Door in the Mountain: New and Collected Poems 1965–2003* (2004) was hailed in the *Harvard Review* as a "beautiful volume" that is "a tribute indeed to one of our most interesting and accomplished poets." The review went on to specify that "Valentine makes a virtue out of spareness, producing increasingly elliptical lyrics to entice readers. The new style, which has its roots in the poems in *Home Deep Blue* from 1989, makes for an art that is less immediately accessible but perhaps all the more powerful for the challenges it puts forth." Of the same volume, John Freeman wrote in the *Seattle Times*, "While her contemporaries have turned the blank page into a confessional, Valentine fashioned a magic carpet out of it instead. Using an eerie sense of poise, she transports readers to cloudy dreamscapes where ordinary things take on secret menace and poignancy."

Responses to Literature

1. Valentine has come to be known for her strikingly brief poems, but her early poem "The Little Flower" is notable for its length and density. Read "The Little Flower" and the more recent, comparatively brief poem "Leaving." Think about how the tightening of her style has changed Valentine's work. Is her poetry stronger for being briefer or has she lost a quality that her earlier work possessed? Explain your response in a brief essay.

2. Much of Valentine's poetry is concerned with social issues. Her poem "Two Poems for Matthew Shepard" is a tribute to a homosexual young man who was murdered by a pair of bigoted men. Read Valentine's poem and explain in a brief essay what you think she is saying about Shepard.

3. Valentine's poem "Seeing You" is considered to be a significant example of contemporary feminist poetry. Read "Seeing You" and explain what you think the message is that Valentine is trying to convey with the poem. Support your response with details from the poem.

BIBLIOGRAPHY

Periodicals

Davis, Ellen. Review of *Door in the Mountain: New and Collected Poems 1965–2003. Harvard Review* (December, 2005).

Koch, Crystal. "Jean Valentine Poetically Enchants Audience." *Praxis* (October 16, 1997).

Muske, Carol. Review of *Growing Darkness, Growing Light. The Nation* (July 21, 1997): 36.

Review of *Growing Darkness, Growing Light. Publishers Weekly* (March 31, 1997): 70.

Web sites

Answers.com. *Jean Valentine*. Accessed November 28, 2008, from http://www.answers.com/topic/jean-valentine.

Harvard University Library. *Valentine, Jean. Papers, 1952–2004 (inclusive), 1970–2004 (bulk): A Finding Aid* . Accessed November 28, 2008, from http://oasis.lib.harvard.edu/oasis/deliver/~sch00369.

Valentine, Jean. *Bio/Books*. Accessed November 28, 2008, from http://www.jeanvalentine.com/bio06.html.

Poetry Foundation. *Jean Valentine*. Accessed November 28, 2008, from http://www.poetryfoundation.org/archive/poet.html?id=7021.

The Poetry Society of America. *A Conversation with Jean Valentine*. Accessed November 28, 2008, from http://www.poetrysociety.org/journal/articles/valentine.html.

Rutgers School of Arts and Sciences. *Writers at Rutgers: Jean Valentine*. Accessed December 12, 2008, from http://english.rutgers.edu/news_events/war/calendar/0405/valentine.html.

Seattle Times *2004 National Book Award Winners: Poetry and Nonfiction*. Accessed December 12, 2008, from http://community.seattletimes.nwsource.com/archive/?date=20041128&slug=nbapoetry28.

✵ Gore Vidal

BORN: *1925, West Point, New York*

NATIONALITY: *American*

GENRE: *Fiction, nonfiction, drama*

MAJOR WORKS:

The City and the Pillar (1946)

Visit to a Small Planet (1955)

Myra Breckenridge (1968)

Burr (1973)

Lincoln (1984)

Overview

A prolific novelist, Gore Vidal is famous for his controversial subject matter and his historical novels. But his versatility extends beyond the world of the novel, as he

Gore Vidal   *Vidal, Gore, photograph. AP Images.*

has also achieved fame as playwright, critic, essayist, mystery writer, and screenwriter.

Works in Biographical and Historical Context

Discord and Politics   Eugene Luther Vidal was born on October 3, 1925, in West Point, New York, where his father was an army instructor of aeronautics at the famous West Point Military Academy. His mother, Nina, was an actress and an alcoholic, who had several affairs during the marriage. She and Vidal's father divorced in 1935.

Vidal became a part of the political life very early. After his parents divorced, his mother married the wealthy and socially prominent financier Hugh D. Auchincloss. After eventually separating from Vidal's mother, Auchincloss went on to marry Janet Lee Bouvier, the mother of future first lady, Jacqueline Bouvier Kennedy Onassis, bringing Vidal into future orbit with the politically powerful Kennedy family.

Vidal spent much of his childhood in Washington, D.C. Because of the discord between his parents, he was heavily influenced by his grandfather, Senator Thomas P. Gore. Thomas, a populist (someone who supports democracy, and the rights of the common people over the elite), who was Oklahoma's first U.S. senator and was also blind. Vidal spent many hours in Gore's extensive library, frequently reading aloud to him. This helped to give Vidal his first understanding of history and politics. Despite the fact that his family was wealthy, he would later describe himself

as a populist, like his grandfather. Through Thomas P. Gore, Vidal met the personalities of Washington. He experienced a stimulating tour of pre-World War II Europe at age fourteen. Inspired by his grandfather, Vidal decided to take the name Gore as his first name.

In 1940, Vidal enrolled in the prestigious Phillips Exeter Academy, where he became interested in writing. By the time Vidal graduated from Exeter and enlisted in the army, World War II (which had begun two years earlier, with the German invasion of Poland), was still years from being over. Trained as an engineer and assigned to an army freighter, Vidal was able to avoid combat. This proved to be a very boring period for him, however. To relieve the boredom of his service responsibilities, he started writing his first novel, *Williwaw* (1946), when he was only nineteen. This success seems to have led to Vidal's decision not to go to college, but to instead embark upon a career of writing.

Homosexual Themes in Vidal's Writing   Vidal had a longtime male companion, Howard Auster, whom he met in 1950. Vidal and Austen were partners until Austen's death in 2003. However, Vidal has never accepted the label "homosexual," and he equally dislikes the term "gay"; he has said, "There are no homosexual people, only homosexual acts."

Gay characters or gay subtexts appear in most of Vidal's work. The publication of Vidal's third novel, *The City and the Pillar* in 1948, resulted in a public and critical clamor over its openly gay main character and depiction of homosexual behavior. The novel was considered scandalous, and several newspapers blacklisted Vidal, refusing to review his future novels. The book was dedicated to Vidal's first romantic partner, Jimmie Trimble, who died in the Battle of Iwo Jima in 1945.

Gore Vidal was not the only person writing about controversial sexual themes during the late 1940s. In the same year that *The City and the Pillar* was published, Alfred Kinsey published his *Sexual Behavior in the Human Male* (1948), which was also a bestseller and similarly, the subject of controversy. Among other things, it suggested that homosexual experiences among males were not uncommon. The appearance of other homosexual characters in popular fiction around this time could also be found in fiction by major authors Tennessee Williams and Truman Capote, among others. It would seem that Vidal was simply tuned into a post–World War II sexual consciousness that would continue through the next decade and soon evolve into the "sexual revolution" of the 1960s. Never behind the times, Vidal wrote another popular novel in 1967 that dealt with gender identity and sexuality. *Myra Breckenridge* featured a male protagonist who becomes female by undergoing a sex change operation.

Dabbling in Film   Vidal's play *Visit to a Small Planet* (1955), about a child-like alien named Kreton trying to understand humans, was a great success. It first appeared on the stage, and was later adapted into a film in 1960. In 1956, Vidal was hired as a screenwriter for Metro Goldwyn

Mayer. He helped rewrite the script for *Ben-Hur* (1959), however, in the course of further rewrites by other scriptwriters, many of his changes were rejected and he was ultimately denied credit. Vidal had a small, uncredited part in Tennessee William's *Suddenly, Last Summer* (1959, for which he also wrote the screenplay). Vidal would continue to work on various television and film productions through the 1980s.

A Bid for Political Office   Vidal ran for Congress in 1960 as a liberal Democrat, and while he was not victorious, neither was his race a disaster; the writer had shown that he possessed the political acumen and the persuasive skills necessary to collect votes. He remained politically active during this period. During President's John F. Kennedy's administration, Vidal served on the Presidential Advisory Committee on the Arts. During the 1968 presidential campaign, he engaged in television debate with author, conservative commentator and one-time CIA deep cover agent William F. Buckley. The exchange became so heated that Buckley threatened to punch Vidal.

Stirring Up Controversy   Vidal's well-regarded historical novels *Burr* (1973) and *Lincoln* (1984), are considered revisionist histories, meaning that they interpret historical events and people differently than have most mainstream accounts. In *Burr*, Vidal portrays Vice President Aaron Burr, who served under Jefferson and was famous for killing Alexander Hamilton in a duel, as a hero. Thomas Jefferson is portrayed as self-centered and hypocritical, someone who does not have the best interests of the country at heart. In *Lincoln*, the sixteenth president of the United States is treated more respectfully than was Jefferson, and yet is portrayed as someone indifferent toward the practice of slavery, and who ignores the constitution when it suits him. These depictions were controversial, because in order to create them, Vidal mixed truth and fact, blurring the line between them

In 1993, Vidal won a National Book Award for his *United States: Essays 1952–1992*. In 1995, Vidal published an autobiography entitled *Palimpsest* that offered details on the various relationships with both men and women that Vidal had over the years. Also in 1995, Vidal attracted criticism by commencing a three year correspondence with Oklahoma City bomber Timothy McVeigh, while McVeigh was in prison. McVeigh had been found guilty of domestic terrorism for bombing the Alfred P. Murrah Federal Building in downtown Oklahoma City. The explosion, on April 19, 1995, killed 168 people, and injured over 800 more. In 2001, Vidal published an article in the magazine *Vanity Fair* in which he suggested that McVeigh had not acted alone in detonating the bomb, and that McVeigh was used as a scapegoat by the press and authorities. Vidal attended McVeigh's execution on June 11, 2001, at the prisoner's request. Although Vidal's explanation was that he wanted to show that a non-violent person (Vidal himself) could disagree with his government, Vidal's sympathy

LITERARY AND HISTORICAL CONTEMPORARIES

Gore Vidal's famous contemporaries include:

Truman Capote (1924–1984): American writer well known for *Breakfast at Tiffany's* and *In Cold Blood* (1966).

Norman Mailer (1923–2007): American novelist, essayist, and political activist who won two Pulitzer Prizes for his books *Armies of the Night* (1968) and *The Executioner's Song* (1979).

Anaïs Nin (1903–1977): Cuban-French author noted for her published diaries and her works of erotica.

Tennessee Williams (1911–1983): American playwright who won the Pulitzer Prize for *A Streetcar Named Desire* (1948) and *Cat on a Hot Tin Roof* (1955).

Charlton Heston (1923–2008): Star of such movies as *Ben-Hur* (1959). Heston won an Academy Award for the film. Vidal wrote the screenplay, though he is uncredited.

toward a terrorist resulted in many people feeling that Vidal was being disloyal to his country.

Another Memoir and Later Year   Vidal and Auster divided their time between Ravello, Italy, and the United States through the 1990s. Auster died in 2003, and in 2006, Vidal published another memoir: *Point to Point Navigation*, which focuses on his later years. Vidal continues to work and make guest appearances at literary events around the country.

Works in Literary Context

Les Enfants Terribles   With the publication of *Williwaw* in 1946, Vidal joined the ranks of the so-called *enfants terribles* (terrible children) who dominated the American cultural scene just after World War II. Such successful writers thrived on deliberately putting forth shocking or unorthodox ideas and stories. Vidal's name was often linked with other post-war prodigies such as Truman Capote, John Horn Burns, James Jones, and—several years later—Norman Mailer. Five years after the release of *Williwaw*, John W. Aldridge wrote in *After the Lost Generation: A Critical Study of the Writers of Two Wars*, "Gore Vidal, at twenty-five, occupies an enviable position in American letters. Not only is he the youngest of the group of new writers whose first books began attracting attention right after the war, but he has already produced as large and varied a body of work as many of his contemporaries may be expected to produce comfortably in a lifetime."

COMMON HUMAN EXPERIENCE

A theme in Gore Vidal's work is the decline of Western civilization. Vidal compares our civilization to ancient Rome just before its disintegration. Here are some other works that treat this theme:

The Waste Land (1922), a long poem by T. S. Eliot. Eliot's poem, set in contemporary London, focuses on the decline of civilization and culture, and the loss of people's ability to find meaning in the modern world.

The Sunlight Dialogues (1972), a novel by John Gardner. A Chief of Police in a small town in New York is called upon to solve a mystery involving a person called the Sunlight Man. This novel has an underlying theme of the collapse of Western civilization, and argues that the values and philosophies of ancient Babylon could be the answer.

Lord of the Flies (1955), a novel by William Golding. Golding's island is a microcosm of civilization in which mankind's natural attraction to evil, when away from societal rules, leads to the inevitable unraveling of civilized behavior among the boys.

Collapse: How Societies Choose to Fail or Succeed (2005), a nonfiction work by Jared Diamond. Diamond examines various cultures across time and geography, and theorizes about why some thrive and some collapse.

Historical Novels Vidal's historical novels, written between 1973 and 2000, are now known as the "Narratives of Empire" (previously called The American Chronicles). They are: *Washington, D.C.* (1967), *Burr* (1973), *1876* (1976), *Lincoln* (1984), *Empire* (1987), *Hollywood* (1990), *The Golden Age* (2000). They cover events in the United States from colonial times to the post–World War II era, and are Vidal's renderings of the worlds of politics and power, worlds to which his grandfather, Thomas Gore, had helped introduce him. While all historical novels take liberties with facts and historical characters in order to produce a compelling story, Vidal has been criticized for bending facts further than most, and for presenting historical figures such as Burr, Jefferson, and Lincoln in ways that do not square with the historical record. Whatever their opinions of the individual novels, most critics feel that this series has been Vidal's greatest achievement.

Sexuality and Gender The themes of homosexuality and gender identity are such an ingrained part of Vidal's writing that William F. Buckley once accused him of being a "pusher" of the gay lifestyle. But for Vidal, his sexuality and his philosophies surrounding sexuality and gender are part of his identity as a human being and a writer, and he has written many essays on these topics. Vidal has indicated that he dislikes the terms "homosexual" and "gay" because he does not like labeling people, and also because he said he believed everyone was bisexual (capable mentally and physically of having sex with either men or women) but some people simply chose to have sex exclusively with one gender or the other.

Works in Critical Context

Vidal has been the subject of critical and media attention for four decades. His work is noted for its eloquence, intelligence, urbane humor, and biting satire, as well as for its attacks on culture and politics. A divisive figure all his life, he has drawn both high praise and scathing criticism.

Myra Breckinridge (1968) Popular as Vidal's historical novels have been, the author's greatest work, say critics, is *Myra Breckinridge*, a campy, satiric look at modern America. A bestseller within weeks of its publication, *Myra Breckinridge* takes satiric aim at almost everything, from uptight heterosexuality to the burgeoning population, from the New American Novel to 1940s movie stars, and from American youth to the American dream. The book is sexually graphic, but most reviewers of the time recognized it as a satire on pornography that had, at the same time, become what it was—satirizing. In May 1968, Margot Hentoff of the *New York Review of Books*, noted that Vidal, "walking on the waters of polymorphous perversity and sexual revolution ... has written the first popular book of perverse pornography—a book for which one does not need even the slightest special taste." *Newsweek*'s Joseph Morgenstern referred to it as "gleefully dirty, wittily dirty, gracefully and intricately dirty in its creation and development of a genuine film freak."

Lincoln *Lincoln* is the third in a series of seven historical novels, written between 1973 and 2000, that focus on American political figures. Critical reviews of the novel were mixed. Harold Bloom, in the July 19, 1984 *New York Review of Books*, wrote, "until now no novelist has had the precision of imagination to show us a plausible and human Lincoln, of us and yet beyond us." Lincoln biographers, on the other hand, were quick to point out that most of what was depicted in the book was wrong and misleading. The novel creates a difficulty for reviewers in being historical, for Gore insisted that his novel was mostly factual, yet it was a work of fiction and not biography.

Lincoln became a tremendously popular novel, partly because its mature depiction of a popular historical figure appealed to a much wider audience than some of the author's earlier works. However, a television miniseries of the novel in 1988 received very poor reviews all around, and was considered to be inferior to the novel.

Responses to Literature

1. Vidal has claimed that "America wanted to be like Greece, but ended up like Rome." Read *Empire*, then, using passages from the book as support, discuss what Vidal meant by this assertion.

2. In at least two cases in which a Vidal novel was brought to the screen, the results were disastrous. One of these was *Myra Breckenridge* (1968), which was made into a film, and the other was *Lincoln* (1984), which was made into a TV miniseries. Read the books, then watch the screen versions. Why do you think they did not translate well? Did it have something to do with Vidal's skills as a screenwriter, or did other factors apply?

3. Vidal wrote the screenplay for the hit Hollywood movie *Ben-Hur*, but later refused to have his name associated with it. The movie is controversial among film historians because of the question of whether or not Vidal introduced homosexual subtext into the plot. Charlton Heston, the film's star, scoffed at the idea. Watch the film, and write a paper in which you argue either for or against the presence of a homosexual theme in the film. Use quotes and examples from the film to support your argument.

BIBLIOGRAPHY

Books

Aldridge, John W. *After the Lost Generation: A Critical Study of the Writers of Two Wars.* New York: McGraw-Hill, 1951.

Baker, Susan, and Curtis S. Gibson, eds. *Gore Vidal: A Critical Companion.* London: Greenwood Press, 1997.

Dick, Bernard F. *The Apostate Angel: A Critical Study of Gore Vidal.* New York: Random House, 1974.

White, Ray Lewis. *Gore Vidal.* New York: Twayne, 1968.

Periodicals

Walter, Eugene. "Conversations with Gore Vidal." In *Transatlantic Review.* 4 (1960): 5–17.

Hentoff, Margot. "Growing Up Androgynous." *New York Review of Books.* vol. 10, no. 9 (1968): 5–17.

Wilhelm, John F., and Mary Ann Wilhelm. "'Myra Breckinridge': A Study of Identity." *Journal of Popular culture.* 3 (Winter 1969): 590–599.

Web sites

PBS American Masters: Gore Vidal. Accessed November 11, 2008, from http://www.pbs.org/.

The Gore Vidal Index. Accessed November 12, 2008, from http://www.pitt.edu/~kloman/vidalframe.html.

⊛ Paula Vogel

BORN: *1951, Washington, D.C.*

NATIONALITY: *American*

GENRE: *Drama*

MAJOR WORKS:

The Baltimore Waltz (1992)

How I Learned to Drive (1997)

Paula Vogel   *Vogel, Paula, photograph. AP Images.*

Overview

Paula Vogel secured her position as a leading voice in the American theater when she won the Pulitzer Prize for Drama in 1998 for *How I Learned to Drive* (1997), a play that explores the relationship between a young girl and the uncle who molests her. Before the success of this play, Vogel's most celebrated work was *The Baltimore Waltz* (1992), for which she won an Obie Award for best play in 1992. Although some scholars rate her plays highly, her unconventional and often intellectual writing style, mixed with potentially offensive subject matter, has relegated much of her work to the margins of mainstream theater. Nevertheless, *How I Learned to Drive*, which has received productions in regional theaters across the United States and on every continent, has thrust her into prominence.

Works in Biographical and Historical Context

Troubles at Home   Paula Anne Vogel was born to a working-class family in Washington, D.C., on November 16, 1951. Her Jewish father, Donald S. Vogel, and her Catholic mother, Phyllis (Bremerman) Vogel, separated when Vogel was ten. Following her parents' divorce, Vogel had very little contact with her father, who remarried, until 1988, when her brother Carl died of AIDS. Vogel's mother raised Vogel and her two older brothers, Mark and Carl, in suburban Maryland until Mark left to live with his father when he was fifteen. Her parents' separation was a difficult adjustment for Vogel, leading her to explore alternative concepts of family in many of her plays.

The most important familial relationship in Vogel's life was the relationship she had with her brother, Carl. Vogel has called him her beloved, her father, and her soul mate. They were close as children and remained supportive of each other as adults. Carl introduced his sister to feminism, the social and political movement that focused on achieving equal rights for women. In 1990, Vogel wrote *The Baltimore Waltz* as a tribute to him, and she said in an interview that all of her plays contain something written specifically for him.

Early Experiences in the Theater Vogel became interested in theater during her sophomore year in high school, primarily because it offered her a way to stay away from home. Because there were few teenage boys in her high-school drama classes, she performed many of the leading male roles in the school plays, but she veered away from acting. She became the stage manager for many of the productions, and in this role, she fell in love with the process of performance. In high school, she was also involved in student government, and she briefly considered pursuing a career in politics. However, as a teenager, she decided to make theater her profession, because it enabled her to live her sexuality openly. She told David Savran she knew she was a lesbian when she was in high school, and she felt the theater "was a home that could include [her] sexuality." Her interest in political structures never faded, and she has remained politically engaged through her work in the theater.

Neither of her parents finished high school, but, with Carl's encouragement, she attended Bryn Mawr College in Pennsylvania on scholarship and later transferred to Catholic University in Washington, D.C. In 1974, she finished her bachelor's degree and then pursued a Ph.D. at Cornell University, where she completed her course work and completed several plays. Her first playwriting honor came in 1977, when she won the American College Theatre Festival's Student Play Writing Award for *Meg*, which examines the relationship between a father and his daughter as she grows into adulthood and begins to see her father, whom she has idealized, as a man with faults and frailties. Though the evolution of this relationship drives the primary action, at its heart, the play explores the absence of women from traditional historical narrative, an interest of many feminist writers and scholars in the late 1970s.

Feminism and the Unconventional Family Vogel continued to explore feminist issues in *The Oldest Profession* (1981), which presents five geriatric prostitutes who pragmatically discuss their failing finances, aging bodies, and fading sexual prowess as they approach death. Set in a New York City park shortly after the election of President Ronald Reagan in 1980, the play depicts the conservative stance toward homelessness and the welfare system of social security. Vogel used elements from her own biography and personal relationships in her characterizations of the women in *The Oldest Profession*. Just before she began writing the play, her grandmother, Vera, had a heart attack. Vera was the youngest and the last surviving of five sisters. Using characteristics and the names of her grandmother and four great-aunts, Vogel re-imagined their lives for her play.

From 1982 to 1985, Vogel served as Artistic Director for Theatre with Teeth, in New York City, which produced *And Baby Makes Seven* (1984). The play examines a nontraditional family made up of the lesbian couple Anna and Ruth, three imaginary adopted children, and Peter, the father of Anna's child, who is born late in the story. During that time, Vogel also worked as a production supervisor at Lincoln Center in New York. In 1984, she was hired to teach playwriting at Brown University in Providence, Rhode Island, where she became a member of the faculty in 1985.

A Fresh—and Controversial—Perspective Vogel's first play of the 1990s was her most explicitly autobiographical work, *The Baltimore Waltz* (1992), which deals with the death of her beloved brother. Although the play stems from personal material, Vogel uses the autobiographical matter to create a humorous and surreal portrayal of a woman's journey as she comes to grips with her brother's death and a satire of the medical profession. All but the last scene in the play takes place in angst-ridden Anna's mind. In her fantasy, she and Carl leave Baltimore and travel throughout a Europe of the American imagination. As the sometimes narrator, Anna guides the audience through a rapid-fire patchwork of language lessons, family vacation snapshots, mysterious encounters, and carefree sexual interludes in twenty-nine highly stylized scenes. Though the play sparked some controversy, it was widely recognized as an important new work responding to the AIDS epidemic in the United States. *The Baltimore Waltz* received several awards in 1992, including the Obie, an award for Off-Broadway productions, for Best Play.

Following *The Baltimore Waltz*, Vogel returned to work on a script she had begun writing in the 1970s, *Desdemona: A Play About a Handkerchief*. The play irreverently adopts the female characters of William Shakespeare's *Othello* in order to offer a critique of gender and class relations in a Western male-dominated culture. Following her skewering of Shakespeare, Vogel wrote *Hot 'N' Throbbing*. Vogel wrote it in response to two disparate frustrations: the devastating statistics on domestic violence in the United States and National Endowment for the Arts grant policies requiring participants to pledge not to create anything offensive to the community. As she explains in the introduction to the play, in 1993, Vogel received an NEA grant, and after signing the obscenity pledge, she wrote *Hot*

'N' *Throbbing* "to see just what would be perceived as pornographic, eager to test the censorship of the NEA pledge." The play draws connections between pornography, erotica, and domestic violence, and questions the pervasiveness of sex and violence in American lives.

Vogel again represents a society out of control in her play *The Mineola Twins* (1996). The action of the play centers on the combative relationship of the twin sisters, Myra and Myrna. Myra, the sexually promiscuous adventurer, represents liberalism, while Myrna, the prudish housewife turned talk-show host, represents conservatism. The play tracks the activities of the sisters across three decades in order to present the pervasiveness and the destructiveness of these polar political attitudes.

Honors and Condemnations Vogel's next play would also receive its share of critical condemnation, but it is also her most honored work. *How I Learned to Drive* (1997), Vogel's unconventional exploration of pedophilia, is less a condemnation of the pedophile than a condemnation of a society that sexualizes children and refuses to properly educate them about sexual relationships. Despite its thematic interests, the exploration of a young woman's sexual awakening, and the strength she gains as a pedophile's victim, lies at the heart of the play. It is also an uneasy and disconcerting love story about a girl and her uncle. The play won the 1997 Lortel, Drama Desk, Outer Critics Circle, New York Drama Critics, and Obie Awards. Vogel also received the 1998 Pulitzer Prize for Drama, and her play was the most produced new play in the United States in 1998.

From the Theater to the Small Screen In addition to her work in the theater, Vogel has been involved in movie projects. She worked on adaptations of *The Oldest Profession* and *How I Learned to Drive*. On January 29, 2000, the cable channel, Showtime, premiered *Common Ground*, three vignettes about being gay in America over the course of three decades. Vogel wrote the first vignette, "A Friend of Dorothy's," set in 1954. Vogel's piece focuses on a woman who has been dishonorably discharged from the navy after being arrested in a gay bar. She returns to her small-town home, where she is dismissed in disgrace by her family and the community. The episode is an exploration of the young woman's sexual awakening and the confusion, fear, and excitement that accompanies it.

Continuing to produce challenging work through the new millennium, Vogel wrote *The Long Christmas Ride Home*, which premiered at The Vineyard Theatre in November 2003. Her *A Civil War Christmas* opened at The Arena Stage in Washington, D.C., in November 2006. That same year, the Vineyard Theatre in New York City initiated the annual Paula Vogel Playwriting Award to an emerging playwright of exceptional promise.

Works in Literary Context

Gay and Lesbian Theater Gay and Lesbian theater largely developed as a result of the AIDS epidemic that

---

LITERARY AND HISTORICAL CONTEMPORARIES

Vogel's famous contemporaries include:

Kate Millett (1934–): Millett is an American feminist activist and writer. She is the author of the highly influential book *Sexual Politics* (1970), which explores the political aspects of feminism.

Terence McNally (1939–): McNally is a Tony Award-winning playwright who often explores gay themes in his work.

David Mamet (1947–): Mamet is an American playwright, author, screenwriter, and film director. He is known for his verbose, often vulgar characters and his penchant for masculine themes. One of his best known works is *Glengarry Glen Ross* (1984).

Anne Bogart (1951–): Bogart is an award-winning American theater director who founded a theatrical technique called "Viewpoints," which is an improvisation method involving physical movements on the stage.

Harvey Fierstein (1952–): Fierstein is an actor and playwright and is one of the most prominent gay celebrities in America. He is perhaps best known for his Tony-award winning plays *Torch Song Trilogy* (1982).

---

rocked the world in the 1980s. The crisis inspired gay playwrights to express their personal concerns, fears, and hopes in theatrical productions. Harvey Fierstein's groundbreaking *Torch Song Trilogy* (1982), which is a triad of plays, was among the first to mainly focus on gay characters. However, it was Larry Kramer's *The Normal Heart* (1985) that first addressed the AIDS crisis and helped bring this issue, which at the time was predominantly considered to be a solely gay one, to a wider spectrum of Americans. Over the years, the specter of AIDS has continued to loom in plays, such as Tony Kushner's *Angels in America: A Gay Fantasia on National Themes* (1990) and Paula Vogel's *The Baltimore Waltz* (1992), but it also simply deals with the lives of gay characters openly, honestly, and humanely.

Feminist Theater The feminist movement developed over the course of the twentieth century with the intent of providing women with all the civil, human, personal, and legal rights afforded to men in the United States and Britain. The feminist movement was integral in winning women the right to vote in the late 1910s, the legalization of abortion in 1973, and numerous workplace rights, such as maternity leave, protection against sexual harassment, and equal pay. In the early 1970s, feminism birthed a movement in theater that often relied on emotional shock and experimentation to deliver its message. Much of Paula Vogel's work, including *The Oldest Profession* and *Desdemona: A Play About a Handkerchief*, are products of the feminist theatrical movement.

COMMON HUMAN EXPERIENCE

In her play *The Baltimore Waltz* (1992), Vogel deals with the AIDS-related death of her dearly loved brother Carl. Other works inspired by the AIDS epidemic include:

> *The Normal Heart* (1985), a play by Larry Kramer. Kramer's play tracks the development of the AIDS crisis in early 1980s New York City.
>
> *And the Band Played On: Politics, People, and the AIDS Epidemic* (1987), a nonfiction book by Randy Shilts. Shilts's journalistic book is a study of the political reasons why the AIDS epidemic was allowed to spread as rapidly as it did during the early 1980s.
>
> *Angels in America: A Gay Fantasia on National Themes* (1990), a play by Tony Kushner. Kushner's lengthy, two-part play focuses on several characters in mid-1980s New York City. The play is an attempt to reconcile the often opposing poles of homosexuality and traditional religion.
>
> *Philadelphia* (1993), a film by Jonathan Demme. The Oscar-winning film *Philadelphia* is based on the true story of an attorney named Geoffrey Bowers, who was fired from his position at a law firm because he had AIDS.

Works in Critical Context

And Baby Makes Seven The often shocking and jarringly humorous nature of Vogel's plays have won her as many advocates as detractors. In response to *And Baby Makes Seven*, some critics felt the play was entertaining in its structural playfulness and fragmented characterizations, while others found the play cumbersome and self-conscious. In *Newsday*, Jan Stuart writes that "Vogel's cerebral brand of clowning feels forced" but commends the playwright for her literate and compassionate voice. Mel Gussow, in *The New York Times*, calls the play whimsical and regressive. Gussow believes that the premise is too thin for a full-length play and feels that Vogel needed to explore the three characters more deeply instead of falling back on "children's games," which he later refers to as "the insufferability of the childish incarnations."

The Baltimore Waltz Diverging critical reaction even greets Paula Vogel's most renowned works, such as *The Baltimore Waltz*. The play's harshest critics were troubled by Vogel's humorous approach to the serious subject matter and condemned her for seemingly valorizing promiscuity. The play's champions welcomed a fresh perspective on the disease and its effects on its victims and their friends and families. Malcolm Johnson writes in *The Hartford Courant*: "Vogel's uproarious, searching, and finally devastating cre-

ation adds up to the very best of theatre. Even to say that this is the theatre's most deeply felt and richly expressed response to the AIDS plague is to diminish its powers." Frank Rich in *The New York Times* writes that he respects Vogel's intent and is fascinated by the play, but he feels the play lacks internal logic and coherence.

Responses to Literature

1. Vogel's play *And Baby Makes Seven* takes a very untraditional view of the American family. Read *And Baby Makes Seven*. In an essay, explain how you think the family in the play is similar to more traditional concepts of the American family.

2. Vogel wrote her play *Desdemona: A Play About a Handkerchief* as a response to William Shakespeare's play *Othello*. Read both Vogel's play and Shakespeare's play. Then, explain what you think Vogel is trying to say about *Othello* with her own work. Support your response with details from both plays.

3. Vogel's plays tend to receive very different reactions from theater critics. Imagine you are a theater critic. Then, read Vogel's play *The Baltimore Waltz* and write your own review of the play. Be sure to refer to specific details from the play in your review.

BIBLIOGRAPHY

Books

Bigsby, Christopher. *Contemporary American Playwrights.* Cambridge, U.K.: Cambridge University Press, 1999, pp. 289–329.

Dolan, Jill. *Amazon All Stars*, Rosemary Curb ed. New York: Applause, 1996, pp. 437–440.

Periodicals

Brustein, Robert. "Robert Brustein on Theatre Homogenized Diversity." *New Republic* (July 7, 1997): 28–29.

———. "What Do Women Playwrights Want?" *New Republic* 10 (April 13, 1992): 28–30.

Coen, Stephanie. "Paula Vogel: No Need for Gravity." *American Theater* (April 1993): 26–27.

Dolan, Jill. "How I Learned to Drive." *Theatre Journal* 50 (1998): 127–128.

Friedman, Sharon. "Revising the Woman's Part: Paula Vogel's 'Desdemona.'" *New Theatre Quarterly* 15 (May 1999): 131–142.

Gussow, Mel. "Review/Theater; Parents-to-Be Regress to Childhood." *The New York Times* (May 7, 1993).

Johnson, Malcolm. "Review of The Baltimore Waltz." *The Hartford Courant* (February 16, 1992).

Rich, Frank. "Review/Theater; Play About AIDS Uses Fantasy World To Try to Remake the World." *The New York Times* (February 12, 1992).

Stuart, Jan. "Review of And Baby Makes Seven." *Newsday* (May 7, 1993).

⚙ Kurt Vonnegut Jr.

BORN: *1922, Indianapolis, Indiana*

DIED: *2007, Manhattan, New York*

NATIONALITY: *American*

GENRE: *Fiction, drama, short stories, essay*

MAJOR WORKS:

The Sirens of Titan (1959)
Cat's Cradle (1963)
Slaughterhouse-Five (1969)
Breakfast of Champions (1973)
Timequake (1997)

Overview

Best known as the author of *Slaughterhouse-Five; or, The Children's Crusade: A Duty-Dance with Death* (1969), Vonnegut is acknowledged as a major voice in modern American literature and applauded for his satirical depictions of modern society.

Kurt Vonnegut Jr.   *Vonnegut, Kurt, Jr., photograph. AP Images.*

Works in Biographical and Historical Context

Growing Up during the Great Depression Vonnegut was born in Indianapolis, Indiana, on November 11, 1922, the son of a successful architect. Both his mother's and father's families were of German heritage and were well established professionally and socially and, as Vonnegut reflects in the introduction to *Slapstick; or, Lonesome No More!* (1976), he and his siblings were born into a large, prosperous family that offered the support of many close relatives and the security of a preserved cultural heritage, things for which he later nostalgically yearned.

The Great Depression, a worldwide economic downturn caused by the collapse of the stock market in 1929, brought a halt to building and hence unemployment for Vonnegut's architect father. Looking back on those years, Vonnegut said that during the Depression his family never went hungry, and although they moved to a new, somewhat smaller house, designed by his father, their lifestyle was not crimped. But his father found no work for ten years and became increasingly withdrawn and tentative. The experience was something Vonnegut seems never to have forgotten, and his fiction abounds with characters who fall into self-doubt when they lose productive social roles. The strains on Vonnegut's mother, Edith, were also considerable, and she perhaps felt the family's financial decline most acutely. With the goal of bringing in money, Edith began taking writing courses in an attempt to become a short-story writer. Though none of her stories was published, her attempt seems to have made an impression on her younger son.

From Prisoner of War to Publicist to Writer After attending Cornell University, where he majored in chemistry and biology, Vonnegut enlisted in the United States Army, serving in World War II. He was taken prisoner by the German army. While a prisoner, he witnessed the Allied firebombing of the defenseless city of Dresden in 1945—an event that heavily influenced his later writing. At least 25,000 people were killed in the bombing raid (some historians estimate more than 100,000 were killed). Because the city had no military or strategic importance, the Allied decision to destroy is has been criticized in the years since the end of the war.

Vonnegut's enlistment in the army had come as a final blow to his mother, who was already becoming increasingly prone to depression. He sought a special leave to return home for Mother's Day the following year, only to have her commit suicide by an overdose of sleeping pills while he was there. His most direct references to this event come in *Breakfast of Champions; or, Goodbye Blue Monday!* (1973), but other indications of its impact may be seen in his recurring references to the mental health of his characters and conceivably in his portrayals of women and marriages.

LITERARY AND HISTORICAL CONTEMPORARIES

Vonnegut's famous contemporaries include:

Doris Lessing (1919–): A British author who won the Nobel Prize in Literature in 2007 at the age of eighty-eight, making her the oldest person to win the award.

William Faulkner (1897–1962): An American author often considered one of the most important "southern" authors; he was awarded the Nobel Prize in Literature in 1945.

Theodore Sturgeon (1918–1985): Most famous for his novel *More than Human (1953)*, this American author was unique in that his science fiction works received attention from the academic community in the 1950s, something unusual for the genre at that time; he was the acknowledged model for Vonnegut's Kilgore Trout.

John F. Kennedy (1917–1963): The thirty-fifth president of the United States until his assassination in 1963, JFK controversially escalated U.S. involvement in the Vietnam War.

Jack Kerouac (1922–1969): An American author and member of the Beat generation whose best-known works include *On the Road* (1957) and *The Dharma Bums* (1958).

Following the war, Vonnegut studied anthropology at the University of Chicago and subsequently moved to Schenectady, New York, to work as a publicist for the General Electric Corporation. During this period, he also began submitting short stories to various journals, and in 1951 he resigned his position at General Electric to devote his time solely to writing.

Early Works Ignored Vonnegut published several novels throughout the 1950s and 1960s, beginning with *Player Piano* in 1952. However, his frequent use of elements of fantasy resulted in his classification as a writer of science fiction, a genre not widely accepted as "serious literature," and his work did not attract significant popular or critical interest until the mid-1960s, when increasing disillusionment within American society led to widespread admiration for his forthright, irreverent satires.

Exploring the Role of Technology in Society Vonnegut focuses on the role of technology in human society in *Cat's Cradle* (1963), widely considered one of his best works. The novel recounts the discovery of a form of ice, called *ice-nine*, which is solid at a much lower temperature than normal ice and is capable of solidifying all water on Earth. Ice-nine serves as a symbol of the enormous destructive potential of technology, particularly when developed or used without regard for the welfare of humanity. In contrast to what he considers the harmful truths represented by

scientific discoveries, Vonnegut presents a religion called Bokononism, based on the concept that there are no absolute truths, that human life is ultimately meaningless, and that the most helpful religion would therefore preach benign lies that encourage kindness, give humanity a sense of dignity, and allow people to view their absurd condition with humor. The motif of the cat's cradle, a children's game played by looping string about the hands in a complex pattern, is used by Vonnegut to demonstrate the harm caused by the erroneous paradigms presented by traditional religions: "No wonder kids grow up crazy. A cat's cradle is nothing but a bunch of X's between somebody's hands, and little kids look at all those X's ... no damn cat, and no damn cradle." In the complex novel *God Bless You, Mr. Rosewater* (1965), Vonnegut declares his admiration for "true" writers of science fiction, introducing the character of Kilgore Trout—a deeply humanistic and almost wholly unappreciated science fiction writer who would make frequent appearances in Vonnegut novels from that point forward.

Dresden in the Context of the Vietnam War Vonnegut's reputation was greatly enhanced in 1969 with the publication of *Slaughterhouse-Five*, a vehemently antiwar novel that appeared during the peak of protest against American involvement in the war in Vietnam. The first printing in March 1969 ran to ten thousand copies, the first Delta printing a year later was twenty-five thousand copies, and the first Dell edition of 1971 was seven hundred thousand copies. The 1972 Universal Pictures' film adaptation, directed by George Roy Hill, also contributed to the popularity of both book and author. Rather suddenly, twenty years into his career as a writer, Vonnegut found himself famous, prosperous, and even something of a guru figure to the Woodstock generation. Simultaneously he was at last earning the acclaim of academics—led by Leslie A. Fiedler, Tony Tanner, and Robert Scholes—and reviewers.

Vonnegut described *Slaughterhouse-Five* as a novel he was compelled to write, since it is based on one of the most extraordinary and significant events of his life. During the time he was a prisoner of the German army, Vonnegut witnessed the Allied bombing of Dresden, which destroyed the city and killed tens of thousands of people. One of the few to survive, Vonnegut was ordered by his captors to aid in the grisly task of digging bodies from the rubble and destroying them in huge bonfires. *Slaughterhouse-Five* is Vonnegut's attempt to both document and denounce the destruction of Dresden. The protagonist of the novel, Billy Pilgrim, is, as Vonnegut was, a prisoner of war in Dresden during the firebombing.

Continued Social Critique During the 1970s and 1980s, Vonnegut continued to serve as an important commentator on American society, publishing a series of novels in which he focused on topics ranging from political corruption to environmental pollution. He also became a prominent and vocal critic of censorship and militarism in the United States. As time went on, he proved to be a remarkably durable author. His recent novels demonstrate that his skills matured while his imagination remained fresh. Such a long, steady career is rare in American letters. In addition to his stories, novels, plays, and nonfiction, he has written many introductions, essays, and commentaries in every conceivable type of book and magazine. He also continued to be in demand as a speaker and to draw large audiences right up until his death in 2007. The heading Vonnegut commonly used for these engagements was "How to Get a Job Like Mine," which served to launch him into an evening of entertainment in which he tended to talk about absolutely anything but what that title suggests.

A Literary Farewell *Timequake*, which Vonnegut declared would be his last novel, proved difficult for him to complete. After several attempts, Vonnegut proved unable to complete it as originally conceived. Eventually he abandoned the original narrator and much of the plot. Calling his original version "Timequake One," he began a new version, narrated in first person, in which he wove together fragments from the old, an account of his struggles with it, and personal memoir. *Timequake* (1997) proved to be Vonnegut's last novel, making it a fitting coda to a successful literary career. Vonnegut died at the age of 84 on April 11, 2007—after several years of conscientious and vehement critique of U.S. foreign policy following the terrorist attacks of 2001.

Works in Literary Context

Vonnegut has come to be recognized as a thoughtful social critic who pondered the impact of technology, science, and social behavior on human existence and the natural environment. As a satirist, he acknowledged his debt to Voltaire and Jonathan Swift, while his brand of humor was influenced by Mark Twain and comedians such as Laurel and Hardy, W. C. Fields, and Bob and Ray. Vonnegut's enduring themes—social injustice, economic inequality, environmental exploitation, and militaristic barbarity—spring from his experiences growing up in the Depression and surviving World War II.

Postmodernism Through his usually damaged, faltering antiheroes his stories search for what gives life meaning in a society in which cultural certainties are absent. The technique in much of his work may be characterized as postmodern; rather than following classical prose models, it instead uses choppy, vernacular sentences and deemphasizes traditional conventions of plot, theme, time, and character development. Like postmodern buildings, which unite the architecture of disparate styles and eras, his novels combine comedy with pathos, fantasy with history, and didacticism with farce. Such forms as poetry, science fiction, satire, drama, graffiti, lyrics, drawings, and even recipes appear in the novels. They deconstruct the social myths on which society often thoughtlessly runs and repeatedly defamiliarize the commonplace daily world to make their audience reexamine its habits of thinking. At the same time, Vonnegut cuts quickly to the issue, actions are reported succinctly, and the prose is geared toward

---

COMMON HUMAN EXPERIENCE

Slaughterhouse-Five examines the harmful impact war can have on a soldier's mental health. Other works that explore the psychic damage caused by warfare include:

The Return of the Soldier (1918), a novel by Rebecca West. This work tells the story of Chris Baldry, who has difficulty rejoining society after his experiences as a soldier in World War I.

Mrs. Dalloway (1925), a novel by Virginia Wolf. Set in post–World War I England, this novel looks at the impact of war on relationships' social structures; Septimus Smith, a veteran, commits suicide after suffering from constant war-related hallucinations.

Johnny Got His Gun (1939), a novel by Dalton Trumbo. A young World War I veteran loses all his limbs and much of his face in a mortar attack, and struggles to keep his sanity while adjusting to a life in which he cannot move, see, hear, or communicate.

Catch-22 (1961), a novel by Joseph Heller. In this popular satiric comedy, Heller follows the path of the reluctant World War II bombardier Yossarian, who wants desperately to avoid flying in any more combat missions.

Ceremony (1977), a novel by Leslie Marmon Silko. *Ceremony* examines the psychological struggles faced by Tayo, a mixed-race Native American World War II veteran traumatized by his combat experiences, as he tries to adjust to life at home on a Laguna Pueblo reservation.

---

moving the story along and holding the reader'ss attention. His style, conspicuous for its short sentences and paragraphs, owes much to his background in journalism.

The Human Condition as Absurd Emphasizing the comic absurdity of the human condition, Vonnegut frequently depicts characters who search for meaning and order in an inherently meaningless and disorderly universe. He focuses in particular on the futility of warfare, the destructive power of technology, and the human potential for both irrationality and evil. He also mocks institutions such as government and religion, which, in his opinion, offer harmful, ill-founded belief systems as remedies to real problems. Although his message is ultimately pessimistic, finding no remedy for the plight of humanity, Vonnegut approaches his subjects with humor and compassion. His works have been described by Richard Giannone as "comic masks covering the tragic farce that is our contemporary life."

After his death in 2007, numerous celebrities paid tribute to Vonnegut's contributions to the world of art and literature. Comedian Jon Stewart ran a television tribute on his program *The Daily Show*, Michael Moore dedicated his 2007 film *Sicko* to Vonnegut, and historian Howard Zinn published an obituary noting Vonnegut's contributions to the socialist movement, amongst many others.

Works in Critical Context

Critics have frequently argued that in his later works Vonnegut tended to reiterate themes presented more compellingly in earlier works. Charles Berryman, for example, writes, "In the novels which follow [*Slaughterhouse-Five*], however, the weight of history is often lacking, and the narrators who suffer a private trauma are apt to appear more absurd than tragic." Many also suggest that Vonnegut's narrative style, which includes the frequent repetition of distinctive phrases, the use of colloquialisms, and a digressive manner, becomes formulaic in some of his later works. While criticized by some as pessimistic, other critics have noted that other aspects of Vonnegut's works counter his gloomy worldview. Edward Haley Foster writes, "Vonnegut can appear sentimental even in his best work, but it may be this, together with his comic sense, that allows his work to escape the bitterness, if not the resignation, that his bleak view of experience would encourage."

Slaughterhouse-Five   While early responses to *Slaughterhouse-Five* sometimes emphasized its initial reception, as seen in the *New York Times Book Review* assertion that "you'll either love it, or push it back in the science-fiction corner," recent criticism has tended to a reading of the work within the historical context of the Vietnam War era and Vonnegut's work as a whole. For instance, critic Charles B. Harris observes, "At its deeper levels of meaning *Slaughterhouse-Five*...posits an uncertain world and, as such, may be perceived as a metaphor for an indeterminate universe." From a historical standpoint, critic Jerome Klinkowitz writes, "*Slaughterhouse-Five* was Vonnegut's first best-seller. [It] catapulted him to sudden national fame, and brought his writing into serious intellectual esteem."

Responses to Literature

1. Where in *Slaughterhouse-Five* does "KV" appear? With which characters does KV sympathize? Do you think this is the voice of the "real" Kurt Vonnegut? Explain why or why not using examples from the text.

2. Do you think *Slaughterhouse-Five* is an antiwar novel? In what ways does it differ from other antiwar novels that you have read? Explain your opinion using detailed analyses of passages from the text.

3. Using examples from a selection of Vonnegut's written works, write a paper explaining Vonnegut's view of the human condition and his perspective on free will.

4. Vonnegut was present during the 1945 Allied bombing of the German city of Dresden, an event he chronicles in *Slaughterhouse-Five*. To find out more about this historical event, read *Apocalypse 1945: The Destruction of Dresden* (2007), by David Irving.

BIBLIOGRAPHY

Books

Allen, William Rodney. *Understanding Kurt Vonnegut.* Columbia: University of South Carolina Press, 1991.

Bly, William. *Kurt Vonnegut's* Slaughterhouse-Five. Woodbury, N.Y.: Barron's, 1985.

Klinkowitz, Jerome. *Kurt Vonnegut.* London & New York: Methuen, 1982.

Lundquist, James. *Kurt Vonnegut.* New York: Ungar, 1977.

Mustazza, Leonard. *The Critical Response to Kurt Vonnegut.* Westport, Conn.: Greenwood, 1994.

Morse, Donald E. *Kurt Vonnegut.* San Bernardino, Calif.: Borgo, 1992.

Reed, Peter J. *Kurt Vonnegut Jr.* New York: Warner, 1972.

———. *The Short Fiction of Kurt Vonnegut.* Westport, Conn.: Greenwood, 1997.

———and Marc Leeds. *The Vonnegut Chronicles: Interviews and Essays.* Westport, Conn.: Greenwood, 1996.

Schatt, Stanley. *Kurt Vonnegut, Jr.* Boston: G. K. Hall, 1976.

✺ Alice Walker

BORN: *1944, Eatonton, Georgia*

NATIONALITY: *American*

GENRE: *Fiction, nonfiction*

MAJOR WORKS:

Meridian (1976)

The Color Purple (1982)

Anything We Love Can Be Saved: A Writer's Activism (1997)

Overview

Since 1968, when *Once*, her first work, was published, Alice Walker has written numerous poems, short stories, novels, and essays expressing with graceful and devastating clarity the relationship between the degree of freedom black women have within and without their communities. Her particular angle of vision is sharpened by her use of the history of black people in the United States, and therefore, of the South, where they were most brutally enslaved. Her works confront the pain and struggle of black people's history, as exemplified in such classic novels as *The Color Purple*.

Works in Biographical and Historical Context

An Outcast Turns to Literature   Walker was born February 9, 1944—the youngest of eight children, five boys and three girls—to Willie Lee and Minnie Tallulah Grant Walker, sharecroppers in Eatonton, Georgia. She

Alice Walker *Araya Diaz / WireImage / Getty Images*

remembers generally hating the southern sharecropper's life with its backbreaking field work and declaring smugly at age two and a half, "I'm the prettiest." However, her sense of self drastically changed one day when she was eight years old. A game of cowboys and Indians with her brothers took a tragic turn as one of them shot her in the eye with his BB gun. The injury left her blind in her right eye, with a scar that she felt made her ugly and disfigured.

When Walker was fourteen, her favorite brother, Bill, paid to have the scar tissue removed. Still she perceived herself as an outcast. In her isolation, she turned to reading and began to write poems. Walker was blessed with a mother who, in spite of the fact that she had never read a book herself, appreciated her youngest daughter's need to do so. Minnie Lou Walker knew the value to her children of the education that she never received and resisted indignantly any white landowner's hints that sharecroppers' children did not need to go to school.

Walker started school at age four, when her mother could no longer take her into the fields with her, and went on to become valedictorian at her high school. Walker recalls her mother's buying her three gifts that gave her increasing degrees of freedom: a sewing machine to provide the independence of making her own clothes, a suitcase to allow her the freedom to travel, and a typewriter to enable her to pursue her art. When, because of her injured eye, the state of Georgia offered Walker a "rehabilitation scholarship" to Spelman, a black women's college in Atlanta, she was able to put all three gifts to use.

The Early Works Walker spent two and a half years at Spelman, where she was an active participant in the civil rights movement, which sought to achieve equal rights for black Americans. She then transferred to Sarah Lawrence, a women's college in Bronxville, New York, where she was one of only six black students. During this period, Walker began writing *Once*. The collection is comprised of her first published poems, which are about love, death, Africa, and the civil rights movement, and her first published story. Walker has often said that all of her poems were a result of her emergence out of a period of despair.

After Walker finished college, she spent a brief time in New York's Lower East Side. Because of her commitment to the Southern revolution, however, it was not long before she returned to the South. From the late 1960s to the middle 1970s, she worked in Mississippi in voter registration and welfare rights. During that time she married Mel Leventhal, a white civil rights lawyer. While in Mississippi, Walker collected folklore from ordinary black women and recorded the details of their everyday lives. Her first collection of short stories, *In Love and Trouble* (1973), powerfully demonstrates the push and pull between the shackles of tradition and the desire for transformation in these black women.

In her first novel, *The Third Life of Grange Copeland* (1970), Walker shows how the racist fabric of the American South affects the black family. Because the Copeland men are thwarted by society in their drive for control of their lives—the American definition of manhood—they vent their frustrations by inflicting violence on their wives. Walker's second novel, *Meridian* (1976), parallels some of her own experiences as a young woman active in the civil rights movement; the main character also experiences an unwanted pregnancy followed by an abortion, much like Walker herself during her years at college.

Walker Composes a Classic In the late 1970s, Walker was back living in New York City, teaching at various colleges and universities in the North as a means of earning a living and of communicating to others the long tradition of black women writers. At this time, she began her third novel, but did not complete it until after she relocated to the San Francisco area in California. Such a move was necessary to the completion of *The Color Purple* (1982) because Walker was having trouble crafting the story of a rural early twentieth-century Southern black woman while in the bustling Big Apple. It was not until she got a place in the country outside San Francisco that her characters' spirit and language came rushing out.

The Color Purple spans generations of one poor black family in the context of rural Southern history. The

LITERARY AND HISTORICAL CONTEMPORARIES

Walker's famous contemporaries include:

Tillie Olsen (1913–2007): Olsen was an American writer and activist who was an influential figure in the American feminist movement of the 1970s.

Julian Bond (1940–): A civil rights leader during the 1960s, Bond served in the Georgia senate from 1975–1986. Bond's work for African Americans was a major influence on Walker.

Steven Spielberg (1946–): Spielberg is an American filmmaker and has directed some of the most popular films of the second half of the twentieth century, including *Jaws* (1975), *Raiders of the Lost Ark* (1981), and *E.T.: The Extraterrestrial* (1982). In 1985, Spielberg's cinematic adaptation of Walker's novel *The Color Purple* was released to great acclaim.

Oprah Winfrey (1954–): Winfrey is one of the most powerful and influential African American media figures in the United States. Although she is best known for her long-running afternoon talk show, *The Oprah Winfrey Show* (1986–), she is also an actress who appeared in the film version of Walker's novel, *The Color Purple*.

Reggie Watts (c. 1972–): Watts is a comedian and jazz singer/musician and is Walker's cousin.

emphases in the novel are on the oppression black women experience in their relationships with black men and the sisterhood they must share with each other in order to liberate themselves. Walker also explores "forbidden" sexual themes, focusing on incest in a black family and portraying a lesbian relationship as natural and freeing. Walker revealed that the novel's protagonist, Celie, was based on the story of her great-grandmother, who at twelve, was raped and abused. Nevertheless, the story ends happily. Walker does not flinch from presenting the sexual abuse, the wife-beatings, and the violence that Celie undergoes in a society that demeans her as a woman. Walker allowed herself five years to write *The Color Purple*. It took her less than one. In 1983, the novel won both the Pulitzer Prize for fiction and the American Book Award for fiction.

In the Wake of The Color Purple Walker's fourth novel, *The Temple of My Familiar*, came out in 1989. Walker has called the book a romance of the past five hundred thousand years. One character, Miss Lissie, has lived through all of those half-million years. Reincarnation provides Walker with a means of encapsulating in one character centuries of the history of black womanhood. She traces both African and South American religions back to goddesses who were dethroned because of

man's jealousy. *The Temple of My Familiar* stayed on *The New York Times* bestseller list for more than four months.

Walker's 1997 collection of essays, *Anything We Love Can Be Saved: A Writer's Activism*, offers her clearest statements yet on her own personal spiritual evolution. Her spiritual journey takes on both public and political overtones when she explains how it has proved to be the source of her activism. In this collection, she makes explicit why traditional Christianity failed to meet the needs of blacks trapped within the Southern sharecropping system that was the world of her childhood, and thus why it failed to offer those of her parents' generation a means of expressing the mystical intimacy with the land that they enjoyed.

Included in *Anything We Love Can Be Saved* under the title, "Treasure," is the acceptance speech Walker gave when she was the recipient of the California Governor's Award for Literature in 1994. Ironically, a few weeks after learning that she was to be designated a "treasure" of the State of California, she learned that her short story "Roselily" and her essay "Am I Blue?" had been removed from the California State Achievement Test for tenth graders. The controversy over the removal of these works from the test became the basis for the slender 1996 volume titled *Alice Walker Banned*. The two works in question are reprinted in the volume, as are letters to the editors of various newspapers and transcripts from the hearings about the ban, as well as an excerpt from *The Color Purple* and an outline of the debate over its appropriateness for young readers.

Walker stormed through the remainder of the twentieth century with the violent, sexually graphic novel *By the Light of My Father's Smile* in 1998, in which she rails against male-dominated society. At the beginning of the twenty-first century with her far more accessible and critically lauded short story collection *Way Forward Is with a Broken Heart* (2000). The novel *Now Is the Time to Open Your Heart* followed in 2005. Widely viewed as a major voice for contemporary black women, Walker continues to blend art and activism while living in Mendocino, California.

Works in Literary Context

Local Color Local color (also known as regionalism) refers to poetry or literature that focuses on a specific region. The work may be written in a local dialect or overly concerned with regional customs, landmarks, or topography. As filtered through the author's worldview, the resulting work is often imbued with a strong sense of sentimentality or nostalgia. William Faulkner is often cited as an important regionalist writer in American literature, with his fictional Yoknapatawpha County—the setting for many of his works—heavily based on the region of Mississippi where he lived. While Walker's work tends to veer away from sentimentality, she often uses local color to conjure a strong sense of the southern regions in which many of her works take place.

Womanism Walker coined the term "womanism" in her book *In Search of Our Mother's Gardens: Womanist Prose* (1983). She used the term to describe a branch of feminism pertaining specifically to black women. The tenets of womanism preach respect for and belief in the ability of women to make worthwhile contributions to society. The womanism movement of the 1980s fully integrated African Americans into the feminism movement, of which they were often excluded.

Works in Critical Context

The Color Purple Although Walker's earlier works received favorable critical response, *The Color Purple* was widely regarded as the author's breakthrough novel. *The New York Times* began its review of the novel by declaring it to be Walker's "most impressive" before stating that this is "[n]o mean accomplishment, since her previous books ... have elicited almost unanimous praise for Miss Walker as a lavishly gifted writer." The *Times* suggests that the book's structure (it is composed of letters) is largely responsible for its effectiveness because "without the intrusion of the author, [it] forces intimate identification with the heroine." However, the *Times* did not ignore the criticism most often voiced about the novel when it mentioned the book's "somewhat pallid portraits of the males."

Now Is the Time to Open Your Heart Walker's *Now Is the Time to Open Your Heart* split critics far more drastically than did *The Color Purple*. While Nicole Moses of *January Magazine* calls the book "entertaining and enlightening" before declaring it "Walker's latest masterpiece," *The New York Times* critic Michiko Kakutani pans this story of a popular writer on a spiritual quest. "If this novel did not boast the name of Alice Walker, who won acclaim some two decades ago with 'The Color Purple,' it's hard to imagine how it could have been published," Kakutani seethes, concluding the novel to be "a remarkably awful compendium of inanities."

Responses to Literature

1. Walker has sometimes been criticized for the way in which she portrays men in some of her novels. Read *The Color Purple* and then explain whether or not you think that Walker's portrayal of men is fair. Support your response with details from the novel.

2. In 1994, Walker's short story "Roselily" was removed from the California State Achievement Test for tenth graders. Read the story and explain why you think it was judged unsuitable for the test. Do you agree with that judgment? Why or why not?

3. Walker has often been praised for the way she writes the speech of Southern black Americans. After reading *The Color Purple*, explain how you think Walker's use of language affects your understanding and

---

COMMON HUMAN EXPERIENCE

Walker coined the term "womanism" to refer to an African American feminist movement. Other womanist works include:

How Stella Got Her Groove Back (1996), a novel by Terry McMillan. One of the more lighthearted examples of womanist fiction, McMillan's novel tells of a career woman's attempt to balance her independence and her career as an investment analyst with motherhood and a budding relationship with a much younger man.

Do They Hear You When You Cry (1998), an autobiography by Fauziya Kassindja. *Do They Hear You When You Cry* is the true story of writer Kassindja's experiences in Togo, West Africa, following the death of her protective father. Afraid she might be forced into an arranged marriage and the barbaric ritual of female genital mutilation, Kassindja dared to stand up for her rights in a region where women are expected to be subservient to men.

Feminine Gospels: Poems (1999), a poetry collection by Carol Ann Duffy. African American poet Carol Ann Duffy offers a selection of her womanist poems, which vary from achingly personal to sweeping and historic.

Baby Love: Choosing Motherhood After a Lifetime of Ambivalence (2007), a memoir by Rebecca Walker. As a young African American girl, Rebecca was told by her own mother, Alice Walker, that she could lose her independence if she decided to have a baby. Now pregnant, Rebecca Walker deals with her womanist beliefs and her impending role as a new mother.

---

appreciation of the story. Support your response with details from the novel.

BIBLIOGRAPHY

Books

O'Brien, John. *Interviews with Black Writers*. New York: Liveright, 1973: 185–211.

Pratt, Louis, and Darnell D. Pratt. *Alice Malsenior Walker: An Annotated Bibliography 1968–1986*. Westport, Conn.: Meckler, 1988.

Tate, Claudia. *Black Women Writers at Work*. New York: Continuum, 1983: 175–187.

Periodicals

Britt, Donna. "Alice Walker and the Inner Mysteries Unraveled." *The Washington Post* (May 8, 1989): B1, B4.

Jaynes, Gregory. "Living by the World." *Life* 12 (May 1989): 61–64.

Kakutani, Michiko. "If the River is Dry, Can You Be All Wet?" *The New York Times* (April 20, 2004).

Moses, Nicole. "Heart Matters." *January Magazine* (August 2004).

Washington, Mary Helen. "Alice Walker: Her Mother's Gifts." *Ms.* 10 (June 1982): 38.

Watkins, Mel. "Some letters Went to God." *The New York Times* (July 25, 1982).

Wilson, Sharon. "A Conversation with Alice Walker." *Kalliope* 6, no. 2 (1984): 37–45.

✸ Margaret Walker

BORN: *1915, Birmingham, Alabama*

DIED: *1998, Chicago, Illinois*

NATIONALITY: *American*

GENRE: *Fiction, poetry*

MAJOR WORKS:

For My People (1942)

Jubilee (1966)

Prophets for a New Day (1970)

Margaret Walker   *Walker, Margaret, photograph. Photographs and Prints Division, Schomburg Center for Research in Black Culture. The New York Public Library. Astor, Lenox and Tilden Foundations. Reproduced by permission.*

Overview

A writer whose career spans five decades, Margaret Walker experienced firsthand two of the most exciting periods in the history of black American literature: the Harlem Renaissance of the 1920s and the Black Aesthetic Movement of the 1960s. She began her career under the guidance of Langston Hughes in the 1930s, and she emerged as a "literary mother" to a group of young writers, including Nikki Giovanni, Alice Walker, and Sonia Sanchez. Walker's reputation as a writer rests chiefly on *For My People* (1942), *Jubilee* (1966), and *Prophets for a New Day* (1970)—three works that reflect Walker's longstanding devotion to the heritage of black American culture.

Works in Biographical and Historical Context

A Child of the Harlem Renaissance "I was born on the seventh day of the seventh month of the year," Walker told an interviewer in 1988. "My mother was her mother's seventh child, and my father was his mother's seventh child.... [M]y grandmother said, 'You are born lucky.'" Margaret Abigail was born in 1915, in Birmingham, Alabama, to Reverend Sigismund C. Walker and Marion Dozier Walker. Sigismund emigrated from Jamaica to study for the ministry; he attended Tuskegee Institute for a time, but he left because of his disagreement with Booker T. Washington's conservative philosophy that industrial and vocational education was the best that African Americans should hope to attain. In 1913, he received a degree from Gammon Theological Seminary in Atlanta. Both he and Walker's mother, a music teacher, propelled their four children toward the highest academic achievements possible.

As a child, Walker developed a deep and abiding interest in books and literature. In the 1920s, she began reading the works of the Harlem Renaissance poets—particularly Langston Hughes—and started writing her first poems when she was twelve years old. According to Walker herself, Hughes had a profound influence on her early development as a writer: "I saw him first when I was about sixteen years old and halfway through college. He read my poetry and encouraged me to write." Walker maintained a friendship with Hughes for the next thirty-five years. W. E. B. Du Bois further encouraged Walker by publishing her poem "I Want to Write" in the *Crisis,* the magazine he founded when Walker was nineteen years old.

Walker attended Northwestern University and, in her senior year, became involved with the WPA Writers' Project—a program instituted by President Franklin Roosevelt to provide employment to writers during the Great Depression—where she developed a friendship with Richard Wright. Both writers benefited greatly from the relationship; Walker helped Wright do research for his novel *Native Son* (1940) and Wright, in turn, helped Walker revise and refine her poetry. In 1939, however, Wright abruptly ended his relationship with the poet. In

A Poetic Equation: Conversations between Nikki Giovanni and Margaret Walker (1974), Walker recalls: "Some mutual 'friends' told him some kind of lie. They said that I had said something. I don't know what they told him, but he became inarticulate with rage." Wright later wrote to Walker, but she refused his letters.

The Poet and the Author After leaving the WPA, Walker returned to school and obtained a master's degree from the University of Iowa. Two years later, in 1942, she published her first collection of poetry, *For My People*. Winner of the Yale Younger Poets Series Award, the poems in *For My People* honor ordinary blacks facing terrible odds.

Walker followed *For My People* with *Jubilee* (1966), a historical novel about a slave family during and after the Civil War. The novel took Walker thirty years to complete. During these years, she married a disabled veteran, raised four children, taught full-time at Jackson State College in Mississippi, and earned a Ph.D. from the University of Iowa. The lengthy gestation, she asserted, partly accounts for the book's quality. As she told Claudia Tate in *Black Women Writers at Work*, "There's a difference between writing about something and living through it.... I did both." The story of *Jubilee*'s main characters, Vyry and Randall Ware, was an important part of Walker's life even before she began to write it down. As she explained in *How I Wrote "Jubilee"* (1972), she first heard about the "slavery time" in bedtime stories told by her maternal grandmother. When old enough to recognize the value of her family history, Walker took initiative, "prodding" her grandmother for more details and promising to set down on paper the story that had taken shape in her mind. Later on, she conducted extensive research on every aspect of the black experience during the Civil War.

In 1977, eleven years after the publication of *Jubilee*, Walker accused Alex Haley of plagiarizing from the work to create his best-selling novel *Roots* (1976). The charges were later dropped, but Walker continued to refer to that incident as the "*Roots* fiasco" and wrote a poem entitled "Ripoff Roots Style."

A Call for Civil Rights Walker's next work, *Prophets for a New Day* (1970), was another book of poetry. Unlike the poems in *For My People*, which name religion an enemy of revolution, *Prophets for a New Day* is deeply religious, drawing parallels between Biblical characters and the current figures in the civil rights movement. In fact, Walker has called *Prophets for a New Day* her civil rights poems, and only two poems in the volume, "Elegy" and "Ballad of the Hoppy Toad," are not about the civil rights movement. In *For My People*, Walker urged that activity replace complacency, but in *Prophets for a New Day*, she applauds the new day of freedom for black people, focusing on the events, sites, and people of the struggle.

Retired but Productive Retirement from Jackson State University in 1979 gave Walker more time for writing and lecturing. She often gave lectures on black

---

---

literature and about the writers she knew: James Weldon Johnson, Langston Hughes, Countee Cullen, Zora Neale Hurston, W. E. B. Du Bois, Richard Wright, and Arna Bontemps. She also completed the book *Richard Wright, Daemonic Genius: A Portrait of the Man, A Critical Look at His Work* (1988), the publication of which was long delayed by legal entanglements from Wright's widow. The following year, she published another poetry collection, *This Is My Century* (1989).

Walker next began work on a sequel to *Jubilee* and an autobiography. Tragically, she died of breast cancer in 1998 and these two projects remain incomplete. Despite this, her position as an important chronicler of the black experience and a leading figure in American letters is assured.

Works in Literary Context

The Harlem Renaissance The Harlem Renaissance was the first major African American artistic movement. The movement was so named because it chiefly grew out of the New York City neighborhood known as Harlem, which boasted a large African American population. The Harlem Renaissance was an encompassing artistic movement,

COMMON HUMAN EXPERIENCE

In her novel *Jubilee* (1966), Walker tells the story of a slave family during and after the Civil War. Other literary works that provide accounts of African American slaves include:

Uncle Tom's Cabin (1853), a novel by Harriet Beecher Stowe. Stowe's anti-slavery novel is the story of Uncle Tom, a long-suffering black slave who ultimately learns to disobey his white owners. While the novel was composed as an anti-slavery message, it has often been accused of establishing certain black stereotypes, and "Uncle Tom" has since come to be used as a term for a black man who allows himself to be subservient to a white.

Roots: The Saga of an American Family (1976), a novel by Alex Haley. Perhaps the most popular and influential novel about slavery written in the twentieth century, Haley's *Roots* follows the life and travails of Kunte Kinte, an African boy who is torn from his home country to be sold into the American slave trade.

Beloved (1987), a novel by Toni Morrison. Tony Morrison's novel is both an unflinching depiction of slavery and a suspenseful ghost story. Sethe is an escaped slave now living in Ohio, but she is perpetually haunted by the torments she suffered as a slave. Compounding her torment is the ghost of her dead baby, which may be haunting her Ohio home.

Fire on the Mountain (1988), a novel by Terry Bisson. Bisson's novel is a re-imagining of history, describing what may have been if the abolitionist John Brown had successfully sparked a slave revolution in 1859, as he actually intended to do. In the novel, the African American slaves successfully take back their freedom after a long and bloody war and form their own government.

influencing everything from music to literature to stage plays to dance to visual art, as well as philosophical thought. The movement intended to express the experience of African Americans during the 1920s and 1930s when the movement was at its peak, yet it remains tremendously influential on all manner of art and literature today. Another facet of the Harlem Renaissance was its euphoric celebration of racial pride and strong challenging of white racism. When she was a young writer, Margaret Walker was heavily influenced by the Harlem Renaissance and mentored by Langston Hughes, one of the definitive writers of the movement.

The Black Aesthetic Movement The black aesthetic movement took place during the 1960s and early 1970s and was defined by the growing prominence of black artists and writers. This artistic movement was a direct result of the contemporary civil rights and black power movements, which both sought to achieve equal rights for African Americans. The black aesthetic movement intended to further these causes and create a distinct black culture separate from that of white artists and writers. According to the movement, the artist was an activist. Among the writers associated with the black aesthetic movement are Alex Haley, Sonia Sanchez, and Margaret Walker.

Works in Critical Context

For My People Walker's poetry collection, *For My People*, was both her first book and her first critically applauded work. Evaluating the title poem some thirty years after it was first published, Roger Whitlow writes in *Black American Literature: A Critical History*, "The poem, written in free verse, rhythmically catalogues the progress of black American experience." In that same volume, Eugenia Collier is more generous in her praise, stating, "It speaks to us, in our words and rhythms, of our history, and it radiates the promise of our future. It is the quintessential example of myth and ritual shaped by artistic genius."

Jubilee Critical reactions to *Jubilee* were mixed. Granting that the novel is "ambitious," *New York Times Book Review* contributor Wilma Dykeman deems it "uneven." Arthur P. Davis, writing in *From the Dark Tower: Afro-American Writers, 1900–1960*, suggests that the author "has crowded too much into her novel." Even so, counter some reviewers, the novel merits praise. Abraham Chapman of the *Saturday Review* appreciates the author's "fidelity to fact and detail." In the *Christian Science Monitor*, Henrietta Buckmaster comments, "In Vyry, Miss Walker has found a remarkable woman who suffered one outrage after the other and yet emerged with a humility and a moral fortitude that reflected a spiritual wholeness." Dykeman concurs: "In its best episodes, and in Vyry, *Jubilee* chronicles the triumph of a free spirit over many kinds of bondages."

Responses to Literature

1. Although Walker's novel, *Jubilee*, is a fictional account of slavery, Frederick Douglass provided the true story of his own experiences as a slave in his autobiography, *Narrative of the Life of Frederick Douglass* (1845). Read both books, and then explain how Douglass's true story is different from Walker's fiction. How are they similar? How do you think each work was affected by the time period in which it was written?

2. Walker wrote her poem, "For My People," using free verse, a poetic form that does not utilize a regular rhyme, rhythm, or metric scheme. Think about how the free verse form of "For My People" affects the message Walker is trying to convey. Does the poem's style improve or lessen your understanding of it? Explain your answer in a short essay.

3. In 1977, Walker accused Alex Haley of plagiarizing her book, *Jubilee*, when he published his own novel, *Roots: The Saga of an American Family*. Read both novels. Do you think Walker was justified in accusing Haley of stealing from her? Why or why not? Use specific examples from both novels to support your response.

BIBLIOGRAPHY

Books

Davis, Arthur. *From the Dark Tower: Afro-American Writers, 1900 to 1960*. Washington, D.C.: Howard University Press, 1974.

Evans, Mari. *Black Women Writers (1950–1980): A Critical Evaluation*. Chicago: Nelson Hall, 1973.

Tate, Claudia. *Women Writers at Work*. New York: Continuum, 1984.

Walker, Margaret. *How I Wrote "Jubilee."* Chicago: Third World Press, 1972.

Whitlow, Roger. *Black American Literature: A Critical History*. New York: Anchor/Doubleday, 1982.

Periodicals

Buckmaster, Henrietta. "*Jubilee* (review)." *Christian Science Monitor* (September 29, 1966).

Chapman, Abraham. "*Jubilee* (review)." *Saturday Review* (September 22, 1966).

Dykeman, Wilma. "*Jubilee* Book Review." *New York Times Book Review* (September 25, 1966).

Web Sites

The Center for Programs in Contemporary Writing. *Margaret Walker, poet and novelist* (obituary). Accessed December 2, 2008, from http://writing.upenn.edu/~afilreis/50s/walker-margaret.html.

Internet Poetry Archive. *Biography*. Accessed December 2, 2008, from http://www.ibiblio.org/ipa/poems/walker/biography.php.

✺ Jeannette Walls

BORN: *c. 1960, Phoenix, Arizona*

NATIONALITY: *American*

GENRE: *Nonfiction*

MAJOR WORKS:

Dish: The Inside Story on the World of Gossip (2000)

The Glass Castle: A Memoir (2005)

Overview

Jeannette Walls is a New York journalist. She spent many years as a gossip columnist, and the gossip industry was the subject of her first book. She is better known, however, for her 2005 memoir, *The Glass Castle: A Memoir*, a shocking and vivid account of her impoverished upbringing by neglectful parents in Arizona and West Virginia in the 1960s and 1970s.

Works in Biographical and Historical Context

Growing Up in Poverty   For a woman who was later to succeed in the highly competitive world of the New York media, Walls had an unlikely start in life. Biographical sources do not list her exact date of birth, but it is believed to have been in 1960, in Phoenix, Arizona. Walls was the daughter of Rex and Rose Marie Walls. Her mother was an artist and writer but seems to have been entirely ill-suited to motherhood. Unable to adjust to the demands of raising four children, she preferred to spend her time on her artistic projects. Her father was a highly intelligent, self-taught man who regarded himself as an inventor, and he was able to teach his children science, as well as how to shoot pistols. He also encouraged them to develop a fearless approach to life. But like his wife, he was hardly an ideal parent. He was an alcoholic and a gambler who, on one occasion, even stole his children's savings in order to go on a drunken binge. Sometimes Rose Marie would work as a teacher and Rex as an electrician, but neither parent was able to keep a job for long, which meant that the family had little money. Walls grew up in extreme poverty; she and her siblings were left to fend for themselves, lacking adequate food or clothing. Sometimes Jeannette fed herself by rummaging through trash cans at school, or even by stealing from the other students, and the children would also eat cat food. All four siblings, one boy and three girls, learned at a young age how to support one another.

During Walls's early childhood, her parents moved around from town to town in the Southwest before deciding to move to Welch, West Virginia, where Rex Walls grew up. Welch was a small, impoverished mining community in the Appalachian Mountains, and the Walls became the poorest of the poor, living in a run-down house without running water and often with no electricity. Jeannette's deprived upbringing, however, did not seem to affect her success at school. Her parents, deeply flawed though they may have been, encouraged their children to read and learn. In high school, Walls wrote for the school newspaper and developed a love of journalism, thus planting the seeds of her later career.

Moving to New York   When Walls was seventeen, she decided to strike out on her own, dropping out of high school and moving from West Virginia to New York City. Her sister, Lori, had already moved there, and the two sisters shared a Bronx apartment. Their brother joined them a year later, and their other sister would soon come to New York, too. Walls finished high school and got an internship and then a job at a Brooklyn alternative newspaper. She was happy with her success but decided that she needed to go to college. After excelling at admission tests, she entered Barnard College in Manhattan. She managed to cram her classes into three days each week, and she worked various jobs during the other four days in order to support herself. During her senior year, her funds were short and she thought she might have to drop out, but her father came up with the money that allowed her to continue her studies. Both her parents had followed their children to New York City; for a while they lived with Lori and Jeannette, but when that did not work out, they lived first in a van and then on the streets. New York City, at the time, had a growing population of homeless people.

Walls graduated from Barnard in 1984 at the age of twenty-four and decided to pursue a career in journalism. Within three years she was employed at *New York* magazine, writing a column that covered the Manhattan cultural and political scene. In 1988, she married a wealthy businessman, Eric Goldberg, and started to live the good life in her husband's Park Avenue apartment. She kept her impoverished background a secret, and people tended to assume that, as a Barnard College graduate and now married to wealth, she had had an easy life of privilege.

Walls's column in *New York* was such a success that two New York newspapers offered her the opportunity to write a daily gossip column. She turned down both offers, preferring instead to join *Esquire* in 1993. Five years later she moved to MSNBC.com, where she wrote the gossip column, "Scoop." She quickly became known as one of the top writers in her field, digging out all the news and secrets that the celebrities might prefer not to be made public.

Publishing Success   Walls's father died in 1994, and her marriage ended in divorce in 1996. However, her career continued on an upward trajectory. In 2000, she published her first book, *Dish: The Inside Story on the World of Gossip*, an account of the role gossip about the rich, the

famous, and the influential has played in the media from the 1950s to the 1990s. *Dish* is a serious book in which Walls examines various issues surrounding gossip: the ambivalent attitude that celebrities have to the invasion of their privacy; the role politics plays in issues of privacy; the distinction, often blurred, between news and gossip; and how, over the decades, the public longing for more and more racy tidbits about the lives of celebrities has increased.

Meanwhile, Walls was preparing to tell the story of her childhood. She had been considering doing this for nearly twenty years and had tried, without success, to write it in fictionalized form. She was persuaded to tackle the project in the form of a memoir by her friend John Taylor, a journalist whom she had first met when they both worked for *New York* magazine. She and Taylor were walking in Central Park when Taylor pointed out to her that whenever he asked her about her family, she changed the subject. She was worried that if she told him, or anyone, about her background, they would not want to be friends with her anymore. But she told Taylor anyway, and he suggested that the story would make an interesting book. She and Taylor married in 2002. Walls worked on the book for several years, keeping it a secret from almost everyone. She described writing it as a cathartic experience for her. The result of her labors, *The Glass Castle: A Memoir*, was published in 2005. The title was taken from the name given to the home that her father claimed he would one day build for his children.

Still insecure about what the consequences of publishing her memoir might be, Walls was pleasantly surprised to find that not only did this not happen, but that she made new friends and deepened existing friendships. Reading her honest confessions about the struggles of her childhood, people opened up to her about their own lives. The novel was a great success with reviewers and the public. Even Walls's mother, at the time living in a dilapidated building in New York with no electricity, read it and reportedly enjoyed it.

In a 2005 interview with Rachel Kramer Bussel of *Gothamist*, Walls commented, "I've never really felt bitter. I'm a really lucky person, I've got a great job, I've got a wonderful husband, I've got a great life."

Works in Literary Context

The Confessional Memoir   The memoir is a literary genre that has existed almost as long as literature has been written. It is similar to autobiography but covers only a portion of the writer's life. The traditional memoir was usually limited to the writer's participation in public affairs. A retired statesman, for example, might write his memoirs concerning the people and the issues he had dealt with during his time in power. In the 1990s a new kind of memoir began to gain popularity in the United States. Written often by people who were not in the public eye, such memoirs featured more intimate, personal, and even sensational elements that, in earlier times, a memoirist would not have considered being worthy of record—not to mention the public embarrassment that might ensue from publishing such revelations. Examples of the new trend in memoir writing, which was sometimes called the confessional memoir, include Mary Karr's *The Liars' Club* (1995), Frank McCourt's *Angela's Ashes* (1996), and Dave Pelzer's *A Child Called It* (1995). Commentators sometimes attributed the rise of such memoirs to the popularity of confessional talk shows on television, in which people spoke about the intimate details of their lives. Another recent example of a confessional memoir is *Prozac Nation* (1994), by Elizabeth Lee Wurtzel, which she published at the age of twenty-six. The book describes her battle with depression while she was a college student. Susanna Kaysen published a similar memoir in the same year, titled *Girl, Interrupted*. The popularity of these memoirs of abuse, mental illness, and various forms of childhood deprivation helped to create the atmosphere in which Walls felt able to write and publish *The Glass Castle* and for it to become a best-seller.

Works in Critical Context

Dish: The Inside Story on the World of Gossip

Dish: The Inside Story on the World of Gossip was well received by reviewers. Noting that "Like it or not, gossip is an integral part of our information-driven world," the reviewer for *Publishers Weekly* concludes, "Provocative and invariably entertaining, Walls gives dishing the dirt its historical, social and political due." In *Library Journal*, Kelli N. Perkins comments that "Walls dishes up plenty of gossip while chronicling the escalating American lust for insider information on celebrities." In Perkins's view, the book is "an entertaining insider's look and a solid history of gossip." For Jonathan Bing, writing for *Variety*, "Walls proves the quintessential insider, and a highly entertaining one at that. Her accounts . . . lay bare the inner workings of the major gossip outlets in their ongoing efforts to somehow balance dish, cronyism and actual news." Bing did, however, have some reservations, claiming that *Dish* "is long on detail and short on analysis." Bing also pointed out some errors and suggested that the book was "likely a rush job, cobbled together at the breakneck speed of a daily columnist with a page to fill."

The Glass Castle: A Memoir

The Glass Castle: A Memoir was far more widely reviewed than Walls's earlier book. There was widespread appreciation of her courage in writing the book, and the spirit with which she dealt with such extreme adversity. The reviewer for *Publishers Weekly* notes that "Walls doesn't pull her punches . . . .in this excellent, unusual book." The reviewer also pays tribute to Walls's "fantastic storytelling knack." In *Newsweek*, Barbara Kantrowitz describes the book as an "unsparing but loving memoir," concluding, "What saves this book from mind-numbing grimness is the family's extraordinary resilience." In *Booklist*, the reviewer observes the dual nature of the

COMMON HUMAN EXPERIENCE

Walls's memoir describes her difficult childhood, and she has said that her favorite books all involve dealing with hardships of one kind or another. The following works are also memoirs in which the authors describe their difficult childhoods:

Angela's Ashes: A Memoir (1996), a memoir by Frank McCourt. This is a best-selling book in which McCourt recalls, often with humor, the abject poverty and misfortune of his childhood in Ireland.

A Childhood: The Biography of a Place (1978), a nonfiction work by Harry Crews. This book is a memoir about Crews's early childhood in rural Bacon County, Georgia, during the Great Depression, when his family lived in a one-room cabin and daily hardships were a matter of course. The memoir has become a classic of its kind.

The Unwanted: A Memoir of Childhood (2001), a book by Kien Nguyen. This is a memoir about the author's childhood in Vietnam. Nguyen was eight years old when Saigon, the capital of South Vietnam, fell to the Communists in 1975. Being half American and half Vietnamese, Nguyen was particularly subject to harassment by the new Communist leaders. He endured poverty and much suffering before immigrating to the United States in 1985.

book, which "speaks candidly about the poverty, hunger, and bullying Walls and her siblings endured as well as surprising affection, the strength of family ties, and the human spirit." In the *New York Times Book Review*, Francine Prose also comments on this aspect of what she called a "chilling memoir," appreciating how, in spite of the horrific childhood Walls endured, she still managed to appreciate, forgive, and love her parents rather than judge them. Prose writes that "Walls has a telling memory for detail and an appealing, unadorned style," and Prose also appreciates the author's "refusal to indulge in amateur psychoanalysis, to descend to the jargon of dysfunction or theorize . . . about the sources of her parents' behavior." *The Glass Castle: A Memoir* was also well received on the other side of the Atlantic. In Britain's *The Spectator*, Olivia Glazebrook comments that she read the book in one sitting and was amazed by it: "Walls and her three siblings survived an upbringing truly stranger than fiction—if it were invented, it would not be credible." Like other reviewers, Glazebrook comments on Walls's skill in creating a balanced account of her extraordinary childhood, declaring that "as she and her siblings did, we must both love and hate her parents."

Responses to Literature

1. Why are people so fascinated by the lives of celebrities? Do you think modern gossip differs much from

the gossip of times past? In your opinion, does gossip consume journalistic resources that could be better spent on "real" news, or should news organizations cater to the desires of their audience?

2. Walls had an extraordinarily deprived childhood, and many readers of *The Glass Castle: A Memoir* might say that her parents were abusive. But Walls grew up to have a successful life and appears to have no bitterness about how she was raised. With this in mind, consider the extent to which our childhoods shape our adult lives. Are children who suffer abuse more likely to have dysfunctional lives as adults?

3. Read *The Glass Castle*. What were the qualities that enabled Walls to survive her childhood? What positive things did Walls and her siblings gain from their upbringing?

4. Research the issue of child poverty in the United States today. How many children live in poverty? What are the causes of their poverty? What can be done to help them? Write an essay in which you examine this question and propose a solution. You may use insights or examples gained from Walls's work to support your proposal.

BIBLIOGRAPHY

Periodicals

Bing, Jonathan. Review of *Dish: The Inside Story on the World of Gossip. Variety* (June 5, 2000): 31.

Glazebrook, Olivia. "Learning How to Swim." *Spectator* (April 30, 2005): 38–39.

Kantrowitz, Barbara. Review of *The Glass Castle: A Memoir. Newsweek* (March 7, 2005): 55.

Perkins, Kelli N. Review of *Dish: The Inside Story on the World of Gossip. Library Journal* (April 1, 2000): 119.

Prose, Francine. "Outrageous Misfortune." *New York Times Book Review* (March 13, 2005): 1.

Review of *The Glass Castle: A Memoir. Booklist* (April 1, 2006): 35.

Review of *The Glass Castle: A Memoir. Publishers Weekly* (January 17, 2005): 41.

Review of *Dish: The Inside Story on the World of Gossip. Publishers Weekly* (February 7, 2000): 74.

Valby, Karen. "Coming Up for Air." *Entertainment Weekly* (March 18, 2005): 32.

Web sites

Bussel, Rachel Kramer. "Jeannette Walls, author, The Glass Castle, gossip columnist, MSNBC.com." *Gothamist.* Accessed November 18, 2008, from http://gothamist.com/2005/05/27/jeannette_walls_author_the_glass_castle_gossip_columnist_msnbccom.php.

"Jeannette Walls Answers Your Questions: A Q + A With the Chronicler of New York's Power Elite." *ABC News.* Accessed November 18, 2008, from http://abcnews.go.com/Primetime/Entertainment/Story?id=552776&page=1.

✸ Robert Penn Warren

BORN: *1905, Guthrie, Kentucky*

DIED: *1989, Stratton, Vermont*

NATIONALITY: *American*

GENRE: *Fiction, nonfiction, poetry, drama*

MAJOR WORKS:
All the King's Men (1946)
Promises: Poems, 1954–1956 (1957)
Now and Then: Poems, 1976–1978 (1978)

Overview

Robert Penn Warren was a twentieth-century American writer closely associated with the Southern Agrarian movement in literature in the 1920s and 1930s, a movement that celebrated the South's rural heritage and bemoaned the damage done to Southern culture by industrialization. Warren achieved widespread fame for his Pulitzer Prize-winning book *All the King's Men* (1946). During his extensive career as a poet, novelist, essayist, and short story writer, Warren received two additional Pulitzer Prizes for his groundbreaking achievements in poetry.

Works in Biographical and Historical Context

Birth of a Southern Agrarian Warren was born and raised in the small southern town of Guthrie, Kentucky, in

Robert Penn Warren   *Warren, Robert Penn, photograph.© Jerry Bauer. Reproduced by permission.*

1905. Traditional core values combined with a rural, agricultural landscape would shape Warren's character during the first decades of the twentieth century. During this time, southern states like Kentucky struggled to maintain an agrarian, or farming, society as technological advancements and industrialization brought progress to the North. Rural communities, such as Guthrie, were afflicted by severe poverty, malnutrition, unemployment, and a lack of adequate roads and electricity. These conditions led to a debate over whether the rural South was being left behind by progress in the North.

These social and technological changes caused tensions in the South that were reflected in political and literary movements of the period. In the 1920s and 1930s, politicians and writers who defended the southern way of life and condemned northern industrialization and secularism as a threat to southern traditions became known as the Southern Agrarians.

In 1921, Warren began contributing to this literary movement not long after enrolling at Vanderbilt University in Nashville, Tennessee, where he studied under renowned poet John Crowe Ransom. Ransom invited Warren to join a select group of young writers that included Donald Davidson and Allen Tate.

From 1922 to 1925, Ransom's group of young writers published the *Fugitive*, a literary journal that included both poetry and criticism. The *Fugitive* served as a forum for the young writers to amplify traditional Southern, agrarian values while underscoring the hazards of the budding industrial economy that was flourishing in the northern states. The pieces collected in Warren's first two volumes, *Thirty-Six Poems* (1935) and *Eleven Poems on the Same Theme* (1942), are based on folk stories of Warren's native Kentucky. The Fugitive group, as these writers came to be labeled, later aligned itself with the Southern Agrarian movement and published *I'll Take My Stand* (1930), a manifesto that defended southern culture and criticized northern modernization as a negative influence on traditional values. In some ways, the Southern Agrarians used this publication to respond to critic H. L. Mencken's essay "The Sahara of the Bozart" (1917), which harshly criticized southern culture for its backwardness and lack of literary production. Warren contributed an essay titled "The Briar Patch," in which he defended racial segregation, reflecting the conservative politics of the Agrarians. Later in life, Warren rejected these early views and supported the civil rights movement of the 1960s.

New Criticism

After completing his studies at Vanderbilt, Warren continued his education at several prominent institutions, including Oxford University in England. In 1930, Warren returned to the United States and married Emma Brescia. A few years later, he accepted a position at Louisiana State University, where he taught English. In 1935, along with fellow faculty members Cleanth Brooks and Charles W. Pipkin, he co-founded the *Southern Review*, an influential literary magazine. Contributors to the *Southern Review* often analyzed a piece of writing as an object of art, independent of outside influences. This form of literary analysis was later referred to as New Criticism. Warren also collaborated with Brooks in editing the textbooks *Understanding Poetry* (1938) and *Understanding Fiction* (1943). Both textbooks introduced future generations of students and teachers to this new, in-depth analysis of text as an art form.

Maturing as a Writer

As he developed his craft and matured as a writer during the 1930s and 1940s, Warren sifted through the surface of human nature and entered into the much darker realm of human corruption. Although Warren did not serve in World War II, the turbulent political situation in the world and the economic upheavals at home, caused by the Great Depression, left marks on his literary work. He focused on the human subject and the forces that influence human behavior, such as society and the idea of God. Warren often targeted his Kentucky upbringing as the setting of his darker works during this time. His first short story "PrimeLeaf" (1930), was published during his final year at Oxford. This piece of historical fiction is set in Kentucky during the Black Patch Tobacco War (1904–1909), a conflict between a large tobacco monopoly and local farmers over price fixing. The farmers could not make a living off the low prices fixed by the tobacco monopoly. The resulting conflict involved violence on both sides, with night attacks on farms, crops, and property. Warren's first novel, *Night Rider* (1939), is set during the same historical conflict.

The novella *Blackberry Winter*, first published in 1946, tells of the loss of innocence. Set during an unseasonably cold June morning, the narrator—nine-year-old Seth—recounts a violent storm that flooded a nearby creek, damaged crops, and left marks of destruction across the countryside. Warren constructs a realm similar to "Prime Leaf" in "The Ballad of Billie Potts," a poem in his collection *Selected Poems, 1923–1943* (1944). The ballad centers on the life of a frontier innkeeper who makes his living by robbing and murdering travelers. The innkeeper's malevolence comes to a climax when he mistakenly kills his son, who had previously gone missing. This theme of human corruption, caused by both external and internal forces, would later appear in his most famous work, *All the King's Men*.

Major Novel Inspired by Huey Long

All the King's Men draws its inspiration from the career of Huey Long, who is often referred to as the Louisiana Kingfish. Long was a controversial political figure who was disliked by the political establishment but supported by the people as a reformer. He was elected governor of Louisiana in 1928, and installed his own people in every level of state government in an attempt to end corruption, but he ultimately fell victim to corruption himself. He served as a U.S. senator from 1932 until 1935, when he was

LITERARY AND HISTORICAL CONTEMPORARIES

Warren's famous contemporaries include:

William Faulkner (1897–1962): Faulkner was one of the most important Southern writers of the twentieth century and won the Nobel Prize in literature in 1949.

Tennessee Williams (1911–1983): Author of *A Streetcar Named Desire* (1947) and *Cat on a Hot Tin Roof* (1955), Williams is considered the most influential Southern playwright of the twentieth century.

John Steinbeck (1902–1968): Steinbeck wrote about social conditions, the working class, and immigrants in such novels as *The Grapes of Wrath* (1939).

Harper Lee (1926–): Lee was influenced by Robert Penn Warren and other Southern writers, and is recognized for her Pulitzer Prize-winning novel, *To Kill a Mockingbird* (1960).

Ralph Ellison (1914–1994): Ellison was a friend of Robert Penn Warren and is known for his novel, *Invisible Man* (1952), about race and alienation in the South.

Huey Long (1852–1937): Long was a controversial reformist politician who served as governor of Louisiana from 1928 to 1932 and later, as U.S. senator.

Franklin Delano Roosevelt (1882–1945): Roosevelt was president of the United States from 1933 to 1945.

assassinated at the Louisiana state capitol. The protagonist of this novel, Willie Stark (based on Long), appears as a simple, earnest farmhand from the South corrupted by power and greed.

Transitions in Life and Literature The 1950s and 1960s mark a transitional period in Warren's life that reflects important changes in American society. The American victory in World War II led to a period of economic expansion and prosperity during the 1950s. Warren and Emma divorced in 1951, and he married Eleanor Clark in 1952. They had two children, Rosanna (born in 1953) and Gabriel (born in 1955). While Warren continued to base his work on his own experiences and emotional turmoil, a reader may identify a break away from figurative darkness. Indeed, many of his most prized writings seem to reflect life experiences that invoke joy, including works that allude to his immediate family.

Promises: Poems, 1954–1956 (1957), for which Warren received his first Pulitzer Prize in poetry as well as the National Book Award, reveals a dramatic shift from his early, darker works. *Promises* has been described by some as a distinctly personal tale from a man who ultimately rediscovered joy.

Taking a New Stand on Race Relations The 1950s were marked by social tensions that resulted in

the birth of the civil rights movement. In 1954, the U.S. Supreme Court ruled in its landmark case, *Brown v. Board of Education*, that segregation in public schools was unconstitutional. In 1957, Martin Luther King, Jr. became president of the Southern Christian Leadership Conference, which organized nonviolent protests against segregation on the church and community level. In 1964, President Lyndon B. Johnson signed the Civil Rights Act, which made it a crime to discriminate against people on the basis of race, color, or religion. During this period of important social changes, Warren abandoned his earlier, conservative views on segregation, and he befriended and supported the work of prominent African American writer Ralph Ellison. He published essays on these social struggles, *Segregation: The Inner Conflict in the South* (1956), and conducted an interview with civil rights leaders titled *Who Speaks for the Negro?* (1965).

Later Life and Works Warren spent the last decades of his life living in Connecticut and in a summer home in Vermont, where he continued to write poetry and a final novel, *A Place to Come To* (1977), a largely autobiographical work. Warren received his second Pulitzer Prize in poetry for *Now and Then: Poems, 1976–1978* (1978). In this collection, he meditates on his life, beginning with his boyhood in rural Kentucky and progressing, in Warren's words, through "sixty years blown like a hurricane past."

In 1986, the Library of Congress appointed Warren Poet Laureate of the United States, a position that he had held from 1944 to 1945 under the title "Consultant in Poetry." Warren is one of the few to hold this honor twice. Warren died in Vermont from complications of cancer in 1989.

Works in Literary Context

The Southern Literary Renaissance In 1917, Baltimore critic H. L. Mencken published an essay titled "The Sahara of the Bozart" that famously derided Southern arts and culture, writing that the South as a whole was "almost as sterile artistically, intellectually, culturally, as the Sahara Desert." There were Southern authors, of course, in the early twentieth century, but they were publishing sentimental books about the pre-Civil War South—so-called "moonlight and magnolia" romances. Mencken mocked such writing and pronounced the South incapable of producing an important, new kind of literature. A generation of young Southerners took Mencken's criticism as a call to arms, and set about creating "Southern" literature. During the 1920s, this produced mostly protest literature, or literature written attacking the old-style books of the South. The founding of *The Fugitive* at Vanderbilt University can be seen as a direct response to Mencken. Warren and other Fugitive poets set out to prove that Southern writers could produce solid work that avoided the pitfalls of sentimentality and romanticism.

The 1920s can be seen as a reactionary phase in Southern writing. During the 1930s, however, Southern literature emerged as a major, mature literary force. The titan of Southern letters was William Faulkner, who published a series of novels in the late 1920s and early 1930s that even Mencken had to admit were impressive. These include *The Sound and the Fury* (1929), *As I Lay Dying* (1930), and *Light in August* (1932). Faulkner steeped his work in the culture and character of the South, representing it in epic scale using a flowing, experimental style. Warren's monumental *All the King's Men* similarly paints the South in tragic terms. By the 1940s, writers like Warren, Flannery O'Connor, Eudora Welty, and Carson McCullers had dispelled any misconceptions the reading public may have had about the artistic abilities of the writers of the American South.

Power and Corruption The human desire for power and its potential for corruption is an enduring literary theme, which Warren introduces into many of his works, including novels like *All the King's Men* and poetry, such as "The Ballad of Billie Potts" and "Brother to Dragons." Even today, media outlets—such as advertisements, infomercials, and other messages—claim that fame and fortune will solve the problems of the common man. While venues have changed and the transmission of messages has improved over time, the false sense of security that comes with blind ambition remains as important a theme in our own day as it was in Warren's time. Warren's ability to construct an American landscape familiar to many, while turning seemingly harmless characters into monsters, is the reason many describe his work as both poignant and timeless.

Works in Critical Context

While critics vary in their interpretation of Warren's major works, many identify a common thread: Warren infused history and his early experiences into fictional characters; these characters yearn for stability and power while residing in a volatile society that tempts and abuses its citizens. Warren illuminates such desires and corruption in perhaps his greatest literary achievement, *All the King's Men*.

All the King's Men *All the King's Men* captures one man's rise and fall from political power as it juxtaposes life and government in a backward American state. Initial criticism of the novel focused on the character of Willie Stark and his corruption by power and greed, while later critics analyzed the important role of Jack Burden, the journalist who narrates the story. As James Hall has noted, "The power of the novel comes from imposing two forms of energy, embodied in Willie and Jack, on the permanent scene of politics." Robert Gorham Davis emphasizes the relationship between action and ideas in this novel, writing, "Warren is fascinated by the strong man of action, as

---

COMMON HUMAN EXPERIENCE

Human corruption caused by the possession of power is a major theme found in many of Warren's works. Other works that center on this same theme include:

Macbeth (1606), a play by William Shakespeare. A nobleman is corrupted by power in one of Shakespeare's most famous plays.

All About Eve (1950), a film directed by Joseph L. Mankiewicz. Regarded as one of the best films of all time, *All About Eve* chronicles the rise of back-stabbing actress Eve Harrington.

The Man Who Would Be King (1975) a film directed by John Huston. This film, based on a tale by Rudyard Kipling, follows two adventurers in Afghanistan who are proclaimed kings but are undone when one of them develops delusions of grandeur and comes to believe he is the reincarnation of Alexander the Great.

Primary Colors (1996), a novel by Joe Klein. Klein presents a fictionalized version of the Bill Clinton 1992 presidential campaign and focuses on human reactions to the achievement of political power.

---

many of our war novelists were fascinated by the Nazis. And the question of *All the King's Men* is solely whether the man of ideas can work with the dictator in the interests of historic change." Davis also comments on the poetic aspects of Warren's prose fiction, describing the novel in the context of Warren's narrative poetry. He contends that "*All the King's Men* is brilliantly done, with magnificent brief set-pieces in which Robert Penn Warren writes prose equivalent to his poems in sound and rhythm and imagery.... Mixed with this pure gold is the brass of slick writing and melodrama that comprises the rest of the novel." Later criticism focuses on aspects of the novel other than its political dimension. Earl Wilcox, for example, sees the many love affairs of Willie Stark as perhaps more important than his one political affair. Wilcox suggests that "the novel is finally about the power of love in the universe to change a man." Wilcox sees in this novel's many themes a complexity that defies easy categorization: "Not all readers find the novel as richly humorous, as politically exciting, or as totally pertinent to humanity.... In a final analysis, the novel resists categorizing... since it depicts many complex matters simultaneously."

Response to Literature

1. Research the life of Huey Long. Write a paragraph about his life, accomplishments, and failures. What

were the forces that drove him on? Did he just long for power or was he idealistic as well?

2. Create a chart on your own paper comparing Huey Long and Warren's fictional character, Willie Stark. Include three similarities and three differences in your chart. Discuss your findings with a partner.

3. Read H. L. Mencken's "The Sahara of the Bozart." Research Warren's reaction to Mencken's writing. Discuss your findings with a partner.

4. Read a few poems written by Warren. Choose your favorite poem then write a paragraph explaining why it is your favorite. Include information about his writing style and themes.

BIBLIOGRAPHY

Books

Berger, Walter. *A Southern Renascence Man: Views of Robert Penn Warren.* Baton Rouge: Louisiana State University Press, 1984.

Blotner, Joseph. *Robert Penn Warren: A Biography.* New York: Random House, 1997.

Bohner, Charles H. *Robert Penn Warren.* New York: Twayne, 1964.

Burt, John. *Robert Penn Warren and American Idealism.* New Haven: Yale University Press, 1988.

Casper, Leonard. *Robert Penn Warren: The Dark and Bloody Ground.* Seattle: University of Washington Press, 1960.

Clark, William Bedford, ed. *Critical Essays on Robert Penn Warren.* New York: Twayne, 1981.

Justus, James H. *The Achievement of Robert Penn Warren.* Baton Rouge: Louisiana State University Press, 1981.

Strandberg, Victor H. *The Poetic Vision of Robert Penn Warren.* Louisville: University Press of Kentucky, 1977.

Periodicals

Ealy, Steven D. "Corruption and Innocence in Robert Penn Warren's Fiction." *Modern Age* 47, Issue 2 (March 22, 2005): 139–147.

Walker, Marshall. "Making Dreams Work: The Achievement of Robert Penn Warren." *London Magazine* 15 (December/January 1976): 33–46.

Web sites

Poets.org. *Robert Penn Warren.* Accessed November 13, 2008, from http://www.poets.org/poet.php/ prmPID/17.

Robert Penn Warren.com. Accessed November 13, 2008, from http://www.robertpennwarren.com.

KYLIT. *Robert Penn Warren.* Accessed November 13, 2008, from http://www.english.eku.edu/ SERVICES/KYLIT/WARREN.HTM.

Literary History.com. *Robert Penn Warren (1905–1989).* Accessed November 13, 2008, from http://www. literaryhistory.com/20thC/WarrenRP.htm.

✸ Booker T. Washington

BORN: *1856, Hale's Ford, Virginia*

DIED: *1915, Tuskegee, Alabama*

NATIONALITY: *American*

GENRE: *Nonfiction*

MAJOR WORKS:
Up from Slavery: An Autobiography (1901)

Overview

A respected educator and founder of the Tuskegee Institute, Booker T. Washington was one of the most important social thinkers of the early twentieth century. His 1895 speech before a racially mixed audience at the Atlanta Cotton States and International Exposition won him national recognition. Washington's *Up from Slavery* (1901) is a classic American autobiography that has long inspired black and white readers alike.

Works in Biographical and Historical Context

Born into Slavery Washington was born in 1856 near Roanoke, Virginia, at Hale's Farm, where his mother was

Booker T. Washington *Washington, Booker T., photograph. The Library of Congress.*

the slave cook of James Burroughs, a minor planter. His father was white and possibly a member of the Burroughs family. As a child, Washington swept yards and brought water to slaves working in the fields. Freed after the American Civil War, he and his mother went to Malden, West Virginia, to join Washington Ferguson, whom his mother had married during the war. Booker later added "Washington" to his name.

In Malden, young Washington helped support the family by working in salt furnaces and coal mines. He taught himself the alphabet, then studied nights with the teacher of a local school for blacks. In 1870 he started doing housework for the owner of the coal mine where he worked. The owner's wife, an austere New Englander, encouraged his studies and instilled in Washington a great regard for education.

Journey to Hampton, and Tuskegee

In the South after the Civil War, blacks—although they were legally free—were often denied access to basic services and institutions. In some cases, special facilities, including schools were created for blacks in order to keep them separated from whites. In 1872 Washington set out for the Hampton Institute, a school set up for blacks by the Virginia legislature. He walked much of the way and worked at menial jobs to earn the fare to complete the five-hundred-mile journey. Washington spent three years at Hampton and paid for his room and board by working as a janitor. After graduating with honors in 1875, he taught for two years in Malden, then returned to Hampton to teach American Indians as part of a special program.

In 1881, General Samuel Chapman Armstrong, the principal at Hampton, recommended Washington to the Alabama legislature for the job of principal of a new school for black students at Tuskegee. Washington was accepted for the position, but when he arrived in Tuskegee he discovered that neither land nor buildings had been acquired for the projected school, nor were there any funds for these purposes. Consequently, Washington began classes with thirty students in a shanty donated by a black church. Soon, however, he was able to borrow money to buy an abandoned plantation nearby and moved the school there.

Building the Tuskegee Institute

Convinced that economic strength was the best route to political and social equality for blacks, Washington encouraged Tuskegee students to learn industrial skills. Carpentry, cabinetmaking, printing, shoemaking, and tinsmithing were among the first courses the school offered. Boys also studied farming and dairying, while girls learned cooking and sewing and other skills related to homemaking. At Tuskegee, strong emphasis was placed on personal hygiene, manners, and character building. Students followed a rigid schedule of study and work and were required to attend chapel daily and a series of religious services on Sunday. Washington usually conducted the Sunday evening program himself.

During his thirty-four-year career as principal of Tuskegee, the school's curriculum expanded to include instruction in professions as well as trades. At the time of Washington's death from arteriosclerosis and extreme exhaustion in 1915, Tuskegee had an endowment of two million dollars and a staff of two hundred. Nearly two thousand students were enrolled in the regular courses, and about the same number in special courses and the extension division. Among its all-black faculty was the renowned agricultural scientist George Washington Carver. So revered was Washington at Tuskegee that he was buried in a brick tomb, made by students, on a hill overlooking the Institute.

A Public Figure

Although his administration of Tuskegee is Washington's best-known achievement, his work as an educator was only one aspect of his multifaceted career. Washington spent much time raising money for Tuskegee and publicizing the school and its philosophy. His success in securing the praise and financial support of northern philanthropists was remarkable. One of his admirers was industrialist Andrew Carnegie, who thought Washington "one of the most wonderful men…who ever has lived." Many other political, intellectual, and religious leaders were almost as approving.

Washington was also in demand as a speaker, and he won national fame on the lecture circuit. His most famous speech was his address at the opening of the Cotton States and International Exposition in Atlanta in September, 1895. Later known as the Atlanta Compromise, the speech contained the essence of Washington's educational and racial views and was, according to the historian C. Vann Woodward, "his stock speech for the rest of his life." Emphasizing to black members of the audience the importance of economic power, Washington contended that "the opportunity to earn a dollar in a factory just now is worth infinitely more than the opportunity to spend a dollar in an opera house." Consequently, he urged blacks not to strain race relations in the South by demanding social equality with whites.

At the Center of Controversy

The Atlanta speech, C. Vann Woodward has noted, "contained nothing [Washington] had not said many times before.… But in the midst of racial crisis," Washington's speech "electrified conservative hopes." Washington was hailed in the white press as leader and spokesman for all American blacks and successor to the prominent abolitionist Frederick Douglass, who had died a few months earlier.

Washington's position, however, was denounced by many black leaders, including civil-rights activist W. E. B. Du Bois, who objected to Washington's emphasis on vocational training and economic advancement and argued that higher education and political agitation would win equality for blacks. According to historian August Meier, a pioneering authority on Washington's place in intellectual history, those blacks who accepted his "accommodation" doctrines "understood that through

LITERARY AND HISTORICAL CONTEMPORARIES

Washington's famous contemporaries include:

W. E. B. Du Bois (1868–1963): Du Bois was a civil-rights leader and the author of *The Souls of Black Folk* (1903).

Emma Goldman (1869–1940): Lithuanian-born Goldman was a prominent American political activist. An anarchist and advocate of violent revolution, she was known popularly as "Red" Emma.

John D. Rockefeller (1839–1937): American industrialist and philanthropist Rockefeller was the founder of Standard Oil, and was the richest man of his era.

Theodore Roosevelt (1858–1919): Roosevelt was an American political leader and president of the United States from 1901 to 1909.

Upton Sinclair (1878–1968): Pulitzer Prize–winning American author Sinclair was famous for such protest novels as *The Jungle* (1906) and *Oil!* (1927).

tact and indirection [Washington] hoped to secure the good will of the white man and the eventual recognition of the constitutional rights of American Negroes."

The contents of Washington's private papers reinforce the later interpretation of the educator's motives. These documents offer evidence that in spite of the cautious stance that he maintained publicly, Washington was covertly engaged in challenging racial injustices and in improving social and economic conditions for blacks. The prominence he gained by his placating demeanor enabled him to work surreptitiously against segregation and disenfranchisement and to win political appointments that helped advance the cause of racial equality. "In other words," Woodward argues, "he secretly attacked the racial settlement that he publicly sanctioned."

Up from Slavery   Among Washington's many published works is his autobiography *Up from Slavery*, an account of his life from slave to eminent educator. Often referred to by critics as a classic, its style is simple, direct, and anecdotal. Like his numerous essays and speeches, *Up from Slavery* promotes his racial philosophy and, in Woodward's opinion, "presents [Washington's] experience mythically, teaches 'lessons' and reflects a sunny optimism about black life in America." Woodward adds, "It was the classic American success story." Praised lavishly, *Up from Slavery* became a best-seller in the United States and was eventually translated into more than a dozen languages.

Even after achieving literary success, Washington continued to focus his time and energy on his duties at the Tuskegee Institute until his death on November 14, 1915, at the age of fifty-nine.

Works in Literary Context

As a literary figure, Washington is remembered today for two works: *Up from Slavery* and the Atlanta Exposition speech (and in fact, the speech is included as a chapter in the former). A reluctant author persuaded to write by his admirers, Washington was not a natural stylist. His books reflect the main concern of his life in the outside world—namely, the "raising up" of his fellow black Americans by means of land ownership and a thorough education, with emphasis on the mastery of skilled trades. As much propaganda as literature, his work launches itself at the consciousness of the reader with the immediacy of speech. An exhortation in writing from one of the greatest public speakers of his time, *Up from Slavery* delves deep into the personal experience of the man who wrote it. This experience sustains its author in the alien terrain of "literature." As a writer, Washington impresses by simplicity of utterance, by a telling use of anecdotes in the building of arguments, and above all by his grasp of practical detail. As he states, "I have great faith in the power and influence of facts."

The Rags-to-Riches Story   Thrift and industry are the solutions Washington preaches, the familiar nineteenth-century gospel of self-help given substance by his own success at Tuskegee. Washington's autobiography thus fits clearly into the tradition of the rags-to-riches story. It has often been compared to Benjamin Franklin's *Autobiography* (1791), an early example of the genre, and with the tales of Horatio Alger, the dime novelist well-known for his stories about impoverished youths who achieve wealth through sheer determination. The title of Washington's narrative suggests his inexorable optimism: he is interested in movement upward, a movement that in Washington's own case was effected by his "struggle for an education." He based his personal confrontation with white America, although at times it scarcely seems to be a confrontation, on the belief that "every persecuted individual and race should get much consolation out of the great human law, which is universal and eternal, that merit, no matter under what skin found, is in the long run, recognized and rewarded." The tension that exists in *Up from Slavery* is between Washington's unwavering self-belief, his tenacious self-reliance and idealism, and the society that excluded him.

The Slave Narrative   *Up from Slavery* is also one of the most famous slave narratives. This genre had its origins in the eighteenth century, and normally features the recollections of a former slave who has escaped from captivity. The genre was most popular in the United States in the first half of the nineteenth century, when a large number were written as part of the political movement to end slavery; famous narratives produced during this era include *Narrative of the Life of Frederick Douglass, an American Slave* (1845) and *Incidents in the Life of a Slave Girl* (1861) by Harriet Jacobs. After the Civil

War and the end of slavery, the genre became less popular, and coming after the turn of the twentieth century, *Up from Slavery* is a late entry. However, it has many of the features of the traditional slave narrative, especially in its focus on education. In the post–Civil War examples of the genre, literacy and education in general is a precious commodity bought by the narrator with some difficulty, and celebrated as a key to freedom. By substituting "progress" for "freedom," Washington's quest for education fits this mold exactly.

Works in Critical Context

Washington's work, especially the politics to be found in his books, has an old-fashioned quality, and many critics have been unwilling to grant him the status of a "great" writer. What keeps people reading him? One answer is his personality, which is appealing on a number of levels. Writing of *Up from Slavery*, one of Washington's first literary advocates, the critic William Dean Howells, wrote of the charming qualities he saw in Washington, "whose winning yet manly personality and whose ideal of self-devotion must endear him to every reader of his book." Geoff Sadler has more recently seen similar qualities in Washington:

> Throughout his writings, one is made aware of Washington's humanity, the genuine concern for his fellows that informs every page. Undoubtedly a man of strongly held opinions, he seems incapable of malice ("No man shall drag me down by making me hate him"). Self-taught himself, he never loses his close affinity with the black working man, whose respect he clearly retained.

Up from Slavery One of the most persistent defenders of Washington as a literary artist is the critic Houston Baker, who has written repeatedly about the qualities he has found in *Up from Slavery* and that others have overlooked. In *Modernism and the Harlem Renaissance* (1987), Baker argues that the book is characterized by a conscious design, an effort to adopt the literary conventions of dominant white culture and use them for political ends: "Given that *Up from Slavery* has sometimes been considered merely an imitative version of Horatio Alger or of Andrew Carnegie's *Gospel of Wealth* (1889), how can one justify an emphasis on self-conscious design" in the book? "One possible answer to this question can be formulated in structural terms. In Washington's work more than forty of two hundred total pages are devoted to oratorical concerns." According to Baker, the book is at one level a public speaking manual, "setting forth strategies of address (ways of talking black and back) designed for Afro-American empowerment." Washington is, however, a subtle enough author to leave the discovery of these strategies to his readers.

COMMON HUMAN EXPERIENCE

Up from Slavery is the story of a young man coming of age. The young man, however, is born a slave, and has to make his way while opposed constantly by the extreme prejudice of his society. Here are some other works in a similar vein:

> *Their Eyes Were Watching God* (1937), a novel by Zora Neale Hurston. This novel tells the story of Janie, a black woman in her forties recalling her younger life.
> *Native Son* (1940), a novel by Richard Wright. In this work, the young black protagonist reacts against the constraints he lives under not with accommodation, but with violence.
> *The Autobiography of an Ex-Coloured Man* (1912), a novel by James Weldon Johnson. This pioneering novel tells the story of an African American man with light skin who must choose which world he wants to live in—white or black.

Responses to Literature

1. Read Benjamin Franklin's *Autobiography*. How is this well-known model for later rags-to-riches tales different from the story Washington tells?

2. Another well-known coming-of-age story by a black author is "The Man Who Was Almost a Man" (1940), by Richard Wright. Dave, the protagonist, begins life just about as poor as did Washington. How do you think Dave would respond to Washington's advice?

3. In books like *The Souls of Black Folk*, W. E. B. Du Bois argues for social equality for black people in the United States. Washington was less aggressive. Who do you think had the better argument? Why?

BIBLIOGRAPHY

Books

Baker, Houston A., Jr. *Turning South Again: Re-Thinking Modernism/Re-Reading Booker T.* Durham, N.C.: Duke University Press, 2001.

Bieze, Michael. *Booker T. Washington and the Art of Self-Representaton.* New York: Peter Lang, 2008.

Harlan, Louis R. *Booker T. Washington: The Wizard of Tuskegee, 1901–1915.* New York: Oxford University Press, 1983.

Meier, August. *Negro Thought in America, 1880–1915: Racial Ideologies in the Age of Booker T. Washington.* Ann Arbor, Mich.: University of Michigan Press, 1963.

West, Michael Rudolph. *The Education of Booker T. Washington: American Democracy and the Idea of Race Relations.* New York: Columbia University Press, 2006.

Periodicals

Ashton, Susanna. "Entitles: Booker T. Washington's Signs of Play." *Southern Literary Journal* 39 (Spring 2007): 1–23.

Gibson, Donald B. "Strategies and Revisions of Self-Representation in Booker T. Washington's Autobiography." *American Quarterly* 45 (September 1993): 370–393.

Hicks, Scott. "W. E. B. Du Bois, Booker T. Washington, and Richard Wright." *Callaloo: A Journal of African Diaspora Arts and Letters* 29 (Winter 2006): 202–222.

Totten, Gary. "Southernizing Travel in the Black Atlantic: Booker T. Washington's *The Man Farthest Down*." *MELUS* 32 (Summer 2007): 107–131.

Web sites

National Park Service. *Booker T. Washington National Monument.* Retrieved November 19, 2008, from http://www.nps.gov/archive/bowa/home.htm.

✹ Wendy Wasserstein

BORN: *1950, Brooklyn, New York*

DIED: *2006, New York City*

NATIONALITY: *American*

GENRE: *Drama*

MAJOR WORKS:

Uncommon Women and Others (1975)

The Heidi Chronicles (1988)

The Sisters Rosensweig (1992)

Overview

In 1989, Wendy Wasserstein became the first woman playwright to win a Tony; that same year she also collected the Pulitzer Prize and the award for best new play from the New York Drama Critics Circle. These accolades for *The Heidi Chronicles*, a play that traces the confusions of a female art historian from the 1960s through the 1980s, suggest that Wasserstein had achieved her goal of writing drama that invites audiences to care about women's lives and dilemmas. Wasserstein frequently identified herself as a member of the generation on the cusp of the women's movement; even though she is gone, her work continues to communicate and analyze the confusion that has accompanied this enormous cultural transition.

Works in Biographical and Historical Context

Early Productions Wasserstein was born on October 18, 1950, in Brooklyn, New York. Her father, Morris W. Wasserstein, was a successful textile manufacturer, who invented velveteen. Her mother, Lola, was a dancer. Wasserstein attended the exclusive Calhoun School on the Upper East Side of Manhattan and studied dancing

Wendy Wasserstein   *Wasserstein, Wendy, photograph. AP Images.*

with June Taylor, whose troupe appeared regularly on the popular comedic variety program *The Jackie Gleason Show*. She also spent many Saturday afternoons at Broadway matinees. Although she loved plays much of her life, the notion of writing them did not occur to her until a friend convinced her to take Leonard Berkman's playwriting course at the neighboring Smith College during her junior year at Mount Holyoke College. She enjoyed the course so much that she later studied creative writing at the City College of the City University of New York with Joseph Heller and Israel Horovitz, receiving her M.A. in creative writing in 1973. The play she wrote as her thesis, *Any Woman Can't* (1973), was produced off-Broadway by Playwrights Horizons. She then moved on to the Yale Drama School, receiving her M.F.A. in 1976.

Her first acclaimed play, *Uncommon Women and Others* (1975), was initially written as a one-act play at Yale; the revised, expanded version appeared in 1977, six years after Wasserstein's graduation from Mount Holyoke. The play opens with a 1978 six-year reunion of women who had graduated from Mount Holyoke in 1972; one of the central characters, Holly Kaplan, is autobiographically based. Shortly after the reunion begins, the play shifts back to the women's final year at Mount Holyoke, setting out their histories.

The play seems a summation of what Wasserstein learned during the first six years after she graduated from

Mount Holyoke. Uncertain about what career to pursue, even after receiving her M.A. and having *Any Woman Can't* produced, she had applied to Columbia Business School and Yale Drama School and was accepted at both. She followed her heart to Yale. When a classmate complained that he could not get interested in the females populating the one-act version of *Uncommon Women and Others*, she wrote that as a student, his remark helped Wasserstein realize how essential it was for her to write plays about women. The critics generally praised *Uncommon Women and Others* for its humor and compassion. It received a *Village Voice* Off-Broadway Award, as well as the Joseph Jefferson and the Boston Critics awards. A year after it appeared off-Broadway it was telecast by PBS.

Bringing Feminism to the Stage   Wasserstein's play *Isn't It Romantic?* (1983) focuses on the relationship between two women trying to make satisfying lives from the new options available to them courtesy of the women's movement. Critics did not like the first version of *Isn't It Romantic?*, and Wasserstein responded to their complaints about its diffusion by continuing to work on the play. Critics praised the revised production first staged in 1983.

Her play *The Heidi Chronicles* (1988) returns to familiar Wasserstein terrain: the issue of how women deal with the new options precipitated by the women's movement. Once again, the central character must choose between pursuing her own needs and desires and having a successful relationship with a man. At the end of the play, Heidi makes a choice that seems to make her happy. She adopts a child, names her Judy, and hopes that the girl will enjoy a world relatively free of the limits that have restrained Heidi's life. The critics praised *The Heidi Chronicles*, and it won several awards, most notably, the Pulitzer Prize and a Tony for best play.

Bachelors and Sisters   In 1990 Wasserstein's book *Bachelor Girls* appeared; it collects essays that had first appeared in periodicals between 1984 and 1990 and that cover a range of topics, including manicures, Geraldine Ferraro, and Wasserstein's deeply disappointing rendezvous with her banker boyfriend in springtime Paris. According to Wasserstein's introduction to *The Sisters Rosensweig* (1992), her next play, she had to struggle to get the right balance between humor and seriousness. The setting for *The Sisters Rosensweig* is Sara Rosensweig Goode's London home. The eldest sister, Sara, has worked hard to transcend her beginnings, transforming herself from a Brooklyn Jewish girl to a passionate Anglophile who will not allow her daughter to attend Harvard or Yale because she sees them as "floundering their way to being second rate." During two days, the four women characters in this play help each other discover a clearer sense of direction.

Wasserstein next wrote a children's book, *Pamela's First Musical* (1996), about a young girl whose glamorous Aunt Louise takes her to a Broadway show. After this, Wasserstein returned to handling more difficult

LITERARY AND HISTORICAL CONTEMPORARIES

Wasserstein's famous contemporaries include:

Joseph Heller (1923–1999): Heller was an American writer who is remembered for his novel *Catch-22*, a satirical novel skewering the absurdities of war set during World War II. Wasserstein studied with Heller when she attended the City College of the City University of New York.

Geraldine Ferraro (1935–): Ferraro was a Democratic politician who made history in 1984 when she became the first woman to run as vice president to a Democratic presidential candidate.

Janet Reno (1938–): Reno was the first female Attorney General of the United States, serving from 1993–2001.

Stephen McCauley (1955–): McCauley is an American novelist and author of the romantic comedy *The Object of My Affection*. Wasserstein wrote the screenplay for the 1998 film based on McCauley's novel.

Frances McDormand (1957–): McDormand is a versatile, Academy Award-winning actress probably best known for her work on her husband Joel Coen's films, such as *Fargo* (1996).

Jennifer Aniston (1969–): Aniston is an American actress who became one of the most recognizable celebrities of the 1990s when she starred on the popular television series *Friends* (1994–2004). Aniston also starred in the film *The Object of My Affection*, scripted by Wasserstein.

issues in her play *An American Daughter* (1997). While *The Sisters Rosensweig* shows the private and family lives of three successful, middle-aged women moving forward, *An American Daughter* argues that when accomplished women attempt to shape the world outside of their living rooms, they run into tall, thick walls, usually put there by a sexism so deeply entrenched that it resists conscious decision and good intentions.

Wasserstein reported in the preface to *An American Daughter* that she had other, more personal encounters with female limits just before writing this play. Her sister, Sandra, developed breast cancer, which soon killed her, and Wasserstein spent years trying unsuccessfully to conceive a child.

The Lights Dim on Broadway   Wasserstein's next project, the script for the 1998 movie *The Object of My Affection*, took more than ten years. She attributes the long struggle to get her rewrite of Stephen McCauley's novel produced to studio executives' reservations about a movie focusing on a relationship between a gay romantic leading man and a pregnant straight woman. The following

COMMON HUMAN EXPERIENCE

In her play *An American Daughter* (1997), Wasserstein deals with the hurdles of sexism that lay in the path of many women. Other works that deal with sexism include:

> *Nine to Five* (1980), a film by Colin Higgins. This popular comedy finds three dissimilar office workers—played by Jane Fonda, Lily Tomlin, and Dolly Parton—bonding over the humiliations they suffer at the hands of their sexist boss. The women hatch a plot to take revenge against him, a scheme that ultimately revolutionizes their office.
> *The Handmaid's Tale* (1985), a novel by Margaret Atwood. Atwood's award-winning novel is set in the post-apocalyptic Republic of Gilead, formerly the United States, where most of the population is sterile; a fertile woman named Offred is enslaved by the nation's dictator, who expects her to bear him a child.
> *Unless* (2000), a novel by Carol Shields. In Shields's feminist novel, Reta Winters is a writer dealing with the increasingly erratic behavior of her nineteen-year-old daughter. Meanwhile, Winters is working on her latest novel, which is in dire straits due to a sexist plot twist her new editor is insisting be grafted onto the book.

year, Wasserstein would finally have a family of her own. In 1999, she gave birth to a baby girl, whom she named Lucy after the Beatles song "Lucy in the Sky with Diamonds." As overjoyed as Wasserstein was to finally have a child, her pregnancy was a difficult one, and the writer chronicled this period in her essay collection *Shiksa Goddess (Or How I Spent My Forties)* (2001).

In December 2005, Wasserstein was hospitalized as a result of lymphoma cancer, an illness she had been intent on keeping private. One month later, Wasserstein died at the age of fifty-five. The following night, the lights on Broadway were dimmed in remembrance of the woman who'd brought so much life to it.

Works in Literary Context

Feminist Theater The feminist movement developed over the course of the twentieth century with the intent of providing women with all the civil, human, personal, and legal rights afforded to men in the United States and Britain. The feminist movement was integral in winning women the right to vote in the late 1910s, the legalization of abortion in 1973, and numerous workplace rights, such as maternity leave, protection against sexual harassment, and equal pay. In the early 1970s, feminism birthed a movement in theater that often relied on emotional shock and experimentation to deliver its message. Wasserstein's earliest work, including *Any Woman Can't*

and *Uncommon Women and Others*, are products of the feminist theatrical movement. Issues related to women and their place in a not entirely equal world remained one of the key themes in her later work as well.

The Regional Theater Movement During the 1930s, professional theatrical companies were limited to New York. Touring theatrical companies did exist, but they did not provide the kind of polished productions one expected to see in Manhattan's famed theater district of Broadway. The stage director, Margo Jones, wanted her work to reach as wide an audience as possible, and she also took issue with the gaudy commercialization of Broadway. So Jones, along with playwrights like Jerome Lawrence and Robert E. Lee (co-writers of the classic play *Inherit the Wind*, 1955), began promoting the development of theaters outside of New York. Jones's own Theater '47 in Dallas, Texas, became the first regional theater, and her work inspired the Ford Foundation to finally offer grants to theaters outside of New York. Today there are regional theaters all over the country, and the movement continues to be championed by theater directors and playwrights such as Wasserstein, who remained a vocal advocate of the regional theater movement until her death in 2006.

Works in Critical Context

The Heidi Chronicles Some critics complained that the wit in the *The Heidi Chronicles* prevented the play from saying anything profound. Gayle Austin of the *Theater Journal* writes that "although it raises serious issues, Wasserstein undercuts serious consideration through facile supporting female characters, sit-com humor and a passive heroine who forms an absence at the center of the play." Austin ties these flaws to a judgment made by many critics that the play is not revolutionary enough: "In this way the play will become part of the system that oppresses women and so highly rewards their creative expressions when they aid in its purposes." Other critics believed that her work has too strong a political dimension. For instance, a critic for *The Hudson Review* argues that "*The Heidi Chronicles* is a lifeless, vulgar play, rendered all the more irritating by the many awards that this non-playwright has won simply because she is a woman writing on fashionable issues." Other reviewers were far more complimentary, such as Mel Gussow of *The New York Times*, who declares the play an "enlightening portrait of [Wasserstein's] generation." Furthermore, Gussow praises the play's humor, a facet of the piece that irked other critics: "Ms. Wasserstein has always been a clever writer of comedy. This time she has been exceedingly watchful about not settling for easy laughter, and the result is a more penetrating play."

The Sisters Rosensweig Critics generally admired *The Sisters Rosensweig*, seeing in it that synthesis of humor and insight Wasserstein has sought throughout her career. John Simon, writing for *New York* magazine, reports, "She is surely one of our wittiest one-liner writers, but under the bubbles and eddies of her wit are real people in deep water resolutely, resonantly trying to keep from drowning." But some critics persisted in measuring Wasserstein's work against their own standards for feminism, as did Richard Hornby of *The Hudson Review*, who judges the play "pseudo-feminist" because the women in the play allow men control over their lives.

Responses to Literature

1. In 1998, Wasserstein wrote a screenplay based on Stephen McCauley's novel *The Object of My Affection*. Read McCauley's book and view the film. What did Wasserstein bring to the story? Do you think she improved it? Explain why or why not in an essay.

2. Wasserstein has said that her play, *An American Daughter*, was inspired by the failed nominations of two women whom President Clinton tried to appoint Attorney General. Read *An American Daughter*, then explain how you think those failed nominations influenced the play. Support your response with details from the play.

3. While the vast majority of Wasserstein's work was intended for an adult audience, she did write a children's book called *Pamela's First Musical*. Read the book; then explain whether or not *Pamela's First Musical* displays any of the themes that Wasserstein deals with in her adult plays. Support your response with details from at least two of Wasserstein's plays.

BIBLIOGRAPHY

Books

Barnett, Claudia, ed. *Wendy Wasserstein: A Casebook*. New York: Garland, 1999.

Periodicals

Austin, Gayle. "Review of *The Heidi Chronicles*." *Theater Journal* (March 1990).
Becker, Becky. "The Theme of Mothering in Selected Dramas." *American Drama* 6 (Spring 1997): 43–57.
Gussow, Mel. "A Modern-Day Heffalump in Search of Herself." *The New York Times* (December 12, 1988).
———. "A review of *The Heidi Chronicles*." *The Hudson Review* (Autumn 1989).
Hornby, Richard. "English Versus American Acting." *The Hudson Review* (Summer 1993): 365–371.
Mandl, Bette. "Feminism, Postfeminism, and *The Heidi Chronicles*." *Studies in Humanities* 17 (December 1990): 120–128.
Rose, Phyllis. "An Open Letter to Dr. Holland." *American Theatre* 6 (October 1989): 26–29, 114–117.

Simon, John. "The Best So Far." *New York* 25, No. 43 (November 2, 1992): 100–101.

Web Sites

America.gov. *Wendy Wasserstein, Articulator of the Modern Woman, Dead at 55*. Retrieved December 13, 2008, from http://www.america.gov/st/washfile-english/2006/January/20060130182221JMreldnaB0.5604364.html. Last updated January 30, 2006.

✸ James Welch

BORN: *1940, Browning, Montana*

DIED: *2003, Missoula, Montana*

NATIONALITY: *American*

GENRE: *Fiction, nonfiction, poetry*

MAJOR WORKS:

Winter in the Blood (1974)

Fools Crow (1986)

The Indian Lawyer (1990)

James Welch *Ulf Andersen / Getty Images*

LITERARY AND HISTORICAL CONTEMPORARIES

Welch's famous contemporaries include:

Eldridge Cleaver (1935–1998): Cleaver was a radical civil-rights leader and key member of the Black Panther party who was also the author of *Soul on Ice* (1968).

N. Scott Momaday (1934–): Momaday is an author of Kiowa descent whose novel *House Made of Dawn* (1968) won the Pulitzer Prize and helped to launch the Native American Renaissance.

Leslie Marmon Silko (1948–): A member of the Laguna Pueblo tribe, Silko is the author of the highly acclaimed novel *Ceremony* (1977).

Hunter S. Thompson (1937–2005): Thompson was an American reporter and book author famous for capturing the atmosphere of the 1960s counterculture in such works as *Fear and Loathing in Las Vegas* (1972).

Kurt Vonnegut Jr. (1922–2007): Vonnegut was a prominent American novelist known for his use of black humor and most famous for the novel *Slaughterhouse-Five* (1969).

Overview

James Welch—poet, novelist, documentary scriptwriter, and historical essayist—was a major voice in the Native American Renaissance, the flowering of literary talent among American Indian writers that took place beginning in the 1960s and 1970s. A contemporary of authors N. Scott Momaday, Leslie Marmon Silko, and Gerald Vizenor, Welch had a variety of different jobs before settling into writing. He worked for the U.S. Forest Service, was a laborer and a firefighter, and at one point was a counselor for the Upward Bound program. He was highly visible as a Native American writer because his themes revolve around the controversial issue of Indian acculturation.

Works in Biographical and Historical Context

A Writer from the Blackfoot Reservation Welch was born on November 18, 1940, in Browning, Montana, on the Blackfoot reservation near Glacier National Park. His parents were James P. Welch Sr. and Rosella O'Bryan Welch, who were predominantly Blackfoot and Gros Ventre Indians, respectively. Welch grew up on Montana's Blackfoot and Fort Belknap Reservations and was an enrolled member of the Blackfoot tribe. His mother worked as a stenographer for the Bureau of Indian Affairs; his father worked as a hospital administrator for the Indian Health Service, and also as a welder.

Welch lived briefly in Minnesota and followed in his father's footsteps when he got a welding job there.

Welch's roots, however, were really in Montana. After attending Northern Montana College in Havre, he transferred to the University of Montana, Missoula, receiving a BA degree in 1965. He then entered the MFA program in creative writing at Missoula under the direction of the poet Richard Hugo. Hugo encouraged him to write about what he knew, especially the reservation and its people. This advice helped steer Welch toward his life work. In 1968, he married Lois Monk, professor of English at the University of Montana, Missoula.

From Poetry to Fiction Following Hugo's advice, Welch's first published work was *Riding the Earthboy 40: Poems* (1971), the title of which refers to his early life riding the range; the "40" refers to a forty-acre piece of land that adjoined the Welch ranch and that belonged to a family with the name Earthboy. After this work, Welch turned from poetry largely to fiction. The move did not go well at first. When Welch showed the draft of his first novel to a friend, the writer William Kittredge, he found problems everywhere. In a short biography of Welch published in the journal *Ploughshares*, Welch recalled this incident: "We stayed up one whole night, and he pointed out all these things to me, and of course I was discouraged and put it away."

Eventually, he did pick the book up again, and it became the novel *Winter in the Blood* (1974). It was followed by the novels *The Death of Jim Loney* (1979) and *Fools Crow* (1986). The last-named work is based on both Welch family history and the wider history of the Indian Wars: it tells the story of the Marias River massacre in 1870, from which Welch's great-grandmother escaped.

On the Parole Board Welch's next novel, *The Indian Lawyer* (1990), was directly concerned with Native American assimilation, a frequent theme in Welch's work. The novel tells the story of Sylvester Yellow Calf, a successful Native American attorney and candidate for a congressional seat. The novel partly revolves around Yellow Calf's service on a parole board.

This aspect of the novel is based on Welch's experience as a member of a parole board, service that was important in his life because of the high Indian prison population in the state. Welch commented on the parole board system to *Ploughshares*: "One of [the parole board's] attitudes had been not to return Indians to the reservation.... But sending them to Billings or Great Falls or wherever, without a tribal support system, would only guarantee trouble." Welch stated of his time on the board: "I think I helped some of the other board members understand Indians better."

Custer and the Little Bighorn Welch's career took a new turn with his next project: he cowrote an *American Experience* documentary for PBS, entitled *Last Stand at Little Big Horn* (1993). During this same period, he wrote a book of historical nonfiction, *Killing Custer: The Battle of the Little Bighorn and the Fate of the Plains Indians* (1994). The book is a personal treatment of events before, during, and after the June 1876 battle. This was done largely from the Indian point of view; Custer himself and the events of the much-celebrated battle are secondary. Covering far more than the Battle of the Little Bighorn, the book was enhanced by photographs of sites and participants, drawings by Indian survivors, and maps.

Welch's last novel was *The Heartsong of Charging Elk* (2000). He was working on a sequel to the novel, and fighting lung cancer, when he died of a heart attack at sixty-two in his home in Missoula.

Works in Literary Context

It is easy to see in Welch's career a tension, one that is present in other Native American authors. He is a master of a modern Euro-American genre, the novel, and he writes in modern English for a contemporary American audience of readers who are mostly not Indians and who do not live on a reservation. At the same time, his work is taken to represent ancient native traditions.

Native American Narrative Traditions Welch's work is partly an effort to reenter the past and revive specifically Native American artistic practices. It is primarily his Gros Ventre and Blackfoot heritage that fuel the literary images he uses to breathe life into his stories. *Winter in the Blood*, for instance, uses dream and vision-quest imagery, and also weaves an epic tale rooted in the mythology and folklore of Indian culture heroes and animal allies and guides. Welch addresses the plight of the modern Indian in light of personal and historical tragedy, moving progressively from an assimilated, European perspective into a more Indian point of view as the tales of his novels progress. The critic Robert F. Gish sees in the novels an effort "to work backward into history, into the times and tellings of older generations, older ways of knowing and perceiving."

The Native American Writer as Native American Leader Like all writers who are taken to represent an ethnic group, Welch had to deal with the expectation that he was a spokesman for his group. As he explained to the journal *Ploughshares*, "I think ethnic and regional labels are insulting to writers and really put restrictions on them. People don't think your work is quite as universal." At the same time, Welch believed that an important role he fulfilled as a Native American novelist was to correct the often skewed image of life on the reservation many Americans have:

> Most people in America have a clichéd idea of Indians, that they're all alcoholics and lazy and on welfare. Maybe through literature, people can gain an understanding of how Indians got the way they are today, and how they differ from one another, as tribes and as individuals.

COMMON HUMAN EXPERIENCE

In Welch's novels, the characters are often torn between the Native American world in which they were raised and the dominant white culture of the United States. Here are some other works in which the characters also struggle in their relationship to the dominant American culture:

> *The Autobiography of an Ex-Coloured Man* (1912), a novel by James Weldon Johnson. This pioneering novel tells the story of an African-American man with light skin who must choose which world he wants to live in— white or black.
>
> *Quicksand* (1928), a novel by Nella Larsen. This novel tells the story of Helga Crane, the child of a Danish mother and a black father. Uncomfortable in the worlds of both black and white people, she travels throughout the nation and beyond, looking for a place where she fits in.
>
> *Ceremony* (1977), a novel by Leslie Marmon Silko. This novel tells the story of Tayo, a member of the Laguna Pueblo tribe. After experiencing the horrors of World War II, he returns to the Laguna Pueblo, where he discovers that turning his back on the dominant culture and immersing himself in the ways of his tribe helps him to heal.

Works in Critical Context

A major issue in Welch's work is the tension between the native past as Welch conceives of it and the native present. Welch has been clear-eyed about the problems of contemporary life in places like the reservations of Montana and other Western states, with their familiar problems of alcoholism and poverty. Critics generally credit Welch for his ability to paint a detailed and complex portrait of reservation life both past and present.

Fools Crow Welch's acclaimed third novel marked a change in direction for the author, telling the story of a band of Blackfoot Indians in Montana Territory in the 1870s. The book follows the life of Fools Crow, who grows from a reckless young warrior to become the tribe's medicine man. Welch's ability to recapture the Blackfoot way of life, especially its spiritual aspects, is a strength of the novel. Reviewing this novel in the *Washington Post Book World*, Dennis Drabelle declares: "If *Fools Crow* succeeds ... it does so because Welch, himself part Blackfoot, manages to convey a sense of his people's world view." Peter Wild of *The New York Times Book Review* agrees, noting that "the book becomes a series of dreams acted out, a chronicle of the Indians' visions as applied to daily life."

Lewis D. Owens, writing in the *Los Angeles Times Book Review*, sees Welch's use of the past as wholly positive: "In this novel, Welch is remembering the world of his ancestors, putting that world together again in a way that will tell both author and reader what has been lost and what saved." Owens argues that Welch's work is significant for other reasons as well. "Perhaps the most profound implication of this novel," Owens suggests, "is that the culture, the world-view brought so completely to life in *Fools Crow*, is alive and accessible in the self-imagining of contemporary Blackfeet and other American Indians."

Responses to Literature

1. Read another well-known novel by a Native American author, for example, *House Made of Dawn* by N. Scott Momaday, or *Ceremony*, by Leslie Marmon Silko. What themes or concerns do these authors share with Welch?

2. Read the novel *Little Big Man* (1964) by Thomas Berger. You can also view the popular movie based on the novel, produced in 1970 and starring Dustin Hoffman. Both tell the story of a white child raised by the Cheyenne, and end with the death of George Armstrong Custer at the Battle of the Little Bighorn. Compare these works to Welch's work *Killing Custer*. Why do you think Custer has been the center of so much controversy? Why does he remain fascinating to so many people? How do the two works differ in their views of Custer?

3. The Indian Wars, of which Custer's battle was a small part, were the struggle between the U.S. Army and the indigenous people of North America. Read *Son of the Morning Star* (1984), by Evan S. Connell. How do these events of over a hundred years ago shape life on the reservation today?

BIBLIOGRAPHY

Books

Lupton, Mary Jane. *James Welch: A Critical Companion.* Westport, Conn.: Greenwood Press, 2004.

McFarland, Ron. *Understanding James Welch.* Columbia, S.C.: University of South Carolina Press, 2000.

Velie, Alan. *Four American Indian Literary Masters: N. Scott Momaday, James Welch, Leslie Marmon Silko, and Gerald Vizenor.* Norman, Okla.: University of Oklahoma Press, 1982.

Wild, Peter. *James Welch.* Boise, Idaho: Boise State University, 1983.

Periodicals

Bevis, William W. "James Welch." *Western American Literature* 32 (Spring 1997): 33–53.

Caldwell, E. K. "History Is Story: An Interview with James Welch." *Bloomsbury Review* 15 (November 1995): 14–15.

Shanley, Kathryn W. "Circling Back, Closing In: Remembering James Welch." *Studies in American Indian Literatures* 18 (Fall 2006): 3–13.

Weltzien, O. Alan. "George Custer, Norman Maclean, and James Welch: Personal History and the Redemption of Defeat." *Arizona Quarterly* 52 (Winter 1996): 115–123.

Wetzel, William. "A Tribute to James Welch" *Studies in American Indian Literatures* 18 (Fall 2006): 43–45.

Web sites

Native American Authors Project. *James Welch, 1940–2003.* Retrieved November 24, 2008, from http://www.ipl.org/div/natam/bin/browse.pl/A7.

✺ Eudora Welty

BORN: *1909, Jackson, Mississippi*

DIED: *2001, Jackson, Mississippi*

NATIONALITY: *American*

GENRE: *Fiction*

MAJOR WORKS:
A Curtain of Green (1941)
The Robber Bridegroom (1942)
Delta Wedding (1946)
The Optimist's Daughter (1972)
One Writer's Beginnings (1984)

Eudora Welty   *Welty, Eudora, 1962, photograph. NYWTS / The Library of Congress.*

Overview

Eudora Welty is renowned for her inventive, insightful, comic works about the Deep South, her native Mississippi in particular. An important tenet of Eudora Welty's fictional theory is that attachment to place, or "regionalism," is not restrictive, but rather it becomes a means to universality in great literature, a way of getting to the roots of what is constant in human experience. Her fiction, including the modern fairytale *The Robber Bridegroom* (1942) and the Pulitzer Prize–winning novella *The Optimist's Daughter*, certainly bears out her theory, as Welty's work is enjoyed by readers around the world.

Works in Biographical and Historical Context

A Home Full of Books and Love Eudora Alice Welty was born on April 13, 1909, the only daughter, with two brothers, of Mary Chestina Andrews and Christian Webb Welty. As a young woman Welty's mother had been a teacher, passionately devoted to books and learning, who rode out on her horse every day to teach in a one-room school in West Virginia. Eudora Welty inherited from her mother a strong independence of spirit, the capacity for risk taking, and the love of tales told within the large mountain family. The Welty home in Jackson, Mississippi, was full of books, and Welty had her own library card at a very young age. The family nurtured Welty's artistic and educational pursuits and supported her pursuit of a degree in English from the University of Wisconsin, which she received in 1929.

Pragmatism Leads to the Big Apple At her father's urging, Welty studied advertising for a year at the Columbia Graduate School of Business in New York during 1930–1931, an attempt on her part to find a means of practical employment. The years in Wisconsin and New York broadened Welty's horizons, and the time she spent in New York City was especially meaningful. The Harlem Renaissance, an artistic movement that rejoiced in the unique identity of the African American culture, was at its height. The movement was centered in the African American neighborhood of Harlem, New York, between the First and Second World Wars. For the first time in the history of the United States, African American art, literature, and music received attention from mainstream America. Jazz was heard on the radio, literature by African American writers such as poet Langston Hughes was widely published, and Harlem clubs featuring African American musicians such as Cab Calloway were popular spots for integrated crowds. Welty and her friends ventured to dances in Harlem clubs and to musical and theatrical performances all over New York City.

Life Doesn't Hold Still Her father's sudden death in 1931 brought an end to Welty's northern adventures. She went home to Jackson to help her mother and brothers. To support herself, Welty first tried various small jobs with local newspapers and with radio station WJDX, which her father had started in the tower of his insurance building. After the stock market crashed in 1929, unemployment and poverty soared, leading the nation into the Great Depression. To help stimulate the economy and put the unemployed to work, the federal government designed a new agency, the Works Progress Administration (WPA). The WPA constructed buildings, built parks, repaired roads, and built thousands of miles of highways. The WPA even had an employment plan for artists in which public buildings were given sculptures or murals, traveling theaters toured the nation, and writers and photographers were commissioned to record the moment for history. In 1933 Welty was offered a position as a publicity agent for the WPA. She traveled for three years around the eighty-two counties of Mississippi doing feature stories on local projects, gathering impressions and photographs of the varied people, groups, landscapes, and towns she visited. These impressions fed her imagination for many years: pictures taken, literally and figuratively, set in "that time, that place" (Mississippi in the Great Depression), formed the basis of much of her fiction. Welty was learning the art of seeing and capturing significant moments in the lives of ordinary people, an art she first practiced with a camera, then with the pen. In reference to the influence that photography had on her works, Welty said in her autobiographical work *One Writer's Beginnings* (1984), "Life doesn't hold still."

Discovery Is Followed by Rapid Success Welty's first modest success came in 1936, when she arranged a one-woman show of her unposed photographs of Mississippi black people. The photos were shown in a small gallery on Madison Avenue in New York City. Seeing firsthand the Depression-struck lives of rural and small-town people in the nation's poorest state, Welty was stimulated to capture their struggles and triumphs in stories, beginning with "Death of a Traveling Salesman," which was published in the literary magazine *Manuscript* in 1936. Other stories followed during the next five years, including some of her most famous: "Why I Live at the P.O.," "Powerhouse," "A Worn Path," "Petrified Man," and "Lily Daw and the Three Ladies." These early works established Welty's characteristic comic touch with dialogue and with recording the incongruous developments of everyday life. Here she also developed a way of treating poverty, loss, and pain with a respectful, discrete lightness.

Welty produced her first three major publications— *A Curtain of Green* (1941), *The Robber Bridegroom* (1942), and *The Wide Net and Other Stories* (1943)— within a three-year period. Together they established the distinguishing marks of her fiction: the importance of place; the impulse to celebrate life; the exploration of human mystery; the theme of love and separateness; the sense of multiplicity in life; and an elusive, changing, and

LITERARY AND HISTORICAL CONTEMPORARIES

Eudora Welty's famous contemporaries include:

John Steinbeck (1902–1968): This American novelist was awarded the Pulitzer Prize in 1940 and the Nobel Prize in Literature in 1962 for his compassionate portrayals of the poor, especially itinerant farm laborers, during the Great Depression and the Dust Bowl years of the 1930s.

William Faulkner (1897–1962): American novelist William Faulkner created a cast of lively and often grotesque characters that revealed the decadence of the South. He was awarded the Nobel Prize in Literature in 1949.

Robert Penn Warren (1905–1989): American poet and novelist, a leading Southern writer and winner of Pulitzer Prizes for fiction (1947) and poetry (1957 and 1979).

Elizabeth Bowen (1899–1973): Bowen, a good friend of Welty's, was an important twentieth-century British writer. Her characters sought to find their complete identity and purpose in an increasingly aggressive world.

Franklin D. Roosevelt (1882–1945): The thirty-second president of the United States, Roosevelt served four terms and led the nation out of the depths of the Great Depression and through most of the Second World War.

Louis Armstrong (1901–1971): An American jazz trumpeter, he was a leader in the development of the jazz idiom in the 1920s and 1930s. He became a world-famous figure of American popular culture.

lyrical style. These stories are mostly about country people, black and white, though others are placed in small towns and cities. Whatever the setting, Welty has been precise in her depiction of the social structures that go with place and time.

Exploring the Depths of the Novel It was the lure of possibilities in form that led Eudora Welty to the writing of longer fictional works. *Delta Wedding* (1946) was Eudora Welty's initial experiment with a full-length novel. Another novella, *The Ponder Heart* (1954), was both a popular and critical success. It is the dramatic monologue of Edna Earle Ponder, small-town hotel manager and niece of her generous, fond, and foolish conveyor of love and money, Uncle Daniel Ponder. He literally tickles his silly little wife to death when a lightning fireball rolls into the room, and his trial turns into farce when he actually throws his money away in the courtroom. Because of its comic high spirits and adroit use of the Southern dialect, the novella won Eudora Welty the William Dean Howells Medal of the American Academy for the most distinguished work of American fiction between 1950 and 1955.

A Best Seller Evolves after Fifteen Years During the next fifteen years, Eudora Welty did not publish any lengthy works. At this time Mississippi and the South were going through the turbulence of the civil rights movement. Welty didn't directly involve herself in the movement but rather remained an observer or chronicler. Welty completed and published her longest novel, *Losing Battles* (1970), and appeared on the best-seller lists for the first time. Welty continued to publish short stories through the eighties, but it was her autobiographical book *One Writer's Beginnings* that became widely popular. Perhaps because she wished to forestall potential biographers, or because she came to accept public interest in how a writer's early experiences shape her vision, Welty provided in the book a re-creation of the world that nourished her own imagination, especially the influence her mother had in her life. Eudora Welty died in Jackson, Mississippi, on July 23, 2001.

Works in Literary Context

Welty's fictional chronicles of Mississippi life add a major comic vision to American literature, a vision that affirms the sustaining power of community and family life and at the same time explores the need for solitude. While much of modern American fiction has emphasized alienation and the failure of love, Welty's stories show how tolerance and generosity allow people to adapt to each other's foibles and to painful change.

Regionalism Welty's stories are almost entirely filled with Southerners, Mississippi Southerners. Black and white both, though mostly white, they are as authentically Southern as they come in their language, gestures, moods, madnesses, everything to the finest detail. With her novel *Delta Wedding*, Welty skillfully chronicles the traditions of the Southern family and community. She works through themes that accompany the emphasis on community, including the precariousness of marriage and the intimate suffering it involves, the weight of family tradition and the accompanying tension caused by the need of the young to break out and affirm their individuality, and the stark and hopeless loss that the living must accommodate after the death of parents and mates. Her depictions of the Southern traditions are often compared to those of her fellow Mississippian, William Faulkner, whose novels such as *The Sound and the Fury* (1929) also chronicle Southern family life.

Folk Tales Welty's fiction also reflects a whimsical and innocent style characteristic of traditional folk tales, like those preserved by the brothers Grimm. The Grimm tales "Hansel and Gretel," "Rapunzel," and "Little Red Riding Hood" reveal the capricious and cruel side of life. Welty's first sustained experiment with folk materials appeared in 1942 with *The Robber Bridegroom*, a bold fusion of Mississippi history, tall tale, and fairytales of mysterious seducers clearly drawn from British and Germanic sources. The innocent tone of the narrative counteracts the dire stuff of robberies, murders, and the depredations of a cruel stepmother. The humor, dialect, and dialogue are reminiscent of the Southern oral tradition captured in Joel Chandler Harris's Uncle Remus stories.

Works in Critical Context

Potential editors were initially reluctant to publish Welty's work because of fear that they were too complex to appeal to the common reader. Later, some critics raised objections to what seemed a needless obscurity, a confusing blend of reality and fantasy in her work. Elaborateness, subtlety, and sophistication of narrative technique are distinguishing marks of Welty's stories. Some critics savored this style, others did not.

A Curtain of Green When *A Curtain of Green* appeared in 1941, it was to generally high critical acclaim, and though the audience was to become larger than predicted, it remained, for many years small and discriminating. One objection was to Southern "gothic" decadence in *A Curtain of Green*. To many critics, Welty's earliest stories remain the best, and her reputation rests on the perennial freshness and lyrical poignancy—or brilliant comedy—of a dozen or more of her early stories. Michael Kreyling declared in *Eudora Welty's Achievement of Order* (1980) that the value of her work is not that it is "primarily regional writing, or even excellent regional writing, but [that it conveys] the vision of a certain artist who must be considered with her peers—[Virginia] Woolf, [Elizabeth] Bowen, and [E. M.] Forster."

The Robber Bridegroom The greater objectivity in narrative method in Welty's novels met with wide approval, and many general readers and critics regarded these works as Welty's finest achievement. *The Robber Bridegroom*, to many early reviewers, was pure magic. In the *New York Times Book Review*, Marianne Hauser calls it "a modern fairy tale, where irony and humor, outright nonsense, deep wisdom and surrealistic extravaganzas become a poetic unity through the power of a pure, exquisite style." Although some other commentators found it lacking in substance, Michael Kreyling defends *The Robber Bridegroom* as a valuable addition to the pastoral tradition in American literature: "Welty seems to be saying that the dream of a pastoral paradise on earth is always one step ahead of the dreamers; it is, sadly, only possible in a dream world removed from contact with human flesh and imperfections. But still worth dreaming."

Responses to Literature

1. Several of Welty's short stories take place on the Natchez Trace in Mississippi. Using your library and the Internet, find out more about the Natchez Trace. What would make the Natchez Trace a good

---

COMMON HUMAN EXPERIENCE

Welty's fiction explored the complexity of community and family relationships and the joy and complications of love between families and between men and women. Here are some other literary works that delve into the complexities of Southern life from various angles:

> *Beloved* (1987), a novel by Toni Morrison. This harrowing story narrates the brutality of slavery and the family love needed to overcome tragedy. *Beloved* won the Pulitzer Prize in 1987 and is considered one of the most outstanding American novels of recent decades.
> "Ballad of the Sad Cafe" (1943), a short story by Carson McCullers that delves into the complexities of a love triangle in a small Southern town.
> *A Long and Happy Life* (1962), a novel by Reynolds Price that carefully details the courtship and love between two Southern youths as they discover the difficulties of growing up.

---

setting for a story? How has Natchez Trace been used throughout history?

2. During the civil rights movement of the sixties, Welty was criticized for not using her writing talent for the cause of the movement. Using your library and the Internet, research the civil rights era and other famous authors who used their talent to crusade for social justice. Do you agree or disagree with Welty's critics that enlightened artists should use their talent to spur social change, or should they be free of such limitations?

3. Many of Welty's works were adapted to the Broadway stage. While reading Welty's stories, describe why her works might be successfully adapted for live audiences. What elements of her narrative would be easy to adapt? What elements would be difficult?

4. Welty attributed her ability to approach her subjects from the outside, and slowly move in closer to reveal the truth, to her years of experience as a photographer. Choose a scene from one of Welty's stories and analyze the photographic vision that slowly develops. What narrative technique is employed to capture the whole scene? How does the narrative change as the reader moves closer to the individual truths?

BIBLIOGRAPHY

Books

Appel, Alfred, Jr. *A Season of Dreams: The Fiction of Eudora Welty.* Baton Rouge: Louisiana State University Press, 1965.

Champion, Laurie, ed. *The Critical Response to Eudora Welty's Fiction*. Westport, Conn.: Greenwood Press, 1994.

Devlin, Albert. *Eudora Welty's Chronicle: A Story of Mississippi Life*. Jackson: University Press of Mississippi, 1983.

Evans, Elizabeth. *Eudora Welty*. New York: F. Ungar, 1981.

Kreyling, Michael. *Eudora Welty's Achievement of Order*. Baton Rouge: Louisiana State University Press, 1980.

Manning, Carol, ed. *The Female Tradition in Southern Literature*. Urbana: University of Illinois Press, 1993.

Marrs, Suzanne. *Eudora Welty: A Biography*. Orlando, Fla.: Harcourt, 2005.

Presnhaw, Peggy Whitman, ed. *Conversations with Eudora Welty*. Jackson: University Press of Mississippi, 1993.

Randisi, Jennifer Lynn. *A Tissue of Lies: Eudora Welty and the Southern Romance*. Washington, D.C.: University Press of America, 1982.

Schmidt, Peter. *The Heart of the Story: Eudora Welty's Short Fiction*. Jackson: University Press of Mississippi, 1991.

Vande Kieft, Ruth M. *Eudora Welty*. New York: Twayne Publishers, 1987.

✵ Nathanael West

BORN: *1903, New York, New York*

DIED: *1940, El Centro, California*

NATIONALITY: *American*

GENRE: *Fiction*

MAJOR WORKS:
Miss Lonelyhearts (1933)
The Day of the Locust (1939)

Overview

Nathanael West was a prominent American novelist whose works portray the despair and alienation that many writers and artists have found to be defining characteristics of twentieth-century existence. When he died at the age of thirty-seven, he had produced four books, at least two of which, *Miss Lonelyhearts* (1933) and *The Day of the Locust* (1939), are regarded as American classics.

Works in Biographical and Historical Context

An Unpromising Student, A New Start   The writer who was to become known as Nathanael West was born Nathan Weinstein on October 17, 1903, in New York City to fairly well-to-do Lithuanian-Jewish immigrants. He was an undistinguished student who failed to graduate from high school and was later dismissed from Tufts College because of poor attendance. However, the illegally obtained transcript of an older student with a similar name and better grades enabled West to transfer to Brown University, from which he graduated in 1924. By this time

he had already written and drawn illustrations for his college and summer camp magazines and was bent upon becoming a writer.

Soon after he graduated, West set out to persuade his family to send him to Paris to work on a novel. Before applying for a passport he decided to change his name, and in August 1926 he took the name Nathanael West. In October 1926 he sailed for Paris, where he remained for three months, fully on his own for the first time. West's experience in Paris had a permanent influence on his understanding of the writer's lifestyle and solidified his preferences in fiction. He began work on his first book, *The Dream Life of Balso Snell* (1931), during this period. This short surrealist novella concerns the adventures of a young skeptic on a dreamlike journey in which he meets and satirizes a number of self-styled artists. West uses the conceit of Snell's travels to parody the work of Jonathan Swift, Fyodor Dostoyevsky, Sigmund Freud, Ernest Hemingway, and many others.

During his brief stay in Paris, West was also influenced by the theories and practice of modern art, especially those of surrealism, the artistic movement that sought to capture the bizarre world of dreams and the subconscious, best remembered today in the work of the painters Salvador Dalí and René Magritte. The influence that surrealism had upon West in Paris is attested to by "The Impostor," a short story that some critics regard as his best but that was not published in West's lifetime. "The Impostor" concerns the doings of expatriate American artists in Paris; in this tale, a painter tells of his meeting with an insane bohemian sculptor named Beano Walsh. In the same spirit as that of *The Dream Life of Balso Snell*, West brings art, deception, and fantasy into violent confrontation.

Perhaps most important of all for West, Paris remained a symbol of liberation, personally and artistically. For years he told stories—mostly fantasies—about his adventures there, and continued to be influenced by French writing and surrealist art for many years.

In the Hotel Business   After dwindling finances compelled him to return to New York, West worked as manager of Kenmore Hall and later the Sutton Club, two hotels owned by his uncles. West allowed writers who found themselves short of funds to lodge at the Sutton for a nominal rent—or for free—and writers James T. Farrell, Erskine Caldwell, Lillian Hellman, and Dashiell Hammett were among those who availed themselves of West's generosity.

While working at the Sutton, West finished *The Dream Life of Balso Snell*. This work was published in a limited edition of five hundred copies and received little critical or popular attention. In 1932 West ventured into magazine publishing, joining poet William Carlos Williams in coediting the journal *Contact*, of which only three issues appeared. The next year West, with the German artist George Grosz, launched a similarly short-lived publication, *Americana*.

On the Farm After the humorist S. J. Perelman married West's sister Laura, the three of them bought a farm in Pennsylvania, where West wrote his second novel, *Miss Lonelyhearts*. Although favorably reviewed, *Miss Lonelyhearts* was one of the last books brought out by Liveright before that publisher declared bankruptcy. As a result, few copies were distributed under the Liveright imprint, and a second printing of the novel sold poorly.

Miss Lonelyhearts is generally considered West's most artistically accomplished work. It is the story of a male newspaper advice columnist who becomes obsessed with the suffering of his correspondents and his inability to help them. West has said that the inspiration for this novel came from actual letters shown to him by an advice columnist and from the lives of the transients he observed as a hotel manager. The novel deals with the loneliness, alienation, despair, and violence that arose from the Great Depression of the 1930s. In 1929 the stock market had collapsed, the first event in a long series of economic disasters that continued until the end of the 1930s. Through much of West's adult life, poverty was the normal condition of life. West's decision to identify his protagonist only as Miss Lonelyhearts also serves to underscore the dehumanizing character of the times by equating the person with his public function.

In Hollywood West found that he required a more regular income than that provided by the sale of his novels and, encouraged by Perelman, who in the early 1930s was a successful Hollywood screenwriter, he began work in the film industry. He was quickly disillusioned by what he had imagined would be a glamorous job; though well paid, he felt he was rudely treated and he resented the fact that his work was subjected to revision without his knowledge.

In his third novel, *A Cool Million; or, The Dismantling of Lemuel Pitkin* (1934), West returned to burlesque comedy, but with an underlying concern with the deceptions fostered by the American myth of success. After the indifferent critical reception and meager sales of *A Cool Million*, West decided to continue screenwriting. Over a period of several years he planned and wrote a novel reflecting his life in Hollywood, *The Day of the Locust*. This novel emphasizes the frustrations of the modern men whose lives are so empty they can find satisfaction only in monstrous fantasies. *The Day of the Locust* has often been called the finest novel about Hollywood to come out of Hollywood, and subsequent books about the film industry are often compared with it. West found in Hollywood a representative sampling of everything he believed was wrong with American culture. Within the microcosm of the film capital, West further narrowed his focus to encompass the lives of those whom critic Edmund Wilson called "nondescript characters on the edges of the Hollywood studios." *The Day of the Locust* differed from other Hollywood novels of the same era, such as F. Scott Fitzgerald's *The Last Tycoon* (1941),

---

LITERARY AND HISTORICAL CONTEMPORARIES

Nathanael West's famous contemporaries include:

John Steinbeck (1902–1968): American novelist, awarded the Pulitzer Prize in 1940 and the Nobel Prize in Literature in 1962 for his compassionate portrayals of the poor, especially itinerant farm laborers, during the Great Depression and Dust Bowl years of the 1930s.

Upton Sinclair (1878–1968): Pulitzer Prize–winning American author, famous for such protest novels as *The Jungle* (1906) and *Oil!* (1927).

F. Scott Fitzgerald (1896–1940): American novelist famous for his portraits of the wealthy elite in works such as *The Great Gatsby* (1925). Like West, Fitzgerald lived as an expatriate in Paris and later worked in Hollywood.

George Orwell (1903–1950): British novelist and essayist known for his journalism and his political novel *1984* (1949).

Ben Hecht (1894–1964): American author and screenwriter; a master of the Hollywood system, he wrote or cowrote the scripts to dozens of films, including many screen classics.

Franklin Delano Roosevelt (1882–1945): American politician and president from 1933 to 1945, elected during the depths of the Great Depression.

---

in that it is not about the rich and famous—the powerful and influential movie stars and studio executives—but about common people whose dreams are manufactured and manipulated by the movies, and who, West believed, harbored a fierce hatred behind their ostensible adoration of movie stars.

Shortly after *The Day of the Locust* was published, West met and married Eileen McKenney, who had served as the subject of Ruth McKenney's popular *New Yorker* magazine sketches that were adapted as the play *My Sister Eileen* (1940). Eight months after their marriage, both were killed in an automobile accident.

Works in Literary Context

Regarded as a stylistic innovator whose works fit no standard literary classification, West combined elements of both traditional literary naturalism and the new technique of surrealism in the two novels for which he is best remembered, *Miss Lonelyhearts* and *The Day of the Locust*. West is known for a distorted, grotesque kind of humor that has led critics to call his novels the forerunners in modern American literature of black humor. West's profoundly negative worldview also acutely reflects the era in which he wrote, the Great Depression.

COMMON HUMAN EXPERIENCE

The Day of the Locust is one of the better-known works about the film industry written by an insider. How does it compare to the following critiques of Hollywood?

> *The Last Tycoon* (1941), a novel by F. Scott Fitzgerald. This novel tells the story of movie executive Monroe Stahr, a character Fitzgerald based on MGM producer Irving Thalberg.
>
> *The Loved One* (1948), a novel by Evelyn Waugh. In 1947 Waugh journeyed to Hollywood and was appalled; this novel records the visit, focusing on a cemetery as a symbol of the film capital.
>
> *Sunset Boulevard* (1950), a film directed by Billy Wilder. Aging silent film star Gloria Swanson played aging silent film star Norma Desmond in this brilliant film noir set in Hollywood, one of the most revered films Hollywood has ever produced.
>
> *The Player* (1992), a film directed by Robert Altman. This film, which tells the story of a sleazy movie executive, is widely regarded as an attack on the Hollywood system—and, strangely, includes cameo appearances by dozens of important Hollywood personalities.

Surrealism Surrealism is the practice of producing fantastic or incongruous imagery in art or literature by means of unnatural juxtapositions and combinations. A movement in visual art and literature based on these principles flourished in Europe between World Wars I and II. The movement represented a reaction against what its members saw as the destruction wrought by the "rationalism" that had guided European culture and politics in the past and that had culminated in the horrors of World War I. According to the major spokesman of the movement, poet and critic André Breton, who published "The Surrealist Manifesto" in 1924, surrealism was a means of reuniting conscious and unconscious realms of experience so completely that the world of dream and fantasy would be joined to the everyday rational world in "an absolute reality, a surreality." West himself identified the influence of surrealism on the novel he planned while living in Paris, *The Dream Life of Balso Snell*. The title itself suggests that the novel is not conventionally "realistic," and the story quickly delivers on this promise. The plot is disjointed. The protagonist encounters the Trojan Horse, enters it through its anus, and wanders through its bowels in a bizarre journey filled with symbolic encounters.

Black Humor The term *black humor* describes writing marked by the use of morbid, ironic, or grotesquely comic episodes that ridicule human folly. Although André Breton published his *Anthology of Black Humor* in 1940, the term did not come into common use until the 1960s. It has often been used to describe the work of novelists Joseph Heller, Kurt Vonnegut, and Thomas Pynchon; outstanding examples of black humor being Heller's novel *Catch 22* (1961) and Vonnegut's novel *Slaughterhouse-Five* (1969). West thus comes toward the beginning of the black humor tradition. Because he was fairly obscure for a long time, and only more recently reevaluated, the extent of West's influence on later writers is not easy to ascertain. Although not generally considered a direct literary influence on subsequent writers, West is noted as one of the progenitors—perhaps the earliest—of black humor in modern American fiction. West's two masterpieces, *Miss Lonelyhearts* and *The Day of the Locust*, suggest his connection to black humor strongly. Both are characterized by fantastic and bizarre situations, and both deal with the alienation typical of the impoverished era in which West wrote.

Works in Critical Context

Until the renewal of interest in West in the late 1950s, most critics considered him a minor novelist. Many still insist upon such a classification because of the narrow range of his themes and subjects. However, Randall Reid has demonstrated that, within the limits allowed by his bleak and pessimistic vision, West is a "complex, wide-ranging, and subtle" author. His experimental style also caused his works to be overlooked during his lifetime by critics and readers who favored literary naturalism. West was neither realistic enough to be classified as a naturalist nor concerned enough with character to have found favor with the proponents of naturalism's successor, the psychological novel. Because his works are innovative and unclassifiable, West has been a difficult author to place within a literary tradition.

Of West's lesser-known novels, *A Cool Million* has received the more thorough critical reexamination. It is most often interpreted as a parody of the classic American success story popularized in the late nineteenth-century novels of Horatio Alger. In the typical Alger story, a young man armed only with complete honesty, a total lack of guile, and an earnest desire to do good, sets out to make his fortune, attaining wealth, love, and happiness through a series of unlikely adventures. In West's reversal of this "luck and pluck" formula, his ingenuous hero is unequal to the obstacles he faces and gradually undergoes his "dismantling"—the loss of an eye, his teeth, a thumb, a leg, his scalp, and eventually his life. *A Cool Million* is written in a pastiche of Alger's style; in fact, one critic has shown that dozens of passages from *A Cool Million* are almost word-for-word re-creations of sections from several of Alger's works. Indeed, some critics have found this novel's greatest fault to be the absence of West's own style.

Miss Lonelyhearts Beyond the confusion over West's place in literary history, his skill as an artist stems from his treatment of the basic human condition. Writing in *New Criterion* on *Miss Lonelyhearts*, Theodore Dalrymple focuses on this side of West. Dalrymple describes the basic plot of *Miss Lonelyhearts*, then notes the universal themes of the book. The central character of the novel

receives letters from uneducated people asking for advice on how to cure suffering that he soon realizes is incurable—at least in the absence of a religious faith that human existence, including or especially its suffering, has a transcendent meaning and purpose. Modern man can neither believe in such a meaning and purpose, nor yet dispense with the need for that belief: this is his tragedy and his predicament, and it is a truth revealed to Miss Lonelyhearts by the letters that he receives daily. He tries nonetheless to resolve the contradiction between the impossibility of and the need for belief by involving himself, Christ-like in his own fevered imagination, in the lives of his correspondents, and is shot dead for his efforts (the title of the chapter in which he dies is "Miss Lonelyhearts Has a Religious Experience"). We live in a world in which no good deed—or compassion and good feeling—goes unpunished.

The Day of the Locust West's final novel is the product of a writer who had been working in Hollywood for some time but not enjoying it much. Writing in *Literature/Film Quarterly*, Robin Blyn notes the influence of cinema on the novel:

The Day of the Locust foregrounds the dilemma of the artist as he confronts the emergent culture industry of the 1930s, an industry which, in the form of the Hollywood studio system, is characterized by its capacity to absorb all that enters its domain.... For even as *Locust* enacts a scathing critique of the Hollywood dream factory, much of its aesthetic remains indebted to the techniques of the Hollywood industry it ostensibly attacks

The novel is filled with dramatic scenes like the scenes from a movie and with what one could call "special effects." To what extent was West attacking the language of movies, and to what extent was he exploiting their power to his own ends? Critics still debate this point.

Responses to Literature

1. The surrealists were intensely interested in dreams. Look at a painting by a famous surrealist, Salvador Dalí. How do West's novels compare to what Dalí does in paint? How are both dreamlike?

2. Analyze the humor in one or more of West's novels. What messages does it contain? How would you describe the viewpoint his humor reveals?

3. Pick one of the other novelists who are often associated with black humor, like Kurt Vonnegut. How is *Slaughterhouse-Five*, for example, similar to West's work? Why do you think critics came to refer to both as practitioners of black humor?

4. Would you consider West to be a "political" writer? Cite examples and build an argument one way or the other.

BIBLIOGRAPHY

Books

Barnard, Rita. *The Great Depression and the Culture of Abundance: Kenneth Fearing, Nathanael West, and Mass Culture in the 1930s.* Cambridge: Cambridge University Press, 1995.

Siegel, Ben, ed. *Critical Essays on Nathanael West.* New York: G. K. Hall, 1994.

Veitch, Jonathan. *American Superrealism: Nathanael West and the Politics of Representation in the 1930s.* Madison: University of Wisconsin Press, 1997.

Periodicals

Edmunds, Susan. "Modern Taste and the Body Beautiful in Nathanael West's *The Day of the Locust*." *MFS: Modern Fiction Studies* 44 (Summer 1998): 306–330.

Greenberg, Jonathan. "Nathanael West and the Mystery of Feeling." *MFS: Modern Fiction Studies* 52 (Fall 2006): 588–612.

Haynes, Doug. "'Laughing at the Laugh': Unhappy Consciousness in Nathaniel West's *The Dream Life of Balso Snell*." *Modern Language Review* 102 (April 2007): 341–362.

Meyers, Jeffrey. "The Battle of Waterloo in West's *The Day of the Locust*." *Notes on Contemporary Literature* 33 (September 2003): 2–4.

Nieland, Justus. "West's Deadpan: Affect, Slapstick, and Publicity in *Miss Lonelyhearts*." *Novel: A Forum on Fiction* 38 (Fall 2004): 57–83.

Rozelle, Lee. "Ecocritical City: Modernist Reactions to Urban Environments in *Miss Lonelyhearts* and *Paterson*." *Twentieth Century Literature* 48 (Spring 2002): 100–15.

Web sites

Lewis, Kevin. *Nathanael West and American Apocalyptic.* Retrieved November 12, 2008, from http://people.cas.sc.edu/lewiske/west.html. Last updated on March 30, 2006.

⊛ Edith Wharton

BORN: *1862, New York City*

DIED: *1937, St. Brice-sous-Foret, France*

NATIONALITY: *American*

GENRE: *Fiction*

MAJOR WORKS:

The House of Mirth (1905)

Ethan Frome (1911)

The Age of Innocence (1920)

Edith Wharton   *Wharton, Edith, 1905, photograph. The Library of Congress.*

Overview

Edith Wharton was the most celebrated American female author of her time. Best known for her novels *The House of Mirth, Ethan Frome,* and *The Age of Innocence,* she also published poetry, criticism, nonfiction about the First World War, travel writing, and several collections of short stories. Her books suffered a period of critical neglect after her death. A revived interest in what they reveal about women's roles in society has brought them back into discussion.

Works in Biographical and Historical Context

A Born Aristocrat   Edith Wharton was born Edith Newbold Jones on January 24, 1862, the third child and first daughter of George Frederic and Lucretia Rhinelander Jones, members of the social hierarchy of aristocratic old New York. Although the family did not live ostentatiously, they enjoyed considerable affluence, with servants, a governess for Edith, carriages, a summer home in Newport, a townhouse in New York, and frequent dinner parties. However, the Civil War caused a decline in New York real estate values and a corresponding decrease in their income. In 1866, taking along their younger son Harry, then sixteen, and Edith, four, the Jones family went to Europe, where they might live more economically, for six years.

Even before she learned to read, Wharton became ardently devoted to what she called "making up." Learning to read only intensified her delight, even though it was not an activity her parents encouraged. Their sensibility, in part determined by their Dutch Reformed and Episcopalian beliefs, did not include a high regard for the world of art. Thus, when the teenaged Edith began to write verse and short stories, her family did not encourage it and later seldom mentioned her literary success.

Understandably shy in this environment, Edith happily traveled Europe with her parents. There she met Henry James, who became her mentor and admiring critic. When not traveling, she spent most of her time in her father's library, only entering the social scene when her parents insisted. In those hours alone, Edith read voraciously and made her first attempts at writing. Walter Berry, a friend of the family, was one of the first to see her early attempts at writing fiction. Berry became a lifelong confidant, sharing with her the intellectual pursuits that few others cared to share.

An Unhappy Marriage   In 1885, Edith married Boston banker Edward Robbins Wharton, known to the family because of his membership in her mother's social circle. He was more than ten years older than Edith and suffered ill health, which, combined with Edith's dissatisfactions with their social life, encouraged her to devote more of her time to writing. They owned a house in Newport, Rhode Island, which she redecorated with the help of the architect Ogden Codman. The book they wrote about the project, *The Decoration of Houses* (1897), explained that a house's decor ought to express the owners' personalities, instead of merely aping aristocratic tastes. The book sold well, to the dismay of her family, and confirmed her in her pursuit of a writing career.

By 1902 the Whartons had sold their house at Newport and built The Mount in Lenox, Massachusetts, where they spent part of each year and entertained such friends as Henry James. It was in Lenox that Edith wrote *The House of Mirth* (1905). The characters in *The House of Mirth* were based on the actual families of aristocratic New York during this era. The Van Osburgh family, for instance, is based on the Astors.

In 1904 the Whartons gave up the annual pilgrimage to Italy they had been making in favor of explorations in France, a significant shift in preference, and one that heralded Wharton's later expatriation. Her residence in

France began in 1907, when she and her husband, who had spent the summer and autumn at The Mount, went to Paris and sublet an apartment in the elite quarter of the Faubourg St. Germain. Teddy, however, became increasingly unstable and volatile. In 1911 Wharton left The Mount for the last time, having decided to separate from Teddy and sell the property. She had hesitated about seeking a separation because of Teddy's unstable state of mind, his attachment to their home, and his pride in overseeing it. After The Mount was sold, she proceeded with her divorce, which was granted in Paris on April 16, 1913. By this time, Europe had become home. During this period, another of Wharton's best-known works appeared, *Ethan Frome* (1911). The book had its genesis on both sides of the Atlantic: begun in French as part of Wharton's effort to learn the language, it had as its inspiration a fatal sledding accident that happened in Lenox in 1904.

Wartime Activist   In August of 1914, most of the nations of Europe became involved in World War I. Wharton's adopted nation of France was locked in a fight for its life against Germany. The onset of World War I brought great disruption to Wharton's life. She used her position as a well-respected public figure to become an impassioned humanitarian, launching major war-relief efforts and seeking material assistance from her countrymen.

In early 1915 Wharton was asked by the French Red Cross to visit military hospitals at the front and report on their needs, a journey that led to several other visits. These expeditions resulted in six magazine articles for Scribner's, calculated to alert her "rich and generous compatriots" to the desperate needs of hospitals and to bring home to her American readers "some of the dreadful realities of war." She collected her articles in a book, *Fighting France, from Dunkerque to Belfort* (1915).

In addition to writing about the cause, Wharton was an energetic fund-raiser and was further aided by "Edith Wharton" committees in New York, Boston, Philadelphia, Washington, and Providence. With her financial support, an ambulance unit, a workroom for female garment workers, and a sanatorium for women and children with tuberculosis were established in France. France recognized her philanthropy by awarding her the Cross of the Legion of Honor.

Return of Peace   In 1919, Wharton acquired the Pavillon Colombe just outside Paris. The same year she leased a second home on the French Riviera. For the rest of her life she divided her time between the two homes. She had all but suspended her fiction writing during the war, but when it ended, was able to return to writing projects that were recognizably similar to her prewar novels. Her greatest success during this era was *The Age of Innocence* (1920), which won the Pulitzer Prize in 1921. Although she had lived in France a long time by this date, she still returned to aristocratic New York for

LITERARY AND HISTORICAL CONTEMPORARIES

Wharton's famous contemporaries include:

Joseph Conrad (1857–1924): Conrad was a British fiction writer, born in Poland, who learned the English language during a career as a sailor. He is best remembered today for his short novel *Heart of Darkness* (1902).

Theodore Dreiser (1871–1945): Dreiser is an American novelist who helped develop the school of naturalism in literature. He is best remembered for his novel *Sister Carrie* (1900).

Charlotte Perkins Gilman (1860–1935): An American writer widely regarded as a founder of literary feminism, Gilman is best known today as the author of the short story "The Yellow Wallpaper" (1892).

H. G. Wells (1866–1946): Wells was a pioneer in the new genre of science fiction. Among the novels he wrote in this field were *The Island of Doctor Moreau* (1896) and *The War of the Worlds* (1898).

Woodrow Wilson (1856–1924): Wilson was an American academic and politician who was president of the United States from 1913 to 1921, and led the nation through World War I.

the setting of the book, which she regarded as an "apology" for the earlier, more satirical novel *The House of Mirth*.

Ten years before her death in 1937, Wharton was nominated to receive the Nobel Prize in recognition that she had become the most distinguished American writer of her generation. That she did not receive the award does not diminish either her achievement in letters or the high esteem granted to her by her contemporaries in both America and Europe.

Works in Literary Context

Wharton is best known as a novelist of manners whose fiction exposes the cruel excesses of aristocratic society in the United States at the beginning of the twentieth century. Her carefully crafted, psychologically complex novels, novellas, and short stories reflect concern for the status of women in society as well as for the moral decay she observed underlying the propriety of the upper classes. While her subject matter, tone, and style have often been compared with those of her friend and mentor Henry James, Wharton has achieved critical recognition as an original chronicler of the conflict between the inner self and social convention.

Gender Roles   Wharton is often regarded as a pioneering literary feminist; this is evident in the novel *The House of Mirth*. Its heroine, Lily Bart, is the quintessence of "the

COMMON HUMAN EXPERIENCE

In *The House of Mirth*, Wharton tells the story of a woman who essentially has to turn herself into a piece of merchandise in order to attract a husband. Here are some other works in which the central female characters also struggle to cope with the institution of marriage:

"The Wife of Bath's Prologue and Tale" in *The Canterbury Tales* (c. 1392), a story by Geoffrey Chaucer. In this tale, a woman who has been married five times, and is eagerly looking for a new husband, gives her opinion of marriage. Often regarded as a feminist hero, the Wife of Bath seems to argue that what women want most is to dominate their partners.

Pride and Prejudice (1813), a novel by Jane Austen. This novel begins with the famous line "It is a truth universally acknowledged, that a single man in possession of a good fortune must be in want of a wife." The novel provides a thorough overview of the politics of betrothal and marriage in Great Britain at the beginning of the nineteenth century.

Their Eyes Were Watching God (1937), a novel by Zora Neale Hurston. This novel tells the story of Janie, who goes through a series of marriages looking for love. Along the way, she experiences most of the marital options open to women at the date that Hurston wrote the novel.

American Girl"—exquisitely beautiful and trained to think of herself not as a woman capable of defining her own goals and making emotional commitments that would give shape and sustenance to her life, but rather as the lovely, passive lady whose future must necessarily be defined by the man who would marry her. She has come to regard herself primarily as a decorative object.

One source of the tragedy lies in Lily's family: her father has died, leaving an almost impoverished wife accustomed to comfort. The widowed Mrs. Bart resolves to recover her lost fortunes through her daughter, whose entire mission in life subsequently becomes defined in terms of bartering her loveliness for a wealthy husband: "She was like some rare flower grown for exhibition, a flower from which every bud had been nipped except the crowning blossom of her beauty." Nor is Lily liberated from this fate by her mother's early death; she must go on, seeking to maintain a luxurious life by living parasitically on the leavings of the newly wealthy, seeking to legitimize her position by achieving the right alliance, not because she wants to, but because she has never learned anything else. She feels that she is "somebody" only when she perceives herself reflected in the admiring mirror of someone else's eyes.

Wharton and Literary Naturalism Among American writers, naturalism is associated with Stephen Crane, Theodore Dreiser, Frank Norris, and others. For the naturalist author, human actions are largely determined by social and hereditary forces that are beyond their control. Wharton had deep knowledge of the forces of heredity and environment, gained from writers like Charles Darwin. While according Lily Bart a measure of freedom and responsibility for her behavior, Wharton could also write of her in such a way as to suggest that Lily is the poignant victim of hereditary and environmental forces that she cannot understand and over which she has little control: "Inherited tendencies had combined with early training to make her the highly specialized product she was: an organism as helpless out of its narrow range as the sea-anemone torn from the rock."

William James, the prominent psychologist of Wharton's era, distinguished between a tender-minded and a tough-minded response to the question of free will and determinism. This distinction is relevant to Wharton's fiction. In her insistence that heredity and environment do strongly influence moral decisions, Wharton must be called a "tender-minded determinist" who realized, like Lily Bart's friend Lawrence Selden, that Lily "was so evidently the victim of the civilization which had produced her, that the links of her bracelet seemed like manacles chaining her to her fate." She learns too late about any alternative order of values based on freedom.

Works in Critical Context

The breadth of Edith Wharton's achievement makes definition of her place in literary history difficult. For fifty years she wrote prolifically, and her audience ranged from scholars to readers of popular magazines. She produced short stories, ghost tales, novellas, novels, autobiography, literary criticism, and books on travel, landscape gardening, Italian architectural history, and interior decorating. This breadth in her career made critical assessment difficult, but by the time Wharton produced her last important novel, *The Age of Innocence*, critics knew what to expect and were able to fit the novel into the context of a long public career.

The Age of Innocence Another novel about Old New York society, *The Age of Innocence* showcases passionate characters hemmed in by their desire to keep their membership in a dispassionate social group. Central among them is the protagonist, Newland Archer, who must give up the woman he loves in order to satisfy the moral demands of his society. "Archer, with his insecurity, his sensitivity, and his passion has obeyed the moral imperatives of his class and time and has given up Ellen and love for the furtherance of the shallow-seeming aims, all amorphous as they are, of his [New York] world," observed Louis O. Coxe. Wharton allows Archer to confess that a life of duty has its rewards, Coxe added—and yet it is a lonely life, since the next generation, represented by Archer's son, enjoys freedom from social pressure and is unable to understand this kind of sacrifice. Other critics stressed the structural qualities of the book. Joseph Warren Beach noted that "The book is remarkable for unity and simplicity of action." Wharton achieves this unity through her development of characters, especially her protagonist: "What more than anything else contributes to the unity and compactness of the drama is that Newland Archer is present in every scene, and that everything is shown from his point of view." This technique "keeps our curiosity and concern at the same white heat as Newland's." The novel was acclaimed as one of Wharton's best, and, according to *The New York Times* writer William Lyon Phelps, was "one of the best novels of the twentieth century" and "a permanent addition to literature."

Responses to Literature

1. Read some of the poetry of Robert Frost, such as "Stopping by Woods on a Snowy Evening" (1922), "Mending Wall" (1914), or "Birches" (1915). Compare these poems to *Ethan Frome*. Both the novel and poems are set in rural New England, which seems a cold and gloomy place on the surface. Are there differences, however, in the way these two writers depict the place? If so, how and why?

2. *The Theory of the Leisure Class* (1899) by the economist Thorstein Veblen introduced the idea of "conspicuous consumption" to the reading public—the idea that people buy things not for their value, but in order to have trophies to show off and confirm their social status. In what ways is Lily Bart in *The House of Mirth* a potential trophy for some future husband? Find other examples in the novel that would qualify as "conspicuous consumption."

3. There have been many books that tell the story of a character who has to choose between following the rules of society or doing what he or she pleases. *The Age of Innocence* centers on this theme. Read another such book, *The Scarlet Letter* (1850) by Nathaniel Hawthorne. How, and why, do the two books develop this theme differently, and what does this indicate about the differences between the two authors?

BIBLIOGRAPHY

Books

Beach, Joseph Warren. *The Twentieth Century Novel: Studies in Technique.* New York: Appleton-Century-Crofts, 1932.

Farwell, Tricia M. *Love and Death in Edith Wharton's Fiction.* New York: Peter Lang, 2006.

Lee, Hermione. *Edith Wharton.* New York: Knopf, 2007.

Sloboda, Noel. *The Making of Americans in Paris: The Autobiographies of Edith Wharton and Gertrude Stein.* New York: Peter Lang, 2008.

Turk, Ruth. *Edith Wharton: Beyond the Age of Innocence.* Greensboro, N.C.: Tudor, 1997.

Wagner-Martin, Linda. The Age of Innocence: *A Novel of Ironic Nostaglia.* New York: Twayne, 1996.

Wright, Sarah Bird. *Edith Wharton's Travel Writing: The Making of a Connoisseur.* New York: St. Martin's Press, 1997.

Periodicals

Coxe, Lewis O. "What Edith Wharton Saw in Innocence." *The New Republic* 132 (June 17, 1955): 16–18.

Kim, Sharon. "Edith Wharton and Epiphany." *Journal of Modern Literature* 29 (Spring 2006): 150–175.

McLoughlin, Kate. "Edith Wharton, War Correspondent." *Edith Wharton Review* 21 (Fall 2005): 1–10.

Phelps, William Lyon. "As Mrs. Wharton Sees Us." *The New York Times Book Review* (October 11, 1920): 1, 11.

Rattray, Laura. "The Unpublished Writings of Edith Wharton." *Edith Wharton Review* 22 (Fall 2006): 1–6.

Web sites

The Edith Wharton Society. *The Edith Wharton Society Homepage.* Retrieved December 8, 2008, from http://www.wsu.edu/~campbelld/wharton/index.html. Last updated on December 8, 2008.

Phillis Wheatley

BORN: *c. 1753, Senegal*

DIED: *1784, Boston, Massachusetts*

NATIONALITY: *American*

GENRE: *Poetry*

MAJOR WORKS:
Poems on Various Subjects, Religious and Moral (1773)

Overview

Phillis Wheatley was the first black person known to have published a volume of writings in North America. Historically significant in American letters, her *Poems on Various Subjects, Religious and Moral* (1773), was used as an exemplar of the power of education by activists against slavery, who hailed the collection as a product of genius. Composed largely of poetry that displays the controlled rhythms and rhyme patterns popularized by Alexander Pope, *Poems on Various Subjects*, has been regarded as both brilliant and artistically inconsequential. Most modern assessments, however, recognize Wheatley's accomplishments as typical of the best poetry of her age.

Phillis Wheatley   *Wheatley, Phillis, engraving. The Library of Congress.*

Works in Biographical and Historical Context

Kidnapped   Wheatley was born sometime around 1753 or 1754—perhaps in Senegal—kidnapped, and brought to New England in 1761. She was purchased by John Wheatley of Boston as a gift for his wife, Susanna, who, according to Margaretta Matilda Odell's *Memoir and Poems of Phillis Wheatley* (1834), "visited the slave market" in order "to make a personal selection from the group of unfortunates offered for sale." Though all sources indicate that the child was frail, Benjamin Brawley, in his *Negro Builders and Heroes* (1937), maintains that "her bright eyes attracted the attention of Susanna Wheatley . . . she was purchased, taken home, and given the name of Phillis."

In those early days, there was nothing in the delicate child to indicate that she would become a well-known poet, but she learned to read and write quickly. She also became competent in Latin. The legend of her precocity has been aided by her biographers' emphasis on her mastery of English, selected classics, and the Bible within sixteen months. It is clear that the Wheatleys took a great interest in the bright youngster, although Odell notes that Phillis "had no brilliant exhibition of feminine genius before her, to excite her emulations," and found the only plausible explanation for her intellectual attainments and poetic gift "in the inspiration of that genius which is the gift of God." Her proficiency in grammar and understanding of style

probably resulted initially from her intense interest in Alexander Pope's translation of Homer.

Along with a handful of male university graduates, she reached a level of education that was extremely rare in colonial society, especially for women. Undoubtedly one of the community's best-educated young women, she profited intellectually from her association with the elite of Boston, which placed her in a cultural atmosphere denied to most young people growing up in colonial America. The Wheatleys took great delight in showing her off, but inherent in this display was evidence of the ambiguous role she had to play.

A Christian Poet   Wheatley became a devout Christian during the waning days of New England Puritanism, the movement of reformist Protestants who sought to create a more spare and rigorous Christianity. Her commitment to religion, as she understood its principles, cannot be minimized. She became a member of the historic Old South Meeting House in 1771, and accepted the interpretation of Christianity preached there. While she was extremely familiar with biblical literature and took delight in the poetry of Pope, the Puritan, John Milton, who wrote *Paradise Lost*, became her favorite. Slavery was not as restrictive for her as for others. She was free to visit the Wheatleys' friends; Odell, however, observes that when Wheatley visited these homes, she requested "that a side-table . . . be laid for her [and] dined modestly apart from the rest of the company," in a position "where she could certainly expect neither to give or receive offense."

Various dates have been given for the beginning of her interest in writing. In a 1772 letter to Phillis's English publishers, John Wheatley indicated that she started writing in 1765. In 1770, her elegy for a famous evangelist, the Reverend George Whitefield, brought her public recognition. First published in the October 11 issue of the *Massachusetts Spy*, it was published as a broadside and a pamphlet in Boston and was also printed in New York, Newport, and Philadelphia before the end of the year. It first appeared in London the following year. In these publications, she was generally identified as "a Servant Girl of 17 Years of Age, Belonging to Mr. J. Wheatley of Boston:—And has been but 9 years in this Country from Africa."

A Respected Public Figure   That she had elected to write of George Whitefield also brought Wheaton to the attention of Selina Hastings, Countess of Huntingdon, an avid supporter of humanitarian causes and an important figure in the eighteenth-century revival movement who had helped Whitefield with his American campaign. Her philanthropic activities were well known, as was her aid in the establishment of both Dartmouth College and the College of New Jersey (now Princeton University). That Wheatley's elegy enjoyed widespread circulation is perhaps a testimony, not only to the greatness of the evangelist and the interest in Phillis Wheatley, but also to the influence of the Countess of Huntingdon.

The elegy for Whitefield was followed by two broadsides that appeared in the March 1772 issue of the *London Magazine*. In an October 10, 1772, letter to the Earl of Dartmouth, whom she considered a friend for his opposition to the Stamp Act, Wheatley enclosed a poem praising his appointment as Secretary of State for the Colonies. During 1773, two more elegies appeared, but by far the most important of her 1773 publications was her collection of verse, *Poems on Various Subjects, Religious and Moral*, published in London and dedicated to the Countess of Huntingdon.

The journey to England that preceded the book's appearance was to provide the high point of her life. The Wheatleys' physician—concerned about her delicate health—had suggested a sea voyage for her, and since one of the Wheatleys was scheduled to go to England on business, it was decided that Phillis would accompany him. Her status at the time of the trip is not clear, although it is known for certain that she had been freed by 1778. In some respects, her status was inconsequential in London, where her African background was considered exotic and contributed to her popularity as well as to her reputation as a poet. She was lionized and showered with presents. Brooke Watson, who became Lord Mayor of London, gave her a copy of *Paradise Lost*. The Earl of Dartmouth reportedly gave her money that she spent buying books. Among her visitors was Benjamin Franklin.

The Revolutionary War While her productivity may not have lessened after 1773, Wheatley's work was published infrequently. In a way, she was a casualty of the Revolutionary War: her book was published at a time when people were more concerned with the political events of the day than with the poetry of a Boston slave. October 1775 found her in Providence, Rhode Island, where John Wheatley had moved his household in order to avoid the military confusion then existing in Boston. Life in war-torn New England was far from stable or pleasant. Mr. Wheatley took the family back to Boston after the British had evacuated the city in March 1776. His death on March 12, 1778, however, effectively broke up the household—his wife had died four years earlier—and on April 1, 1778, Wheatley married John Peters, a free black Bostonian. Biographers have often said that Peters was "worthless," maintaining that he caused an estrangement between his wife and her white friends, behaved in a superior manner, and lacked the ability to support her and their three children. It is difficult to determine the validity of the charges made against him, for he undoubtedly suffered from the negative attitude toward assertive free blacks in northern cities. Whatever the truth may be, the marriage failed, and Wheatley— abandoned, lonely, and destitute—was forced to spend her last days as a scullery maid in a rooming house.

She continued to write after her marriage, although few of her poems were published. The poems that she did write do not allude to her misery—as is to be expected

LITERARY AND HISTORICAL CONTEMPORARIES

Wheatley's famous contemporaries include:

Patrick Henry (1736–1799): Henry was governor of Virginia and a radical leader of the American Revolution who is remembered for saying, "Give me liberty or give me death!"

Thomas Jefferson (1743–1826): Jefferson was an American political leader, author of the Declaration of Independence, and later, president of the United States from 1801–1809.

Samuel Johnson (1709–1784): Johnson was a British writer of poetry and prose who produced one of the earliest dictionaries of the English language.

Betsy Ross (1752–1836): Ross was a supporter of the American Revolution and is popularly believed to have designed the first national flag.

Richard Brinsley Sheridan (1751–1816): Sheridan was an Irish playwright remembered for the comedies *The Rivals* (1775) and *The School for Scandal* (1777).

from a poet raised in the tough-minded Puritan tradition. She died in Boston on December 5, 1784.

Works in Literary Context

Scholarly understanding of Wheatley is evolving all the time; coming to understand her better has partly been a matter of simply unearthing more of her work. Recently, scholars have uncovered poems, letters, and more facts about her life and her association with eighteenth-century black abolitionists. They have also charted her notable use of classicism and have weighed in on the sociological intent of her biblical allusions. All this research and interpretation has proven Wheatley's disdain for the institution of slavery and her use of art to undermine its practice.

Biblical Imagery Early twentieth-century critics of black American literature were not very kind to Wheatley because of her supposed lack of concern about slavery. Wheatley, however, did have a statement to make about the institution of slavery, and she made it to the most influential segment of eighteenth-century society—the institutional church. Two of the greatest influences on her thought and poetry were the Bible and eighteenth-century evangelical Christianity, but until fairly recently, Wheatley's critics did not consider her use of biblical allusion, nor its symbolic application, as a statement against slavery. She often spoke in explicit biblical language designed to move church members to decisive action. For instance, in an outspoken letter to the Reverend Samson Occom, written after Wheatley was free and published repeatedly in Boston

COMMON HUMAN EXPERIENCE

The most important feature of Wheatley's personality is her Puritan faith. One needs to keep in mind that her stern Puritanism is the central element of her life; for instance, her Christianity is more important to her than her racial identity. Here are some other works that center on the requirements of a demanding Puritan faith:

> *Paradise Lost* (1667), an epic poem by John Milton. This work retells the story of the Garden of Eden and the fall of man; it also intends to "justify the ways of God to men," a goal that Wheatley also often set for herself.
>
> *The Scarlet Letter* (1850), a novel by Nathaniel Hawthorne. This novel, set in colonial Boston, tells the story of a pair of adulterous lovers. One is a Puritan clergyman who hides his guilt, but is consumed by it.
>
> "The Minister's Black Veil" (1836), a short story by Nathaniel Hawthorne. This short story also tells the tale of a New England Puritan minister who is consumed by guilt, but the source of his guilt becomes the central question. In the context of the story, it appears to have no source, and yet is overwhelming.

newspapers, she equates American slaveholding to that of pagan Egypt in ancient times. Freedom is a necessity, she explains:

> Otherwise, perhaps, the Israelites had been less solicitous for their Freedom from Egyptian Slavery: I don't say they would have been contented without it, by no Means, for in every human Breast, God has implanted a Principle, which we call Love of freedom; it is impatient of Oppression, and pants for Deliverance; and by the Leave of our modern Egyptians I will assert that the same Principle lives in us.

Neoclassicism   At one level, appreciating Wheatley's work is a matter of understanding her mastery of the forms and themes of neoclassicism, the seventeenth- and eighteenth-century literary tradition often associated with Alexander Pope. One element commonly found in neoclassical poetry—especially in the work of Pope—is the heroic couplet, rhyming pairs of lines in which each line has ten syllables of alternating stressed and unstressed syllables. The fact that Wheatley's work shows so little emotion must be considered as a further characteristic of a neoclassical aesthetic, which did not permit the poet the luxury of displaying great personal feeling. Like most poems in the genre, her many funeral elegies are stilted, sophisticated, and detached. She seldom explored her own thoughts on death, even when she knew the deceased well. Her letters demonstrate that she was capable of expressing emotion, but even in these instances, it is restraint that seems the paramount characteristic of her writing.

Works in Critical Context

In black American literary history, one of the central questions is the place of the author in the wider community. Should the work of black writers function as propaganda for community causes, or are they free to write about any subject they wish—even subjects that may make the community look bad? Wheatley's reputation has suffered because of this controversy. Even though it arose long after her lifetime, critics have focused on her work as ammunition in this continuing debate, in ways that have been hard on Wheatley.

Wheatley and Race   Wheatley has, in fact, been dealt an extraordinary amount of abuse for her apparent failure to be an advocate for her race. Angelene Jamison, for instance, argues that that author had become "so engulfed in the education, religion, values, and the freedom of Whites that she expressed no strong sentiments for those who had been cast into the wretchedness of slavery by those she so often praised with her pen." J. Saunders Redding gives a classic statement of this attitude, writing that it is the "negative, bloodless, unracial quality in Phillis Wheatley that makes her seem superficial, especially to members of her own race." More recently, however, Margaret Perry has argued that Wheatley's poetry was largely constrained by her environment and the style in which she wrote: "Her efforts to project herself away from the individual to the universal was part of the artistic detachment imposed by the form of poetry she loved, and the Puritan world in which she lived and believed." Positive assessments like this one have recently become more common.

Responses to Literature

1. Wheatley was known for using the heroic couplet as her main poetic form. Read some of her poems, or those of Alexander Pope, to get a feel for the form. Then try writing your own poem, at least ten lines long, using only heroic couplets. You can write about any subject you wish.

2. Wheatley is a master of the elegy, a formal poem of mourning. Read another famous elegy in the classical tradition, "Lycidas" (1638) by John Milton. What features of the classical elegy do both Milton and Wheatley use?

3. Read the essays in the posthumous collection of Zora Neale Hurston's shorter work, *I Love Myself When I Am Laughing* (1979), focusing especially on the essay, "How It Feels to Be Colored Me" (1928). How is Hurston's perspective similar to Wheatley's? How is it different?

BIBLIOGRAPHY

Books

Redding, J. Saunders. *To Make a Poet Black*. Chapel Hill, N.C.: University of North Carolina Press, 1939.

Richmond, Merle A. *Bid the Vassal Soar: Interpretive Essays on the Life and Poetry of Phillis Wheatley (ca. 1753–1784) and George Moses Horton (ca. 1797–1883).* Washington, D.C.: Howard University Press, 1974.

Robinson, William H. *Phillis Wheatley and Her Writings.* New York: Garland, 1984.

Periodicals

Black, Daniel P. "Literary Subterfuge: Early African American Writing and the Trope of the Mask." *CLA Journal* 48 (June 2005): 387–403.

Chiles, Katy L. "Becoming Colored in Occom and Wheatley's Early America." *PMLA: Publications of the Modern Language Association of America* 123 (October 2008): 1398–1417.

Franke, Astrid. "Phillis Wheatley, Melancholy Muse." *New England Quarterly* 77 (June 2004): 224–251.

Slauter, Eric. "Neoclassical Culture in a Society with Slaves: Race and Rights in the Age of Wheatley." *Early American Studies* 2 (Spring 2004): 81–122.

Thompson, Gordon E. "Methodism and the Consolation of Heavenly Bliss in Phillis Wheatley's Funeral Elegies." *CLA Journal* 48 (September 2004): 34–50.

Thorn, Jennifer. "'All Beautiful in Woe:' Gender, Nation, and Phillis Wheatley's Niobe." *Studies in Eighteenth-Century Culture* 37 (2008): 233–258.

Web sites

Perspectives in American Literature. *Phillis Wheatley (1753–1784).* Retrieved December 1, 2008, from http://www.csustan.edu/english/reuben/pal/chap2/wheatley.html. Last updated November 13, 2008.

⊛ E. B. White

BORN: *1899, Mount Vernon, New York*

DIED: *1985, Brooklin, Maine*

NATIONALITY: *American*

GENRE: *Fiction, nonfiction*

MAJOR WORKS:

Stuart Little (1946)

Charlotte's Web (1952)

The Trumpet of the Swan (1970)

Overview

Few writers have achieved recognition in as many fields as did E. B. White. He was regarded as one of the finest essayists of the twentieth century; he was the author of two classics of children's literature, *Charlotte's Web* (1952) and *Stuart Little* (1946); and his extensive contributions to *The New Yorker* were instrumental in making that magazine a success.

E. B. White   *MPI / Getty Images*

Works in Biographical and Historical Context

Developing a Love of Writing   Elwyn Brooks White was born in Mount Vernon, New York, on July 11, 1899, the youngest of six children. The family was well off, White's father having risen from somewhat humble beginnings to become president of Horace Waters and Company, a New York piano firm. As White has stated, there was nothing exceptionally luxurious about his background. There were pianos and other instruments in the house, though, and lots of music, performed with enthusiasm rather than professional dedication. Although White played the piano, his main love was writing. When he was a teenager, his poems, essays, and short stories were published in the Mount Vernon High School *Oracle*.

In the fall of 1917, White entered the Liberal Arts College at Cornell University. He made the board of the student newspaper, the *Cornell Daily Sun*, his freshman year and became editor-in-chief at the end of his junior year. In early May of 1920, he won first prize for an editorial submitted to the Convention of Eastern College Newspapers.

White officially began his writing career in 1921 after graduating from Cornell. He worked for a time as a reporter with two news services in New York City, then drove a Model T cross-country with his friend Howard Cushman. Ending up in Seattle, White took a job as a reporter for the *Seattle Times*, but having trouble adjusting to his new job, he lasted less than a year. White next worked for a short time as a mess boy on a ship bound for Alaska but soon returned to New York, where he spent two years as an advertising copywriter.

Observing the World Around Him

It was while working as a copywriter that White began to submit short pieces to the fledgling magazine, *The New Yorker*, barely a few months old at the time. Editor Harold Ross was so impressed by these articles that he hired White to write the opening "Talk of the Town" section for the magazine. Both Ross and Katharine Angell, the magazine's literary editor who later became White's wife, found White's style ideal for *The New Yorker*. Over the next forty years, White contributed poems, essays, sketches, stories, and even photo captions to the *New Yorker* and wrote the "Talk of the Town" section for eleven years.

In 1929 White collaborated with a colleague from *The New Yorker*, writer and artist James Thurber, on *Is Sex Necessary?; or, Why You Feel the Way You Do*, a spoof of sex manuals. The book made both White and Thurber well-known. The two authors parody other serious writers on the subject, making light of complexities, taking a mock-serious attitude toward the obvious, delighting in reducing the case-history technique to an absurdity. Thurber's drawings, turned out in a few hours, illustrate the book, which has gone through more than twenty-five printings since it first appeared. White's share of the royalties enabled him to marry Katharine Angell on November 13, 1929.

Over the years, it has been White's essays for *The New Yorker*—many of which are collected in 1977's *Essays of E. B. White*—that have done the most to build his literary reputation. White's essays are personal and informal, seem to happen upon their subject as they ramble along, and have a gentle humor about them. New York City, where *The New Yorker* has its offices, and the Maine countryside, where White owned a farm, are the two most common settings of his essays. White often began with a small incident in his own life and then extrapolated larger implications from it. In all of his essays, White's style is clear, personal, and unaffected. Although they cover a wide range of topics—from observations of nature to the problems of city living, and from political commentary to literary parody—they invariably display a gentle humor, which White saw as a necessary counterbalance to everyday life.

When White turned his attention to political matters, he often focused on the international race for bigger and better weapons and the tensions between the world's nations. White was known as a forceful advocate of world government, which he recommended for democratic nations only, and as a defender of individual privacy. A concern for the environment, inspired by Henry David Thoreau's book *Walden* (1854) was also evident in White's life and work. Following the example of Thoreau, who lived close to the land, White bought a saltwater farm in North Brooklin, Maine, in 1934. He and his wife moved there permanently in 1938 and took to raising geese, chickens, and sheep. The essays collected in *One Man's Meat* (1942), originally written as monthly columns for *Harper's* magazine, are set on White's farm and chronicle his daily life in the country.

A Master of Children's Literature

Although most critics praise White for his work as an essayist, he is more popularly known as the author of *Charlotte's Web* and *Stuart Little*, two classics of American children's literature. Inspired by a vivid dream, White began to write a children's story about a small, mouse-like character in 1939. Whenever one of his eighteen nieces and nephews wanted to be told a story, White improvised new adventures for his hero, whom he named Stuart Little. In 1945, he gathered these adventures together into a book-length manuscript, which he sent to Harper & Row for consideration. Children's book editor, Ursula Nordstrom, found the book to be as moving as it was humorous and accepted *Stuart Little* for publication. The book has since sold more than two million copies in English and has been translated into twenty other languages.

White's next children's book, *Charlotte's Web*, was published in 1952. *Charlotte's Web* is set on a farm much like the one White owned in Maine. Feeling pangs for a soon-to-be-slaughtered pig on his farm, and moved by the artistry of a spider spinning its web he had been watching, White began to formulate a story. Wilbur is destined to die, but he is saved by his friend Charlotte, a spider, when she weaves the words "Some Pig" into a web above his pen. People who see this miraculous message are so impressed by it that Wilbur is spared and even put on display at the local fair. During their stay at the fair, Charlotte dies. David Rees, writing in *The Marble in the Water: Essays on Contemporary Writers of Fiction for Children and Young Adults*, called *Charlotte's Web* "the one great modern classic about death."

It wasn't until 1970 that White published his third and final children's book, *The Trumpet of the Swan*. It has much in common with his earlier efforts. Like the previous two books, *The Trumpet of the Swan* grew out of an experience in White's own life. His fascination with the trumpeter swans at the Philadelphia Zoo, initiated by a story in the *New York Times*, led White to tell the story of Louis, a voiceless trumpeter swan. Because he cannot speak, his human friend, Sam Beaver, takes Louis to school with him to learn to read and write. Thereafter, Louis carries a chalkboard and chalk with him to write out his messages. His father, wanting him to be able to communicate with other swans as well, steals a trumpet for him to play. Soon Louis's trumpet playing leads to nightclub work and to a meeting with Serena, a female swan with whom he falls in love.

White is also known for his updates and revisions to *The Elements of Style* (1959), a grammar guide originally written by one of his Cornell professors, William Strunk Jr. Although White wrote little after *The Trumpet of the Swan*, he received a Pulitzer Prize in 1978 in acknowledgement of his overall contribution to American literature. White died at his home in Maine on October 1, 1985.

Works in Literary Context

Talking Animals The concept of animals capable of human speech has been an element of various forms of mythology, folklore, and fairy tales for as long as stories have been told. From ancient Greek mythology to Native American folk tales to Aesop's Fables to the famed fairy tales of the Brothers Grimm, talking animals have been used symbolically to offer pearls of wisdom, deceive human characters, or feature as stand-ins for different aspects of human emotions and behaviors. The biblical Book of Genesis features one of the most famous examples of a talking animal as a serpent in the Garden of Eden deceives Adam into eating a forbidden apple from the Tree of Knowledge, which leads to humankind's expulsion from Paradise. In contemporary use, the talking animal has found its most regular home in the realm of children's literature. Numerous classics of children's literature, including C. S. Lewis's *The Chronicles of Narnia* and Lewis Carroll's *Alice's Adventures in Wonderland*, feature talking animals.

White used talking animals in each of his children's books, but his depiction of them differed in each book. *In Charlotte's Web*, the animals are only capable of speaking to each other, while the mouse in *Stuart Little* is able to talk to people. In *The Trumpet of the Swan*, all of the animals can speak except for the swan Louis, who is born mute.

Satire Satire is an approach to any literary, graphic, or performing art that intends to ridicule humanity's follies, vices, and shortcomings. Although satire is distinguished by a humorous, ironic tone, the end result of satire is not always intended to be merely comedic. Often the satirist uses satire to make a social or political point by pretending to adopt a viewpoint she or he opposes and presenting it in a ridiculous manner. The term was first applied to a collection of poetry by the ancient Roman poet, Quintus Ennius, that ridiculed his fellow poet, Accius. Throughout literary history, writers, including Jonathan Swift, Mark Twain, and Charles Dickens, have composed satirical works. Although White is best known for his children's books, he wrote a number of satirical works for an adult readership. His first published book, *Is Sex Necessary?; or, Why You Feel the Way You Do*, was a satire of romantic advice manuals. During the Great Depression, he wrote a satirical essay about the U.S. economy called "Alice Through the Cellophane" for *The New Yorker*.

LITERARY AND HISTORICAL CONTEMPORARIES

White's famous contemporaries include:

A. A. Milne (1882–1956): Milne was a British writer. He will forever be remembered as the creator of a beloved children's book series featuring a bear named Winnie-the-Pooh.

James Thurber (1894–1961): Thurber was an American short story writer and cartoonist. He is best known for the cartoons he created for *The New Yorker* magazine and *My Life and Hard Times* (1933), a book of stories and illustrations.

Eudora Welty (1909–2001): Welty was an American writer best known for her Southern-flavored short stories. She won the coveted Pulitzer Prize for her novel *The Optimist's Daughter* (1972).

Garth Williams (1912–1996): Williams was an American illustrator who achieved his greatest fame for his work on children's books, including work on White's *Stuart Little* and *Charlotte's Web*.

John Updike (1932–2009): Updike is an American writer who received his greatest acclaim for a series of books about a former high school basketball player named Harry "Rabbit" Angstrom.

Works in Critical Context

Charlotte's Web Critical evaluation of *Charlotte's Web* places it among the very best of its genre. It is "outstanding among post-war American children's fiction," John Rowe Townsend writes in his *Written for Children: An Outline of English Language Children's Literature* (1965). Similarly, Eudora Welty writes in her review for *The New York Times* that "[a]s a piece of work, [*Charlotte's Web*] is just about perfect, and just about magical in the way it is done." The reviewer for the *Chicago Sunday Tribune* judges *Charlotte's Web* to be a "rare story of a beautiful friendship," as well as "witty and wise, lively and tender." Since its initial publication in 1952, *Charlotte's Web* has become a classic of American children's literature and has sold well over three million copies.

The Trumpet of the Swan Writing in the *New York Times Book Review*, John Updike expresses his opinion that *The Trumpet of the Swan* joins *Stuart Little* and *Charlotte's Web* "on the shelf of classics." Although it differs from the previous books, Updike finds that *Trumpet*

has superior qualities of its own; it is the most spacious and serene of the three, the one most imbued with the author's sense of the precious instinctual heritage represented by wild nature,... yet [the book] does not lack the inimitable tone of the two earlier works—the simplicity that never condescends, the straight and earnest telling that happens upon, rather than veers into, comedy.

COMMON HUMAN EXPERIENCE

In his book *Stuart Little*, White follows Stuart's quest to find Margalo, the bird he loves who has flown away from his house to escape the clutches of his family's cat. Other works that follow a character's quest include:

Alice's Adventures in Wonderland (1865), a book by Lewis Carroll. Alice's adventures begin when she follows a white rabbit down into its hole and winds up in a bizarre, confusing world, from which she must then find her way home.

The Wonderful Wizard of Oz (1900), a book by L. Frank Baum. One of the most famous children's books of all time, this work tells the tale of a Kansas farm girl named Dorothy who is whisked off to an enchanting fantasyland called Oz during a tornado. As Dorothy ventures to return home, she meets a friendly trio of characters and is pursued by a wicked witch.

The Hobbit (1937), a novel by J. R. R. Tolkien. Tolkien's fantasy introduces Bilbo Baggins, a small, elf-like creature called a hobbit who embarks on a quest to find a treasure, which is guarded by a fire-breathing dragon named Smaug.

Star Wars (1977), a film by George Lucas. *Star Wars*, which began one of the most successful film series of all time, is the story of Luke Skywalker, a young man who must leave his home to rescue an imprisoned princess and defeat the forces of evil that intend to control the galaxy.

Responses to Literature

1. Although *Stuart Little* is widely considered to be a classic of children's literature, many critics find the ending of the story to be unsatisfying. After reading *Stuart Little*, write an essay explaining whether or not you agree with these critics. Explain why you did or did not find the ending to be satisfying, using details from the book to support your response.

2. Both *Stuart Little* and *Charlotte's Web* feature talking animals, but these animals are presented in decidedly different ways in White's two books. Read both books; then explain how White's depictions of talking animals differ between the two books.

3. In White's works, as with many fables and folktales, animals are given qualities similar to humans. Choose an animal character from one of White's works and identify the specific human traits he gives to that character. How would the work be changed if the character were actually human?

BIBLIOGRAPHY

Books

Kramer, Dale. *Ross and the New Yorker*. Garden City, N.Y.: Doubleday, 1951, pp. 68–77.

Rees, David. *The Marble in the Water: Essays on Contemporary Writers of Fiction for Children and Young Adults*. Boston: Horn Book, 1980, pp. 68–77.

Townsend, John Rowe. *Written for Children: An Outline of English Language Children's Literature*. Colwall, Malvern, Herefordshire: Garnet Miller, 1965.

Periodicals

Beck, Warren. "E.B. White." *College English 7* (April 1946): 367–373.

Geismar, Maxwell. "Go Climb a More Meaningful Tree." *Commonweal 51* (March 10, 1950): 573.

Griffith, John. "*Charlotte's Web*: A Lonely Fantasy of Love." *Children's Literature 8* (1980): 111–117.

Maloney, Russell. "Tilley the Toiler." *Saturday Review of Literature 30* (August 30, 1947): 7.

Review of *Charlotte's Web*. *Chicago Sunday Tribune* (October 19, 1952).

Updike, John. "The Trumpet of the Swan (review)." *The New York Times* (June 28, 1970).

Welty, Eudora. "Life in the Barn Was Very Good." *The New York Times* (October 2, 1985).

✸ Walt Whitman

BORN: *1819, West Hills, New York*

DIED: *1892, Camden, New Jersey*

NATIONALITY: *American*

GENRE: *Poetry*

MAJOR WORKS:
Leaves of Grass (1855)
Drum-Taps (1865)
Sequel to Drum-Taps (1865–1866)

Overview

Walt Whitman's *Leaves of Grass* (1855) is hailed as a masterpiece of American literature. Published in nine editions between 1855 and 1892, the collection pioneered a vision of humanity based on Whitman's radically democratic ideals and unveiled an ambitious poetic persona designed to serve as the embodiment of America. The poems of *Leaves of Grass* glorify America through evocations of its citizenry, landscape, and history as filtered through the "self" of the longest and most highly regarded poem, "Song of Myself." Eschewing conventional verse forms and diction, Whitman wrote in an unrestrained and idiosyncratic style that reflected the iconoclasm of his personal outlook. Though deemed obscene by some when it was published, the influence of *Leaves of Grass* on American literature has been pronounced and lasting.

Walt Whitman   *Whitman, Walt, photograph. The Library of Congress.*

Works in Biographical and Historical Context

From Undistinguished Beginnings   There is nothing in Whitman's life prior to 1855 to indicate future greatness. Born on May 31, 1819, to Walter Whitman and Louisa Van Velsor, young Walt passed his early years in undistinguished fashion. Shortly before his fourth birthday, the family moved from its home at West Hills, Long Island, to Brooklyn. Whitman's father, a carpenter, hoped to find employment in the town, for there had been few opportunities to ply his craft on Long Island, and he had been reduced to farming and cutting firewood to earn money for his family.

Whitman received a rudimentary education during the six years he attended the public schools in Brooklyn, beginning about 1825. He obtained even more important lessons from his parents. His mother taught him the value of family ties, and Whitman remained devoted to his family throughout his life, becoming, in a real sense, its leader after the death of his father. Whitman inherited the liberal intellectual and political attitudes of a free thinker from his father.

Whitman's formal education ended in his eleventh year, when he went to work as an office boy. He was fortunate in his first choice of employment, the lawyers James B. Clark and his son, Edward. The younger Clark took a liking to Whitman, assisting him with his hand-writing and composition and treating him to a subscription in a local circulating (or lending) library, where he was introduced to a new, vast world of romance as he devoured the writings of Sir Walter Scott. Whitman was then employed in a physician's office before landing another job that would greatly influence his life.

Walt Whitman: Newspaperman   In the summer of 1831, Whitman joined the office staff of the *Long Island Patriot*, a four-page weekly whose editor, Samuel E. Clements, shared the liberal political views of his father. It was here that Whitman first broke into print with "sentimental" bits of filler material. The following summer, Whitman went to work for another printer, Erastus Worthington, and in the autumn he moved on to the shop of Alden Spooner, the most successful publisher-printer in Brooklyn.

Although his family moved back to the area of West Hills in 1834, Whitman stayed on in Brooklyn. He published a few pieces in the *New York Mirror*, attended the Bowery Theater, continued subscribing to a circulating library, and joined a local debating society. In his sixteenth year, Whitman moved to New York City to seek work as a compositor. His move was poorly timed: a wave of Irish immigrants had contributed to the already unruly behavior in the city's streets; anti-abolitionist and anti-Irish riots often broke out; unemployment was high; and the winter was miserably cold. Whitman could not find satisfactory employment and, in May 1836, he rejoined his family, now living in Hempstead, Long Island.

In June, Whitman began to teach school in nearby Norwich. In days when a high school diploma (or its equivalent) was the exception and not the rule, and when teacher certification was unknown, Whitman's apparent choice of profession was not unusual. During the next phase of his life, Whitman would alternate between teaching and printing, his public vacillation in profession reflecting his private indecision about where his future lay. Whitman taught at various schools until the spring of 1838, when, with the financial support of friends, he began his own newspaper, the weekly *Long Islander*, in Huntington.

Whitman's stint as an independent newspaperman lasted until May 1839, when he sold the paper and his equipment and went again to New York. He subsequently edited numerous papers for short periods, including the New York *Aurora* and the Brooklyn *Eagle*. During this time, Whitman also published poems and short stories in various periodicals. Generally undistinguished, sentimental, and educational, these early pieces are considered typical of the pious attitudes of the era. The verse, written in conventional rhyme and meter, gives no indication of the dynamic, free-flowing style Whitman later developed in *Leaves of Grass*. His first separately published work was an anti-alcohol novel titled *Franklin Evans; or, The Inebriate* (1842). He later called it "rot" and claimed that it was written only as hackwork.

LITERARY AND HISTORICAL CONTEMPORARIES

Whitman's famous contemporaries include:

Ralph Waldo Emerson (1803–1882): Emerson was an American poet and philosopher and leading member of the philosophical movement called transcendentalism. He was a great supporter of Walt Whitman when he was a struggling poet.

Abraham Lincoln (1809–1865): The sixteenth president of the United States, Lincoln led the country during the bloody American Civil War (1861–1865) between the North and the South. Lincoln was assassinated in 1865, a tragic event that inspired Whitman's poem "O Captain! My Captain!"

James Harlan (1820–1899): Harlan served as a senate representative of Iowa (1855–1857) and later served as the United States Secretary of the Interior (1865–1866). After being appointed Secretary of the Interior, Harlan fired Whitman from his job at the Department of the Interior.

Emily Dickinson (1830–1886): Dickinson was an American poet and was virtually unknown as a poet during her lifetime. She has since achieved lasting fame due to the vast collection of private poetry discovered and published after her death.

Mark Twain (1835–1910): Twain, whose real name was Samuel Langhorne Clemens, was a noted American humorist whose works include the novels *The Prince and the Pauper* (1882) and *Adventures of Huckleberry Finn* (1884).

The Radical Poet Whitman's sudden transformation from a conventional journalist to a radical poet remains unexplained, though commentators have suggested causes ranging from writer Ralph Waldo Emerson's 1842 lecture, "The Poet"—in which Emerson called for an American poet to capture the spirit of the burgeoning republic—to the emotional freedom resulting from Whitman's discovery of his homosexuality. Whatever the motivation, critics note that from the publication of the first edition of *Leaves of Grass*, Whitman actively promoted himself as a representative of the common people. The first edition of *Leaves of Grass*, published when Whitman was thirty-five years old, contains twelve untitled poems and no indication of its author, aside from the copyright notice, in which the holder is identified as "Walt Whitman, an American, one of the roughs, a kosmos," a phrase that is echoed in one of the poems.

In a preface that has come to be regarded as one of literature's most influential expositions of artistic aims, Whitman outlined the methods and concerns of a new mode of poetry, centered on simplicity and nature: "[To] speak in literature with the perfect rectitude and insouciance of the movements of animals and the unimpeachableness of the sentiment of trees in the woods and grass by the roadside is the flawless triumph of art." In accordance with the preface, the poems in *Leaves of Grass* sharply break from the American verse tradition, employing unrhymed and unmetered lines, blending poetic and unpoetic speech, and addressing subjects that had been considered unfit for poetry, most conspicuously, the body and human sexuality. Many Americans were shocked by the first poem of *Leaves of Grass*, to be called "Song of Myself" in later editions of the book. Although Ralph Waldo Emerson congratulated Whitman on *Leaves of Grass* in a letter stating, "I greet you at the beginning of a great career," biographers note that he, too, disapproved of the sexually explicit passages in Whitman's work.

In the subsequent editions of *Leaves of Grass*, Whitman included new poems, revised and combined existing ones, added and altered titles, and shifted poems into thematic groupings. He once referred to the different editions of *Leaves of Grass* as "a succession of growths like the rings of trees." In such poems as "Scented Herbage of My Breast" and "City of Orgies," Whitman articulated his dream of democracy founded on the existence of close bonds between men. "As I Ebb'd with the Ocean of Life," another important poem that was added to *Leaves of Grass* in 1860, is filled with anxiety about writing, death, and the "self," and as is characteristic of Whitman, the "self" becomes a metaphor for humanity as a whole. Often cited as one of his most moving poems, "As I Ebb'd with the Ocean of Life" has been read as a process of confronting fears and striving to transform them into hope.

Serving America During the American Civil War, Whitman tended wounded soldiers in army hospitals in Washington, D.C., while working as a copyist in the army paymaster's office. He described some of his wartime experiences in the collections *Drum-Taps* (1865) and *Sequel to Drum-Taps* (1865–1866). The latter contains his eulogy for Abraham Lincoln, "When Lilacs Last in the Dooryard Bloom'd," which Whitman later incorporated into the "Memories of President Lincoln" section of *Leaves of Grass*. The poem is an attempt to come to terms with the loss of the president on a collective level. Though another work occasioned by Lincoln's death, "O Captain! My Captain!," is Whitman's best-known poem, it is also the one he most regretted writing, as he felt it was too formally rigid and distant in emotion.

Following the war, he worked for the Department of the Interior until the secretary, James Harlan, discovered that Whitman was the author of *Leaves of Grass* and dismissed him on grounds of immorality. He was immediately rehired as a clerk at the Justice Department and remained in this position until he suffered a paralytic stroke in 1873, two years after publishing his philosophical essay *Democratic Vistas* (1871) and the fifth edition of *Leaves of Grass*. Although he lived nearly twenty more years and published four more editions of *Leaves of Grass*, Whitman produced little significant new work following his stroke. Primarily, he reworked and rearranged previous editions of *Leaves of Grass* and collected his early writings. Whitman died on March 26, 1892, in Camden, New Jersey.

Works in Literary Context

Transcendentalism   The philosophical, cultural, and literary movement of transcendentalism posited that a spiritual reality exists beyond the observable world. This spiritual reality can be experienced through intuition. The movement emerged during the mid-nineteenth century as a protest against scholastic intellectualism. The first important work of transcendentalist thought is generally considered to be Ralph Waldo Emerson's essay *Nature* (1836), which views nature as a divine entity. Following the publication of Emerson's essay, the transcendentalism movement began to spread through New England and spawned significant works by the writers Henry David Thoreau and Margaret Fuller. While Whitman was not officially linked with the transcendentalism movement, he was influenced by it, and several of his poems, including "Song of Myself" and "Out of the Cradle Endlessly Rocking," can be read as latter-day examples of transcendentalism. Whitman is often considered to be responsible for merging transcendentalism with realism.

Realism   Unlike those who espoused transcendentalism, followers of realism strived to depict the world objectively, unsentimentally, and unromantically. The movement began during the mid-nineteenth century and was distinguished by a refusal to indulge in overly dramatic literary climaxes and exaggerated celebrations of heroism. Both the good and the bad aspects of everyday life are portrayed in realist works, and its down-to-earth sensibility was championed by writers Robert Frost, Thomas Hardy, and Philip Larkin. Whitman's *Leaves of Grass* was considered to be a work that helped paved the way for the transition from transcendentalism to realism.

Works in Critical Context

Leaves of Grass   Despite initial negative critical judgments of its frank approach to sex, *Leaves of Grass* has come to be recognized as a remarkable accomplishment. The poet, Galway Kinnell, has written about Whitman's "transformation, in the world of letters, from freak to master," theorizing that, except for a few perceptive minds—Emerson and Henry David Thoreau in the nineteenth century, Carl Sandburg and Vachel Lindsay in the first half of the twentieth century—mainstream critics were generally too shocked or puzzled by *Leaves of Grass* to give it a fair and thoughtful reading. By the middle of the twentieth

---

COMMON HUMAN EXPERIENCE

Whitman's poem "O Captain! My Captain!" was composed as a tribute to the recently slain President Abraham Lincoln. Other poems written in tribute to Abraham Lincoln include:

The Death of Lincoln (1865), a poem by William Cullen Bryant. Published the very year that Lincoln was murdered, Bryant's poem is steeped in sadness, yet there is also a tone of peaceful resignation in the work.

"To Abraham Lincoln" (1906), a poem by John J. Loud. Loud's poem is a sensitive, sweet tribute to Lincoln's memory that describes the fallen president as a "kindly, loving, whole-souled man." The poem celebrates Lincoln as a defender of the oppressed and compares him to the Biblical leader, Moses.

"Poem" (1909), a poem by Julia Ward Howe. Howe, ninety years old at the time, unveiled her poem on the one hundredth anniversary of Lincoln's birth. "Poem" is a concise but poignant retelling of Lincoln's story from his birth in "A cabin of the western wild" to the "treacherous shot" that ended his life.

"Abraham Lincoln" (1919), a poem by Berton Bellis. Bellis's endearing poem recalls Lincoln's famously "awkward appearance" that housed a "heavenly made heart."

---

century, however, Whitman's poetry had gained wide acceptance, due in part to more open societal attitudes towards sex. It has been the task of critics to sort out the large quantity of myths generated by Whitman's detractors, his disciples, and the poet himself. In particular, critics have sought to explain the significance of sexual imagery in his poetry. Textual analyses continue to reveal complexities in Whitman's work, and such investigations contribute to an evolving appreciation of his powers as a poet. Perhaps *The New York Times* best summed up the work in a 2005 article stating, "Whitman's poem is one of those literary mazes, with passages brilliant and tedious, through which it is possible to follow dozens if not hundreds of ideas."

Democratic Vistas   Hardly as celebrated as *Leaves of Grass*, Whitman's prose collection *Democratic Vistas, and Other Papers* was still well regarded by critics. In a review published in 1888 in *The Academy*, Walter Lewin writes that the title piece "is quite the best thing Whitman has produced in prose" after stating that "there is plenty of excellent matter in the present volume." However, Lewin does not view the book as flawless: "Whitman's essays do not mark him out as a master of style in prose. . . . But what they may lack in style is more than compensated by the abundance of thought they contain." Meanwhile, a supportive review in *The Sunderland Times* concludes,

Walt Whitman hails with joy the oceanic, variegated, intense practical energy, the clamorous demand for facts, even the business material isms of the current age.... The mark of progress is the growing mastership of the general inferior self by the superior self, in the individual, the nation, the race. And this is what he thinks, and we concur with him in thinking, America is destined to do, is doing, and will accomplish.

Responses to Literature

1. One of Whitman's most famous works is "Song of Myself." Think about the poem's meaning as you read it and then write an analysis of the work. Be sure to support your conclusions with specific details from the poem.

2. Whitman composed two tributes to President Abraham Lincoln, "When Lilacs Last in the Dooryard Bloom'd" and "O Captain! My Captain!" Read each poem and explain which one you believe to be the more effective tribute to Lincoln. Be sure to be specific as you explain why you think one poem does a better job of paying tribute to Lincoln than does the other one.

3. Whitman spent thirty-five years revising and re-issuing his *Leaves of Grass* in order to improve it. In modern times, creators such as George Lucas (*Star Wars*, 1977) and Steven Spielberg (*E. T. the Extra-Terrestrial*, 1982) have been criticized for revisiting their earlier works and altering them. Do you think a creator should be able to alter one of their existing creations at their own discretion? Why or why not?

BIBLIOGRAPHY

Books

Bucke, Richard Maurice. *Walt Whitman*. Philadelphia, Penn.: McKay, 1883.

Burroughs, John. *Notes on Walt Whitman as Poet and Person*. New York: American News, 1867.

Clark, William. *Walt Whitman*. London: Swan Sonnenschein, 1892.

Krieg, Joann P. *A Whitman Chronology*. Iowa City, Iowa: University of Iowa Press, 1998.

O'Connor, William Douglas. *The Good Gray Poet: A Vindication*. New York: Bunce & Huntington, 1866.

Perry, Bliss. *Walt Whitman*. Boston: Houghton, Mifflin, 1906.

Reef, Catherine. *Walt Whitman*. New York: Clarion, 1995.

Periodicals

Frank, Michael. "Whitman's Multitudes, for Better and Worse." *The New York Times* (November 18, 2005).

Lewin, Walter. "Review of *Democratic Vistas, and Other Papers*." *The Academy*, 33 (June 30, 1888): 441–442.

Review of *Democratic Vistas*. *The Sunderland Times* (May 21, 1872).

Web Sites

Virginia Commonwealth University. *Whitman and Transcendentalism*. Accessed November 13, 2008, from http://www.vcu.edu/engweb/transcendentalism/roots/legacy/whitman/index.html.

✺ John Greenleaf Whittier

BORN: *1807, Haverhill, Massachusetts*

DIED: *1892, Hampton Falls, New Hampshire*

NATIONALITY: *American*

GENRE: *Poetry*

MAJOR WORKS:

Voices of Freedom (1846)

Songs of Labor, and Other Poems (1850)

Home Ballads and Poems (1860)

The Tent on the Beach and Other Poems (1867)

Overview

In the long struggle to abolish slavery, the Quaker, John Greenleaf Whittier played an important role. Whittier knew that much of the poetry he had written for the

John Greenleaf Whittier   *Whittier, John Greenleaf, photograph. Public Domain*

anti-slavery movement had been hastily composed and for purely political reasons, but there is in his collected poetry a core of excellent work, at the head of which stands his masterpiece, "Snow-Bound," a lovingly imaginative re-creation of the good life in rural New England.

Works in Biographical and Historical Context

Discovering Journalism and Politics Whittier's youth was deeply rooted in the values, history, and traditions of rural Essex County, Massachusetts. Born in 1807, in Haverhill, Massachusetts, Whittier lived in a farmhouse that his great-great-grandfather had built in the seventeenth century. Whittier grew up in a poor but respectable household characterized by hard work and warm family affection. The Whittiers were also devout Quakers, a Christian religious sect devoted to simplicity in their everyday lives and their religious worship. The Essex County area was rich with folklore; tales of witches and ghosts told on winter evenings by the fire exercised the young Whittier's imagination, but it was his discovery of the Scottish poet, Robert Burns, who could speak the beauty of the commonplace circumstances of a rural environment, that made him wish to be a poet.

In 1829, at the age of twenty-two, Whittier accepted the editorship of the *American Manufacturer*, a political weekly in Boston. This position had been secured for him by William Lloyd Garrison, himself a young newspaper editor who was just then beginning his long career as a reformer. Whittier entered journalism for the opportunity to write; what he learned from the experience, however, was politics.

In February 1831, while at Hartford, Whittier published a collection of tales and poems entitled *Legends of New-England*. Although the volume received little attention at the time, it is significant as a pioneering effort to define New England folklore. Whittier was never entirely comfortable with the melodramatic style, however, and suppressed the book in later life. On one occasion, he paid five dollars for the privilege of destroying a copy of this rare early volume.

Choosing the Path of Abolition Toward the end of 1831, Whittier retired in ill health to Haverhill and spent the winter recuperating. He knew that he was at a crossroads in his life and wished to settle, finally, on a career. Poetry hardly paid at all, but he had come to like politics and found that his editorials had made him a popular man in Massachusetts. His friend and patron, William Lloyd Garrison, who had begun publishing his *Liberator* two years before, wrote to Whittier urging him to enlist in the gathering struggle against slavery. Whittier knew that to enlist in this cause, unpopular as it then was in New England, would be tantamount to giving up all hope of gaining elected office. Still, Whittier had been slowly coming to the very conclusion that Garrison now sought to force on him—that the evil of slavery had to be resisted actively.

Whittier took up the cause of abolition and was able, in 1835, to gain a seat in the state legislature from his small home district of Haverhill. There, he was an effective spokesman for his cause, winning over many to his views on the slavery question, sending petitions to the Congress, trying to get a bill through the state house granting trial by jury in cases involving the return of runaway slaves, and even organizing opposition to the death penalty. He continued all the while to express his abolitionism in poems published in Garrison's *Liberator* and in the editorial columns of the *Gazette*, but opposition to his moral stand was mounting. He was forced out of the *Gazette* and was threatened with violence in September 1835 by a mob in Concord, New Hampshire. In 1838, Whittier moved to Philadelphia to edit the *Pennsylvania Freeman*, which he succeeded in turning into a vigorous tool of the abolitionist movement. Although politics had become the central focus of Whittier's life, his boyhood love of poetry had not abated.

The Political Poet In 1838, Whittier's first authorized collection of poetry, called *Poems*, which was published in Philadelphia. Included in this collection is some of his most heartfelt arguments, such as "Clerical Oppressors," a poem attacking the hypocrisy of the Southern clergy in lending the support of Christianity to the slave system. In such poems as "Stanzas," Whittier noted the irony of America's apparent commitment to slavery in light of its historic dedication to freedom.

Though he remained politically active, the publication in 1843 of *Lays of My Home* marked his return to the poetic treatment of regional materials. Included in this collection are "The Merrimack," which treats the local scenery with the touch of the pastoral landscape artist; "The Ballad of Cassandra Southwick," which explores New England history; and "The Funeral Tree of the Sokokis," which is based on Indian lore. The near relation of Whittier's regional and abolitionist poetry is indicated, not only in the consistent advocacy of tolerance and brotherhood in the regional poems, but also in the appeal to New England pride that so often forms the basis of his anti-slavery expressions. The finest poem of this sort, "Massachusetts to Virginia," makes its appearance in this volume. After the overwhelming enthusiasm of the 1830s had dissipated in division and anger within the anti-slavery ranks, Whittier was able, during the next two decades, to maintain a healthier, more mature balance between his commitments to poetry and reform.

The Lyrical Abolitionist In 1846, Whittier published his last collection of anti-slavery poems, *Voices of Freedom*, and in 1847, brought out a collection of prose sketches entitled *The Supernaturalism of New England*.

The decade of the 1850s opened with a shock. On the seventh of March 1850, U.S. Secretary of State Daniel Webster affirmed his support of compromise with the Southern slave power. Whittier, shocked and saddened by the unexpected defection of this former reformer,

LITERARY AND HISTORICAL CONTEMPORARIES

Whittier's famous contemporaries include:

Henry Clay (1777–1852): American politician, Clay, helped form the now-defunct Whig political party and co-founded the American Colonization Society. Whittier was an early supporter of Clay but was a staunch opponent of the American Colonization Society, which sought to send freed slaves to Africa.

Nathaniel Hawthorne (1804–1864): Hawthorne was a New England writer whose stories often included supernatural themes. One of his most famous works is the novel *The Scarlet Letter* (1850).

Abraham Lincoln (1809–1865): The sixteenth president of the United States, Lincoln led the country during the bloody American Civil War (1861–1865) between the North and the South. Lincoln also played a crucial role in the abolition of slavery when he issued the Emancipation Proclamation (1863), which called for the freeing of slaves in Confederate territories in the South.

Oliver Wendell Holmes (1809–1894): Holmes was an American doctor and writer who became one of the most beloved poets of the nineteenth century. His enduring works include "The Last Leaf" and "Old Ironsides."

Walt Whitman (1819–1892): Whitman was a poet famed for his rather radical poetic style and subject matter. He is best known for his collection *Leaves of Grass* (1855), which he revised and updated throughout his life.

"The Garrison of Cape Ann," and "The Swan Song of Parson Avery." All of these poems were first collected in *Home Ballads and Poems*, published in 1860. One of the volume's very few hints that a civil war was coming was the poem Whittier wrote in response to John Brown's raid on Harper's Ferry, "Brown of Ossawatomie."

Whittier's Quaker pacifism did not prevent him from being an ardent supporter of the Union cause when the American Civil War broke out. He admired Abraham Lincoln and was particularly proud of having voted for him four times, as a citizen and as an elector in 1860 and 1864. He wrote a number of patriotic poems during the war, of which "Barbara Frietchie" is certainly the most famous. *In War Time and Other Poems*, published in November 1863, contained several better examples of Whittier's public poetry, in addition to several more "home ballads." This volume was reissued in 1865 under the title, *National Lyrics*, and included "Laus Deo," in which Whittier joyously recorded the death-knell of slavery, the moment for which so much of his career had been a preparation.

Achieving Success With the war over and slavery outlawed, a part of Whittier's public life came to a close. Whittier's whole mood was retrospective as he set to work on "Snow-Bound," his masterpiece, published in February 1866. The poem recalls a winter storm at the old Whittier homestead when the poet was a child. A day and a night of driving snow had transformed everything, and the threat of isolation, of freezing or starving, is countered by the family at the wood fire on the hearth, the warmth of which is a symbol of life and family affection. The poem was Whittier's first genuine commercial success, as well as his most complete artistic success. He earned $10,000 from the sale of the first edition and was never to want for money again.

The Tent on the Beach and Other Poems, which followed a year later, continued the success. "The Wreck of the Rivermouth," "The Changeling," and "Abraham Davenport"—all first collected in this volume—show Whittier's abiding fondness for legendary and historical New England material, while "The Eternal Goodness" and "Our Master" indicate the new importance, which the liberal religious tradition of the Quakers was coming to assume, in his later poetry.

The remainder of the poet's long life was spent quietly and uneventfully in Amesbury and, after 1876, in a spacious home in Danvers, Massachusetts. He continued to write, almost up to the time of his death. Whittier's last book of poems, *At Sundown*, was privately printed in 1890 for close friends and was reissued for the public, with additions, at about the time of the poet's death on September 7, 1892. Whittier's reputation was never higher than at the time of his death. For years his birthdays had virtually been public holidays and were marked by celebrations throughout New England and the West. Whittier was essentially a public poet, a poet speaking to a large segment of the American people.

responded with his powerful protest poem "Ichabod." Whittier's books of poetry were appearing at fairly regular intervals, but sales continued to be moderate at best. In 1850, *Songs of Labor, and Other Poems* appeared and included not only "Ichabod," but also "Calef at Boston," "On Receiving a Quill…," and the series of occupational poems that gives the volume its title. Two more volumes of poetry followed by 1856.

From the Political to the Personal An important turn in Whittier's career occurred in 1857. The founding of the *Atlantic Monthly* in that year gave him a forum where he appeared regularly with all the most prominent writers of New England. His contributions to the earliest issues were better poems than he had ever written. The poetry of this period shows Whittier's increasing disengagement from broadly political issues. His attention was turning more and more to his own personal past, as shown in the nostalgic, quasi-autobiographical poems "Telling the Bees" and "My Playmate"; he was also increasingly drawn to the larger, but still personal past, of New England history, as shown in the many fine ballads that he wrote at this time, including "Skipper Ireson's Ride,"

Works in Literary Context

Abolitionist Literature   In the nineteenth century, members of the anti-slavery abolitionist movement made a considerable cultural, political, and social impact through the literature they published. Abolitionist literature spanned the forms of poetry, autobiography, literary fiction, and essay. While the literary movement achieved prominence during the nineteenth century, its roots can be traced back to the previous century during the Age of Enlightenment, the era in which human rights issues arose. The seeds of anti-slavery sentiments can be found sporadically in certain examples of English poetry and literature of the late 1700s, such as Thomas Chatterton's poems, the *African Eclogues* (1770). The most memorable, influential, and focused examples of abolitionist literature would arise during the nineteenth century in America, as former slaves, such as Harriet Tubman, Frederick Douglass, and Sojourner Truth provided harrowing, but literate, first-person accounts of their own experiences as slaves. White abolitionists, such as Whittier, expressed their anti-slavery stance in poetry and prose at this time.

Pastoral Poetry   As the term applies to literature and poetry, a "pastoral" is a work concerned with rural subject matter, which is often romanticized to an almost fantastical degree. The pastoral poem dates back to the ancient Greek poet Theocritus, whose poems were structured as dialogues between animal herders. The folksy simplicity and celebration of farm-life present in Theocritus's poems inspired other poets of the period to mimic his style, and a longstanding poetic genre was born. However, the first English-language pastoral would not appear until the early sixteenth century when the Scottish poet Alexander Barclay composed his *Eclogues*. For the next two hundred years, the pastoral was a tradition in English-language poetry. As a formal genre, the pastoral came to an end in the early eighteenth century, around the time Alexander Pope wrote his *Pastorals* (1709). Afterward, the pastoral persisted informally, but elements of the genre were still strongly felt in such works as Whittier's "Snow-Bound."

Works in Critical Context

Voices of Freedom   A collection of Whittier's strong anti-slavery sentiments, *Voices of Freedom* (1846) was typically judged by its political content as much as its poetic content. William J. Long writes in his book *Outlines of English and American Literature* (1917) that the collection represents Whittier as "no longer an echo but a voice, a man's voice, shouting above a tumult," but said of the poems contained therein that, "it was inevitable that his reform lyrics should fall into neglect with the occasions that called them forth. They are interesting now not as poems but as sidelights on a

---

COMMON HUMAN EXPERIENCE

Whittier's poem "Clerical Oppressors" was a powerful statement of abolitionist beliefs. Other anti-slavery works include:

"The Bereaved Mother" (1845), a poem by Jesse Hutchinson. Hutchinson's moving poem is a lament for the mother who grieves for her enslaved child. The poem chillingly details the tortures and humiliations the bereaved mother witnesses.

The Bigot Fire (1848), a poem by George Latimer. Latimer's poem draws a direct correlation between slavery and the bigotry that fanned its flames.

"I Am an Abolitionist" (1848), a song by William Lloyd Garrison. Set to the tune of the popular song "Auld Lang Syne," Garrison's is a celebratory exclamation of pride from an abolitionist. Each stanza begins with the title exclamation, driving its political point home unashamedly.

"Your Brother Is a Slave" (1848), a poem by D. H. Jaques. Jaques's concise three-stanza poem is a plea to those who espouse America's freedoms and the word of God to recognize the inhumanity of slavery.

---

critical period of our history." Regardless of this "inevitability," Long comments that "[t]here is a fine swinging rhythm in these poems" and more provocatively that "[i]f words could kill a man, these surely are the words." He also reserves special praise for the Daniel Webster-attacking "Ichabod," describing it as "the most powerful poem of its kind in our language" though also "fearfully unjust to Webster."

"Snow-Bound"   Still remembered as Whittier's finest poem, the pastoral "Snow-Bound" continues to stir poetry lovers. At the time of its publication, an assessment in *The North American Review* stated that the work was "a very real and very refined pleasure. It is true to nature and local coloring, pure in sentiment, quietly deep in feeling, and full of those simple touches that show the poetic eye and the trained hand." William J. Long describes the poem as a "masterpiece" and suggests that the "beautiful idyl placed him in the front rank of American poets." The poem's simplicity, grace, and sublime evocativeness have endured through the ages. In 2003, Linda Sue Grimes wrote in *American Poetry*, "The charm of the poem captivates the reader and shows the beauty that Whittier was able to relate."

Responses to Literature

1. While much of Whittier's early poetry was concerned with social issues, his most famous work is "Snow-Bound," which is personal and pastoral. Read

"Snow-Bound" and his earlier work "Clerical Oppressors." Do you notice anything in these two very different poems that link them both to the same creator? Explain your answer in a brief essay.

2. During the American Civil War, Whittier wrote a poem called "Barbara Frietchie." Read the poem; then explain what message you think Whittier is trying to convey through the poem. Support your response with examples from the poem.

3. Whittier wrote his poem, "Ichabod," as a criticism of Daniel Webster, a politician who was willing to compromise on the issue of slavery. Read the poem, and then explain what you think Whittier is trying to say about Webster. Support your response with specific details from the poem.

BIBLIOGRAPHY

Books

Bennet, Whitman. *Whittier: Bard of Freedom.* Chapel Hill, N.C.: University of North Carolina Press, 1941.

Carpenter, George Rice. *John Greenleaf Whittier.* Boston: Houghton, Mifflin, 1903.

Higginson, Thomas Wentworth. *John Greenleaf Whittier.* New York: Macmillan, 1902.

Long, William Joseph. *Outlines of English and American Literature.* Boston: Ginn and Company, 1917.

Mordell, Albert. *Quaker Militant: John Greenleaf Whittier.* Boston: Houghton, Mifflin, 1933.

Pollard, John A. *John Greenleaf Whittier: Friend of Man.* Boston, Mass: Houghton, Mifflin, 1949.

Periodicals

Grimes, Linda Sue. "Snow-Bound." *American Poetry* (March 31, 2003).

Hall, Donald. "Whittier." *Texas Quarterly* 3 (Autumn 1960): 165–174.

"Whittier's Snow-Bound." *The North American Review* (April 1866): 631–632.

Web Sites

Poets.org. *John Greenleaf Whittier.* Accessed December 5, 2008, from http://www.poets.org/poet.php/prmPID/720.

✸ John Edgar Wideman

BORN: *1946, Washington, D.C.*

NATIONALITY: *American*

GENRE: *Fiction*

MAJOR WORKS:

The Hiding Place (1981)

Sent for You Yesterday (1983)

Brothers and Keepers (1995)

John Edgar Wideman   *Wideman, John Edgar, photograph. © Jerry Bauer. Reproduced by permission.*

Overview

John Edgar Wideman is best known for his novels and short stories set in the town of Homewood, the working-class, predominantly black neighborhood near Pittsburgh, Pennsylvania, where he was raised. The overarching theme of his fiction is the individual's quest for self-discovery. In his later works this general theme is expressed through an exploration of memory and a focus on more specifically African American issues. Kermit Frazier has commented that the "characters in Wideman's fiction can escape neither collective nor personal history and memory, so they are forced to deal with them in some way—be it successfully or ineffectually."

Works in Biographical and Historical Context

Rhodes Scholar Wideman was born in 1946 in Washington, D.C., though he grew up in Pittsburgh, Pennsylvania. His youth was spent during a time of unrest and increased agitation for civil rights in America. During the 1950s and 1960s, the civil rights movement spurred reforms to end racial discrimination against African Americans in the United States. The turmoil of growing up in the inner city prompted Wideman to excel at school and in sports. After graduation from Peabody High School in Pittsburgh, Wideman attended the University of Pennsylvania on a basketball scholarship where he became an All-American forward for the team. In 1963, he was selected as the first black Rhodes scholar—since 1905, a highly prized international award for postgraduate study at the University of Oxford. In England, he attended Oxford and studied eighteenth-century European literature and the early development of the novel. In 1965 he was married to Judith Ann Goldman, an attorney, with whom he has three children. After graduating from Oxford in 1966, Wideman was awarded a fellowship to the University of Iowa Writer's Workshop for creative writing.

His first two novels, *A Glance Away* (1967) and *Hurry Home* (1969), reflect his formal training, as well as his own experiments with narrative technique. In *A Glance Away*, a rehabilitated drug addict returns to his home, where he renews family and social ties while trying to avoid relapse; in *Hurry Home*, a black law school graduate seeks cultural communion with white society by traveling to Europe, then reaffirms his black heritage in Africa. These characters find hope for the future only by confronting their personal and collective pasts. In *The Lynchers* (1973), four embittered African American men plan to kill a white policeman in hopes of sparking widespread racial conflict; they are defeated, however, by their own hatred and distrust of one another.

Shifting Themes Wideman has attributed his shift toward black-oriented themes and increased use of myth and dialect in his later novels to his growing awareness of such prominent black authors as Richard Wright and Jean Toomer. In *The Homewood Trilogy*, which comprises the short story collection *Damballah* (1981) and the novels *Hiding Place* (1981) and *Sent for You Yesterday* (1983), Wideman uses deviating time frames, black dialect, and rhythmic language to transform Homewood into what Alan Cheuse described as "a magical location infused with poetry and pathos." *Hiding Place*, published simultaneously with *Damballah*, is about a boy's strong ties to his family and his involvement in a petty robbery that results in an accidental killing. With *Sent for You Yesterday*, Wideman won the 1984 PEN/Faulkner Award for fiction. Through the characters of Doot, the primary narrator, and Albert Wilkes, an outspoken blues pianist, Wideman asserts that creativity and imagination are important means to transcend despair and strengthen the common bonds of race, culture, and class.

The year 1986 brought much upheaval to the Wideman family when his eighteen-year-old son was involved in a camping trip murder in Arizona, for which he was later convicted. Perhaps reflecting this turmoil, Wideman's novel *Reuben* (1987) deals with violence and the legal system. As the narrator, Reuben, an ambiguous figure who is a lawyer, provides inexpensive legal aid to the residents of Homewood. Among his clients are Kwansa, a young black woman whose brutal ex-husband, a recovering drug addict, kidnaps

and seeks legal custody of their illegitimate child; and Wally, an assistant basketball coach at a local university who comes to Reuben because he fears he will be blamed for the illegal recruiting practices of his department. Wally, who may have actually murdered a white man, is possessed by an ingrained hatred of white society that leads him to fantasize about committing violence against middle-aged white males. As Madison Smartt Bell notes, "[*Reuben*] is perhaps most importantly a detailed and sensitive portrait of the inner life of its characters."

In the novel *Philadelphia Fire* (1990), Wideman combines fact and fiction to explore an actual incident involving MOVE—a militant, heavily-armed black commune that had repeatedly refused police orders to vacate its house in Philadelphia in 1985. With the approval of the mayor, police bombed the house from a helicopter, killing eleven commune members—including five children—and creating a fire that destroyed more than fifty houses. In juxtaposition to the novel's narrative content, Wideman includes in *Philadelphia Fire* an address to his imprisoned son.

Continued Focus on Race and Community The *Cattle Killing* (1996) weaves together memories from the narrator's childhood in Philadelphia with the plight of blacks in the city in the late eighteenth century, as well as the story of the South African Xhosa tribe. Wideman's next novel, *Two Cities* (1998), incorporates elements from *A Tale of Two Cities* (1859), a historical novel by Charles Dickens that follows characters in Paris and London

COMMON HUMAN EXPERIENCE

Wideman's novels and memoirs are written with innovative narratives that bring to light the tensions involved in the heritage of enslavement and abuse that has been the experience of African Americans. Some other works that deal with the dilemma of coming to terms with familial and communal heritage are:

The Piano Lesson (1936), a play by August Wilson (1945–2005). This play tells the story of an African American family grappling with their painful legacy.

The Fire Next Time (1963), a novel by James Baldwin (1984–1987). Baldwin's text, based on a slave song based on the Bible, expresses concern for young black men.

The Souls of Black Folk (1903), a multi-genre work by W.E.B. DuBois. In this complex, and multilayered work, DuBois articulates the dilemma of African Americans living in a state of "double-consciousness."

Live from Death Row (1995), a memoir by Mumia Abu Jamal. Jamal, sentenced to death for the 1981 killing of a police officer, records his memories and experiences while imprisoned on death row.

Breaking Ice (1990), an anthology edited by Terry McMillan. This collection contains work by both established and emerging African-American authors.

during the French Revolution. In Wideman's novel—set in Philadelphia and Pittsburgh—the author tells the story of Kassima, a woman who is tentatively stepping back into a social life after the grief of losing two sons to gang-related crime and an imprisoned husband to AIDS.

In 2001, following the end of his first marriage, Wideman published the memoir *Hoop Roots: Basketball, Race, and Love* (2001). In an interview with Lisa Baker in the *African American Review*, Wideman describes this book as a study of race and culture. *God's Gym* (2005), published the year after his marriage to journalist Catherine Nedonchelle, continues the exploration of race and community in a collection of short stories. The ten stories delve into topics spanning from family and basketball to illness and death, and are written in a style that weaves jazz rhythms with dreamlike, stream-of-consciousness style, wandering seemingly far from the original story, but eventually resolving back to the starting elements.

Wideman's latest novel, *Fanon* (2008), mixes fiction, biography, and memoir to tell the story of Franz Fanon—a psychiatrist, philosopher, revolutionary, and author of *Black Skin, White Masks* (1952)—told through three narratives. Besides writing a string of novels and nonfiction works, he frequently pens commentaries for *Harper's*. Novelist Charles Johnson called Wideman "easily the most acclaimed black male writer of the last decade," and the renowned critic, Robert Bone, author of *The Negro Novel in America*, designates Wideman as "perhaps the most gifted black novelist of his generation."

Works in Literary Context

According to Reggie Young, "African American writers... are generally so well defined as social realists that few critics take them seriously as practitioners of what some call 'extreme fiction'—that is, fiction that treads non-traditional formal territories." In his innovative and modernist writing, Wideman offers modern prose that illustrates the alienation and loss resulting from conflicting demands that self and community make upon the individual in contemporary America, with special emphasis on his native African American community. This is especially evident in Wideman's exploration of the relationship between the writer, his family, and the larger community.

Social Dichotomy Wideman's writing exposes the tensions between the individual and the community. His characters negotiate the terrain between independence and the necessity of interdependence in familial and communal connections. In his writing, as in his life, Wideman deals with alienation from those with whom he has close ties. Yet, *Brothers and Keepers*, written during encounters with his imprisoned brother, exemplifies interdependence and connection, through the very act of writing. Contrasting his brotherly relationship with Robby coexisting with an estrangement, he writes in the book, "So Robby and I faced each other in the prison visiting lounge as familiar strangers." In another of his books, *Philadelphia Fire*, Wideman exposes the distance of his life as a successful academic, from that of his family and community, resolved when the protagonist returns from a Greek isle to rejoin his Philadelphia community that has been violated by a bomb.

African American Academic Wideman's compositions are frequently autobiographical, though they are fictionalized and thus semi-autobiographical. In Wideman's work, James Marcus contends that there has been a struggle with "the question: What kind of fiction does a black man write from the predominantly white groves of academe?" Wideman has faced in his writing what he has acknowledged as the multiple traditions that ground his work, European and Afro-American, the Academy and the Street. His ability to mediate between these cultures in his writing lends uniqueness to his voice. Through his memoirs and other works of fiction, Wideman offers readers personal insight into minority culture and the way in which the harsh experience of racism transforms the members of those communities. While telling very personal stories that are particular to his cultural milieu, he strikes cords of universality that speak to a wide audience extending beyond the boundaries of culture.

Works in Critical Context

Critic Keith Byerman questions why Wideman's writing "has not received the attention given to other contemporary writers despite the quality and range of his work." A response to that question may be as Bonnie TuSmith comments, "No one claims that Wideman is an easy read. On the contrary, the writer challenges his readers on every level." Christopher Weber writes of Wideman, "He has brilliantly extended the long-running emphasis among African American writers on rendering black speech and rhythms. His prose can be scanned like poetry or, better, performed as a song or slam before a microphone." No matter what genre he uses primarily in any given work, most of Wideman's books are what James Olney has identified as metaphors of self through thinly veiled autobiographical fictional depictions, described as "the mingling of fiction and nonfiction."

Sent for You Yesterday Wideman's PEN/Faulkner winning novel *Sent for You Yesterday* (1983) is the last in his Homewood trilogy. Mbalia comments that it "brings together into one whole all the pieces of Wideman's family history to show the connection between and within generations" and the responsiblities of each generation. The African tradition, emphasizing continuity of family, is illustrated in Wideman's novel with the question posed, "How come you a family man?" In response to the question from his single friend, a father evokes, "an image of a man's love for his family that is profoundly moving in its simplicity and accuracy" according to TuSmith and Byerman. Wideman's further uses music in *Sent for You Yesterday* to bridge the distance between generations of his family. With music and lyrical prose, he juggles bits of memories and emotions in search of understanding of and identity with his heritage.

Hoop Roots: Basketball, Race, and Love Wideman, in an interview with Lisa Baker in the *African American Review*, said of his book *Hoop Roots: Basketball, Race, and Love* that it is "really a study of race and culture—using sport as a way of getting people's attention." *Hoop Roots* follows Wideman's "lifelong love affair with basketball," comments David L. Ulin in the *Atlantic Monthly*, at times "yielding to reflections on family, racial tension, memory, and the nebulous territory of storytelling itself." A *Publishers Weekly* reviewer calls the book a "brilliant tribute to basketball, survival and families linked by blood, joy, and tragedy." Tracy Grant, a reviewer for *Black Issues Book Review*, finds the book a challenge to read because of Wideman's free-flowing style, but comments that *Hoop Roots* demonstrates Wideman's "unique voice and his true gift for capturing a slice of black life from the past."

Responses to Literature

1. Read *Sent for You Yesterday*. How does Wideman use shifts in time to convey the story? Why do you think Wideman uses this technique?

2. In *Sent for You Yesterday*, how does the story illustrate the fragility of life and relationships?

3. Read *Hoop Roots: Basketball, Race, and Love*. How does the title relate to Wideman's memoir? Why do you think the author chose this title for his remembrance?

4. Using the Internet and your library, research the incidents that inspired *Philadelphia Fire*. Who were the participants in this historical incident? Why was violence used? Describe what you believe is the author's view of the event?

BIBLIOGRAPHY

Books

Byerman, Keith. *John Edgar Wideman: A Study of Short Fiction.* New York: Twayne, 1998.

Mbalia, Doreatha. Drummond *John Edgar Wideman: Reclaiming the African Personality.* Cranberry, N.Y.: Associated University Presses, 1995.

TuSmith, Bonnie, and Keith E. Byerman Eds. *Critical Essays on John Edgar Wideman.* Knoxville, Tenn.: University of Tennessee Press, 2006.

TuSmith, Bonnie. Ed. *Conversations with John Edgar Wideman.* Jackson, Miss.: University Press of Mississippi, 1998.

Periodicals

Baker, Lisa. "Storytelling and Democracy: A Conversation with John Edgar Wideman." *African American Review* 34.2 (2000): 263–272.

James, Marcus. "The Homewood trilogy: Damballah. Hiding place. Sent for you yesterday." *The Nation* 243 (October 4, 1986): 321–323.

Law, Violet. "John Edgar Wideman." *The Progressive* 72.4 (April 2008): 33–36.

Pearsall, Susan. "Narratives of Self and the Abdication of Authority in Wideman's Philadelphia Fire." *MELUS* 26.2 (2001): 15–46.

Varsava, Jerry. "The Quest for Community in American Postmodern Fiction." *International Fiction Review* 243 (January 2003): 1–11.

Web Sites

Basketball, Race, and Love. Retrieved December 5, 2008, from www.alternet.org/story/15704/?page=entire. Last updated on April 22, 2003.

⊛ Richard Wilbur

BORN: *1921, New York City*

NATIONALITY: *American*

GENRE: *Poetry*

MAJOR WORKS:
Things of This World (1956)
New and Collected Poems (1988)
Collected Poems (2004)

Richard Wilbur   *Wilbur, Richard, 1954, photograph. AP Images.*

Overview

Richard Wilbur has long been recognized as a major literary talent and as an important man of letters—a poet, critic, translator, and editor. Wilbur, a two-time Pulitzer Prize winner, has said of his poetry that it was not until World War II "that I began to versify in earnest. One does not use poetry for its major purposes, as a means of organizing oneself and the world, until one's world somehow gets out of hand." His poetry published in *Things of This World* (1957) was honored with a Pulitzer Prize and a National Book Award. Wilbur, additionally, has excelled as a translator of Molière (1622–1673), a French dramatist celebrated for his comedies, and of Jean Racine (1639–1699), a preeminent French tragedian. His translation of Moliere's *Tartuffe* (1964), televised in 1971 and 1978, has become the foremost of the English versions of the play.

Works in Biographical and Historical Context

Child Poet   Richard Wilbur was born in New York City, one of two children of Lawrence L. and Helen Purdy Wilbur. His father was a portrait painter. When Wilbur was two years old, the family moved to a pre-Revolutionary stone house in North Caldwell, New Jersey. Although he did not live far from New York City, he and his brother,

Lawrence, grew up in rural surroundings, which, he later speculated, led to his love of nature.

Wilbur showed an early interest in writing, which he has attributed to his mother's family, because her father was an editor of the *Baltimore Sun* and her grandfather was an editor and a publisher of small papers aligned with the Democratic party. At Montclair High School, from which he graduated in 1938, Wilbur wrote editorials for the school newspaper. At Amherst College he was editor of the campus newspaper, the *Amherst Student*. He also contributed stories and poems to the Amherst student magazine, the *Touchstone*, and considered a career in journalism.

Marriage and World War II   Immediately after his graduation in June 1942, Wilbur married Charlotte Hayes Ward of Boston, an alumna of Smith College. It was a time of war, the United States having just recently joined the Allied Forces as an active participant fighting against the Axis Powers of Germany, Italy, and Japan. As a member of the Enlisted Reserve Corps, Wilbur went on active duty in the army in 1943, in the midst of World War II, and served overseas with the 36th (Texas) Division, first in Italy at Monte Cassino, later at Anzio, then along the Siegfried Line in Germany. It was during the war that he began writing poems, as he later said, borrowing Robert Frost's phrase, as "a momentary stay against confusion" in a time of disorder. When the war ended, he found himself with a drawer full of poems, only one of which had been published.

Prized Poet   Wilbur went to Harvard University for graduate work in English to become a college teacher, and he decided to submit additional poems for publication only after a French friend read his manuscripts, "kissed me on both cheeks and said, 'You're a poet!'" as Wilbur said in a 1970 interview. In 1947, the year he received his master's from Harvard, his first volume of poems, *The Beautiful Changes and Other Poems* (1947), appeared.

With the appearance of his second book of poems, *Ceremony and Other Changes* (1950), Wilbur was appointed an assistant professor of English at Harvard, where he remained until 1954, living in Lincoln, Massachusetts, with his wife and three (later four) children. He spent the academic year 1952–1953 in New Mexico on a Guggenheim Fellowship to write a poetic drama. When his attempts at a play did not work out to his satisfaction, he turned to translating Molière's *Le Misanthrope* (1666) instead, beginning his distinguished career as a translator. A grant from the Prix de Rome permitted Wilbur to live at the American Academy in Rome for a year. On his return to America, his translation of *The Misanthrope* (1955) was published and performed at the Poets' Theatre in Cambridge, Massachusetts.

In 1954 Wilbur was appointed an associate professor of English at Wellesley College, where he taught until 1957. His third volume of poetry, *Things of This World* (1956), was published and was his most honored book: he received the Edna St. Vincent Millay Memorial Award, the National Book Award, and the Pulitzer Prize. That same year a musical version of Voltaire's *Candide* (1759), with lyrics by Wilbur, book by Lillian Hellman, and score by Leonard Bernstein was produced in 1957 at the Martin Beck Theater in New York City.

Televised Translation In 1957 Wilbur began a long tenure as professor of English at Wesleyan University and as advisor for the Wesleyan Poetry Series. He received a Ford Foundation grant in drama and worked with the Alley Theater in Houston. *Advice to a Prophet and Other Poems*, his fourth book of poetry, appeared in 1961, and his translation of Molière's *Tartuffe* (1963) earned him an award as corecipient of the Bollingen Poetry Translation Prize. The Lincoln Center Repertory Theatre brought his translation of *Tartuffe* to the stage in New York City in 1964. His collected poems, *The Poems of Richard Wilbur*, had appeared in 1963, and his fifth book of poetry, *Walking to Sleep: New Poems and Translations*, followed in 1969. In 1976 his sixth volume of poems, *The Mind-Reader*, was published, and in 1977 he moved to Smith College as writer-in-residence. He won a second Pulitzer Prize in 1989 for *New and Collected Poems* (1988), next publishing a book of poetry in 2004, *Collected Poems, 1943–2004*. A Chancellor Emeritus of The Academy of American Poets, Wilbur currently lives in Cummington, Massachusetts.

Works in Literary Context

The Poetry of Everyday Experience Wilbur's vigorous defense of traditional patterns, metrics, and rhyme early on achieved accolades for him as he poeticized to express "the splendor of mere being." As the chaotic times of the 1960s evolved, there was less critical approval of his "controlled" poetry. He continued, though, to compose his delicate verse, making poetry of the mundane—as in "A Hole in the Floor," which alludes to the archeological discovery of Troy. Wilbur's praise for being and nature is heard in his tributes to crickets ("Cigales") and love ("Love Calls Us to the Things of This World"). A reviewer for the *Washington Post* comments, "Throughout his career Wilbur has shown, within the compass of his classicism, enviable variety. His poems describe fountains and fire trucks, grasshoppers and toads, European cities and country pleasures."

American Realists and Experimentation Following World War II, American writers and poets began to create innovative and self-aware works reflexively shaped by and shaping the texture of popular culture. From stylistic abstractions of matters elite, poetry increasingly employed exactness of observed detail that reflected influences of lives of the masses. Wilbur's poetry, though maintaining elements of traditional poetic form, echoes this realism in aspects of his poems, such as "The Pardon" (1947) where he recounts the death of his dog.

Works in Critical Context

Wilbur has always been recognized as a major literary talent but he has never quite been ranked as one of the two or three best contemporary American poets. Early in his career he was overshadowed as a poet by Robert Lowell, who won the Pulitzer Prize for *Lord Weary's Castle* in 1947 (the year Wilbur's first book of poems, *The Beautiful Changes and Other Poems*, was published) and whose *Life Studies* (1959) was given principal credit for important new directions in poetry that Wilbur chose not to take. In the 1960s comparisons between Lowell and Wilbur gave way to comparisons between Lowell and James Dickey as the country's most important poets. Since the 1970s, more critical attention has been given to such poets as John Ashbery, A. R. Ammons, James Wright, W. S. Merwin, and James Merrill than to Wilbur.

Things of This World *Things of This World* (1956) is widely regarded as containing Wilbur's most mature, popular, and critically acclaimed work. Wilbur received both the National Book Award and the Pulitzer Prize for Poetry for the collection. Horace Gregory, in his critique for *Partisan Review*, concludes with his conviction "that *Things of This World* will be regarded by many as the best single book of poems published this year; and I believe that Wilbur's charm should not be underrated." Anthony Hecht of the *New Republic* writes, "Wilbur's government

COMMON HUMAN EXPERIENCE

Wilbur's poetry conveys his expressed liking for the natural world. Other works that reflect a fondness for nature are:

Life Studies (1959), a poetry collection by Robert Lowell. This collection is considered a watershed in its dramatic turn toward deeply personal work with a loosened adherence to meter and form.

Harmonium (1904), a poetry collection by American poet Wallace Stevens. Now considered a groundbreaking contribution to Modernism, this collection of poetry was not fully recognized until the last years of Stevens's life.

"Everything That Acts Is Actual" (1957), a poem by Denise Levertov. This work praises the wonder of life itself.

The Complete Poems of Emily Dickinson (1960), a poetry collection by Dickinson. This poet led a reclusive life and published very little, and her poems earned wide acclaim only after her death.

of his enormous resources" is what makes these poems triumph. Further analysis of Wilbur's poems by William Bell written for *America* emphasizes that *Things of This World* exemplifies Wilbur as "a poet of far-ranging and intriguing ideas, and one who practices the fusion of thought and feeling. The reader who takes up Wilbur embarks on exciting adventures of both mind and heart."

The Mind-Reader Anthony Hecht of the *New Republic* writes the following about "The Mind-Reader," the long title poem of Wilbur's collection of the same name: "This new work bears all the hallmarks of excellence that have stamped Wilbur's previous work: a kinetic imagination that is rare among poets, as well as an unusually rich and fertile gift for metaphor." Charles Woodward writes of the work in *Contemporary Poetry*, "Between the two poles of sensation and knowledge, Wilbur's mind functions as mediator." Wilbur's poetry recalls that the mind's reflections are not less "substantial or valid than the objects of its perceptions." To the critics who fault the classicism of Wilbur, Rebecca Faery writes, "The technical virtuosity is dazzling…his polish and craftsmanship enable him to use traditional forms without their seeming stale or dated. It is a delight to read Wilbur's work, and to discover that pleasure is still a legitimate aim of poetry."

Responses to Literature

1. Read *The Beautiful Changes*. Cite three examples of how the title of the collection relates to individual poems. What is the author's point of view toward change?

2. Read *A Baroque Wall Fountain in the Villa Sciarra*. Compare the fountains that are described in this poem. How do these fountains relate to the poetic themes of pleasure and joy, acceptance and transcendence?

3. After reading "The Mind-Reader," review the lines, "I am not/Permitted to forget." What do these lines reveal about the speaker's idea of himself?

BIBLIOGRAPHY

Books

Ellmann, Doug and Robert O'Clair, eds. *The Norton Anthology of Modern Poetry*. New York: W. W. Norton, 1973, pp. 1000-1010.

Engle, Paul and Joseph Langland, eds. *Poet's Choice*. New York: Dial Press, 1962.

Rosenthal, M. L. *The Modern Poets*. Oxford: Oxford University Press, 1960.

Periodicals

Bell, William F. "At Play on the Shore: Richard Wilbur" *America* 171 (October 15, 1994): 18–21.

Faery, Rebecca B. "The Mind Reader: New Poems." *Hollins Critic* 14.2 (April 1977): 15–16

Gregory, Horace. "The Poetry of Suburbia." *Partisan Review* 13 (Fall 1956): 545–553.

Hecht, Anthony. "Master of Metaphor." *The New Republic* 2 (May 16, 1988): 23–32.

Woodward, Charles R. "Richard Wilbur's Critical Condition" *Contemporary Poetry: A Journal of Criticism* 2 (Autumn 1977): 16–24.

Web Sites

Poets.org: from the Academy of American Poets. *Richard Wilbur*. Retrieved November 29, 2008 from http://www.poets.org/poet.php/prmPID/202.

✸ Laura Ingalls Wilder

BORN: *1867, Pepin, Wisconsin*

DIED: *1957, Mansfield, Missouri*

NATIONALITY: *American*

GENRE: *Fiction*

MAJOR WORKS:
Little House in the Big Woods (1932)
Little House on the Prairie (1935)
Little Town on the Prairie (1941)
On the Banks of Plum Creek (1937)

Overview

Laura Ingalls Wilder is one of the best-known and beloved American writers of literature for children. Her "Little House" series, which chronicles her childhood as a pioneer in nineteenth-century America, has earned her popular and critical praise since its publication in the

Laura Ingalls Wilder   © *Bettmann / Corbis.*

1930s and 1940s; the books continue to be popular with today's children. Her historically accurate stories combine storytelling with autobiography, both entertaining children and contributing to their knowledge of American history and the conditions pioneers faced while settling the Midwest and plains.

Works in Biographical and Historical Context

Indian Country and Dakota Homestead   Wilder was born February 7, 1867, in Pepin, Wisconsin, to Charles Philip Ingalls, a carpenter, and Caroline Lake Quiner, a former schoolteacher. Wilder's father favored living close to the edge of the frontier where he did not have to suffer the influence of his neighbors. When Wilder was one year old, the family journeyed west to Missouri and then to Kansas, settling in "Indian Country." The family was stricken with malaria and accosted by Native Americans. In 1871, the Ingalls were informed that they were trespassing on native lands and were forced to move back to Wisconsin. Several years later, after suffering devastating setbacks, the family moved to Burr Oak, Iowa, where they managed a hotel before returning to Walnut Grove, Minnesota. Taking advantage of the Homestead Act of 1862—which granted land to families who built a house and

resided on the land for at least six months each year for five years—the Wilder family ventured to De Smet in what became South Dakota. Initially, the Ingalls family dwelled in a small house during the summer and wintered in town.

Teacher at Fifteen   In 1882, at the age of fifteen, Wilder earned her teacher's certificate and moved to a nearby settlement to teach school. She was forced to reside with a local family, an experience made difficult by her landlady's constant depression. During the next three years, Wilder taught school and courted Almanzo James Wilder, a local homesteader, ten years her senior. In 1885, the two married and in 1886, their daughter Rose was born. Disaster struck the family repeatedly: a son died in 1889; Almanzo and Laura contracted diphtheria, forcing them to send their daughter to Minnesota to stay with relatives; Almanzo suffered a debilitating stroke as a result of the diphtheria; crops failed; and their house burned. Between 1889 and 1894, the family lived with Wilder's in-laws in Minnesota, resided in Florida for two years, and returned to De Smet. However, after saving one hundred dollars, the family relocated to Mansfield, Missouri. Here, Wilder and her husband slowly built a more stable and prosperous life.

Published at Sixty-Five   Following her daughter's departure to pursue a successful career as a writer and journalist, and as economic pressures increased with the loss of the family investments in the Wall Street Crash of 1929, Wilder began writing her stories. Her first attempt was *Pioneer Girl*, a first person account of her life, which was rejected by publishers. With the help of her daughter, Rose, Wilder revised her style, shifting to third person and broadening her focus to encompass her entire family. In 1932, while the United States was in the midst of a severe economic downturn known as the Great Depression, her first book, *Little House in the Big Woods*, was published. Publishers counted on the book, which chronicled a simple and more self-sufficient time, to appeal to Depression-era readers; they were right. The next year, she published *Farmer Boy* (1933), an account of her husband's youth in rural New York, before returning to the developing story of her own childhood.

The best known of the Little House books is probably *Little House on the Prairie* (1935), after which the television series was named. The series ran from September 1974 to March 1983 and introduced a new generation of young readers to the books. The semi-autobiographical novel is comprised of events that actually occurred in Wilder's life before those outlined in her first novel; however, exercising creative license, Wilder alters the order of events.

Wilder published five additional books in the series between 1937 and 1943. In 1949 her husband died, leaving Wilder alone on their farm, spending her days answering fan mail. After several heart attacks, Wilder died on her farm in Missouri on February 10, 1957. During her life, she garnered several awards, including

LITERARY AND HISTORICAL CONTEMPORARIES

Wilder's famous contemporaries include:

Edith Wharton (1862–1937): Wharton was an American author who was famed for documenting the lives of the upper class in works like *The House of Mirth* (1905) and *The Age of Innocence* (1920).

Katherine Anne Porter (1890–1980): Porter was an American writer best known for her novel *Ship of Fools* and the work *Flowering Judas* (1930), which showcased Porter's modernist style.

Willa Cather (1873–1947): Cather was an American novelist famous for her novels of the Great Plains, such as *O Pioneers!* (1913).

Sinclair Lewis (1885–1951): Lewis was an American novelist and winner of the 1930 Nobel Prize in Literature with particular note for his novel, *Babbitt* (1922).

William Faulkner (1897–1962): Faulkner was a Southern writer who won the Pulitzer Prize and is considered to be one of the greatest of all American writers. His works include *Light in August* (1932) and *The Reivers* (1962), which formed the basis of a feature film in 1969.

the first Laura Ingalls Wilder Medal from the American Library Association in 1954.

Works in Literary Context

In her writing, Wilder tells the story of her youth growing up on the American frontier realistically and without sentimentality. However, the books are not strictly autobiographical. Wilder edits her life story in order to create a coherent storyline and promote her interpretation of American history. Although she does not shy away from difficult subjects such as grave illnesses, her sister's blindness, drought and plague, she omits both her brother and her son's deaths as infants.

American Ruralists After raising her family, Wilder became increasingly involved in farm organizations, serving on the Missouri Development Association and writing for the Missouri Ruralist and the St. Louis Star. Then, as the cultural and artistic exuberance of the Roaring Twenties, with its focus on modernity, ebbed with the 1930s economic downturn, the Wilder family suffered loss along with other Americans. However, with the turn in financial fortunes, Wilder found an audience for her stories of pioneering that featured a simple and family-centered rural life. Wilder wrote fondly of her memories as a girl being raised on the American frontier where honesty, hard work and enterprise were hallmarks of success. Wilder's attempt to faithfully transfer her experience into fictional forms met with success from the

masses who were reeling in the midst of a down-spiraling economy. The nature of Wilder's narratives and characters returned traditional values associated with rural life to the attention of readers. Her stress on the importance of self-reliance, family loyalty, understanding, compassion, and, most importantly, determination, innovation and hard work met with popular interest. Wilder's best-selling novels described life fraught with danger but nonetheless a simpler life in which gifts were handmade and where family companionship and her father's fiddle music provided nightly entertainment.

Mother and Daughter Team Wilder's works are based on her childhood experiences in the American frontier, though they are fictionalized accounts. It was only after Wilder's daughter, Rose, grew to adulthood and left home to become a writer that Wilder began writing her narratives. Then, during a trip west to see her daughter, Wilder began to work even more purposefully on improving her writing. After her return to Missouri, she and Rose exchanged letters regarding writing and Wilder's stories. However, it was not until the mid-1920s when Rose moved back to Missouri that Wilder began preparing her stories for publication. With Rose there to edit the manuscripts, Wilder novelized her memories. Rose and Wilder, sharing similar traditional values, worked together diligently to form narratives that educate young readers about historical conditions that led to the development of the United States as it now exists and to capture a time period that has vanished.

Works in Critical Context

Wilder encountered approval from her readers and critics with the publication of her first novel, approval which increased with the publication of each subsequent book. Scholars note that Wilder's plot and character development and the sophistication of the stories increase throughout the series. And noted children's author, E. B. White, states: "[Wilder] speaks to us directly and brings her affectionate memories alive by the power of overwhelming detail and with a dramatic force that derives from honesty and accuracy." However, other critics note that despite the appeal of Wilder's writing, the author is presenting a personal interpretation of the frontier and, given her editorializing of her life events, not a strictly accurate account, even of her own life. The most notable controversy surrounding Wilder's writing is the source. Scholars debate the extent to which Wilder's daughter, a famous and respected writer herself, contributed to her mother's books. While there is little doubt that Wilder's daughter edited her mother's writing, scholars concur that Wilder was the chief contributor.

Little House on the Prairie Little House on the Prairie begins with the Ingalls family leaving their comfortable home and making their way westward. The life of pioneering, though harsh, is an adventure that highlights the family and, comments Claire Fellman, "its ability to survive all kinds of crises on its own." This emphasis on the individualist and strong family reflected Wilder's strong opposition to the New Deal, which she saw as endangering the American farm families. Ann Romines critiques another political aspect of the novel, revealing that the characteristic of Ma as an Indian-hater gives voice to the fear and frustration that was felt on the frontier by the women who were not allowed to directly oppose the men. In contrast to her mother, Laura is sympathetic to the Indians. Janet Spaeth, in her perceptive study of Wilder's work, suggests in *Laura Ingalls Wilder* (1987) that Laura's response to the Indian baby signals that Laura has begun, "to be aware of the complexity of language, particularly its inadequacy as a means of relaying one's innermost feelings . . . ; the baby is, to her, a symbol of a part of herself that she does not know how to acknowledge. She has discovered an aspect of her own being that is inexpressible through language: it cannot be touched by the intellect, only by the heart."

The Long Winter Her novel *The Long Winter* (1940) was originally titled "The Hard Winter," but the publishers feared such a negative title might discourage young readers, so they insisted that Wilder change it. But the story of the way the Ingalls family and their fellow citizens of De Smet, Dakota Territory, survived the winter of 1880–1881 is based on historical fact. *The Long Winter* is considered to be among her finest writing; commentators praise her ability to evoke the mood of the endless snow and wind and the growing desperation of the characters. The main theme that emerges during the blizzard tale, as delineated by Anita Fellman, is that of the "sense of the family as a solitary unit." Rounding out that solitude of the family is the theme of its ability to thrive and prosper in the midst of harsh circumstances. Eileen H. Colwell shares this view, commenting that Wilder's female characters . . . demonstrate courage and resourcefulness. Virginia Wolf conveys that Wilder's antagonism toward towns described as "a sore on the beautiful, wild prairie" is nonetheless contradicted in *The Long Winter*, wherein she narrates the necessity of living in a town. Colwell and reviewers such as May Hill Arbuthnot and Anne Thaxter Eaton posit that, not only does Wilder paint a realistic and vivid portrait of pioneer life, but she offers important life lessons about the necessity for honesty, hard work and integrity.

Responses to Literature

1. In *Little House on the Prairie*, how does Wilder characterize her life? Would you like to live as she did? Why or why not?

2. View the television adaptation of Wilder's *Little House on the Prairie*. Which elements of her original work are most evident in the show? Why do you think viewers in the 1970s—and even more recent

---

COMMON HUMAN EXPERIENCE

Wilder's semi-autobiographical novels furnish lively historical detail of her surroundings and family life. Some other famous works with autobiographical foundations are:

The Glass Menagerie (1945), a play by Tennessee Williams. Williams, a renowned Southern playwright, insightfully captured the desolation of his family life in this melancholy play.

Dakota: A Spiritual Geography (2001), a memoir by Kathleen Norris. Norris chronicles life on the Great Plains, the intriguing ways that people become metaphors for their land, and the ways that that environment influences the human spirit.

Roots (1976), a novel by Alex Haley. Haley researched his own African American ancestors across many generations in preparing to write this work.

What I Think I Did (2000), a memoir by Larry Woiwode. Woiwode intermingles his life story with a running narrative of a North Dakota blizzard in 1996.

---

viewers—have responded so positively to a show about nineteenth-century prairie life?

3. In *The Long Winter*, what are the dangers faced by the Wilder family? How does the family respond to each life and death situation? What values undergird their survival?

4. Using the Internet and your library, research pioneer experiences in America. What was the cultural background of the pioneers who settled in North America? Why do you think these pioneers chose to face the hardships of frontier life?

BIBLIOGRAPHY

Books

Fellman, Anita Clair.*Little House, Long Shadow*. Columbia, Missouri: University of Missouri Press, 2008.

Romines, Ann.*Constructing the Little House: Gender, Culture and Laura Ingalls Wilder*. Amherst, Mass.: University of Massachusetts Press, 1997.

Spaeth, Janet.*Laura Ingalls Wilder*. Boston: Twayne, 1987.

Wolf, Virgina L. *Little House on the Prairie: A Reader's Companion.*. New York: Twayne, 1996.

Periodicals

Hines, Stephen W. "Laura Ingalls Wilder: Farm Journalist: Writings From the Ozarks." *Capper's* 130.2 (February 2008): 42–44.

Web Sites

Laura's History. Retrieved December 3, 2008, from http://www.lauraingallswilderhome.com/history1.htm.

Laura Ingalls Wilder. Retrieved December 4, 2008, from www.lauraingallswilder.com. Last updated on September 3, 2002.

⚙ Thornton Wilder

BORN: *1897, Madison, Wisconsin*

DIED: *1975, Hamden, Connecticut*

NATIONALITY: *American*

GENRE: *Fiction, drama*

MAJOR WORKS:

The Bridge of San Luis Rey (1927)

Our Town (1938)

The Skin of Our Teeth (1942)

The Matchmaker (1955)

Overview

Thornton Wilder was a student of the human condition. His plays in particular were concerned with both the timely and the timeless, and he most distinguished himself in the theater, although his first literary success was as

Thornton Wilder   *Wilder, Thornton, 1968, photograph. AP Images.*

a novelist. Wilder was the first major American playwright to discard realism in favor of a more modernist, experimental theatrical style. The full-length plays *Our Town* (1938) and *The Skin of Our Teeth* (1942), and the one-act plays *The Happy Journey to Trenton and Camden*, *The Long Christmas Dinner*, and *Pullman Car Hiawatha*, all published in 1931, influenced American playwrights from Tennessee Williams and Arthur Miller to Edward Albee and John Guare.

Works in Biographical and Historical Context

A Young Artist Encouraged by His Mother Thornton Niven Wilder was born in Madison, Wisconsin, on April 17, 1897, to Amos Parker Wilder and Isabella Niven Wilder. His father was the editor of *The Wisconsin State Journal*, and his mother was a devotee of world literature and music. When Wilder was nine years old, his father uprooted the family after being appointed consul general in Hong Kong, where he was responsible for representing the commercial interests of the United States in the region.

Wilder's first exposure to theater occurred before he reached his teens. Isabella Wilder and the children had returned to the United States while Amos Wilder remained in Hong Kong. Living near the University of California in Berkeley, Wilder learned of a theater in need of extras for the chorus. Isabella encouraged her ten-year-old son's participation by sewing costumes appropriate for his roles. Amos Wilder did not approve of such activities, but because he was thousands of miles away, Isabella had the greater influence upon Wilder's development.

Travels Abroad and Early Success in Fiction While studying at Oberlin College, Wilder's love of world literature continued to grow, and his first publication as a creative writer came when some of his pieces appeared in the college literary magazine. However, he would produce his most ambitious writing project to date after enrolling at Yale University. *The Trumpet Shall Sound* (1926), a four-act play, won him the Branford Brinton Award from the university.

Following a year abroad at the American Academy in Rome, Wilder returned to America in 1921 to take a position teaching French at the Lawrenceville School, a private preparatory academy in central New Jersey. During his time in Rome, Wilder had filled his notebooks with character sketches, which he first called "Memoirs of a Roman Student" but subsequently rewrote as his first novel, *The Cabala*, published in 1926. The book was reviewed favorably and sold well enough that he was able to take a leave of absence and write a second novel: *The Bridge of San Luis Rey*. This work won Wilder the first of his three Pulitzer Prizes and made him a literary celebrity.

While teaching at the University of Chicago in 1930, Wilder was able to work on the more socially relevant *The*

Long Christmas Dinner and Other Plays in One Act (1931). Three of the plays in the piece display the kinds of theatrical experiments that would make Wilder famous. *The Long Christmas Dinner* takes place over ninety years, and the rapid passage of time is signified by actors donning white wigs and adjusting their delivery of lines and movement on the stage in accordance with their characters' advancing age. In *Pullman Car Hiawatha*, Wilder makes use of a character identified as the Stage Manager who calls characters forth, dismisses them, and even prompts them with their lines. He also performs minor roles, and he and other characters address the audience directly about the purposes of the play. No scenery is used apart from chalk lines on the floor and pairs of chairs to represent the berths of a Pullman car. The last of these nonrealistic plays is *The Happy Journey to Trenton and Camden*.

A Hit on Broadway and in London   In 1936 Wilder resigned from his teaching position to concentrate more on writing. This move resulted in the creation of his most celebrated work. The play *Our Town* dramatizes life in a small New England town around the turn of the century. The audience is introduced to the town, Grover's Corners, New Hampshire, and the two families that serve to represent the townsfolk, the Webbs and the Gibbses, by the Stage Manager, who addresses the audience and the actors directly, telling the latter which scenes to play. As in *Pullman Car Hiawatha*, the Stage Manager character acts some of the minor roles himself and frequently comments on the action. There was no set for the play aside from some chairs, tables, and ladders. Such abstract theatrical style was, for the most part, new to American theatergoers in 1938.

Wilder's next play, *The Merchant of Yonkers* (1938), opened while *Our Town* was in the middle of its long run. However, *The Merchant of Yonkers* suffered the opposite fate of *Our Town*, and closed after only thirty-nine performances to almost unanimous derision by theater critics. Retitled *The Matchmaker* and staged by a new director, the play went on to run in London for nearly a year. *The Matchmaker* was revived on Broadway in 1955, where it enjoyed the longest run of any Wilder play (486 performances). *The Matchmaker* tells the tale of Horace Vandergelder, a domineering, tight-fisted sixty-year-old businessman in conflict with Ambrose Kemper, a young artist who wants to marry Ermengarde, Vandergelder's niece and ward. The play was adapted as a Broadway musical called *Hello, Dolly!* in 1964. A successful film version of the musical was released in 1969. *The Matchmaker*, unlike *Our Town*, is a lighthearted work of conventional realism.

Wilder's next play, *The Skin of Our Teeth*, was written at the time of the U.S. entry into World War II. Inspired by that harrowing global conflict, *The Skin of Our Teeth* is Wilder's attempt to reassure his audience that although the human race is forever facing extinction, it ultimately survives each crisis, if only just barely. In each

---

LITERARY AND HISTORICAL CONTEMPORARIES

Thornton Wilder's famous contemporaries include:

Max Reinhardt (1873–1943): An Austrian theater director and actor. Thornton Wilder was a longtime fan of Max Reinhardt, who directed the failed first production of Wilder's *The Merchant of Yonkers*.

Gertrude Stein (1874–1946): Stein, an American writer of fiction, biographies, memoirs, and critical analysis, established a strong friendship with Wilder after meeting him at the University of Chicago in 1934.

Edmund Wilson (1895–1972): The influential American literary critic and writer. After Thornton Wilder was accused of plagiarizing James Joyce's novel *Finnegan's Wake* when writing his *The Skin of Our Teeth*, Wilson defended Wilder.

James Joseph "Gene" Tunney (1897–1978): Tunney, an American heavyweight boxing champion, took a walking tour of Europe with Wilder in 1928. The tour was widely publicized by American and European newspapers and magazines. Tunney's defense of his title against Jack Dempsey in 1927, is known as "The Long Count Fight" and is one of the most famous boxing bouts in history.

Alfred Hitchcock (1899–1990): Hitchcock, a British filmmaker famously dubbed "The Master of Suspense," hired Wilder to pen his 1943 thriller *Shadow of a Doubt*. Hitchcock thought so highly of Wilder's screenplay that he rode with him cross-country on a train to Florida (where Wilder was to begin his World War II military training) so that they could work together on the script as long as possible.

---

of the three acts Wilder dramatizes a different threat at different times in human history: a colossal glacier advances down the North American continent during the Ice Age; a great flood rises to wipe out decadent humankind, as in the Book of Genesis in the Bible; and a modern global war lasting years saps humanity of its will to live. Though not as frequently produced as *Our Town*, *The Skin of Our Teeth* remains in the repertory of the professional and amateur American theater.

Troubled Times for the Writer and the World   In the late 1940s and early 1950s, Wilder's writing was not going well, partly because of his postwar malaise and the death of his mother in 1946. After a brief return to teaching, *The Merchant of Yonkers* was successfully revived, as noted above, as *The Matchmaker*, and Wilder resolved to revisit the theater. *The Alcestiad*, an adaptation of Euripides' tragedy *Alcestis* that Wilder had begun before the war, was retitled *A Life in the Sun* and staged at Edinburgh in

COMMON HUMAN EXPERIENCE

In *Our Town*, the character Emily dies in childbirth. In the third act, the deceased Emily is able to revisit her own past and see her family living on without her for a short time. Other works with dead narrators, or with characters who examine their lives by supernatural means, include:

The Lovely Bones (2002), a novel by Alice Sebold. The best-selling novel *The Lovely Bones* is narrated by Susie Salmon, a teenage girl who has been raped and murdered. She is now in heaven, keeping an eye on her family and friends and struggling to come to terms with both her life and her meaningless death.

A Christmas Carol (1843), a story by Charles Dickens. This holiday classic features the miser Ebenezer Scrooge, who is visited on Christmas Eve by a series of ghosts who show him scenes from his past, present, and future that prompt him to change his ungenerous, unkind ways.

My Name Is Red (2004), a novel by Orhan Pamuk. Turkish Nobel Prize winner Pamuk presents a murder mystery set in sixteenth-century Istanbul. The book has ten different narrators, one of whom is the murder victim.

The Penelopiad (2005), a novella by Margaret Atwood. In this retelling of the myth of Odysseus and his loyal wife Penelope, Penelope herself is able to tell her side of the story from her vantage point as a twenty-first-century resident of Hades, the ancient Greek underworld.

1955. Wilder mixed and matched characters and actions from Greek mythology to allegorize Christian doctrine and theology. The first production of *The Alcestiad* was universally condemned by critics as dull and heavy-handed.

In the late 1950s and early 1960s Wilder worked on two cycles of one-act plays, "The Seven Deadly Sins" and "The Seven Ages of Man." Taken as a whole, the eleven one-act plays differ radically from Wilder's earlier plays, most strikingly in the darker tone created by characters who are bitter, cynical, resentful, and, in some cases, even criminal. "The Seven Deadly Sins" and "The Seven Ages of Man," which turned out to be Wilder's finale as a dramatist, portray an America that is, underneath its sunny surface, corrupted by materialism. Even more surprising is the suggestion that human nature itself is too divided, aggressive, and selfish to make lasting relationships. American playwright John Guare, in his introduction to volume 1 of *The Collected Short Plays of Thornton Wilder*, suggests Wilder's earlier optimism was dampened by the rising tension of the Cold War, particularly the nuclear arms race between the United States and the Soviet Union.

Renewed Optimism at Life's End

In his final two literary efforts, the novels *The Eighth Day* (1967) and *Theophilus North* (1973), Wilder resurrected his faith in the gradual progress of the human race and his affirmation of America leading the way. The title character of the second novel, which is thinly disguised but also highly idealized autobiography, is nothing less than Christlike, as he heals the sick, raises the dead, saves marriages, and uncovers counterfeiters. Both novels stayed on the best-seller lists for a long time, and *The Eighth Day* won the National Book Award. In fact, during the last two decades of his life, Wilder received several honors and awards for his long career as a playwright, novelist, teacher, essayist, and literary scholar. Unfortunately, his health was beginning to fail, but his creativity never flagged. Even at the time of his death in 1975, Wilder was at work upon a sequel to his last novel.

Works in Literary Context

Epic Theater Developed by German playwright, director, and essayist Bertolt Brecht during the early 1900's, Epic Theater presents an artificial representation of reality. The intention of this theatrical movement was to force the audience to take an active role in interpreting the play, rather than merely viewing it as passive spectators. Brecht achieved this through techniques that constantly prevented the audience from forgetting that they were watching a play. Actors might abandon their characters to comment on the plot or address the crowd directly, a technique known as "breaking the fourth wall" (the "fourth wall" being the barrier between performance and audience). The influence of Epic Theater on Thornton Wilder is evident in such plays as *The Long Christmas Dinner*, in which actors only pantomimed eating and drinking rather than using props or real food to create a greater illusion of reality. Jumps in time and the symbolic birth and death set pieces also prevented the audience from forgetting that they were watching a play. The influence of Epic Theater is present in much of Wilder's work, including *Pullman Car Hiawatha*, *Our Town*, and *The Matchmaker*.

The Cyclical Nature of Existence Much of Wilder's work views time as an ever-revolving wheel. The very structure of *Our Town* is cyclical, tracing the process of birth to death as Dr. Gibbs delivers twins at dawn in the opening scene, leading to the final scene in which death is addressed in the form of Emily's nighttime funeral. By associating birth with day and death with night, Wilder is suggesting that the two are as natural and regular as the revolving hands of a clock. Life continues, the Earth keeps spinning on its axis. *The Skin of Our Teeth* also addresses this cyclical theme by showing that human beings are constantly faced with the possibility of their own extinction, but always manage to escape oblivion. Throughout history, potentially devastating threats to humankind seem to arise as regularly as the turning of centuries.

Works in Critical Context

Our Town   Although reviewers were at first highly critical of much of Wilder's work, his reputation has grown considerably in subsequent years. For example, Wilder's *Our Town* was enormously successful, running for 336 performances and winning the Pulitzer Prize for drama. But initial reviews by critics were mixed, both in regard to its mundane content and abstract form. Scholarly studies of Wilder and American drama have since acknowledged the importance of *Our Town* to the development of modern American theater, however. In a 2007 study of *Our Town* in *The New York Times Book Review*, Jeremy McCarter wrote that while Wilder may not be "our greatest playwright, but if we really understand him, he seems by far the most essential: the homegrown writer who made the largest claims for the theater, who put its special capacities to better use than his contemporaries—or his successors." The universal popularity of the play is evidenced by the many professional and amateur productions at home and abroad and by its remaining continuously in print.

The Matchmaker   Though *Our Town* is generally regarded as Wilder's most artistically significant piece of work, *The Matchmaker* was his biggest crowd-pleaser, enjoying the longest Broadway run of any of his plays (486 performances). Despite its popularity, further evidenced by its adaptation into a very successful musical titled *Hello Dolly!*, the play's initial run was a disaster. Under its original title *The Merchant of Yonkers*, the play closed after a mere thirty-nine performances. Critics largely blamed director Max Reinhardt, who approached the light comedy with heavy-handed execution. Today the play remains popular, but critical reaction is mixed. In *Drama for Students*, David Kelly wrote, "*The Matchmaker*, which Wilder meant as an examination of theatrical conventions, reads like just another comedy of manners today, because modern audiences are more accustomed to satire that is sharper and more obvious"

Responses to Literature

1. Thornton Wilder used a "Stage Manager" character in several of his plays, including *Pullman Car Hiawatha*, *The Happy Journey to Trenton and Camden*, and *Our Town*. Read two of these three plays, and then write a short essay comparing the way the Stage Manager functions in both plays. What do you think the purpose of the Stage Manager is and why is he a unique character?

2. Wilder's most famous play, *Our Town*, features an act in which a character named Emily reflects on her life after she has died. How does Emily's unusual situation affect the way she views her past and what kind of emotions does this stir up in you as the reader? Compose your response to these questions in a short essay.

3. The Epic Theater movement was an unusual approach to theater, but it was not an entirely new one. Research and explain its origins and what influenced the movement. Then discuss how Thornton Wilder adapted this theatrical movement to suit his own worldview.

BIBLIOGRAPHY

Books

Ballet, Arthur H. *"Our Town" as a Classical Tragedy*. San Diego: Greenhaven Press, 2000.

Fergusson, Francis. *Three Allegorists: Brecht, Wilder, and Eliot*. New York: G. K. Hall & Co., 1996.

Periodicals

Cardullo, Bert. *Whose Town Is It, Anyway? A Reconsideration of Thornton Wilder's "Our Town"*. *CLA Journal* (September 1998): 71–86.

Erstein, Hap. "Remarkable *Our Town* Dispenses Its Wisdom." *Washington Times* (Nov. 23, 1990): p.1.

Kelly, David. "Critical Essay on *The Bridge of San Luis Rey*." *Novels for Students* 16 (2007): vol. 24.

Kelly, David. "Critical Essay on *The Matchmaker*." *Drama for Students* 16 (2003): vol. 16.

Kreger, Erika M. "A discussion of *The Skin of Our Teeth*." *Drama for Students*.

McCarter, Jeremy. "'Our Town'-Great American Tragedy?" *Contemporary Literary Criticism* (Feb., 1959): 258–264.

Stephens, George D. "'Our Town'-Great American Tragedy?" *Modern Drama* (February 1959): 258–264.

⊛ Tennessee Williams

BORN: *1911, Columbus, Mississippi*

DIED: *1983, New York City*

NATIONALITY: *American*

GENRE: *Drama*

MAJOR WORKS:

The Glass Menagerie (1944)

A Streetcar Named Desire (1947)

Cat on a Hot Tin Roof (1955)

The Night of the Iguana (1961)

Overview

Tennessee Williams is acknowledged as one of the greatest American dramatists of the post–World War II era. His stature is based almost entirely upon works he completed during the first half of his career. He earned Pulitzer Prizes for *A Streetcar Named Desire* (1947) and *Cat on a Hot Tin Roof* (1955) and New York Drama Critics Circle Awards for these works as well as *The Glass Menagerie* (1944) and *The Night of the Iguana* (1961). Williams's lyrical style and his thematic concerns are distinctive in American theater; his material came almost exclusively from his inner life and was little influenced by

Tennessee Williams   *Williams, Tennessee, 1955, photograph. AP Images.*

and his boisterous, highly masculine father, who, according to Williams, nicknamed his son "Miss Nancy."

When Williams was eight years old, his father's promotion to a managerial position uprooted the family from the safe and serene world of small-town Mississippi. Negative effects of the move to industrialized St. Louis were felt by Williams, his mother, and his sister. His brother, Dakin, was born soon after the relocation. A few years later, the unhappy young Williams turned to writing as a means of both escape and recognition. Through poetry and short stories, he won prizes from advertising contests, school publications, and women's clubs.

The Beginnings of a Career   Williams's first published work came in 1927. The essay answering the question "Can a Good Wife Be a Good Sport?" was awarded third prize in a contest sponsored by *Smart Set* magazine. The next year his short story "The Vengeance of Nitocris" was published in *Weird Tales;* he received thirty-five dollars.

In 1929 Williams entered the University of Missouri, where he won small prizes for poetry and prose, pledged a fraternity, and discovered alcohol as a cure for the extreme shyness that had thus far kept him in virtual isolation. When he failed the Reserve Officers' Training Corps (ROTC), a military officer training program, during his third year, his father withdrew him from school and set him to work in the International Shoe Company warehouse. Williams's days were spent in the monotony and drudgery of dusting shoes and typing order forms; during the nights, he turned to writing. The tedium and repression of his job led to a nervous breakdown in 1935, from which he recovered by spending a year in Memphis with his sympathetic grandparents.

During the year in Memphis, Williams was introduced to drama. A farce about two sailors on shore leave, *Cairo, Shanghai, Bombay!* (1935), was his first produced play. Returning to Saint Louis to enroll at Washington University, he had decided that writing would be his career, and he proceeded through the next several years writing a number of works, such as *Candles in the Sun* (1937), *Orpheus Descending* (1937), and *The Long Goodbye* (1940). However, his breakthrough would not be staged until nearly a decade after his debut.

Universal Acclaim   In 1944 Williams captured the public's attention with his first major play, *The Glass Menagerie.* Tom, the narrator of the play, dreams of being a writer and is said to represent Williams. Tom's sister, Laura, is crippled both physically and socially. His mother, Amanda, is a fading Southern belle who lives in the past. The action of the play concerns Amanda persuading Tom to bring to the house a "gentleman caller," whom she hopes will marry Laura and provide for her future. Tom brings a man who is already engaged, upsetting his mother and causing Laura to retreat more deeply into her fantasy world of records and her glass animal collection. Tom then leaves his family, as his father had before him, to pursue his own destiny. The simplicity of *The Glass Menagerie* is

other dramatists or by contemporary events. One critic notes, "Williams has remained aloof from trends in American drama, continuing to create plays out of the same basic neurotic conflicts in his own personality."

Works in Biographical and Historical Context

A Child Escapes into Writing   Williams was born Thomas Lanier Williams on March 26, 1911, in Columbus, Mississippi. His mother, Edwina Dakin Williams, prim daughter of an Episcopal minister, had been "swept off her feet" by robust salesman Cornelius Coffin Williams, descended from a line of East Tennessee frontiersmen and political officeholders. During Williams's early years, his father was on the road a great deal, so he, his mother, and his older sister, Rose, lived in the rectory— or living quarters attached to a church—with his maternal grandparents. The family moved to Clarksdale, Mississippi, when young Williams entered school.

An early childhood plagued by illness—a near-fatal bout with diphtheria left him convinced that he had suffered irreparable heart damage—kept him from the company of other children. A weak physical condition, combined with the influence of his delicate and protective mother, earned him the ridicule of both other children counterbalanced by lyrical language and a great deal of symbolism, which some critics consider overwhelming. However, this emotionally compelling play was extremely popular, and Williams followed its formula in his later work. Laura is the typical Williams heroine in that she is too fragile to live in the real world. Laura and Amanda's escapes from the world through fantasy and living in the past, respectively, foreshadow later plays where the characters escape through alcohol and sex.

Williams established an international reputation in 1947 with *A Streetcar Named Desire*, which many critics consider his best work. The play begins with the arrival of Blanche DuBois at the home of her sister, Stella, and her brother-in-law, Stanley Kowalski, a lusty, crude, working-class man. Blanche has presided over the decay and loss of her family's estate and has witnessed the suicide of her young husband. She comes to Stella seeking comfort and security, but clashes with Stanley. While Stella is in the hospital giving birth, Stanley rapes Blanche, causing her to lose what little is left of her sanity. At the end, Blanche is committed to a sanitarium. In *A Streetcar Named Desire*, Williams uses Blanche and Stanley to illustrate conflicts that recur in his plays: illusion versus truth, weakness versus strength, and the power of sexuality to both destroy and redeem.

Although none of Williams's later plays attained the universal critical and popular acclaim of *The Glass Menagerie* and *A Streetcar Named Desire*, several works from the 1940s and 1950s are considered significant achievements in American drama. In *Summer and Smoke* (1947), Williams continues his exploration of the tension between the spirit and the flesh begun in *A Streetcar Named Desire*. In *The Rose Tattoo* (1950), one of his most lighthearted plays, he celebrates the life-affirming power of sexuality. *Cat on a Hot Tin Roof*, which is set on a Mississippi delta plantation, revolves around lies and self-deception. This play involves some of Williams's most memorable characters: Brick, a homosexual, who drinks to forget his guilt over the death of a lover; Maggie, his wife, who struggles "like a cat on a hot tin roof" to save their marriage; and Big Daddy, whose impending death from cancer prompts his family to compete for the inheritance. *The Night of the Iguana*, which Williams said is about "how to get beyond despair and still live," was his last play to win a major prize and gain critical and popular favor.

Fading from Glory   Later in his career, the "emotional currents" of Williams's life were at a low ebb. Such plays as *Suddenly, Last Summer* (1958) and *Sweet Bird of Youth* (1956), which are filled with violence, grotesquerie, and black comedy, reflect Williams's traumatic emotional state at the time of their composition. In his *Memoirs* (1975), he referred to the 1960s as his "Stoned Age," and he explained in an interview that "I needed [drugs, caffeine, and alcohol] to give me the physical energy to work.... But I am a compulsive writer. I have tried to stop working and I am bored to death." Williams continued to produce plays until his death, but critical

LITERARY AND HISTORICAL CONTEMPORARIES

Williams's famous contemporaries include:

Eugene O'Neill (1888–1953): O'Neill was widely considered to be the finest American playwright of his era, having written such venerable works as *Anna Christie* (1920) and *The Iceman Cometh* (1940).

Elia Kazan (1909–2003): Greek-American filmmaker Kazan created powerful classics like his adaptation of *A Streetcar Named Desire* (1951) and his realization of Williams's screenplay for the film *Baby Doll* (1956).

Arthur Miller (1915–2005): Miller was an American playwright whose works, such as *Death of a Salesman* (1949) and *The Crucible* (1953), are regarded as some of the defining works of American theater.

Marlon Brando (1924–2004): Academy Award–winning actor Brando starred as Stanley Kowalski in the 1951 film version of *A Streetcar Named Desire*. Brando also starred in *The Fugitive Kind*, the film adaptation of Tennessee Williams's play *Orpheus Descending* (1957).

Gore Vidal (1925–): American writer Vidal is famed for his plays, screenplays, novels, essays, and short stories, as well as his outspokenness regarding his homosexuality. His debut novel, *The City and the Pillar* (1948), was the first significant American novel to openly address homosexuality.

Diane Ladd (1932–): Second cousin to playwright Williams, acclaimed actress Diane Ladd has distinguished herself on both film and stage, including a performance in *Orpheus Descending*.

reception became increasingly negative. Much of Williams's later work consisted of rewriting his earlier plays and stories, and his new material showed little artistic development, according to critics. Writer Gore Vidal said in 1976: "Tennessee is the sort of writer who does not develop; he simply continues.... I am not aware that any new information (or feeling?) has got through to him in the [past] twenty-eight years." It was not only a lack of new themes that caused critics to denounce Williams's later work, but the absence of freshness and dramatic soundness in his treatment of these themes.

Williams was subject to much negative and even hostile criticism during his lifetime. Many of the qualities for which he is faulted are praised in his other works. His lyricism and use of symbols are hallmarks of such plays as *A Streetcar Named Desire*, but in other plays, critics accuse him of being overly sentimental or heavy-handed. Williams is lauded for his compassionate understanding of the spiritually downtrodden, but he has also been accused of crossing the line between sympathetic interest and

COMMON HUMAN EXPERIENCE

Williams's play *Cat on a Hot Tin Roof* is concerned with the deep denial and secrets of a family affected by death, alcoholism, and concealed homosexuality. Other literary works that involve family secrets include:

"The Fall of the House of Usher"(1839), a short story by Edgar Allan Poe. Poe's chilling tale of terror is set in a mansion, crumbling as a result of its ruinous physical state and the psychological state of Roderick Usher, the man who lives in the house and may harbor a terrible secret involving his dead sister.

Jane Eyre (1847), a novel by Charlotte Brontë. Brontë's classic novel of one English family's very dark secrets finds a lonely governess named Jane Eyre, who begins to see a ghostly woman roaming the home where she works. The truth behind this woman provides the novel's main twist.

Rebecca (1938), a novel by Daphne du Maurier. The new bride of a rich Englishman moves into his mansion, Manderley, only to realize that his deceased wife, Rebecca, continues to hold a spooky sway over all those who enter it. The truth behind Rebecca's death eventually comes to light in this decidedly dark novel written in the Gothic tradition.

Middlesex (2003), a novel by Jeffrey Eugenides. Eugenides's sprawling Pulitzer Prize-winning novel follows Calliope Stephanides, a hermaphrodite who comes to learn about the strange history of her family that led to her unusual sex.

Castle of Otranto (1764). American Southern Gothic literature picked up on the gloomy combination of horror and romance that defined its English equivalent, but used these elements more to comment on the strangeness of the American South than to create suspense. Writers of Southern Gothic works also use the uniquely grotesque character of the genre to draw attention to social issues by depicting grotesque stereotypes. Among the defining writers of the Southern Gothic genre are William Faulkner, Flannery O'Connor, Truman Capote, and Williams.

Works in Critical Context

A Streetcar Named Desire The tremendous reputation of *A Streetcar Named Desire* did not take long to earn. Upon its first staging in 1947, the play was praised by critics and adored by theatergoers. A review in *The New York Times* wastes no time in stating the critic's evaluation of the play. The review opens by declaring, "Tennessee Williams has brought us a superb drama." The reviewer goes on to describe the playwright as "a genuinely poetic playwright whose knowledge of people is honest and thorough and whose sympathy is profoundly human." The raves of *The New York Times* were echoed in the *New York Daily News*, *The Saturday Review*, and *The New Republic*. However, some periodicals took issue with the play's frankly sexual themes, which many considered shocking at the time. The *New York Journal American* sarcastically referred to the play as, "*The Glands Menagerie*," while declaring its subject matter "unpleasant." A similarly mocking review also appeared in *Partisan Review*, but such assessments were few. Overall, *A Streetcar Named Desire* was greeted with applause from the critical community.

Suddenly, Last Summer Some of Williams's early works like *A Streetcar Named Desire* and *Cat on a Hot Tin Roof* were often deemed shocking for their depictions of sexuality, but in terms of the sheer bizarre, they could not compare to the playwright's *Suddenly, Last Summer*. Williams expected the play, which sports one of the weirdest climaxes in his catalog, to be too much for critics to stomach. He said that he expected to be "critically tarred and feathered and ridden on a fence rail out of the New York theatre." Much to Williams's surprise, the tense, one-act play was reviewed quite favorably. A year after its stage debut, a film version of *Suddenly, Last Summer* (with a screenplay by celebrated writer Gore Vidal) was released. In spite of the film's all-star cast (Katharine Hepburn, Elizabeth Taylor, Montgomery Clift), the film received some mixed notices. *The New York Times* wrote, "Whatever horrifying import there may have been in Tennessee Williams's short play . . . has been drained out of it through tedious talking and a terminal showdown that is irritatingly obscure." *Variety* was similarly critical, comparing the film unfavorably to

perverse sensationalism. Although critics are nearly unanimous in expressing their disappointment and sadness that the mastery of Williams's early work was not continued in his later plays, they are quick to point out that the writer's contributions to American theater has been remarkable. He died in New York on February 24, 1983.

Works in Literary Context

Local Color Local color (also known as regionalism) refers to literature that hones in on a specific region. The work may be written in a local dialect or overly concerned with regional customs, landmarks, or topography. As filtered through the author's worldview, the resulting work is often imbued with a strong sense of sentimentality or nostalgia. Williams often used local color to conjure a strong sense of the southern regions in which his works take place.

Southern Gothic The Southern Gothic genre is an American development upon the English Gothic fiction genre, which dates back to Horace Walpole's novel *The*

the play: "Nothing that's been added is an improvement on the original; they stretch the seams of the original fabric without strengthening the seamy aspects of the story."

Responses to Literature

1. The title of Williams's *A Streetcar Named Desire* is somewhat enigmatic, yet it is a very appropriate title for the play. Read *A Streetcar Named Desire* and explain, in a short essay, why its title is appropriate.

2. Brick, the hero of *Cat on a Hot Tin Roof*, is disabled. Why do you think Tennessee Williams chose to do this and what do you think Brick's physical condition says about him as a character? Support your response with details from the play.

3. Amanda is the mother of the troubled Wingfield family in *The Glass Menagerie*. Read the play and think about the way Williams portrays Amanda in it. Do you think Williams believes she has good qualities or does he portray her as merely foolish? Write your response in an essay.

BIBLIOGRAPHY

Books

Adler, Thomas P. *"A Streetcar Named Desire": The Moth and the Lantern.* Boston: Twayne, 1990.

Boxill, Roger. *Tennessee Williams.* New York: Macmillan, 1987.

Donohue, Francis. *The Dramatic World of Tennessee Williams.* New York: Ungar, 1964.

Griffin, Alice. *Understanding Tennessee Williams.* Columbia, S.C.: Univeristy of South Carolina Press, 1995.

Hayman, Ronald. *Tennessee Williams: Everyone Else is An Audience.* New Haven, Conn.: Yale University Press, 1993.

Leavitt, Richard. *The World of Tennessee Williams.* New York: Putnam, 1978.

Leverich, Lyle. *Tom: The Unknown Tennessee.* New York: Crown, 1995.

Pagan, Nicholas. *Rethinking Literary Biography: A Postmodern Approach to Tennessee Williams.* Rutherford, N.J.: Fairleigh Dickinson University Press, 1993.

Spoto, Donald. *The Kindness of Strangers: The Life of Tennessee Williams.* Boston: Little, Brown, 1985.

Williams, Edwina Dakin and Lucy Freeman. *Remember Me to Tom.* New York: Putnam's, 1963.

Periodicals

Atkinson, Brooks. "First Night at the Theater." *The New York Times* (December 4, 1947).

Crowther, Bosley. "Suddenly, Last Summer (1959)." *Variety* (January 15, 1959).

McCarthy, Mary. "Oh, Sweet Mystery of Life: A Streetcar Named Desire." *Partisan Review* 15 (March 1948): 49–53.

Nathan, George Jean. "The *Streetcar* Isn't Drawn by Pegasus." *New York Journal American* (December 15, 1947): 14.

"Suddenly, Last Summer." *The New York Times* (December 23, 1959).

✸ William Carlos Williams

BORN: *1883, Rutherford, New Jersey*

DIED: *1963, Rutherford, New Jersey*

NATIONALITY: *American*

GENRE: *Poetry*

MAJOR WORKS:

"The Red Wheelbarrow" (1923)

The Knife of the Times and Other Stories (1932)

Paterson (1946–1958)

Autobiography (1951)

William Carlos Williams   *Alfred Eisenstaedt / Time Life Pictures / Getty Images*

Overview

Best known as a poet, William Carlos Williams was an accomplished writer in many genres. He produced twenty-three volumes of poetry, five collections of short fiction, six novels, seven books of nonfiction, five plays, and four translations. His work, in all genres, is characterized by a direct treatment of reality, creating an artistry of immediacy and freshness. Williams was also a doctor in continuous practice for four decades.

Works in Biographical and Historical Context

The Physician and the Poet   William Carlos Williams was born and lived his entire life in Rutherford, New Jersey. His father, William George Williams, was English by birth and remained a British citizen his entire life, even though he left England at age five. Williams's mother, Raquel Helene Rose Hoheb (called Elena by her family), born in San Juan, Puerto Rico, was partly French, Dutch, Spanish, and Jewish. An exotic and romantic personality, she exerted a strong influence on her son, as did his paternal grandmother, Emily Dickinson Wellcome. As a youth, Williams was passionately devoted to sports, especially track, until, at age sixteen, he began to suffer from an ailment diagnosed as adolescent heart strain. He then channeled his abundant energy into literature. From 1902 to 1906, Williams attended medical school at the University of Pennsylvania, where he befriended the poet, Ezra Pound. After his internship in New York hospitals, he pursued two professions—medicine and writing—with equal vigor. Much to his satisfaction, he found that these two careers complemented, rather than contradicted, one another: in his *Autobiography* (1951), Williams insists, "As a writer, I have been a physician, and as a physician a writer."

While Ezra Pound and a small group of English and American poets in London met informally, and plotted the first steps of a new literary trend they christened, Imagism, Pound's old school friend, William Carlos Williams, remained at home, practicing obstetrics in Rutherford, New Jersey, but listening intensely to the news from abroad, Pound regularly reported to him in his letters. Although Imagism, under Pound's direction, lasted but a few short, intense years, the style became the unique property of Williams, who exploited its every potential and possessed it so thoroughly in his work of the next four decades, that today the abbreviated lyric is nearly indistinguishable from his name.

Williams also passionately pursed a purely American mode of verse to distinguish him from Pound and his cohorts, who accepted the European verse tradition and made it the basis of their work. Williams's quest may have arisen from his own troubled sense of identity: the son of a British father who never changed his citizenship, and a Puerto Rican mother with whom he was rarely close. Imagism attracted Williams because of its shift of emphasis from idea to image in the poem. Pound and Williams

both were opponents of hazily suggestive language for poetry, but Williams saw in Imagism an opportunity to reclaim verse language as a vehicle of direct comment on American life. He saw the free verse method—which rejected conventional rhyme, rhythm, and metric schemes—as a way of expressing this sense of freedom, evident in his most famous poem, "The Red Wheelbarrow" (1923).

Williams's long use of the sketchy Imagist poetic may have no other cause than that he found it suitable to his imagination. It may also have been a matter of necessity, since after marrying Flossie Herman in 1912, and beginning his medical practice in earnest, Williams had little free time in which to write. He thought of himself as first a writer, only second as a provider and family man. In *Autobiography* he records how he would often pull up his typewriter between patients and dash out a poem, quite often in its first and only draft. The very brevity of the lyric, in other words, expressed the condition of the poet's harried life, as much as it staked out his unique position on the making of poetry.

Williams paid a price for his unchanging mode of poetry. After having a number of slight texts published, including the privately printed *Poems* of 1909, his first book, the more mature work of *Al Que Quiere!* (1917), the bold improvisatory sequence *Kora in Hell* (1920), *Sour Grapes* (1921), and his best early book, *Spring and All* (1923), he fell into obscurity and had only one other work of poetry, *Go Go* (1923), published during the rest of the decade.

Sketches in Prose   In the 1930s, Williams expanded his literary repertoire to include short stories, publishing the collections *The Knife of the Times and Other Stories* (1932) and *Life Along the Passaic River* (1938). He seems to have turned to fiction, at this point, because of the consistent discouragement he met with in his attempts to be recognized as a poet. In his frustration, he found the short story to be a more direct vehicle for his ideas and emotions. Williams's short stories are not traditional in form, but are sketches or fragments of his experience and imagination that begin and end on impulse. Many of these stories are autobiographical, having to do with a doctor-narrator and his patients. His characters are revealed objectively by their responses to their immediate environment, and are raised to the level of individuals in the midst of depraved insensitivity. Often designed as casual, spontaneous conversations in which Williams is a participant, his stories evolve from nascent speech patterns, or what he calls "the American idiom," a narrative technique that heightens the intensity and immediacy of his short fiction.

Williams published *The Knife of the Times and Other Stories* in 1932, at the darkest moment of the Great Depression. Williams's stories dramatize the fortitude and perseverance of his characters in spite of the oppression ("the knife") of the times. Most of these stories (only one of which was first published in a periodical) illustrate the power of love and identity as forms of survival. One of the first reviews of this publication praises these stories for their "clinical calm" and "even-colored tone."

Williams claimed that *Life Along the Passaic River* was a continuation of the stories in *The Knife of the Times and Other Stories.* He admitted, however, that he was a more mature writer at this stage, seldom needing to revise his work. Among these stories are some of Williams's most incisive social comments. His autobiographical narrator becomes even more deeply involved in the lives of the people he knows along the banks of the Passaic. With passionate authenticity, Williams writes about their hopes, their fears, their weaknesses, their strengths, shifting the point of view from tough to tender, and from indifferent to sympathetic.

The most frequently anthologized of Williams's stories is "The Use of Force" (1933), which dramatizes a struggle between life and death, or more specifically, between control and loss of control. In this story, the doctor-narrator is called upon to diagnose the problem of a child with a fever; but the child, Mathilda, refuses to let the doctor look at her throat. A strong sense of distrust between doctor and child at the beginning of the story sets the scene for the different levels of conflict that take place.

During the 1930s, Williams also published *A Novelette and Other Prose* (1932) and the first installment (*White Mule*, 1937) of what is known as the "Stecher trilogy." This particular novel represented Williams's first real public success. During this period, he also published four new books of poetry, two collections of his poems, and his first play.

A Productive Period The 1940s were especially productive for Williams: he continued the Stecher trilogy with *In the Money: White Mule—Part II* (1940); he wrote three plays; and in 1946, he began to produce, over a period of eight years, the epic poem he had prepared his whole life to write, *Paterson*. In addition, he wrote five new books of poems.

In 1948 Williams suffered the first in a series of heart attacks, which were accompanied by serious depression. However, he remained focused enough to publish two award-winning works the following year: *Selected Poems* and *Paterson (Book Three)*. At this time, Williams was simultaneously working on a libretto for an opera, book four of *Paterson*, his autobiography, a novel, and an edition of his collected short stories. *Make Light of It* (1950) includes the stories collected in Williams's first two volumes of short fiction and a third group of twenty-one stories, entitled "Beer and Cold Cuts."

Williams's Decline After 1950 Williams entered a period of physical decline, though this did not restrict his productivity. In 1951 he published *Paterson (Book Four)*, *Autobiography*, and *The Collected Earlier Poems*.

LITERARY AND HISTORICAL CONTEMPORARIES

Williams's famous contemporaries include:

Wallace Stevens (1879–1955): Stevens was an American poet and a major figure in the modernist cultural movement. He is known for his poems "Anecdote of the Jar" (1919) and "The Emperor of Ice Cream" (1922). Stevens met Williams during a summer retreat in 1915.

James Joyce (1882–1941): Joyce was an Irish author and one of the most influential, original writers of the twentieth century. Joyce's dense classic *Ulysses* (1919) appeared serially in *Little Review* alongside Williams's prose "improvisations." *Ulysses* had a significant influence of Williams's writing.

Ezra Pound (1885–1972): Pound was one of the forerunners of the modernist movement and a codeveloper of the Imagist movement. Pound befriended Williams at the University of Pennsylvania and the two remained friends for many years.

Charles Demuth (1883–1935): Demuth was an American painter who was a master of watercolors and oils and the originator of Precisionism, a form of painting that was geometric in style and industrial in subject matter. Demuth and Williams were close friends until Demuth's diabetes-related death in 1934.

Marcel Duchamp (1887–1968): Duchamp was a French artist and a leading surrealist, practicing a form of art that emphasized the dream like and the bizarre. Duchamp met Williams during a summer retreat in 1915.

T.S. Eliot (1888–1965): Eliot was a leading modernist, and his poem "The Waste Land" (1922) is regarded as a prime example of that literary movement. Certain critics have argued that Williams's *Paterson* is a response to Eliot's poetry series *Four Quartets* (1935–1942).

In 1952, though Williams completed the Stecher trilogy with *The Build-Up*, he suffered a serious depression and a heart attack, accompanied by a loss of speech. At this point, Williams retired from medicine and devoted the rest of his life to writing. Williams was invited to serve as consultant in poetry at the Library of Congress. The appointment was delayed by Williams's health and then abandoned by the Library of Congress after a traumatic investigation into Williams's political association with Ezra Pound. Pound was facing treason charges because of time he spent in Italy while the country was in conflict with the United States during World War II. This unfortunate episode was followed, in March 1953, by yet another heart attack and depression that sent Williams to a mental hospital until June.

In 1961 Williams published final collections of his stories, (*The Farmers' Daughters: The Collected Stories*)

COMMON HUMAN EXPERIENCE

Williams's epic poetry series *Paterson* explores the history and citizens of Paterson, New Jersey, a city near his hometown of Rutherford. Other works inspired by the people of New Jersey include:

> *Goodbye, Columbus* (1959), a novella by Philip Roth. Neil Klugman is a graduate of Rutgers University and is now living with his aunt and uncle in the working-class neighborhood of Newark. After falling for Brenda Patimkin, a resident of the wealthy Short Hills, he becomes painfully aware of the class resentments boiling in the New Jersey suburb.
>
> "In a Prominent Bar in Secaucus One Day" (1961), a poem by X. J. Kennedy. In a New Jersey bar, a ragged woman stands up and declares that she once lived a life of glory before announcing that beauty is fleeting and warning the women in the bar to not waste their youths drinking. Sadly, the poem ends with the bartender calling the police, who take the drunkenly effusive woman away.
>
> *The Sopranos* (1999–2007), a television series created by David Chase. Tony Soprano is a murderous mob boss struggling to balance his rocky family life with his position as the head of a New Jersey crime organization. In an attempt to come to terms with his troubled life and overcome the panic attacks that have plagued him his entire life, Tony seeks solace on the couch of psychiatrist, Dr. Melfi.
>
> *Five-Finger Discount* (2002), a book by Helene Stapinski. The true story of journalist Helene Stapinski is an account of her rise from a tumultuous childhood in New Jersey with her out-of-control family members—some of whom were criminals—to her position as a writer for such respected publications as *The New York Times* and *New York* magazine.

filters thoughts, observations, and perceptions through the imagination, thus creating an imaginative view of life that improves upon reality. In his attempt to come to terms with his surroundings, Williams created a body of tightly structured works that are poignant and vital to an understanding of human nature's basic drive for survival.

Works in Literary Context

Modernism The artistic movement called modernism is essentially characterized by its fragmented, experimental approach to literature, music, and the visual arts. The movement reflected a shift away from previously held concepts of societal norms and attempts at capturing realism in the arts. Modern art and literature emerged from the development of urban, industrial, technological civilization in the early twentieth century. Experimentation was paramount to the modernists, who strived to annihilate anything they considered to be holding back human progress. The first wave of modernism began around 1910 and lasted into the 1940s. Among the original modernists were the poets T. S. Eliot, Wallace Stevens, Ezra Pound, and William Carlos Williams.

Imagism The poetic doctrine of imagism grew out of the modernist movement. Imagist poets, such as Ezra Pound, Amy Lowell, and Williams, used vivid, precisely described visual images to bring their poems to life. They composed concise, clear verses, focused on a specific visual image. Early imagists rejected the romanticism and sentimentality of the Victorian poetry of the late nineteenth century. While the official movement only lasted a few years, its influence lasted many years, seeping into movements such as the objectivist poetry of the 1930s (which treated poems as objects) and the Beat poetry of the 1950s (which rejected traditional American values in favor of drug and sex experimentation and Eastern spirituality). Williams was a mentor to many younger poets, including Kenneth Rexroth, who became a leader of the San Francisco Renaissance, and Allen Ginsberg, the preeminent Beat poet.

Works in Critical Context

"The Red Wheelbarrow" Of all his work, Williams's brief poem "The Red Wheelbarrow" has proven to be the most enduring and has achieved a legendary status among critics as an exemplar of the principles of imagism. Cleanth Brooks and Robert Penn Warren, two leading members of the New Criticism movement, suggest in their book, *Understanding Poetry* (1938), that "The Red Wheelbarrow" was nothing less than "a new vision of the ordinary."

Paterson Williams's sprawling series of epic poems, *Paterson*, is regarded as a masterpiece of long-form poetry. A 1953 assessment of the first book in the series by poet-critic Randall Jarrell lauded, "There has never been a poem more American... if the next three books are as good as

and his plays, (*Many Loves and Other Plays: The Collected Plays*), and released his last book of poetry, *Pictures from Brueghel and Other Poems*, the following year. He died on March 4, 1963.

In his brief tapestries of fiction and fact, Williams is searching for those characteristics that enable the human being to survive, the threads of human fortitude that make the difference between health and disease, life and death. Throughout his career he became intensely involved in his patients' conditions, then worked, through his short fiction, to give those experiences meaning and significance. Williams reveals the psychological complexities of his characters with the detachment of a scientist, developing, in the process, a deep respect and concern for them that is aesthetically convincing. A work of art, says Williams, has the potential to save the world because it this one...the poem will be the best very long poem that any American has written." Contemporary critics rate *Paterson* with equal awe. A 1995 edition of the series was greeted with wild applause. *The Library Journal* deemed the book "a modernist classic" before stating that "*Paterson* is a nativist's answer to the cosmopolitan Pound and Eliot." In a more mixed review, *Publisher's Weekly* concluded that "Williams at his strongest is as good an American poet as there has been; still, it must be noted that not all of the five books of *Paterson* (plus fragments of a sixth) are up to that level."

Responses to Literature

1. The goal of the imagist poet is to create a strong sense of an object. How does the arrangement of stanzas in "The Red Wheelbarrow" help to convey the image that poet Williams is trying to conjure in the mind of the reader?

2. Williams was both a literary artist and a medical doctor, a rare combination. How do you think his medical knowledge and experience found its way into his poetry? Write an essay providing evidence for your claims.

3. Williams wrote *Paterson* as a tribute to a city in his home state of New Jersey. Read the book; then explain what you think Williams is trying to say about the city. Support your response with details from the book.

4. In his poem, "Winter Trees," Williams creates an image of a specific scene, but he also conjures a particular feeling. Read the poem and explain the feeling you think Williams was trying to convey. How does the poem make you feel?

BIBLIOGRAPHY

Books

Breslin, James E. *William Carlos Williams: An American Artist*. New York: Oxford University Press, 1970.

Brinnin, John Malcolm. *William Carlos Williams*. Minneapolis: University of Minnesota Press, 1963.

Brooks, Cleanth, and Robert Penn Warren. *Understanding Poetry*. New York: Henry Holt, 1938.

Guimond, James. *The Art of William Carlos Williams: A Discovery and Possession of America*. Urbana: University of Illinois Press, 1968.

Jarrell, Randall. *Poetry and the Age*. New York: Knopf, 1953.

Koch, Vivienne. *William Carlos Williams*. Norfolk, Conn.: New Directions, 1950.

Mariani, Paul. *William Carlos Williams: A New World Naked*. New York: McGraw-Hill, 1981.

Whittemore, Reed *William Carlos Williams: Poet from Jersey*. Boston: Houghton Mifflin, 1975.

Periodicals

Mottram, Eric. "The Making of *Paterson*." *Stand 7* (1965): 17–34.

Web Sites

Barnes & Noble.com. *Paterson*. Accessed December 8, 2008, from http://search.barnesandnoble.com/Paterson/William-Carlos-Williams/e/9780811212984/?itm=5.

✵ August Wilson

BORN: *1945, Pittsburgh, Pennsylvania*

DIED: *2005, Seattle, Washington*

NATIONALITY: *American*

GENRE: *Drama*

MAJOR WORKS:
Ma Rainey's Black Bottom (1982)
Fences (1985)
The Piano Lesson (1989)
Two Trains Running (1990)
King Hedley II (2001)

August Wilson   *Wilson, August, photograph. AP Images.*

Overview

August Wilson was a phenomenally successful American playwright who won two Pulitzers, five New York Drama Critics Circle awards, and several Tony Awards. In a rare occurrence, in 1988 Wilson had two plays running simultaneously on Broadway—*Fences* (first performed in 1985) and *Joe Turner's Come and Gone* (1986). Dedicated to representing blacks from every decade of the century in a ten-play cycle, Wilson completed the cycle before his untimely death due to liver cancer in 2005. Wilson's plays expanded the range of American theater by documenting and celebrating black historical experience, thereby showing that embracing African spiritual and cultural heritage could promote individual and collective healing for blacks.

Works in Biographical and Historical Context

Childhood Poverty and Dropping Out August Wilson was born Frederick August Kittel on April 27, 1945, to an African-American mother, Daisy Wilson Kittel, and a white German father, Frederick August Kittel, who all but abandoned the family soon after August was born. August was one of six children and grew up in poverty in Pittsburg, in a two-room apartment above a grocery store. His mother, whom he idolized, supported her family with cleaning jobs and encouraged her children to read, teaching August to read at age four.

When Wilson was an adolescent, his mother married an African American named David Bedford, who moved them to Hazelwood, a mostly white suburb; there Wilson and his family were victims of racist vandalism and abuse. Wilson dropped out of high school at age fifteen following false charges of plagiarism on a paper he had written. After dropping out of school, Wilson spent much of his time in the library, and prepared himself to be a writer, hoping for several months that his mother would not find out that he was not in school. He was largely self-taught, and educated himself by reading all that he could by the writers in the black literature section of the library. These authors included Richard Wright, Ralph Ellison, Langston Hughes, and Amiri Baraka. He also eagerly read books on black anthropology and sociology.

Influences of Blues Music and Black Power His twentieth year, 1965, was a pivotal one for Wilson. He moved out of his mother's home into a rooming house and joined a group of young black intellectuals, poets, and playwrights. That same year, Wilson bought his first typewriter and a used Victrola, on which he played several jazz and blues records, purchased for five cents each from a nearby resale store. He often speaks of the profound impact of listening to the blues, and specifically Bessie Smith, for the first time. Hearing her voice gave him realization of the nobility and spirituality of African-American folk expression and increased his own self-esteem as a member of the black community.

Later in the fall of 1965, Wilson heard Malcolm X's recorded voice for the first time. Although the media has tended to downplay this aspect of Wilson's career and life, the Black Power movement was, as he says in "The Ground on Which I Stand" (1996), "the kiln in which I was fired." He was drawn to the Black Power and Nation of Islam messages of self-sufficiency, self-defense, and self-determination, and appreciated the origin myths espoused by the controversial leader of the Nation of Islam, Elijah Muhammad. In 1969 Wilson married Brenda Burton, a Muslim, and briefly converted to Islam in an unsuccessful attempt to sustain the marriage. They had a daughter, Sakina Ansari-Wilson, and divorced in 1972.

Wilson's poetic work developed his expertise with metaphor and eventually evolved into effective playwrighting. In his preface to *Three Plays* (1991) Wilson reflects on his first empowering experiences in writing drama: "When I sat down to write I realized I was sitting in the same chair as Eugene O'Neill, Tennessee Williams, Arthur Miller, Henrik Ibsen, Amiri Baraka, and Ed Bullins." He asserts that regardless of race, all playwrights face the same problems of crafting convincing drama and characters. After moving to St. Paul, Minnesota, in 1978 to write plays for the Science Museum of Minnesota, Wilson became the recipient of a fellowship with the Minneapolis Playwrights Center in 1980, and, in 1981 he married Judy Oliver, a social worker.

Broadway Success Wilson's Broadway success began in 1984 with *Ma Rainey's Black Bottom.* (The title is a reference to a popular dance of the 1920s.) The drama takes place during an imaginary recording session in 1927 where the musicians and singer Ma Rainey confront verbal abuse they have encountered and discuss other forms of abuse, most notably the various experiences of racism that all of them have suffered. First staged in 1984 by the Yale Repertory Theater in New Haven, Connecticut, it garnered such glowing reviews that before the end of the year it had opened on Broadway. Wilson was hailed as a "promising new playwright" for American theater. Meanwhile, the play itself went on to win several awards, including the New York Drama Critics Circle Award.

Wilson's next drama, *Fences* (1985), also had its first performance with the Yale Repertory Theater then opened on Broadway in 1987. From the first, *Fences* received rave reviews. It grossed eleven million dollars in its first year and won the 1987 Pulitzer Prize for Drama as well as the New York Drama Critics Circle Award and four Tony Awards. Wilson confirmed his talent with his next drama, *Joe Turner's Come and Gone*, which opened on Broadway in 1988 and was yet another winner of the New York Drama Critics Circle Award. The play is about an ex-convict's efforts to find his wife. It is also an allegory for all uprooted black Americans.

A Second Pulitzer Prize In 1990, after the end of his second marriage, Wilson moved west to Seattle, Washington. While still on the East Coast, though, he triumphed with the Broadway opening of *The Piano Lesson* (1990), which won him a second Pulitzer Prize. In this drama, a brother and sister quarrel over a piano that has been in the family for generations. Boy Willie wants to sell the piano to buy the land on which their ancestors were slaves, but his sister Berenice wants to keep the piano because of the family history carved on it.

Also in 1990, the Yale Repertory Theater continued the tradition of introducing Wilson's plays by staging the first production of *Two Trains Running*, which opened on Broadway in 1992. Set in Pittsburgh in 1968, *Two Trains Running* takes place at a lunch counter, where the regulars discuss the issues of the times, including the civil rights movement and the Vietnam War. Wilson's success as a playwright continued throughout his life as his plays were produced on stage and in film. In 1995 a film version of *The Piano Lesson* was televised on Hallmark Hall of Fame, and it featured four members of the original Broadway cast. *Seven Guitars* (1996) won the New York Drama Critics Circle Award and *King Hedley II* debuted on Broadway in 2001. A revival of *Ma Rainey's Black Bottom* opened on Broadway in 2003 with Whoopi Goldberg and Charles Dutton. Though his art was at times controversial and his life was shortened by cancer, Wilson's place in American theatrical history was secured by his passionate writing and activism that moved African-American theater to the forefront of national attention and to the mainstream of Broadway.

Works in Literary Context

Wilson enlivened the American theater by creating plays that celebrated the African-American historical experience. His success resulted in part from his ability to translate the specifics of black life into the conventions of realism and naturalism within his themes of the search for identity, racial exploitation and injustice, empowerment through the blues, and spiritual regeneration. While he adheres to traditional dramatic form, his plays imply no easy answers. Embracing the spiritual, Wilson's plays give voice to the mystical as integral to everyday life and experience. Complex and mysterious, his plays show the poisonous effects of a bitter legacy on black individuals and their communities and include thrilling if infrequent moments of personal liberation.

American Realists and Experimentation Following World War II, American writers began to create innovative and self-aware works that reflected popular culture. From chronicling the elite classes of society, writers increasingly experimented with influences of media and oral language from popular culture. Wilson's plays and characters echoed this realism in the landscape of their everyday life. Audience members recognized and identified with Wilson's use of language to define his black

---

LITERARY AND HISTORICAL CONTEMPORARIES

Wilson's famous contemporaries include:

Amiri Baraka (1934–): American poet, novelist and playwright Baraka is the author of *Somebody Blew Up America* (2001).

Malcolm X (1925–1965): Malcolm X was an African-American Muslim minister, public speaker, and human rights activist best known for works such as *The Autobiography of Malcolm X* (1965).

Nikki Giovanni (1932–): A Grammy-nominated American poet, activist and author, Giovanni is author of *Black Feeling, Black Talk/Black Judgement* (1970) and *The Collected Poetry of Nikki Giovanni* (2003).

Derrick Bell (1930–): Bell is an American professor of law and a major figure within the legal studies discipline of Critical Race Theory. He recently authored *Race, Racism & American Law* (2008).

Jack Kerouac (1922–1969): The charismatic American author of the Beat Generation, he is best known for the novel *On the Road* (1957).

---

characters. In an interview with Heather Henderson in *Theater*, actor James Earl Jones states, "Few writers can capture dialect as dialogue in a manner as interesting and accurate as August's."

Naturalism In contrast to the middle-class settings of American Realism, the naturalist dramaturgy gave voice to more working-class and impoverished characters enmeshed in a struggle against their own desperate circumstances. An example of such a character is Laura Wingfield in Tennessee Williams's play *The Glass Menagerie* (1944). Wilson's characters are also generally concerned with economic struggles, as in *Fences*, where the action significantly begins on payday. Writing in the *Village Voice*, a reviewer called Wilson a mythmaker, a folk ethnologist, "collecting prototypical stories, testimonies, rituals of speech and behavior" while working with "basically naturalistic panorama plays" to create complex characters, none of whom are "unindicted or unforgiven."

Works in Critical Context

The widespread critical acclaim of August Wilson's art has assisted in establishing his stature as the foremost African-American playwright of the late twentieth century. Critics and scholars have written extensively on Wilson's portraits of African Americans. As the poet/playwright, he employed the "language of his community, as an on-sight storyteller, to place us magically into the field of play on the regional and national stages of America and abroad. This is a part of August Wilson's legacy," writes Haki R.

COMMON HUMAN EXPERIENCE

Wilson's success rests in part with his artful expression of the struggle of African Americans to find their place in the mainstream culture. Here are some other works that involve individual struggles with identity:

Roots (1976), a television miniseries, based on a book by Alex Haley, that chronicles an African-American family across many generations, from the kidnapping of an African warrior by slave traders to the family life in post–Civil War America.

The New World (1969), a poem by Amiri Baraka. This poem explores the relationship between self and the modern world.

The Glass Menagerie (1944), a play by Tennessee Williams, dramatizes the struggles of a brother and sister to find their way in a broken world symbolized by a collection of glass figurines.

The Odyssey (c. 720 B.C.E.), an epic poem by Homer. A central work in world literature, this Greek epic recounts the journey of a heroic king to find his place in his world as he fights to regain what is rightfully his.

American Pastoral (1997), a novel by Philip Roth. This Pulitzer Prize-winning novel traces the life of a contented and conventional Jewish-American businessman from Newark, New Jersey, whose life is devastated by political tumult in the 1960s.

Madhubuti. According to Elizabeth Alexander, professor of African American Studies at Yale University, Wilson's

> characters with historical integrity talk, really talk, about profound issues of black progress. No matter the decade, no matter the characters, all of August Wilson's plays ask black people: Where do we go from here? What is progress? Can we do it together? What is our inheritance? Lest you imagine that talk as dissertational, however, August Wilson makes characters named Slow Drag and Levee and Toledo and Cutler lie, woof, and signify, in the great oral tradition of Negro talk in the spaces we've made our own.

Fences   The critical reception of *Fences* was almost unanimously positive when it opened on Broadway. Clive Barnes, who had been somewhat critical of Wilson's first Broadway play, fully embraced *Fences*, calling it in *New York Theatre Critics Reviews* "the strongest, most passionate American writing since Tennessee Williams." Barnes, writing for the *New York Post*, praised *Fences* as "one of the richest experiences I have ever had in the theater." A critic for *New York Magazine* praised the work for its universal qualities, calling it an "elegant play" not only because of its artful and fluid composition but also because in it "race is

subsumed by humanity." The play "marks a long step forward for Wilson's dramaturgy."

The Piano Lesson   *The Piano Lesson* won Wilson his second Pulitzer Prize in 1990 as it further developed his familiar theme of overcoming the bitter legacy of slavery through a revitalized connection with an African heritage. A reviewer for *Time* called the play "the richest yet of dramatist August Wilson" and the piano "the most potent symbol in American drama since Laura Wingfield's glass menagerie." Clive Barnes, writing for the *New York Post*, stressed the significance and power of the piano as a living symbol of the family's past and emphasized the effective confrontations in the play between the living and the dead, between the real and the supernatural. In contrast, an unnamed reviewer for *New York Magazine* was largely critical of the Broadway production for having too many confusing subplots and contradictions and for the "uncompelling" use of the supernatural. Writing for *The New York Times*, Frank Rich notes that the music enhances the mystical aspects of the play, concluding, "That haunting music belongs to the people who have lived it, and it has once again found miraculous voice in a play that August Wilson has given to the American stage."

Responses to Literature

1. Using your library and the Internet, find out more about how Western literature and popular culture have portrayed the identity of blacks in America and analyze whether these portrayals were accurate. How do they treat the history of African-American spiritual and cultural heritage? How are the emotional battles with injustice and racism represented?

2. After reading *Fences*, use your library and the Internet to research real-life cases of high-school dropouts in America. Write a paper detailing the potential social, physical, and emotional impact of dropping out of school.

3. Most of Wilson's characters are black Americans living in Pittsburgh. White Americans figure in the plots of his plays but do not appear on stage. Why do you think that Wilson designed his plays and characters in this way? How do his plays represent white Americans?

4. August Wilson has expressed his indebtedness to the art and expression in blues music. He was particularly inspired by Bessie Smith. Find out more about Bessie Smith and her blues performances by listening to such recordings as her *Downhearted Blues* (1923).

5. Read *The Piano Lesson*. Describe the ghosts of the past that Boy Willie and Berniece must confront. How does Wilson employ the piano to assist them in resolving the issues with their legacy?

BIBLIOGRAPHY

Books

Wilson, August. *Three Plays.* Pittsburgh, Pa.: University of Pittsburgh Press, 1991.

Periodicals

Alexander, Elizabeth. "The one who went before: remembering the playwright August Wilson, 1945–2005." *American Scholar* 75.1 (Winter 2006): 122.

Brookner, Anita. "A Disturbing Absence of Disturbance." *Spectator* 294 (January 3, 2004): 29–30.

Brustein, Robert. "Subsidized Separatism." *American Theatre* 13 (October 1996): 27, 100–101.

Glover, Margaret E. "Notes on August Wilson: The Songs of a Marked Man." *Theater* 19 (Summer–Fall 1988): 69–70.

Madhubuti, Haki R. "In Memoriam: August Wilson: 1945–2005." *Diverse Issues in Higher Education* 22 (November 2005): 19.

Parks, Suzan-Lori. "Interview." *American Theatre* (November 2005): 22.

Saunders, James. "Essential Ambiguities in the Plays of August Wilson." *The Hollins Critic* 32 (December 1995): 1–12.

Üsekes, Çigdem. "American Drama." *American Drama* 37 (2003): 115–125.

Wessling, Joseph H. "Wilsons Fences." *The Explicator* (Winter 1995): 123–128.

Wilson, August. "The Ground on Which I Stand." *American Theatre* 7 (September 1996): 14–16, 71–74.

———. "August Wilson Responds." *American Theatre* 13 (October 1996): 101–107.

Web Sites

August Wilson. Retrieved November 19, 2008, from www.augustwilsoncenter.org. Last updated on November 20, 2008.

✺ John Winthrop

BORN: *1588, Suffolk, England*

DEATH: *1649, Boston, Massachusetts Bay Colony*

NATIONALITY: *English*

GENRE: *Nonfiction*

MAJOR WORKS:

A Model of Christian Charity (1630)

A Short Story of the Rise, Reign, and Ruin of the Antinomians, Familists & Libertines (1692)

A Journal of the Transactions and Occurrences in the Settlement of Massachusetts and the Other New England Colonies, from the Year 1630 to 1644 (1790)

John Winthrop   *Winthrop, John, photograph. The Library of Congress.*

Overview

John Winthrop, leader of the Great Migration to New England, was one of the most important first-generation chroniclers of New England's evolution. Repeatedly serving as governor of Massachusetts, he stood out among those responsible for the shaping of the events recorded in the journal that was first published as *A Journal of the Transactions and Occurrences in the Settlement of Massachusetts and the Other New-England Colonies* (1790). However, he is best known for a sermon he gave prior to the Puritan arrival in the New World. That sermon, *A Model of Christian Charity* (1630), has served as a fundamental statement of the philosophy of America for nearly four centuries. Its vision of the new Puritan colony as "a city on a hill" has been adopted by many political figures, including Ronald Reagan, as a vision for the United States as a whole, and it confirms the special place of leadership the country holds even among the world's greatest powers.

Works in Biographical and Historical Context

Birth and Tragedy in England Winthrop was born in 1588, the year of the defeat of the Spanish Armada by English naval forces. His grandfather, Adam

Winthrop, had raised the family to the level of the gentry in Suffolk and had established it at Groton Manor, an estate formed from lands confiscated from church holdings in the reign of Henry VIII. Winthrop's father, also named Adam, was an auditor of the accounts of Trinity College in nearby Cambridge, and in 1602 he enrolled his son in that college. After less than two years at Trinity— a typical stay for a young gentleman—Winthrop returned to Groton and wed Mary Forth in 1605. He then assumed more responsibilities on the family estate, became a father, and spent time in London studying law at the Inns of Court. In 1617 he was serving as a justice of the peace in Suffolk. About the same time his father transferred supervision of the manor to him.

Life was not without disappointments for Winthrop. His wife Mary died in 1615 after having borne six children. Winthrop's second wife, Thomasine Clopton, died a year after their 1616 wedding. In 1618, at the age of thirty, Winthrop took a third wife, Margaret Tyndal. Paralleling these family upheavals was the growth of a regional economic crisis that, by 1627, made it increasingly difficult for Winthrop to support his growing family adequately.

Winthrop's Puritanism Brings Conflict with the King

At some point during these years of challenge and growth, John Winthrop became a Puritan—one of a group of men and women who felt lifted above their base human nature by God's aid. The Protestant Reformation, begun in 1517 when Martin Luther criticized the Catholic Church and the Pope, had spread throughout Europe to reformers intent on changing the organization, liturgy, and theology of the established Church of England. These reformers avoided excess in the use of worldly things and dedicated themselves to soldiering on behalf of the God's providential design. Such militancy brought them into conflict with the established authorities after Charles I, a devout supporter of the Church of England, assumed the English throne in 1625.

Winthrop was but one of many who became increasingly uncomfortable with the compromises necessary to stay in favor with England's civil and religious authorities. Some Puritans, looking for a chance to demonstrate the wisdom of their way, organized the New England Company in 1628, with the notion of establishing their own colony in America, far from the reach of the Church of England, where they could worship as they wished. The following year the group was reorganized and chartered as the Massachusetts Bay Company, and Winthrop was chosen governor.

Writing the Famous "Blueprint" for Massachusetts

During the Puritans' crossing of the Atlantic, Winthrop delivered a lay sermon, *A Model of Christian Charity* (1630), which explained to his fellow passengers the nature of the task before them. He told them that they had been specially called by God to be an example to all mankind.

They were to be "as a City upon a Hill; the eyes of all people" would be upon them. By virtue of sailing to New England they had entered into a covenant with God. If they adhered strictly to the divine will they would be rewarded with prosperity, security, and success, and those evidences of God's favor would inspire England and other nations to emulate the New England way. If they settled for less than perfection in themselves and in those residing among them, then they would suffer God's wrath.

The physical challenges encountered in the new colony necessitated treaties with some Native American tribes and protection from others. In 1636, the Massachusetts Bay Colony organized three militia regiments to defend the colony against the Pequot Indians. This organization is recognized today as the founding of the United States National Guard.

Religious Dissenters Challenge Winthrop

In addition to external forces, the colonists faced social and ideological challenges within their communities. Anne Hutchinson—pushing a familiar Puritan doctrine to its logical conclusion—exceeded the acceptable limits of thought in the colony. All Puritans agreed that people were saved by the free gift of grace bestowed on them by God, and that they could not earn salvation by performing good works (as Catholics believed). Hutchinson argued that this doctrine was being deserted in Massachusetts as many ministers placed undue emphasis on the necessity of obedience to law. This stress on behavior, she continued, suggested that the ministers believed in salvation through works. Even more intolerable was her belief that obedience to the law was irrelevant because God's grace exempted the saved from the demands of the law, a view that Winthrop regarded as a direct challenge to the structure of authority in the colony. (The leaders called her an "antinomian," a Greek word meaning "opposed to law.")

Quite aside from her arguments, however, there were other reasons to silence her. First, she was a woman challenging a male hierarchy; her actions, as Winthrop said, were not considered "fitting for ... [her] sex." Second, her challenge—unlike that of another dissenter, Roger Williams—began to draw substantial support. And third, that support came largely from merchants who were already challenging Winthrop's orthodoxy and would gladly have seen it overturned because of its hostility to trade. In 1637, Hutchinson was tried before the magistrates and, after two grueling days of questioning, was banished to Rhode Island. Six years later, she was killed in a raid by Native Americans. Her death, said Winthrop, was "a special manifestation of divine justice."

In his last years, Winthrop continued to deal with a long line of religious and political dissenters, whom he consistently outmanuevered. Personal tragedy struck again when Margaret, his wife of twenty-nine years, died in the summer of 1647. Never one to wait, he had remarried by the spring of 1648 and Martha Coytmore, his new wife, was expecting a child. Winthrop lived to see his last son born, but not by much: he died at home in Boston on March 26, 1649, two months after King Charles I was executed and the Puritans seized control of the government in England.

Works in Literary Context

Journal Writing The journal tradition of literature encompasses day-to-day accounts of events, along with a record of personal impressions. John Winthrop was the great political leader of early New England, and his writing furnishes valuable information on that colonization period. He has never been treated as a literary figure, though influential nineteenth-century educator Moses Coit Tyler provided his readers with selections from Winthrop's journal and from *A Model of Christian Charity*, along with admiring comments, in *History of American Literature during the Colonial Time, 1607–1765* (1878). More recently, this sermon has become the most quoted document for describing Puritan aspirations. What Winthrop's record of his New World experiences is to be called has yet to be decided; the journal is clearly one of the two most important sources of information about early New England. Winthrop himself called his work a history; that is, while he gave no name to the first volume of his manuscript, he called each of the other two *A Continuation of the History of New England*.

Remaining in manuscript form for over a century, Winthrop's observations formed the basis for important histories by Thomas Prince (A *Chronological History of New-England*, 1736) and William Hubbard (*A General History of New England*, 1815) and a valuable source for Cotton Mather and all subsequent students of the period. Winthrop's journal, more than any other document, succeeds in revealing extensive details of state and domestic affairs in early America.

Documenting History Winthrop acted as historian as well as governor to the Bay Colony. Implicit in *A Model of Christian Charity* was a view of history as a process evolving from beginnings in the Garden of Eden and progressing toward the climactic millennium and the second coming of Christ. This Christian theory of history has its roots in the four gospels and the Book of Revelation. As a philosophy of history it received its most famous statement in Saint Augustine's *City of God* (413–426). The *Magdeburg Centuries* (1559–1574) represented an effort to use this approach to develop the first comprehensive history of the Christian church from a Protestant viewpoint.

Works in Critical Context

Although Winthrop's works have been subject to critical debate over their status as literature, there remains no doubt that they have a historical significance matched by

LITERARY AND HISTORICAL CONTEMPORARIES

Winthrop's famous contemporaries include:

Anne Hutchinson (1591–1643): A religious leader and pioneer in Puritan New England who was banished for her activism in religious ideology termed Antinomianism by its opponents.
Rembrandt van Rijn (1606–1669): Rembrandt was a Dutch artist best known for works such as *The Night Watch* (1642) and *Bathsheba at Her Bath* (1654).
Rene Descartes (1596–1650): The French philosopher, mathematician, scientist, and writer of *Discourse on the Method* (1637) and *Meditations on First Philosophy* (1641).
Massasoit (1600–1661): Massasoit was a powerful Native American chief who visited Plymouth in 1621 to negotiate a treaty with the English.
Diego Rodriguez Velazquez (1599–1660): A preeminent Spanish painter whose paintings include *Las Meninas* (1656).

few others in the early decades of American settlement. Winthrop's sermon *A Model of Christian Charity* continues to be quoted by modern political figures, and his idea of the early American colony at Massachusetts as "a city upon a hill" is one of the most enduring metaphors in American literature.

Incidents in the Journal Written the years 1630–1649, the *Journal* detailed people and events of the Massachusetts Bay Colony's formation of a theocracy—a form of civil government based on the Bible with God at its head. Moses Coit Tyler (1835–1900), critiqued the import of Winthrop's writings

> As John Winthrop, while upon the voyage, wrote this discourse to prepare the spirits of himself and his associates for the toils and frets and depressions of their pioneer life, so also immediately upon going on board ship he began another piece of writing, which he continued to work at not only during the rest of the voyage but during the rest of his life, and which is a treasure beyond price among our early historic memorials.

Despite the inspirational voice and pen of Winthrop, there was an increasing support in colonial America for the separation of church and the tolerance of different religious beliefs. Winthrop assiduously battled these ideas and was succeeded in this effort by defenders of the theocratic ideal such as Increase Mather and his son Cotton.

A Model of Christian Charity Hailed one of the most famous and influential speeches in United States

COMMON HUMAN EXPERIENCE

Winthrop chronicles the extraordinary historical events that reflected and influenced national and world government, religion and philosophy. Here are some other works that address similar issues of history and social consciousness:

Emile (1762), a novel by Jean-Jacques Rousseau. This work tells the story of Emile and his tutor in order to illustrate how one might educate the ideal citizen to live in corrupt society.

The Prosperity Agenda (2008), a nonfiction book by Nancy Soderberg and Brian Katulis that is an argument against the United States' promoting democracy, encouraging market reforms, or giving financial support to faltering governments.

"First Love" (1943), a short story by Eudora Welty. This work relates the story of a Mississippi orphan who encounters an enigmatic Aaron Burr following his tragic historic duel with Alexander Hamiliton.

The Bonfire of the Vanities (1987), a novel by Tom Wolfe. This story reveals a corrupt court system and social injustice as it chronicles the downfall of a multimillionaire Wall Street bond trader.

The Piano Lesson (1936), a play by August Wilson. *The Piano Lesson* tells the story of an African American family grappling with their painful legacy.

history, Winthrop's *A Model of Christian Charity* inspired the settlers as he envisioned the colony a beacon of godliness for the world. Moses Coit Tyler characterizes it accordingly: "It is an elaborate exposition of the Christian doctrine of unselfishness, and bears especially upon the condition awaiting the colonists in the new, perilous, and struggling life toward that they were going." Winthrop's proclamation, "We must consider that we shall be a city upon a hill. The eyes of all people are upon us" gave voice to the potential magnitude of what awaited them in the New World.

Responses to Literature

1. In *A Model of Christian Charity*, Winthrop sets out a vision for New England. Read this text to discover the details of the vision expressed. What is the basis for the vision? To whom is the passage addressed and what is its purpose?

2. To find out more about the Massachusetts Colony, read *The Paradise of All These Parts: A Natural History of Boston* (2008), by John Hanson Mitchell.

3. After reading *The Journal of John Winthrop*, use your library and the Internet to research another colony settled in the New World. Write a paper comparing

the religious, social and physical environments in the two colonies.

4. In *The Journal of John Winthrop*, locate the passage where he discusses the banishment of Anne Hutchinson. In what ways, if any, does Winthrop's account of events seem biased?

5. Read *A Model of Christian Charity*. Also locate and read the five points of Calvinism that form a basis for Winthrop's writing. How are they addressed in Winthrop model? Why do you think Calvinism might be appealing to the people who founded the Massachusetts Bay Colony?

BIBLIOGRAPHY

Books

Aronson, Marc. *John Winthrop, Oliver Cromwell, and the Land of Promise.* New York: Clarion Books, 2004.

Dunn, Richard S. *Puritans and Yankees: The Winthrop Dynasty of New England, 1630–1717.* Princeton, N.J.: Princeton University Press, 1962.

Lawrence Shaw Mayo. *The Winthrop Family in America.* Boston: Massachusetts Historical Society, 1948.

Periodicals

Dunn, Richard S. "John Winthrop Writes His Journal." *William and Mary Quarterly* 41 (April 1984): 185–212.

Gray, Stanley. "The Political Thought of John Winthrop." *New England Quarterly* 3 (October 1930): 681–705.

Johnson, E. A. J. "The Economic Ideas of John Winthrop." *New England Quarterly* 3 (April 1930): 234–250.

Web Sites

Today in Massachusetts. Retrieved November 25, 2008, from www.historyorb.com/countries/usa/massachusetts.

The National Women's Hall of Fame. *Anne Hutchinson.* Retrieved November 25, 2008, from http://greatwomen.org/women.php?action=viewone&id=84.

✹ Larry Woiwode

BORN: *1941, Carrington, North Dakota*

NATIONALITY: *American*

GENRE: *Fiction*

MAJOR WORKS:
What I'm Going to Do, I Think (1969)
Beyond the Bedroom Wall (1975)

Overview

With two award-winning novels and works published in *The New Yorker, Esquire, The Atlantic Monthly,* and *The Paris Review,* Larry Woiwode has attracted critical and

Larry Woiwode   *University of North Dakota*

popular attention. Writing in a distinctly mannered, traditional style with realistic autobiographical detail, his writing evokes surprising emotional responses in his readers. Woiwode's work often reflects the biblical view of covenant families resting on God's grace or rebelling against it.

Works in Biographical and Historical Context

Childhood and Tragedy Woiwode was born October 30, 1941 and was the second child in a family of three sons and two daughters. Religion was woven into the fabric of their lives. His father, Everett, was a devout Catholic; Audrey, his mother, was raised Protestant but later converted to Catholicism. Both parents were schoolteachers, and while the boys were growing up in Sykeston, North Dakota, Everett served at the local school as athletic coach, teacher, and superintendent.

When Woiwode was nine, his father moved the family to Illinois. This event, as Woiwode later reflected, seemed to bend his life in two. His mother, who never adjusted to the move, lost the will to fight her recurrent kidney problems. On January 30, 1951, she died. Her death made her son—who had never understood her disease—fear that his years of negative thoughts about her had brought on her death.

The family rearranged itself after its center dropped out. His father worked odd jobs for a while before going back into teaching, and he shared the children's upbringing with various relatives. Woiwode spent summers with his maternal grandparents in Minnesota, and he later hired himself out for farm work. Hours of turning rows with a tractor gave him a feel for the contours of land and

a habit of listening—to the clattering machinery, to the breathing earth, and to his own thoughts.

Walt Whitman and the Big Apple In time he followed his brother Dan to the University of Illinois in Urbana. By then, the faith of his father had lost its relevance. Not because of atheism—"I can't remember a time when I didn't basically believe,"he has said—but other matters came to the foreground: girls and goals, alcohol and angst, drama and literature. He was not sure of his direction, and this led to his changing his academic major several times (and finally leaving the university, four and a half years later, without a degree). However, Woiwode had read and written poetry ever since his high school days. And as he read Walt Whitman, he came to recognize the character of a writer's voice, and was launched on a quest for his own vocabulary and rhythm.

Stung by the end of a romance in his senior year of college, the young Woiwode moved to New York City in the World's Fair year of 1964. Pursuing writing and acting, he allowed himself one year to become established as a writer and pursued that goal with an important advantage: a professor had already introduced him to William Maxwell, fiction editor of *The New Yorker*. Maxwell was always receptive to talent, but he shared another bond with his new protégé: he, too, was deeply affected by the loss of his mother at an early age.

Over the next several months, Woiwode supported himself with a part-time job at a small press and public-relations firm, while he worked on stories and met Maxwell for sandwiches in Central Park. On Maxwell's side, their relationship became a struggle to save the young writer's work from becoming overly intellectual. Woiwode himself recognized his tendency to try to be profound rather than honest, and he finally realized the impossibility of such a thing.

First Novel Wins Faulkner Award Woiwode made a decision, with Maxwell's encouragement, to write what he knew, and he turned to his own family for inspiration. His first submitted story to *The New Yorker* was a tenderly drawn portrait of his grandmother, "a woman who influenced me more than any writer." One late afternoon in November 1964, Maxwell called him into his office and announced, "You're in." The story had been accepted for publication. With more financial stability assured, he reunited with his university sweetheart, Carole, and they were married in 1965.

What I'm Going to Do, I Think (1969), is both the title of Woiwode's first novel and a description of its character Chris's unsettled state of mind after he is forced into marriage. It was written in the years before abortion was legal—*Roe v. Wade*, the landmark Supreme Court decision that nullified all state and federal laws against abortion, would not be decided until 1973. The story follows the protagonist as he decides whether to break up, or to stay with his new wife; to welcome the child or recommend an abortion; and to accept the ecstasy and grief of commitment or run

LITERARY AND HISTORICAL CONTEMPORARIES

Larry Woiwode's famous contemporaries include:

Madeleine L'Engle (1918–2007): American novelist and church librarian L'Engle won the Newbery Medal for *A Wrinkle in Time* (1963).

John Updike (1932–2009): Updike is an American novelist who was awarded the Pulitzer Prize for *Rabbit Is Rich* (1981) and again for *Rabbit at Rest* (1990).

Nikki Giovanni (1932–): Giovanni is a Grammy-nominated American poet, and the author of *The Collected Poetry of Nikki Giovanni* (2003).

Saul Bellow (1915–2005): American novelist and Nobel Prize winner Bellow is best known for works such as *The Adventures of Augie March* (1953) and *Humboldt's Gift* (1975).

Robert De Niro (1943–): De Niro is an acclaimed American actor, director, producer and two-time Academy Award winner for *The Godfather, Part II* (1974) and *Raging Bull* (1980).

away. The novel won the William Faulkner Foundation Award the year of its publication.

A Family Chronicle With his appointment as writer-in-residence at the University of Wisconsin–Madison in 1973, Woiwode continued work on his second novel, *Beyond the Bedroom Wall*, written in the tradition of the family chronicle. The work is a scrapbook bulging with newspaper clippings, journal entries, and countless snapshots in prose, and it spans four generations of a family whose individual members appear and grow and bleed into each other.

Once an "agnostic humanist, a hedonist roarer," and later a writer with critical success and money but no peace, Woiwode began a spiritual odyssey that led him to settle with his family on a farm in North Dakota in 1978. His growing religious passion lost him some friends but helped him see his writing as a form of Christian service. As he continued writing, he also engaged in teaching in several university writing programs and continued to win awards for his prose.

Later Works With his later novels—*Born Brothers* (1988), *Poppa John* (1991), and *Indian Affairs* (1992)—Woiwode found himself confronted with a thinning audience. His voice was undiminished in power and even more polished in craft, but it was too explicitly religious for a world steeped in skepticism. Not surprisingly, his later novels were not as well-received as his earlier ones. Woiwode's *What I Think I Did* (1998), though classified as a memoir, includes novelistic recollections of his early life that are trained along a running narrative of the blizzard of 1996, a once-in-a-lifetime

storm that threatened the safety of his family and reduced him to burning construction timbers, broken furniture, and even old books for warmth.

A more recent foray into nonfiction, *A Step From Death* (2008), continues the meditative, autobiographical narrative written in the nonchronological and scattered way of memory. This memoir extends Woiwode's story of starting out as an actor in New York City, where he became a lifelong friend of "Bob" DeNiro before shifting to writing. This work, based on a near-death experience, is the tale of almost losing his life as the result of a horrendous accident where he became entangled with a spinning tractor shaft that jerked him to the ground and resulted in a two-hour desperate struggle. During the agony, recalling how field mice sometimes die of sheer panic with only a forepaw caught in a trap, he thus persisted to free himself from the shaft. His memoir has been recognized as a portrait that is "full of wisdom, generosity, humility, love of wife and family and reverence for the earth." Woiwode continues crafting his memoirs, indicating in this latest that he has several other books nearing readiness for publication.

Works in Literary Context

Woiwode, like other Great Plains writers—Willa Cather, Wright Morris, Sharon Butala, and Kathleen Norris—articulates the absolute necessity of the residents of the Plains to establish and maintain a connectedness to place and to understand the relationship between one's existence and place. A demanding environment that challenges survival wraps his recurrent themes of the meaning and impact of death and the intricate negotiations between one's psyche and personal moral code within the demands of family and society. His religious and intellectual prose achieves a powerful psychological realism and depth of insight in an intensely imagined, lyrical style remarkable for its clarity and precision. Woiwode's view of art as a vehicle for access to truth places in him the company of artists and writers such as Madeleine L'Engle and C. S. Lewis.

American Realists and Experimentation Following World War II, American writers began to create innovative and self-aware, or reflexive works that reflected the shape and texture of everyday life and popular culture. From chronicling the elite classes of society, writers increasingly rooted their work in the landscape of everyday existence. Woiwode's stories and characters echo this realism as they depict everyday struggles of family life. Recognizing Woiwode's unique use of language in his characterizations, he is acclaimed for his ability to paint authentic characters with distinctive sensibilities through the use of thought and consciousness.

Family Chronicle Woiwode's writing often reflects complex and historical family relationships that encompass alternately resisting or resting in God's grace. Critic Brent MacLaine comments that in *Beyond the Bedroom Wall*,

Woiwode explores the literary tradition of the family chronicle utilizing

> the metaphor of the family photo album as a narrative device to explore the tensions between the public, immediately accessible meaning of the photograph and its private, often mysterious and inaccessible meaning, which, when revealed, shows or tells a quite different picture.

Works in Critical Context

"At his best," say critics Paul Marx and Loretta Cobb, "Woiwode renders the commonplace with such emotional and psychological truth that all the reader's capacity for empathy and compassion is tapped." They also note his powers of description, stating that "at his best, his readers see and feel and learn with him, making easy transfers of their fictional experience to their own lives."

Beyond the Bedroom Wall After *What I'm Going to Do, I Think* earned Woiwode critical success, *Beyond the Bedroom Wall* extended that success to mainstream readers, ultimately selling over two million copies. Author John Gardner, reviewing the work for *The New York Times Book Review*, is generous with his praise, stating, "It seems to me that nothing more beautiful and moving has been written in years." Gardner acknowledges that the writing is "patently sentimental" and even sometimes embarrassing, yet he still credits the author's work as "simply brilliant." An unnamed reviewer for *The New Yorker* declares that "Mr. Woiwode's voice is a strong and clear one, and his sense of the intricacy of family ties is extraordinary." Peter S. Prescott, in a review for *Newsweek*, notes that Woiwode "writes very well about the big subjects," but points out that the book "is better in its parts than in its whole. As long as three ordinary novels, it need have been no longer than two."

Acts An informal commentary on the New Testament, *Acts* (1992) gained praise as a "tough, moving personal testament" by Kirkus Reviews. However, as noted by J. B. Cheaney, the novel "was also dismissed as shaky in scholarship and naive in its insistence on a literal interpretation of scripture." Paul Marx and Loretta Cobb write that *Acts* "is applied apologetics, a book ready to put into the hands of those who ask why we act in the way we do." Having headed university writing programs, Woiwode has noted that with *Acts* he tried to "address students who might be hearing about the church and biblical concepts for the first time."

Responses to Literature

1. Read *Beyond the Bedroom Wall*, and then find out more about the literary tradition of the family chronicle. What are some other famous examples of this tradition in America? What about in other cultures? How do the families in these stories compare and contrast?
2. Watch the movie version of *The Red Badge of Courage* (1951), based on a book by Stephen Crane.

COMMON HUMAN EXPERIENCE

Woiwode's success rests in part with his artful expression of human struggles within and against the natural world. Some other works with similar themes include:

Dakota: A Spiritual Geography (2001), a nonfiction book by Kathleen Norris. Norris chronicles life on the Great Plains, the intriguing ways that people become metaphors for their land and the ways that that environment influences the human spirit.

Jungle Rudy: Chronicle of a Family (2006), a documentary directed by Rob Smits. Using correspondence, audio recordings and home movie footage, this film reveals a portrait of an elusive man who went off the grid in 1953 to find a rainforest home in the shadow of Venezuela's spectacular Angel Falls.

Nanook of the North (1922), a documentary by Robert Flaherty. This historic film set in the far north of Canada presents gripping images of Inuit (Eskimo) life.

The Mosquito Coast (1982), a novel by Paul Theroux. In this book, a rebellious American inventor moves his family to the Honduran jungle in an attempt to create a utopian community there.

Describe the meaning of courage in this story. How does the main character respond when he feels his life is threatened? Compare this with the main character in Woiwode's *What I Think I Did*.

3. After reading *What I Think I Did*, use your library and the Internet to research real-life blizzard-survival experiences in America. Write a paper detailing the potential physical and emotional impact of this type of experience.
4. Woiwode, writing of the Great Plains and rural America, portrays rural life and the families who understand and value the land on which they live and make their living. Do you think this differs from writing found in other parts of the country? Why or why not?
5. Using your library and the Internet, research the history of Native American tribes of the Great Plains. Find out more about the ways that they coped with life in that challenging environment. What tales of their courage in the face of the harsh winter weather can you locate?

BIBLIOGRAPHY

Books

Cole, Kevin L. *In The Gift of Story: Narrating Hope in a Postmodern World*. Waco, Tex.: Baylor University Press, 2006.

Marx, Paul and Loreta Cobb. "Woiwode, Larry." *Contemporary Novelists*. Detroit: St. James Press, 2001.

Periodicals

Cheaney, J. B. "Taming Memory—The Fiction of Larry Woiwode." *World and I* 17.10 (October 2002): 256.

Cockrell, Eddie. "Jungle Rudy: Chronicle of a Family." *Variety* 407.8 (July 16, 2007): 35.

Gardner, John. Review of *Beyond the Bedroom Wall. The New York Times Book Review* (September 28, 1975): 1–2.

Hansen, Ron. "A Crazy-Making Existence." *America* 199.4 (August 18, 2008): 26.

MacLaine, Brent. "Photofiction as Family Album: David Galloway, Paul Theroux and Anita Brookner." *Mosaic* 24 (Spring 1991): 131–149.

Prescott, Peter S. "Home Truths." *Newsweek* (September 29, 1975): 85–86.

Publishers Weekly 240.13 (March 1993): 44.

Review of *Beyond the Bedroom Wall. The New Yorker* (December 29, 1975): 55–56.

✹ Thomas Wolfe

BORN: *1900, Asheville, North Carolina*

DIED: *1938, Baltimore, Maryland*

NATIONALITY: *American*

GENRE: *Fiction*

MAJOR WORKS:

Look Homeward, Angel (1929)

Of Time and the River (1935)

The Web and the Rock (1939)

You Can't Go Home Again (1940)

Thomas Wolfe   *Thomas C. Wolfe, photograph by Carl Van Vechten. Reproduced by permission of the Carl Van Vechten Trust.*

Overview

Thomas Wolfe is best known for his four novels—*Look Homeward, Angel* (1929), *Of Time and The River* (1935), *The Web and The Rock* (1939), and *You Can't Go Home Again* (1940). Despite his premature death at the age of thirty-eight, he was also the author of an impressive body of short fiction, published in collections including *From Death to Morning* (1935), *The Hills Beyond* (1941), *The Short Novels of Thomas Wolfe* (1961), and *The Complete Short Stories of Thomas Wolfe* (1987). Much of Wolfe's short fiction is autobiographical in nature and poetic in impulse, and it depicts Wolfe's vision of human isolation and estrangement. Unlike the longer fiction, the shorter works demonstrate Wolfe's increased ability, in his later years, to impose order and form upon his materials. Indeed, the artistic merit of some of his novellas exceeds that of any of the novels, with the possible exception of *Look Homeward, Angel.*

Works in Biographical and Historical Context

Asheville Home and World's Fair in St. Louis

Wolfe was born in Asheville, North Carolina, the eighth child of William Oliver, a stonecutter from Pennsylvania, and Julia Elizabeth Westall Wolfe, a native North Carolinian. In 1904 he went with his mother and some of the other children to St. Louis, where his mother kept a boardinghouse during the World's Fair, and where his brother, Grover, died. Wolfe would reference this event with distinction in his fiction. In 1905 he began attending public school in Asheville and in 1912, moved to a private school operated by Mr. and Mrs. J. M. Roberts. Margaret Roberts was his teacher, mentor, and a major influence on his life and work.

From University Student to University Instructor

Wolfe enrolled in the University of North Carolina in 1916, and in 1918 took a course in playwriting that resulted in the 1919 performance of his one-act play, *The Return of Buck Gavin*, with Wolfe in the title role. In June 1920, he graduated from the university with a B.A. degree, and in September entered the Graduate School for Arts and Sciences at Harvard University. He completed his M.A. in English in 1922, the year of his father's death. In February 1924, he began teaching English at the Washington Square College of New York University, a task that he continued to perform intermittently until

January 1930. He sailed for England in October 1924 for the first of seven European trips. After touring France, Italy, and Switzerland on his return voyage in 1925, he made the acquaintance of Aline Bernstein. Though she was eighteen years his senior and married, a stormy affair ensued. Bernstein was one of the powerful influences on his life and he dedicated his first novel to her, though he ended the affair shortly thereafter.

Publication of First Novel In 1928 Wolfe completed the manuscript for the novel *Look Homeward, Angel*, which was published by Scribner's, where he began a difficult working relationship with editor Maxwell Perkins. The book was based heavily upon his own experiences growing up in Asheville, with the main character of Eugene Gant standing in for the author. Wolfe had worried that in the autobiographical backdrop of the novel he had exposed himself too greatly, and he was relieved when most critics hailed the book with surprised superlatives. He was, however, unprepared for the howls of outrage that arose from his home town. He was irrevocably hurt when he heard that the book had been denounced from the pulpits and reviled on street corners, even though copies of the book sold there faster than they could be shipped into town. Wolfe's trepidation increased as his close personal and working relationship with his editor, Maxwell Perkins, deteriorated. While he benefited greatly from Perkin's faith in his writing and from his editorial expertise, Wolfe eventually sought another publisher, due to feeling that he had become too dependent on Perkins.

With the descent of the booming economy of the twenties into the Great Depression, Wolfe's struggle to find ways to support himself so that he could write became more difficult. However, six months after publication, he was awarded a Guggenheim Fellowship and went abroad again. In Paris he felt a great wave of homesickness and, in "the almost intolerable effort of memory and desire," recreated and enlarged the entire progress of his life. The past came back to him "loaded with electricity, pregnant, crested, with a kind of hurricane violence." He says that the second book was not really written; it wrote him. The onrushing memories bore him along on a "torrential and ungovernable flood," thus he decided on the inevitable title *Of Time and the River*.

Writing and Travels In March 1935, after the author had worked on the continuation of his (or Eugene Gant's) story for almost six years, *Of Time and the River* appeared. His next novels continue the saga of the writer's life. Wolfe's four autobiographical novels are actually one towering autobiography.

In 1936 as he was on tour in Germany, an encounter with a Jew trying to escape Germany brought the cruel nature of the Nazi state to his attention. Upon his return to the States, the incident was transformed into one of his most powerful short works, "I Have a Thing to Tell You," a strong indictment of Germany, which was serialized in the *New Republic*. Like many of his shorter works,

LITERARY AND HISTORICAL CONTEMPORARIES

Wolfe's famous contemporaries include:

F. Scott Fitzgerald (1896–1940): Fitzgerald was a highly praised American novelist who, like Wolfe, died at a relatively young age. He was known for his portrayals of America during the Jazz Age in novels like *The Great Gatsby* (1925).

William Faulkner (1897–1962): Faulkner was a Pulitzer Prize–winning Southern author considered to be one of the greatest of all American writers. His works include *The Sound and the Fury* (1929) and *As I Lay Dying* (1930).

Sinclair Lewis (1885–1951): Lewis was an American novelist and the author of *Main Street* (1920) and *Babbitt* (1922). He was the winner of the 1930 Nobel Prize in Literature.

Dorothy Parker (1893–1967): Parker was a humorist known mainly for her stories, poems, and columns in *The New Yorker*.

John Dos Passos (1896–1970): Dos Passos was an American novelist considered one of the Lost Generation, American literary figures who lived abroad in France and other parts of Europe after World War I. He was best known for his trilogy *U.S.A.* (1938).

it was later incorporated in expanded form in one of his novels, in this case *You Can't Go Home Again*.

Terminal Illness In 1938 he embarked on a western tour after depositing a large collection of manuscripts with a new editor. While visiting Seattle in the summer of 1938, he became ill and was sent to the Johns Hopkins University Hospital in Baltimore, where he died of tubercular meningitis, just before his thirty-eighth birthday. After Wolfe's death, his editor assembled and published two novels from existing manuscripts, *The Web and the Rock* and *You Can't Go Home Again*. Subsequently, a collection of short stories and sketches was published in 1941 as *The Hills Beyond*.

Works in Literary Context

Though his life was short, Wolfe's literary accomplishments were exceptional, despite the critical approbation toward his somewhat robust rhetoric. Writing prose based on his life and his search for fulfillment, Wolfe develops strong characterizations and memorable protagonists who are reflections of himself. He is represented initially by Eugene Gant, the main character in his first two novels, and subsequently by George Webber in his final two books. Wolfe's egocentric exaggerations and overextended raptures are generally accepted as stylistic

COMMON HUMAN EXPERIENCE

Wolfe's novels are set in a provincial South, alive with dialects, parodies, and local color. Other famous works set in the South are:

Blackberry Winter (1947), a short story by Robert Penn Warren. Warren depicts the life of a young boy living on a Tennessee farm.

The Optimist's Daughter (1972), a novel by Eudora Welty. Welty explores the difficulties that ensue when a Southern family patriarch marries a much younger woman.

Member of the Wedding (1946), a novel and play by Carson McCullers. McCullers's well-known work chronicles the life of a young girl in Alabama.

A Man in Full (1998), a novel by Tom Wolfe. Wolfe offers a modern portrait of the South in the novel. Its protagonist is an aging man from Atlanta whose real estate empire has begun a dismal slide toward bankruptcy.

manifestations of the author and man. In balance, the defects are minor when weighed against Wolfe's major accomplishments that offer an indelible portrayal of the voice of alienated adolescence and the artful search for fulfillment.

Dixieland Home Southern provincialism of post Civil War North Carolina is the setting and occasional subject of Wolfe's fond memories of his youth. In his first novel, *Look Homeward, Angel*, Wolfe details life in the thinly disguised town of Asheville. His eye for nuanced description and his ear for dialect present powerfully drawn narratives of his Southern home and heritage. Using satire and caricature, he attacked, yet reveled in the richness of his life in the South. However, by his final novel, *You Can't Go Home Again*, the idealistic Libya Hill has also been infected by the march of materialistic progress.

Autobiographical Novel Wolfe's writing was described by John Chamberlain in a 1929 issue of *The Bookman* as "a rich, positive grappling with life, a remembrance of things past untinged by the shadow of regret, of one who has found his youthful experiences full of savor." Mark Schorer appraises Wolfe's thinly disguised autobiographical works as "extraordinary books" that will remain, at minimum, literary curiosities. He continues, "In fiction there has never been such a protracted demonstration of frank self-involvment." As other modernists like Henry James's *The Portrait of an Artist as a Young Man* (1916), Wolfe's tetralogy illustrates the isolation of modern man and the search for something lost in the prevailing milieu of displacement. Wolfe's final novel deals with the ultimate loss of innocence and idealism in America due to the corruption by economic opportunism of the booming twenties followed by the depression years.

Works in Critical Context

Writing came easily—often too easily—to Wolfe. Wolfe tried too hard and stretched himself too far for perfection, but perfection was scarcely his aim. His furious desire to outreach time and space was bound to fail. But, as William Faulkner, Wolfe's fellow Southerner and in many ways his opposite, contended, "Wolfe made the best failure because. . . . [h]e was willing to throw away style, coherence, all the rules of preciseness, to try to put all the experience of the human heart on the head of a pin."

In order to affect this all-encompassing experience within the modernist literature of memory, Wolfe utilized frame-breaking tendencies that shattered the traditional literary bounds of time and order according to John Rowan Raper. Furthermore, Raper, writing in the *Southern Literary Journal*, notes that the narratives of Wolfe embrace and witness the modern "surrealism and expressionism that were flourishing literary movements," which Wolfe would have encountered in his European travels. In the *Mississippi Quarterly* Joseph M. Flora elaborates on the modernism of Wolfe's supernatural narrative elements, "Harry Potter fans will be amused to discover in 'The Plumed Knight,' Wolfe's satire of post-bellum military schools, that Theodore Joyner's academy is called Hogwart; Wolfe does seem to have regarded Lost Cause fanatics like Joyner as practicing a kind of witchcraft and wizardry."

Wolfe's short life afforded him time to paint his expansive narratives in with vivid color, jarring prose and memory for detail, yet ever short of his quest to capture "the full flood and fabric of . . . life itself." Daniel Young, Floyd Watkins and Richmond Beatty, writing in *The Literature of the South*, note that among his final passages, "To lose the earth you know, for the greater knowing" is his wistful evocation of the Wordsworthian concept of a Lost Paradise.

Look Homeward, Angel Wolfe's first novel achieved critical acclaim as it displayed the immense and exuberant talent of the author. John Chamberlain termed it as substantially rich: "*Look Homeward, Angel* has its faults, but they are not those springing from a poverty of material. Mr. Wolfe gives the impression of being inexhaustible." Raper critques Wolfe's novel as one "that overwhelms readers and biographers with its loyalty to real life" Furthermore, Raper notes that Wolfe then bursts the established realism upon entering the "fantastical realm where the boy encounters the avatars of his past life . . . confronts the ghost of his dead brother, Ben, and receives instruction from beyond the grave that clarifies the quest lying ahead."

You Can't Go Home Again In reviewing the last of Wolfe's autobiographical novels, Cliff Fadiman, writing for the *The New Yorker*, praises the author "as one inspired. No one of his generation had his command of language, his passion, his energy." *You Can't Go Home*

Again has often been critiqued as a more restrained, more socially conscious, and more satirical book than any of its predecessors. This novel chronicles protagonist George Webber's step-by-step break with all forces in his past which have a claim on him. Albrecht Strauss writes of the idealism inherent in Wolfe's heightened lyrical prose that, "Just as Stephen Dedalus, in Joyce's *A Portrait of the Artist as a Young Man*, must turn his back on home, so George Webber must cast off the spell of family, romantic love, the dream of glory and fame, escape to a self-indulgent aesthetic European exile." However, that exile is tainted in Germany with the realization of the evil behind the mask of the Nazi's and the incompatibility of anti-Semitism and humanity. Upon returning to America, he embraces and rediscovers his home country with love, sorrow and hope. *New York Times Book Review* proclaimed that "*You Can't Go Home Again* will stand apart from everything else that he wrote because this is the book of a man who had come to terms with himself, who has something profoundly important to say."

Responses to Literature

1. Read *The World Came to St. Louis: A Visit to the 1904 World's Fair* or view the film *Meet Me in St. Louis* to learn more about the world in which Wolfe lived and wrote. Where in Wolfe's writing does he reflect aspects of St. Louis during this period? How does the author integrate his experience in St. Louis into his works?

2. In *Look Homeward, Angel*, how does the young Wolfe portray race relations? Is the novel's treatment of African Americans offensive? What do the critics write of Wolfe's racial views?

3. Read Wolfe's *I Have A Thing to Tell You*. Describe the author's point of view in this story. Why do you think Wolfe wrote this story?

4. Read *Of Time and the River*. How would you describe the author's writing style? What are the realistic elements of the story? How does Wolfe use fantasy in the book?

BIBLIOGRAPHY

Books

Aswell, Edward G. *In the shadow of the giant, Thomas Wolfe: correspondence of Edward C. Aswell and Elizabeth Nowell, 1949-1958, edited by Mary Aswell Doll and Clara Stites*. Athens: Ohio University Press, 1988.

Mauldin, Joanne Marshall. *Thomas Wolfe: When Do the Atrocities Begin?*. Knoxville: University of Tennessee Press, 2007.

Mitchell, Ted. Ed. *Thomas Wolfe: An Illustrated Biography*. New York: Pegasus Books, 2006.

Young, Daniel, Floyd Watkins, and Richmond Beatty, eds. *The Literature of the South*. Glenview, Ill.: Scott, Foresman and Company, 1968, pp. 610–612, 974–1008.

Untermeyer, Louis, ed. "Thomas Wolfe (1900–1938)." *Makers of the Modern World: The Lives of Ninety-two Writers, Artsits, Scientists, Statesmen, Inventors, Philosophers, Composers, and Other Creators Who Formed the Pattern of Our Century*. New York: Simon & Schuster, 1955, 726–735.

Periodicals

Chamberlain, John. Review of *Look Homeward, Angel*. *The Bookman* (December 1929): 31–34.

Fadiman, Cliff. Review of *You Can't Go Home Again*. *The New Yorker* (April 1940): 89.

Flora, Joseph M. After the New Critics: Reading Thomas Wolfe. *Mississippi Quarterly* (June 22, 2006).

Raper, John Rowan. "Inventing Modern Southern Fiction: A Postmodern View." *Look Homeward, Angel. Southern Literary Journal* 22.2 (Spring 1990): 3–18.

Strauss, Albrecht. "You Can't Go Home Again - Thomas Wolfe and I." *Southern Literary Journal* 27.2 (Spring 1995): 107–117.

Web Sites

Thomas Wolfe Web Page. Retrieved December 2, 2008, from http://library.uncwil.edu/wolfe/wolfe.html.

Thomas Wolfe Memorial. Retrieved December 2, 2008 from www.wolfememorial.com. Last updated on September 3, 2002.

✸ Tom Wolfe

BORN: *1930, Richmond, Virginia*

NATIONALITY: *American*

GENRE: *Fiction, nonfiction*

MAJOR WORKS:
The Right Stuff (1979)
The Bonfire of the Vanities (1987)
A Man in Full (1998)

Overview

Tom Wolfe's writings have produced penetrating social and cultural insights, raised intriguing journalistic questions, and suggested the vast potential of nonfiction writing when exercised by a stylistically inventive, perceptive author committed to investigative reporting. For these accomplishments Tom Wolfe ranks as one of the premier literary journalists in America.

Works in Biographical and Historical Context

Southern Tradition Wolfe was born on March 2, 1931, in Richmond, Virginia, to Helen Hughes and Thomas Kinnerly Wolfe Sr., an agronomist, college professor, and editor of the *Southern Planter*. Raised in a traditional

Tom Wolfe   *Wolfe, Tom, photograph. AP Images.*

and stable Southern family structure, the younger Thomas would later say: "I was lucky, I guess, in my family in that they had a very firm idea of roles: Father, Mother, Child. Nothing was ever allowed to bog down into those morass-like personal hang-ups."

Sports and Education   Wolfe attended public school until the seventh grade, when he entered Saint Christopher's School, where he achieved academic honors, coedited the campus newspaper, and chaired the student council. In 1947 he entered Washington and Lee University, where he divided his extracurricular time between pitching for the baseball team and writing for the school newspaper. An English major, he graduated cum laude in 1951. That same year, after a brief, unsuccessful attempt to become a professional baseball player, Wolfe enrolled at Yale University, where he earned a doctorate in American studies in 1957.

Newspaper Reporting—United States and Latin America   In December 1956 he began as a reporter on the *Springfield Union* in Massachusetts. For ten years he worked for newspapers, including a six-month assignment in 1960 where he served as Latin American correspondent for the *Washington Post* and won the Washington Newspaper Guild's foreign news prize for his coverage of Cuba.

In 1962 Wolfe became a reporter for the *New York Herald-Tribune* and *New York* magazine, and the following year he began an article about custom-car aficionados in Southern California for *Esquire* magazine. He had great difficulty trying to arrange his notes into a traditional article, and when he reached his deadline, he simply provided his notes as they were—a mixture of fact, personal observation, opinion, and literary-style description—to the magazine editor. The editor ran the notes untouched, and a new style of journalism—referred to as "New Journalism"—was born. Quite by accident, Wolfe realized that what would otherwise have been a bland and structurally rigid form-magazine article was transformed into an exciting and creative literary journalism that, while still factual, sounded like a novel. By applying the stylistic techniques usually associated with fiction writing to factual data collected from exhaustive research, Wolfe could produce an audience-involving, realistic nonfiction.

Wolfe continued to create sensation when in 1968 he published two bestsellers on the same day: *The Pump House Gang*, composed of articles about life in the sixties, and *The Electric Kool-Aid Acid Test*, a nonfiction story of a LSD-fueled, cross-country trip in the summer of 1964 aboard a psychedelic-painted school bus during the hippie era. His highly controversial book about racial friction in the United States, *Radical Chic & Mau-Mauing the Flak Catchers*, was published in 1970. The book described a party, given by Leonard Bernstein for the Black Panthers—formed in 1966 by African Americans to promote black power and self-defense—in his Park Avenue duplex, juxtaposed with a portrayal of the inner workings of the government's poverty program.

Again, Wolfe generated additional furor with the 1975 release of his book on the American art world, *The Painted Word*. Wolfe's depiction of the "art village" as a network of no more than three thousand people, with hardly more than three hundred living beyond the New York metropolitan area, was highly controversial. In 1976 he published his well-known essay "The Me Decade and the Third Great Awakening" in the collection *Mauve Gloves & Madmen, Clutter & Vine*.

The Right Stuff

In 1979, a year after his marriage to Sheila Berger—art director of *Harper's Magazine*—Wolfe completed a book he had been at work on for more than six years. The book recounted the early American space program and its goal, set by President Kennedy, of landing a man on the moon before Soviet Russia. This work focused on the psychology of the rocket-plane pilots and the astronauts, and the competition between them. The book, *The Right Stuff*, became a best-seller and won the American Book Award for nonfiction, the National Institute of Arts and Letters award for prose style, and the Columbia Journalism Award. In 1983, the work formed the basis of a feature film starring Sam Shepherd and Dennis Quaid.

"The right stuff," "radical chic," and "the Me Decade" (sometimes altered to "the Me Generation") all became popular phrases, but Wolfe has expressed the most pride in "good ol' boy," which he contributed to written language in a 1964 article in *Esquire* called "The Last American Hero," about a North Carolina stock car racing driver.

Wolfe began illustrating his own work in newspapers and magazines in the 1950s, and in 1977 he launched a monthly illustrated feature for *Harper's Magazine*. *In Our Time*, published in 1980, the birth year of his first child, daughter Alexandra, featured these drawings and many others. In 1981 he wrote a companion to *The Painted Word* entitled *From Bauhaus to Our House*, about the world of American architecture.

Writing for Rolling Stone

In 1984 and 1985 Wolfe wrote his first novel, *The Bonfire of the Vanities*, in serial form for *Rolling Stone* magazine. It was published as a book in 1987, whereupon it became number one on the New York Times bestseller list for two months and remained on the list for more than a year.

Wolfe's second novel, *A Man in Full*, published in November 1998, has as its protagonists an aging man from Atlanta whose real estate empire has begun a dismal slide toward bankruptcy and a twenty-three-year-old manual laborer in Alameda County, California, working at a property owned by the developer. These men come to face the question of what is it that makes "a man in full" now, in view of the beginning of a new millennium. With the tremendous commercial (if not critical) success of *A Man in Full*, Wolfe appeared on the cover of *Time* magazine in his trademark white suit, white homburg hat, and white kid gloves.

New Works in the New Millennium

In October 2000 Wolfe published *Hooking Up*, a collection of fiction and nonfiction pieces concerning the turn of the new century. His novel *I Am Charlotte Simmons* (2004) was followed by the 2005 publication of *Carves Down-Home Angels*. His latest novel, *Back to Blood*, is scheduled for a 2009 release.

Works in Literary Context

Wolfe's works reveal familiarity with a modern literary tradition, spanning influences from the naturalism popularized by French journalist and novelist Émile Zola (1840–1902) to candid journalism and newspaper reporting.

LITERARY AND HISTORICAL CONTEMPORARIES

Wolfe's famous contemporaries include:

Truman Capote (1909–2001): Capote was an American novelist and short story writer best known for *Breakfast at Tiffany's* (1958) and *In Cold Blood* (1965).

Saul Bellow (1915–2005): American novelist and Nobel Prize winner Bellow was best known for works such as *The Adventures of Augie March* (1953) and *Humboldt's Gift* (1975).

John Updike (1932–2009): Updike is an American novelist who has been awarded the Pulitzer Prize twice, for *Rabbit Is Rich* (1981) and *Rabbit at Rest* (1990).

Nora Ephron (1941–): Ephron is an American film producer, screenwriter, novelist, and journalist. She has earned three Academy Award nominations for screenwriting on films such as *Silkwood* (1983), *When Harry Met Sally* (1989), and *Sleepless in Seattle* (1993).

Hunter S. Thompson (1937–2005): American practitioner of "gonzo" journalism and author of *Hell's Angels* (1966) and *Fear and Loathing in Las Vegas* (1972).

COMMON HUMAN EXPERIENCE

Wolfe chronicles life and characters with wry, streetwise language and keen insight. Here are some other works written in forms of naturalistic journalism:

The White Album (1981), an essay collection by Joan Didion. This collection, nominated for a National Book Award, is named for the legendary Beatles album that serves as a metaphor for the 1960s.

The Naked and the Dead (1948), a novel by Norman Mailer. Based on his military service in World War II, it tells the story of an infantry platoon on a barren, Japanese-held island in the South Pacific.

J'accuse (1898), a letter by Émile Zola published in a French newspaper. Zola risked his life to publish this exposé of the French government's cover-up and anti-Semitism in the Dreyfus Affair.

In Cold Blood (1971), a nonfiction novel by Truman Capote. This work, straddling the line between fact and fiction, is a true crime exposé of two drifters who murder a Kansas family and flee to Mexico.

Naturalism   Writing with an eye to examining characters in the context of natural and social history, literary naturalists focus on influences of heredity and environment, unflinchingly portraying the darker side of life while "scientifically" offering insight on the determinants and underlying forces that shape human behavior. Wolfe has argued that the only hope for the future of the American novel is a Zolaesque naturalism in which the novelist becomes the reporter, as Wolfe had done in writing *The Bonfire of the Vanities*, which was recognized by many as the seminal novel of America in the 1980s.

The "New Journalism"   Wolfe brought a new style of writing to the forefront of American literature, a style that blends fictional techniques with journalistic writing. According to Wolfe, New Journalists are motivated by their desire to provide a fuller, more realistic prose than traditional journalism—a style that both excites and informs readers. Theoretically, a writer can practice New Journalism neutrally on any topic; the form prescribes neither a subject matter nor a posture of advocacy. New Journalists, Wolfe explains, "do analyze and evaluate their material, although seldom in a moralistic fashion."

Works in Critical Context

The foremost theorist and best-known practitioner of New Journalism, Tom Wolfe has become almost synonymous with the journalistic movement he helped foster in the mid-1960s. After several books and numerous articles, Wolfe's writings continue to provoke and sustain debate. Whatever his future literary offerings, Wolfe thus far has delivered a bursting portfolio of provocative observations and thoughts. When students of American culture look back on the last third of the twentieth century, Wolfe may well be the person toward whom they turn. More than any other fiction or nonfiction writer, he has recorded in detail the popular mentality of the period.

The Bonfire of the Vanities   Wolfe's *The Bonfire of the Vanities* garnered praise for his incisive portrayal of New York's criminal-justice system and the city's turbulent social and ethnic divisions. Infused with immensely realistic detail, *The Bonfire of the Vanities* is, according to Chris Katterjohn of the *Indianapolis Business Journal*, "at its best, art that throws a mirror up to humanity and challenges us to take a look at ourselves."

Christopher Lehmann-Haupt of *The New York Times* writes, "The plot of *Bonfire* is an astonishingly intricate machine that manages to mesh at every turn despite its size and complexity." He also applauds the author's ability to create characters that "remain sympathetic enough when it matters to hold our interest and keep us rooting, an amazing feat considering how contemptible most of them can be." Lehmann-Haupt notes that the novel is in some ways "what Mr. Wolfe has been doing all along. But in other important ways his embrace of fiction has liberated him. All things considered, it allows him to outperform himself."

The Right Stuff   Of *The Right Stuff*, Christopher Lehmann-Haupt of *The New York Times* writes: "What fun it is to watch Mr. Wolfe put the antiseptic space program into the traces of his inimitable verbal cadenzas." Many other critics found both positive and negative in the book. Laurie Stone, writing for *The Village Voice* compliments the "splendid opening chapters on aviation history and the birth of the space program," but notes that "the middle of the book sags dully." Michael Collins, in his review for *Washington Post Book World*, suggests that the book displays the work of a less experimental and daring writer than previous works: "To a large extent the Wolfe has been tamed, his fangs worn down to the gumline." However, Collins does note that Wolfe excels at portraying the individual personalities of the astronauts, as well as the details of the space program. Regardless of critical opinion, *The Right Stuff* remains Wolfe's most commercially successful nonfiction work.

Responses to Literature

1. In what ways does *The Kandy-Kolored Tangerine-Flake Streamline Baby* reflect the traits and tenets of New Journalism? Provide specific examples from the work to support your statements.

2. After reading *The Bonfire of the Vanities*, use your library and the Internet to research the real historical event known as the Bonfire of the Vanities, which took place in 1497 in Italy. What are the details of the event? How does this event relate to Wolfe's novel?

3. *The Bonfire of the Vanities* is the tale of the downfall of multimillionaire and Wall Street bond trader Sherman McCoy. Give three specific examples from the story that demonstrate Sherman's sense of entitlement.

4. View the film version of Wolfe's *The Right Stuff*. How does this film treat the notion of heroes? What role does competition play in Wolfe's characterizations of the astronauts?

BIBLIOGRAPHY

Books

Weingarten, Marc. *Who's afraid of Tom Wolfe?: How New Journalism Rewrote the World*. London: Aurum, 2005.

Shomette, Doug, ed. *The Critical Response to Tom Wolfe*. Westport, Conn.: Greenwood Press, 1992.

Periodicals

Collins, Michael. "So You Want to Be an Astronaut." *Washington Post Book World* (September 9, 1979): 1, 8.

Crawford, Sheri F. "Tom Wolfe: Outlaw Gentleman." *Journal of American Culture* 13 (Summer 1990): 39–50.

Harvey, Chris. "Tom Wolfe's Revenge." *American Journalism Review* (October 1994): 40–46.

Katterjohn, Chris. "Welcome to Wall Street, the Sequel." *Indianapolis Business Journal* 29.30 (Sept 29, 2008): 10.

Lehmann-Haupt, Christopher. "Books of the Times." *The New York Times* 16 (October 27, 1987).

Macdonald, Dwight. "Parajournalism, or Tom Wolfe and His Magic Writing Machine." *New York Review of Books* (August 26, 1965): 3–5.

Newfield, Jack. "Is There a New Journalism?" *Columbia Journalism Review* (July/August 1972): 45–47.

Stone, Laurie. "Spaced Out." *The Village Voice* vol. XXIV, no. 37 (September 10, 1979): 71, 73, 76.

Web Sites

Tom Wolfe. Retrieved November 24, 2008, from www.tomwolfe.com.

✸ Tobias Wolff

BORN: *1945, Birmingham, Alabama*

NATIONALITY: *American*

GENRE: *Fiction*

MAJOR WORKS:

In the Garden of the North American Martyrs (1981)

The Barracks Thief (1984)

This Boy's Life: A Memoir (1989)

Our Story Begins: New and Selected Stories (2008)

Tobias Wolff *Wolff, Tobias, photograph. AP Images.*

Overview

Tobias Wolff, best known for *This Boy's Life: A Memoir* (1989), provided a definition of the guiding principles behind his own stories in explaining his preference for works of others that "speak to us, without flippancy, about things that matter. They write about what happens between men and women, parents and children.... They are, every one of them, interested in what it means to be human." What his reviewers have consistently understood, and what Wolff himself implies, is that his is a genuinely humanistic fiction—both human and humane.

Works in Biographical and Historical Context

Broken Home and Abuse Wolff was born on June 19, 1945, in Birmingham, Alabama, to Rosemary Loftus Wolff and Arthur Saunders Wolff. Wolff hardly knew the compulsive liar and con man that was his biological father. "Duke" Wolff was many things during his lifetime: a car thief, a heavy drinker, forger, and absent father. Tobias Wolff, who was raised as a Catholic, only learned of his father's Jewish heritage following the elder Wolff's death. "Duke" carefully concealed his Jewish origins and prevented relations with his family; Wolff was introduced to his cousins only after his father's passing. Following his parents' divorce, his older brother Geoffrey—who

LITERARY AND HISTORICAL CONTEMPORARIES

Wolff's famous contemporaries include:

Raymond Carver (1938–1988): Carver was an American short story writer and author of *What We Talk About When We Talk About Love* (1981), a collection known for its minimalist style.

Tim O'Brien (1946–): O'Brien is an American author famed for documenting the experiences of those who, like himself, fought in Vietnam. In 1979, he received the National Book Award for his second novel *Going After Cacciato* (1978).

Larry Heinemann (1946–): Heinemann is an American novelist and winner of the 1986 National Book Award for *Paco's Story* (1987). His novel tells the story of a soldier during the Vietnam War and follows him upon his return home as a veteran.

John Updike (1932–2009): Updike, an American novelist, was awarded the Pulitzer Prize for *Rabbit Is Rich* (1981) and *Rabbit at Rest* (1990).

Geoffrey Wolff (1937–): Professor, author, and brother of Tobias Wolff, Geoffrey Wolff documented his difficult childhood with his father in the book *Duke of Deception* (1979).

Oliver Stone (1946–): Stone is an American screenwriter, director, producer, and winner of three Academy Awards, including one for *Born on the Fourth of July* (1989).

authored the memoir *The Duke of Deception* (1979)—lived with their father. The younger Wolff and his mother moved to Washington where he was forced to deal with a sadistic new stepfather. Wolff, desiring to escape his miserable home life, gained entrance to The Hill School—a prestigious preparatory boarding school located in Pottstown, Pennsylvania—by falsifying admission documents, but he was later expelled. Later, after spending years as a victim of his stepfather's vicious behavior, he chronicled the struggle in *This Boy's Life: A Memoir*.

Special Forces Service in the Vietnam War
Emerging from his adolescence, Wolff joined the military and became a member of the United States Army Special Forces. He was taught the Vietnamese language and spent a year as an advisor to Vietnamese troops during the Vietnam War, a military conflict between North Vietnam and its communist allies and South Vietnam, the United States, and their allies. His experience in the military from 1964–1968 was later the foundation of his memoir *In Pharaoh's Army* (1994).

Oxford University and Marriage After his stint in the military, Wolff earned his bachelor's degree in English in 1972 from Oxford University. In 1975 he received the

Wallace Stegner Fellowship in Creative Writing, published his first novel, *Ugly Rumors* (1975), and married Catherine Delores Spohn, an art-history teacher and a social worker, with whom he subsequently had two sons, Michael and Patrick. He then received a master's degree from Stanford University in 1978.

Breaking Through In 1984 Wolff published *The Barracks Thief*, a novella of seventy-three pages, which won the PEN/Faulkner Award for Fiction in 1985. Reviewer Mona Simpson defined Wolff's achievement in this piece as a deftly staged "small-scale moral drama." The novella seems to take up where Wolff's later autobiography *This Boy's Life: A Memoir* leaves off: it introduces a protagonist, Philip, whose defining youthful experiences of paternal abandonment relate him to the young Toby Wolff (in *This Boy's Life: A Memoir*), and it follows him from basic training to service in Vietnam.

Publication of *This Boy's Life: A Memoir* marked a significant change in Wolff's career as it vaulted him into a role as a force in American literature. In this memoir of himself as a youngster, he drew critical success for his horrific coming of age narrative that recounts his struggles with a disrupted home and family life. In addition to becoming a successful novelist, Wolff gained added prestige in 1993 when his memoir became a Hollywood film starring Leonardo DiCaprio and Robert De Niro.

Author and Professor Wolff, while teaching creative writing at university, has written and edited several collections of short stories, including *Best American Short Stories* (1994) and *The Night in Question* (1997). His novel *Old School* (2003) is narrated by a student attending an exclusive private school, much like The Hill School Wolff briefly attended, and continues Wolff's exploration of identity and class.

Works in Literary Context

Wolff's stories offer up human and moral themes often chronicling status seekers and the ways they go about ordering their lives to create and manipulate their image. Wolff has stated that "you could say that all of my characters are reflections of myself, in that I share their wish to count for something and their almost complete confusion as to how this is supposed to be done."

Undoubtedly a great influence on Wolff's writing has been that of his older brother, Geoffrey, whose intervention and example gave Wolff his first glimpse of the possibilities beyond the narrow world evoked in *This Boy's Life: A Memoir*. He described his brother as "the first person I'd ever met for whom books were the only way in which you could in good conscience spend your life." Wolff recounts another nurturing relationship with the late Raymond Carver, a friend with whom Wolff taught at Goddard and Syracuse: "Ray's work gave me a sense of confirmation about what I was doing. I felt an immediate affinity for his standards of honesty and exactness, his refusal to do anything cheap in a story, to destroy his characters with irony that proved his own virtue."

Wolf's fiction is realistic with an edge, sometimes termed "dirty realism"—a movement derived from minimalism characterized by description in exquisite detail with minimal words. Critic Brina Caplan takes exception with cases in his writing where mirroring events has become an end in itself, resulting in sterile flashes of likeness. She also lauds Wolff who, when he chooses, "can do more than find the words for things; at his best, he can use words to test lives against accidental and self-selected conditions. When he concentrates on the interpenetration of mind and circumstance, then his perspective—however trivial the situation or purposefully alien the character—fixes our attention.?

American Realists and Experimentation Following World War II, American writers began to create innovative and self-aware, or reflexive works shaped by the texture of popular culture. From chronicling the elite classes of society, writers increasingly experimented with influences of lives of the masses. The autobiographical nature of Wolff's narratives and characters echo this realism in the terrain of their everyday life. In realistic fiction, events do not speak for themselves; they require both a shaping grammar that controls incident and explains the convergence of circumstance and personal necessity.

Memoir The connection between family and the search for identity is inherent in the critical discussion of the memoir, placed within the literary tradition of the autobiography though less structured or comprehensive. "As Wolff is in print, so he is in person," comments arts reporter Nadine Oregan succinctly characterizing Wolff the author with his memoirs. She notes that even when he is telling a horrific story from his own youth, he is "rarely less than humorous and warm." Wolff doesn't allow himself the luxury of complaint or negativity as, "That's what has got me through life," he comments, that it is the "sense of hilarity that lies just beyond the edge of the awful. The two are so mingled sometimes."

Works in Critical Context

Tobias Wolff sees his fiction as "inquisitive" rather than preachy, though some critics would disagree. "I don't always have answers to the questions I raise, and I don't feel that I always ought to have answers," Wolff declares in an interview with Nadine O'Regan. Writing in *The New York Times*, Christopher Lehmann-Haupt notes that Wolff's outlook in at least some of his stories "seems almost old-fashioned in its morality and its concern for the great wrongs." Erin McGraw observes in *The Georgia Review* that "Wolff isn't interested in exalting his characters; he's interested in judging them, and his stories typically have a sharp moral edge."

In the Garden of the North American Martyrs In a review of Wolff's first collection, *In the Garden of*

COMMON HUMAN EXPERIENCE

Wolff's memoirs of his military service in Vietnam are laced with optimism and told with subtle humor. Here are some other works that address topics related to the military:

Paco's Story (1971), a novel by Larry Heinemann. This work portrays a soldier's experiences in the Vietnam War and the subsequent challenges he faces upon his return to the United States.

"The Father of My Country" (1968), a poem by Diane Wakoski. This poem speaks to the military facets of nationhood.

For Whom the Bell Tolls (1942), a novel by Ernest Hemingway. The book chronicles a young American who becomes involved in military maneuvers during a civil war in Spain.

The Things They Carried (1990), a novel by Tim O'Brien. This book, which resembles a collection of individual stories, relates the experiences of a United States military platoon fighting the Vietnam War.

---

the North American Martyrs (1981), Brina Caplan describes his writing as engaging in scrutiny of "the disorders of daily living to find significant order." These stories, often concerning middle-class men and women rather than impoverished boys, impressed critic Lee Anne Schrieber of *The New York Times*. In her review, she declares that Wolff's intention with these stories is to "undermine our complacency."

This Boy's Life: A Memoir This chronicle of his troubled youth is his best-known and clearest work of autobiography. Wolff admits to occasionally altering the facts to suit the needs of the narratives, although his mother did say that the account was probably "about 85 percent true." According to Joel Connaroe, the "book reads very much like a collection of short stories, each with its own beginning, middle and end." *This Boy's Life: A Memoir* garnered high praise from most who reviewed it. Connaroe hails it as "literate and consistently entertaining—and richer, and darker, and funnier than anything else Tobias Wolff has written."

Responses to Literature

1. In *This Boy's Life: A Memoir*, the young Wolff embarks on a plan to create an identity acceptable to the admissions staffs of upper-class prep schools. Why does he feel the need to change his identity? How does he do so in order to be accepted by admissions officers?

2. View the film version of *This Boy's Life: A Memoir*. How does the film differ from the memoir? Are there

any ways in which you think the film is better at portraying the author's troubled childhood?

3. Read *The Duke of Deception*, written by Tobias Wolff's brother, Geoffrey Wolff. Compare his story with *This Boy's Life: A Memoir*. Describe the problems that the brothers have in common. In what ways do they view their family life differently? Do their accounts appear to reinforce each other when taken as a whole?

4. Read *Sister* (1985) a story about a young woman searching for her identity. What are the goals of the protagonist? Does her search relate to her brother? Do you think her goals are worthy? Why or why not?

BIBLIOGRAPHY

Periodicals

Begley, Ann. "No Dimmin His Light." *America* 198 (April 28, 2008): 31–34.

Caplan, Brina. "Particular Truths." *The Nation* 234 (February 6, 1982): 29–30.

Connaroe, Joel. Review of "Particular Truths." *The Nation* 234 (February 6, 1982): 29–30.

Hellman, David. Review of *This Boy's Life*. *New York Times Book Review* (January 15, 1989).

O'Gorman, Farrell. "Tobias Wolff's Back in the World." *CRITIQUE: Studies in Contemporary Fiction* 48.1(Fall 2006): 71–90.

Simpson, Mona. Review of *The Barracks Thief*. *New Republic* (December 9, 1985).

Wolff, Tobias. "Winter Lights." *The New Yorker* 84.17 (June 9, 2008): 70.

"The Barracks Thief." *Forbes* 136 (July 15, 1985): 19–20.

Web Sites

O'Regan, Nadine. *Tobias Wolff Interview*. Retrieved November 28, 2008, from http://nadineoregan.wordpress.com/2008/07/06/tobias-wolff-interview-sbp. Last updated on July 6, 2008.

■ Edward Irving Wortis

SEE *Avi*

◉ Herman Wouk

BORN: *1915, New York City*

NATIONALITY: *American*

GENRE: *Fiction*

MAJOR WORKS:
The Caine Mutiny (1951)
Marjorie Morningstar (1955)
The Winds of War (1971)
War and Remembrance (1978)

Herman Wouk   *Wouk, Herman, photograph. © Jerry Bauer. Reproduced by permission.*

Overview

Herman Wouk, a prolific novelist and dramatist, has written nine novels and three plays. Though the critical response to his works vary as much as the subject matter, at least five of the novels that Wouk wrote between 1947 and 1978 were best-sellers. A reading of his works makes the reasons for their popularity apparent: each displays his expertise at composing a compelling narrative. Wouk first gained prominence with his Pulitzer Prize-winning novel *The Caine Mutiny* (1951) and has since written several best-selling novels, including *The Winds of War* (1971) and *War and Remembrance* (1978). His best-selling American novels, which have been translated into some thirty languages, portray significant moral dilemmas. Wouk is best known for his epic war novels that have been the source of popular movies and television programs.

Works in Biographical and Historical Context

From Gag Writing to War Wouk was born May 27, 1915, in New York City, to Abraham Isaac and Esther Wouk, Jewish immigrants from Russia. His father was an industrialist in the power laundry field who started as an immigrant laundry laborer. Wouk was raised in the

Bronx area of New York City where he attended school, graduated from high school and then enrolled in college at Columbia University. In 1934 he received his B.A. from Columbia with honors. Following graduation, Wouk wrote for radio comedians in New York City during 1934 and 1935 before becoming a scriptwriter for a top radio show, hosted by the very influential comedian, Fred Allen, from 1936 through 1941.

Wouk began writing fiction in 1943 while serving in the navy during the global military conflict of World War II. During the war between the Allies and the Axis powers that began when Hitler invaded Poland in 1939, Wouk was on sea duty on the Pacific Ocean. He later used his Navy experience aboard the USS *Zane* and USS *Southard* as background for his third novel, *The Caine Mutiny* (1951). In 1945 he married Betty Sarah Brown, with whom he had three sons. Wouk made his debut as a novelist a year later with *Aurora Dawn* (1946), a satire about the New York advertising business, which was inspired by a wave of post–World War II experimentation. It was followed by *City Boy* (1948), a partly autobiographical story of a Bronx boy.

Upon publication, *The Caine Mutiny* was acclaimed by critics, who considered Wouk's treatment of the military affair insightful and carefully constructed. The novel was awarded the 1952 Pulitzer Prize for Fiction and was made into a hit Broadway play starring Henry Fonda, and a film starring Humphrey Bogart. Harry Gilroy, writing for *The New York Times*, commented that Wouk "has a profound understanding of what Navy men should be, and against some who fell short of the mark he has fired a deadly broadside." The book is not concerned with battles at sea, but with adherence to appointive authority. The conflict centers around Lieutenant Commander Philip Francis Queeg, who, according to W. J. Stuckey in *The Pulitzer Prize Novels*, "manifests a professional incompetence that will probably remain unparalleled in or out of fiction." When it appears that Queeg is too terrified to issue the necessary orders to save the ship during a typhoon, Lieutenant Maryk, the ship's executive officer, is persuaded by Lieutenant Keefer and his followers to seize control. Maryk is subsequently tried for creating a mutiny, but he is acquitted through the efforts of Lieutenant Barney Greenwald, an adept trial lawyer. At a party celebrating Maryk's acquittal, Greenwald tells Maryk that it is he, Maryk (and not Queeg), who is morally guilty, for he deserted a military system that had, despite its flaws, protected America from foreign fascists.

Embracing Jewish Faith The drowning death of Wouk's oldest son, Abraham Isaac, in 1951, "deepened his father's position against 'the fashionable, unthinking agnosticism of the age.'" His religious faith is expressed in *This Is My God* (1959), an informal but detailed account of Judaism for "the many Jews who do not observe the religion, who yet would like to know a lot more about it." Wouk extended his writing on the Jewish

faith with his fourth novel, *Marjorie Morningstar* (1955), as in previous novels, the story focuses on rebellion, but this time, in a civilian context rather than military. The book traces the life of a beautiful, intelligent girl who renounces the values and authority of her hard-working Jewish parents only to end up, years later, affirming them as a suburban matron and community servant. The journey of Marjorie parallels Wouk's own conflicts with his Jewish heritage. Wouk's protagonist, Marjorie Morgenstern, faces the duplicity inherent in attempting to live by both Jewish and American standards and the struggle young American Jews experience in coming to terms with the traditions of their elders. E. W. Foell notes in the *Christian Science Monitor* that Wouk "has not flinched at what he sees in his characters' thoughts, [but] many of his readers are likely to." Critics aside, *Marjorie Morningstar* was a best-selling novel and became the basis of a popular film in 1958, starring Natalie Wood and Gene Kelly.

After *Marjorie Morningstar*, Wouk interrupted his career as a novelist to be a visiting professor at Yeshiva University and to write a short, clear account of the Jewish faith from a personal viewpoint—something he had been thinking of doing for years. Dedicated to the memory of his grandfather, Mendel Leib Levine, a rabbi from Minsk, *This Is My God* (1959) became a best-seller. In his next novel, *Youngblood Hawke* (1962), based on the life of the American writer Thomas Wolfe, Wouk depicts the obsession of a writer who is caught up in the intrigue of the publishing world.

A Jewish History of War and Independence Wouk then decided to write a panoramic novel about World War II. Having begun reading standard histories of the war in 1962, Wouk moved to Washington two years later in order to utilize the National Archives and Library of Congress, as well as to interview surviving military leaders. His quest for information also led him to England, France, Italy, Germany, Poland, Czechoslovakia, Israel, Iran, and the Soviet Union. Because of the scope of his task, Wouk ended up writing not one, but two novels: *The Winds of War* (1971) and a sequel, *War and Remembrance* (1978). During the writing of *War and Remembrance*, he spent time as scholar-in-residence at Aspen Institute, Colorado, in 1973–74. Generally praised by critics for their depth and accuracy of detail, the two books may be described as the history of World War II seen through the eyes of an American family and their immediate friends and contacts.

Wouk's 1985 novel *Inside, Outside* "comes as close to being an outright autobiography as he is likely to write," declares John Eisenhower in the *Chicago Tribune Book World*. It tells of a Jewish man who, like Wouk, was born in New York City in 1915, the son of immigrant parents who established a commercial laundry business. Like Wouk, protagonist Israel David Goodkind—"Yisroelke" to his friends and family on the "inside"—

LITERARY AND HISTORICAL CONTEMPORARIES

Wouk's famous contemporaries include:

Saul Bellow (1915–2005): Bellow was an American novelist and Nobel Prize winner best known for works such as *The Adventures of Augie March* (1953) and *Humboldt's Gift* (1975).

Martin Luther King Jr. (1929–1968): King was an African American preacher and civil rights leader who was awarded the 1964 Nobel Peace Prize. He is perhaps most famous for his speech *I Have a Dream* (1963).

Ingmar Bergman (1918–2007): Bergman was a Swedish director who depicted bleakness and despair, as well as wit and hope in his works, including *The Seventh Seal* (1957) and *Winter Light* (1962).

John F. Kennedy (1917–1963): Kennedy was the president of the United States from 1961–1963. He was also the author of the Pulitzer Prize–winning *Profiles in Courage* (1955).

Madeleine L'Engle (1918–2007): L'Engle was an American children's novelist and church librarian. She was the winner of the Newbery Medal for *A Wrinkle in Time* (1963).

worked as a gag writer, although Goodkind becomes a lawyer rather than a novelist.

Nearly a decade later, Wouk produced two expansive historical novels on the founding of the modern state of Israel. *The Hope* (1993) picks up at the end of World War II, and recounts the creation and early development of Israel through the lives of several military men and their families. The central character is Zev Barak, an Israeli officer who participates in the 1948 War of Independence, the 1956 Suez Campaign, and the Six Day War of 1967, and who is privy to political and diplomatic intrigue involving David Ben-Gurion, Yitzhak Rabin, and Menachem Begin. In *The Glory* (1994), the sequel, Wouk continues his story of Israel's struggle for nationhood through the experiences of the Barak family, covering the period from 1967 to the early 1980s.

Recent Work   *A Hole in Texas* (2004) recounts the adventures of a physicist involved with a super collider project who learns that the Higgs boson, an electromagnetic particle for which he has been searching, has already been discovered by a Chinese physicist. On September 11, 2008, The Library of Congress honored Wouk as the first recipient of the Library of Congress Award for Lifetime Achievement in the Writing of Fiction. Wouk, 93, has published more than a dozen novels. "Though underappreciated by literary types," writes Arnold Beichman in the *National Review*, "Herman Wouk is one of our outstanding historical novelists."

Works in Literary Context

Wouk's novels uphold such traditional values as respect for religion, belief in honor and valor, patriotism, and deference toward authority and order. Wouk rejects modernist devices in favor of traditional storytelling with several of his novels, recalling narrative techniques of other authors. His first novel, *Aurora Dawn* (1946), a satire on the advertising industry, is reminiscent of Henry Fielding's novel *Tom Jones* (1749); *The City Boy* (1948) and *Marjorie Morningstar* (1955), both initiation novels about Jewish youths, echo Sinclair Lewis and Mark Twain; and *The Winds of War* (1971) and *War and Remembrance* (1978) were compared to Upton Sinclair's "Lanny Budd" stories. His fiction is characterized by a direct narrative style in which the protagonists describe the events they experience.

Moral Dilemmas   Wouk's work, in contrast to the mainstream of contemporary novelists, draws thematic dimensions based on traditional morality and virtue. His moral perspective is evident in his stories of characters grappling with everyday life judgments. The best-selling status of Wouk's novels evidences wide identification with the difficult and universal quandaries presented, for example, in deference to authority, seeking love or dealing with graft and corruption. Through his direct narrative structures, Wouk's stories are told in straightforward prose and acclaimed for exceptional perception into the human psyche of people dealing with dilemmas in life, love, and war.

Historical Fiction   Wouk's best-known works, though fictionalized accounts, are renowned for their historical accuracy. Wouk's bestsellers, with their portrayal of human drama elaborated with historical accuracy, have made it "likely that more Americans have learned about, or remembered, the war through Wouk's account than from any other single source in the last decade," claims Michael Mandelbaum in *Political Science Quarterly*. He has been acknowledged by some critics, also, as a social historian with a strong commitment to established values. A critic describes the outcome of this plotting: "When the book is done, the rebels emerge as villains and the evils rebelled against as blemishes on the face of a healthy world."

Works in Critical Context

Wouk's novels have spanned a broad range of subject matter, from life and mutiny on a World War II minesweeper in *The Caine Mutiny*, through coming of age in New York City and suburbia in *Marjorie Morningstar*, to the World War II epic of *The Winds of War* and *War and Remembrance*. Wouk continues to be lauded and attract a large readership, while enduring critical attacks for essentially the same reasons. The narratives of Wouk recount action from the protagonist's point of view, and though less experimental than some modern literature, his very popular novels have been adapted for stage, feature film and television. Beichman, in his analysis of Wouk's plays and novels, surmises that they exemplify an exceptionally perceptive concern with American society in war and in peace. Situating Wouk in the same literary tradition as Miguel de Cervantes, Honore de Balzac, and Charles Dickens, Beichman highlights the strong plots, moralist outcomes, and active characters that are the stuff of Wouk's novels. Beichman asserts that Wouk's work counters the mainstream of contemporary American novelists by its focus on virtue, in contrast to those who have disavowed traditional narrative elements such as invention, coincidences, suspense, and a moral perspective.

The Caine Mutiny Many critics consider Wouk's treatment of the military affair in *The Caine Mutiny* as exceptionally insightful and carefully constructed. Harry Gilroy, for example, writes in the *New York Times* that Wouk "has a profound understanding of what Navy men should be, and against some who fell short of the mark he has fired a deadly broadside." Edmund Fuller points out in his *Man in Modern Fiction* that the book's ability "to view the problem within the inescapable military premise without oversimplifying it" distinguishes *The Caine Mutiny* from other World War II novels. Discussing the justification of the mutiny in his *In My Opinion*, Orville Prescott says that it is "the crux of [the novel, and] Mr. Wouk develops it extremely well, with racy wit and genial humor, with lively pace and much ingenuity of incident and with unexpected subtlety." Similarly, a reviewer for the *Times Literary Supplement* concludes: "So convincingly has Mr. Wouk created his officers, so subtly has he contrived the series of incidents that culminate in the final drama, that, given both the characters and the situations, the climax is perfectly acceptable."

The Winds of War Michael Mandelbaum asserts that Wouk's aim with *Winds of War* was to create something not purely fictional and that his "hybrid literary genre" of historical romance "turns out to be singularly appropriate." Reviewing *The Winds of War* in the *Midwest Quarterly*, Richard R. Bolton writes: "Critics who have castigated the book for failing in various ways as a novel have seemingly overlooked the author's description of it as a romance." If one accepts Wouk's idea of what *The Winds of War* is, it will be viewed as a historical romance, with a didactic purpose of dramatizing the his themes of; how the evil emerged and how "men of good will"have been involved with it. Augmenting the personal romantic narrative, the links of the protagonist to the military powers involved in the war lend an in depth military perspective to the novel. Paul Fussel compliments the expertise evident: "The quality of the military reasoning . . . is impressive, and so is Wouk's scholarship . . . in contemporary history."

Responses to Literature

1. Read *The Caine Mutiny*. Describe the character of the protagonist and the antagonist. How do these characters mature over the course of the story? What are the plot points that inspire or prompt their growth.

2. In *The Caine Mutiny*, identify the moral dilemmas faced by the protagonist? What are the effects of the choices made by the protagonist? Based on the novel' s resolution, how do you think the author views the protagonist?

3. Watch the film version of *The Winds of War*. In what ways does the story relate to the author' s life? What moral values surface in the story? Where do you find these values in the life of the author?

4. Using the Internet and your library, research memoirs of World War II in America. What are the varying points of view on the war? Describe examples of citizens or events that exhibit a perspective of the war similar to that of the author. What instances do you find that conflict with the author's view of the war?

BIBLIOGRAPHY

Books

Beichman, Arnold. *Herman Wouk: The Novelist as Social Historian*. New Brunswick, N.J.: Transaction Publishers, 2004.

COMMON HUMAN EXPERIENCE

Wouk's war novels and memoirs are acclaimed for their historical accuracy, though the narratives are fictional. Some other famous works related to wartime are:

For Whom the Bell Tolls (1942), a novel by Ernest Hemingway. This book chronicles the adventures of a young American who becomes involved in military maneuvers during the Spanish Civil War.

Paco's Story (1978), a novel by Larry Heinemann. Heinemann relates the story of a soldier during the Vietnam War, and follows him upon his return home as a veteran.

In the Shadow of the Alamo (2001), a novel by Sherry Garland. The novel tells the story of fifteen-year-old Lorenzo Bonifacio who never intended to be a soldier, but finds himself forced to join General Santa Anna's army.

The Things They Carried (1990), a novel by Tim O'Brien. This work tells the story of a United States military platoon, fighting the Vietnamese War, whose members are characterized by items in their gear and what those items symbolize.

Catch 22 (1955), a novel by Joseph Heller. This satiric novel, set during World War II, focuses on a reluctant bombardier named Yossarian.

Fussell, Paul. *A Boy Scout Handbook and Other Observations.* Oxford: Oxford University Press, 1982.

Geismar, Maxwell. *American Moderns from Rebellion to Conformity.* New York: Hill and Wang, 1958.

Hyman, Stanley Edgar. *Standards: A Chronicle of Books for Our Time.* New York: Horizon Press, 1966.

Mazzeno, Laurence W. *Herman Wouk.* New York: Macmillian, 1994.

"Herman Wouk." *Contemporary Novelists.* Sixth edition. Detroit: St. James Press, 1996.

Periodicals

Bolton, Richard R. *Midwest Quarterly* (July 1975).

Dreifus, Erika. "Herman Wouk Honored with Career Award." *The Writer* 122.1 (January 2009): 9.

Fussell, Paul. Review of "War and Remembrance" *The New Republic* 179 (October 14, 1978): 32–33.

King, Florence. "Shock, Shock Over." *National Review* 60.13 (July 2008): 47.

Osburne, Robert. "Schwimmer Raises 'Caine' in N.Y. Return." *Hollywood Reporter* 393.47 (April 11, 2006): 21.

Web Sites

Herman Wouk's Spellbinding Ways. Retrieved December 6, 2008, from http://www.dailypress.com/entertainment/la-et-wouk10-2008sep10,0,2142009.story. Last updated on October 7, 2008.

Herman Wouk Features. Retrieved December 6, 2008, from http://www.eilatgordinlevitan.com/kurenets/k_pages/stories_wouk.html. Last updated on February 7, 2006.

☸ Richard Wright

BORN: *1908, Roxie, Mississippi*

DIED: *1960, Paris, France*

NATIONALITY: *American*

GENRE: *Fiction, nonfiction*

MAJOR WORKS:
Uncle Tom's Children (1938)
Native Son (1940)
Black Boy (1945)

Overview

Richard Wright occupies a unique place in African American literature. He was the first black novelist to describe the plight of the urban masses and the first to present this material in the naturalistic tradition. Not only is he the father of the post–World War II black novel, he is also the main precursor of the black arts movement of the 1960s. Wright was influential on the

Richard Wright   *Richard Wright, 1943, photograph. The Library of Congress.*

work of other prominent African American writers like Ralph Ellison and James Baldwin.

Works in Biographical and Historical Context

A Dislocated Early Life in Mississippi   Wright was born on September 4, 1908, on a plantation in Roxie, Mississippi, twenty-two miles east of Natchez, to sharecropper Nathan Wright and teacher Ella Wilson Wright. Nathan Wright was extremely poor. In 1911, Ella Wright went to Natchez to live with her family while Nathan became an itinerant worker. Later that year, in an effort to improve their economic status, Nathan Wright moved his family to Memphis, Tennessee, but then deserted his family. Richard lived in Memphis until he was almost eight. As small children, he and his younger brother Leon were often hungry; the menial jobs that Ella Wright had to take did not provide adequate income to support the family. In 1914, Ella Wright became ill, and the two brothers were sent to a Methodist orphanage.

Mrs. Wright and her sons moved to Elaine, Arkansas, to live with her sister, Maggie, and Maggie's husband, Silas Hoskins, in 1916. Soon after this, Hoskins was murdered by whites who coveted his property, and the family fled to West Helena, Arkansas, where they lived in fear for several weeks. Mrs. Wright took the boys to Jackson, Mississippi, but they returned to West Helena by the winter of 1918. Further family disintegration occurred after Mrs. Wright suffered a stroke in 1919. Wright chose to live with an uncle and aunt in Greenwood, Mississippi, where he could be near his mother, but restrictions they placed on him made him an emotional wreck, and he was permitted to return to Jackson in 1920, where he lived with his grandmother.

Wright's education was disrupted by family disorganization, which made regular school attendance impossible. In 1920, he enrolled at the Seventh Day Adventist school in Jackson, Mississippi, with his Aunt Addie, the only teacher. Wright felt stifled by his aunt and his maternal grandmother, who tried to force him to pray. He later threatened to leave home because his grandmother refused to permit him to work on Saturdays, the Adventist Sabbath. This strife left him with an uncompromising hostility toward religious solutions to mundane problems.

Wright's formal education started in 1921, and he attended public schools in Jackson for several years. He was interested in writing, and his first story, "The Voodoo of Hell's Half Acre," was published in 1924 in the *Southern Register*, a black Jackson newspaper. In 1925, Wright was made class valedictorian. Determined not to be called an "Uncle Tom," he refused to deliver the assistant principal's prepared valedictory address that would not offend the white school officials and convinced the black administrators to let him read essentially what he had written.

In November 1925, Wright returned to Memphis where he indulged his passion for reading. Through subterfuge, he was able to borrow books from the white library, at a time when public services were segregated; though the standard was supposed to be "separate but equal" services for whites and blacks, the facilities for blacks were generally pitiful or nonexistent. Of special importance to Wright when it came to reading were H. L. Mencken's *A Book of Prefaces* (1917) and one of his six volumes of *Prejudices* (1919–27). Wright was particularly impressed with Mencken's vision of the South as hell.

Literary Success in Chicago

In 1927, Wright arrived in Chicago, where he worked as a postal clerk, reading extensively during his time off. His job at the post office was eliminated during the Great Depression, and he received government relief in 1931. In 1932, he began attending meetings of the Chicago John Reed Club, a Communist literary organization, and in 1933 Wright formally joined the Communist party. Along with many intellectuals of the day, he was disillusioned with the failures of capitalism, and the atrocities committed in the communist Soviet Union by the dictator Joseph Stalin were not yet generally known.

By 1935, Wright had completed his first novel, "Cesspool," which was published after his death as *Lawd*

Today (1963). In February 1936, Wright began working with the National Negro Congress, and the following year, after a quarrel with a Communist party leader, he went to New York to become Harlem editor of the *Daily Worker*. He helped organize *New Challenge*, a quarterly for works of progressive black authors, and wrote for the first issue "Blueprint for Negro Writing," a statement of his theories on Afro-American writing. Wright also developed a friendship with Ralph Ellison.

In 1938, four of Wright's short stories were published by Harper under the title *Uncle Tom's Children*. In one of the stories, "Big Boy Leaves Home," Wright uses natural setting, varied points of view, and thematic richness to make an apparently simple tale about truancy, murder, lynching, and flight one of high artistic merit. *Uncle Tom's Children* was favorably received, and excellent sales provided him with enough money to move to Harlem, where he began writing *Native Son*. In August 1939, Wright married Dhimah Rose Meadman with Ralph Ellison as best man. The marriage ended quickly, however, and Wright married Ellen Poplar in March 1941.

First Novel: Native Son

In 1939, Wright was awarded a Guggenheim Fellowship, which enabled him to complete *Native Son* (1940). The novel marked the beginning of a black literature that refused to compromise with many white expectations. Set in Chicago, *Native Son* centers around a doomed young black man, Bigger Thomas. Desperate to escape poverty, Bigger, with his street gang, considers robbing a white man's delicatessen, but then gets a job as a chauffeur with a wealthy white couple, Mr. and Mrs. Dalton. Late one night, the blind Mrs. Dalton enters the bedroom of her rebellious young daughter, Mary, as Bigger is trying to help the drunken girl into bed before her parents realize her misbehavior. Terrified of the consequences if he is discovered in Mary's room, Bigger covers her face with a pillow to keep her from answering her mother's calls. In the process, he unwittingly kills her; then, panic-stricken, he decapitates the body and burns it in the Daltons' furnace. Bigger tries to implicate Mary's Communist boyfriend in her disappearance but then decides to flee with his lover Bessie. In his mounting terror, he decides she is a burden and murders her. Bigger then terrorizes the tenements until police finally capture him. In Wright's unvarnished depiction of the hopeless and tragic fate of a black youth in a racist society, Wright contributed for the first time in the canon of white American literature a relentlessly honest view of black life in the United States.

Native Son sold two hundred thousand copies in under three weeks. The following year, Wright's sociological study, *Twelve Million Black Voices: A Folk History of the Negro in the United States* was published to critical acclaim. Wright fully identifies with the black experience and convincingly analyzes the roles of blacks in the total American experience.

LITERARY AND HISTORICAL CONTEMPORARIES

Wright's famous contemporaries include:

Thurgood Marshall (1908–1994): Marshall was an African American civil rights lawyer who later became a Supreme Court justice.

Langston Hughes (1902–1967): Hughes was the leading poet of the Harlem Renaissance during the 1920s and 1930s.

W. E. B. Dubois (1868–1963): American writer, historian, and civil rights activist DuBois was one of the most influential figures in African American history. His most renowned work is *The Souls of Black Folk* (1903).

James Baldwin (1924–1987): Baldwin was an African American novelist, playwright, and civil rights activist. His most noted work is the autobiographical novel *Go Tell It on the Mountain* (1953).

Ralph Ellison (1914–1994): An African American novelist and short-story writer, Ellison is most famous for his novel *Invisible Man* (1952).

Autobiographies *Black Boy* followed in 1945. It is an autobiography, an episodically structured yet richly thematic work, similar to a movie documentary, with Wright as the narrator. It focuses on significant events in his life from the age of four (1912) through nineteen (1927). Wright describes, from an adult perspective, the economic, familial, educational, and racial handicaps he faced.

Black Boy reached the bestseller lists and received critical praise. The second part of Wright's autobiography, *American Hunger*, like *Black Boy*, explores many of Wright's recurrent themes: manhood, freedom, flight, oppression. Wright focuses on his experiences in Chicago, and he becomes critical of the entire American system, not just the South. Unlike *Black Boy*, whose ending suggests a success story, *American Hunger*, which was not published until 1977, represents the culmination of Wright's disappointment with America. In the author's view, moral, economic, and racial conditions in Chicago and New York City are but additional proof of the country's failures.

A Move to Paris Wright visited Paris in 1946, where he became friends with Gertrude Stein and many French intellectuals, including Jean-Paul Sartre. Later that year, in London, Wright was introduced to the progressive, militant leaders of the Third World, who were shaking off centuries of colonial rule. These meetings significantly affected Wright's political thinking and his interest in Africa. In 1947, Wright and his family became permanent citizens of France, and France was his home base until his death in 1960.

The last fourteen years of Wright's life are notable for a shift in ideological emphases: instead of determinism he explored choice; along with racism he emphasized a more metaphysical isolation; in place of colonialism in the Deep South he focused on global oppression. Existentialism and identification with the people of the Third World are outgrowths of his earlier experiences. Though no longer a card-carrying Communist, his writings still reflected Marxist ideals and sympathies.

Wright remained productive during the 1950s, although none of his works from this period equal the mastery of his earlier work. His later works include the existentialist novel *The Outsider* (1953); *Black Power: A Record of Reactions in a Land of Pathos* (1954), which was written as a result of a trip to the Gold Coast (now Ghana); and *White Man, Listen!*, Wright's last book of nonfiction, a series of lectures delivered between 1950 and 1956 in Italy, Germany, France, and Sweden. Wright died of a heart attack in Paris on November 28, 1960.

Works in Literary Context

Racism and Escape Wright felt victimized by racial discrimination and racial prejudice throughout his life in the United States. It is therefore not surprising that racism, and the possible responses to it, form a consistent theme in his work. In "Big Boy Leaves Home," for example, Big Boy Morrison, Bobo, and two fellow truant adolescents are enjoying the idyllic countryside until a white woman discovers them naked, resting after a swim in a creek forbidden to blacks. Black and white fears suddenly translate the Edenic setting into one of violence and murder, terminating with Big Boy killing the white woman's fiancé, after which he hides in a kiln overnight hoping to be taken by truck to Chicago the next morning. His hope of safety barely survives the lynching and burning of Bobo by white citizens.

Many of Wright's major themes—fear, initiation into violence, flight, survival, and freedom—appear in this story, all related to the tension between the black and white races. Wright uses a setting and action reminiscent of the story of the Fall in Genesis, but here violent white racism drives Big Boy from the southern garden to uncertain freedom in the North; his initiation into violence and flight add poignancy and depth. There is irony in the title, for Big Boy is not simply leaving home. His survival depends on his flight from home to escape life-threatening racial tensions in his search for justice and freedom.

Fear In "Big Boy Leaves Home," the protagonist achieves adulthood through rebellion motivated by fear, and fear is also a prominent theme in *Native Son*. Three key scenes in Book 1 dramatize this theme. The opening, fear-filled scene illustrates the emotional violence manifested by the four members of the Thomas family against one another. All are afraid of a huge rat, and Bigger prolongs the fear (even after he kills it) by swinging the dead rat in front of his sister Vera until she faints. When Bigger joins his street-gang friends until it is time for a job interview at the residence of the wealthy Daltons, another kind of fear surfaces. The gang plans to rob Blum's Delicatessen, a white man's business, and each gang member becomes afraid. Bigger demonstrates his fear through violence, terrifying Gus with kicks and threats of murder until he thinks the hour set for the robbery has passed. Hired by the Daltons, Bigger's fears mount to hysteria when Mary Dalton's blind mother enters Mary's bedroom, where Bigger has taken her after an evening out drinking with her boyfriend, during which she has become drunk. Fear remains the central motif throughout the novel, including Book 3, in which Wright now focuses not on Bigger's individual fears but on those of other individual blacks and the black and white communities in general.

Whiteness and Blindness Dominant symbols in *Native Son* include whiteness and blindness. Wright uses whiteness to represent Bigger's fear and anxieties. Upon meeting Mrs. Dalton, he observes "that her hair and face were completely white; she seemed to him like a ghost." When Bigger returns to the kitchen to get some water, "What he saw made him suck his breath in; Mrs. Dalton in flowing white clothes was standing stone stiff in the middle of the kitchen floor." Later, at Mary's bedroom door, Mrs. Dalton appears an "awesome blur...silent ghost-like." Bigger is never at ease in the presence of Mrs. Dalton and her ubiquitous white cat. Even the weather takes on symbolic overtones. It begins to snow when Bigger flees the Dalton residence. The ice and snowstorms in Book 2 are perpetual reminders of the hostile white environment.

The blindness motif is also pervasive. Wright makes all his characters blind in some way. Mrs. Dalton is physically blind. Racism impairs the moral vision of state prosecutor Buckley. Bigger's limited perception leads him to label all others, especially whites, as blind.

Works in Critical Context

The publication of Wright's *Uncle Tom's Children* (1938) and *Native Son* (1940), within two years of each other made it clear that a new voice had entered American literature. Wright was able to give expression to the black experience in America in a way that few whites had considered.

Wright's reputation ebbed during the 1950s as younger black writers such as James Baldwin and Ralph Ellison rejected his naturalistic approach and the ideological preoccupations of his fiction. In the 1960s, with the growth of the militant black consciousness movement, there was a resurgence of interest in Wright's work. Wright's place in American literature remains controversial: some contend that his writing is of sociological and historical, rather than literary, interest; his defenders believe that his books of the early 1940s are as important in the American naturalist tradition as they are in the history of black literature, and that Wright is properly ranked with such writers as Theodore Dreiser, James T. Farrell, and John Steinbeck.

COMMON HUMAN EXPERIENCE

Wright explores issues of racial oppression and the search for freedom. In *Black Boy*, he moves north to Chicago in a bid to escape from virulent Southern racism. The following works all explore aspects of the long African American quest for freedom:

Why We Can't Wait (1964), a nonfiction work by Martin Luther King Jr. The great American civil rights leader traces the history of the fight for equality, assesses the situation as it stood in 1964, and details the change that must happen in the near future.

Amistad (1997), a movie directed by Stephen Spielberg. This film dramatizes the story of a slave ship that, in 1839, was heading for the United States when the slaves rebelled and took over the ship. Much of the film concentrates on the courtroom drama that followed, in which the case for the slaves' freedom is made.

The Fire Next Time (1963), an essay collection by James Baldwin. This book includes the notable essay "Letter from a Region of My Mind," in which Baldwin rejects the idea of separatism as preached by the Black Muslims and declares that the way to racial healing and harmony is through love.

Harriet Tubman (2004), a nonfiction book by Catherine Clinton. This book is a biography of one of the great heroes of African American history. Harriet Tubman escaped slavery and often returned to the South to lead others to freedom, using the network of sympathizers and safe houses known as the Underground Railroad.

Native Son The new ground broken by *Native Son* was apparent in the enthusiasm of the reviews it received. Clifton Fadiman in the *New Yorker* compares Wright to Theodore Dreiser and John Steinbeck and praises his "passion and intelligence" that examines "layers of consciousness only Dostoyevski and a few others have penetrated." Henry S. Canby in *Book of the Month Club News* writes that, "like *Grapes of Wrath* it is a fully realized story...uncompromisingly realistic and quite as human as it is Negro." Ralph Ellison in *New Masses* finds in it "an artistry, penetration of thought and sheer emotional power that places it in the first rank of American fiction." The few dissenting voices, among them Howard Mumford Jones and David Cohn, had objections that were more personal than literary. While there is yet much critical debate over the place that *Native Son* should occupy in the corpus of great literature, there is a consensus that the novel is one of the classic works of American literature.

Black Boy *Black Boy* (1945) met with a similarly positive response. Critics from the *New York Times*, the *New*

York Herald Tribune, and the *St. Louis Post Dispatch* were among those who wrote glowing reviews. Dorothy Canfield Fisher places the work on the level with Jean-Jacques Rousseau's *Confessions* and St. Augustine's *Confessions*. Among the thousands of congratulatory letters to Wright was one from William Faulkner, who writes that "Wright said it well, as well as it could have been in this form." Some blacks expressed mixed acceptance. They felt that Wright spent too much time documenting black despair. A few southern critics made extremely negative remarks concerning the book's account of race relations in the South. Most critics and readers concurred that *Black Boy* merits a place on the shelf next to the autobiographies of Benjamin Franklin, Frederick Douglass, and Henry Adams.

Responses to Literature

1. As you read *Native Son*, describe how you respond to the character, Bigger Thomas. Are you sympathetic to him? Do your feelings change as the novel progresses? Is Bigger to blame for what he does or is he a victim?

2. As you read *Black Boy*, consider the importance of reading in Richard's life. What does he read? What is his family's attitude toward reading? How does reading shape his ideas and his response to life?

3. Read Wright's short story "Big Boy Leaves Home" and compare it to *Native Son*. In what ways are these two works similar in subject and theme? Is there any optimism or hope in these works, or are they both unrelentingly pessimistic?

4. In *Black Boy*, when Richard moves to Chicago, he appears to have achieved his goal, but life in the North is not all he wanted or expected it to be. Show how in Part II of this autobiography, Richard encounters some of the same problems he wanted to escape. What has he gained by his move and what stays the same in his life?

BIBLIOGRAPHY

Books

Bakish, David. *Richard Wright*. New York: Ungar, 1973.

Butler, Robert. *Native Son: The Emergence of a New Black Hero*. Boston: Twayne, 1991.

Brignano, Russell Carl. *Richard Wright: An Introduction to the Man and His Works*. Pittsburgh, Pa.: University of Pittsburgh Press, 1970.

Fabre, Michel. *The World of Richard Wright*. Jackson: University Press of Mississippi, 1985.

Felgar, Robert. *Student Companion to Richard Wright*. Westport, Conn.: Greenwood Press, 2000.

Gomes, Peter J. *Richard Wright: Critical Perspectives Past and Present*. New York: Amistad, 2000.

Hakutani, Yoshinobu, ed. *Critical Essays on Richard Wright*. Boston: G. K. Hall, 1982.

Margolies, Edward. *The Art of Richard Wright*. Carbondale: Southern Illinois University Press, 1969.

Reilly, John M. *Richard Wright: The Critical Reception*. New York: Burt Franklin, 1978.

Rowley, Hazel. *Richard Wright: The Life and Times*. Chicago: University of Chicago Press, 2008.

Walker, Margaret. *Richard Wright: Daemonic Genius*. New York: Amistad, 2000.

✴ Hisaye Yamamoto

BORN: *1921, Redondo Beach, California*

NATIONALITY: *American*

GENRE: *Fiction*

MAJOR WORKS:

Seventeen Syllables: 5 Stories of Japanese American Life (1985)

Overview

Yamamoto's stories chronicle the tensions between first- and second-generation Japanese-Americans, the racism that has affected and continues to affect their lives, and the universal kinds of marital and family conflicts that are sometimes exacerbated in their experience by cultural factors.

Works in Biographical and Historical Context

Internment Camp Influences Childhood Hisaye Yamamoto is a *nisei*, or child born to Japanese immigrants. She was born on August 23, 1921 in Redondo Beach, California, to Kanzo and Sae Tamura Yamamoto, a Japanese couple from Kumamoto, Japan. She spoke mainly Japanese as a child. Yamamoto's parents sought to make their way in California as tenant smallholders, cultivating strawberries and other fruit. Yamamoto came early and enthusiastically to authorship, writing throughout her school years. She received her first rejection slip at age fourteen as she was working through Los Angeles' Excelsior High School and Japanese language school. She later attended Compton Junior College, where she majored in European languages and Latin, earning an associate of arts degree.

In 1941, Yamamoto and her parents were interned in the wake of the Japanese attack on Pearl Harbor, which ushered in American involvement in World War II. President Franklin D. Roosevelt's Executive Order 9066 called for the detention of 120,000 people of Japanese heritage, nearly 60 percent of whom were American-born *nisei*. The Yamamoto family was sent to Poston Relocation Center in Arizona, a camp that eventually held 18,000 internees, situated within the Colorado Indian Tribes Reservation. Replete with armed guards and watchtowers, the camp was a defining experience for Yamamoto, as it was for many other prominent Americans of Japanese descent.

Yamamoto became a regular contributor to the camp newspaper, *Poston Chronicle*, where she published her serialized murder mystery, "Death Rides the Rails to Poston." In 1944, she briefly moved eastward with her brother to Springfield, Massachusetts, where she worked as a cook (an experience that inspired a short story, "Pleasure of Plain Rice"), but she returned to Poston on learning that her brother Johnny had been killed on military duty in Italy.

From Writer to Mother From 1945 to 1948 Yamamoto again took up residence in Los Angeles, this time working as subeditor and columnist for the *Los Angeles Tribune*, a weekly black newspaper. This experience spurred an interest in African-American history and culture that has long and deeply affected her. Yamamoto's first major publication, "The High-Heeled Shoes, A Memoir," was accepted by *Partisan Review*, where it appeared in October 1948. That year, Yamamoto adopted an abandoned boy a few months old, Paul, the first phase in what became a busy and full family life. In 1950, having recently completed stories, such as "Seventeen Syllables," Yamamoto won a John Hay Whitney Foundation grant, giving her a year to focus on her storytelling. In 1953, she turned down a chance at academic study at Stanford in favor of a move to the Catholic Worker community farm in Staten Island, with its mission of helping rehabilitate the poor and dispossessed. In 1955, Yamamoto married an Italian-American man, Anthony DeSoto; she drew on her relationship with DeSoto for her story "Epithalamium." She and her husband moved back west to California, where she once again took up full-time residence in Los Angeles. There Yamamoto gave birth to four children: Kibo, Elizabeth, Anthony, and Claude.

Through all of her experiences, Yamamoto continued to write. Her stories, poetry, and essays have been published in numerous American and Canadian periodicals, in Japanese and English. Additionally, her works have been anthologized in books ranging from *Best American Short Stories 1952* to *Charlie Chan Is Dead: An Anthology of Contemporary Asian American Fiction* (1993), and they have been reprinted or extracted in a host of college and high-school textbooks. In 1986, Yamamoto received a lifetime achievement award from the Before Columbus Foundation, established by Ishmael Reed, Victor Hernández Cruz, Rudolfo A. Anaya, and the Chinese-American novelist, Shawn Wong, in the 1970s, to recognize and promote America's multicultural literary traditions. Further testament to the power of her stories came in 1991, when "Seventeen Syllables" and "Yoneko's Earthquake" were adapted for the screen as *Hot Summer Winds*, an hour-long PBS movie for *American Playhouse*.

Yamamoto's only collection of stories, *Seventeen Syllables*, was first published in 1985, and then republished several times before a revised and enlarged edition appeared

LITERARY AND HISTORICAL CONTEMPORARIES

Yamamoto's famous contemporaries include:

Doris Lessing (1919–): Lessing is a British author who capped a brilliant career by winning the Nobel Prize in Literature in 2007.

Cesar Chavez (1927–1993): Chavez protested unfair working conditions for migrant laborers and eventually succeeded in gaining reforms.

Martin Luther King Jr. (1929–1968): King was an American civil rights leader and led grassroots groups in the Southern United States to nonviolently protest racial segregation. He won the Nobel Peace Prize in 1964 and was assassinated in 1968.

Pat Morita (1932–2005): Morita was a Japanese-American actor. He is best remembered for his roles in the television show *Happy Days* and in the *Karate Kid* film series.

Maxine Hong Kingston (1940–): Kingston is a Chinese-American writer. She writes about being a child of immigrant parents. Her autobiography *The Woman Warrior: Memoirs of a Girlhood Among Ghosts* (1976) is studied widely in college classrooms.

Michiko Kakutani (1955–): Kakutani is a Japanese-American journalist and Pulitzer Prize winner. She has worked as book critic for *The New York Times* since 1983. Her reviews are famous for being critical of even notable authors.

in 2001. Her work continues to be reprinted and taught at universities, and her reputation in Japanese-American literature is cemented.

Works in Literary Context

Japanese-American Literature Yamamoto's stories regularly deal with the struggles that Japanese-American families have juggling the Japanese and American cultures. Several stories, for instance, illustrate the dynamics of the terms *issei* and *nisei*. *Issei* is the Japanese term immigrant families use to name the immigrant parents themselves, referring to them as the first generation. *Nisei* means second generation and refers to the children of *issei*. *Nisei* and *issei* have very different perspectives on Japanese and American cultures because of their very different experiences. Yamamoto's work also refers to the traditional practice of the "picturebride," in which the betrothed couple has only seen each other in photographs before their wedding. This practice was popular in the Japanese community due to the turn-of-the-century immigration of a large number of Japanese men looking for financial opportunity. Once settled,

COMMON HUMAN EXPERIENCE

Yamamoto writes about her experience as the child of Japanese-American immigrants. Other works that focus on the experience of children who are the first generation to grow up in a new country include:

> *Brown Girl, Brownstones* (1959), a novel by Paule Marshall. Marshall's novel tells the story of a young girl growing up in New York, in a family from Barbados.
>
> *The Woman Warrior: Memoirs of a Girlhood Among Ghosts* (1976), an autobiography by Maxine Hong Kingston. Using a series of different narrative techniques, Kingston describes her childhood struggles integrating her gender and ethnicity into her identity.
>
> *The House on Mango Street* (1984), a novel by Sandra Cisneros. A young Latina girl grows up in a poor Chicano neighborhood in Chicago.
>
> *Breath, Eyes, Memory* (1994), a novel by Edwidge Danticat. The young protagonist in Danticat's story must face a sometimes brutal past as she embarks on her new life in New York.
>
> *White Teeth* (2000), a novel by Zadie Smith. British author Smith incorporates several different characters from several different ethnic backgrounds into this novel about generations and identity, set in modern-day London.

many became engaged to Japanese fiancées with only a photograph and letter of introduction. Yamamoto presents these various Japanese-American cultural specificities throughout her work with all of their beauty and conflict. One of Yamamoto's greatest accomplishments in "Seventeen Syllables," for instance, is her use of point of view to show how father, mother, and daughter struggle with the immigration experience, generational conflicts, and ideas about gender roles, all arising from the family's shared Japan-to-America history.

Mothers and Daughters Yamamoto's stories often illustrate the struggles between mothers and daughters, relationships that are even more strained due to the cultural issues involved with Japanese-American immigrant families. Among the particular elements of conflict between Yamamoto's characters is the appropriate role of women. Several of Yamamoto's mother figures, for instance, are part of difficult marriages to overbearing husbands. These marriages were often chosen for reasons other than love; in "Seventeen Syllables" for instance, security and financial stability were the already-pregnant wife's key concerns. "Yoneko's Earthquake" further illustrates tense relationships between mother and daughter, as the mother in this narrative has an affair to alleviate her

desperate situation with her abusive husband. Her paramour has a strong relationship with the daughter, and the ensuing difficulties hurt both mother and daughter significantly. Yamamoto's stories contend with coming of age in households in which fathers are the weaker parents and in a society rife with racism and cultural conflict.

Works in Critical Context

Though the body of Yamamoto's work is slim, critics laud its polish and perception, as well as its depiction of the Japanese-American experience. In the view of C. Lok Chua in *Studies in Short Fiction*, however, Yamamoto's stories transcend the ethnic; they "seem to build up to moments of epiphany (or satori) that reverberate with penetrating questions about human nature and societal structure."

Seventeen Syllables *Seventeen Syllables* has been widely anthologized and appreciated as a rich collection of short stories about both Japanese-American culture and universal human experience. Charles L. Crow writes, "Yamamoto writes of the great theme of Japanese-American literature, the conflict of the first two generations, *Issei* and *Nisei*, and the painful gulf that grew between them." He continues, "These are rich, emotionally complex and tightly controlled stories." Valerie Miner points to the stories' wider scope than specifically Japanese-American experience. She writes:

> *Seventeen Syllables* is a book, not just about Japanese-Americans, but also about Chicanos, blacks, Filipinos, Eskimos and whites of various classes. The collection reflects Yamamoto's rich variety of experiences growing up in California and speaking English as a second language, being interned in Arizona during World War II, reporting for the black weekly *Los Angeles Tribune*, becoming active in Catholic Worker projects in the 1950s, and then raising a family with her husband, Anthony De Soto.

Responses to Literature

1. One of the frequent issues causing family conflict in Yamamoto's stories is miscommunication. Look at two instances of such conflict. How much of these dilemmas are caused by language disconnects, and how much are generational? Discuss how Yamamoto's characters face both unique challenges as immigrant families in a new country, as well as normal parent/child generational misunderstandings.

2. Conflicted parent relationships appear often in Yamamoto's writing. Write about a similar relationship in your family, either one you've participated in or one you've observed. How does the tension between family members cause problems? How does it also foster growth?

3. Research the Japanese internment camps of World War II, using your library and the Internet. Be sure to avoid biased or invalid information. How did the United States justify this policy? Do you see safeguards

in place today that might keep the government from detaining ethnic groups in a similar fashion?

4. Restricted creativity is a theme in Yamamoto's stories. Choose one character who would like to be an artist but who faces resistance. What form does that resistance take? How might the character express creativity within those limitations? What hope does Yamamoto place in the urge to create?

BIBLIOGRAPHY

Books

Cheung, King-Kok. *Articulate Silences: Hisaye Yamamoto, Maxine Hong Kingston, Joy Kogawa.* Ithaca, N.Y.: Cornell University Press, 1993.

Davis, Rocío G. *Transcultural Reinventions: Asian American and Asian Canadian Short-Story Cycles.* Toronto: TSAR, 2001.

Kim, Elaine H. *Asian American Literature: An Introduction to the Writings and Their Social Context.* Philadelphia: Temple University Press, 1982.

Periodicals

Cheng, Ming L. "The Unrepentant Fire: Tragic Limitations in Hisaye Yamamoto's Seventeen Syllables." *MELUS: The Society for the Study of the Multi-Ethnic Literature of the United States* 19 (1994): 91–107.

Crow, Charles L. "A review of *Seventeen Syllables: 5 Stories of Japanese American Life.*" *Western American Literature* 22 (Aug 1987): 167.

Miner, Valerie. "The Daughters' Journey." *The Nation* (Apr 24, 1989): 566–69.

Osborn, William P. and Sylvia A. Watanabe. "A Conversation with Hisaye Yamamoto." *Chicago Review* 39 (1993): 34–8.

Usui, Masami. "Prison, Psyche, and Poetry in Hisaye Yamamoto's Three Short Stories: 'Seventeen Syllables,' 'The Legend of Miss Sasagawara,' and 'The Eskimo Connection,'" *Studies in Culture and the Humanities* 6 (1997): 1–29.

✺ Laurence Yep

BORN: *1948, San Francisco, California*

NATIONALITY: *American*

GENRE: *Fiction, drama*

MAJOR WORKS:

Dragonwings (1975)

Child of the Owl (1977)

The Serpent's Children (1984)

Sea Glass (1979)

The Case of the Goblin Pearls (1997)

Laurence Yep   *Joanne Ryder / Writer Pictures*

Overview

The novelist, short-story writer, and playwright Laurence Yep is one of the first Asian-American writers to dedicate himself to bringing the cultural values and historical significance of Chinese Americans into literature for young readers. Themes of tolerance, acceptance, and the struggle to balance the expectations of others with one's own desires, as well as strong female characters and a dedication to historical accuracy, are all found in his works.

Works in Biographical and Historical Context

Growing Up between Cultures Yep was born in San Francisco on June 14, 1948. His grandfather, Yep Lung Gon, had been born in San Francisco in 1867; this meant that Yep's father, Thomas Gim Yep, was born an American citizen in 1914 even though his birthplace was Kwangtung Province, China. Thomas Gim Yep was brought to the United States when he was ten. Yep's mother, Franche Lee Yep, was born in Lima, Ohio, in 1915. They had one son, Thomas, before Yep was born. The parents owned a grocery store, La Conquista, in an

African-American neighborhood. Yep worked in the store while attending a bilingual elementary school in Chinatown and, later, a predominantly Caucasian Catholic high school.

Giving up his early desire to become a chemist, Yep enrolled in the journalism program at Marquette University in 1966. As a student there he wrote science-fiction short stories that were published in *Galaxy* magazine and the anthology *World's Best Science Fiction of 1969*. He was introduced to children's literature by his fellow journalism student and future wife, Joanne Rose Ryder.

Yep transferred to the University of California at Santa Cruz in 1968 and received his BA in 1970. In 1973 he published his first novel, *Sweetwater*, a science-fiction work set on the planet Harmony. The young protagonist, Tyree Priest, is a member of a racial minority, the half-amphibian Silkies. Against his father's wishes he forms a friendship with one of the majority Argans, who opens his eyes to the reality of prejudice. Yep earned his PhD from the State University of New York at Buffalo in 1975 and took part-time positions as an instructor of English at the satellite campus of Foothill College in Mountain View, California, and at San Jose City College.

Juvenile Writing Earns Recognition

In 1975 Yep published the historical novel *Dragonwings*, the first in his Golden Mountain Chronicles series about several generations of the Young family of Chinese immigrants to the United States—the "Land of the Golden Mountain," as the Chinese called it. The product of more than six years of research into Chinese-American history, *Dragonwings* depicts the immigrant culture of the 1900s, including the bachelor societies created by Chinese men bereft of their families because of immigration restrictions and financial concerns. The main character is based in part on Fung Joe Guey, who built and flew a biplane in 1909; the character's obsession with achieving flight is based on Yep's father's desire for a garden in their barren backyard when Yep was a child and on his talent for building kites. *Dragonwings* won a Newbery Honor Book Award, a Children's Book Award from the American Library Association, an International Reading Association Award, and the Carter A. Woodson Award from the National Council of Social Studies, all in 1976.

In 1976 Yep left his position at San Jose City College to devote himself full-time to his writing. Over the next thirty years, Yep wrote prolifically, producing individual novels, fantasy series, plays, and collections of folktales. Among his better known works is the second novel of the Golden Mountain Chronicles series, *Child of the Owl*. This narrative is set in San Francisco's Chinatown in 1965. The story reflects Yep's feelings when he was growing up and struggling with being too Chinese to be considered American and with being too American to be considered Chinese. The novel won the *Boston Globe-Horn Book* Award in 1977 and the Jane Addams Award of the Women's International League for Peace and Freedom in 1978.

Writing Series, Folktales, Plays

Yep then continued the Golden Mountain Chronicles in 1979 with *Sea Glass*. When his family moves from San Francisco's Chinatown to the mostly white coastal village of Concepcion, Craig Chin becomes an outsider in his mostly Anglo school. Overwhelmed by these changes and by his father's obsession with turning him into a superior athlete, Craig escapes the pressures by visiting his Uncle Quail. His uncle helps him to choose between being himself and being the person others want him to be. Craig's physical description, ineptitude at sports, and the pressure he feels from his father are autobiographical; Yep's Uncle Francis is the model for Uncle Quail's knowledge of sea life and scuba diving. The work won the Commonwealth Club of California Silver Medal in 1979.

Yep returned to the Golden Mountain Chronicles in 1984 with *The Serpent's Children*, which begins during the Taiping Revolution in China in 1849. After her mother's death, Cassia, her brother Foxfire, and their father struggle with poverty as they try to protect their lands from the invading Manchus and rival clans, and to honor their mother's dying wish to keep the family together. Yep shows how the Chinese were forced to send male relatives off to America, the "Land of the Golden Mountain," to survive.

Yep and Ryder were married on February 14, 1985. From 1987 through 1989 Yep was a lecturer in Asian-American studies at the University of California at Berkeley. In 1987 he had two one-act plays produced in San Francisco.

In 1989 Yep published *The Rainbow People*, in which he retells twenty Chinese folktales that had been gathered in Oakland's Chinatown in the 1930s as part of a federal government Works Progress Administration project, a part of Franklin Delano Roosevelt's economic-recovery program during the 1930s Depression. Yep's introduction describes the time and place from which the stories come and the way people lived during the period, and he prefaces each story with an explanation of how it relates to the Chinese-American experience. The book won Yep his second *Boston Globe-Horn Book* Award in 1989. In 1990, Yep was made writer-in-residence at the University of California, Santa Barbara, and won a fellowship from the National Endowment for the Arts.

More Asian Inspirations

Yep returned to the Golden Mountain series in 1993 with *Dragon's Gate*; the second of his books to win a Newbery Honor Book Award, it is the prequel to the previous winner, *Dragonwings*. Yep published a Chinese version of the novel under the title *Lung Men* in 1995.

Aimed at younger readers, Yep's anthology *American Dragons: Twenty-Five Asian-American Voices* (1993) comprises short stories, poems, and excerpts from plays about growing up Asian-American by authors with cultural roots throughout Southeast Asia, from Japan to India. The selections raise questions about identity as the youthful protagonists either embrace or reject their Asian heritage.

Yep's next story, a novella called *Hiroshima* (1995), recounts a young girl's life after the American atomic bomb is dropped on her city on August 6, 1945.

Mysteries and Recognition Another of Yep's better-known works is the first in another series, the Chinatown Mysteries: *The Case of the Goblin Pearls.* For his many contributions to young-adult literature, Yep won the Laura Ingalls Wilder medal from the American Library Association in 2005.

With his positive emphases on families and interpersonal relationships, on the search for identity and the importance of cultural heritage, and on tolerance and strength of character, Laurence Yep is a key writer in Asian-American literature for children and young adults. He creates works set in both modern and past times that interest younger readers while maintaining historical integrity. His versatility and range of material, from science fiction and Chinese folktales to historical novels and modern-day adventures, mark him as a major writer.

Works in Literary Context

Chinese Folktales Yep has often used Chinese fables as the basis for his engaging stories. *The Boy Who Swallowed Snakes* (1994), for example, tells of a boy named Little Chou who gets rid of a dangerous magic snake by swallowing it. The snake doesn't kill the virtuous boy, as legend predicts, but instead multiplies a thousand-fold, until the greedy man who planted the snake thinking it would bring him riches returns to claim it and is destroyed. Equally engaging is *The City of Dragons* (1995), about a young boy with the world's saddest face who leaves his family in disgrace to travel with a band of giants to the City of Dragons. The giants tell sad tales to make the dragons cry, for dragon tears turn to pearls, but to no avail. When the dragons see the boy's face, however, they are overcome with sorrow, and their tears provide the boy with the riches that return him to his family a hero. In *The Ghost Fox* (1994), an evil fox spirit comes to poison the soul of Little Lee's mother, turning her against the boy in his father's absence. The mother grows angry and cruel, turning Little Lee from their home, but Lee proves to be even more clever and courageous than the crafty fox, and he eventually banishes the fox and reclaims the love of his mother. The tale exploits every child's fear of losing their mother's love, but offers the pleasing moral that love conquers in the end.

Children's Literature Yep has made significant contributions to several genres of children's fiction. During the 1980s he wrote three mysteries, two of which—*The Mark Twain Murders* (1982) and *The Tom Sawyer Fires* (1984)—feature as their main character nineteenth-century American writer Mark Twain as a young reporter in San Francisco. In 1997 Yep introduced the Chinatown Mystery series with *The Case of the Goblin Pearls.* In this captivating novel twelve-year-old Lily joins forces with a

LITERARY AND HISTORICAL CONTEMPORARIES

Yep's famous contemporaries include:

Amy Tan (1952–): Tan is a Chinese-American novelist famous for her novel *The Joy Luck Club* (1989), a tale of relationships between Chinese-American mothers and daughters.

Wayne Wang (1949–): Wang is a Chinese-American director who has directed films such as *Anywhere But Here* (1999) and *Because of Winn-Dixie* (2005).

J. K. Rowling (1965–): Made internationally famous by her financially lucrative fantasy series about a young wizard named Harry Potter, Rowling became an even greater commercial success through successful films and merchandising.

Yo-Yo Ma (1955–): An internationally famous cello player of Chinese descent, Ma has won several Grammy Awards and spends time educating children about classical music.

Laura Bush (1946–): Two-term First Lady to President George W. Bush, Laura Bush championed children's reading during her time in the White House. She is trained as a librarian and a teacher.

great aunt named Tiger Lil, a character actress with a forceful personality, to solve the mystery behind a series of gang robberies. Yep is an avid proponent of the power of children's literature. "To write for children, one must try to see things as they do; and trying to look at the world with the fresh, inexperienced eyes of a child enables the writer to approach the world with a sense of wonder," he wrote in *Reading Teacher.* Yep's empathetic understanding of young people has brought him acclaim from critics and readers alike. "There are scenes in *Child of the Owl*," Maxine Hong Kingston writes in *Washington Post Book World*, "that will make every Chinese-American child gasp with recognition. 'Hey! That happened to me. I did that. I saw that.'"

Works in Critical Context

Many critics agree that Yep's success as a writer is due more to his imaginative, well-paced writing style than to his subject matter, which covers a broad range of topics.

Dragonwings Yep provides the reader with a new way of viewing Chinese Americans, not as yellow men living in white society but as ordinary—as well as extraordinary—people. In his afterword to *Dragonwings*, he states: "I wanted to show that Chinese-Americans are human beings upon whom America has had a unique effect." Having been described by critics as sensitive, adventurous, and original, *Dragonwings* remains Yep's most acclaimed and

COMMON HUMAN EXPERIENCE

Yep often writes about the difficult relationship between fathers and sons. Other works that consider this relationship include:

Hamlet (c. 1602), a play by William Shakespeare. Danish Prince Hamlet must decide if he will avenge his father's death after he learns his uncle murdered him. Indecision and self-doubt overcome the protagonist in this classic tragedy.

Fathers and Sons (1862), a novel by Ivan Turgenev. Set in Russia, this story shows the generational clash when a young medical student disavows his father's traditional thought in favor of his own path.

"A River Runs Through It" (1976), a short story by Norman Maclean. Exploring the difficult relationship between himself, his brother, and his Presbyterian father, Maclean weaves trout fishing and the Montana landscape into his autobiographical narrative.

The Kite Runner (2003), a novel by Khaled Hosseini. An Afghani immigrant to America returns home to rescue the son of a childhood friend, whom he betrayed. Once in war-torn Kabul, the narrator not only learns about the fate of his friend's family but also learns much about his own father.

The Pursuit of Happyness (2006), a film starring Will Smith. Based on the true story of successful Wall Street businessman Chris Gardner, this film follows as Gardner struggles in a competitive stockbroker internship while caring for his son.

successful work, chosen as an ALA Notable Children's Book in 1975 and selected as a Newbery Honor Book for 1976. Critics applauded the complexity of Yep's characters and his sensitive portrayal of the prejudice they faced in the United States. Frank Chin, for instance, writes, "In *Dragonwings*, Yep has written an Asian-American folklore that will someday be as deeply rooted in American folklore as Paul Bunyan and Johnny Appleseed." Additionally, Ruth H. Pelmas writes that, "as an exquisitely written poem of praise to the courage and industry of the Chinese-American people, *Dragonwings* is a triumph."

Responses to Literature

1. To write *Dragonwings*, Yep conducted extensive research on Chinese-American history. What part of your family background is less familiar to you? Find ways to research this history, using the Internet and your librarian. How can this element of your background influence your perception?

2. Read one of Yep's series of books, such as the Golden Mountain Chronicles. Trace the theme of individual identity through the books. How do Yep's characters grow into a stronger sense of themselves? How does community help and hinder that discovery?

3. Yep includes many different cultural heritages and racial backgrounds for his characters. Do you think Yep's portrayals are fair and balanced? Do you find any elements of stereotype? Write an essay about the effects of diversity in Yep's novels.

4. Yep writes about the Chinese immigrant experience in California. Choose another immigrant group in the United States, such as the Mexican or the Irish. Using the Internet and your library, research its experience in America, including the challenges it has faced. Compare your research with the experiences detailed in Yep's writing. How does the Chinese-American experience compare with other immigrants' lives in the United States?

BIBLIOGRAPHY

Books

Kim, Elaine. *Asian American Literature: An Introduction to the Writings and Their Social Context*. Philadelphia.: Temple University Press, 1982.

Lim, Shirley Geok-lin and Amy Ling, eds. *Reading the Literatures of Asian America*. Philadelphia.: Temple University Press, 1992.

Wong, Sau-ling Cynthia. *Reading Asian American Literature: From Necessity to Extravagance*. Princeton, N.J.: Princeton University Press, 1993.

Periodicals

Bush, Margaret A. "Laurence Yep the Traitor." *The Horn Book Magazine* (March–April 2003): 219.

Chin, Frank. Review of *Dragonwings*. *Interracial Books for Children Bulletin* 7.2 & 3 (1976).

Kingston, Maxine Hong. "Middle Kingdom to Middle America." *Washington Post Book World* (May 1, 1977): E1, E8.

Pelmas, Ruth H. Review of *Dragonwings*. *New York Times Book Review* (November 16, 1975).

Yep, Laurence. "Writing *Dragonwings*." *Reading Teacher* (January 1977): 359–363.

⊛ Anzia Yezierska

BORN: *1885, Plinsk, Russia*

DIED: *1970, New York, New York*

NATIONALITY: *American*

GENRE: *Fiction*

MAJOR WORKS:

Hungry Hearts (1920)

Salome of the Tenements (1923)

Bread Givers (1925)

Anzia Yezierska   *Yezierska, Anzia, c.1885-1970, photograph. Culver Pictures, Inc.*

Overview

Anzia Yezierska's special contribution to Jewish American literature lies in her depiction of the immigrant experience from the point of view of the Jewish woman, whose struggles to achieve autonomy, both within the family and in the larger American society she describes sympathetically and persuasively.

Works in Biographical and Historical Context

Russian Immigrant Finds Education the Key

Born in a mud hut in Plinsk, on the Russian-Polish border, to Bernard and Pearl Yezierska, Anzia's family came to America in 1890. Their immigration was part of a mass arrival to the United States of people ready to work, many from southern and eastern Europe. As America's economy was becoming more and more industrialized, both skilled and unskilled workers were needed in the newly formed factories throughout the northern U.S. At the immigrants' portal of Ellis Island, each Yezierska family member was given a new name that was easier to pronounce and spell in America. Yezierska became Hattie Mayer.

The family settled in a tenement on the Lower East Side of New York. Yezierska's sisters went to work in sweatshops, while the young Anzia sold paper bags to pushcart peddlers when she was not in school. The

Yezierska family quickly learned that America held opportunities for an individual with an education. All the brothers were given the opportunity for schooling, which enabled them to secure stable jobs and earn their own livings, while the sisters supported their rabbi father until they married and had children. By day Yezierska worked at menial jobs and in a sweatshop, so-called because of its dangerous and unregulated factory environment. Because the Industrial Revolution was still a relatively new phenomenon in America, government regulations about proper work environments had not yet been established. For example, laws preventing child labor were not instituted until the Fair Labor Standards Act of 1938.

Searching for Fulfillment

Though she worked all day, Yezierska spent her nights attending school to learn to read and write English. Three years after her arrival in America she obtained a scholarship to study domestic science at Columbia University. However, her subsequent career as a teacher of that subject was short-lived; she found herself to be temperamentally unsuited to the job of teaching. In or about 1910, she married an attorney, but after only a few months this marriage was annulled. Shortly thereafter she married Arnold Levitas, a teacher and author of textbooks, and gave birth to a daughter, Louise. However, finding domestic chores and maternal responsibilities oppressive, Yezierska left Levitas and soon after surrendered her daughter to his care. She devoted the remainder of her life to pursuing a career as a writer.

In her fiction, Yezierska repeatedly describes the attempt of a spirited Jewish female protagonist from the ghetto to bridge the chasm between the chaotic though vital immigrant milieu and the orderly but ultimately repressed world of the uptown Jews and WASPs (White Anglo-Saxon Protestants). Seeking to capture the essence of ghetto life and to approximate both the rhythms of her native Yiddish tongue and the fractured English of her immigrant characters, she fashioned a series of novels and short stories that delineate the metamorphosis of the immigrant girl from naive to educated young lady and her subsequent liaison with either an urbane and assimilated Jewish young man or a scholarly WASP who serves as her mentor. Several of her short stories focus on the daily experiences of middle-aged and older women from the ghetto. Writing about her own literary efforts, Yezierska said, "Writing about the Ghetto, I found America." To Yezierska, America was a miraculous country that afforded those immigrants possessing determination and intelligence the opportunity to "make a person" of themselves. By becoming educated, they would be able to escape the squalor and ugliness of the ghetto; in turn, they could infuse their warmth and vitality into the sterile, restrained Anglo-Saxon culture. Frequently in her works, however, the protagonist, once she has become Americanized, finds herself suspended uncomfortably between the restrictive but colorful ghetto culture and the antiseptic uptown world for which she had once yearned.

Writing Career Focuses on Popular Immigration Issues With the publication of her short story "The Free Vacation House" 1915, Yezierska's literary career was launched. In 1917 Yezierska made the acquaintance of prominent intellectual John Dewey, who is best known for his work in pragmatic philosophy and psychology. Yezierska obtained permission to audit his seminar in social and political thought at Columbia University. During the course of this year, a romantic relationship developed between the fifty-eight-year-old Dewey and Yezierska, who was then in her thirties. Included in *The Poems of John Dewey* (published posthumously, 1977) are several poems that he wrote to and about Yezierska in 1917 and 1918. Dewey was to serve as the prototype for the supportive though austere Anglo-Saxon male appearing again and again in her fiction, in the role of mentor and sometimes lover of the young Jewish immigrant female protagonist. When Dewey's seminar concluded, he asked Yezierska to serve as translator for a group of graduate students who were conducting a study of the Polish community in Philadelphia. This experience is treated fictionally in Yezierska's novel *All I Could Never Be* (1932). Dewey and Yezierska parted in 1918, when he left for an extended trip abroad. Recognition for her realistic fictional representation of immigrant life came to Yezierska when Edward J. O'Brien not only included her short story "The Fat of the Land" in *Best Short Stories of 1919* but also dedicated the volume to her.

The next year Yezierska published a volume of short stories about Jewish immigrant life, *Hungry Hearts*. With the appearance of this book, she became a celebrity, for Hollywood producer Samuel Goldwyn purchased the film rights to the work and with much fanfare brought her out to Hollywood. Called "The Sweatshop Cinderella" by publicists of the day, Yezierska settled in California with the intention of pursuing her writing career there, but within the year she returned East because she discovered that when she was no longer living in the familiar milieu of New York's Lower East Side she could not write. After her return, she began her first novel, *Salome of the Tenements*, which depicts the difficulties immigrants encounter in the process of becoming American. The rise of settlement houses in this period provides one of the main historical contexts for Yezierska's novel. In particular, the novel is a critique of settlement-house education projects aimed at Americanizing immigrants by assimilating them into the so-called American melting pot, a process that replaced the customs that immigrants had brought from the Old World with those of the dominant Anglo-Saxon culture.

The short stories and sketches that subsequently appeared in Yezierska's *Children of Loneliness* (1923) and in the novels *Arrogant Beggar* (1927) and *All I Could Never Be* also deal with the immigrant experience, and describe the female version of the American Dream while delineating the tensions between the values of the Old World and the New World. Though Yezierska's early works were on the whole favorably reviewed by the critics, those who had applauded the emotional power of her early fiction soon began to speak negatively of her unvarying style and subject matter.

Depression and Anti-Immigration Sentiment Dampen Later Career The Great Depression years brought economic hardship to Yezierska, as they did to many other writers. The royalties from her published books were negligible, and her modest savings disappeared with the 1929 stock-market crash. Like many other unemployed writers of this era, she was fortunate to find both a job and a community through the W.P.A. Writers' Project, a work program implemented by President Franklin Delano Roosevelt to give struggling artists paying positions. The work assigned to her—cataloguing the trees in Central Park—hardly made effective use of her creative talents though. This period in her life, as well as the early years of her career, is vividly described in her autobiographical novel *Red Ribbon on a White Horse* (1950). The novel also recounts her brief sojourn in a small New Hampshire town after a ghetto acquaintance willed her some money and thus freed her for a time from the pressing necessity of earning a living. However, realizing once again, as she had during the year she lived in Hollywood, that she could not write when she was too far removed from the familiar ghetto world of her youth, she soon returned to New York City, where she lived until her death. For many years, Yezierska's writing grew less popular as a growing hatred for immigrants arose in mainstream America, demonstrated by the restrictive immigration laws of 1924 and culminating in the 1927 executions of Italian anarchists Nicola Sacco and Bartolomeo Vanzetti, who had been convicted of murder in a trial that revealed an undercurrent of anti-immigrant prejudice.

Though she had no novels published after 1950, she continued to write short stories and book reviews. Her last published story, "Take up Your Bed and Walk," which describes the experience of an elderly Jewish woman, appeared in *Chicago Jewish Forum* in 1969, a year before her death, and has recently been republished in a volume of her collected fiction, *The Open Cage: An Anzia Yezierska Collection* (1979), edited by Alice Kessler Harris. With the publication of this collection and the republication of *Bread Givers*, Yezierska's fiction is now available to a new generation of readers.

Works in Literary Context

Immigrant Writing Over a career of more than fifty years, Yezierska was a prominent part of the vanguard in the literary treatment of the immigrant experience. As she stated in stories, essays, and interviews, Yezierska felt her mission as a writer was to "build a bridge of understanding between the American-born and myself," essentially to translate the experience of the Jewish ghetto for all America. Her work demonstrates not only her conviction that she could build this bridge, but also her belief in America as the promised land. Finding a common language through which to describe herself and her people was no easy task, however. While her tales express a belief in this land of opportunity, her female protagonists just as often articulate Yezierska's feeling of being "in" America but "not of them." The bridge between the Old World and New often seems like an illusion, with Yezierska and her characters caught between "worlds of difference that no words could bridge over."

Feminism and the "New Woman"   With the passing of the Nineteenth Amendment in 1920, women had gained the right to vote. In its attention to the experiences of the immigrant woman, Yezierska's work also addresses the specific concerns of women. The stereotype of the New Woman was extremely popular, rejecting the traditional domestic sphere in favor of more public lives including both working and social involvement. While there is no evidence that Yezierska knew any of the "New Women" who dominated the New York scene in the 1920s, such as entertainment celebrities, she certainly subscribed to similar individualistic, self-reliant ideals. Many of the female characters she created exhibit a sense of self-reliance, looking to their own individuality to find happiness rather than relying on a husband or other family member for fulfillment. Yezierka's sister Annie also proved to be a source of inspiration. Although burdened with poverty and many children, Annie was not discouraged. Her self-reliant activities, such as organizing the women of the tenement for social change, and the vivid stories of her life provided the material for Yezierska's stories, including her first, "The Free Vacation House," which focused on the problems of an immigrant wife and mother.

Works in Critical Context

When Yezierska emerged on the literary scene in the 1920s, the American public was generally interested in the immigrant experience. She was not the first voice to speak about the struggles of the Jewish immigrant. Writers such as Abraham Cahan and Israel Zangwill had already found success with stories that depict life on the East Side of New York City. The positive reception of Yezierska's work was based on another historical factor as well. Yezierska persisted in her efforts to bring the Jewish immigrant experience to other Americans. The themes of her stories—immigrant anguish, poverty, and the cultural negotiation between the Old World and the New—were common to many immigrants in America.

Bread Givers   *Bread Givers* (1925) earned Yezierska critical acclaim and respect as a mature artist. The subtitle— *A Struggle Between a Father of the Old World and a Daughter of the New*—indicates the conflicts between traditions, cultures, and genders that form the theme of the novel.

In its attention to these tensions *Bread Givers* is perhaps Yezierska's most autobiographical work. Women readers of the suffrage decade must certainly have been drawn to the self-reliant, proto-feminist Sara Smolinsky. Yet the novel, although widely read and admired for several years after its publication in 1925, went out of print and into obscurity with the onset of the Great Depression in 1929. The end of the 1920s marked a decline of interest in Yezierska's work. Previously praised for its realism, her style was criticized as sentimental and melodramatic. Her characters and plots were described as limited and overused. The Jewish community in particular resented her criticism of their beliefs, customs, and language. Public interest in the plight of immigrants had also declined. In 1975 *Bread Givers* was rediscovered by Alice Kessler Harris, who edited a new edition of the novel. This rediscovery came on the heels of the revival of the women's movement in the United States, and the novel has found a new audience of female readers. In 1991, Elizabeth Ammons states, for instance, "The achievement of *Bread Givers* stems directly from this impulse to forcibly combine clashing elements. . . . The book does not at all behave the way a nice middle-class novel should. But it works."

Responses to Literature

1. Research immigrant labor in the early twentieth century using your library and the Internet. Compare the working conditions that Yezierska faced

COMMON HUMAN EXPERIENCE

Yezierska writes about the female immigrant experience in the United States. Other works that portray the concerns of similar women in cultural transition include:

"The New Colossus" (1883), a poem by Emma Lazarus. Lazarus was a Jewish American poet who promoted Russian immigrants' rights. In this, her most famous poem, are the famous lines engraved on the Statue of Liberty: "Give me your tired, your poor / Your huddled masses yearning to breathe free."

Annie John (1986), a novel by Jamaica Kincaid. Kincaid's novel focuses on the British colonial background of her childhood life in Antigua, as she learned British traditions in the context of the larger Caribbean culture.

How the García Girls Lost Their Accents (1992), a novel by Julia Alvarez. Alvarez's story follows the lives of a family from the Dominican Republic living in New York.

Breath, Eyes, Memory (1994), a novel by Edwidge Danticat. The young protagonist in Danticat's story must face a sometimes brutal past as she embarks on her new life in New York.

Seventeen Syllables: 5 Stories of Japanese American Life (1985), a short story collection by Hisaye Yamamoto. Yamamoto writes stories about her experiences as the daughter of Japanese immigrants, including her family's prison experiences in a World War II internment camp.

with today's conversations about sweatshops in developing countries. How are American's views of sweatshops different when they are not within their own borders?

2. Yezierska found writing difficult when she was not in the place she grew up, the busy New York area. At different times, she chose to pursue either more lavish or more secluded residences, but found she could not write under different conditions. What circumstances allow you to write? Make a list of environmental circumstances that make writing difficult for you, and circumstances that encourage it. What is surprising on that list?

3. Yezierska concluded that her own ethnicity was not something to try to avoid. In fact, she found that the sterile middle-class life she once desired brought her little pleasure. What elements make your family's culture different than others? Write an essay considering what your life would actually be like without those differences. At what point do you imagine you might miss them?

BIBLIOGRAPHY

Books

Ammons, Elizabeth. "Slow Starvation: Hunger and Hatred in Anzia Yezierska, Ellen Glasglow, and Edith Summers" in *Conflicting Stories: American Women Writers at the Turn of the Twentieth Century*. New York: Oxford University Press, 1991, 161–182.

Harris, Alice Kessler. Introduction. *Bread Givers*. New York: Braziller, 1975.

Schoen, Carol B. *Anzia Yezierska*. Boston: G. K. Hall, 1982.

Periodicals

Ferraro, Thomas. "'Working Ourselves Up' in America: Anzia Yezierska's *Bread Givers*." *South Atlantic Quarterly* 89.3 (1990): 547–581.

Salvatori, Mariolina. "Women's Work in the Novels of Immigrant Life." *MELUS* 9.4 (1982): 39–58.

Shoen, Carol B. "Anzia Yezierska: New Light on the 'Sweatshop Cinderella.'" *MELUS* 7.3 (1980): 3–11.

Wilentz, Gay. "Cultural Mediation and the Immigrant's Daughter: Anzia Yezierska's *Bread Givers*." *MELUS* 17.3 (1991–1992): 33–41.

✸ Jane Yolen

BORN: *1939, New York, New York*

NATIONALITY: *American*

GENRE: *Fiction, nonfiction, poetry*

MAJOR WORKS:

The Emperor and the Kite (1967)

Friend: The Story of George Fox and the Quakers (1972)

The Girl Who Cried Flowers (1974)

Dragon's Blood: A Fantasy (1982)

Owl Moon (1987)

Overview

Jane Yolen is one of the most prolific contemporary writers of children's stories. Since 1963, she has written hundreds of books, including poetry collections, realistic stories, animal tales, ABC books, and fantasies. Her special talents, however, lie in the writing of literary folktales, noted for their beauty of language and imagery and their abstract, philosophic mode.

Works in Biographical and Historical Context

Multi-Talented in School, Yolen Chooses Writing
Jane Yolen was born in New York City but, because of the Second World War, spent two years in Virginia, living with her grandparents while her father worked in England for the government. After the war, the family moved

Jane Yolen   *Yolen, Jane, photograph by Jason Stemple. Copyright © 2000 Jason Stemple. Reproduced by permission.*

ical sketch: "In *The Magic Three of Solatia*, the ceremony of Thrittem is a kind of bar mitzvah crossed with a silent Quaker meeting. In *Cards of Grief*, I worked in storytelling, seders, and the Mass, along with Communion, Confession, and the Viaticum."

When Yolen was thirteen, her family moved to Westport, Connecticut, where she attended Staples High School. Although she was captain of the girls' basketball team, served on the newspaper staff, was active in the jazz, Spanish, and Latin clubs, won the school's English prize, and performed with the choir, her greatest inspiration during these years came from the woman whom she always called a cousin, the sister of one of her aunts-by-marriage. Her name was Honey Knopp, and she really introduced Yolen to Quakerism and pacifism. She and her husband, Burt, also hosted music festivals, called hootenannies, and helped Yolen realize another, more poetic side of her character. The folk music she was exposed to has also influenced her work, and she writes music to accompany many of her stories.

From Publishing House to Publishing Her Own Books

Yolen attended Smith College, developing her writing skills there, and having her stories published in magazines and newspapers. She had hoped to be a journalist but found herself too emotional to do cold, pitiless interviews. However, she won a journalism award at Smith as well as many poetry prizes. She even earned money at college by writing poetry and singing folk songs. After graduation, eager to see if she could be a successful writer, Yolen moved to Greenwich Village and began to work for various publishers in New York City. In 1962 she started a job with Alfred A. Knopf as an assistant editor of children's books. She had already started writing books for children on her own. Her first effort, *Pirates in Petticoats*, was published in 1963. In 1968 she researched, wrote, and published a book called *World on a String: The Story of Kites* for her father, a kite enthusiast.

In 1962 Yolen married David Stemple, a computer programmer and photographer. Her book *The Girl Who Loved the Wind* (1972) is dedicated to him and celebrates their meeting. After five years of marriage, the couple ordered a Volkswagen camper and went adventuring in Europe, where they toured for nine months. Yolen recalls that during this time they climbed a mountain in Greece and worked in an orange grove in Israel, then back in the United States, she "mushed" on a dog sled in Alaska and went rafting down the Colorado River. Yolen and her husband have three children.

As her children grew older, Yolen's output broadened from children's books to include young adult and adult fiction; her first book for adults, *Cards of Grief* (1984), was a selection of the Science Fiction Book Club. Interestingly, she does not see a sharp distinction between books for children and books for adults.

back to New York and lived there until Jane was a teenager. Her parents gave her a strong literary bent—her father, who wrote books and radio scripts, came from a line of Russian/Ukrainian storytellers. Her mother wrote short stories and created crossword puzzles, and both parents read to Yolen as soon as she was old enough to listen. She learned to read before starting school at New York's PS 93.

Yolen studied ballet for eight years, played fantasy games in Central Park, and loved music, especially folk songs. While in the sixth grade, she scored highly on a test and was accepted at Hunter, a school for gifted girls. At Hunter, she wrote her eighth-grade social studies paper in rhyme and eventually wrote her first two books (unpublished), a nonfiction one on pirates and a seventeen-page novel about the pioneer West.

In the summers of her twelfth and thirteenth years, Yolen attended a Quaker camp in Vermont, where she first became acquainted with pacifism and storytelling. Between high school and college she spent a summer working in an American Friends Service Committee work camp in Yellow Springs, Ohio. These experiences led to an interest in Quaker beliefs. Her religious horizons were also broadened in her teenage years when she was introduced to Catholicism by a friend. Many rituals in her fairy tales reflect this exposure; she writes in her autobiograph-

LITERARY AND HISTORICAL CONTEMPORARIES

Yolen's famous contemporaries include:

Jimmy Carter (1924–): The thirty-ninth president of the United States, Carter's administration was largely unsuccessful due to difficulties including the Iran hostage crisis in 1979, in which Iranian militants held fifty-two American diplomats hostage for over a year. His work after he left the White House, including international diplomacy and involvement with Habitat for Humanity, earned him the 2002 Nobel Peace Prize.

Jim Henson (1939–1990): The beloved creator of characters for the educational children's television show, *Sesame Street* and "The Muppet Show," Henson died unexpectedly of pneumonia at age fifty-one.

Judy Blume (1938–): Prolific writer of adolescent fiction, Blume is best known for her sensitive portrayals of the difficulties of the childhood and preteen years. *Are You There God? It's Me, Margaret* (1970) and *Flubber* (1974) are among her best-known titles.

Ezra Jack Keats (1916–1983): A distinguished children's author, Keats is best known for his stories about a young African American boy named Peter. His books were some of the first to focus on a black character, and include *The Snowy Day* (1963).

Marlo Thomas (1937–): Thomas is a film and television actor and is the daughter of similarly accomplished actor, Danny Thomas. Marlo has written several well-received children's books, including *Free to Be You and Me* (1974).

Continuing to write, turning out one or more books a year, Yolen believes that constant composition prevents one from turning stale. Though she has written realistic stories and fantasies, her major interest is in the literary folktale, for she believes that a child, like an adult, "needs a mythology." She also believes that effective language is an important requisite for a good book: she has written that "an excellent book is a powerful book, an excellent writer is one who uses words powerfully." Yolen taught children's literature at Smith College and is a frequent lecturer at conferences throughout the country, as well as a book reviewer. In 1981, she received an honorary Doctor of Laws degree from Our Lady of the Elms College, Chicopee, Massachusetts. She was elected president of the Science Fiction Writers of America in 1986.

Works in Literary Context

Folklore Yolen is probably best known for her literary folk and fairy tales, drawing on elements of old stories to illustrate modern themes. She rebuilds, and in some cases

creates from fragments, mythologies that apply to modern times while maintaining a timeless sense of wonder and beauty. In particular, Yolen draws on the long tradition of reinterpreting and embellishing the legend of King Arthur in her *Merlin Trilogy*. Sir Thomas Malory's *Le Morte D'Arthur* (1485) codified much of the popular portions of the legend of Arthur and Merlin. Other popular books in this tradition include *The Once and Future King* (1958) by T. H. White and *The Mists of Avalon* (1982) by Marion Zimmer Bradley.

Wordplay and Metaphor Yolen has written several Beginning-to-Read books, in which she typically reveals her fascination for words. *The Giants' Farm* (1977) and *Spider Jane* (1978) are two such books. In these, as well as in others of the same type, Yolen tries not to oversimplify the language and works to provide stories that will amuse and interest beginning readers. She deplores what she calls "Coffee Break Books," which she considers "simple-minded non-books" that are turned out "in short order." Yolen's own stories involve much wordplay and metaphor; they delight because of the intriguing combinations of sounds.

Works in Critical Context

Yolen's many writings include fiction, poetry, nonfiction, and plays for young adults and children. For her creations ranging from ABC books to texts on kite flying to stories about vampires and novels about Merlin, she has won many awards.

The Wild Hunt In *The Wild Hunt* (1995) two boys, Jerold and Gerund, both read about and pursue the title quest in what a *Kirkus Reviews* writer calls "parallel realities." This structurally complex tale turns on a ritual enacted between the Horned King and his wife, the White Goddess: she must choose a hero (Jerold), whom the King must name and capture. Some reviewers found the multilayered chapters too abstract, but Joan Zahnleiter of *Magpies* found the structure "tantalising" and evidence of "Yolen's superb skills in writing fantasy." Frances Bradburn in *Booklist* described it as an "intense novella, which suggests a violence that only barely materializes. Despite its deceptively simple format, the story is a complex, yet entertaining melding of a variety of European myths, legends, and folklore." Bradburn also commented on the book's format: "An intriguing chapter format—Chapter One, Chapter One-Sort of, Chapter One-Almost, Chapter Two, etc.—harks back to the uneasy boundaries between reality and perception much as they are in *Through the Looking Glass*."

The Merlin Trilogy Yolen's *The Merlin Trilogy* (2004) (*Passager*, *Hobby*, and *Merlin*) was assessed as "an enjoyable introduction to Arthurian fantasy," by Ann A. Flowers in *Horn Book*. In *Passager*, the first book, the eight-year-old Merlin, living on his own in the forest as a wild child after being abandoned, is "captured"by a kindly falconer, who slowly reintroduces the boy to language and civilized behavior. *School Library Journal*'s Susan L. Rogers believes this slender book would be equally effective in attracting reluctant readers and in delighting others with its "rich language and poetic phrasing." In the second book, *Hobby*, Merlin's adventures continue after his adopted family dies in a fire and he must leave to make his own way. Among those he encounters is Ambrosius, whose deceptive magic does not appeal to him. Indeed, as Flowers puts it in her *Horn Book* review, Merlin "realizes that only truth will serve him and his dreams in the future."

Queen's Own Fool At times, critics find Yolen's historical work straying into the simplicity of her children's work, as Jane Resh Thomas did in her review of *Queen's Own Fool* (2000), a novel about Queen Mary of Scotland, told through the eyes of her female jester:

> Although the story bursts with romance and intrigue, the authors, Jane Yolen and Robert J. Harris, never overcome the daunting hazards inherent in setting a novel in the maelstrom of dynastic Reformation politics. While acknowledging the folly of Mary's romantic choices, the authors excuse her and simplify history in furthering her legend.

Anne, St. John, however, in *Horn Book*, took a different view. She wrote,

> The two authors have woven fiction and historical fact into a seamless tapestry. The details of Mary's life are accurate, and most of the characters are based on real people. By choosing to have one of the queen's female fools—about whom few facts are known—narrate the story, Yolen and Harris have imbued history with personality.

Responses to Literature

1. Yolen sometimes includes original music with her stories. Choose and listen to some of Yolen's compositions. How do they add to her narratives? Describe why you think her music fits, or doesn't fit, the accompanying story.

2. Yolen's tone has been called melancholy even though she writes for children. Is it appropriate to write more serious stories for younger readers? Choose a story that you think is especially sad. How do you think a child might respond to the text? Why would Yolen choose this kind of tone as opposed to a more light, happy narrative voice?

3. Yolen has produced hundreds of books over her career. She attributes her success to writing every day. For one week, write at least one page of any kind of text—from journal entries to poetry—every day. How difficult is it to maintain that pace? What did you notice about your writing as the week went on?

COMMON HUMAN EXPERIENCE

Yolen does not condescend to her younger readers. Other children's books that tell substantial and mature stories include:

Harold and the Purple Crayon (1955), a children's book by Crockett Johnson. A young boy named Harold takes readers on a magical walk in the moonlight as he draws whatever he needs with his trusty purple crayon.

Alexander and the Terrible, Horrible, No Good, Very Bad Day (1972), a children's book by Judith Viorst. A day full of troubles begins with Alexander finding bubble gum in his hair. He must watch as others have seemingly better luck, leaving him to hope the day will end quickly.

Tar Beach (1988), a children's book by Faith Ringgold. A young girl dreams that she can fly over the Brooklyn Bridge, and help ease her family's financial worries.

Owl Babies (1996), a children's book by Martin Waddell. Three child owls must keep each other calm when they think their mother has left them.

The Giving Tree (1964), a children's book by Shel Silverstein. In this book, a young boy learns important life lessons as he grows up but continues to visit a favorite tree throughout his lifetime.

---

4. Many of Yolen's books are fantasies, from stories about dragons to those about sea creatures. How do her novels compare to other fantasies you have read? How are they similar and different? How would you describe Yolen's style of fantasy compared to another writer?

BIBLIOGRAPHY

Books

Yolen, Jane. *Touch Magic: Fantasy, Faerie, and Folktale in the Literature of Childhood*. New York: Philomel. 1981.

Periodicals

Estes, Cheri. Review of *Here There Be Unicorns*. *School Library Journal* (Jan 1995): 110.

Flowers, Ann A. Review of *Passager*. *Horn Book* (July/Aug 1996): 466.

Rogers, Susan L. Review of *Passager*. *School Library Journal* (May 1996): 118–19.

Scanlon, Donna L. Review of *Here There Be Witches*. *School Library Journal* (Dec 1995): 110.

Sherman, Chris. Review of *Here There Be Unicorns*. *Booklist* (Nov 1, 1994): 492–93.

Web sites

Yolen, Jane. Retrieved December 12, 2008, from http://www.janeyolen.com.

⚙ Paul Zindel

BORN: *1936, Staten Island, New York*

DIED: *2003, New York, New York*

NATIONALITY: *American*

GENRE: *Drama, fiction*

MAJOR WORKS:

*The Effect of Gamma Rays on Man-in-the-Moon
    Marigolds* (1964)
The Pigman (1968)
My Darling, My Hamburger (1969)

Overview

Zindel's informal narrative style and candid approach to
subjects of interest to young people made him one of the
most popular writers of contemporary young adult literature. Though also a Pulitzer-prize winning dramatist for his
play *The Effect of Gamma Rays on Man-in-the-Moon Marigolds* (1964), he was most acclaimed for his novels *The
Pigman* (1968) and *My Darling, My Hamburger* (1969),
as well as for his numerous other young adult novels.

Works in Biographical and Historical
Context

Financial Hardship Leads to Numerous Moves
Zindel was born on Staten Island, New York, in 1936.

Paul Zindel   *Zindel, Paul, photograph. AP Images.*

His father left the family early in the marriage, leaving his
wife to raise Zindel and his sister on her own without
much money. Their mother tried numerous schemes to
support the family. The family lived through World War
II (1940–1945), during which the Allied forces defeated
the Axis powers, including Hitler and the Nazis. The
general economic boom following the war did not help
the Zindel family, as Zindel's mother variously served as a
private duty nurse, a hot dog vendor, a real estate salesman, and even as a dog breeder, with none of her jobs
bringing in much cash. Almost every six months the
family moved, through a series of apartments on Staten
Island and finally, into a ramshackle house in Travis, New
York. Zindel began writing at an early age, preparing
short sketches for high school functions, and continued
to write in college, composing two original plays by the
time he received his master of science degree from Wagner College in Staten Island in 1959. He remained in his
hometown for the next ten years, working at a local high
school as a chemistry and physics teacher while continuing to write on the side.

Zindel's first success came in 1964 when his play *The
Effect of Gamma Rays on Man-in-the-Moon Marigolds*
had its premiere at Houston's Alley Theatre. *Marigolds*
is the story of a young girl, Tillie, who lives with her
epileptic sister and her abusive mother, Beatrice. "*Marigolds* was written when I was twenty-five-years-old,"
Zindel has commented:

> One morning I awoke and discovered the manu-
> script next to my typewriter. I suspect it is autobio-
> graphical, because whenever I see a production of
> it I laugh and cry harder than anyone else in the
> audience. I laugh because the play always reminds
> me of still another charmingly frantic scheme of my
> mother's to get rich quick.

Though similarities exist between Beatrice and his
own mother, Zindel has noted his mother's compassion
and dedication to her family. The play went on to be
produced on Broadway in 1970 and to win the 1971
Pulitzer Prize for Drama.

Realistic Adolescent Novels Make Waves Zindel's
success continued when, in 1966, Charlotte Zolotow, an
editor for Harper & Row, saw a television production of
Marigolds produced by National Educational Television.
Moved by his understanding depiction of Tillie, Zolotow
contacted Zindel and convinced him to write a work for
young adults, which became his first novel. *The Pigman*
was instrumental in establishing the realistic teenage
novel as a distinct genre. *The Pigman* garnered the *Boston
Globe–Horn Book Award* for fiction and was selected as
one of *School Library Journal*'s most influential books of
the twentieth century. In 1969, Zindel quit his teaching
position to write dramas and young adult novels full time.
In his second novel, *My Darling, My Hamburger*, he tells
the story of a high school girl with abusive parents who,

when she discovers she is pregnant, turns to an illegal abortionist.

The 1960s and 1970s produced a counterculture movement in the United States in which the younger generation questioned the standard traditions of family, gender roles, and authority. Zindel's work comes out of this movement in its refusal to condescend toward teenagers because of their youth. But, because Zindel's young adult novels have recurring themes of abusive adults and desperate teenagers, he has met with criticism. He believes, however, that he is confronting the reality of teenage life.

> Teenagers *have* to rebel. It's part of the growing process. In effect, I try to show them they aren't alone in condemning parents and teachers as enemies or ciphers. I believe I must convince my readers that I am on their side; I know it's a continuing battle to get through the years between twelve and twenty—an abrasive time. And so I write always from their own point of view.

Zindel continued to write prolifically during the 1980s and 1990s, writing a book nearly every year. He also wrote the screenplay for the film *Runaway Train* (1985), starring John Voigt. Between 2001 and 2003, Zindel published no less than fourteen books. He died of cancer on March 27, 2003, while living in New York.

Works in Literary Context

Realism in Teenage Novels Zindel is a best-selling author of young adult works who has pioneered the genre's break with romanticism toward a more realistic mode. Zindel's characters are often desperately unhappy. His stories do not have tidy endings or shallow platitudes about a perfect world. Quite the contrary, as Zindel deals honestly with loneliness, eccentricity, escapism, sexual tension, and drug and alcohol abuse. Many of Zindel's stories are concerned with teenagers who are alienated from their parents and teachers, young people who struggle to find meaning and self-worth in a society that batters them. In *Elementary English*, Beverly A. Haley and Kenneth L. Donelson note that Zindel

> looks at the world through the eyes of adolescents, many kinds of adolescents, all trying to find some meaning in a world apparently gone mad, all concerned with man's cruelty and "matters of consequence." By selecting an adolescent point of view, Zindel forces the reader to look at the world as if he were awakening to it for the first time, a kind of rebirth.

Zindel's message is not hopelessly grim, however. His young heroes and heroines discover their worth, connect with one another, and learn important lessons about life—sometimes the hard way. In facing ugly reality, they see beyond the ugliness to something better, and they strive for that better vision.

LITERARY AND HISTORICAL CONTEMPORARIES

Zindel's famous contemporaries include:

Allen Ginsberg (1926–1997): One of the founders of the American Beat poetry movement of the 1950s and 1960s, Ginsberg is best known for his poem *Howl* (1956).

Bono (1960–): Lead singer and front man for the Irish rock band U2, Bono became a world presence at the turn of the twenty-first century with his pioneering work to engage Western countries in the global threat of extreme poverty and AIDS. He retains a loyal youth audience.

Heath Ledger (1979–2008): A well-respected actor from Australia, Ledger began his career as a teen heart throb. He died of complications due to the mixing of prescription drugs at the age of twenty-eight.

Tipper Gore (1948–): Gore is the wife of former vice president Al Gore. Tipper Gore publicly campaigned to increase awareness about issues concerning children and families. She received much public attention for her efforts to institute warning labels on music with questionable content.

John Hughes (1950–): Film director and writer, Hughes became well known for his movies about teenage life, including *The Breakfast Club* (1985).

Overcoming Abuse Zindel examines adolescents' relationships with adults through a variety of realistic characters. Michael J. Meyer points out in *Children's Literature Association Quarterly* that "Zindel's sympathetic portraits of abused male adolescents are especially valuable because he offers not only a picture of why such abuse occurs but also provides hope that the situation can be resolved positively." For example, in *The Amazing and Death-Defying Diary of Eugene Dingman* (1987), Zindel's protagonist is more or less ignored by his dysfunctional parents. But, during his summer as a waiter at an Adirondack resort, he finds surrogate mentors to learn from. In *David and Della* (1993), David Maholy's parents fax him messages from throughout the world but have a difficult time conversing with him in person. However, David still manages to find ways of expressing his creativity and affirming the value of life.

Works in Critical Context

Ever since the appearance of his first two books, Zindel's novels have been the objects of a extensive controversy and evaluation. On the one hand, they have been described as humorous and honest, and on the other hand, they have been condemned as "hack work" and slick "con jobs."

COMMON HUMAN EXPERIENCE

Zindel shows the real difficulties adolescents can face in their teen years. Other works that explore the challenges that teenagers face include:

Fame (1980), a film directed by Alan Parker. Set in a New York high school for the performing arts, this film shows the struggles of a group of teenaged dancers, musicians, and actors.

Juno (2007), a film written by Diablo Cody. An offhandedly humorous story about a high school girl who becomes pregnant, the film follows the girl's placement of her baby into an adoptive family, as well her own search for identity and love.

To Kill a Mockingbird (1960), a novel by Harper Lee. Now a classic of Southern literature, the story involves conflicted race relations in the South, and is told through the eyes of a young girl.

The Outsiders (1983), a film directed by Francis Ford Coppola. A gang of teenagers is challenged by a rival gang, but their real desire is to fit in.

The Catcher in the Rye (1951), a novel by J. D. Salinger. About a young boy trying to find authenticity in an artificial world, the book has become a classic despite many groups' attempts to censor it.

The Pigman Zindel's first novel has been the subject of extensive critical and largely favorable discussion. For critic Loretta Clarke, in an article in *College English*, "As a swift moving narrative, the story works well. Its lack of complexity fits the statement of intent made by the narrators in the opening oath 'to record the facts, and only the facts.'" James T. Henke observed a depth in the novel that is unusual for young adult fiction. He described it as

> rich in provocatively suggestive metaphor and symbol. For instance, Mr. Pignati's beloved zoo is a symbol of the plight of modern man in our impersonal society. Each of us, so Zindel says, lives in his own cage of indifference, boredom, or self-absorption. As do the creatures in the zoo, we may live in close proximity, but we do not live together. At the zoo, Mr. Pignati delights in tossing peanuts to Bobo the gorilla, and John delights in teasing Bobo by attempting to "speak" like an ape. Both acts, one pathetic, the other comic, are symbolic of modern man's need to communicate with someone, something, anything.

Critic Diane Farrell offers a similar view about the novel's uncompromising approach to its subject matter: "Few books that have been written for young people are as cruelly truthful about the human condition. Fewer still accord the elderly such serious consideration or perceive

that what we term senility may be a symbolic return to youthful honesty and idealism."

Critic David Rees was of the opinion that *The Pigman* is Zindel's finest book. He went on to say:

> It is a somber and chastening story that gets better and better as it goes on, and despite the linguistic irritations, it deserves its high reputation and wide readership. More than any other of his novels, it has coherent shape and direction, and its climax is particularly good: a chilling, sobering, morality-tale conclusion. It also has several finely-wrought verbal felicities. . . . Lorraine and John are credible realistic characters, telling us more, strangely, about each other in their first-person narrations than about themselves. Effective, too, is the emphasis laid by the author on the fact that it is a combination of their own selfishness and Mr. Pignati's that leads to the old man's death—not some vague malevolent adult world outside that is responsible.

Lavinia Russ was also enthusiastic about the novel. She praised Zindel as being "one of the brightest stars in the children's book sky. When Paul Zindel's first book, *The Pigman* appeared, it was so astonishingly good it made your reviewer feel like some watcher of the skies when a new planet swims into his ken."

My Darling, My Hamburger *My Darling, My Hamburger* was generally not as well received as Zindel's first novel. Indeed, some of the criticism directed at it was quite harsh. Josh Greenfeld criticized Zindel for a lack of honesty:

> How do you reach the young, the teenagers? In books, as in life, I do not know. But neither, I think, does Mr. Zindel. For I do know that fiction must offer truth in the guise of illusion, not illusion instead of the truth. And the one thing our Now children can sense most assuredly, as they peer across that well-known gap at their generators, is the scent of adult con.

Writing in 1980, over a decade after the publication of the book, David Rees offered a mixed assessment:

> The main theme of the book—Liz's abortion—is dealt with fairly well; the whole business comes over, as it should, as an ugly, emotionally messy, squalid experience. But the dice are far too heavily loaded against Liz. Quirks of fate play a large role in what happens, and her encounters with the unbelievably nasty Rod Gittens seem a little too much when added to the chain of circumstantial events that leads to her and Sean Collins making love without any contraceptive precautions. Also, the book seems, ten years later, rather unmodern. The horror of the back-street abortion, even if still with us, is not now necessarily the outcome of an unwanted pregnancy, and the whole atmosphere of the teenage romance as portrayed here has a passe feeling to it with its formal dates and dances. It's as if the author felt as unrelaxed as his characters. Maybe the trouble is that the book

is too didactic, and that not enough space is devoted to developing what goes on inside the characters: one feels curiously uninvolved with them, unlike, say, in *The Pigman*.

Responses to Literature

1. Zindel presents teenage life as serious, and full of very real problems. How are teenagers usually perceived? What shapes those perceptions? Are they true or false? How do Zindel's books treat teenagers as mature?

2. Zindel deals with mature issues in his novels, like child abuse, abortion, and underage alcohol use. Do you think it is appropriate for these topics to be in young adult books? If so, where would you draw the line? What topics would be inappropriate for inclusion in a young adult book?

3. Choose a teenage character from one of Zindel's novels. Write a short character description. Now consider that character as an adult, ten years later. Write a second character description, imagining what that character's life is like, and how he or she has changed and stayed the same over the years.

4. Using your library and the Internet, research underage drinking, being sure to avoid biased sources. What are some of the dangers of teenage drinking? What are some of the motivations for youth to drink alcohol? How can underage drinking, and the dangers that accompany it, be minimized?

BIBLIOGRAPHY

Books

Forman, Jack Jacob. *Presenting Paul Zindel*. Boston: Twayne, 1988.

Zindel, Paul. *The Pigman and Me*. New York: HarperCollins, 1992.

Periodicals

Farrell, Diane. Review of *The Pigman*. *Horn Book* (Feb. 1969).

Haley, Beverly A., and Kenneth L. Donelson. "Pigs and Hamburgers, Cadavers and Gamma Rays: Paul Zindel's Adolescents." *Elementary English* (Oct. 1974): 941–945.

Janeczko, Paul. "An Interview with Paul Zindel." *English Journal* (1977): 20–21.

Meyer, Michael L. Review. *Children's Literature Association Quarterly* (1992): 11.

Maholy, David. Review. *Washington Post Book World* (May 8, 1994): 20.

Russ, Lavinia. Review. *Publishers Weekly* (Apr 13, 1970).

Scales, Pat. "The Pigman and He: Paul Zindel's Stories are Full of Fear, Self-Loathiing, and Unconditional Friendship. No Wonder They're So Popular with Teens" *School Library Journal* Vol. 48, no. 6 (June 2002): 52–55.

Web sites

Random House, Inc. *Paul Zindel*. Retrieved December 8, 2008, from http://www.randomhouse.com/author/results.pperl?authorid=34133.

Glossary of Literary Terms

The glossary contains terms found in various entries throughout the *Gale Contextual Encyclopedia of American Literature*. This glossary includes terms for various literary components or techniques relevant to the work of the authors, terms for important artistic movements or groups discussed in relation to the authors, and terms for social, political, or philosophical ideas that profoundly impacted American literature. Definitions for more basic literary terms, such as "figurative language," have not been included.

ALLEGORY: A work in which the entire narrative serves as a symbol for something beyond the surface-level story.

ANACHRONISM: A thing or idea mentioned in a work of art that occurs outside its normal place in time. In William Shakespeare's play *Julius Caesar*, for example, the author mentions the striking of a clock to indicate time passing—even though no such clocks existed in ancient Rome, the time period in which the play is set.

ANTI-HERO: A main character in a literary work whose actions and ideals would not generally be regarded as heroic, though the character may still be portrayed sympathetically by the author. Holden Caulfield, the protagonist of J. D. Salinger's novel *The Catcher in the Rye* (1951), is an example of an anti-hero.

AVANT-GARDE: Meaning "advance guard" in French, a term used to describe artists or artistic works that are considered innovative or nontraditional.

BALLAD: A poetic work written in the form of a traditional song that commonly relates a folk tale, myth, or legend. Ballads are often written in four-line stanzas with alternating lines of eight and six syllables, in which the lines with six syllables contain end-rhyme.

BEAT GENERATION: A collective term for a group of writers who rose to prominence in the late 1940s and

1950s. Their work and their lifestyles were marked by defiance of legal and cultural authority, experimentation with drugs and unconventional sexual relationships, interest in Eastern religions, and an affinity for improvisational jazz music. Famous Beat writers include: Allen Ginsberg, Jack Kerouac, and William S. Burroughs.

BILDUNGSROMAN: Taken from a German term meaning "novel of formation," a novel that documents the maturation of the protagonist. The bildungsroman is also commonly known as a "coming of age" novel.

BLANK VERSE: A type of poetry which follows a set pattern of stressed and unstressed syllables in each line, but does not feature consistent rhyme. Poet Robert Frost wrote many of his poems in blank verse.

CAPTIVITY NARRATIVE: A first-hand, nonfiction account of the captivity of a white American settler by Native Americans.

COMEDY: In classical Greek drama, a play that ends happily for its major characters; many ancient comedies poked fun at political figures or cultural stereotypes, which inspired the laughter modern audiences now associate with the term.

CONFESSIONAL POETRY: Confessional poetry is a kind of poetry popularized in the 1950s and 1960s characterized by revelations of extremely intimate, often unflattering details of the poet's private life. Subjects often include sex and drug use. Major confessional poets include Sylvia Plath and Anne Sexton.

ENJAMBMENT: In poetry, the splitting of a continuous phrase or sentence into two or more lines. The result is that a single line may appear to express an incomplete thought, though the work as a whole is afforded a more complex rhythm and structure. Poet e. e. cummings made frequent use of enjambment.

EPIC: A literary work, originally a work in poetic form, that focuses on large-scale events and themes, and often takes place over a long period of time. *The Odyssey*, an ancient Greek epic by Homer, is one of the earliest examples. The term is now often applied to long works that cover a time span of many years, such as Margaret Mitchell's 1936 novel *Gone With the Wind*.

EPIGRAM: A short, clever statement—often in the form of a couplet—intended to impart humor and insight. Dorothy Parker was famous for her witty epigrams.

EPISTOLARY NOVEL: A novel in which the story is told through letters written by one or more characters. Samuel Richardson was an early practitioner of the epistolary novel, with works such as *Pamela* (1740) and *Clarissa* (1748). Alice Walker produced a more recent version with her 1982 novel *The Color Purple*.

EXISTENTIALISM: A philosophical movement that gained popularity in the first half of the twentieth century, thanks to literary works by Jean-Paul Sartre and Simone de Beauvoir, among others. Existentialism is characterized by the idea that life does not have a greater meaning or purpose beyond that which people choose to create for themselves. Many prominent African American writers have been labeled existentialist, including Ralph Ellison and Richard Wright.

EXPERIMENTAL NOVEL: A work which defies the traditional structure or subject matter of a novel, and emphasizes style or technique over content. Thomas Pynchon's 1973 novel *Gravity's Rainbow*, for example, is considered an experimental novel.

FABLE: A short tale whose purpose is to impart a message or lesson, usually featuring animals as characters. "The Tortoise and the Hare" is a well-known example of a fable. James Thurber and Joel Chandler Harris are known for their fables.

FARCE: A dramatic work characterized by characters being put into comedic situations that are unlikely or improbable, as in Thornton Wilder's *The Matchmaker* (1954).

FLASH FICTION: Short fiction, usually under one thousand words, that despite its length contains all the traditional elements of story such as a protagonist and conflict that is somehow resolved. O. Henry and Ray Bradbury are both authors of flash fiction.

FRAME NARRATIVE: A literary device in which the main story being told to the reader is presented as a story being told by one of the characters within the work, as in "The Celebrated Jumping Frog of Calaveras County," an 1865 short story by Mark Twain.

GONZO JOURNALISM: A subjective style of journalism in which events are described from the reporter's point of view. Gonzo journalism originated with Hunter S. Thompson.

GOTHIC FICTION: A literary sub-genre that emerged in the last half of the eighteenth century and was characterized by eerie atmosphere, melodrama, mystery, and romance.

IMAGISM: A poetic movement of the early twentieth century that emphasized direct expression through concise imagery and non-standard structure. Ezra Pound was instrumental in the development of the Imagist movement, and poet Amy Lowell was a leading practitioner.

IMPRESSIONISM: An artistic movement that emerged during the latter half of the nineteenth century, and focused on artistic impression over realistic representation. In literature, impressionism was characterized by a focus on the depiction of the interior, mental landscapes of characters, and was associated with other literary movements such as Symbolism.

IRONY: A literary device in which a character's perception of reality differs from actual reality, or in which a character's words do not express their true feelings. Sarcasm is a well-known form of irony. Dramatic irony occurs when an audience is given information that is not known by one or more characters in the play.

LIBRETTO: A text for the vocal portion of an opera or other musical work, often written in verse form. Composers frequently employ well-known writers to write libretti for their works, and writers such as Paul Laurence Dunbar, Langston Hughes, and Gertrude Stein sometimes worked as librettists.

LOST GENERATION: A term used to describe a loosely defined group of American writers who spent time in Europe—especially Paris—following World War I. These writers, including Ernest Hemingway, F. Scott Fitzgerald, and Sherwood Anderson, were notable for themes of disillusionment in their works.

MAGICAL REALISM: A literary style developed primarily in South America in which fantastic or supernatural elements are woven into otherwise realistic tales. Writers commonly associated with magic realism include Jorge Luis Borges, Alejo Carpentier, Gabriel García Márquez, and Carlos Fuentes; however, the work of some North American writers has been labeled magical realist, including Toni Morrison's 1987 novel *Beloved* and John Cheever's famous 1947 short story "The Enormous Radio."

MELODRAMA: A literary work which contains heightened or exaggerated emotions from the characters. The term originally applied to theatrical productions in which music (or melody) was used to accentuate the drama occurring on the stage.

MODERNISM: An artistic movement during the early twentieth century influenced by the rapid industrialization, scientific advancements, and devastating warfare of the time. Modernist writers were noted for their radical departure from traditional literary forms, with notable Modernist works including T. S. Eliot's poem "The Waste Land" (1922) and James Joyce's novel *Ulysses* (1922).

MUCKRAKERS: A term applied to journalists and fiction writers of the late nineteenth and early twentieth century whose work uncovered corruption in the government and big business. Authors Frank Norris and Upton Sinclair were both considered muckrakers.

NATURALISM: A literary movement of the late nineteenth century that focused on realistic portrayals of people and situations, and specifically dealt with the effects of heredity and environment on a characters's personality and development. Stephen Crane is widely regarded as a Naturalist.

NEOCLASSICISM: A term describing art that sought inspiration in ancient Greek and Roman forms, with emphasis on rationalism and proportion. Phillis Wheatley is considered a neoclassical poet.

NEW JOURNALISM: A style of journalism popularized in the 1960s and 1970s in which the journalist employed such literary techniques as setting scenes, presenting subjects as fleshed out "characters," and offering details of setting and scene.

NIHILISM: A philosophical movement that first appeared in the nineteenth century and is characterized by the belief that life has no objective purpose, moral code, or value. Writers associated with nihilism include Ivan Turgenev, whose novel *Fathers and Sons* (1862) described the Russian Nihilist movement and popularized the concept. More recent fiction has also been labeled Nihilist, including Bret Easton Ellis's 1985 novel *Less Than Zero*.

PARABLE: A short tale meant to impart a message or lesson to the reader. Parables are similar to fables, but do not include supernatural or fantastic elements such as talking animals.

PARODY: A literary work designed to mock or criticize another, usually well-known literary work or genre. An early example is *Shamela* (1741), Henry Fielding's parody of the successful Samuel Richardson novel *Pamela* (1740). Wendy Wasserstein's *Sloth* (2006) is a recent example of a parody.

PASTORAL: Literature that depicts rural life, nature, and the people of a rural region in a highly idealized way. The *Eclogues* (c. 40 B.C.E.) by the ancient Roman poet Virgil are among the oldest examples of pastoral poetry. Some works by Willa Cather and Wallace Stegner contain pastoral elements.

PICARESQUE: A type of novel first developed in Spain that focuses on the adventures of a rogue, or clever antihero. Among many others, James Branch Cabell's 1919 novel *Jurgen* exhibits the key traits of the picaresque.

POSTMODERNISM: A post-World War II literary movement characterized by nonlinearity, or a nonstandard narrative timeline, as well as metafiction, in which the author shows awareness of the story as a work of fiction and may even appear as a character within it.

PSEUDONYM: An alternate name used by a writer, often to hide the writer's identity. For example, William Sydney Porter used the pen name O. Henry when writing his celebrated short stories.

PSYCHOLOGICAL FICTION: A type of fiction in which a great deal of attention is paid to the thoughts and feelings of the characters, as opposed to external action. Henry James was well known for his psychological fiction.

REALISM: An artistic movement characterized by a desire to portray characters and environments as objectively, or as close to reality, as possible. Realism relies heavily upon physical descriptions, and Gustave Flaubert's novel *Madame Bovary* (1856)—with its almost grotesque precision to detail—is considered a landmark work of realism. Prominent American realists include Mark Twain and Edith Wharton.

ROMAN À CLEF: A literary work containing fictionalized depictions of real people and events. The work may be autobiographical, as in Sylvia Plath's *The Bell Jar* (1963), or it may refer to thinly disguised versions of well-known people, as in Truman Capote's *Answered Prayers* (1987).

ROMANTICISM: An artistic and philosophical movement that developed throughout Europe in the late eighteenth and early nineteenth centuries, and was popular in the United States throughout the nineteenth century (thought it reached its peak near the middle of the century). Romantic literature is notable for its expression of powerful emotions and use of natural settings. The work of Walt Whitman, Ralph Waldo Emerson, and Harriet Beecher Stowe is considered Romantic.

SATIRE: A type of literature intended to attack a person, group, institution, or idea through parody or irony. Very often, the satirist exposes the shortcomings of its subject by ironically expressing a position in support or praise of the subject. Benjamin Franklin, Stephen Crane, and Dorothy Parker are a few of the many American writers known for their satires.

SERIAL PUBLICATION: The printing of consecutive portions of a novel or other lengthy work of literature in successive issues of a periodical. Some of Mark Twains's works were first printed through serial publication.

SOCIAL REALISM: An artistic movement of the nineteenth century defined by sympathetic yet realistic depictions of the working class and the poor conditions in which they lived. Upton Sinclair's 1906 novel *The Jungle* is an example of social realism.

SONNET (ELIZABETHAN): A poetic form typically consisting of fourteen ten-syllable lines and an alternating rhyme scheme. William Shakespeare is perhaps the most famous practitioner of English-language sonnets.

SOUTHERN GOTHIC FICTION: A type of Gothic fiction (see definition) in which grotesque, supernatural, melodramatic, and mysterious elements are deployed for the sake of exploring the culture of the American South. Prominent authors of Southern Gothic literature include Flannery O'Connor, William Faulkner, Carson McCullers, and Tennessee Williams.

STREAM OF CONSCIOUSNESS: A literary technique meant to emulate the flow of thought in a character's mind. This is sometimes expressed through disjointed or run-on sentences, repetitions of words or phrases, or tenuous associations between different subjects. Notable works that use the stream of consciousness technique include *The Sound and the Fury* (1929) by William Faulkner and *On the Road* (1957) by Jack Kerouac.

SURREALISM: An artistic movement of the early twentieth century noted for its embrace of the irrational. Surrealist literary works often contained jarring juxtapositions of unrelated things, seemingly random or nonsensical phrases, and dreamlike situations. William Burroughs is considered a surrealist.

TRAGEDY: In classical Greek drama, a play that focuses on themes such as love, fate and betrayal, and does not end happily for one or more of the main characters. The play *Antigone* (c. 442 B.C.E.) by Sophocles is a typical Greek tragedy. Eugene O'Neill wrote several famous tragedies that drew heavily on ancient Greek models.

TRANSCENDENTALISM: A philosophical movement that originated in New England in the first half of the nineteenth century, Transcendentalism prized individualism and forwarded the idea that each individual has the ability to achieve a transcendent spirituality by communing with nature and remaining true to his or her essential self.

VERNACULAR: The casual and natural speech of a group of people or culture. Mark Twain's 1884 novel *Adventures of Huckleberry Finn* makes masterful use of the American vernacular of the 1830s.

Index

B

C

D

E

F

G

H

H

I-J

K

M

M

N

O

P

Q-R

R

S

S

T

U-W

W

Y-Z

Nationality/Ethnicity Index